GHANA

in the
Humanities and Social Sciences
1900-1971

A Bibliography

by

Christian Chukwunedu Aguolu

The Scarecrow Press, Inc.
Metuchen, N. J.   1973

Library of Congress Cataloging in Publication Data

Aguolu, Christian Chukwunedu, 1940–
    Ghana in the humanities and social sciences,
1900–71.

    1. Ghana—Bibliography. 2. Africa—Bibliography.
I. Title.
Z3785.A65   016.91667   73-9519
ISBN 0-8108-0635-5

Dedicated to

my entire

family

FOREWORD

David Brokensha

Ghana, as Mr. Aguolu points out, is "bibliographically better off than almost all other black African states." This present bibliography will find an honored place among its predecessors, from Cardinall's pioneering work of 1932 to the many intervening collections. Not only does this bibliography supplement the earlier ones, but it goes further, in several important ways. First, it covers the years 1900-1971, which include most of the colonial period as well as the first fourteen years of independence. Second, there are numerous references to unpublished material: this inclusion will be welcomed by many scholars, as will the third feature, the most useful descriptive and critical annotations. Finally, readers will appreciate the inclusion of over 500 works on Africa in general.

The bibliography reflects the wealth of publications about Ghana in the humanities and social sciences. Few other nations of comparable size--or even of much larger population--can boast the quality and quantity of the material which is listed here. From the early days, Ghanaian authors were important: today they predominate in fields such as Ghanaian history, an indication of the contribution of the University of Ghana. However, expatriates continue to produce works on Ghana, and to be welcomed as fellow-scholars by their Ghanaian colleagues. As one who has enjoyed this hospitality, I can attest to its warmth and to its rarity.

Christian Aguolu is eminently qualified for his formidable task. After attending Government College at Umuahia in his native Eastern Nigeria, he studied classics at Ibadan University, but took the honors degree of the University of London in 1965. He obtained his master's degree in librarianship in 1968 at the University of Washington, Seattle. His academic career has been marked by an impressive series of distinguished scholarly awards, prizes and fellowships, and he has also studied several European languages. From 1968 to 1972 we were fortunate in having Mr. Aguolu as a reference librarian and bibliographer at the University of California, Santa Barbara: as I know from my own courses, many students received considerable help, especially when working on African topics.

Mr. Aguolu is presently a Ph.D. student in library science at the University of California, Berkeley. He has completed two

v

other bibliographies which will shortly be published by G. K. Hall: one on <u>Nigeria in the Humanities and Social Sciences, 1900-71</u>, the other on <u>The Nigerian Civil War, 1967-70</u>.

All of us who have a scholarly interest in Ghana will welcome this major contribution.

Dr. Brokensha is professor of anthropology, University of California, Santa Barbara.

TABLE OF CONTENTS

ACKNOWLEDGMENTS

Many people contributed in various ways to bring this work to fruition. Lack of mention of a name should not be taken as a mark of ingratitude, for I am deeply grateful to all. But I cannot fail to mention a few names. The first is Donald Fitch, head of the Reference Department, University of California Library, Santa Barbara, who personally supported the production of this work, by constantly advising and encouraging me and editing it. The second is Professor Irving Lieberman, Director of the School of Librarianship, University of Washington, Seattle, my former adviser, for his useful suggestions at every stage of the work. The third group are the members of my family for their encouragement and faith in my work: Jerry and Wanda Aguolu of University of California Medical School at Davis; Senior Magistrate S. I. Aguolu of Senior Magistrate's Court, Afikpo, Nigeria; G. N. Z. and Mary Umezulike of Divisional Office, Amawbia-Awka, Nigeria; Basil and Edith Lebechuku of the Ministry of Trade and Industry, Aguata, Nigeria; the Rev. Dr. & Mrs. Elliott Mason of the Trinity Baptist Church, Los Angeles, California.

The fourth group are Professor David Brokensha of the University of California, Santa Barbara, who let me see part of his unpublished manuscript on Ghana; J. K. T. Kafe, of the Balme Library, University of Ghana, who provided me with the most information on Ghana by correspondence; A. N. de Heer, librarian of the Research Library on African Affairs at Accra for helping to identify some material; Hans E. Panofsky, Curator of Africana, Northwestern University, for his suggestions and the material he was kind enough to send me; Afari-Gyan, a Ghanaian doctoral student in political science at the University of California, Santa Barbara, for helping me identify dubious Ghanaian family names and tribes; Dr. Okechukwu Odita, of Ohio State University; Dr. Herbert Cole, of the University of California, Santa Barbara; Dr. Sunday Ogbonna Anoxie of the State University of New York at New Paltz, publisher of the Conch Magazine; Professor John Harris, Vice-Chancellor of the University of Benin, Nigeria, for sending me useful material; Eugene Graziano, assistant university librarian, University of California, Santa Barbara; Dr. Rolf Güsten of IFO (Institut für Wirtschaftsforschung), Munich, Germany; and Dr. Donald C. Davidson, librarian, University of California, Santa Barbara, for their encouragement.

Finally, I am very grateful to the Research Committee of the University of California, Santa Barbara, for their generous sponsorship; to the Reference Department, especially the Inter-Library

Loan Section, of the University of California Library, Santa Barbara, for calling my attention to many valuable items which I would otherwise have missed; to the Board of Editors of the <u>Dictionary of International Biography</u>, London, for awarding me a Distinguished Service Certificate of Merit in "bibliographical studies" even when this work had not been completed; and to my typists, especially Mrs. Mary Gill, Sherry Self, Beth McIsaac, and Joyce Ferman, for their interest in the work and the useful suggestions they gave me.

Christian Chukwunedu Aguolu

University of California
Berkeley

April 1973

INTRODUCTION

A Brief Political History

The study of the political history of any former colonial territory in Africa consists of the examination of the administrative steps taken by the colonial master to amalgamate peoples in a certain geographic area who might be culturally, linguistically and philosophically dissimilar, into a single administrative unit, and of the subsequent demand by these peoples for independence. This artificial method of creating nations, which was only a political expedient, sowed the seeds of future tribal and political unrest in post-independence Africa in the 1960's. Ghana is no exception.

Known as the Gold Coast until it gained its independence on March 6, 1957 (the first British colony in Africa to do so), it is composed of many ethnic groups with different languages and dialects. The 1970 census set its population at 8,543,561 with a density of 90 per square mile. In this mostly agricultural country, English is the official language owing to the complexity of local languages and dialectal differences.

The principal tribes belong to the Kwa linguistic family: Akan (40 per cent), Ewe, Ga, Dagbani, Hausa and Nzima. Evidence as to their origin based mostly on oral traditions and archaeological findings is conflicting and conjectural. Especially so is the disagreement among archaeologists and historians over the origin of the Akan people who constitute the principal group. They are traditionally believed to have arrived in what was the Gold Coast in three successive waves. The first comprised the Guans and kindred peoples, who came down the Volta Valley as early as A.D. 1200. The second wave brought the Fantis down the rivers Offin and Pra, reaching the coast about A.D. 1300 and spreading eastward through Cape Coast until they came into contact with the Guans. The third group, the Twi people, came between the earlier settlers filling up Ashanti and Akim. The Ga and Ewe states are believed to have been founded by settlers from what is now Nigeria.

Subsequent missionary activities in the colonial period converted many of them to Christianity. Christians constitute 42.8 per cent of the population, practitioners of traditional religions 38.2 and Moslems 12 per cent.[1] However, the typical Ghanaian maintains animist beliefs.

The Portuguese were the first Europeans to arrive in the Gold Coast in the second half of the fifteenth century in search of

1

gold, ivory, spices and slaves. The name "The Gold Coast" was given to this part of the West African coast because these European traders found gold to be in common use amongst the local inhabitants. The first recorded arrival of an Englishman was in 1553. The Danes, the Dutch and the French followed later to compete in the material and human trade originally monopolized by the Portuguese, and by 1750 the English, the Danes, and the Dutch had secured settlements on the coast. In 1824 the government of the United Kingdom assumed control of the British trading settlements, and in 1844 goaded the local chiefs into signing the bond by which they agreed to acknowledge the authority of the British Queen and abolish some of their tribal practices considered repugnant by the British.

In 1850 and 1871 the Danes and the Dutch, respectively, re-linquished their settlements to the British who mounted a series of military campaigns against the raiding Ashantis of the inland. In 1874 the Gold Coast was declared a British colony and after bloody battles with the inland Ashanti Kingdom, the British protectorates were established over the Ashanti (South Central) and the Northern Territories. With Germany's defeat in the World War I, its terri-tory of Togoland was shared between France and the United King-dom, the western part becoming first a British mandate and after the World War II, a British "trust territory."

A series of constitutional revisions from 1946 to 1957 paved the way for Gold Coast independence. In 1946 the Legislative Council had for the first time an African majority representing Ashanti and the colony. Following the constitutional committee of 1949 under the chairmanship of Justice Henley Coussey, elections which included the Northern Territories were held in February 1951.

Thus this new legislature for the first time represented the whole country. By this time nationalist movement had begun to receive strong impetus from Dr. Kwame Nkrumah on his return from studies in the United States and Britain. Nationalism and aspirations for independence were sweeping over the African con-tinent after the World War II. Nkrumah's Convention People's Party won the 1951 elections with Nkrumah as prime minister when that office was created in 1952 and also won the 1954 elections.

On March 6, 1957 the Gold Coast became independent and was renamed Ghana after the ancient empire which existed in West Africa from the 4th to 13th centuries. Some historians claim that the original Gold Coast peoples came from that kingdom. This traditional name carries a marked national and emotional appeal. The British Togoland voted to be amalgamated with the Gold Coast, although the Ewe people who formed the southern part of the trust territory preferred to remain under the British. The result is that this powerful ethnic group seems to remain in Ghana today as a resentful minority. On July 1, 1960 Ghana became a republic with Nkrumah as president. In 1962 he was made a life president, and the political referendum held in 1964 turned Ghana into a single party state, making Nkrumah all-powerful and dictatorial.

Presidential actions were unimpeachable; all political opposition was banned. Political opponents were either clamped in jail or sent into a voluntary exile. The two outstanding victims were Dr. Joseph Boakye Danquah, an erudite lawyer and author, who languished in jail until his death in 1965; and Dr. Kofi Busia, a noted sociologist and university professor who preferred a voluntary exile in Holland. The press was suffocated and no articles or editorials critical of the government could be published, and community development organizations were infused with the ideology of Nkrumahism. A charismatic, brilliant man, well groomed in rhetoric, Nkrumah created a kind of emperor-worship for himself-- an imperial cult reminiscent of the days of Roman Emperors. His people gave him the title of "Osagyefo" or the "Redeemer"; court decisions were ridiculed; Supreme Court judges were removed from office for not voting in accordance with his wishes. Democracy was in fact dead in Ghana.

He called for a Pan-African union of states, perhaps with himself their leader--a "primus inter pares." Despite his leftist policies, the United States and Britain financed the great Volta hydroelectric project and other industrial and agricultural works. The Soviet Union and China participated in many construction projects to further Ghana's industrial growth. However, much money was squandered on many ostentatious projects. Ghana's economy deteriorated until the country was faced with an instant economic disaster.

On February 24, 1966 Nkrumah's regime was overthrown in a coup jointly organized by the army and police while he was on his way to China. He then went into a voluntary exile in the neighboring leftist country of Guinea--where he unceasingly nourished the hope of returning to Ghana one day and continuing his rule-- until his death on April 27, 1972.

He loved his country; he loved Africa and he loved the black man. Uniquely confident in his ability, Nkrumah believed that it was his destiny to redeem the lost pride of the black man. He won the admiration of the blacks in the United States and the Caribbean. His political philosophy and ideological orientation are clearly reflected in his numerous publications in which he called for an end to all vestiges of colonialism in Africa and for economic and political independence for all black African states. However controversial he may have been, his contributions to his country and to Africa are undeniably great. It is debatable whether Ghana could have gained its independence on March 6, 1957, without him, or whether the name "Ghana" would have been so widely heard of in spite of the smallness of the country itself. His major works include, Ghana; The autobiography of Kwame Nkrumah (1957), I speak of freedom: A statement of African ideology (1961), Africa must unite (1963), Neo-colonialism: The last stage of imperialism

(1965), <u>The challenge of the Congo</u> (1967), <u>Handbook of revolutionary</u>
<u>warfare: A guide to the armed phase of the African revolution</u>
(1968), <u>Axioms of Kwame Nkrumah: Freedom fighters' edition,</u>
new edition (1969), <u>Dark days in Ghana,</u> new edition (1969), and
<u>Consciencism: philosophy and ideology for decolonization,</u> rev.
ed. (1970).

The leaders of the 1966 coup established a National Liberation Council as the government, with Lt. General Ankrah, former
army chief of staff, as chairman.   A political election, held in
August 1969, was won by the Progress Party of Dr. Busia who had
returned from exile on the fall of Nkrumah.   Ghana returned to a
democratically constituted government in October 1969 with Busia as
prime minister.   Ironically, however, this government was swept
away on January 12, 1972 in Ghana's second military coup led by
Lt. Colonel Ignatius K. Acheampong who felt that the Busia regime
had been unable to tackle the pressing national economic problems.
Once again Busia retired into an exile, but this time, in the Ivory
Coast.   A National Redemption Council was set up as the government with Acheampong as head of the Military Government.   The
political stability of Ghana rests chiefly on its economic stability
and on the ability of the present government to devise a constitutional system or formula acceptable to the country's disparate
tribal units.   Whether the Acheampong regime can do these things
remains to be seen.

<u>Bibliographic Problems</u>

Bibliographically, Ghana is better off than almost all other
black African states, and this is due to the early interest its
government took in library development.   In 1928 Bishop John
Aglionby of Accra laid the foundation of the Gold Coast future
library development by opening a library of some 6, 000 books in
Bishop's Boys' School.   The question of establishing a public library was first raised at the Legislative Council in 1933.   In 1939
the Carnegie Corporation of New York appointed Hanns Vischer,
joint secretary of the Advisory Committee on Education in the
Colonies, and Margaret Wrong, secretary of the International Committee on Christian Literature for Africa, to study and report on
the expansion of the West African libraries.   Another study was
conducted in West Africa by Ethel Fegan for the Carnegie Corporation in 1940.

The first library school in West Africa was opened at
Achimota College in September 1944 by Miss Fegan, with twelve
students, six from the Gold Coast, five from Nigeria and one from
Sierra Leone.   The British Council opened a library in 1945 in
Accra.   On January 1, 1950 the British Council Library Committee,
recognized by the Gold Coast government, became the Gold Coast
Library Board responsible for public library services throughout
the country.   The Central Library was opened in Accra in 1956.

Up to this time, the government's interest had focused upon

public and school libraries. There was no national library, no national bibliography or any kind of bibliographical activity. It was not until the death of Nkrumah's adviser on African affairs, George Padmore, a West Indian, author of numerous works that were critical of colonial administration in Africa and called for African unity, in 1959, that the need for a research library and a coordinated bibliographical work first dawned upon the Ghanaians. It was Prime Minister Nkrumah himself who set the tone during the opening of the George Padmore Library on June 30, 1961, by declaring:

> A good national library is at once the repository of a nation's culture and wisdom and an intellectual stimulant. In this library, there shall be no national frontiers, for here shall be stored the cumulative experience, the collective wisdom and knowledge about the entire continent of Africa and the assessment, revaluations and studies of observers from all over the world.... National bibliographic and documentation services have not yet received serious consideration in Ghana. An annual publication listing all books and government reports published in this country as well as books written about Ghana from other countries would be an invaluable service, and the foundation of the George Padmore Memorial Library should make this possible. We look forward to the time when a unified bibliography of Africa outlining the progress and achievements of the African peoples will be made possible. [2]

To the books and government reports mentioned by Nkrumah should be added theses, periodical articles, conference papers, pamphlets and all other items of research value. He was, perhaps, the first African leader to realize that libraries are not inert repositories of artifacts or documents of the past but living agencies of progress, intellectual enrichment and public enlightenment. Such a realization is the key to any effective bibliographical activity in a nation, which has to be funded by the government. Besides, the government has to encourage and train the personnel to do the work. Government and public apathy, lack of funds and shortage of man-power constitute the most serious obstacles to library development and bibliographical work in Africa. This is confirmed by a recent study conducted by Samuel I. Kotei, lecturer in library studies, University of Ghana, on the state of national bibliography in Africa. [3]

Many African states have no national libraries, but some African university libraries act in that capacity. In Nigeria, for example, the University of Ibadan Library carried out the responsibility of a national library from 1953 to June 1970 when the National Library created in 1962 began to assume its proper role. The Ibadan University Library published Nigerian Publications; a current national bibliography.

In Ghana the Research Library on African Affairs carries out this function; it issued the country's first national bibliography in 1968 covering material published in 1965 and 1966. Each issue of the Ghana National Bibliography attempts to list all publications, official and non-official, published in Ghana or abroad and written by Ghanaians or other nationals during the period covered. It includes books, periodical articles, theses, official publications, and works in the vernacular languages. Hans E. Panofsky, curator of Africana, Northwestern University, has observed, "National libraries are usually the source of the most comprehensive bibliographies prepared in a country. Indeed, the most significant function of a national library is to prepare the national bibliography."[4]

To obtain an effective control of materials published locally, most countries have a depository law by which publishers are required to deposit a copy or a certain number of copies of any book published in that country with a specified library or institution. In spite of the law, no country can claim to have a complete record of every book published in it. Not even the Bibliothèque Nationale of France, the Library of Congress of the United States, or the British Museum can make such a claim, in spite of the clarity and specificity in the legal deposit clause.

More than 200 new titles of books are published every year in Ghana. The trend today is towards more indigenous publishing, especially in regard to educational material for primary and secondary schools, to reflect national needs. John Nottingham, director of the East African Publishing House in Nairobi, notes also that "This will lead to significant savings in foreign exchange and will have other obvious beneficial economic effects."[5]

The Book and Newspaper Registration Act of 1961 (Act 73) as amended in 1963 (Act 193) requires that a copy of every book published in Ghana be delivered to the following institutions:

(1)   The Ghana Library Board
(2)   The Library of the University of Ghana
(3)   The Library of Kumasi University of Science and Technology
(4)   The Library of the University College of Cape Coast
(5)   The Library of the Ghana Academy of Science
(6)   The Registrar-General's office.

Even this amended act excludes government publications with only a vague proviso, "except as directed by the minister," but includes all reports of commissions and committees of inquiry. There is no clear distinction between a publisher and a printer, thus providing a convenient loop-hole for depository evasions. Many local printers are also publishers but claim no knowledge of the law. Unfortunately, the failure of many publishers to comply with it is chiefly due to lack of realization of the fact that such a deposition of the book helps to advertise it through its listing in the national bibliography or in other published bibliographies.

In his paper presented at the International Conference on African Bibliography in Nairobi in December 1967, Professor John Harris, former librarian of the University of Ibadan, indicates that non-compliance with the requirements of the legal deposit is a common practice in Africa, and in Nigeria he discovered that persuasion and diplomacy proved more effective in making publishers deposit their books than a legal threat, and "this has done much to dispel any feeling that the deposit legislation is a coercive bureaucratic measure."[6]

There is a striking contrast between the Nigerian National Library Decree of 1970, (the amended form of the 1950 Publications Ordinance), and the Book and Newspaper Registration Act of 1963. In Nigeria only three copies of the book are sent to the National Library at Lagos, one of which is sent to the University of Ibadan. In Ghana six copies are required but sent to different institutions. The Nigerian legislation is more specific in its definition of a publisher and a book; whereas in Ghana there is no depository requirement for government publications. In Nigeria, every federal government department is required to send twenty-five copies of its publication to the National Library, while the departments of state government send ten copies, unless the National Library Director prefers a smaller number.

Of all black African countries, Ghana is perhaps best equipped with retrospective bibliographies. There are two most important of these: A. W. Cardinall's A Bibliography of the Gold Coast (1932), was issued by the Gold Coast chief census officer as a companion volume to the Census Report of 1931. It lists over 5,000 unannotated works of great historical value covering the period from the first European arrival in West Africa to the ultimate control of the Gold Coast by the British. A. F. Johnson's A Bibliography of Ghana, 1930-1961 (1964) is a classified listing of some 2,608 items in the arts and sciences, including books, periodical articles, government publications and few unpublished materials. These two major works are supplemented by a listing of about 700 items classified by subject and covering the period 1958-1964 which was published in African Studies Bulletin, X (September 1967), 35-79, compiled by David Brokensha and Samuel I. Kotei. It includes books, periodical articles and government publications. G. M. Pitcher's Bibliography of Ghana, 1957-1959 (1960) which includes pamphlets is confined to publications in the first three years of Ghana's independence.

The problem of official publications has been mitigated by the publication of Ghana: a guide to official publications, 1872-1968 (1969), compiled by Julian Witherell and Sharon Lockwood of the U. S. Library of Congress. Equally important is D. O. Bampoe's A Guide to the official publications of Ghana (Gold Coast), 1600-1966 (1967?), originally completed as a thesis for the Fellowship of the Library Association (Great Britain). Two other valuable general works originally submitted as requirements for the same

Library Fellowship are S. A. Afre's Ashanti and Brong-Ahafo: An annotated bibliography (1967) and E. Y. Amedekey's The Culture of Ghana: A Bibliography (1966).

The Research Library on African Affairs, besides compiling the Ghana National Bibliography, has been publishing useful subject bibliographies. Choice of subject depends chiefly on the availability of bibliographical and library resources and on the permanence of interest. A few notable works in this series are Ghanaian writers and their works (1962); The Akan of Ghana: A selected bibliography (1962); A select bibliography of folklore, legends and tradition of African peoples. 2nd ed. (1964); Dr. W. E. B. Du Bois, 1868-1963; A bibliography (1964); and A select annotated bibliography of Ghana (1965).

Although the Ghana National Bibliography includes theses, primarily those accepted in Ghana, there is urgent need for a more comprehensive bibliography of theses done by Ghanaians everywhere and on any subject and those done by non-Ghanaians on Ghana. J. K. T. Kafe of the Balme Library, University of Ghana, has compiled an annotated bibliography on Ghana covering the period, 1920-1970, but it is limited to works in the English language submitted in American and British Commonwealth universities. Such a limitation is surprising in that Ghana has never had any single bibliography of academic theses. One wishes that Kafe had included non-English language titles submitted in countries other than America and the British Commonwealth countries even if they were not annotated.

Serial publications and works in the vernacular languages have received considerable attention. The chief serial bibliographic publications include List of periodicals in the Balme Library (1961), issued by the Balme Library; Catalogue of Serial publications (1961) and List of periodicals currently received (1964), both issued by the Library of Kumasi University of Science and Technology; and A list of Ghanaian Newspapers and periodicals (1970), compiled by A. N. de Heer, librarian of the Research Library on African Affairs at Accra. Many of the current Ghanaian periodicals are listed in Sub-Saharan Africa: A guide to serials (1970), compiled by the U. S. Library of Congress; so are many Ghanaian newspapers and periodicals covered in Hans Behn's Die Presse in Westafrika (1969) and in Africa: A guide to newspapers and magazines (1970), by Fritz Feuereisen and Ernst Schmacke.

The inclusion of works in the vernacular languages in the Ghana National Bibliography has been a significant feature of that bibliography. The Ghana Bureau of Languages published in 1967 a 161-page work--Bibliography of works in Ghana languages--that included some 1, 200 items classified by the ethnic division, with titles in English and descriptive annotations. This might serve as a model for other African states. Mrs. F. A. Ogunsheye, Professor of Library Studies, University of Ibadan, is engaged in a similar work but limited to those works in the Yoruba language.

Nor should one ignore the role of archives in bibliographical control. Unpublished materials, especially personal letters or papers of natives who have made significant contributions to their country should be deposited with their country's archives; preservation and organization of these materials may be even more challenging than books or serials. Archival management is a comparatively young profession in Africa and archivists generally receive on-the-job training and might go to England for further training. It is incontestably true that they should work cooperatively with librarians since both are concerned with preserving, organizing and retrieving graphic records. The professional knowledge and experience of both should be exchanged between them. Fortunately, this is already happening in Ghana where the director of Library Services is a member of the Permanent Committee on Public Archives and the chief archivist is in turn a member of the Ghana Library Board--a symbiotic arrangement mutually rewarding.

By the Public Archives Ordinance, No. 35 of 1965, public records are periodically transferred to the National Archives of Ghana, from the archives of ministerial departments and other state institutions; so also are the originals of the Acts of Parliament and State Agreement Contracts in accordance with 1960 Act of Parliament and the State Property and Contracts Act of 1960.

Despite the pessimism of Marshall McLuhan about the survival of print in our electronic age, [7] the typographic man will continue to be a vital force in our technologically dependent society. The amount of information disseminated daily is staggering and the power of the printed word is not likely to be diminished for some time to come. Even if the attainment of complete bibliographical control is only a visionary concept, at least "the ideal is an intelligible one. "[8]

How does Ghana compare with other West African countries, such as Sierra Leone and Nigeria? With regard to retrospective works, Ghana is better off than either of those two countries, and Sierra Leone better off than Nigeria. Sierra Leone has Harry Luke's A Bibliography of Sierra Leone (1925)--a 230-page work listing some 1, 103 items covering the period up to 1924. In 1970 another comprehensive bibliography, by G. J. Williams and entitled A Bibliography of Sierra Leone, 1925-1967, was published. It is classified by subject including 3, 049 items in the arts and sciences. Even at her independence in 1960, Nigeria had nothing except the list of references that appeared as an appendix to The Nigeria handbook (1953), and many of these references are now dated and even inaccurate.

John Harris' Books about Nigeria, first published in 1959 was the first real attempt to produce any sort of retrospective work for Nigeria. Limited to works designed for the general reader in

its four previous editions, it includes scholarly works in its present
fifth edition.   It does not attempt to include periodical articles,
pamphlets or other unpublished works such as theses.   However,
Nigeria has Margaret Amosu's Nigerian theses (1965), a comprehensive list not limited by language or geographic area, containing
theses written by Nigerians and non-Nigerians on Nigeria.   A new
edition is in progress.   There are other subject monographic works,
such as J. A. Ombu's Niger Delta Studies, 1927-1967 (1970); B. A.
Oni-Orisan's A Bibliography of Nigerian history (1968); and N. O.
Ita's Bibliography of Nigeria: A survey of anthropological and
linguistic writings from the earliest times to 1966 (1971), A. O.
Ike's Economic development of Nigeria 1950-1964; A bibliography
(1966), and Ike's A list of books, articles and government publications on the economy of Nigeria, published annually since 1953 by
the Nigerian Institute of Social and Economic Research, Ibadan.

        The National Library of Nigeria at Lagos has been turning
out a great number of subject bibliographies and bibliographies of
serial publications.   Ghana, Sierra Leone and Nigeria are all
well covered in West Africa: general, ethnography, sociology,
linguistics (1958) compiled by Ruth Jones of the International African Institute, London.

        The publication of Nigeria's current national bibliography,
Nigerian Publications, weekly since 1953, with quarterly and annual
cumulations, puts Nigeria ahead of any black African state with
regard to current national bibliography.   The Ghana National Bibliography was first published only in 1968, covering works published
in 1965 and 1966, and its time lag of two to three years is rather
too long in the light of the number of works published yearly in
Ghana and on Ghana abroad.

        However, Ghana has the potentialities and the manpower
compared with Nigeria and Sierra Leone to improve its retrospective and current bibliographies more easily than the other two
countries; its librarians need only be financially supported by the
government.   The survey recently conducted by John Harris on professional librarians and the ratio of library books to the population
of Ghana, Nigeria and Sierra Leone shows Ghana to be better off
than the other two countries.

        The striking advance of Sierra Leone since 1961/62 is chiefly
due to the growth of its National Library Service.

        The future of the Ghanaian bibliography rests mainly on the
Ghanaian librarians and bibliographers.   An American or European
librarian or bibliographer working on an African bibliography has
many serious problems to face.   In the first place he may be un-
familiar with the complexities of the local languages and differences
in ethnic distribution, and this is bound to retard his work and
even affect its quality.   Secondly, spellings of family names are so

PROFESSIONAL LIBRARIANS PER CAPITA[9]

| | 1961/2 | | 1967/8 | |
	Number	Ratio	Number	Ratio
Ghana	26	1:257,690	72	1:109,700
Nigeria	44	1:1,227,000	164	1:390,000
Sierra Leone	3	1:727,000	14	1:184,000

NUMBER OF BOOKS PER CAPITA[10]

Ghana	1:12	1:6.75
Nigeria	1:106	1:46
Sierra Leone	1:68	1:6.8

inconsistently used in various bibliographical sources that the bibliographer is left wondering which spelling is right.   The present
writer, although an African, found this the most disturbing problem
in this study.   There are many hyphenated or compound family
names in Ghana, and owing to the lack of standardization of African
names for bibliographical or classificatory purposes, many Western
scholars have not bothered about uniformity in the use of these names
in their works.   Is it De Graft Johnson, J. C.; Johnson, De Graft
J. C.; De Graft-Johnson, J. C., or De Graft, Johnson J. C.?   Is it
Kole, Nene Azzu Mate or Mate-Kole, Nene Azzu?   The availability
of an authoritative biographical directory could save the day; otherwise whichever one the bibliographer chooses, he must make cross
references from the ones not used to the one used, since different
people might look under different entries.   Such idiosyncracies in
genealogical nomenclature are not likely to bother a Ghanaian bibliographer who is familiar with them.

    Here are a few recommendations for the improvement of
Ghana's bibliographical activity which should be well coordinated.
The Book and Newspaper Registration Act should be amended again
and points of confusion clarified.   A unambiguous line should be
drawn between a printer and a publisher and the term book itself
should be clearly defined.   Government departments should also
deposit their publications with the same institutions that receive
depository items from publishers.   The Department of Library
Studies, University of Ghana, should give more bibliographical
training to its students, and the government should encourage librarians with bibliographical interests and reward their achievements.   Efforts should be made to avoid duplication of bibliographical
work, and this could be achieved by having more effective inter-
library cooperation.   The Ghana Library Association, the Balme
Library, The Research Library on African Affairs, the Library of
Kumasi University of Science and Technology, and University College of Cape Coast Library have important roles to play in this.
The production of the two union catalogues in science and technology,

and in the humanities and social sciences is only an auspicious beginning.

Notes

1. Africa '71 (New York: Africana Pub. Corp. , 1971), p. 266.

2. Evelyn J. Evans.   A Tropical library service: The story of
    Ghana's libraries (London: Deutsch, 1964), p. 134.

3. S. I. A. Kotei.   "Some notes on the present state of national
    bibliography in English-speaking Africa, " Africana Library
    J. , II (Winter 1971), p. 13-17.

4. Miles M. Jackson, ed.   Comparative and the international
    librarianship: essays on themes and problems (Westport,
    Conn. :   Greenwood Pub. Corp. , 1970), p. 230.

5. "Establishing an African publishing industry: a study in de-
    colonization, " African Affairs, 68 (1969), p. 139.

6. J. D. Pearson and Ruth Jones, eds.   The Bibliography of
    Africa (London: Cass, 1970), p. 38.

7. Herbert Marshall McLuhan.   The Gutenberg galaxy; The
    making of typographic man (London: Routledge, 1962);
    Understanding media: The extensions of man (London:
    Routledge, 1962).

8. Patrick Wilson.   Two kinds of power: an essay on biblio-
    graphical control (Berkeley: University of California
    Press, 1968), p. 40.

9. John Harris, Patterns of library growth in English-speaking
    West Africa (Legon: Dept. of Library Studies, University
    of Ghana, 1970), p. 6.

10. Ibid. , p. 5.

SCOPE, PURPOSE, AND ARRANGEMENT

This bibliography, comprehensively selective, is designed to complement and supplement two major retrospective bibliographies of Ghana, namely: A. W. Cardinall's A Bibliography of the Gold Coast (1932) and A. F. Johnson's A Bibliography of Ghana, 1930-1961 (1964). But it differs from these works in several ways. Serious efforts are made to include unpublished material such as master's theses or doctoral dissertations, conference papers, research reports, and pamphlets of research value. Entries have full bibliographic data except prices which are very unstable, and could be easily found in trade book or publishers' catalogs. Many of the entries are both descriptively and critically annotated, especially the reference works, and review sources are given for many items. Reference works have longer annotations.

It is limited to material published since 1900, the year during which the British were trying to establish their protectorates over the Ashanti and the Northern Territories, which they finally did in 1901. But some classic works published before 1900, but reprinted since 1900 are included, especially in linguistics. As this work was continued into 1972, the author decided to include a very few relevant works published that year. However, the essential period covered is 1900-1971. It includes, in general, books, periodical articles, theses or dissertations, conference papers and pamphlets, official publications, a select annotated list of newspapers and periodicals published outside Ghana with substantial bibliographic material on Africa, and a directory of major publishers, booksellers, printers and book trade organizations in Ghana. Children's literature generally neglected by previous bibliographers is given full attention here. There is a separate section for Children and Young People's Literature. Appended is a list of major sources consulted that could be useful to anyone who wants to find more information on a specific subject of interest. The entries are classified chiefly by subject with some subdivisions, and are numbered consecutively.

This work is intended for the university student and the scholar. However, there are many works of interest to the general reader. The choice of items was governed principally by such factors as permanence of interest, relevance, availability for personal examination, and authoritativeness of the source. Classification by subject has been difficult, as many works tend to cut across disciplines, especially in the fields of anthropology, religion and sociology. Items listed under one subject may also be appropriately listed under another. The author has tried to avoid

13

repetition of entries as much as possible, unless a work specifically deals with two subjects, e. g. , R. S. Rattray's Religion and art in Ashanti (1927); or if the subjects treated in a work are such that the work is very likely to be very much missed by a user if listed under one subject.   Psychology is given a peripheral treatment, since not much has been written on African psychology, and most existing works on the subject are written from an educational or sociological viewpoint and are thus listed under education or sociology.

Although this work is confined to works in the humanities and social sciences, material on agriculture is included if it deals with Ghana's economic development.   There are also many entries on Africa in general which are considered relevant to Ghana, either listed in the first part of this bibliography (AFRICA) or under the appropriate subject in the classified GHANA sections.   Another distinguishing feature of this bibliography is the indication in GHANA, Section 12, "Literature," of works written by Ghanaians where known.   This would help the user know quickly Ghana's contribution in the field of creative works.

Owing to the scope and nature of this work, the author was not able to examine personally all the items included but had to rely sometimes on authoritative bibliographical sources.   The research is based chiefly on the resources of the University of California Libraries, especially the Santa Barbara campus, and considerable material was obtained from the University of Ghana. Efforts were made to be as representative as possible in the selection of material on each subject.   There was no work consulted that did not contain errors in it, and the author would be glad if any user of this work could report any wrong citations to him for correction in the next edition since the errors in the original bibliographical sources used will be transferred to this.   Part one of this bibliography (AFRICA) is the same as that in the Bibliography of Nigeria in the Humanities and Social Sciences, 1900-71, which was begun and completed simultaneously with this work.

LIST OF ABBREVIATIONS AND FULL TITLES

Adm. Sci. Q.	Administrative Science Quarterly (New York)
Adult Educ.	Adult Education (London)
Adv. Sci.	Advancement of Science (London)
Afr. Act.	L'Afrique Actuelle (Paris)
Afr. Dev.	African Development (London)
Afr. Hist. Stud.	African Historical Studies (Brookline, Mass.)
Afr. Lit. Art.	L'Afrique Littéraire et Artisque; Revue Culturelle sur l'Afrique et le Monde Noir (Dakar, Senegal)
Afr. Music Soc. Newsletter	African Music Society Newsletter (Johannesburg)
Afr. Rev.	African Review (Accra)
Afr. Stud.	African Studies (Johannesburg)
Afr. Stud. Bull.	African Studies Bulletin (Boston)
Afr. Stud. Rev.	African Studies Review (East Lansing, Mich.)
Afr. Urban Notes	African Urban Notes (East Lansing, Mich.)
Africa Q	Africa Quarterly (New Delhi)
Africana Library J.	Africana Library Journal (New York)
Afro-Asian Econ. Rev.	Afro-Asian Economic Review (Cairo)
Afro-Asian Theatre Bull.	Afro-Asian Theatre Bulletin (Lawrence, Kansas)
ALA Bull.	The American Library Association Bulletin (Chicago)
Amer. Anthrop.	American Anthropologist (Washington, D.C.)
Amer. Arch.	American Archivist (Washington, D.C.)
Amer. Bar. Assoc. J.	American Bar Association Journal (Chicago)
Amer. Bk. Coll.	American Book Collector (Chicago)
Amer. Econ. Rev.	American Economic Review (Providence, R.I.)
Amer. Hist. Rev.	American Historical Review (Washington, D.C.)
Amer. J. Comp. Law	American Journal of Comparative Law (Ann Arbor, Mich.)
Amer. J. Econ. Soc.	American Journal of Economics and Sociology (New York)
Amer. J. Int. Law	American Journal of International Law (Washington, D.C.)
Amer. J. Soc.	American Journal of Sociology (Chicago)

Amer. Lit.	American Literature (Durham, N. C.)
Amer. Pol. Sci. Rev.	American Political Science Review (Washington, D. C.)
Amer. Psych.	American Psychologist (Washington, D. C.)
Amer. Scholar	American Scholar (Washington, D. C.)
Amer. Soc. Rev.	American Sociological Review (Washington, D. C.)
Ann. Amer. Acad. Pol. Soc. Sci.	Annals of the American Academy of Political and Social Science (Philadelphia)
Ann. Assoc. Amer. Geogr.	Annals of the Association of American Geographers (Lawrence, Kansas)
Ann. Fac. Droit. Istanbul.	Annales de la Faculté de Droit d'Istanbul (Istanbul)
Ann. N. Y. Acad. Sci.	Annals of the New York Academy of Sciences (New York)
Arch. Rev.	Architectural Review (London)
Asian Afr. Stud.	Asian and African Studies (Jerusalem)
Assoc. Bar City N. Y. Rec.	Association Bar City New York Record (New York)
Brit. J. Educ. Psych.	British Journal of Educational Psychology (London)
Brit. J. Educ. Stud.	British Journal of Educational Studies (London)
Brit. J. Psychol.	British Journal of Psychology (Cambridge)
Brit. J. Soc.	British Journal of Sociology (London)
Bull. Afr. Stud. Canada	Bulletin of African Studies in Canada (Edmonton, Alta.)
Bull. Assoc. Afr. Lit. Eng.	Bulletin of the Association for African Literature in English (Freetown, Sierra Leone)
Bull. Doc. Bibliog.	Bulletin de Documentation Bibliographique (Montrouge, France)
Bull. Ghana Geogr. Assoc.	Bulletin of the Ghana Geographical Association (Accra)
Bull. IFAN	Bulletin d'Institut Français d'Afrique Noire (Dakar, Senegal)
Bull. Inst. Afr. Stud.	Bulletin of the Institute of African Studies (Legon)
Bull. Inst. Hist. Res.	Bulletin of the Institute of Historical Research (London)
Bull. Sch. Orient. Afr. Stud.	Bulletin of School of Oriental and African Studies (London)
Bull. Soc. Afr. Church Hist.	Bulletin of the Society for African Church History (Nsukka, Nigeria)
Bus. Educ. World	Business Education World (New York)

Cahiers Econ. Soc.	Cahiers Economiques et Sociaux (Lovanium, Zaire)
Cahiers Etud. Afr.	Cahiers d'Etudes Africaines (Paris)
Canadian Geogr. J.	Canadian Geographical Journal (Ottawa)
Canadian J. Afr. Stud.	Canadian Journal of African Studies (Montreal)
Canadian Library J.	Canadian Library Journal (Ottawa)
Canadian Psych. J.	Canadian Psychiatric Journal (Ottawa)
Christian Cent.	Christian Century (Chicago)
Coll. & Res. Lib.	College and Research Libraries (Chicago)
Coll. Univ.	College and University (Wash., D.C.)
Colonial Rev.	Colonial Review (London)
Comm. Dev. J.	Community Development Journal (Lon.)
Comm. Emp. Rev.	Commonwealth and Empire Review (London)
Community Dev. Bull.	Community Development Bulletin (London)
Comp. Dr.	Comparative Drama (Kalamazoo, Mich.)
Comp. Educ. Rev.	Comparative Education Review (Madison, Wis.)
Comp. Pol.	Comparative Politics (Chicago)
Comp. Stud. Soc. Hist.	Comparative Studies in Society and History (London)
Cult. Events Afr.	Cultural Events in Africa (London)
Curr. Dig. Soviet Pr.	Current Digest of the Soviet Press (Columbus, Ohio)
Current Hist.	Current History (New York)
Dev. Civil.	Développement et Civilisations (Paris)
East Afr. J. Rural Dev.	East African Journal of Rural Development (Kampala)
Econ. Bull. Afr.	Economic Bulletin for Africa (Addis Ababa)
Econ. Bull. Ghana	Economic Bulletin of Ghana (Legon)
Econ. Dev. Cult. Change	Economic Development and Cultural Change (Chicago)
Econ. Geogr.	Economic Geography (Worcester, Mass.)
Econ. Hist. Rev.	Economic History Review (Herts., England)
Econ. Journal	Economic Journal (Cambridge, England)
Edinburgh Rev.	Edinburgh Review (Edinburgh)
Edit. Res. Rpts.	Editorial Research Reports (Washington, D.C.)
Educ. Leadership	Educational Leadership (Washington, D.C.)
Educ. Panorama	Educational Panorama (Washington, D.C.)

English Hist. Rev.	English Historical Review (London)
English Stud. Afr.	English Studies in Africa (Johannes-burg)
Ethnog-Archäol. Z.	Ethnographische-Archäologische Zeitschrift (Leipzig)
F. A. O. Rev.	F. A. O. Review (Rome)
Food Res. Inst. Stud.	Food Research Institute Studies in Agricultural Economics, Trade and Development (Stanford, Cal.)
Foreign Affairs Rpts.	Foreign Affairs Reports (New Delhi)
Foreign Comm. Wkly.	Foreign Commerce Weekly (Washington, D. C.)
FRI Res. Bull.	FRI Research Bulletin (Accra)
Fund. Educ.	Fundamental Education (Paris)
Geo. Rund.	Geologische Rundschau (Stuttgart, Germany)
Geogr. J.	Geographical Journal (London)
Geogr. Magazine	Geographical Magazine (London)
Geogr. Rev.	Geographical Review (New York)
Geogr. Rev. India	Geographical Review of India (Calcutta)
Ghana Bull. Theol.	Ghana Bulletin of Theology (Legon)
Ghana J. Agr. Sci.	Ghana Journal of Agricultural Science (Accra)
Ghana J. Child Dev.	Ghana Journal of Child Development (Legon)
Ghana J. Education	Ghana Journal of Education (Accra)
Ghana J. Sci.	Ghana Journal of Science (Accra)
Ghana J. Soc.	Ghana Journal of Sociology (Legon)
Ghana Med. J.	Ghana Medical Journal (Accra)
Ghana Teachers' J.	Ghana Teachers' Journal (Accra)
Ghana Library J.	Ghana Library Journal (Accra)
Gold Coast Rev.	Gold Coast Review (Accra)
Gold Coast Teachers' J.	Gold Coast Teachers' Journal (Accra)
Govt. Opp.	Government and Opposition (London)
Harvard Educ. Rev.	Harvard Educational Review (Cambridge, Mass.)
Howard Law J.	Howard Law Journal (Washington, D. C.)
Illus. Lond. News	Illustrated London News (London)
Industrial and Labor Rel. Rev.	Industrial and Labor Relations Review (Ithaca, N. Y.)
Inst. Int. Educ. News Bull.	Institute of International Education News Bulletin (New York)

Inst. Brit. Geogr. Trans.	Institute of British Geographers Transactions (London)
Int. Affairs	International Affairs (London & Moscow)
Int. Comm. Jurists Bull.	International Commission of Jurists Bulletin (Geneva)
Int. Commerce	International Commerce (Washington, D. C.)
Int. Comp. Law Q.	International and Comparative Law Quarterly (London)
Int. Folk Music Council J.	International Folk Music Council Journal (Cambridge, England)
Int. J. Adult Youth Educ.	International Journal of Adult and Youth Education (Paris)
Int. J. Amer. Ling.	International Journal of American Linguistics (Baltimore)
Int. J. Comp. Soc.	International Journal of Comparative Sociology (Toronto)
Int. J. Psych.	International Journal of Psychology (Paris)
Int. J. Soc. Psychiatry	International Journal of Social Psychiatry (London)
Int. Labour Rev.	International Labour Review (Geneva)
Int. Rev.	Interracial Review (New York)
Int. Rev. Adm. Sci.	International Review of Administrative Sciences (Brussels)
Int. Rev. Missions	International Review of Missions (London)
Int. Soc. Sci. Bull.	International Social Science Bulletin (Paris)
Int. Theatre Inf.	International Theatre Informations
Inter-African Labour Inst. Bull.	Inter-African Labour Institute Bulletin (London)
Irish Ecc. Rec.	Irish Ecclesiastical Record (Dublin)
J. Adm. Overseas	Journal of Administration Overseas (London)
J. Afr. Adm.	Journal of African Administration (London)
J. Afr. Hist.	Journal of African History (London)
J. Afr. Lang.	Journal of African Languages (London)
J. Afr. Law	Journal of African Law (London)
J. Afr. Soc.	Journal of African Society (London)
J. Amer. Stat. Assoc.	Journal of the American Statistical Association (Washington, D. C.)
J. Asian Afr. Stud.	Journal of Asian and African Studies (Leyden)
J. Asian Stud.	Journal of Asian Studies (Coral Gables, Fla.)
J. Business Law	Journal of Business Law (London)
J. Commonwealth Pol. Stud.	Journal of Commonwealth Political Studies (Leicester, England)

J. Crim. Law	Journal of Criminal Law, Criminology and Police Science (Baltimore)
J. Dev. Areas	Journal of Developing Areas (Macomb, Ill.)
J. Dev. Stud.	Journal of Development Studies (London)
J. Doc.	Journal of Documentation (London)
J. Econ. Hist.	Journal of Economic History (New York)
J. Educ. Libr.	Journal of Education for Librarianship (Albany, N. Y.)
J. Farm Econ.	Journal of Farm Economics (Lexington, Kentucky)
J. Folklore Inst.	Journal of Folklore Institute (The Hague)
J. Gen. Educ.	Journal of General Education (University Park, Pennsylvania)
J. Higher Educ.	Journal of Higher Education (Columbus, Ohio)
J. Hist. Soc. Nigeria	Journal of the Historical Society of Nigeria (Ibadan)
J. Home Econ.	Journal of Home Economics (Washington, D. C.)
J. Hum. Rel.	Journal of Human Relations (Wilberforce, Ohio)
J. Int. Affairs	Journal of International Affairs (New York)
J. Kumasi Coll. Tech.	Journal of Kumasi College of Technology (Kumasi, Ghana)
J. Libr.	Journal of Librarianship (London)
J. Local Adm. Overseas	Journal of Local Administration Overseas (London)
J. Management Stud.	Journal of Management Studies (Achimota, Ghana)
J. Marketing	Journal of Marketing (Chicago)
J. Mental Sci.	Journal of Mental Science (London)
J. Mod. Afr. Stud.	Journal of Modern African Studies (Cambridge, England)
J. Negro Educ.	Journal of Negro Education (Washington, D. C.)
J. Negro Hist.	Journal of Negro History (Washington, D. C.)
J. New Afr. Lit. Arts	Journal of the New African Literature and the Arts (Stanford, Cal.)
J. Nursing Educ.	Journal of Nursing Education (New York)
J. Personality	Journal of Personality (Durham, N. C.)
J. Pol. Econ.	Journal of Political Economy (Chicago)
J. Res. Crime Delinq.	Journal of Research in Crime and Delinquency (Davis, Cal.)
J. Roy. Afr. Soc.	Journal of the Royal African Society (London)

J. Roy. Anthrop. Inst.	Journal of the Royal Anthropological Institute (London)
J. Soc. Africanistes	Journal de la Société des Africanistes (Paris)
J. Soc. Issues	Journal of Social Issues (Ann Arbor, Mich.)
J. Soc. Comp. Leg.	Journal of the Society of Comparative Legislation
J. Soc. Psych.	Journal of Social Psychology (Provincetown, Mass.)
J. Soc. Pub. Teachers Law	Journal of the Society of Public Teachers of Law (London)
J. Trop. Geogr.	Journal of Tropical Geography (Singapore)
J. W. Afr. Sci. Assoc.	Journal of the West African Science Association (Ibadan, Nigeria)
J. West Afr. Lang.	Journal of West African Languages (London)
Jr. Lib.	Junior Libraries (New York)
L. C. Inf. Bull.	Library of Congress Information Bulletin (Washington, D. C.)
Labor Law J.	Labor Law Journal (Chicago)
Land Econ.	Land Economics (Madison, Wis.)
Law Cont. Problems	Law and Contemporary Problems (Durham, N. C.)
Law Q. Rev.	Law Quarterly Review (London)
Legon J. Agric.	Legon Journal of Agriculture (Legon)
Libn. & Bk. World	Librarian and Book World (New York)
Library Assoc. Rec.	Library Association Record (London)
Library J.	Library Journal (New York)
Library Mat. Afr.	Library Materials on Africa (London)
Library Q.	Library Quarterly (Chicago)
Library Rev.	Library Review (Glasgow)
Makarere J.	Makerere Journal (Makerere, Uganda)
Malayan Law Rev.	Malayan Law Review (Singapore)
Malayan Library J.	Malayan Library Journal (Kuala Lumpur)
Mém. IFAN	Mémoirs de l'Institut Français d'Afrique Noire (Dakar, Senegal)
Merrill-Palmer Q. Beh. Dev.	Merrill-Palmer Quarterly of Behavior and Development (Detroit)
Mitt. Inst. Orient.	Mitteilungen des Institut für Orientforschung (Berlin)
Mod. Law Rev.	Modern Law Review (London)
Music Jl.	Music Journal (New York)
N. Y. Rev. Bks.	New York Review of Books (New York)

N. Y. Times Bk. Rev.	New York Times Book Review (New York)
N. Y. Times Magazine	New York Times Magazine (New York)
Nat. Hist.	Natural History (New York)
Nat. Rev.	National Review (New York)
Negro Hist. Bull.	Negro History Bulletin (Washington, D. C.)
Nigerian Geogr. J.	Nigerian Geographical Journal (Ibadan)
Nigerian J. Econ. Soc. Stud.	Nigerian Journal of Economic and Social Studies (Ibadan)
Oil and Gas J.	Oil and Gas Journal (Tulsa, Okla.)
Ont. Library Rev.	Ontario Library Review (Toronto, Canada)
Oriental Geogr.	Oriental Geographer (Dacca, Pakistan)
Oversea Educ.	Oversea Education (London)
Oversea Q.	Oversea Quarterly (London)
Oxford Econ. Papers	Oxford Economic Papers (Oxford)
Oxford Univ. Inst. Econ. Stat. Bull.	Oxford University Institute of Economics and Statistics Bulletin (Oxford)
Parl. Affairs	Parliamentary Affairs (London)
Penn. Sch. J.	Pennsylvania School Journal (Harrisburg, Penn.)
Poetry Rev.	Poetry Review (London)
Political Q.	Political Quarterly (London)
Pol. Sci. Q.	Political Science Quarterly (New York)
Pop. Stud.	Population Studies (London)
Public Opinion Q.	Public Opinion Quarterly (New York)
Rechts. Weekblad	Rechtskundig Weekblad (Antwerp, Belgium)
Ref. Presb. World	Reformed and Presbyterian World (Geneva)
Ref. Q.	Reference Quarterly
Renaissance & Mod. Stud.	Renaissance and Modern Studies (Nottingham)
Research Rev.	Research Review (Legon)
Rev. Econ. Stat.	Review of Economics and Statistics (Cambridge, Mass.)
Rev. Econ. Stud.	Review of Economic Studies (Edinburgh)
Rev. Estud. Musicales	Revista de Estudios Musicales (Mendoza, Argentina)
Rev. Litt. Comp.	Revue de Littérature Comparée (Paris)
Rev. For. Hist. a'Outre-Mer.	Revue Française d'Histoire d'Outre-Mer (Paris)
Rev. Fr. Sci. Pol.	Revue Française de Science Politique (Paris)

Rev. Ghana Law	Review of Ghana Law (Accra)
Rev. Int. Educ. Adult. Jeunesse	Revue Internationale de l'Education des Adultes et de la Jeunesse (Paris)
Rev. Jur. Pol.	Revue Juridique et Politique (Paris)
Rev. Psych. Peuples	Revue de Psychologie des Peuples (Le Havre)
St. Louis Univ. Law J.	St. Louis University Law Journal (St. Louis, Mo.)
Sat. Rev.	Saturday Review (New York)
Sci. Amer.	Scientific American (New York)
Scottish Geogr. Mag.	Scottish Geographical Magazine (Edinburgh)
Sierra Leone Bull. Rel.	Sierra Leone Bulletin of Religion (Freetown)
Sierra Leone Stud.	Sierra Leone Studies (Freetown)
Soc. Educ.	Social Education (Washington, D.C.)
Soc. Stud.	Social Studies (Brooklawn, N.J.)
Sociol. Educ.	Sociology of Education (Washington, D.C.)
Solicitors' J.	Solicitors' Journal (London)
Soundings	Soundings; Collections of the University Library (Santa Barbara, Cal.)
South Afr. Arch. Bull.	South African Archaeological Bulletin (Claremont, Cape Town)
South Afr. J. Econ.	South African Journal of Economics (Johannesburg)
Southwestern J. Anthrop.	Southwestern Journal of Anthropology (Albuquerque, N.M.)
Statistical & Econ. Rev.	Statistical and Economic Review (London)
TLS	Times Literary Supplement (London)
Teacher Educ.	Teacher Education (London)
Teacher Educ. New Countries	Teacher Education in New Countries (London)
Teachers Coll. Rec.	Teachers College Record (New York)
Times Educ. Supp.	Times Educational Supplement (London)
Trans. Gold Coast & Togoland Hist. Soc.	Transactions of the Gold Coast and Togoland Historical Society (Accra)
Trans. Hist. Soc. Ghana	Transactions of the Historical Society of Ghana (Legon)
Trans. Inst. Brit. Geogr.	Transactions of the Institute of British Geographers (London)
Trans. N.Y. Acad. Sci.	Transactions of the New York Academy of Sciences (New York)
Trans. Royal Hist. Soc.	Transactions of the Royal Historical Society (London)

UCLA Law Rev.	University of California Los Angeles Law Review (Los Angeles)
UNESCO Bull. Lib.	UNESCO Bulletin for Libraries (Paris)
U. S. Dept. State Bull.	U. S. Department of State Bulletin (Washington, D. C.)
Univ. Ghana Law J.	University of Ghana Law Journal (Legon)
Univ. Ghana Reporter	University of Ghana Reporter (Legon)
Univ. Kansas Law Rev.	University of Kansas Law Review (Lawrence)
Univ. Quarterly	Universities Quarterly (London)
Univ. Rev.	Universities Review (Bristol)
Ver. Recht in Ubersee	Verfassung und Recht in Ubersee (Hamburg)
W. Afr. Arch. Newsletter	West African Archaeological Newsletter (Ibadan, Nigeria)
W. Afr. J. Archaeol.	West African Journal of Archaeology (Ibadan, Nigeria)
W. Afr. J. Educ.	West African Journal of Education (Ibadan, Nigeria)
W. Afr. Lib.	West African Libraries (Ibadan, Nigeria)
W. Afr. Rel.	West African Religion (Nsukka, Nigeria)
W. Afr. Rev.	West African Review (London)
WALA News	The West African Library Association News (Ibadan, Nigeria)
Western Pol. Q.	Western Political Quarterly (Salt Lake City, Utah)
Wis. Law Rev.	Wisconsin Law Review (Madison)
World Year Bk. Educ.	World Year Book of Education (New York)
Wilson Lib. Bull.	Wilson Library Bulletin (New York)
Yale Law J.	Yale Law Journal (New Haven, Conn.)

AFRICA

(A) REFERENCE WORKS

(1) DICTIONARIES, DIRECTORIES, HANDBOOKS, ETC.

1 Africa Contemporary record: annual survey and documents,
1968/69- . Edited by Colin Legum and John Drysdale.
London: Africa Research Limited, 1969- . 1970-71 ed.
1, 100 p.
    Intended for anyone interested in contemporary African
affairs and edited by two well-known British journalists
assisted by the staff of the Africa Research Bulletin. Arrangement of each issue is essentially the same. In three parts:
Part 1 consists of topical essays on current issues in various
African countries, by different authorities, as well as annual
surveys of the relations between Africa and foreign powers by
the editors and other experts. Part 2: country by country
review of events of the year. Part 3: Articles and documents on international relations, including foreign policy
statements by different African states. Extensive maps, subject and name indexes, lacking in the 1968/69 edition.
    Rev: Africana Library J., II (Spring 1971), 17-18.

2 Africa '71: a reference volume on the African continent. Compiled and edited by the Editorial Staff of Jeune Afrique. New
York: Africana Publishing Corp., 1971. 440 p.
    An annual reference work first published in 1968. The
first part gives a general survey of Africa--political, economic, linguistic, sociological and geographical. The second
part comprises topical essays by informed writers. The
third section deals with Africa's relations with the developed
countries. The fourth part consists of country by country
analysis of recent political events, economic development,
social and linguistic situation, with detailed maps, extensive
tables and charts. An authoritative encyclopedia intended for
the student of African affairs and the teacher, and a valuable
reference tool in libraries, schools, universities and corporations.

3   African-American Institute. African colleges and universities:
     a digest of information. New York: African-American Insti-
     tute, 1970. 123 p.
          Published in collaboration with the Association of African
     Universities and the Agency for International Development, it
     provides much needed information on entrance and degree re-
     quirements, fields of study and areas of specialization in
     various African institutions of higher learning.
          Rev: Africana Library J., II (Summer 1971), 14.

4   Alman, Miriam, ed. Periodicals published in Africa: a list
     and a union list. London: Crosby Lockwood (forthcoming).

5   Balandier, Georges et J. Maquet. Dictionnaire des civilisations
     africaines. Paris: F. Hazan, 1968. 448 p.
          Deals with various aspects of African life, analyzing cul-
     tural characteristics of different ethnic groups. Beautifully
     illustrated.

6   Benveniste, Guy and William E. Moran. Handbook of African
     economic development. New York: Praeger for the Stanford
     Research Institute, 1962. 178 p. (Books that matter)
          "The principal external factors considered are government
     assistance in men and money, foreign investment, and trade.
     An interrelated improvement of all four required of African
     development is to be assisted effectively" (Preface). Appendix
     A: International economic cooperation in Africa. Appendix B:
     Selected African hydro-electric and mineral development pro-
     jects being studied or initiated.

7   Bradbury, R. E. Directory of African studies in United King-
     dom universities. Birmingham: African Studies Association
     of the United Kingdom, 1969. 73 p.
          Entries for the 38 universities and university colleges
     listed are alphabetical except for the universities of Hull,
     St. Andrews, Strathclyde listed separately on pp. 64-65.
     Only a general guide to the courses and programs relating to
     African studies recently or currently available at the univer-
     sities, and does not provide comprehensive information on
     entrance requirements better obtainable from the applicable
     institutions themselves. Emphasis is on the humanities and
     social sciences. Appendix I: Newly appointed staff members.
     Appendix II: Societies, institutes and organizations on Africa.
     Appendix III: Africanists with non-university addresses. In-
     dex of discipline represented in staff lists, and abbreviations
     to names of countries.

8   Dictionary of African biography. 1st ed. London: Melrose
     Press, 1970- . 340 p. Annual.
          Sketchy biographical data arranged alphabetically by the
     biographee. Criteria for inclusion, which accord with the
     principles of the charter of the Organization of African Unity,

appear somewhat arbitrary. Many "persons of contemporary achievement" are omitted, e.g., Dr. Nnamdi Azikiwe, a noted Nigerian politician and former President of Nigeria and Wole Soyinka, the best known African playwright, while much less known figures find their way into the dictionary. Includes the text of the charter of the Organization of African Unity, but excludes any reference to South Africa, Rhodesia and Portuguese colonies. The compiler and Hon. General Editor, Dr. Ernest Kay, is editor and publisher of London, as well as the General Editor of the Dictionary of International Biography.
> Rev: Africana Library J., II (Spring 1971), 21.

9 Duignan, Peter. Handbook of American resources for African Studies. Stanford, Calif.: Hoover Institution, Stanford University, 1967. 218 p. (Hoover Institution bibliographical series, No. 29)
> Describes the African resources of 95 library and manuscript collections, 108 church and missionary libraries and archives; 95 art and ethnographic collections, and 4 business archives.
> Rev: Amer. Arch., XXXI (Jan. 1968), 69-70. Library Q., XXXVII (Oct. 1967), 397-9.

10 Feuereisen, Fritz and Ernst Schmacke, eds. Africa: a guide to newspapers and magazines. New York: Africana Publishing Corp., 1970. 251 p.
> The most up-to-date directory of African newspapers and magazines arranged in a chart form by country. Data given include title of the newspaper or magazine, political orientation, address, circulation, language of publication, frequency, readership, etc. Title and geographic indexes. Highly recommended.

11 "Government printers in Africa: a directory (Part I: English Speaking nations)," Africana Library J., I (Spring 1970), 16.
> Government printers of some 18 countries, grouped alphabetically by country with addresses.

12 Herdeck, Donald E. and R. Alain Everts. African authors: A bibliographical companion to black African writing, 1550-1971. Rockville, Md.: Black Orpheus Press, 1972. 430 p. (Dimensions of the black intellectual experience.)
> Provides biographical and bibliographical information on writers in European and African languages. Includes black writers of South Africa, detailed cross references by country and linguistic groups. Dr. Herdeck, former lecturer in the African Studies and Research Program at Howard University, teaches at Georgetown University. Everts is a specialist in South African literature.

13 Kitchen, Helen, ed. A Handbook of African Affairs. New York: Praeger for the African-American Institute, 1964. 311 p.

In four parts: I: For each independent country, it gives
the latest, political, economic, demographic, fiscal and
linguistic information. II: Armies, police and other security
forces, by country. III: The Organization of African Unity.
IV: Critical essays by Africans on contemporary African
creative writing and a chart of African universities.
Rev: N. Y. Times Bk. Rev., LXX (Feb, 7, 1965), 41.
TLS (Feb. 11, 1965), 113.

14 Luttwak, Edward. Coup d'état: a practical handbook. London:
Penguin Press, 1968. 209 p.
Discusses various methods of toppling governments and the
appropriate situations for doing so, with practical examples
from African, Latin American and Asian states.
Rev: N. Y. Rev. Bks, XIII (Aug. 21, 1969), 12-15.
West Africa, No. 2689 (Dec. 14, 1968), 1471-2.

15 Matthews, Sharlynn E. Abbreviations for use in African
studies: a preliminary guide. New York: Negro Universities Press, 1969. 19 p. Bibliog. (African Bibliographic
Center. Special bibliographic series, v. 4, no. 2.) Reprint of the 1966 edition.

16 Melady, Thomas Patrick. Profiles of African leaders. New
York: Macmillan, 1961. 186 p.
The leaders described: Haile Selassie of Ethiopia; William
Tubman of Liberia; Leopold Senghor of Senegal; Sekou Touré
of Guinea; Felix Houphouet-Boigny of the Ivory Coast; Kwame
Nkrumah of Ghana; Abubakar Balewa of Nigeria; Tom Mboya
of Kenya and Julius Nyerere of Tanganyika (Tanzania). In-
cludes quotations from their speeches illustrative of their
positions on important issues.
Rev: N. Y. Times Bk. Rev. (Feb. 26, 1961), 3+.

17 Panther House Ltd. Black list: the concise reference guide
to publications and broadcasting media of black America,
Africa and the Caribbean. New York: Panther House Ltd.,
1970. 289 p.
In two sections. I: Afro-American section. Lists separately, black newspapers, periodicals, broadcasting stations,
colleges and universities, publishers, book clubs, book stores,
literary agents, etc. with their addresses, names of editors
and other relevant data where applicable. II: International
Section, dealing with Africa and the Caribbean. Material included here is mostly similar to that in Section I, but contains
in addition foreign embassies and their addresses and UN
representatives grouped alphabetically by country. No index.
It would have been more useful to subdivide clearly the entries
in sections by country, with the name of the country preceding
the items rather then put the country at the end of the entry;
thus making it confusing and retarding quick reference.

18 Pearcy, George Etzel and Elvyn A. Stoneman. A Handbook of
    new nations. Cartography by Frank J. Ford and Clare Ford.
    New York: Crowell, 1968. 327 p.
        With an excellent introductory essay, the new nations are
    discussed in separate chapters arranged in chronological order
    by the date of independence. Topics examined include history
    of the country, physical features, population, languages, re-
    ligions, education, politics and economy.
        Rev: Library J., XCIII (March 15, 1968), 1125. National
    Rev., XX (June 4, 1968), 563.

19 "Publishers in Africa: a select directory, " Africana Library J.,
    I (Summer 1970), 11-16. Supplement in I (Winter 1970), 33-
    4.
        "Aims to provide a highly selective check list of the more
    significant publishers in Africa South of the Sahara. They are
    the publishers producing a fairly regular book program, from
    whom catalogues or listings of available titles can usually be
    obtained on request. " Grouped alphabetically by country
    with addresses, including research institutes, university book
    stores known to distribute books for their university or insti-
    tute, and African offices of major British publishers that pro-
    duce books occasionally under a separate imprint for local
    consumption. Other British and U.S. distributors are indi-
    cated when known. Excludes national library boards, archives
    and government printers.

20 Roe, John. SCOLMA directory of libraries and special collec-
    tions on Africa. 3rd ed. London: Crosby Lockwood (forth-
    coming). 1st ed. 1963.
        2nd ed. 1967 by Robert L. Collison, with 160 entries for
    libraries and special collections in the British Isles, grouped
    by town, A-Z, and indicating address, hours open, publications,
    availability of items, etc. SCOLMA is the Standing Conference
    on Library Materials on Africa.

21 Segal, Ronald. Political Africa: a who's who of personalities
    and parties. London: Stevens, 1961. 475 p.
        Assesses the importance of 400 African leaders in Section
    I, arranged alphabetically by name and describes more than
    100 political parties of various countries in Section II, arranged
    alphabetically by country with cross references from each
    country to the relevant names in Section I. Includes useful
    information, at the beginning of each country section, on area
    and population. Up-dated by Sidney Taylor's The New Africans:
    a guide to the contemporary history of emergent Africa and
    its leaders (1967). No bibliography or index.
        Rev: J. Afr. Hist., III (1962), 168-9. Library J.,
    LXXXVI (Dec. 15, 1961), 4279.

22 Seidenspinner, Gundolf. Museums in Africa: a directory.
    New York: Africana Publishing Corp., 1970. 594 p.

Published in association with the German Africa Society,
it surveys 506 museums established or being established in
49 countries, noting gardens and collections of particular
interest in Africa. In two parts. I: The directory itself
indicating address, administrator in charge; hours of work;
admission fee, type of museum, number of exhibits, publications, etc. II: Appendix in which the museums are classified by subject and type. A key-word index.

23   Taubert, Sigfred, ed. African book trade directory 1971.
      Munich: Verlag Dokumentation, 1971. 319 p.
         The first comprehensive book trade directory for the
      African continent, the Canary Islands and Mauritius published
      as a result of the UNESCO "Meeting of Experts on Book De-
      velopment in Africa" held in Ghana in 1963. Booksellers
      and publishers are listed separately by country and then by
      city with their addresses, which are sometimes incomplete.
      Includes printers, statistical data on each country's area,
      population, book production, book trade organizations with
      their addresses. City index.
         Rev: Africana Library J., II (Summer 1971), 13.

24   Taylor, Sidney, ed. The New Africans: a guide to the con-
      temporary history of emergent Africa and its leaders. New
      York: Putnam, 1967. 504 p.
         A well-produced reference work with data up to 1966 con-
      taining about 600 biographies of African leaders in 33 countries,
      arranged alphabetically by country. Updates Ronald Segal's
      Political Africa: a who's who of personalities and parties
      (1961).
         Rev: Coll. & Res. Lib., XXIX (Jan. 1968), 72. Wilson
      Lib. Bull., XLII (Dec. 1967), 426.

25   United Nations. Economic Commission for Africa. Directory
      of Government printers and prominent bookshops in the African
      region. Addis Ababa, Ethiopia, 1970. 48 p. (E/CN.14/Lib. /
      Ser. D. 1.)

26   United Nations Educational, Scientific and Cultural Organiza-
      tion. Secretariat. Social Scientists specializing in African
      studies: a directory. Africanistes spécialistes de sciences
      sociales repertoire. The Hague: Mouton, 1963. 375 p.
      (Monde d'outre mer passé et présent. 4 sér. 5. Bibliogra-
      phies et instruments de travail.)
         A biographical directory of 2,072 social scientists from
      Africa and other countries, specializing in African studies.
      Data given include career, specialty, past and present activity,
      membership of learned societies, publications and postal
      address. The term "social science" is here widely inter-
      preted; Text in English and French; Geographic and subject
      specialty indexes.

(2) BIBLIOGRAPHY

GENERAL

27 Africa Institute of the Academy of Sciences, Moscow. List of
    books, pamphlets and articles on Africa published in the
    U.S.S.R., 1963- . Moscow, 1963- .
        A series publication arranged by subject in the first part
    and by geographical area in the second part. Material is
    listed in Russian followed by English and French translations,
    and includes also book reviews, translations and works in
    non-Russian languages. The 1969 issue in 2 volumes, 163 p.,
    and 199 p. available on exchange, covers material published
    in the Soviet Union on Africa during the period, July-Dec.
    1966.

28 The African Bibliographic Center. A Current bibliography on
    African Affairs. New York: Greenwood Periodicals, Inc.,
    1963- . Monthly.
        "Aimed primarily at assisting you in keeping abreast in
    the field of African studies. Publications listed are generally
    within a three year period with the emphasis on the most cur-
    rent." (Introduction, June 1965.) Grouped into three major
    parts: I. Features, including book reviews, forthcoming
    books, bibliographical essays. II. General subject section.
    III. Geographical section. Author index. Includes docu-
    ments published by governments and international organizations,
    and original bibliographies.

29 African encounter: a selected bibliography of books, films and
    other materials for promoting an understanding of Africa
    among young adults. With a foreword by Mennen Williams.
    Chicago: American Library Association, 1963.   69 p.
        The entries evaluatively annotated are arranged by author
    under broad topics. Recreational and informational books,
    fiction and non-fiction, are included. Listed at the end are
    the organizations dealing with Africa; organizations with
    Africa in their programs and African embassies. Author and
    title index.

30 American Universities Field Staff. A Select bibliography: Asia,
    Africa, Eastern Europe, Latin America. New York, 1960.
    534 p.
        Over 7,000 items, many of them briefly annotated, designed
    for the American college student and the general reader, ar-
    ranged in regional sections, with subdivisions by country and
    then by subject for major regions. Symbols are used for
    rating. Author and title indexes. The chapter on Africa com-
    piled by Professor L. Gray Gowan of Columbia University and
    Edwin S. Munger of the American Universities Field Staff.

31 Besterman, Theodore. A World bibliography of bibliographies
    and bibliographical catalogues, calendars, abstracts, digests,
    indexes and the like. 4th ed. rev. enl. Geneva: Societas
    Bibliographica, 1965-66. 5 vols. 1st ed. 1939/40 (2 v.)
    3rd ed. 1955-66 (4 v.)
        Alphabetical subject listing of over 117, 000 separately
    collated volumes of bibliographies in more than 40 languages.
    The unannotated entries of this edition "this time really the
    last" (Preface), are arranged under more than 16, 000 head-
    ings. Excludes general library catalogues, but includes
    patent abridgements and lists of manuscripts. It is rather
    weak on items in Oriental and Slavic languages; location of
    material is often slowed down by its use of forenames be-
    fore surnames (all in caps) and it does not always give
    names of publishers, only place of publication. Author, edi-
    tor, etc. anonymous title index.
        Rev: (3rd ed.) J. Doc. , XII (March 1956), 44-6.

32 Bibliographic index; a cumulative bibliography of bibliographies,
    1937- . New York, H. W. Wilson, 1938- .
        Alphabetical subject list of both separately published bib-
    liographies and those included in books and periodicals in
    various foreign languages. Issued quarterly with cumulative
    annual and multi-annual volumes.

33 Bibliothèque du Musée de l'Homme, Paris. Catalogue systé-
    matique de la Section Afrique. Boston, Mass.: G. K. Hall,
    1971. 2 v.
        Contains about 24, 000 index cards for approximately 8, 000
    works and pamphlets with many analytics.

34 Bloomfield, B. C. and M. Mckee. Africa in contemporary world.
    London: National Book League, 1967. 30 p.
        Designed for the intelligent general reader, it contains 189
    numbered items critically annotated and grouped by country
    within five regions. Appendix lists some leading African
    authors. No index.

35 Bogaert, Jozef. Sciences humaines en Afrique noire; guide bib-
    liographique, 1945-1965. Bruxelles: Centre de Documentation
    Economique et Sociale Africaine (CEDESA), 1966. 226 p.
        In two parts with subdivisions, 1, 494 numbered and anno-
    tated items are listed. The first section includes general
    bibliographies and general works of reference and in the second
    section, subject or special bibliographies and works on specific
    subjects are arranged by subject. Author, geographic and sub-
    ject indexes. The earlier edition, published by Editions de
    l'Université Lovanium, Léopoldville, 1964, has 593 entries.

36 Books about Africa South of the Sahara, 1958-62: a reading
    list. New York: Missionary Research Library, 1963. 68 p.
        834 unannotated entries grouped by subject under country or

geographic area, with an appendix of centers for African
Studies in the United States and an author index.

37 Boston. University. Library. Catalog of African government
documents and African area index. 2nd ed. rev. enl. Boston, Mass.: G. K. Hall, 1964. 471 p. 1st ed. 1960.
An author catalog of monographs and serials from 4, 300
cards photolithographically reproduced covering all areas of
Africa. The arrangement is based on the L. C. Schedule
J700-881 for African states. The sub-numbering, locally
devised, accords with other schemes that provide for arrangement by departments within a government: The index is an
A-Z list of all items on Africa in the Boston University
Library. Emphasis is on economics, history, sociology and
anthropology.

38 _____. List of French doctoral dissertations on Africa,
1884-1961. Compiled by Marion Dinstel and with indexes by
Mary Darrah Herrick. Boston: G. K. Hall, 1966. 336 p.
The numbered entries are arranged by author under country
or geographic area, with author, area and subject indexes.
Emphasis on French-speaking countries.

39 De Benko, Eugene and Patricia L. Butts. Research sources
for African studies: a checklist of relevant serial publications based on library collections at Michigan State University.
East Lansing: African Studies Center, Michigan State University, 1969. 384 p.
Alphabetical listing of some 2, 100 serials with annotations.
Official publications entered under the name of the issuing
agency unless they have distinctive titles. Subject and geographic index.
Rev: Africana Library J., I (Summer 1970), 23.

40 Deutsche Afrika-Gesellschaft. Schöne Schriften aus Afrika:
ein Verzeichnis von Werken zeitgenossischer afrikanischer
Autoren. Bonn, 1962. 88 p.
Includes biographical notes, and vernacular titles often
translated into German.

41 Downs, Robert B. and Frances Jenkins, eds. Bibliography:
current state and future trends. Urbana: University of
Illinois Press, 1967. 611 p.
Scholarly bibliographic essays on the current status and
future trends of general and special bibliography in the United
States and in other countries in the humanities, social,
natural, physical and medical sciences. The scope and limi-
tations of the major existing bibliographies in each field are
noted. The material in this book was originally published in
the January and April 1967 issues of the Library Trends.
Extensive bibliography at the end of each chapter, author,
title and subject index.

Rev: J. Doc., **XXIV** (Sept. 1968), 214-5. <u>Library J.</u>,
XCIII (March 15, 1968), 1118.

42 Duignan, Peter, et al., eds. <u>Africa south of the Sahara: a</u>
    <u>bibliography for undergraduate libraries.</u> Williamsport,
    Pennsylvania: Bro-Dart, 1971. 105 p. (New York State
    University. Foreign Area Materials Center. Occasional
    publication, No. 12.)
        1, 328 unannotated entries of books grouped by region or
    country, and then by subject, with full bibliographic data
    and review sources. Includes items mostly in English and
    published in the last 25 years and a few government publica-
    tions. Each entry is graded by a symbol, A, B or C. Cri-
    teria for inclusion are rather arbitrary; items included are
    not most representative of the area concerned. The repe-
    tition of the full bibliographic data in the index unnecessarily
    augments the bulk of the book.
        Rev: <u>Africana Library J.</u>, III (Spring 1972), 23.

43 _____ and Kenneth M. Glazier. <u>A Checklist of serials for</u>
    <u>African studies.</u> Based on the libraries of the Hoover Insti-
    tution and Stanford University. Stanford, Calif.: Hoover
    Institution, 1963. 104 p. (Hoover Institution bibliographical
    series, 13.)
        1, 417 numbered items divided into two parts. I. African
    serials, including periodicals, monographic series, annual
    reports, government debates, etc. II. African newspapers.
    Indicates the holdings of the libraries of Stanford University.

44 Flint, John E. <u>Books on the British Empire and Common-</u>
    <u>wealth; a guide for students.</u> London: Oxford University
    Press for the Royal Commonwealth Society. 1968. 65 p.
        Classified by country, beginning with a general section,
    it excludes works on sport, travel, mining, biological sciences
    and official reports but emphasizes historical and political
    literature. No index.

45 Fontvieille, Jean Roger. <u>Guide bibliographique du monde noir,</u>
    <u>I: histoire littérature, ethnologie.</u> Yaoundé Cameroun:
    Ministère de l'Education de la Jeunesse et de la Culture,
    1969. 1250 p. (Université fédéral du Cameroun, Yaoundé.
    Publication. Sér. Bibliographies et catalogues, 1.)
        Text in French and English.

46 Garling, Anthea. <u>Bibliography of African bibliographies.</u> Cam-
    bridge: African Studies Centre, Cambridge University, 1968.
    138 p.

47 Glazier, Kenneth M. <u>Africa south of the Sahara 1964-68: a</u>
    <u>select and annotated bibliography.</u> Stanford, Calif.: Hoover
    Institution Press, Stanford University, 1969. 139 p. (Hoover
    Institution bibliographical series, XLII.)
        Continuing the 1964 edition which covered 1958-1963, it

lists 220 books on African studies, literature and arts, well annotated and arranged alphabetically by author with a subject index. Only works in English are listed, and review sources are also given, though mostly favorable ones.

Rev: Africana Library J., I (Summer 1970), 23.

48 _____. "Recent reference works on Africa," Afr. Stud. Bull., VIII (Sept. 1965), 63-8.

Lists titles under the following categories--archives;--bibliographies;--Catalogues, directories;--handbooks, etc.

49 Gutkind, Peter Claus and John B. Webster. A Select bibliography on traditional and modern Africa. Syracuse, New York: Bibliographic Section, Program of Eastern African Studies, Syracuse University, 1968. 323 p. (Typescript) (Occasional bibliography, No. 8.)

An excellent general bibliography with some 2,921 entries for books and periodical articles in the humanities and social sciences. Periodical articles are mostly in English and French.

50 Hewitt, Arthur Reginald. Union list of Commonwealth newspapers in London, Oxford and Cambridge. London: The Athlone Press for the Institute of Commonwealth, University of London, 1960. 101 p.

Entries, based on the holdings of the British Museum, are arranged alphabetically by title under the country or territory of origin. Title index.

51 Hoehn, R. Philip and Jean Judson. "Theses on sub-Saharan Africa accepted by the University of California at Berkeley," Afr. Stud. Bull., XII (Sept. 1969), 157-66.

Part I: General; Central Africa; East Africa; and West Africa. Part II: Titles by country. Entries arranged alphabetically by author.

52 Holdsworth, Mary. Soviet African studies, 1918-59: an annotated bibliography. London: Royal Institute of International Affairs, 1961. 2 v. (Chatham House memoranda.)

Analyzes the Soviet works in Africa up to the end of 1958. Part I: General functional studies. Part II: Regional Studies. Entries mostly annotated are classified by subject with author and subject indexes to each part. Supplemented by the Central Asian Research Centre's Soviet writing on Africa, 1959-61: an annotated bibliography (1963).

53 Hoselitz, Berthold Frank, ed. A Reader's guide to the social sciences. Rev. ed. New York: The Free Press, 1970. 425 p.

First published 1959. Intended to serve "not only as a guide to libraries but also an introduction to the general reader interested in the literary output of the different social

sciences and even to social scientists in one discipline who
wish to obtain a general overview of the literature of a sister
discipline, " (Preface, 1959). Subjects discussed by different
authorities: sociology, anthropology, psychology, political
science, economics, geography. General bibliography and no
index.

54 Howard University. Library. The Moorland Foundation.   A
    Catalogue of the African Collection in the Moorland Foundation.
    Compiled by students in the Program of African Studies and
    edited by Dorothy B. Porter.   Washington, D.C.: Howard
    University Press, 1958.   398 p.
       4, 865 books and pamphlets arranged by regions with
    supplementary lists of periodicals and newspapers.

55 Kelley, Douglas C.   Africa in paperbacks; 199 paperbound
    books in Africa south of the Sahara in print, May 1960.
    East Lansing: Bureau of Social and Political Research,
    Michigan State University, 1960.   37 p.
       A classified annotated list, half of which deals with higher
    education in Africa.   Publisher's addresses and prices are
    given, and specially recommended titles are marked with an
    asterisk.

56 Koehler, J.   Deutsche Dissertationen über Afrika; ein Ver-
    zeichnis für die Jahre, 1918-1959.   Bonn: Schroeder, 1962.
       A classified listing of about 800 items with catchword
    and author indexes.

57 Kotei, S. I. A.   "Some notes on the present state of national
    bibliography in English-speaking Africa, " Africana Library J.,
    II (Winter 1971), 13-17.
       Outlines the main impediments to national bibliography in
    English-speaking Africa and briefly describes the major bib-
    liographic activities in specific countries.   The author is a
    Lecturer in Library Studies, University of Ghana.

58 McAree, James.   "A Select bibliography of paperback books on
    Africa for secondary school use, " Soc. Stud. (Dec. 1966),
    304-7.

59 MacKnight, V. R.   Bibliography on sources of information for
    the study of the advancement of women in emerging nations of
    Africa, Washington, D.C.: Catholic University of America,
    1964.

60 Malclès, Louise-Noelle.   Les Sources du travail bibliographique.
    Geneva: Droz, 1950-58.   3 v. in 4.
       Lists and evaluates outstanding bibliographies and standard
    reference works of the more important countries, many of
    which are found in Winchell's Guide to reference books and
    Walford's Guide to reference material.   International in scope,

although emphasizing European works, particularly those published 1940-1950. Entries are classified under broad cate-
gories with sub-divisions. v. 1: General bibliographies.
v. 2 (in 2 parts): Specialized sources in the humanities and
social sciences, covering pre-history, anthropology, linguistics, geography, music, art, etc. v. 3: Specialized sources
in the natural and applied sciences. Author, subject and title
index in each volume.

61 Matthews, Daniel G. "African bibliography today: selected
and current bibliographical tools for African studies, 1967-
68," Curr. Bibliog. Afr. Affairs, New Series, I (Nov. 1968),
4-17.

62 National Book League, London. Commonwealth reference books
and bibliographical guide. London, 1965. 54 p.
Lists about 590 annotated items grouped by region and
country. Includes bibliographies, dictionaries, directories,
yearbooks, encyclopedias, etc. No introduction or index.

63 _____, et al. Reader's guide to the Commonwealth. London,
1970. 210 p.
An excellent annotated list of books prepared by the National
Book League, the Commonwealth Institute and the Foreign Aid
Commonwealth Office for the Commonwealth Book Fair held at
the Commonwealth Institute of Sept. 1970. Beginning with a
general section, the arrangement is primarily topical under
broad geographic areas. Includes children's books and prices,
and indicates author's nationality where necessary. No index.

64 New York Public Library. Dictionary catalog of the Schomburg
Collection of Negro Literature and History. Boston, Mass.:
G. K. Hall, 1962. 9 v.
"Includes books by authors of African descent, regardless
of subject matter or language ... and all significant materials
about peoples of African descent." (Preface)

65 Northwestern University, Evanston, Ill. Library. Catalog of
the Melville J. Herskovits Library of African Studies. Boston,
Mass.: G. K. Hall, 1972. 8 v.
An author-title catalog of over 60,000 volumes, including
600 periodicals and newspapers, rare books, microfilms,
microfiche, manuscripts, maps, recordings, photographs,
literary and political ephemera, reproduced from about
118,000 cards by offset on permanent/durable acid-free paper
with 21 cards per 10" x 14" page. Materials in European and
African languages are included with emphasis on sub-Saharan
Africa, particularly former German Africa, Zaire and West
African countries of Ghana, Nigeria, Gambia and Sierra Leone.
The catalog constitutes a significant bibliographic source of
contemporary literature on Africa. Professor Melville Jean
Herskovits (1895-1963), an anthropologist, established the

first African studies program in the United States in 1948.
For his obituary see Amer. Anthrop., LXVI (Feb. 1964),
83-109.   por., bibliog.

66   Royal Commonwealth Society, London. Library. Subject cata-
     logue of the Library of the Royal Empire Society, by Evans
     Lewin.   v. 1:   The British Empire generally and Africa.
     London, 1930.   582 p.
          A comprehensive catalog very strong in history, and de-
     scription and administration, geographically arranged and sub-
     divided by subject under each country.   Entries, chronological
     under subject, include books, pamphlets, periodical articles
     and government publications, most of which were published by
     the end of the 19th century and early 20th century.

67   South African Public Library.   A Bibliography of African bib-
     liographies, covering territories south of the Sahara.   4th ed.
     Cape Town, 1961.   79 p.   (Grey bibliographies no. 7.)
          Classified by the Universal Decimal Classification scheme,
     it lists both separately published bibliographies and those in-
     cluded in books.   Very strong in linguistic and ethnographic
     studies.

68   Spitz, Allan A.   Developmental change: an annotated bibli-
     ography.   Lexington: Univ. of Kentucky Press, 1969.   316 p.
          Covers materials published on Africa, Asia, Latin America
     between 1945 and summer 1967 with emphasis on post-1960
     publications.   Entries are alphabetically arranged by author
     under the topic.   Author and journal indexes and a list of
     books cited.   Lack of a geographic or country index makes
     it very difficult to know what has been written on any specific
     country.
          Rev: Choice, VII (May 1970), 370.   Library J., XCIV
     (Jul. 1969), 2593.

68a Staatsbibliothek Preussischer Kulturbesitz.   Catalogue of
     African official publications available in European libraries
     as of 1 May 1971.   Berlin, 1971.   251 p.
          Lists 1186 titles of monographic and periodical publications
     from 38 African countries.   Cooperating libraries include the
     Federal Republic of Germany, Hungary, Czechoslovakia,
     France, Britain, Italy and Sweden.

69   Standing Conference on Library Materials on Africa.   Theses
     on Africa accepted by the universities in the United Kingdom
     and Ireland.   Cambridge: Heffer, 1964.   74 p.
          Lists 1,142 theses presented 1920-62, arranged by region
     and country and subdivided by subject, with an author index.
     Continued in SCOLMA's United Kingdom publications and
     theses on Africa 1963-   , which published annually, includes
     books, periodical articles and some newspaper articles, ar-
     ranged by author alphabetically under country.   Theses are
     listed separately.

70   U. S. Dept. of the Army.   Africa: problems and prospects;
     a bibliographic survey.   Rev. ed.   Washington, D. C., 1967.
     226 p.   1st ed. 1962.
        Most of the materials are available in the U. S. Army
     Library, Pentagon, selected from "more than 900 unclassified
     items from several thousand documents, books, and periodical
     articles in order to shed light on the problems facing Africa,
     as well as to present the emerging economic, political and
     sociological picture of the continent for the future." Arrange-
     ment is both geographical and topical.   Includes 16 appendices
     of good maps and tables.   Section VIIA lists reference books
     and bibliography of bibliographies.   Entries are annotated or
     consist of excerpts from journals or books.   No index.

71   U. S. Library of Congress.   General Reference and Bibliography
     Division.   African Section.   Africa south of the Sahara: a
     selected annotated list of writings.   Compiled by Helen F.
     Conover, Washington, D. C., U. S. Govt. Printing Office,
     1963.   354 p.
        A critical bibliography, which supersedes two earlier
     L. C. bibliographies: Introduction to Africa (1952) and Africa
     south of the Sahara ... 1951-56 (1957).   2, 173 numbered
     items are mostly for English language material covering
     various subjects.   General index.

72   .   Africa south of the Sahara.   Index to periodical
     literature, 1900-1970.   Boston: G. K. Hall, 1971.   4 v.
        Primarily designed as a working tool for the African
     Section of the Library of Congress, it includes over 84, 000
     entries arranged by country and region and subdivided by
     ethnic group.   There is an author index to poetry and short
     stories published in African literary journals and in other
     periodicals devoted to African cultural studies.   Emphasis is
     on material published in the past three years, but efforts
     are made to cover material published in African journals
     from their beginning dates of publication.   Excludes articles
     specifically on North Africa.
        Rev: Africana Library J., II (Winter 1971), 28-9.

73   .   African libraries, book production, and archives:
     a list of references.   Compiled by Helen Conover.   Washing-
     ton, D. C., 1962.   64 p.
        Organized into three parts. I: Libraries. II: Book
     production. III: Archives. Parts I and III are geographically
     subdivided and Part II arranged by author.   Author index.
     Though dated, it is still available.

74   .   A List of American doctoral dissertations on Africa.
     Washington, D. C., 1962.   69 p.
        Arranged alphabetically by author with a catchword index of
     titles with regional breakdowns.

75 _____. Sub-Sahara Africa: a guide to serials. Washington,
     D.C., 1970. 409 p.
     The most up-to-date comprehensive reference work on
     African serials. 4,670 annotated entries and alphabetically
     arranged by title or issuing agency, with subject and organ-
     ization indexes. Data given include beginning date; place of
     publication, publisher, frequency, L.C. call number, cessa-
     tions, suspensions and mergers. Includes periodicals,
     monographic series, annual reports of institutions, yearbooks
     and directories. Supersedes Conover's Serials for African
     Studies (1961).
     Rev: Africana Library J., II (Spring 1971), 19 & 21.

76 U.S. Library of Congress. Serial Division. Reference Dept.
     African newspapers in selected American libraries: a union
     list. Compiled by Rozanne M. Barry, 3rd ed. Washington,
     D.C., 1965. 135 p. 1st ed. 1956.
     Arranged by country and then by place of publication, with
     a title index.

77 U.S. and Canadian publications on Africa, 1960- . Stanford,
     Calif., Hoover Institution, 1962- Annual.
     Books, pamphlets and periodical articles are topically and
     geographically arranged in two sections, with an author index.

78 Walford, Albert J., ed. Guide to reference material, v. 2-3.
     2nd ed. London: The Library Association, 1968-70. 1st
     ed. 1959. v. 2: 543 p. (1968); v. 3: 585 p. (1970).
     Both volumes are designed "to provide a signpost to refer-
     ence books and bibliographies published mainly in recent
     years. It is international in scope, with some emphasis on
     items published in Britain." (Introduction) v. 2: Philosophy
     and psychology, religion, social sciences, geography, biography
     and history. v. 3: Generalities, languages, the arts and
     literature. Entries in both volumes are classified according
     U.D.C. scheme, with volume 2 containing about 3,300 items
     and volume 3 about 3,700 items, and all are evaluatively
     annotated, and review sources are given for some. The
     avowed British slant is much less evident in these volumes
     than in the original 1959 edition, "except in such subjects as
     law, social services and local history, where the national
     element is bound to have prominence. Less developed
     countries in Africa, Asia and Latin America receive more
     attention." Each volume has an author, title and subject index.

79 White, Carl M. et al. Sources of information in the social
     sciences: a guide to the literature. Totowa, New Jersey:
     Bedminster Press, 1964. 498 p. Preliminary ed. 1959.
     Intended for graduate library school students but valuable
     to all researchers in the social sciences especially for many
     specialized sources not included in Winchell's Guide to refer-
     ence books and Walford's Guide to reference material. In

each of its 8 chapters a specialist provides "a bibliographical
review of basic monographic works for a collection of sub-
stantive material.   This review is followed by a list of reference works [compiled by librarian]. " (Preface) There are
2, 741 numbered items on the whole and a good author and title
index.   Law is omitted, the contents list is insufficiently detailed and inclusion of a subject index would have enhanced its
usefulness.

80   Winchell, Constance M.   Guide to reference books.   8th ed.
     Chicago: American Library Association, 1967.   741 p.
          First edition 1902, by Alice Bertha Kroeger, published as
     Guide to the study and use of reference books.   A general
     reference work international in scope, systematically arranged
     by discipline with informed and evaluative annotations though
     not uniformly provided.   Africa is fairly well represented.
     Numerous cross references; author, title and subject index.

ARCHAEOLOGY, ETHNOLOGY, RELIGION, SOCIAL STUDIES

81   Bibliographie ethnographique de l'Afrique sud-Saharienne, 1925/
     30.   Tervuren, Belgie: Koninklijk Museum voor Midden-
     Africa, 1932- .   Annual.   (irregular)
          Includes books and periodical articles in various languages
     on life and culture in Sub-Saharan Africa, but annotated in
     French and arranged alphabetically by author.   Subject index
     refers one not to the item number or page but to the author.
          Rev: (1970 ed)   Africana Library J. , II (Summer 1971),
     13.

82   "A Bibliography of anthropological bibliographies: Africa, "
     Current Anthropology, X (Dec. 1969), 527-66.
          872 partially annotated entries topically and geographically
     arranged.   Author index.   Anthropology, here interpreted
     broadly, comprises ethnology, ethnography, social and
     physical anthropology, culture history, archaeology, linguis-
     tics, religion, etc.

83   COWA surveys and bibliographies.   Areas 9-14:   Africa.   Cam-
     bridge, Mass. :   Council for Old World Archaeology, 1957-
     series 1- .   Biennial.
          Each series consists of 22 area booklets on the archaeology
     of the entire Old World from the palaeolithic to the recent
     times, and each area report covers the last two to three
     years of archaeological activity, and comprises a survey of
     current work and an annotated bibliography of the most im-
     portant books and periodical articles.

84   Edinburgh. University. Dept. of Social Anthropology.   African
     urbanization: a reading list of selected books, articles and
     reports.   London: International African Institute, 1965.   27 p.

(Africa bibliography series, 3.)

"Intended as a guide to research into urban problems and urbanization in African countries south of the Sahara." (Foreword) Some 996 annotated entries grouped by country with separate sections for bibliographies and general works. Index to towns cited.

85 International African Institute. Africa bibliography series; ethnography, sociology, linguistics and related subjects, v. 4: West Africa. Based on the bibliographical card index of the International African Institute. Compiled by Ruth Jones, London, 1958. 116 p.

Strongest in ethnography, anthropology and linguistics it is one of the most authoritative comprehensive bibliographic sources of retrospective publications on West Africa. Entries which include books and periodical articles are first grouped geographically and then subdivided by subject. Author index and index of ethnic and linguistic names.

86 Mitchell, Robert C. and Harold W. Turner. A Comprehensive bibliography of modern African religious movements. Evanston, Ill.: Northwestern University Press, 1966. 132 p.

Attempts "to include every available reference in any language to modern African religious movements that has been published and achieved more than local circulation." Omits Islamic religious movements. 1,313 entries briefly annotated are primarily grouped geographically with a general section. Indexes of authors and of people.

87 Wieschhoff, Heinrich Albert. Anthropological bibliography of Negro Africa. New York: Kraus Reprint, 1970. 461 p. Reprint of ed. New Haven, 1948.

Alphabetical arrangement by name of tribe and geographic area.

88 Zaretsky, Irving I. Bibliography on spirit possession and spirit mediumship. Berkeley: Dept. of Anthropology, University of California, 1966. 106 p.

With emphasis on sub-Saharan Africa, most of the entries are annotated. Ethnic group index.

Rev: Canadian J. Afr. Stud. III, No. 3 (1970), 660-1.

ECONOMICS, LAW, POLITICS

89 Alderfer, Harold F. A Bibliography of African governments, 1950-1966. 2nd ed. Lincoln University Press, 1967. 163 p. 1st ed. 1964.

Unannotated books and periodical articles, listed separately under geographic divisions. Author index. Professor Alderfer is Director of the Institute of African Government, Lincoln University, U.S.A.

90 Ballard, John A. "Politics and government in former French
    West and Equatorial Africa: a critical bibliography." J. Mod.
    Afr. Stud., III, No. 4 (1964), 589-605.
    Includes many references relevant to English West Africa.

91 Commission for Technical Cooperation in Africa South of the
    Sahara. Inventory of economic studies concerning Africa
    South of the Sahara: an annotated reading list of books,
    articles, and official publications. London, 1960. 301 p.
    (Its publication, No. 30.)
    Over 1,300 items topically arranged under nine main geo-
    graphic areas with an author index. Titles are listed in
    both English and French, but annotations in English or French.
    Supplement I issued in 1963 (159 p.) adds nearly 900 items,
    including official publications.

92 D'Hertefelt, Marcel. African government and systems in static
    and changing conditions: a bibliographical contribution to
    political anthropology. With an introduction by M. Fortes
    and E. E. Evans-Pritchard. Tervuren, Belgique: Musée
    Royal de l'Afrique Centrale, 1968. 178 p.
    1,269 unannotated entries--books and periodical articles
    mostly published after 1940. Indexes of peoples and subjects.
    A country index rather than that of peoples would have been
    more useful. The introductory essay examines some political
    concepts.

93 Friedland, William H. Unions, labor and industrial relations
    in Africa: an annotated bibliography. Ithaca, New York:
    Center for International Studies, Cornell University, 1965.
    159 p.
    "Attempts to accumulate references to publications dealing
    with the subject of trade unions, industrial and labor relations
    and related subjects in Africa" (Introduction). 683 entries
    almost all annotated, arranged alphabetically by author or
    issuing agency, followed by 41 titles of technical papers deal-
    ing with specific aspects of labor problems in Africa issued
    by the International Labour Office, Geneva. Subject, geo-
    graphic and major publications indexes.

94 Glickman, Harvey. "The Military in African politics: a bib-
    liographic essay," African Forum, II (Summer 1966), 68-75.

95 Hanna, William and Judith Lynne Hanna. Politics in black
    Africa: a selective bibliography of relevant periodical litera-
    ture. East Lansing: African Studies Center, Michigan State
    University, 1964. 139 p.
    "Concerned with the resources relevant to African studies
    which were available in the Michigan State University Library,
    we decided to compile a list of all periodicals which would be
    of particular use to the social scientist specializing in African
    affairs" (Introduction).

1, 283 unannotated entries for articles in English and French
topically arranged with an author index. A country or geographic index would have enhanced its usefulness.

96   Karal, Gulgun. African legal and constitutional materials: an
     annotated bibliography. Los Angeles: University of California,
     1969. 125 p.
     A research project jointly financed by the University of
     California, Los Angeles, and the United States Peace Corps.
     Entries are arranged by country under topical grouping. Has
     neither an introduction nor an index.

97   McGowan, Patrick J. African politics: a guide to research
     resources, methods, and literature. Syracuse, New York:
     Maxwell Graduate School of Citizenship and Public Affairs,
     Syracuse University, 1970. 130 p. (Syracuse University
     Program of Eastern African Studies. Occasional Paper, No.
     55.)
     1, 443 entries divided into 2 main sections. Part I--Refer-
     ences to guides; handbooks, bibliographies, etc. Part II--
     Select bibliography on political change in Africa. Its special
     features include a list of sources for biographical information;
     notes on guides to libraries; special collections and various
     union lists for locating materials. Very valuable despite
     several typographical errors, especially on names of authors,
     lack of indexes and incomplete bibliographic data.
     Rev: Africana Library J., I (Summer 1970), 24.

98   Martin, Jane. A Bibliography on African regionalism. Boston:
     African Studies Center, Boston University, 1969. 121 p.
     Unannotated listing of books and periodical articles divided
     into six sections, each with sub-divisions. Part I deals with
     general theories of economic integration and its implications;
     Part II: Political regionalism and the organization of African
     Unity; Parts III, IV and V: Case studies of East, West and
     North Africa. Part VI: Aids to further research. Each
     section has a useful introductory essay and most entries are
     for works published in the 1960's. No index.
     Rev: Africana Library J., II (Summer 1971), 15.

99   Patrikios, Vaptistis-Titos. Development--a bibliography.
     Rome: FAO, 1969. 136 p.
     469 entries for post-1960 publications primarily on food
     and agriculture. Divided into sections covering both economic
     and social development. Includes annotated bibliographies and
     unannotated lists of periodicals and introductory works on
     problems of hunger and development. The annotations are in
     French or English.
     Rev: Africana Library J., II (Summer 1971), 15.

100 Sufrin, Sidney C. and F. E. Wagner. A Brief annotated bib-
     liography on labour in emerging societies. Syracuse: Syra-
     cuse University Press, 1961. 64 p.

EDUCATION, GEOGRAPHY, HISTORY, PSYCHOLOGY

101   Altbach, Philip G.   Higher education in developing countries:
a select bibliography.   Cambridge, Mass.:   Center for International Affairs, Harvard University, 1970.   119 p.   (Occasional papers in international affairs, No. 24.)
    Beginning with a long useful introductory essay on higher
education in developing countries, covering Africa, Asia and
Latin America, followed by a general section it is organized
mostly by geographic area or country.   Entries are unannotated and books and periodical articles are listed separately.
Many official publications and reports are included.   No historical cut off date was used, and some references go back
to the nineteenth century.   No index.

102   Bederman, Sanford Harold.   A Bibliographic aid to the study
of the geography of Africa: a selected listing of recent literature in the English language.   Atlanta: Bureau of Business and Economic Research, Georgia State University,
1970.   212 p.
    Lists some 1,900 items, books and periodical articles,
and organized into general and regional sections with a
topical index to each section, and author and geographic
indexes for the whole book.
    Rev: Afr. Stud. Rev., XIII (Sept. 1970), 330-1.

103   Brembeck, Cole Speicher and John P. Keith.   Education in
emerging Africa: a select and annotated bibliography.   East
Lansing: College of Education, Michigan State University,
1962?   153 p.   (Michigan State University Education in
Africa series, 1.)
    Classified by topic, it includes books, official publications
and periodical articles.   No index.

104   Couch, Margaret.   Education in Africa: a select bibliography.
Part I: British and former British territories in Africa.
London: Institute of Education, University of London, 1962.
121 p.   (Education libraries bulletin supplement 5.)
    Based on the catalogue of the Library of the Education
Dept., London University, it excludes South Africa, listing
about 1,300 items arranged by country and subdivided by
kind of education and then arranged chronologically.   Country
and author indexes.

105   Dahlberg, Richard and Benjamin E. Thomas.   "An analysis
and bibliography of recent African atlases," Afri. Stud. Bull.,
V (Oct. 1962), 23-33.

106   Dolan, Eleanor F.   Higher education in Africa south of the
Sahara: selected bibliography, 1945-1960.   Washington,
D.C.:   American Association of University Women, Educa-
tional Foundation, 1961.   80 p.

Classified by form of material it includes annual publications, bibliographies, newspapers, periodicals, books and
pamphlets, United States publications, Government publications geographically grouped. Emphasis is on the education
of women and on the English language sources. Author and
title index.

107 Drake, Howard. A Bibliography of African education, south
of the Sahara. Aberdeen: Aberdeen University Press, 1942.
97 p.
Unannotated entries, arranged chronologically, are classified by subject and subdivided by region and country. Author
and subject indexes. Of great historical value.

108 Geoffrion, Charles A., ed. Africa: a study guide to better
understanding. Bloomington: Bureau of Public Discussion
and African Studies Program, Indiana University, 1970.
33 p. (African studies continuing education series.)
A guide to books, films and other recordings topically
organized. Each section includes bibliography, suggested
questions for analysis and discussion.
Rev: Africana Library J., I (Winter 1970), 28.

109 Hanson, John W. and Geoffrey W. Gibson. African education
and development since 1960: a select and annotated bibliography. East Lansing: Institute for International Studies
in Education and African Studies Center, Michigan State
University, 1966. 327 p. (Education in Africa series, 2.)
Books, periodical articles and government documents
arranged by topic with some geographic subdivisions.
Author index.

109a Hoorweg, J. C. and H. C. Marais. Psychology in Africa: a
bibliography. Leyden: Afrika-Studencentrum, 1969. 139 p.
Entries are grouped, except for a preceding general section, under nine topics such as methodology and research
technology; experimental psychology; physiological psychology;
developmental psychology; social psychology; personality;
clinical psychology; educational psychology; military personnel
psychology. A geographic or country index would have enhanced its usefulness.

110 Kay, Stafford and Bradley Nystrom. "Education and colonialism in
Africa: an annotated bibliography," Comp. Educ. Rev.,
XV (June 1971), 240-59.
Annotated entries topically arranged.

111 Klingelhofer, E. L. A Bibliography of psychological research
and writings on Africa. Uppsala: Scandinavian Institute of
African Studies, 1967. 33 p.
Entries are topically arranged, with no author or geographic index, which would have aided the user in knowing

easily what has been written on a specific region or country. The author is Professor of Psychology at Sacramento State University, California and former Visiting Professor of Educational Psychology at the University College, Dar es Salaam, Tanzania.

112 Matthews, Daniel G. , ed. Current themes in African historical studies: a selected bibliographical guide to resources for research in African history. Westport, Conn.: Negro Universities Press, 1970. 389 p. (African Bibliographic Center. Special bibliographic series, v. 7, No. 2.)
   Part I: "Towards a bibliography of medieval West Africa," compiled by S. M. Zoghby, with a general index. Part IIA covers selected current literature, 1967- mid 1969 and some selected periodical resources, subdivided by subject and geographic area, with author and title index. Part IIB contains selected materials 1960-1969 with an author index. Part III comprises two bibliographic essays dealing mainly with aspects of African diaspora. Part IIIB: a bibliographic sources of Brazilian influence on Africa. A valuable work for the serious history student and the scholar.

113 Munger, Edwin S. A Selected, current, annotated bibliography on the geography of Sub-Saharan Africa drawn from reasonably accessible English sources. Chicago: Dept. of Geography, University of Chicago, 1954? 28 p.
   Confined to materials in English, entries are primarily arranged by geographic area or country with brief annotations, emphasizing post-1950 publications. No index.

114 Parker, Franklin. African education: a bibliography of 121 U. S. A. doctoral dissertations. Washington, D. C.: World Confederation of Organizations of the Teaching Profession, 1965? 48 p.
   Entries mostly annotated are arranged alphabetically by author with subject index and an index of degree granting institutions.

115 Project Africa. Africa south of the Sahara: a resource and curriculum guide. Compiled by Barry K. Beyer. New York: Crowell, 1969. 137 p.
   Intended for school teachers it includes books, journals and audio-visual materials and contains addresses of consulates, publishers, etc.

116 Sommer, John W. Bibliography of African geography, 1940-1964. Hanover: Dartmouth College, 1965. 139 p. (Geography publications at Dartmouth College, No. 3.)
   1,724 unannotated numbered entries arranged by topic with an author index. Includes only periodical articles but lacks a country index which would have made it more useful. Intended for the scholar.

117 Tolman, L. E. , et al. "Africa: a selected bibliography with
     related instructional aids for the elementary and secondary
     school, " J. Educ. , No. 144 (Oct. 1961), 1-90.

118 Yates, Barbara. "A Bibliography on special problems in
     education in Tropical Africa, " Comp. Educ. Rev. , VIII
     (Dec. 1964), 307-19.

119 _____. "Educational policy and practice Tropical Africa,
     a general bibliography, " Comp. Educ. Rev. , VIII (Oct.
     1964), 215-28.

                  LANGUAGE, LITERATURE, THE ARTS

120 Abrash, Barbara. Black African literature in English since
     1952: works and criticism. With an introduction by John F.
     Povey. New York: Johnson Reprint Corporation, 1967.
     91 p.
        A valuable reference work with an excellent introduction
     by the Chairman of the African Language and Literature
     Committee, African Studies Association of America. Lists
     463 entries, including individual works of authors, criti-
     cisms, and anthologies indicating the nationality of the writer,
     selected periodicals and author index.
        Rev: Wilson Lib. Bull. , XLII (March 1968), 736.

121 Chicorel, Marietta and Veronica Hall, eds. Chicorel theater
     index to plays in anthologies, periodicals, discs and tapes,
     v. 1. New York: Chicorel Library Publishing Co. , 1970.
     573 p.
        "Consists of just one alphabetical list comprehending four
     types of entry: author's name, play title, anthology title,
     editor's name, each with all the significant data required
     by the user. " Includes over 500 anthologies and 8, 500
     entries; projected to be kept up to date. Some African
     writers are listed. There are author, title, editor and
     subject indexes, and a directory of publishers.
        Rev: Amer. Lit. , XLII (Jan. 1971), 618. Library J. ,
     XCV (Dec. 1, 1970), 4157.

122 East, N. B. African theatre: a checklist of critical materials.
     New York: Africana Publishing Corp. , 1970. 47 p.
        Unannotated entries arranged alphabetically by author and
     organized into 7 sections: Bibliographies; General subjects;
     films and regional areas.
        Rev: Africana Library J. , I (Fall 1970), 23.

123 Eliet, Edouard. Panorama de la littérature négro-africaine,
     1921-1962. Paris: Présence Africaine, 1965. 263 p.
        Rev: J. Mod. Afr. Stud. , III, No. 4 (1965), 640-5.

124   Gaskin, L. J. P.   A Bibliography of African Art.   London:
      International African Institute, 1965.   120 p.   (Africa bib-
      liography series B.)
         The most comprehensive existing bibliography of African
      art with over 5,300 unannotated entries and arranged in 6
      main sections--geographic and by form of material.   Author,
      geographic and ethnic, and subject indexes.
         Rev: Amer. Anthrop., XL (Feb. 1967), 659.

125   _____.   A Select bibliography of music in Africa.   London:
      International African Institute, 1965.   83 p.   (Africa bib-
      liography series B.)
         More than 3,000 unannotated entries excluding works on
      Afro-American music.   The main section is geographically
      subdivided.   Author index; geographical and ethnic index.
      Intended for the scholar.
         Rev: Africa, XXXVI (April 1966), 219-20.

126   Gillis, Frank and Alan P. Merriam.   Ethnomusicology and
      folk music: an international bibliography of dissertations
      and theses.   Middletown, Connecticut: Wesleyan Univer-
      sity Press, 1966.   148 p.
         Includes numerous references to African music.

127   Jahn, Janheinz.   A Bibliography of neo-African literature from
      Africa, America and the Caribbean.   New York: Praeger,
      1965.   359 p.
         Published simultaneously in German and English, it re-
      mains the most comprehensive single-volume bibliography of
      neo-African literature in existence.   3,566 unannotated
      numbered entries grouped under such headings as Anthologies;
      East Africa; Southern Africa; America; Latin America;
      Forgeries, etc., with an author index.   Attempts to list the
      whole of black creative writing in Europe, Africa, Western
      hemisphere from the 16th century to the present day, in-
      dicating the vernacular languages used and the nationality of
      the writer and providing English, French and German ver-
      sions of all titles.   His African geographical classification
      is rather unsatisfactory; country grouping would have been
      preferable; besides the work is incomplete.   Lesotho and
      Ethiopia, for example, are either inadequately represented
      or ignored; no critical works, folk tales or transcribed
      oral literature.   See Bernth Lindfors' additions and correc-
      tions to this bibliography in Afr. Stud. Bull., XI (Sept.
      1968), 129-48.   The African section of this work has been
      updated and improved in Bibliography of Creative African
      writing (1971), by Janheinz Jahn and C. P. Dressler, which
      also now includes critical works.
         Rev: Africa Report, XI (March 1966), 45.   J. Mod.
      Afr. Stud., III (Dec. 1965), 640-5.

128 _____ . The Black experience: 400 years of black literature from Africa and the Americas. Nendeln, Liechtenstein:
Kraus Reprint, 1970. 56 p. (Series 1)
    "Offers a means of tracing the many aspects of the Negro
struggle for freedom, and fills a gap in the search for material with which to demonstrate the history of an independent
black literary heritage. " (Preface). Entries chiefly consist
of brief informative notes on black authors from Africa, the
Caribbean, the United States, South America or Europe.
Contents: I: Journals and magazines. II: Books/writers of
the late 19th century. III: Books/literature from the Caribbean; Books/literature from South America; Books/modern
African literature. Author index.

129 _____ and Claus Peter Dressler. Bibliography of creative
African writing. Nendeln, Liechtenstein: Kraus-Thomson,
1971. 446 p.
    Attempts to list all authors whose books appeared before
1900 and after 1900, only creative works. Excludes political
writings and essays but includes political autobiographies.
Only the original works are numbered continuously. Bibliographies, journals, secondary literature and anthologies are
separately numbered. Theses are included and nationality of
the writer indicated for the original works. Lists over
2,176 numbered items grouped geographically with general
and forgeries sections. Author index. The introduction,
instructions for use, and the appendices are in English,
French and German and original works are accompanied by
critical or review sources.
    Rev: Africana Library J. , II (Winter 1971), 26-7.

130 Lindfors, Bernth. "Additions and corrections to Janheinz
Jahn's Bibliography of neo-African literature, 1965, " Afr.
Stud. Bull. , XI (Sept. 1968), 129-48.
    Corrects a few errors in Jahn's work and adds some new
titles, arranged in a similar way. Lack of explanatory notes
on the abbreviations used means that the user must either
remember what the abbreviations mean in Jahn's bibliography
or go and consult it.

131 Mercier, Roger. "Bibliographie africaine et malgache; écri-
vains noirs d'expression française, " Rev. Litt. Comp. ,
XXXVII, No. 1 (1963), 145-71.
    Limited to works in French, it is classified according to
literary genres--anthologies; poetry; novels; drama; folk
tales; short stories; essays; history, etc. and includes many
critical works. No indication of the nationality of the author.

132 Merriam, Alan P. African music on LP: an annotated dis-
cography. Evanston: Northwestern University Press, 1970.
200 p.
    LP is "Long Playing. " The work is an outcome of a

project carried out under the auspices of the Committee of
Fine Arts and the Humanities of the African Studies Association in U.S.A.   Not a selective bibliography though it lists
only commercially issued records arranged alphabetically
under the record companies of producing organizations.
Recordings are listed as individual items following alphabetical and numerical order from lowest to highest.   18
indexes including those to record companies, producing
organizations, album titles, tribal groupings, music types,
etc.

133   Murphy, John D. and Henry Goff.   A Bibliography of African
      languages and linguistics.   Washington, D.C.:   Catholic
      University of America Press, 1969.   147 p.
          "Not only works relating to the so-called 'Negro-African'
      languages are included, but also those dealing with the
      African varieties of Arabic, the Hamitic languages (Berber,
      etc.), Malagasy (an Indonesian language), Afrikaans (a de-
      velopment of Dutch) and the various Creoles" (Introduction).
      1,218 unannotated entries divided by linguistic areas with
      language and author indexes.
          Rev: Africana Library J., I (Summer 1970), 23-4.

134   Paricsy, Pal.   A New bibliography of African literature.
      Budapest: Center for Afro-Asian Research, Hungarian
      Academy of Sciences, 1969.   108 p.
          Modeled on Jahn's Bibliography of neo-African literature
      (1965) which it is designed to update and complement, it
      adds in part 1,361 new entries to Jahn's bibliography and
      continuing from 1965 it lists 377 items in part 2.   Author,
      editor and translator index.   Paricsy is Fellow of the
      Hungarian Academy of Sciences.

135   _____.   Studies on modern African literature.   Budapest:
      Center for Afro-Asian Research, Hungarian Academy
      of Sciences, 1971.   121 p.   (Studies on developing countries,
      No. 43.)
          Rev: Africana Library J., II (Winter 1971), 26-7.

136   _____.   "A Supplementary bibliography to J. Jahn's Bib-
      liography of neo-African literature from Africa, America
      and the Caribbean," J. New Afr. Lit. and the Arts (Fall
      1967), 70-82.
          Divided into two parts.   1: Anthologies.   2: Works.
      Bibliographic entry follows Jahn's pattern.

137   Ramsaran, John A.   New approaches to African literature: a
      guide to Negro-African writing and related studies.   2nd ed.
      Ibadan: Ibadan University Press, 1970.   168 p.   1st ed.
      1965.
          An authoritative reference work on Negro-African creative
      expression, oral and written.   Chapter I: Oral literature--

vernacular and translation. Chapter II: Modern African
literature. Chapter III: West Indian and French Caribbean
literature. Chapter IV: American Negro novel. Each
chapter has other literary subdivisions and each section is
preceded by an introductory bibliographic essay. Author and
title indexes. The entries are unannotated. Pagination is
not given nor even the nationality of the author.
　　　Rev: (1965 ed.) J. Mod. Afr. Stud., III (Dec. 1965),
640-5.

137a　Scheub, Harold. Bibliography of African oral narratives.
　　　Madison: African Studies Program, University of Wisconsin,
　　　1971. 160 p. (African Studies Program. Occasional paper,
　　　No. 3.)
　　　　　The first comprehensive work of its kind on African oral
　　　literature.

138　U. S. Library of Congress. Music Division. African music; a
　　　briefly annotated bibliography. Compiled by Darius L.
　　　Thieme. Washington, D.C., 1964. 55 p. Superseded by
　　　Gaskin's A select bibliography of music in Africa (1965).
　　　　　It includes items mainly published between 1930 and
　　　1963. Section I: Periodical articles; Section II: Books.
　　　All geographically grouped. Excludes works by peoples of
　　　non-African extraction.

139　Varley, Douglas H. African native music: an annotated bib-
　　　liography. London: Dawsons of Pall Mall, 1970. 116 p.
　　　Reprint of the 1936 edition.
　　　　　Confined to the Negro and Bantu cultures roughly south of
　　　the Sahara, entries for the most part are arranged geo-
　　　graphically with an author index.

140　Zell, Hans M. and Helene Silver, eds. A Reader's guide to
　　　literature of Africa. New York: Africana Publishing Corp.,
　　　1971. 232 p.
　　　　　Comprises over 600 annotated books on contemporary
　　　black African literature in English and French, including
　　　criticisms, anthologies, bibliographies and review excerpts.
　　　Complete bibliographic data are given for each entry with
　　　indications of out-of-print or unavailable material. Includes
　　　biographies of authors and a detailed author index. An ex-
　　　cellent work--a "must" for all libraries with African col-
　　　lections and students of African literature.
　　　　　Rev: Africana Library J., II (Winter 1971), 26-7.

(B) CLASSIFIED SUBJECTS

Items listed here are confined to works published since 1960--the year of independence for many African states. The general section includes publications on library, bibliographic and archival organization in Africa.

(1) GENERAL

141 Aiyepeku, Wilson O. "Problems of complete bibliographic control: the position of geography in relation to the social sciences," Nigerian Libraries, VII (April/Aug. 1971), 1-11. The author is Lecturer, Dept. of Library Studies, University of Ibadan, Nigeria. Includes extensive bibliography.

141a Benge, Ronald Charles. Bibliography and the provision of books. London: Association of Assistant Librarians, 1963. 240 p.
Written primarily as a textbook for students studying for the Final Examination of the British Library Association, it is organized into seven chapters covering the following topics: reading; writing; library service, publishing, bibliography, bibliographic location of items and professional responsibility. References follow each chapter.
Rev: Bull. Doc. Bibliog., IX (Aug. 1964), 448-9. Library Assoc. Rec., LXVI (Jan. 1964), 43.

142 Bousso, A., et al. "A Library education policy for the developing countries," UNESCO Bull. Lib., XXII (July/Aug. 1968), 173-88.

143 Bown, Lalage and Michael Crowder, eds. First International Congress of Africanists: proceedings, Accra, 11-18 December 1962. With a foreword by Kenneth Onwuka Dike. London: Longmans for the International Congress of Africanists, 1964. 368 p.

144 Brokensha, David and Michael Crowder, eds. Africa in the wider world: the inter-relationship of area and comparative studies. New York: Oxford University Press, 1967. 219 p. (Commonwealth and international library.)
Papers presented at the conference held in Sierra Leone in 1966 sponsored by the Institute of International Studies of the University of California and the Institute of African Studies of Fourah Bay College, Sierra Leone.

145   Carter, Gwendolen M. and Ann Paden, eds. Expanding hori-
      zons in African studies; Program of African Studies, North-
      western University; proceedings of the twentieth anniversary
      conference, 1968. Evanston, Ill.: Northwestern University
      Press, 1969. 364 p.
         Subjects discussed include religion, archaeology, art,
      music, linguistics, economics, geography, politics, etc.
      Contributors are authorities in their own fields.
         Rev: Choice, VII (July 1970), 738. Library J., XCV
      (May 15, 1970), 1857.

146   Collier, Robert Gordon. "The Cooperative Africana Microform
      Project," Africana Library J., II (Autumn 1971), 12-14.

147   Ferguson, John and L. A. Thompson. Africa in classical
      antiquity. Ibadan: Ibadan University Press, 1969. 222 p.

148   Fraser, Donald. The Future of Africa. Westport, Conn.:
      Negro Universities Press, 1970. 309 p.
         Reprint of the 1911 ed.

149   Gardner, Frank. "UNESCO and library and related services
      in Africa," UNESCO Bull. Lib., XX (Sept./Oct. 1966),
      212-8.

150   Institute of Commonwealth Studies, London. The Impact of
      African issues on the Commonwealth. London: University
      of London Institute of Commonwealth Studies, 1969. 70 p.
      (Collected seminar papers series, No. 6.)

151   Jackson, Miles M., ed. Comparative and international li-
      brarianship; essays on themes and problems. Westport,
      Conn.: Greenwood Publishing Corp., 1970. 307 p.
         Beginning with a useful introductory essay by the editor,
      it brings together original essays on different kinds of
      libraries and library problems by well-informed writers
      from different nationalities and is designed "to give to both
      students and practitioners of librarianship and the related
      sciences a composite view of the problems, progress, and
      prospects for librarianship ... [and] provides an assessment
      of recent and historical developments that have taken place
      on a worldwide basis" (Introduction). Each chapter is fol-
      lowed by valuable references. The appendix provides
      statistical information on books in the National Libraries
      of the U.S.S.R., Latin America and Africa. General index.
         Rev: J. Doc., XXVII (June 1971), 162-3. Library
      Assoc. Rec., LXXIII (June 1971), 121-2. Ont. Library
      Rev., LV (June 1971), 132-3.

151a Landheer, Bartholomeus. Social functions of libraries. New
      York: Scarecrow Press, 1957. 287 p.
         Surveys various aspects of social functions of the library;

importance of reading in personality development; and the
role of the writer in different cultural situations. Select
bibliography and index.
  Rev: Coll. & Res. Lib., XIX (May 1958), 255. J. Doc.,
XIV (June 1958), 79-80.

152 Line, Maurice B. "Information requirements in the social
     sciences: some preliminary considerations," J. Libr., I
     (Jan. 1969), 1-29.

153 Miner, Horace, ed. The City in modern Africa. New York:
     Praeger, 1967. 364 p.
       Consists of studies by scholars of different disciplines--
     anthropology, economics, political science, psychology,
     sociology and geography. Countries studied include Ghana,
     Nigeria, the Ivory Coast, Uganda, Zambia, etc.
       Rev: J. Asian Afr. Stud., V (Jan./April 1970), 130-1.

154 Molnos, Angela. "Whither African bibliographies, an observer's
     afterthoughts to a recent conference," East African Journal,
     V (Feb. 1968), 17-25.

155 Moore, Clark and Ann Dunbar, eds. Africa yesterday and
     today. New York: Praeger, 1968. 394 p.
       Comprises excerpts from books and periodicals, with
     emphasis on politics and history. Organized into six sec-
     tions. I. A geographical view of the continent. II. The
     structure of African cultures. III. Survey of the past.
     IV. The development of colonial systems between World
     War I and World War II. V. Africa since World War II.
     VI. The future of Africa. Bibliography.

156 Panofsky, Hans E. "African studies in American libraries."
     In Tsuen-Hsuin Tsien and Howard W. Winger, eds. Area
     studies and the library. Chicago: University of Chicago
     Press, 1966, pp. 96-105.
       Paper delivered at the Thirteenth Annual Conference of
     the University of Chicago Graduate Library School, 1965.

157 _____. "Cooperative acquisitions efforts in Africana."
     In Annette Hoage Phinazee, ed. Materials by and about
     American Negroes. Atlanta: School of Library Service,
     Atlanta University, 1967, pp. 55-61.
       Paper presented at an institute sponsored by the Atlanta
     University School of Library Service with the cooperation of
     the Trevor Arnett Library, 1965.

158 _____. "National libraries and bibliographies in Africa."
     In Miles M. Jackson, ed. Comparative and international
     librarianship: essays on themes and problems. Westport,
     Conn.: Greenwood Publishing Corp., 1970, pp. 229-55.
       "Attempts to describe briefly the present state of national

libraries and national bibliographies in Africa, as well as
bibliographical work pertinent to Africa performed else-
where. "

159 "Periodicals and magazines on African literature," Africana
     Library J. , I (Fall 1970), 14-20.
          A survey in two parts. I: Major literary and cultural
     periodicals. II: Little magazines and other general African-
     ist periodicals that frequently include creative writing from
     Africa, essays, book reviews, bibliographies, etc. on
     African literature. All entries are well annotated, specify-
     ing editorial policy and office.

160 Rieger, Morris. "Statement of objectives and functions of
     the working group for technical assistance to developing
     countries of the International Council of Archives," Africana
     Library J. , II (Autumn 1971), 7-8.

161 "A Report on the meeting of the Archives-Libraries Committee
     of the African Studies Association--U. S. A. , held in Denver,
     Colorado, November 3, 1971," Africana Library J. , II
     (Winter 1971), 23-5.

162 SCOLMA. Conference on the acquisition of material from
     Africa, Birmingham University, 1969; reports and papers.
     Compiled by Valerie Bloomfield. Zug, Switzerland: Inter
     Documentation Co. , 1969. 154 p.

163 Seck, A. Dakar: métropole ouest-africaine. Dakar: IFAN,
     1970. 535 p.

164 "Study sessions on African historical archives," UNESCO Bull.
     Lib. , XX (Nov. 1966), 327.

165 Taylor, Alan R. "Library and archival resources for African
     studies: present state and future needs," Paper presented
     at the Eleventh Annual Meeting of the African Studies Asso-
     ciation, Los Angeles, 1968.

166 Varley, Douglas Harold. "Conference of University Libraries
     in Tropical Africa," UNESCO Bull. Lib. , XIX (March/
     April 1965), 73-6.

167 _____. "University library cooperation in tropical Africa,"
     Libri, XV, No. 1 (1965), 64-71.
          Paper given at the Leverhulme Library Conference, Salis-
     bury, 1964.

168 _____. The Role of the librarian in the new Africa. Lon-
     don: Oxford University Press, 1963.
          An inaugural lecture given in the University College of
     Rhodesia and Nyasaland (Malawi), 1962.

169 Wattenberg, Ben and Ralph Lee Smith. The New nations of
     Africa. New York: Hart, 1963. 479 p.
         Surveys the geographical, cultural, political and economic
     conditions in the new nations and assesses their position in
     the Cold War.

170 Webster, John B. "Toward an international automated biblio-
     graphic system for Africana, " Paper presented at the
     Eleventh Annual Meeting of the African Studies Association,
     Los Angeles, 1968.

171 Willemin, Silvère. "The Training of librarians in Africa, "
     UNESCO Bull. Lib., XXI (Nov. /Dec. 1967), 291-300.

172 Williams, G. Mennen. Africa for the Africans. Grand
     Rapids, Michigan: Euerdmans, 1969. 218 p.
         An account of author's five years service as U. S.
     Assistant Secretary for African Affairs. In part I, he
     describes democracy, socialism, one-party government
     and non-alignment policy, communism, etc. In part 2,
     White supremacist governments of Rhodesia, South Africa
     and Portugal in its African territories. In part 3: U. S.
     policy towards Africa-trade investment, assistance and
     Peace Corps.
         Rev: New Republic, CLXII (Jan. 24, 1970), 24.

172a Wilson, Patrick. Two kinds of power: an essay on biblio-
     graphical control. Berkeley: University of California
     Press, 1968. 155 p. (University of California Publica-
     tions: Librarianship, No. 5.)
         A scholarly, philosophical examination of the problem of
     bibliographic control in which the philosopher-librarian dis-
     tinguishes between two kinds of bibliographic power--"de-
     scriptive power" and "exploitative power. " He states, "two
     notions [are] singled out for particular discussion, largely
     critical: the notion of relevance, central to the study of
     information retrieval, and the notion of the subject of a
     writing, central to library practice" (p. 2). Professor Wil-
     son is the Dean of the School of Librarianship, University
     of California, Berkeley.
         Rev: J. Doc., XXV (June 1969), 158-9. Library J.,
     XCIV (Feb. 1, 1969), 517-8. Library Q., XXXIX (Jan.
     1969), 112-4.

(2) ANTHROPOLOGY, ARCHAEOLOGY, PHILOSOPHY, RELIGION,
     SOCIOLOGY

173 Abraham, William E. The Mind of Africa. London: Weiden-
     feld & Nicolson, 1962. 206 p.
         Contending that every society has an ideology, this Oxford-
     trained philosopher examines the metaphysical, rational and

spiritual world view of Africa and contrasts it with the
materialistic and scientific philosophies of the developed
Western and Eastern countries.
> Rev: Commonweal, LXXVII (May 31, 1963), 286. TLS,
> (Dec. 7, 1962), 948.

174 African Research Group. African Studies in America: the
extended family. A tribal analysis of U. S. Africanists; who
they are, why to fight them. Cambridge, Mass., 1970.
93 p.

175 Ardrey, Robert. African genesis: a personal investigation
into animal origins and nature of men. New York: Atheneum, 1961. 380 p.
> Rev: New Statesman, LXII (Dec. 1, 1961), 846. N. Y.
> Times Bk. Rev. (Nov. 19, 1961), 4.

176 Arnott, Kathleen. African myths and legends. Illus. by Joan
Kiddell-Monroe. London: Oxford University Press, 1962.
211 p. (Myths and legends series.)
> Various aspects of African life--abuse of justice; belief
> in witchcraft; power of patience and endurance, etc. In-
> tended for young people.

177 Balandier, Georges. Sens et puissance; les dynamiques
sociales. Paris: Presses Universitaires de France, 1971.
312 p. (Bibliothèque de Sociologie contemporaine.)

178 Barrett, David. Schism and renewal in Africa: an analysis
of six thousand contemporary religious movements. New
York: Oxford University Press, 1968. 363 p.

179 Beattie, John H. and John Middleton, eds. Spirit mediumship
and society in Africa. New York: Africana Publishing
Corp., 1969. 310 p.
> A set of thirteen studies by noted psychologists and
> anthropologists on the phenomena of spirit possession and
> mediumship, and on the impact of spirit cults on social
> change.
> Rev: Library J., XCIV (Dec. 1, 1969), 4441. TLS
> (March 5, 1970), 261.

180 Briggs, L. C. Tribes of the Sahara. Cambridge: Harvard
University Press, 1960. 295 p.

181 Brokensha, David. Applied anthropology in English-speaking
Africa. Lexington, Ky: Society for Applied Anthropology,
1966. 31 p. (Society for Applied Anthropology, monograph,
No. 8.)

182 _____ and M. Pearsall, eds. The Anthropology of development in sub-Saharan Africa. Lexington: Kentucky University
Press, 1969. 100 p.

183 Brooks, Hugh and Yassin El Ayouty, eds. Refugees south of
     the Sahara: an African dilemma. Westport, Conn.: Negro
     Universities Press, 1970. 307 p.
         Rev: African Affairs, LXXI (Jan. 1972), 89-90.

184 Bunbury, Isla. "Women's position as workers in Africa
     south of the Sahara," Civilisations, XI, No. 2 (1961), 159-
     67.

185 Carey, Margaret. Myths and Legends of Africa. Feltham:
     Hamlyn, 1970. 160 p.

186 Carlston, Kenneth S. Social theory and African tribal organ-
     ization: the development of socio-legal history. Urbana:
     University of Illinois Press, 1968. 462 p.
         Rev: Amer. Anthrop., LXXI (Aug. 1969), 757. Science,
     CLXIV (June 6, 1969), 1158.

187 Clignet, Remi. Many wives, many powers: authority and
     power in polygamous families. Evanston, Ill.: North-
     western University Press, 1970. 380 p.
         Attempts to clarify the meaning of polygamy in modern
     Africa in the light of the western missionary's belief that
     the practice has been an instrument of domination of women
     by men.
         Rev: Africa Report, XVI (April 1971), 39-40.

188 Desai, Ram, ed. African society and culture. New York:
     M. W. Lads, 1968. 130 p.
         Examination of different African folktales.

189 Edinburgh. University. Centre of African Studies. Witchcraft
     and healing: proceedings of a seminar. Edinburgh, 1969.
     87 p.

190 Egbuna, Obi Benue. Destroy this temple: the voice of Black
     Power in Britain. London: MacGibbon & Kee, 1971. 157 p.
         "This book is a love-letter, perhaps the most sincere
     love-letter I have ever written ... motivated by love which
     I feel for all the oppressed peoples of the world.... It is
     a love letter to my people, a record of my experiences so
     that those who will come after us will not have to run the
     gauntlet my generation has been through in order to learn
     the black--and--white facts of life" (Introduction). The
     author, a Nigerian novelist and playwright, compares racial
     discrimination in the United States with that in Britain.

191 Evans-Pritchard, E. E. The Position of women in primitive
     societies. London: Faber & Faber, 1965. 260 p.
         Rev: Ann. Amer. Acad. Pol. Soc. Sci., CCCLXIII
     (Jan. 1966), 206. Book Week, X (April 10, 1966), 8.

192   Fagan, Brian M. In the beginning: introduction to archaeol-
      ogy. Waltham, Mass.: Little, Brown, 1972.
      Dr. Fagan is Professor of Anthropology and Archaeology
      at the University of California, Santa Barbara.

193   _____. Iron age cultures in Zambia. London: Chatto &
      Windus, 1967-69. 2 v. (Robins series, No. 5.)

194   _____. Southern Africa during the iron age. New York:
      Praeger, 1965. 222 p. (Ancient peoples and places, 46.)
      Rev: Nat. Hist., LXXV (Aug. 1966), 11. TLS (Aug. 4,
      1966), 711.

195   Fagg, William. Divine kingship in Africa. London: British
      Museum Publications, 1970. (unpaged) (59 p.) plates 40 p.

196   Gatewood, Richard. Some American Protestant contributions
      to the welfare of African countries in 1963. New York:
      National Council of the Churches of Christ, 1964. 88 p.

197   Gelfand, Michael. The African witch; with particular refer-
      ence to witchcraft beliefs and practice among the Shona of
      Rhodesia. London: E. & S. Livingstone, 1967. 227 p.
      Rev: J. Asian Afr. Stud., V (1970), 315-6.

198   Hamrell, S., ed. Refugee problems in Africa. Uppsala:
      Scandinavian Institute of African Studies, 1968. 121 p.

199   Hance, William A. Population, migration, and urbanization
      in Africa. New York: Columbia University Press, 1970.
      450 p.
      Rev: Choice, VII (Feb. 1971), 1702. Library J., XCV
      (Aug. 1970), 2704.

200   Hanna, William John and Judith Lynne Hanna. Urban dynamics
      in black Africa: an interdisciplinary approach. Chicago:
      Aldine-Atherton, 1971. 390 p.
      Contents include patterns of urban growth, urban migra-
      tion and commitment; impact of migration and town life
      upon the individual; urban conditions; urban ethnicity; non-
      ethnic perspectives and practices; bases of political conflict;
      bases of political integration; patterns of change. Extensive
      bibliography, pp. 209-378. William Hanna is Professor of
      Political Science at the City University of New York, and
      Judith Hanna is Adjunct Professor of Liberal Arts, Fordham
      University, Lincoln Center.

201   Harris, F. J. Social casework: an introduction for students
      in developing countries. London: Oxford University Press,
      1971. 185 p.

202   International Labour Office. Women workers in a changing
      world. Geneva, 1963. 133 p.

203 King, Noel Q. Religions of Africa: a pilgrimage into traditional religions. New York: Harper & Row, 1970. 116 p.

204 Lacouture, Jean. The Demi-gods: charismatic leadership in
the third world. Translated from the French by Patricia
Wolf. New York: Knopf, 1970. 300 p. French ed., by
Editions du Seuil, Paris, 1969.

205 Lambo, T. A. African traditional beliefs, concepts of health
and medical practice. Ibadan: Ibadan University Press,
1963. 11 p.
Dr. Lambo is a noted Nigerian psychiatrist.

206 Leakey, Louis Seymour. The Progress and evolution of man
in Africa. London: Oxford University Press, 1961. 50 p.

207 _____. Stone age Africa: an outline of prehistory in
Africa. Westport, Conn.: Negro Universities Press, 1970.
21 p. Reprint of ed. London, 1936.

208 Legum, Colin. "Tribal survival in the modern African political
system," J. Asian Afr. Stud., V (Jan./April 1970), 102-12.

209 Little, Kenneth. Some contemporary trends in African urbanization. Evanston, Ill.: Northwestern University Press,
1966. 15 p. (Melville J. Herskovits memorial lecture, 2.)
Paper delivered under the auspices of the Program of
African Studies, Northwestern University on April 20, 1965.

210 Lloyd, Peter C. The new elites of tropical Africa; studies
presented and discussed at the Sixth International African
Seminar at the University of Ibadan, Nigeria, July 1964.
Foreword by Daryll Forde. Lon.: Oxford Univ. Press, for the
International African Institute, 1966. 390 p. Bibliog.
Includes contributions in French.
Rev: New Statesman, LXXII (Aug. 26, 1966), 294; TLS
(Sept. 15, 1966), 854.

211 Lystad, Robert, ed. African world: a survey of social research. New York: Praeger, 1965. 575 p.
Consists of 18 bibliographical essays, each summarizing
the present state of knowledge and research in a specific
field--the humanities, social or medical sciences. Emphasis
is on sub-Saharan English and French publications.
Rev: Choice, II (Feb. 1966), 853. Library J., XC
(June 15, 1965), 2835.

212 McGee, Terence Gary. The Urbanization process in the
third world: exploration in search of a theory. London:
Bell, 1971. 179 p.

213 Maistriaux, Robert. La Femme et la destin de l'Afrique:
les sources psychologiques de la mentalité dite "primitive."

Pref. de Edouard Morot--Sir. Elisabethville: Editions CEPSI, 1964. 534 p. (Centre d'étude des problèmes sociaux indigenes. Collection de memoires, V, No. 16.)

214 Maquet, Jacques Jerome. Africanité, traditionnelle et moderne. Paris: Présence Africaine, 1967. 180 p.

215 _____. Power and society in Africa. London: Weidenfeld & Nicolson, 1971. 256 p.

216 Miller, Norman N., ed. Research in rural Africa. East Lansing: African Studies Center, Michigan State University, 1970. 341 p.

217 Mullin, Joseph. The Catholic Church in modern Africa: a pastoral theology. London: Chapman, 1966. 256 p.

218 Neill, Stephen Charles. Christian faith and other faiths: the Christian dialogue with other religions. 2nd ed. London: Oxford University Press, 1970. 245 p.

219 _____. The Church and Christian union. New York: Oxford University Press, 1968. 423 p. (The Bampton lectures, 1964.)

220 _____. Twentieth Century Christianity: a study of modern religious trends by leading churchman. Garden City, New York: Doubleday, 1963. 432 p.

221 Oosthuizen, G. C. Post-Christianity in Africa: a theological and anthropological study. London: Hurst, 1968. 273 p.
    Chiefly a theological but critical examination of independent churches.
    Rev: Africa, XLI (April 1971), 175-6.

222 Ottenberg, Simon and Phoebe Ottenberg, eds. Cultures and societies of Africa. New York: Random House, 1960. 614 p.
    Rev: Amer. Anthrop., LXIII (April 1961), 431. Amer. Soc. Rev., XXVI (April 1961), 332.

223 Parrinder, E. Geoffrey. African mythology. London: Hamlyn, 1967. 139 p.

224 Paulme, Denise. Women of tropical Africa. London: Routledge, 1963. 308 p.

225 Scobie, Alastair. The Women of Africa. London: Cassell, 1960. 184 p.

226 Shinnie, P. L., ed. The African iron age. London: Oxford University Press, 1971. 320 p.

227 Southall, Aidan, ed. Social change in modern Africa. With
a foreword by Daryll Forde. New York: Oxford University
Press for the International African Institute, 1963. 337 p.

228 Thomas, Louis Vincent, et al. Les Religions d'Afrique noire.
Textes et traditions sacrés. Paris: Fayard, 1969. 407 p.
(Coll. Le Trèsor spirituel des l'humanité.)

229 Thurnher, Majda Theresia. "A Comparative study of marriage
stability in African societies," Doctoral Dissertation, University of California, Berkeley, 1966. 197 p.

230 United Nations. Commission on the Status of Women. United
Nations assistance for the advancement of women in developing countries. New York, 1962. 17 p. (E/CN. 6/
395)

231 Williams, G. Mennen. "Women in the new Africa: address,
September 24, 1963," U.S. Dept. State Bull., XLIX (Oct.
21, 1963), 636-9.

232 Zahan, Dominique. Religion, spiritualité et pensée africaines.
Paris: Payot, 1970. 248 p. (Bibliothèque scientifique.)

233 Ziegler, Jean. Sociologie de la nouvelle Afrique. Paris:
Gallimard, 1964. 380 p. (Coll. idées 59.)

(3) ECONOMICS, LAW, POLITICS

234 Adie, W. A. C. "China and Africa today," Race, V (April
1964), 3-25.

235 "Africa in the seventies: population, investment," Afr. Dev.
(London), (Jan. 1970), 10-13.

236 "Africa, the United States and the future," In Nancy Hoepli,
ed. West Africa today, New York: H. W. Wilson, 1971,
pp. 156-84.

237 African Communist, London. Ten years, 1959-1969 of the
African communist. London: Unkululeko Publications (30
Goodge Street), 1969. 104 p.

238 "African Socialism," African Forum, I (Winter 1966), 3-71.
Six articles by various contributors including Kwame
Nkrumah and Leopold Sedar Senghor.

239 Akpan, Moses E. "African strategies in the United Nations,
1960-1966." Doctoral Dissertation, Southern University,
1970. 183 p.

240 Alderfer, Harold Freed. Local government in developing
     countries. New York: McGraw-Hill, 1964. 251 p. (Mc-
     Graw-Hill series in international development.)
       Rev: J. Asian Stud., XXIV (Feb. 1965), 313.

241 _____. Public administration in newer nations. New York:
     Praeger, 1967. 206 p. (Praeger special studies in inter-
     national politics and public affairs.)
       Rev: Choice, V (Nov. 1968), 1218.

242 Almond, Gabriel Abraham and Sidney Verba. The Civic cul-
     ture: political attitudes and democracy in five nations; an
     analytic study. Boston: Little, Brown, 1965. 379 p.
     (The Little, Brown series in comparative politics.)
       Rev: Journal of Politics, XXVII (Feb. 1965), 206.

243 _____ and James S. Coleman, eds. The Politics of the
     developing areas. Princeton: Princeton University Press,
     1960. 591 p.
       Rev: Amer. J. Soc., LXVI (July 1960), 96. Current
     Hist., XXXIX (July 1960), 45.

244 Andic, Fuat, et al. A Theory of economic integration for
     developing countries. London: Allen & Unwin, 1971.
     168 p. (University of York Studies in economics, 6.)

245 Andrain, Charles Franklin. "The Pan-African movement:
     the search for organization and community in twentieth
     century Africa," Master's Thesis, University of California,
     Berkeley, 1961. 166 p.

246 _____. "Political concepts of African leaders," Doctoral
     Dissertation, University of California, Berkeley, 1964.
     334 p.

247 Andreski, Stanislav. The African predicament; a study in
     the pathology of modernization. London: Michael Joseph,
     1968. 237 p.
       Primarily on West Africa, it attempts to explain why
     the lofty hopes put on Africa by the Western powers have
     not been fulfilled, and criticizes the Western conception of
     tribalism and nationalism in Africa.
       Rev: Economist, CCXXVIII (Sept. 7, 1968), 60. TLS
     (Oct. 10, 1968), 1143.

248 "The Armies of Africa," Africa Report, IX (Jan. 1964).
     Entire issue.
       Country by country analysis--size of the armed forces;
     sources of external military assistance, defense pacts, etc.

249 Austin, Dennis and Ronald Nagel. "The Organization of
     African Unity," World Today, XXII (Dec. 1966), 520-9.

250 Baade, Hans Wolfgang, ed. African law; new law for new
     nations. Dobbs Ferry, New York: Oceana, 1963. 119 p.
     (Library of law and contemporary problems.)

251 Barnes, Leonard. African renaissance. New York: Bobbs-
     Merrill, 1969. 304 p.
     Political instability and lack of economic progress in
     Africa emanate primarily from a misplaced emphasis on
     African governmental policy.
     Rev: TLS (Feb. 6, 1969), 139.

252 Baum, E. "The United States, self-government and Africa:
     an examination of the nature of the American policy on self-
     determination with reference to Africa in the post-war era,"
     Doctoral Dissertation, University of California, 1964.

253 Beling, Willard A., ed. The Role of labor in African nation-
     buildings; proceedings of the Institute of World Affairs. New
     York: Praeger, 1968. 204 p.
     All chapters except one are derived from the papers pre-
     sented at the conference sponsored by the University of
     Southern California, 5-7 Dec. 1965. Many of the contribu-
     tors, American experts in labor, are political scientists.
     Rev: Choice, V (Nov. 1968), 1180. Library J., XCIII
     (Oct. 15, 1968), 3779.

254 Bell, M.J. "Military assistance to independent African
     states," Adelphi Papers (London, Institute for Strategic
     Studies), No. 15 (1964).

255 Benet, Yves. Idéologies des independences africaines. Paris:
     F. Maspero, 1969. 431 p. (Cahiers libres, 139-140.)

256 Berg, Elliot. "Recruitment of a labor force in Sub-Saharan
     Africa," Doctoral Dissertation, Harvard University, 1960.

257 Bienen, Henry. "Military assistance and political develop-
     ment," Paper presented at the International Sociological
     Association Meeting, London, Sept. 1967. 90 p.

258 _____, ed. The Military intervenes; case studies in po-
     litical development. New York: Russell Sage Foundation,
     1967. 175 p.

259 Bipoun-Woum, Joseph-Marie. Le Droit international africain:
     problèmes generaux-règlement des conflits. Paris: Li-
     brairie Générale de Droit et de Jurisprudence, 1970. 327 p.
     (Bibliothèque africaine et malgache droit et sociologie po-
     litique, Vol. V.)

260 Blumenfeld, F.Y. "Tribalism vs. nationalism," Edit. Res.
     Rpts., II (Nov. 2, 1960), 803-21.

261   Bohannan, Paul, ed.   Law and warfare; studies in anthro-
      pology of conflict.   Garden City, New York: National
      History Press for the American Museum of Natural History,
      1967.   441 p.   (American Museum source books in anthro-
      pology.)
          Examination of the two basic forms of conflict resolution.
      Rev: Amer. Anthrop., LXX (June 1968), 579.

262   Boutros-Ghali, Boutros.   L'Organization de l'Unité Africaine.
      Paris: A. Colin, 1968.   197 p.

263   Bozeman, Adda Bruemmer.   The Future of law in multicul-
      tural world.   Princeton, N.J.:   Princeton University Press,
      1971.   229 p.

264   Brice, Belmont.   "The Nature and the role of the military in
      Sub-Saharan Africa," African Forum, II (Summer 1966),
      57-67.

265   Büttner, T., ed.   Revolution und Tradition.   Zur Rolle der
      Tradition im antiimperialistisvhen Kampf der Völker Afrikas
      und Asiens.   Leipzig: Scientifique Review of the Karl-Marx
      University, 1971.   224 p.

266   Butwell, Richard, ed.   Foreign policy and the developing
      nation.   Lexington, Ky.:   University of Kentucky Press,
      1969.   236 p.

267   Cervenka, Zdenek.   The Organization of African Unity and
      its Charter.   2nd ed. With an introduction by Diallo Telli.
      New York: Praeger, 1969.   253 p.
          Describes the origin, structure, and the activities of the
      body.
          Rev: Choice, VII (March 1970), 150.   Library J., XCV
      (Jan. 1, 1970), 74.

268   Coleman, James Smoot, ed.   Political parties and national
      integration in tropical Africa.   Berkeley: University of
      California Press, 1964.   730 p.
          Rev: Journal of Politics, XXVII (Nov. 1965), 892.   TLS
      (April 15, 1964), 297.

269   _____ and Belmont Brice.   "The Role of the military in
      Sub-Saharan Africa," In John Johnson, ed.   The Role of
      the military in underdeveloped countries.   Princeton, N.J.:
      Princeton University Press, 1962, pp. 359-405.

270   Collins, John.   "Foreign conflict in behavior by African

states," Doctoral Dissertation, Northwestern University, 1967.

271 Cowan, Laing Gray. The Dilemmas of African independence. Rev. ed. New York: Walker, 1968. 167 p. 1st ed. 1965. Rev: Library J., XCIII (Oct. 15, 1968), 3792. Soc. Stud., LX (Dec. 1969), 337.

272 _____. "The Military and African politics," International Journal (Toronto), XII (Summer 1966), 289-97.

273 Crocker, Chester A. "Military and security problems in the international relations of Africa," Doctoral Dissertation, Johns Hopkins University, 1968?
     Emphasis is on the historical development of military forces in former French and British colonies in Africa and the different methods used by France and Britain in transferring defense powers to those countries.

274 Daggs, Elisa. All Africa; all its political entities of independence or other status. New York: Hastings House, 1970. 824 p.
     Designed as an introduction to Africa, giving a chapter to each country, with a discussion of its history, geography, economy and politics.
     Rev: Africana Library J., I (Fall 1970), 23. Library J., XCV (Aug. 1970), 2652.

275 Damman, Ernst. Wort und Religion; Studien zur Afrikanistik, Missionswissenschaft, Religionswissenschaft. Stuttgart: Evangelischer Missionsverlag, 1969. 384 p. Bibliog.

276 Debrah, E.M. "Will most uncommitted nations remain uncommitted?" Ann. Amer. Acad. Pol. Soc. Sci., CCCXXXVI (July 1961), 83-97.
     A discussion of foreign policy of developing nations by a Ghanaian diplomat.

277 Doorn, Jacques van. Military profession and military regimes: commitments and conflicts; papers from a conference held in London on Sept. 14-16, 1967. The Hague: Mouton, 1968. 304 p.

278 Doro, Marion E. and Newell M. Stultz, eds. Governing in black Africa; perspective on new states. Englewood Cliffs, N.J.: Prentice-Hall, 1970. 362 p.
     Examines ethnicity and national integration in West Africa; monarchical tendency in African political culture; African nationalism; decision-making on international affairs; African socialism, etc.

279 El-Ayouty, Yassin. The United Nations and decolonisation: the role of Afro-Asia. The Hague: Martinus Nijhoff, 1971. 286 p.

280 Ellis, William W. "National configuration and international policies: African voting in the United Nations General Assembly; a case study," Doctoral Dissertation, New York University, 1966.

281 Emerson, R. Africa and United States policy. Englewood Cliffs, N. J.: Prentice-Hall, 1967. 117 p.

282 Euben, J. Peter. "Nationalist and communist Chinese foreign policy in Asia, Africa and Latin America," Master's Thesis, University of California, Berkeley, 1964. 229 p.

283 Ferkiss, Victor C. Africa's search for identity. New York: Braziller, 1966. 346 p.
   Rev: J. Mod. Afr. Stud., V (May 1967), 145. Library J., XC (Dec. 1, 1965), 5287.

284 Foell, Earl W. "Africa's vanishing act at the U. N.: where does the United States stand on African questions," Africa Report, XIV (Nov. 1969), 31-3.
   The author is U. N. correspondent for the Los Angeles Times.

285 Fortes, Meyer and E. E. Evans-Pritchard, eds. African political systems. London: Oxford University Press for the International African Institute, 1970. 302 p.

286 Friedland, William H. Unions and industrial relations in underdeveloped countries. Ithaca, New York: New York State School of Industrial and Labor relations, 1963. 66 p. (New York State School of Industrial & Labor Relations at Cornell. Bulletin 47.)

287 Friedmann, Wolfgang. Joint international business ventures in developing countries: case studies and analysis of recent trends. New York: Columbia University Press, 1971. 448 p.

288 Genoud, Roger. Nationalism and economic development. London: Pall Mall Press, 1969.
   Rev: West Africa, No. 2718 (July 5, 1969), 772-3.

289 Glickman, Harvey. "Regionalism and micro-politics: dialogues on the theory of African political development, Part II," African Report, XII (June 1967), 31-2.

290 Gluckman, Max, ed. Ideas and procedures in African customary law; studies presented and discussed at the Eighth

International African Seminar at the Haile Selassie I University, Addis Ababa, January 1966. With an introduction by A. N. Allott and others. London: Oxford University Press for the International African Institute, 1969. 361 p.

291 Gormerly, Patrick J. "The Population obstacle to economic transformation in Sub-Saharan Africa," J. Mod. Afr. Stud., VIII (Oct. 1970), 471-7.

292 Green, Reginald Herbold and Ann Seidman. Unity or poverty? The economics of Pan-Africanism. Harmondsworth: Penguin, 1968. (Penguin African library, AP23.)

293 _____ and K. G. V. Krishna. Economic cooperation in Africa: retrospect and prospect. Nairobi: Oxford University Press, for University College, Nairobi, 1967. 160 p.
     Based on the International Seminar on Economic Cooperation in Africa, 1965.

294 Greene, Fred. "Toward understanding military coups," Africa Report, XI (Feb. 1966), 10-11, 14.
     Contends that "a military takeover can be viewed as a step in the arduous search for order and progress, but at the same time it may be a setback in the process of maturation." Examines various motives for military coups in Africa.

295 Gutteridge, William. Armed forces in new states. London: Oxford University Press, 1962. 68 p.

296 _____. The Military in African politics. London: Methuen, 1969. 166 p. (Studies in African history, 4.)
     Rev: Afr. Stud., XXX, No. 1 (1971), 61-2.

297 _____. Military institutions and power in the new states. New York: Praeger, 1965. 182 p.

298 Hanna, William John, ed. Independent black Africa; the politics of freedom. Chicago: Rand McNally, 1964. 651 p.
     Rev: Choice, II (June 1965), 266.

299 Hannah, Harold Winford and Robert R. Caughey. The legal base for universities in developing countries. Urbana: University of Illinois Press, 1967. 455 p.
     Rev: J. Higher Educ., XXXIX (June 1968), 355. Library J., XCII (Nov. 15, 1967), 4150.

300 Harris, P. B. Studies in African politics. London: Hutchinson, 1970. 192 p.

301 Hazlewood, Arthur, ed. African integration and disintegration case studies in economic and political union. London:

Oxford University Press, 1967. 414 p.
   Rev: Africa Report, XIII (June 1968), 60-2. J. Adm.
Overseas, VII (Oct. 1968), 563.

302 Hempstone, Smith. Africa--angry young giant. New York:
     Praeger, 1961. 664 p. (Books that matter.) London ed.
     by Faber, under title: The new Africa.
        Rev: New Statesman, LXII (Sept. 22, 1961), 397. TLS
     (Sept. 22, 1961), 626.

303 Hopkins, Keith. "Civil-military relations in developing
     countries," Brit. J. Soc., XVII (June 1966), 165-82.

304 Hovet, Thomas. Africa in the United Nations. Evanston,
     Ill.: Northwestern University Press, 1963. 336 p.
     (African Studies, No. 10.)

305 Huff, Curtis E. "Political development and foreign policy:
     problems in the African countries," Doctoral Dissertation,
     Michigan State University, 1968?

306 Institut für Wirtschaftsforschung. German economic research
     in Africa: Summarizing report on the work of the African
     Studies Centre, 1961 to 1969. Munchen, 1970. 19 p.

307 Institute of Commonwealth Studies, London. Opposition in the
     new African states. London: University of London Institute
     of Commonwealth Studies, 1969. 129 p. (Collected Seminar
     papers series, No. 4.)

308 _____. Post-independence constitutional changes. London:
     University of London Institute of Commonwealth Studies,
     1969. 138 p. (Collected seminar papers series, No. 5.)

309 Inter-African Labour Institute. The Human factors of produc-
     tivity. 2nd ed. London, 1960. 159 p.

310 Italiaander, Rolf. The New leaders of Africa. Translated
     from the German by James McGovern. Englewood Cliffs:
     Prentice-Hall, 1961. 306 p.

311 Jackson, Barbara Ward. Nationalism and ideology. New
     York: Norton, 1966. 125 p.

312 _____ and P. T. Bauer. Two views on aid to developing
     countries. London: Institute of Economic Affairs, 1966.
     58 p. (Its occasional papers, No. 9.)
        Contents: The Decay of development--a study in frustra-
     tion, by Barbara Ward Jackson; Foreign aid: an instrument
     of progress, by P. T. Bauer.

313 Janowitz, Morris. The Military in the political development
     of new nations: an essay in comparative analysis. Chicago:
     University of Chicago Press, 1964. 134 p.
     Civil-military relationships in the new states.

314 Jones, D. M. V. The Time shrinkers: aviation between
     Britain and Africa. London: Rendel, 1971. 273 p.

315 Kabia, Zeinhom Mohamed. "African economic integration as
     a stimulus for economic development," Doctoral Dissertation,
     University of Illinois, 1969. 250 p.

316 Kamarck, A. M. "African economic development: problems
     and prospects," Africa Report, XIV (Jan. 1969), 16-20+.

317 Kapil, Ravi L. "On the conflict potential of inherited bound-
     aries in Africa," World Politics, XVIII (July 1966), 656-73.

318 Karioki, James N. "The Philosophy and politics of Julius
     K. Nyerere: an analysis of African statesmanship," Doc-
     toral Dissertation, American University, Washington, D. C.,
     1970. 283 p.

319 Kay, D. A. The New nations in the United Nations, 1960-67.
     New York: Columbia University Press, 1970. 254 p.

320 Kedourie, Elie, ed. Nationalism in Asia and Africa. With
     an introduction by Elie Kedourie. New York: World Pub-
     lishing Co., 1970. 573 p.

321 Klineberg, Otto and Marisa Zavolloni. Nationalism and tri-
     balism among African students: a study of social identity.
     Paris: Mouton, 1969. 324 p. (International Social Science
     Council, No. 2.)

322 Klümper, Per. Die Chemische Industrie in Afrika. Hamburg:
     Deutsches Institut für Afrika-Forschung, 1970. 173 p.
     (Afrika Branchenberichte, No. 2.)

323 Krishnamurthy, S. "The African Development Bank," Africa
     Quarterly, VI (April/June 1966), 60-5.

324 Kuper, Hilda and Leo Kuper, ed. African law; adaptation and
     development. Berkeley: University of California Press,
     1965. 275 p.
     A scholarly analysis of the process of adaptation in
     African jural systems.
         Rev: Choice, III (Nov. 1966), 837. Soc. Rev., XV
     (July 1967), 251.

325 Lee, J. M. African armies and civil order. New York:
     Praeger, 1969. 198 p. (Institute for Strategic Studies.

Studies in international security, 13.)
Rev: Amer. Pol. Sci. Rev., LXIV (June 1970), 599.
Choice, VI (Dec. 1969), 1484.

326 Legum, Colin. "Nationalism's impact on Pan-Africanism,"
East African Journal, II (April 1965), 5-16; 38-40.

327 Legvold, Robert. "Moscow's changing view of Africa's
revolutionary regimes," Africa Report, XIV (Mar./April
1969), 54-8.

328 Lloyd, Peter J. International trade problems of small
nations. Durham, N.C.: Duke University Press, 1968.
140 p.
Rev: Choice, V (Oct. 1968), 1010. Library J., XCIII
(June 1, 1968), 2234.

328a Lofchie, M.F., ed. The State of the nations: constraints
on development in independent Africa. Berkeley: University of California Press, 1971. 305 p.

329 Loken, R. De L. Manpower development in Africa. New
York: Praeger, 1969. 152 p.

330 McKay, Vernon, ed. African diplomacy; studies in the de-
termination of foreign policy. New York: Praeger, 1966.
210 p.
Rev: Amer. Pol. Sci. Rev., LXI (Sept. 1967), 839.

331 Manigat, M. "L'Organisation de l'Unité Africaine (Les conflicts internationaux)," Rev. Fr. Sci. Pol. (April 1971),
382-401.

331a Maquet, Jacques. Power and society in Africa. London:
Weidenfeld & Nicolson, 1971. 254 p.
A good introduction to African politics written by a French
anthropologist.
Rev: Africa, XLII (Oct. 1972), 346.

332 Matthews, Ronald. African powder-keg: revolt and discontent
in six emergent nations. London: Bodley Head, 1966.
223 p.
Deals with Algeria, Ghana, Congo (Brazzaville), Gabon,
Dahomey and Malawi.

333 Mazrui, Ali A. "Political hygiene and cultural transition in
Africa," J. Asian Afr. Stud., V (Jan./April 1970), 113-25.

334 Mboya, Tom J. "The Party system and democracy in Africa,"
Foreign Affairs, XLI (1963), 650-8.

335   Mendes, Joao. La Revolution en Afrique; problèmes et per-
        spectives. Paris: The Author (5 rue Auguste-Simon),
        1970. 285 p.

336   Mosely, Philip E. "Soviet policy in the developing countries,"
        Foreign Affairs, XLIII (Oct. 1964), 87-98.

337   Nader, Laura, ed. Law in culture and society. Chicago:
        Aldine Pub. Co., 1969. 454 p.
        Papers presented at a 2nd Wenner-Gren Conference held
        at Burg Wartenstein, Gloggnitz, Austria, Aug. 3-13, 1966.

338   Nicol, Davidson, ed. Black nationalism in Africa 1867; ex-
        tracts from the political, educational, scientific and medical
        writings of Africanus Horton. New York: Africana Publish-
        ing Corp., 1970. 186 p.
        Dr. James Africanus Horton, a distinguished physician
        and versatile writer, was considered one of the most informed
        spokesmen for African culture in Victorian Europe. He
        was also known for his passionate defense of Africans'
        capacity for self-government.
        Rev: Afr. Hist. Stud., IV (1971), 449-50; West Africa,
        No. 2752 (March 7, 1970), 261.

339   Nottingham, John. "Establishing an African publishing in-
        dustry: a study in decolonization," African Affairs, LXVIII
        (April 1969), 139-44.
        The need for indigenous publishing in Africa stressed by
        the Director of the East African Publishing House in Nairobi,
        Kenya. The article was originally a paper delivered to the
        Conference of the U. K. African Studies Association at Sussex
        on 19 September, 1968.

340   Nyerere, Julius K. "One-party rule," Atlas, III (1962), 185-7.

341   Organization for Economic Cooperation and Development. In-
        vesting in developing countries; facilities for the promotion
        of foreign private investment in developing countries. Paris:
        O. E. C. D., 1970. 120 p.

342   Ostrander, F. Taylor. "U. S. private investment in Africa,"
        Africa Report, XIV (Jan. 1969), 38-41.
        Includes 4 tables: I: Total U. S. direct investment in
        Africa. II: U. S. direct investment in Africa by type of
        activity. III: Total U. S. direct investment abroad.
        IV: Total U. S. investment abroad by principal areas.

343   Payne, Denis, ed. African independence and Christian free-
        dom: addresses delivered at Makarere University College,
        Uganda, in 1962. London: Oxford University Press, 1965.
        89 p. (A Three crown book.)

344   Perham, Margery. "The Psychology of African nationalism,"
      Optima, X (March 1960), 27-36.

345   Pistrak, Lazar. "Soviet views on Africa," Problems of Com-
      munism, XI (March/April 1962), 24-31.

346   Quigg, P. W. "The Changing American view of Africa,"
      Africa Report, XIV (Jan. 1969), 8-11.

347   Rothchild, Donald. "The Limits of federalism: an examina-
      tion of political institutional transfer in Africa," J. Mod.
      Afr. Stud., IV (Nov. 1966), 275-93.

347a _____. "New trends in African integration," Africa Today,
      XV (Nov. /Dec. 1968), 6-8.

348   Rubinstein, G. "Aspects of Soviet-African economic relations,"
      J. Mod. Afr. Stud., VIII (Oct. 1970), 387-404.

349   Sampson, Anthony. Common sense about Africa. New York:
      MacMillan, 1960. 175 p.
      The theme is African nationalism.
      Rev: TLS (Feb. 5. 1960), 75.

350   Sandler, Bea. The African cookbook. New York: World
      Publishing Co., 1970. 232 p.

351   Scalapino, Robert A. "Sino-Soviet competition in Africa,"
      Foreign Affairs, XLI (July 1964), 640-54.

352   Schapiro, Leonard. "The Soviet dream in Africa," Encounter,
      XXIV (Feb. 1965), 49-53.

353   Segal, Aaron. "Africa newly divided?" J. Mod. Afr. Stud.,
      II (May 1964), 73-90.
      Discusses the association of some independent African
      states with the European Economic Community or 'Common
      Market' and the relations of Britain and France and their
      respective African dependencies in the pre-independence
      period following World War II.

354   _____. "External impact on African integration," Africa
      Today (Oct. /Nov. 1968), 13-15.
      Minority and integration problems in independent African
      states.

355   Sigmund, Paul E., ed. The Ideologies of the developing
      nations. With a foreword by Reinhold Niebuhr. Rev. ed.
      New York: Praeger, 1967. 428 p. Reprint of the 1963 ed.
      The anthology of the political theories and ideologies of
      the leaders of the new nations, divided into four parts.
      I: Asia, II: The Islamic world, III: Africa, IV: Latin

America. Includes a select bibliography grouped by geographic area. No index.
Rev: Choice, V (Sept. 1968), 874.

356 Shearer, John Jordan. "Africa's new role in world politics,"
Master's Thesis, University of California, Berkeley, 1961.
107 p.

357 Sinha, Surya. "New nations and the law of nations," Doctoral
Dissertation, University of Illinois, 1966.
Examines the attitudes of Asian and African states to-
wards the existing rules of international law.

358 Sklar, Richard L. "Political science and national integration--
a radical approach," J. Mod. Afr. Stud., V (May 1967),
1-11.

359 Smith, Thomas. Elections in developing countries: a study of
electoral procedures used in Tropical Africa, South-East
Asia and the Caribbean. London: Macmillan, 1960. 278 p.

360 Stevenson, Robert F. Population and political systems in
tropical Africa. New York: Columbia University Press,
1968. 306 p.

361 Sufrin, Sidney C. Unions in emerging societies: frustration
and policies. Syracuse: Syracuse University Press, 1960.
124 p.
Includes an annotated bibliography.

362 Szentes, T. Introduction to the economy of tropical Africa.
Budapest: Hungarian Academy of Sciences, 1968. 69 p.

363 Telli, Diallo. "The Organization of African Unity in historical perspective," African Forum, I (Aug. 1965), 7-28.

364 United Nations. Economic Commission for Africa. The Impact
of Western European integration on African trade and development. New York, 1960. (E/CN. 14/72)

365 U.S. Dept. of Commerce. Digest of African countries' economic development plans. Washington, D.C. Supt. of Docs.,
U.S. Govt. Printing Office, 1970.

366 U.S. Agency for International Development. U.S. foreign aid
in Africa; proposed fiscal year 1971 program. Washington,
D.C., 1970.

367 Wallerstein, Immanuel. Africa; the politics of a contemporary
social movement. New York: Random House, 1967. 274 p.
Rev: Book Week (May 7, 1967), 14. Amer. Soc. Rev.,
XXXII (Dec. 1967), 1031.

368 _____. "African unity reassessed," Africa Report, XI
       (April 1966), 41-7.

369 Welch, Claude Emerson. "Soldier and state in Africa,"
       J. Mod. Afr. Stud., V, Nov. 3 (1967), 305-22.

370 _____. Soldier and state in Africa: a comparative analysis
       of military intervention and political change. Evanston, Ill.:
       Northwestern University Press, 1970. 320 p.
       The roots and implications of military intervention; the
       military and politics; the military and political change in
       Africa. Appendix A: Armed strength and defense expendi-
       tures of various African states in 1966. Appendix B: Vio-
       lence and military involvement in African politics from in-
       dependence through 1968. Selected bibliography.

371 Widstrand, C. G., ed. African boundary problems. Uppsala:
       Scandinavian Institute of African Studies, 1969. 202 p.
       Papers presented at the seminar organized by the Scandi-
       navian Institute of African Studies.

372 Wilson, Dick. "China's economic relations with Africa,"
       Race, V (April 1964), 61-71.

373 Woddis, Jack. Africa, the roots of revolt. New York:
       Citadel Press, 1962. 285 p.

374 Wraith, Ronald and Edgar Simpkins. Corruption in developing
       countries. New York: Norton, 1963. 211 p.
       Rev: Economist, CCIX (Dec. 1, 1963), 1274. TLS
       (Dec. 26, 1963), 1059.

375 Wriggins, William Howard. The Ruler's imperative: strate-
       gies for political survival in Asia and Africa. New York:
       Columbia University Press, 1969. 275 p. (Southern Asia
       Institute publication.)
       Rev: Library J., XCIV (Nov. 1, 1969), 4014. Pacific
       Affairs, XLIII (Fall 1970), 422.

376 Ziegler, Jean. Le Contre-révolution en Afrique. Paris:
       Payot, 1963. 242 p. (Etudes et documents Payot.)

(4) EDUCATION, GEOGRAPHY, HISTORY, PSYCHOLOGY

377 Abernethy, David and Coombe Trevor. "Education and poli-
       tics in developing countries," Harvard Educ. Rev., XXXV
       (Summer 1965), 287-302.
       "Education and politics are inextricably linked. A govern-
       ment's education policy reflects and sometimes betrays its
       view of society or political creed."

378 African-American Institute, New York. "Factors contributing
     to prolongation of students' U. S. stay or failure to return to
     Africa, " Paper presented at a Conference on Admission and
     Guidance of African Students, Howard University, March
     1967.

379 "African education South of the Sahara, " J. Negro Educ. , XXX
     (Summer 1961), 173-364.
          Various articles by different contributors on the educational
     problems in the area, with emphasis on the difficulties of
     obtaining adequate finances and personnel.

380 African Studies Association of the United Kingdom. Education
     in Africa: proceedings the third (1968) Conference. Nai-
     robi: East African Publishing House, 1969.

381 "African studies in the United States, " Afr. Stud. Bull. , XI
     (April 1968), 83-127.
          A classified listing of American universities with African
     studies centers, giving information on faculty, courses,
     fellowships, summer programs, etc.

382 Anumonye, Amechi. African students in alien cultures. Buf-
     falo: Black Academy Press, 1970. 148 p.

383 Ashby, Eric. African universities and western tradition. Cam-
     bridge, Mass;: Harvard University Press, 1964. 113 p.
     (The Godkin lectures at Harvard University, 1964.)
          Rev: Harvard Educ. Rev. , XXXV (Winter 1965), 104.
     J. Higher Educ. , XXXVI (May 1965), 295.

384 _____. Patterns of universities in non-European societies.
     London: School of Oriental and African Studies, University
     of London, 1961.

385 _____. Universities: British, Indian, African: a study in
     the ecology of higher education. Cambridge, Mass. : Harvard
     University Press, 1966. 558 p. Bibliog.
          Rev: Harvard Educ. Rev. , XXXVII (Spring 1967), 281.
     TLS (Feb. 2, 1967), 77.

386 Beeby, C. E. The Quality of education in developing countries.
     Cambridge, Mass. : Harvard University Press, 1966. 139 p.
          Examines the concept of quality and describes the relative
     functions of the educator and the economist in educational
     planning.
          Rev: Harvard Educ. Rev. , XXXVI (Fall 1966), 533.

387 Benveniste, Guy and Warren F. Ilchman, eds. Agents of
     change: professionals in developing countries. New York:
     Praeger, 1969. 252 p.
          "Based on the papers presented at an international

conference held at the University of California, Berkeley, in
May 1968, under the auspices of the university's Professional
Schools' Program ... its main purpose is to provide new
opportunities for the professional schools at the university,
to internationalize their outlook and to expand their research
and training activities in other societies and cultures, " the
editors state.   Includes biographical notes on the contributors.

388   Beyer, Barry K.   "Teaching about Africa south of the Sahara
       in American secondary schools--a survey and a challenge, "
       Afr. Stud. Bull. , XI (April 1968), 18-27.
            The author is Director of Project Africa, a Social Studies
       curriculum Development, Ohio State University.

389   Blumenfeld, F. Y.   "Education for Africans, " Edit. Res. Rpts. ,
       II (Sept. 28, 1960), 705-20.

390   Boyd, Andrew Kirk.   An Atlas of world affairs.   6th rev. ed.
       New York: Praeger, 1970. 176 p.

391   Brown, Godfrey N.   Living history: a guide for teachers in
       Africa.   London: Allen & Unwin, 1967. 160 p.   (Education
       for development, the teacher's bookshelf.)

392   Brunschwig, Henri.   L'Avènement de l'Afrique noire, du XIXe
       Siècle á nos jours.   Paris: Librairie A. Colin, 1963.
       247 p.   Bibliog.

393   "The C. I. A. and the Peace Corps in Africa, " Curr. Dig.
       Soviet Pr. , XX (Jan. 24, 1968), 24-5.

394   Cell, John W.   British colonial administration in the mid-
       nineteenth century.   The policy-making process.   New
       Haven: Yale University Press, 1970. 344 p.
            Rev: Amer. Hist. Rev. , LXXV (Dec. 1970), 2058.
       Choice, VII (June 1970), 604.

395   Chabas, Bernard and Louis Montoy.   Geographie de l'Afrique
       noire.   Paris: Bordas, 1970. 303 p.

396   Chesswas, John D.   Methodologies of educational planning for
       developing countries.   Paris: UNESCO, Institut international
       de planification de l'education, 1969. 2 v. 106 p. ; 84 p.

397   Coleman, James Smoot.   Education and political development.
       Princeton: Princeton University Press, 1965. 620 p.
       (Studies in political development, 4.)
            Rev: Soc. Stud. , LVII (Oct. 1966), 231.

398   Collins, Robert O. , ed.   African history: text and readings.
       New York: Random House, 1971. 594 p.
            Excellent selections from the works by and about prominent

African figures designed as an introduction to African history,
and attempt to "embrace the full time span of documentary
records pertaining to Africa [and] to cover the vast geographical sweep of sub-Saharan Africa." Sources are indicated in footnotes; includes an index and no bibliography.

399 _____. Europeans in Africa. New York: Knopf, 1971.
168 p. (Studies in world civilization.)
    Contents: Portuguese in Africa; Africa before the
Scramble; partition and pacification; European rule; dis-
mantling the empires. Bibliography, chronology of events
and index.

400 _____. The Partition of Africa: illusion or necessity?
New York: Wiley, 1969. 239 p. Bibliog. (Major issues
in history.)
    Designed for university courses in African history. No
index. The author is Professor of History at the University
of California, Santa Barbara.
    Rev: Choice, VI (Jan. 1970), 1639.

401 _____, ed. Problems in African history. Englewood
Cliffs, N.J.: Prentice-Hall, 1968. 374 p.

402 _____. Problems in the history of colonial Africa, 1860-
1960. Englewood Cliffs, N.J.: Prentice-Hall, 1970.
389 p.

403 Cowan, L. Gray, et al., eds. Education and nation-building
in Africa. New York: Praeger, 1965. 403 p.
    Rev: Catholic World, CCII (Mar. 1966), 378. J. Negro
Educ., XXXV (Summer 1966), 276.

404 Cross, Colin. The Fall of the British Empire, 1918-1968.
London: Hodder & Stoughton, 1968. 359 p.
    Rev: Ann. Amer. Acad. Pol. Soc. Sci., CCCLXXXIV
(July 1969), 158. TLS (Oct. 3, 1968), 1131.

405 Cyr, Leo G. United States policy toward Africa. Athens:
Center for International Studies, Ohio University, 1966.
23 p. (Papers in international studies, No. 1.)

406 Dalby, David, ed. Language and history in Africa. New
York: Africana Publishing Corp., 1970. 159 p.
    A collection of inter-disciplinary papers presented at
the 1967-69 London Seminar on Language and History in
Africa designed to explore opportunities for collaboration
between linguists and historians concerned with African
studies.

407 Dammann, Ernst. "Afrikasprachliche Literatur in Russischer
Sprache," Afrika und Ubersee, XLIV, No. 3 (1961), 262-85.

List of major publications in Russian relating to African
linguistics.

408   Davidson, Basil. Africa: History of a continent.   New York:
      Macmillan, 1966.   320 p.
          Rev: N. Y. Times Bk. Rev. (Dec. 4, 1966), 70.   TLS
      (Jan. 12, 1967), 22.

409   _____.   The African genius: an introduction to African
      cultural and social history. Boston: Little, Brown, 1969.
      367 p.
          Rev: Economist, CCXXXIII (Dec. 27, 1969), 41.   N. Y.
      Rev. Bks. , XV (Dec. 17, 1970), 44.

410   _____.   The African past: chronicles from antiquity to
      modern times. Boston: Little, Brown, 1964.   392 p.
          Rev: J. Afr. Hist. , VI, No. 1 (1965), 121-3.

411   _____.   Which way Africa?   The Search for a new society.
      Rev. ed. Harmondsworth: Penguin, 1967.   229 p.

412   Edinburgh. University. Centre of African Studies.   The Theory
      of imperialism and the European partition of Africa, proceed-
      ings of a seminar held in the Centre of African Studies, Uni-
      versity of Edinburgh, 3rd and 4th November, 1967.   Edin-
      burgh, 1967? 187 p.

413   Edstrom, Lars-Olof, et al. , eds. Mass education; studies in
      adult education and teaching by correspondence in some de-
      veloping countries. New York: Africana Publishing Corp. ,
      1971.   380 p.
          Rev: Africana Library J. , III (Spring 1972), 25.

414   Engholm, Eva. Education through English: the use of English
      in African Schools. Cambridge: Cambridge University
      Press, 1965.   182 p.

415   Ferguson, John. Roma aeterna: the value of classical studies
      for the twentieth century. Ibadan: Ibadan University Press,
      1961.   14 p.

416   Gavin, R. J. Documents relating to "The Scramble for Africa. "
      Ibadan: Dept. of History, University of Ibadan, 1966.
      276 p.

417   Great Britain. Commonwealth. Secretariat. Education in rural
      areas; report of the Commonwealth Conference on Education
      in Rural Areas, held at the University of Ghana, Legon,
      Accra, Ghana, 23 March-2 April 1970. London: Common-
      wealth Secretariat (Printing Section, Marlborough House,
      S. W. 1), 1970.   314 p.

418   Gregory, Robert G.   "Africana archives and innovative teach-
       ing; the teacher-scholar's new need for research materials, "
       Africana Library J. , II (Winter 1971), 18-19.

419   Hance, William A.   The Geography of modern Africa.   New
       York: Columbia University Press, 1964.   653 p.
       Rev: Library J. , LXXXIX (June 15, 1964), 2592.
       Science, CLXV (Sept. 25, 1964), 1424.

420   Hatch, John.   A History of post-war Africa.   New York:
       Praeger, 1965.   432 p.
       Rev: Amer. Hist. Rev. , LXXI (April 1966), 1030.

421   Hannah, Harold Winford.   Resource book for rural univer-
       sities in the developing countries.   Urbana: University of
       Illinois Press, 1966.   375 p.
       Prepared under contract with U. S. Agency for Interna-
       tional Development.
       Rev: Ann. Amer. Acad. Pol. Soc. Sci. , CCCLXVII
       (Sept. 1966),   208.

422   Hanson, J. W.   Imagination and hallucination in African educa-
       tion.   East Lansing: Michigan State University, 1965.   55 p.

423   Hornby, William Frederic and Peter Newton.   Africa.   London:
       University Tutorial Press, 1971.   462 p.   (Advanced Level
       geography series.)

424   Horrut, C. Frédéric.   Lugard et la pensée coloniale britan-
       niques de son temps.   Bordeaux: Centre d'Etude d'Afrique
       Noire, 1970.   83 p.

425   Hugot, Henry J.   L'Afrique préhistorique.   Paris: Hatier,
       1970.   128 p.

426   Jackson, Barbara Ward, et al.   The Legacy of imperialism:
       essays.   Pittsburgh: Chatham College, 1960.   94 p.

427   Jacqz, Jane W.   African students in U. S. universities: re-
       port of a conference on the admission and guidance of
       African students, held at Howard University, Washington,
       D. C. , March 17-18, 1967.   New York: African-American
       Institute, 1967.   88 p.

428   Jolly, Richard.   Planning education for African development.
       Nairobi: East African Publishing House, 1969.   168 p.

429   July, Robert.   A History of the African people.   New York:
       Scribners, 1970.   650 p.
       A textbook for University students, divided into 2 parts.
       I: Ancient Africa.   II: Modern Africa.   Each section is
       subdivided partly by topic, partly by geographic area.   A

list of references for further reading follows each chapter
and there is a separate bibliography at the end.
Rev: <u>Africa,</u> XLI (Jan. 1971), 71-2.

430 Kamm, Josephine. <u>Explorers into Africa.</u> London: Gollancz,
1970. 160 p.

431 Kirkman, W. P. <u>Unscrambling an empire; a critique of
British colonial policy, 1956-1966.</u> London: Chatto &
Windus, 1966. 214 p.

432 Lacour-Gayet, Robert. <u>Histoire de l'Afrique du Sud.</u> Paris:
Fayard, 1970. 487 p. (Les Grandes études historiques.)

433 Lee, J. M. <u>Colonial development and good government: a
study of the ideas expressed by the British official class</u> in
<u>planning decolonization, 1939-1964.</u> Oxford: Clarendon
Press, 1967. 311 p.
Rev: <u>Economist</u> (Dec. 16, 1967), 1149. <u>TLS</u> (April 25,
1968), 419.

434 Lewis, Leonard John. <u>Education and political independence
in Africa and other essays.</u> London: Nelson, 1962. 128 p.
The author is Professor and Head of the Dept. of Education in Tropical Areas at the University of London.

435 _____ and A. J. Loveridge. <u>The Management of education:
a guide for teachers to the problems in new and developing
systems.</u> New York: Praeger, 1965. 124 p.

436 Lewis, Roy and Yvonne Foy. <u>The British in Africa.</u> London:
Weidenfeld & Nicolson, 1971. 238 p.

437 Mabileau, Albert and Jean Meyriat, eds. <u>Decolonisation et
regimes politiques en Afrique noire.</u> Paris: Colin, 1967.
280 p.

438 McNown, John C., ed. <u>Technical education in Africa.</u> Nairobi: East African Publishing House, 1971.

439 "Man-power, education and training in Africa," <u>Econ. Bull.
Afr.,</u> X (June 1970), 63-74.

440 Miller, J. D. B. <u>Britain and the old dominions.</u> London:
Chatto & Windus, 1966. 286 p. (Britain in the world
today.)
Considers the social and economic situation in individual
British colonies before World War I; their experiences in
war and peace between 1918 and 1945; their military, political and economic development since 1945 and their relations with Britain.
Rev: <u>Tablet</u> (Dec. 10, 1966), 1386. <u>TLS</u> (April 20,
1967), 330.

441 Moumouni, Abdou. Education in Africa. Translated from the
     French by Phyllis Y. Nauts Ott. New York: Praeger,
     1968. 319 p. French ed. , by Maspero, Paris, 1964.
     399 p.
         Education in French Africa, 1816-1960 and problems after
     independence.

442 Mwase, George Simon. Strike a blow and die: a narrative of
     race relations in colonial Africa. Edited and with a new
     introduction by Robert I. Rotberg. Cambridge, Mass.:
     Harvard University Press, 1970. 135 p.

443 N'Diaye, Jean Pierre. La Jeunesse africaine face à l'impéri-
     alisme. Paris: Maspero, 1971. 186 p. (Cahiers libres,
     199-200.)

444 O'Connor, A. M. The Geography of tropical African develop-
     ment. Oxford: Pergamon, 1971. 207 p.
         Examines the major changes in the geography of tropical
     Africa chiefly during the period, 1956-1968; with special
     reference to the geographical pattern of recent and current
     economic development.

445 Oliver, Roland, ed. The Dawn of African history. 2nd ed.
     London: Oxford University Press, 1968. 112 p.
         The material included here is derived from unwritten
     sources in many languages and unwritten lore of pre-
     colonial times. This edition includes an index.

446 _____ . The Middle age of African history. London: Ox-
     ford University Press, 1967. 112 p.
         A companion volume to The Dawn of African history, it
     consists of essays covering the period from the Arab in-
     vasion of the seventh century to the arrival of the European
     settlers in the nineteenth century.

447 Omer-Cooper, John D. , et al. The Making of modern Africa.
     New York: Humanities Press, 1969-1970. 2 v. (The
     Growth of African civilisation series.)

448 Perham, Margery Freda. The Colonial reckoning; the end of
     imperial rule in Africa in the light of British experience.
     New York: Knopf, 1962. 203 p.
         Rev: New Statesman, LXIV (Aug. 3, 1962), 147. Pol.
     Sci. Q. , LXXVII (Sept. 1962), 459.

449 Pollock, Norman Charles. Studies in emerging Africa. London:
     Butterworths, 1971. 342 p.

450 Porter, Arthur T. "University development in English-speak-
     ing Africa: problems and opportunities, " African Affairs,
     LXXI (Jan. 1972), 73-83.

A slightly abridged version of a talk given to a joint
meeting of the Royal African Society and the Royal Society
of Arts, held on 22 April, 1971. Professor Porter is Head
of the Planning Unit, Kenya Ministry of Education.

451 Povey, John. "Education through the eyes of African writers, "
     Educ. Forum (Nov. 1966), 95-102.

452 Pritchard, J. M. Africa: geography of a changing continent.
     New York: Africana Publishing Corp., 1971. 247 p.
          Written in a textbook fashion with chapter-end questions
     and exercises, it describes the land, climate, soils, and
     national regions of Africa, and examines land and water use
     in agriculture; mining and industry; population--its growth,
     distribution and resettlement patterns; transportation and
     communications.

453 Ranger, T. O., ed. Emerging themes of African history:
     proceedings of the International Congress of African his-
     torians held at University College, Dar es Salaam, October
     1965. Nairobi: East African Publishing House, 1968.
     230 p.

454 Richards, Audrey. "The Adaptation of universities to the
     African situation, " Minerva, III (Spring 1965), 336-42.

455 Ross, Murray, ed. New Universities in this modern world.
     London: Macmillan, 1966. 190 p.

456 Rotberg, Robert I., ed. Africa and its explorers: motives,
     methods and impact. Cambridge, Mass.: Harvard Univer-
     sity Press, 1970. 351 p.
          Rev: Africa Report, XVI (Oct. 1970), 34-6.

457 _____. A Political history of tropical Africa. New York:
     Harcourt, Brace & World, 1965. 450 p.
          A study of the sub-Saharan Region from the mid-nine-
     teenth century to the present. Topics examined include
     resistance to European conquest and rebellion against alien
     rule; religious, political, economic and literary forms of
     protest, revolution, protest against racism and neo-colonial-
     ism.
          Rev: Amer. Anthrop., LXIX (Feb. 1967), 122. J.
     Negro Hist., LII (Jan. 1967), 66.

458 _____. Rebellion in black Africa. London: Oxford Univer-
     sity Press, 1971. 320 p.

459 Ruth Sloan Associates. The Educated African: a country by
     country survey of educational developments in Africa. Edited
     by Helen Kitchen. New York: Praeger, 1962. 542 p.
          Rev: Economist, CCVI (Mar. 9, 1963), 908. Sat. Rev.,
     XLV (Oct. 20, 1962), 87.

460 Sasnett, Martena Tenney, ed. Foreign students look at the
     U. S. Los Angeles: Cole-Holmquist, 1960. 100 p.
     The result of a project carried out with the cooperation
     of the National Association of Foreign Student Advisers.

461 _____ and Inez Sepmeyer. Educational systems of Africa;
     interpretations for use in the evaluation of academic creden-
     tials. Berkeley: University of California Press, 1966.
     1550 p.
     A comprehensive study of the educational institutions and
     patterns of education in 44 African states, covering primary,
     secondary and university education; vocational, technical
     and teacher training. Arrangement is by country and each
     national study is prefaced with a brief historical, cultural
     and educational background. Courses offered, admission
     requirements, degrees, etc., with necessary statistical
     data are clearly set out. Extensive, select bibliography.
         Rev: Choice, IV (July/Aug. 1967), 522. Library J.,
     XCII (April 15, 1967), 1610.

462 Scanlon, David, ed. Traditions of African education. New
     York: Teachers College, Columbia University, 1964. 184 p.

463 Selltiz, Claire, et al. Attitudes and social relations of foreign
     students in the United States. Minneapolis: University of
     Minnesota Press, 1963. 434 p.
         Rev: Amer. Anthrop., LXVI (Dec. 1964), 1461.

464 Sillery, Anthony. Africa: a social geography. London:
     Duckworth, 1961. 244 p.
     Deals with the topography, climate, vegetation, peoples,
     agricultural and mineral products, etc.

465 Stamp, L. Dudley. Africa: a study in tropical development.
     London: John Wiley, 1964. 534 p.
         Part 1. Africa in general, discussed under topics: soils,
     forests, peoples, culture, etc. Part 2. Treatment by
     country or region.

466 Stravianos, Leften Stavnos, ed. The Epic of man to 1500; a
     collection of readings. Englewood Cliffs, N. J.: Prentice-
     Hall, 1970. 366 p.

467 Touval, Saadia. "Africa's frontiers: reactions to a colonial
     legacy," Int. Affairs (London) (Oct. 1966), 279-93.

468 Thornton, A. P. Doctrines of imperialism. New York: Wiley,
     1965. 246 p. (New dimensions in history: essays in
     comparative history.)
         Rev: Amer. Hist. Rev., LXXII (Oct. 1966), 125. TLS
     (June 23, 1966), 551.

469   _____ . The Imperial idea and its enemies a study in
           British power. New York: St. Martins, 1963. 372 p.

470   Tinbergen, Jan.   The Financing of higher education in Africa.
           Paris: UNESCO, 1962.   78 p.

471   Turner, V. , ed.   Colonialism in Africa, 1870-1960.   Vol. III:
           Profiles of change: African society and colonial rule.   Lon-
           don: Cambridge University Press, 1971.   455 p.

472   UNESCO.   Practical guide to in-service teacher training in
           Africa.   Paris, 1970.   81 p.

473   Unoh, S. O.   The Study of reading.   Ibadan: Ibadan University
           Press, 1968.   43 p.

474   van Rensburg, P.   Education and development in an emerging
           country.   Uppsala: Scandinavian Institute of African Studies,
           1967.   48 p.

475   Vansina, Jan.   "Once upon a time: oral traditions as history
           in Africa, " Daedelus, C (Spring 1971), 442-68.

476   Wickert, F. R. , ed.   Readings in African psychology.   East
           Lansing: African Studies Center, Michigan State University,
           1967.   381 p.
               Emphasis is on the post-colonial studies in sub-Saharan
           Africa.
               Rev: J. Asian Afr. Stud. , V (Oct. 1970), 314-5.

477   Woddis, Jack.   An Introduction to neo-colonialism.   London:
           Lawrence & Wishart, 1967.   133 p.

(5) LANGUAGE, LITERATURE, THE ARTS

478   African-Scandinavian Writers' Conference, Stockholm, 1967.
           The Writer in modern Africa.   Edited by Per Wästberg.
           Uppsala: Scandinavian Institute of African Studies, 1968.
           123 p.

479   Ainslie, Rosalynde.   The Press in Africa: communications
           past and present.   New York: Walker, 1966.   264 p.
               Traces the development of various African newspapers
           under broad geographic areas, noting their political impact
           on the countries in which they are published, followed by a
           topical treatment of different effects of the press.   Includes
           bibliography and a list of African broadcasting stations,
           news agencies, daily newspapers and index.
               Rev: Choice, V (Sept. 1968), 760.   TLS (Nov. 24, 1966),
           1065.

480   The Arts and man: a world view of the role and functions of
      the arts in society.   Englewood Cliffs, N. J.:   Prentice-Hall,
      1969.   171 p.

481   Atkins, Guy, ed.   African language studies (presented to Mal-
      colm Guthrie).   London: School of Oriental and African
      Studies, University of London, 1970.   435 p.

482   Barton, Frank.   The Press in Africa.   Nairobi: East African
      Publishing House, 1966.   80 p.
      Discusses the qualities and qualifications of a journalist;
      freedom of the press; relations between the press and the
      politicians, etc.   Includes schools of journalism in Africa.

483   Bascom, W.   African arts.   Berkeley: Lowie Museum of
      Anthropology, University of California, 1967.   90 p.

484   Bebey, Francis.   Musique de l'Afrique.   Paris: Horizons de
      France, 1969.   208 p.   (Collections "Expressions")

485   Berrian, Albert H. and Richard A. Long, eds.   Negritude:
      essays and studies.   Hampton: Hampton Institute Press,
      1967.   115 p.

486   Brench, Anthony Cecil.   The Novelists' inheritance in French
      Africa: writers from Senegal to Cameroon.   London: Ox-
      ford University Press, 1967.   146 p.   (A three crown book.)
      Rev: English Stud. Afr. (Sept. 1967),   201.

487   Brentjes, Burchard.   African rock art.   New York: Clarkson
      V. Potter, 1970.   116 p.   57 line drawings.

488   Dalby, David, ed.   Language and history in Africa.   New
      York: Africana Publishing Corp., 1971.   160 p.

489   Deutsche Afrika-Gesellschaft, Bonn.   The Commercial radio
      in Africa.   Bonn, 1970.   307 p.

490   Fagg, William.   Miniature wood carvings of Africa.   Bath,
      England: Adams and Dart, 1970.   104 p.   8 plates.

491   Finnegan, Ruth.   Oral literature in Africa.   London: Oxford
      University Press, 1970.   580 p.   (Oxford Library of African
      Literature.)

492   Furay, Michael, ed.   Critical approaches to modern African
      literature.   New York: Africana Publishing Corp.   (forth-
      coming).

493   Hachten, William A.   Muffled drums: the news media in
      Africa.   Ames: Iowa State University Press, 1971.   314 p.
      A general survey of the news media in contemporary

Africa with specific case studies of Ghana, Nigeria, the
Ivory Coast, Senegal, Kenya, Zambia and South Africa.
Emphasis is the news media as institutions.

494 _____. "Newspapers in Africa: change or decay?" Africa
Report, XV (Dec. 1970), 25.

495 Hanna, Judith Lynne. "Africa's new traditional dance, "
Ethnomusicology (Jan. 1965), 13-21.

496 _____. "The Status of African dance studies, " Africa,
XXXVI (July 1966), 303-7.

497 _____. "What is African dance?" J. New Afr. Lit. Arts
(Fall 1966), 64-6.

498 Heine, Bernd. Status and use of African Linguas francas.
Munchen: Weltforum Verlag, 1970. 206 p. (Afrika-
Studien, No. 49.)

499 Hughes, Langston, ed. An African treasury: articles, essays,
stories, poems by black Africans. New York: Crown,
1960. 207 p.
Rev: Black Orpheus, No. 9 (1961), 67-8. Présence
Africaine, Eng. ed., VI-VII, Nos. 34-35 (1960), 239-40.

500 Jahn, Janheinz. "African literature, " Présence Africaine,
Eng. ed., XX, No. 48 (1963), 47-57.

501 _____. Manuel de littérature neo-africaine du 16e siècle à
nos jours de l'Afrique à l'Amerique. Traduit par Gaston
Bailly. Paris: Editions Resma, 1969. 293 p.
Originally published in German under title: Geschichte
der neo-afrikanischen Literatur, by Eugen Diederichs Verlag,
Dusseldorf-Koln. Surveys the whole range of neo-African
literature, with biographical notes on major writers in this
field. Each chapter is devoted to a specific theme and includes numerous bibliographical references.

502 [No entry]

503 _____. Muntu: an outline of the new African culture.
Translated from the German by Marjorie Grene. New York:
Grove, 1961. 267 p.
Analysis of African philosophy, religion and the arts.
Rev: Black Orpheus, No. 9 (1961), 63-5. TLS (Aug. 11,
1961), 498.

504 Kerine, Jane. African crafts. New York: Lion Press, 1970.
64 p.

505 Kesteloot, Lilyan. Les Ecrivains noirs de langue française;

naissance d'une littérature. 3rd ed. Bruxelles: Institut de
Sociologie, Université de Bruxelles, 1967. 343 p. (Etudes
africaines) 1st ed. 1963.
Originally submitted as doctoral dissertation, University
of Brussels.

506 _____. Négritude et situation coloniale. Yaoundé: Editions
CLE, 1968. 95 p. (Coll. Abbia)

507 Killam, G. D. Africa in English fiction, 1874-1939. Ibadan:
Ibadan University Press, 1968. 206 p.
A critical, analytical survey of the African fiction writing,
followed by sources, a bibliography arranged by geographic
area and index.

508 Landeck, Beatrice. Echoes of Africa in folk songs of the
Americas. 2nd rev. ed., New York: D. McKay, 1969.
184 p.

508a Lang, D. M. and D. R. Dudley, eds. Penguin companion to
classical, oriental & African literature. New York: Mc-
Graw, 1971. 359 p.

509 Laude, Jean. The Arts of Africa. Translated from the French
by Jean Decock. Berkeley: University of California Press,
1971. 289 p. 201 illus.
French ed. 1966, by Le Livre de Poche, Paris, 1966.

510 Lindfors, Bernth. "American university and research library
holdings in African literature," Afr. Stud. Bull., XI, No. 3
(1968), 286-311.

511 Lloyd, Joan E. Barclay. African animals in renaissance literature and art. London: Oxford University Press, 1971.
96 p. 93 plates. (Oxford studies in art and architecture.)

511a McGregor, Gordon Peter. English in Africa; a guide to the
teaching of English as a second language with particular reference to the past-primary scholl stages. London: Heinemann
Educational, 1971. 214 p. (UNESCO. Source books on curricula and methods.)

512 Makeba, Miriam. The World of African song. Chicago:
Quadrangle, 1970. 128 p.

513 Markovitz, I. L. Leopold Sedar Senghor and the politics of
négritude. London: Heinemann, 1969. 300 p.

514 Merriam, Alan. "Examples of western impact on African
music," Paper presented at the Ninth Annual Meeting of
African Studies Association, Bloomington, Indiana University, 26-29 Oct., 1966.

515   Moore, Gerald, ed. African literature and the universities.
      Ibadan: Ibadan University Press, 1965. 148 p.

516   _____ . "The Arts in the new Africa," African Affairs,
      LXVI (April 1967), 140-8.
            A critical analysis of the themes of some major con-
      temporary African writers with emphasis on Nigerians, in-
      cluding Chinua Achebe, Christopher Okigbo, J. P. Clark.

517   Mphahlele, Ezekiel. The African image. London: Faber &
      Faber, 1962. 240 p.
            Topics discussed include negritude; the position of Africans
      in South Africa; the "nationalist" in politics and society,
      etc.
            Rev: J. Mod. Afr. Stud., I (March 1963), 117-8.

518   _____ . African writing today. Baltimore: Penguin, 1967.
      347 p.
            Rev: Choice, V (May 1968), 351.

519   _____ . "The Language of African literature," Harvard Educ.
      Rev., XXXIV (Spring 1964), 298-306.

520   _____ . "Writers in search of themes," W. Afr. Rev.,
      XXXII (Aug. 1962), 40-1.

521   Mutiso, Gideon C. "Social and political ideas in African lit-
      erature, 1945-1967," Doctoral Dissertation, Syracuse Univer-
      sity, 1969, 280 p.

522   Opubor, Alfred. Critical approaches to African literature.
      Ibadan: Jonala Publications, 1970.

523   Radford, W. L., ed. African poetry for schools. Nairobi:
      East African Publishing House, 1970.

524   Rajana, Rozina. "Understanding and enjoying African music,"
      Negro Digest (May 1968), 38-45.

525   Robbin, Judith Powers. "Three traditions of African wall
      decoration," Master's Thesis, University of California,
      Berkeley, 1965. 133 p.

526   Segy, Ladislas. African sculpture speaks. 3rd enl. ed.
      New York: Hill & Wang, 1969. 292 p. 1st ed. 1952.
            Rev: Africa, XLI (April 1971), 178-80.

527   Shapiro, Norman R., ed. Negritude: black poetry from
      Africa and the Caribbean. Edited and translated from the
      French by Norman R. Shapiro. With an introduction by
      Wilfred Cartey. New York: October House, 1970. 247 p.

528 Sommerlad, Ernest Lloyd. The Press in developing countries.
London: Methuen, 1966. 189 p.
"The first volume to take a hard look at problems of the
press in developing regions of the world, and to place those
problems in the world-wide perspective" (Foreword). The
author is in charge of UNESCO's programs for the training
of journalists throughout the world.
Rev: Economist, CCXXIV (Aug. 12, 1967), 581. TLS
(Nov. 2, 1967), 1033.

529 Spencer, John, ed. Language in Africa: Leverhulme Conference on Universities and the Language Problems of Tropical
Africa, Ibadan, Nigeria, 1961-62. London: Cambridge University Press, 1963. 167 p.
Examines the linguistic problems in Africa and suggests
further research in this area.

530 Stokke, O. Reporting Africa. Uppsala: Scandinavian Institute
of African Studies, 1971. 224 p.

531 Tibble, Anne, ed. African-English literature: a short survey
and anthology of prose and poetry up to 1965. New York:
October House, 1965. 304 p.
Part I: Surveys African literature by geographic area--
East Africa, South Africa, West Africa--with a brief historical outline of African writings. Part II: Comprises
selections from works of fiction, drama and poetry of
major African writers. Includes bibliography.

532 Vieyra, Paulin S. Le Cinéma et l'Afrique. Paris: Présence
africaine, 1969. 220 p.

533 Warren, Fred Anthony and Lee Warren. The Music of Africa:
an introduction. Englewood Cliffs, N. J.: Prentice-Hall,
1970. 87 p.
Juvenile.

534 Wassings, R. S. African art: its backgrounds and traditions.
Translated by Diana Imber. Photos by Hans Hinz. New
York: Abrams, 1968. 300 p. 254 illus.
Rev: N. Y. Rev. Bks., XIII (Dec. 18, 1969), 36.

535 Wauthier, Claude. L'Afrique des Africains: inventaire de la
négritude. Paris: Editions du Seuil, 1964. 314 p. (Coll.
L'histoire immédiate). English ed., translated by Shirley
Kay under title: The Literature and the thought of modern
Africa, published by Pall Mall Press, London, 1966. 323 p.
Rev: Nation, CCIV (June 26, 1967), 822. TLS (Aug.
3, 1967), 705.

536 Weman, Henry. African music and the church in Africa.
Uppsala: Svenska Institutet for Missionsforskning, 1960.
296 p. (Studia missionalia Uppsaliensia, 3.)

537 Whiteley, W. H. <u>A selection of African prose.</u>   London: Ox-
        ford University Press, 1964. 2 v.
            v. 1: Traditional oral texts. 200 p.   v. 2: Western
        prose, comprising representative examples of the works of
        African authors from different parts of the continent. 185 p.
            Rev: <u>J. Mod. Afr. Stud.</u>, II (Nov. 1964), 464-8.

(A) REFERENCE WORKS

Specific subject bibliographies, handbooks, directories and dictionaries are entered under the appropriate subject in the main classified section. The publications listed here are of general reference
value.

(1) DICTIONARIES, DIRECTORIES, HANDBOOKS, ETC.

538 Behn, Hans Ulrich. Die Presse in Westafrika. Hamburg:
     Deutsches Institut für Afrika-Forschung, 1969. 267 p.
     (Hamburger Beitrage zur Afrika-Kunde, Band 8.)
         Written in German, it deals with various aspects of the
     press in both English- and French-speaking countries.
     Specially useful as a reference tool is its appendix which
     groups by country current newspapers and periodicals,
     giving their frequency, circulation, editorial addresses. In-
     cludes an extensive bibliography and no index.

539 Brokensha, David, ed. Akwapim handbook. With an intro-
     duction by David Brokensha.   Accra: State Publishing Corp.
     1972. 310 p.
         An authoritative reference work on the small area of
     former Akwapim Local Council covering just over 300 square
     miles with a population of 80,000. It is divided into five
     main sections dealing with ecology, history, society, economy
     and recent developments. Different contributors discuss the
     main aspects of one subject within each section in different
     chapters. A product of several years of research primarily
     intended for students, scholars and the Akwapim people
     themselves, "this handbook is not merely a record of 'tradi-
     tions' or 'customs;' all of us who wrote chapters are inter-
     ested in the past, because we believe that an understanding
     of our history can aid our handling of contemporary prob-
     lems" (Introduction). Extensive bibliography with over 330
     items. The editor, Professor of Anthropology at the Uni-
     versity of California, Santa Barbara, is author of Social
     Change at Larteh Ghana (1966).

93

540   Ghana. Central Bureau of Statistics. Statistical yearbook.
      1st ed. 1961+ Accra, 1962+ Annual.

541   _____. Ministry of Information and Broadcasting. Ghana;
      an official handbook, 1961+ Accra, 1962+ Annual.
            Contains directory information, with notes on government
      departments, statutory boards and corporations, land and
      people of Ghana, arts, culture, the press, etc.

542   _____. Ministry of Trade and Industry. Handbook of Com-
      merce and industry. Accra, 1968. 321 p.
            Issued in 1951-52 by the Ministry of Commerce and In-
      dustry and in 1955 by the Ministry of Trade and Labour,
      these early volumes were published as handbooks of trade
      and commerce.

543   Ghana yearbook; a Daily Graphic publication. Accra: Ghana
      Graphic Co. , 1957+ Annual.
            Continuing the Gold Coast yearbook 1953-56, it gives
      directory information on Ghana's politics, economics,
      schools and colleges. Includes a list of officials; diplomatic
      missions and representatives; trade directory, organizations,
      personalities, etc.

544   The Gold Coast handbook. Edited by John Maxwell. London:
      Crown Agents for the Gold Coast Government, 1928. 525 p.
            Includes a survey of native population by R. S. Rattray.

545   The Gold Coast handbook 1937. London: West Africa Publicity
      for Gold Coast Government, 1937. 442 p.

546   Trade directory of the Republic of Ghana, including classified
      trade index. 1st ed. 1959+ London: Diplomatic Press and
      Publishing Co. , 1954+ Annual.
            Title varies: 1959-62, Directory of Ghana. A valuable
      reference tool with directory information and textual material
      on government ministries, agencies, offices, etc. There is
      a supplementary list of business firms and a brief biographical
      section.

547   U. S. Dept. of the Army. Special warfare area handbook for
      Ghana. Washington, D. C. , 1962. 533 p.
            Gives the sociological, economic, political and military
      background of Ghana. Various aspects of national security
      are examined--criminal law and procedure, national police
      service; the Army, the Navy and Air Force, logistics and
      foreign influence, etc. and Ghana's strategic importance is
      also evaluated. Bibliography.

(2) BIBLIOGRAPHY

548 Afre, Sampson Andrews. Ashanti and Brong-Ahafo: an anno-
      tated bibliography. Cape Coast: University College Library,
      1967. 539 p.
      Originally submitted as thesis for the Fellowship of
      Library Association (Great Britain).

549 Amedekey, E. Y. The Culture of Ghana: a Bibliography.
      London: Library Association, 1966. 634 p.
      Author's thesis for the Fellowship of Library Association
      (Great Britain).
      Rev: Ghana Library J., IV, No. 1 (1970), 49-50.

550 Bampoe, D. O. A Guide to the official publications of Ghana
      (Gold Coast), 1600-1966. London: The Library Assoc., 1967?
      Submitted as the Library Association (Great Britain)
      Fellowship thesis. Lists some 5,000 titles.

551 Bowyer, T. H. "The Ghana National Bibliography, 1965,"
      Library Mat. Afr., VI (Nov. 1968), 62-5.
      Review of the first issue of the Ghana National Bibliography
      compiled by E. Oko Oddoye and Teresa Gyedu of Research
      Library of African Affairs and published in 1968.

552 Brokensha, David and S. I. A. Kotei. "A Bibliography of Ghana,
      1958-1964," Afr. Stud. Bull., X (Sept. 1967), 35-79.
      Supplements A. W. Cardinall's A Bibliography of the Gold
      Coast (1932) and A. F. Johnson's A Bibliography of Ghana,
      1930-61 (1964). Following the latter's general plan, the
      entries are arranged under broad subject groupings. No
      explanatory notes for the periodical abbreviations used.

553 Bureau of Ghana Languages. Bibliography of works in Ghana
      languages. Accra, 1967. 165 p.

554 Cardinall, Allan Wolsey. A Bibliography of the Gold Coast.
      Accra: Govt. Printer, 1932. 384 p.
      The most comprehensive retrospective bibliography of
      Ghana in existence, compiled by Gold Coast's Chief Census
      Officer and issued as a companion volume to the census
      report of 1931. Its 5168 unannotated numbered items are
      grouped under 15 sections, some in a broad chronological
      order, others by subject or form. Author index. Includes
      references on Togoland, Dahomey, the Upper Volta and the
      Ivory Coast because the Gold Coast "is only an artificial
      creation, and its political boundaries cut across not only
      tribal areas and national features but pass through cultivated
      fields and even houses."

555 Commonwealth Institute. Library. Ghana, Sierra Leone, the
      Gambia: selected reading lists for advanced study. London,
      1967. 25 p.

556 de Heer, A. N.   A List of Ghanaian newspapers and periodicals.
     Accra: Research Library on African Affairs, 1970.   16 p.

557 Ghana National Bibliography, 1965+ Accra: Ghana Library
     Board, 1968+ Annual.
          The first issue for works published in 1965 was a general
     lumping together of books irrespective of the subject arranged
     by author with no subject index, followed by official and
     serial publications.   Subsequent issues show considerable
     improvement, as items are now classified by subject; peri-
     odical articles, theses and doctoral dissertations included,
     with an author index.   Entries are based chiefly on the
     acquisitions of the Research Library on African Affairs, on
     material deposited with the Ghana Library Board under the
     defective Book and Newspaper Registration Act, 1961 amended
     in 1963.   The aim in each issue of this annual publication
     "has been to list all publications both official and non-offi-
     cial published in Ghana or elsewhere, and written by a
     Ghanaian or other nationals" during the period covered.   Its
     time lag of roughly two years is too long for a current
     national bibliography.
          Rev: Library Mat. Afr., VI (Nov. 1968), 62-5.

558 Ghana writers and their works.   Accra: Ghana Library Board,
     Padmore Research Library, 1962.   49 p.   (Special subject
     bibliography, No. 1.)

559 Johnson, Albert Frederick.   A Bibliography of Ghana, 1930-
     1961.   Evanston, Illinois: Northwestern University Press
     for the Ghana Library Board, 1964.   210 p.
          "In some respects a continuation of A. W. Cardinall's
     A bibliography of the Gold Coast which appeared as a sup-
     plement to the Census Report of 1931, it attempts "to list
     all publications on the Gold Coast and Ghana during the
     formative years 1930-61 with selected periodical articles.
     This list is intended to be comprehensive, including works
     of technical and scientific interest, translations and pure
     literature but vernacular texts have been omitted" (Introduc-
     tion).   The entries for the 2608 numbered items are es-
     sentially unannotated and classified by subject or form with
     an author index.

560 _____.   Books about Ghana: a select reading list.   Accra:
     Ghana Library Board, 1961.   32 p.

561 Kotei, S. I. A.   The Akan of Ghana: a select bibliography.
     Accra: Ghana Library Board, Padmore Research Library on
     African Affairs, 1963.   17 p.   (Special subject bibliography,
     No. 3.)
          Books and periodical articles arranged alphabetically by
     author.

562 _____ . Select annotated bibliography of Ghana. Accra:
Ghana Library Board, Padmore Research Library on African
Affairs, 1965. 47 p. (Special subject bibliography, No. 5
July 1965.)
One of the series of the subject bibliographies issued by
the Padmore Research Library intended to update Albert
Johnson's Bibliography of Ghana, 1930-1961 (1964), and
"tries, by being selective and annotated, to assist all those
who are desirous of building a standard stock of books about
Ghana. " Entries are arranged alphabetically by author
under broad subject groupings. Three appendices; bibliographies; Ghanaian periodicals in print; a note on the
Padmore Research Library on African Affairs, now simply
called Research Library on African Affairs. Author index.

563 List of periodicals in the Balme Library. Legon: Balme
Library, University of Ghana, 1961. 168 p.

564 Pitcher, G. M. Bibliography of Ghana, 1957-1959. Kumasi:
The Library, College of Technology, 1960. 177 p.
A classified listing of books, periodical articles, pam-
phlets published in the first three years of Ghana's inde-
pendence. Author and title index.
Rev: WALA News, IV (Oct. 1961), 32.

565 Rydings, H. A. The Bibliographies of West Africa. Ibadan:
Ibadan University Press for the West African Library Asso-
ciation, 1961. 36 p.
Lists 50 bibliographies with excellent annotations including
general African bibliographies with material on West Africa.
Author index.

566 U. S. Library of Congress. General Reference and Bibliography.
African Section. Ghana: a guide to official publications,
1872-1968. Compiled by Julian W. Witherell and Sharon B.
Lockwood. Washington, D. C. , 1969. 110 p.
1, 283 entries covering selected documents issued by the
Gold Coast (1872-1957) and Ghana (1957-1968), British
official publications, League of Nations and United Nations
materials on British Togoland. Indicates sources and includes an author and subject index.
Rev: Africana Library J. , I (Fall 1970), 23. L. C.
Inf. Bull. , XXVIII (Sept. 25, 1969), 492.

566a Warren, Dennis M. The Akan literature of Ghana: a bib-
liography. Edited by Alan Taylor. Boston: African
Studies Association, 1972. 46 p.
Lists 492 items.

567 Wolfson, Freda. "Ghana in books, " West Africa (Feb. /March
1957), 2080-3.

568 Chantler, Clyde. The Ghana story. London: Linden Press,
     1971. 214 p. 17 plates; 2 maps.

569 Foster, Philip and Aristide R. Zolberg, eds. Ghana and the
     Ivory Coast; perspectives on modernization. With an intro-
     duction by Immanuel Wallerstein. Chicago: University of
     Chicago Press, 1971. 303 p.
         The first comprehensive, comparative study of the trans-
     formation and modernization of both countries by authorities
     from several social science disciplines. Contents include
     Political change, conflict and development in Ghana, by Jon
     Kraus; The grassroots in Ghanaian politics, by Martin
     Kilson; Attempts to change the marriage laws in Ghana and
     the Ivory Coast, by Dorothy Dee Vellenga; The moderniza-
     tion of law in Ghana, by Beverley Pooley; Structural trans-
     formation versus gradualism; recent economic development
     in Ghana and the Ivory Coast, by Elliot J. Berg; Reflections
     on economic strategy, structure, implementation, and
     necessity: Ghana and the Ivory Coast, 1957-67, by Reginald
     Green; Convergence and divergence in educational develop-
     ment in Ghana and the Ivory Coast, by Remi Clignet and
     Philip Foster. Author and subject index. Dr. Foster is
     Professor of Education and Sociology at the University of
     Chicago and author of Education and Social change in Ghana
     (1965). Dr. Zolberg is Professor and Chairman, Dept. of
     Political Science, University of Chicago and author of
     Creating political order: the party states of West Africa
     (1966).

570 Ghana Academy of Arts and Sciences. Proceedings 1969.
     Accra, 1970. 116 p.

571 "Ghana," African Affairs, LXXI (Jan. 1972), 84-6.
         An abridged version of the talk given to the Royal African
     Society and the Royal Commonwealth Society on 10 June,
     1971, by A. B. Attafua, Ghana's High Commissioner in Lon-
     don. It focuses on Ghana's constitution and economy.

572 "Ghana." In David Rowe, ed. New nations: a student hand-
     book. Hamden, Connecticut: Shoe String Press, 1968.
     pp. 37-9.
         Includes brief notes on Ghana's history, constitutional
     development, government, economy, education, etc., con-
     taining valuable statistical data.

573 "Ghana," In Etzel Pearcy and Elvyn Stoneman. A handbook
     of new nations. New York: Crowell, 1968, pp. 102-6.
         Chiefly historical and political.

574 "Ghana." In Louis Barron, ed. Worldmark encyclopedia of
     the nations. v. 2: Africa New York: Harper & Row,
     1967, pp. 93-104.
         Excellent authoritative survey of various aspects of the
     country--geography, ethnic groups, languages, religion, his-
     tory, government, economy, education, etc. Includes
     bibliography and a map.

575 Harman, H. A. "The Gold Coast, 1931," Africa, VII (Jan.
     1934), 60-9.
         Review of A. W. Cardinall's The Gold Coast, 1931; a
     review of conditions in the Gold Coast as compared with
     those of 1921-(1932).

576 Kimble, George H. T. "Ghana," Focus, IX (April 1959), 1-6.
         A general survey.

577 MacDonald, G. The Gold Coast, past and present; a short
     description of the country and the people. Westport, Con-
     necticut: Negro Universities Press, 1969. 352 p.
         Reprint of the 1898 edition.

578 Marie Louise, Princess. Letters from the Gold Coast. Lon-
     don: Methuen, 1926. 240 p.

579 Mayer, Emerico Samassa. Ghana: past and present. The
     Hague: Levision Press, 1965. 112 p.

580 Redmayne, Paul. The Gold Coast, yesterday and today.
     London: Chatto & Windus, 1938. 128 p.

581 Royal Institute of International Affairs. Ghana: a survey of
     the Gold Coast on the eve of its independence. London,
     1957. 62 p.

582 Zemba, Lydia Verona. Ghana in pictures. London: Oak
     Tree Press, 1968. 64 p. (Visual geography series.)
         History, government, people and economy of Ghana.

(C) CLASSIFIED SUBJECTS

(1) ANTHROPOLOGY

583 Abruquah, J. W. "Kinship and national efficiency," Insight (Cape Coast), I (Nov. 1966), 86-9.

584 Ackah, C. A. "An Ethical study of the Akan tribes of Ghana," Doctoral Dissertation, London University, 1958/59.

585 Acquaye, Joseph R. "Fanti: native customs about conception and birth," Anthropos, XXIII, Nos. 5-6 (1928), 1051-3.

586 Adaye, J. J. Tales and customs of the natives. Akropong: Bere Adu, 1913.

587 Adjaye, Nana Annor. Nzima land. With a new introductory note by R. S. Blay. 2nd ed. New York: Humanities Press, 1971? 1st ed. 1931, by Headley Bros., London. 294 p.
        Based chiefly on oral traditions, it is the only literary work of an Omanhene of Nzima which records author's independent thoughts during the British rule. He not only foresaw Ghanaian independence, although he thought it would not come about until 2030, but also he laid the foundation of the history and customs of Nzimaland.

588 Adjei, Ako. "Mortuary usages of the Ga people of the Gold Coast," Amer. Anthrop., XLV (Jan./March 1943), 84-98.

589 Adjetey, P. A. "Some consequences of polygamous marriages," Universitas, IV, No. 6 (June 1961), 168-71.

590 Adu, A. L. The Role of chiefs in the Akan social structure: an essay. Accra: Govt. Printer, 1949. 18 p.

591 Akesson, Sam K. "The Secret of Akom," African Affairs, XLIX (July 1950), 237-46; (Oct. 1950), 325-33.
        A pioneer study of the Gold Coast rites of fetish priests by a Methodist Minister.

592 Akrofi, C. A. Twi mmebusem--Twi proverbs with English translations and comments. London: Macmillan, 1958. 173 p.

593 Akyeampong, H. K. The Akim Abuakwa crisis. With a foreword by Dr. J. B. Danquah. Accra: The Author, 1958. 63 p.

594 Aldous, J.   "Urbanization, the extended family and kinship
     ties in West Africa," Social Forces, XLI (1962), 6-12.

595 Alicoe, T.   The Evolution of Gold Coast chiefship.   Sheffield:
     Telegraph and Star, 1953.

596 Amoo, J. W. A.   "The Effect of western influence on Akan
     marriage," Africa, XVI (Oct. 1946), 228-37.

597 Anomako III, Nana Kodwo.   "The Place of the chiefs in the
     new Ghana," Insight (Cape Coast), I (Nov. 1966), 38-44.

598 Antubam, Kofi.   Ghana's heritage of culture.   Leipzig: Koeh-
     ler & Amelang, 1963.   222 p.

599 Arhin, Kwame.   "Diffuse authority among the coastal Fanti,"
     Ghana Notes and Queries, No. 9 (Nov. 1966), 66-70.

600 Armitage, Cecil H.   "Notes on the Northern territories of the
     Gold Coast," United Empire, No. 4 (Aug. 1913), 634-9.

601 Armstrong, Robert G.   "The Development of complex societies
     in West Africa," Proceedings of the Nigerian Institute for
     Social and Economic Research.   Ibadan, 1960, pp. 20-7.

602 Badu, N. A.   "The Position of the traditional authority in
     modern Ghana," B. Litt's Thesis, Oxford University,
     1963/64.

603 Balmer, W. T.   A History of the Akan peoples of the Gold
     Coast.   London: Atlantis Press, 1926.   208 p.

604 Beckett, W. H.   Akokoaso: a survey of a Gold Coast village.
     London: Lund Humphries, 1944.   95 p.   (L. S. E.: mono-
     graph on social anthropology, 10.)

605 Beier, Horst Ulli, ed.   The Origin of life and death: African
     creation myths.   London: Heinemann, 1966.   65 p.

606 Breffit, G. V.   "Ashanti living legend: the history of the sacred
     stool of Ashanti," W. Afr. Rev., (Nov. 1960), 40-3.

607 Berry, Jack.   "A Ga folktale," Bull. Sch. Orient. Afr. Stud.,
     XII, Part 2 (1948), 409-16.

608 Bittle, William E. and Gilbert Geis.   The Longest way home;
     Chief Alfred C. Sam's back-to-Africa movement.   Detroit:
     Wayne State University Press, 1964.   229 p.
         The activities of "Alfred C. Sam, self-proclaimed Gold
     Coast chieftain and leader of what apparently was the first
     large-scale and negro-inspired back-to-Africa movement."
     Bittle is an anthropologist and Geist a sociologist.
         Rev: Amer. Soc. Rev., XXX (Aug. 1965), 642.

609   Brokensha, David.   "Akwapim studies," Universitas (Accra),
       V (Jan. 1962), 4-7.

609a   _____ .   "Anthropological enquiries and political science:
       a case study from Ghana," Paper presented at the Annual
       Meeting of the African studies Association, Philadelphia,
       Oct. 27-30, 1965.
            The author is Professor of Anthropology, University of
       California, Santa Barbara.

610   _____ .   "Influence and authority in rural Ghana," Paper
       presented at the Annual Meeting of the African Studies Asso-
       ciation, New York, November 1967.   10 p.

610a   _____ .   "Labadi: a Ghanaian sub-culture," New African. ,
       I (Aug. 1962), 8-11.

611   _____ .   "Problems in fieldwork: a study of Larteh, Ghana,"
       Current Anthropology, IV (Dec. 1963), 533-4.

611a   _____ .   "The Resilient chieftaincy at Larteh, Ghana."   In
       Michael Crowder and Obaro Ikime, eds.   West African
       chiefs; the changing status under colonial rule and inde-
       pendence.   New York: Africana Publishing Corp. , 1970,
       pp. 393-406.
            Divided into three periods.   I: The precolonial period.
       II: The colonial period. III: Independence 1957 and on.
       Extensive bibliographical references.

612   _____ .   Social change at Larteh, Ghana.   Oxford: Claren-
       don Press, 1966.   294 p.
            A study of a small town in Southern Ghana which "is still
       based on agriculture" and "has numerous links with the city
       and the wider world. "   Includes the examination of the im-
       pact of Christianity and economic changes engendered by
       the introduction of cocoa on the town; community develop-
       ments stimulated by cocoa and mission education.
            Rev: J. Asian Afr. Stud. , IV (April 1969), 155-7.
       Social Forces, XLVI (June 1968), 578.

612a   _____ .   "Training community development workers in
       Ghana. "   In Raymond Apthorpe, ed.   Social research and
       community development; proceedings of the 15th conference
       of Rhodes- Livingstone Institute for Social Research.
       Lusaka, 1961, pp. 134-40.

612b   _____ .   Volta resettlement, ethnographic notes of Southern
       areas.   Legon: Dept. of Sociology, University of Ghana,
       1962.   125 p.

613 Brown, Paula S. "Patterns of authority in West Africa,"
     Africa, XXI (Oct. 1951), 261-74.

614 Busia, Kofi Abrefa. "The Ashanti." In Daryll Forde, ed.
     African worlds. London: Oxford University Press, 1954,
     pp. 190-209.

615 _____. The Place of the chief in the Gold Coast. Achi-
     mota: Achimota Press, 1949. 10 p.

616 _____. The Position of the chief in the modern political
     system of Ashanti: a study of the influence of contemporary
     social changes on Ashanti political institutions. London:
     Oxford University Press, for the International African Insti-
     tute, 1951. 233 p.

617 Caldwell, John C. "Extended family obligations and education:
     a study of an aspect of demographic transition amongst
     Ghanaian university students," Population Studies, XIX, No.
     2 (1965), 183-99.

618 Cardinall, Allan W. "The State of our present ethnographical
     knowledge of the Gold Coast peoples," Africa, II, No. 4
     (1929), 405-12.

619 _____. The Nature of the Northern territories of the Gold
     Coast, their customs, religion and folklore. London: Rout-
     ledge, 1920. 158 p.

620 _____, ed. Tales told in Togoland. London: Oxford
     University Press, 1931. 290 p.

621 Chardey, F. "Résurrection d'un mort et apparitions de morts
     chez les Ewe," Anthropos, XLVI (Sept. /Dec. 1951), 1005-6.

622 Christensen, James Boyd. Double descent among the Fanti.
     New Haven: Human Relations Area Files, 1954. 145 p.
     (Behavior Science monographs.)

623 _____. "Marketing and exchange in a West African tribe,"
     Southwestern J. Anthrop., XVII (Summer 1961), 124-39.

624 _____. "The Role of proverbs in Fante culture," Africa,
     XXVIII (July 1958), 232-42.

625 Cohen, Abner. "Politics of the Kola trade: some processes
     of tribal community formation among migrants in West
     African towns," Africa, XXXVI (Jan. 1966), 18-36.

626 Courlander, Harold and Albert Prempeh. The Hatshaking
     dance and other tales from the Gold Coast. New York:
     Harcourt, Brace, 1947. 115 p.

627   Clarke, K. W. "A Motiv-index of the folk-tales of culture
      area V, West Africa," Doctoral Dissertation, Indiana Uni-
      versity, 1958.

628   Dodoo, Robert. "Ashanti cultural resource elements and their
      relevance to the perception and utilization of resources,"
      Afr. Stud. Rev., XIV (April 1971), 55-81.

629   Danquah, Joseph B. The Akim Abuakwa handbook. London:
      Forster, Groom, 1928. 128 p.

630   _____. "The Culture of the Akan," Africa, XXII, (Oct.
      1952), 360-6.
      Review of The sacred state of the Akan, by E. L. R.
      Meyerowitz.

631   _____. The Gold Coast Akan. London: United Society for
      Christian Literature, 1945. 62 p. (Africa's own library
      series, no. 11.)

632   De Graft-Johnson, J. C. "Akan land tenure," Trans. Gold
      Coast & Togoland Hist. Soc., I, (1954), 99-103.

633   _____. "The Fanti Asafu," Africa, V (July 1932), 307-22.
      A warrior organization "found in almost every town or
      village in the Gold Coast in a more or less developed state,
      but no where has the organization been so fully developed
      or does it play so important a part in the social and po-
      litical life of the people as among the Fantis of the Coast
      towns."

634   _____. "The Significance of some titles," Gold Coast
      Review, II (July/Dec. 1926), 208-23.

635   Debrunner, Hans. Witchcraft in Ghana: a study on the be-
      lief in destructive witches and its effects on the Akan tribes.
      Kumasi: Presbyterian Book Depot, 1959. 210 p.

636   Dennett, Richard Edward. At the back of the black man's
      mind; or notes on the kingly office in West Africa. London:
      Cass, 1967. 288 p. A reprint of the Macmillan 1906 edi-
      tion.
      The British author states that it is designed to show that
      in Africa "there is a religion giving us a much higher con-
      ception of God than is generally recognized by writers on
      African modes of origin." Includes an appendix of religious
      beliefs and social laws of the Yoruba.
      Rev: West Africa, No. 2670 (Aug. 3, 1968), 895.

637   Denteh, A. C. "Birth rites of the Akans," Research Review
      (Legon), III, No. 1 (1966), 78-81.

638   Dieterlen, Germaine.   Les âmes des Dogons.   Paris: Institut
       d'Ethnologie, 1941.   272 p.

639   Duncan-Johnston, A. and H. A. Blair.   Enquiry into the Con-
       stitution and organization of the Dabgon kingdom.   Accra:
       Govt. Printer, 1932.   68 p.

640   Dunn, J. S.   "Fante star lore, " Nigerian Field, XXV (April
       1960), 52-64.

641   Eisenstadt, S. N.   "African age groups: a comparative study, "
       Africa, XXIV (April 1954), 100-13.
            Attempts to determine some of the main structural differ-
       ences between the various age-set systems and the conditions
       or types of societies in which the systems arise and the
       functions they fulfill.

642   Ellis, A. B.   The Tshi-speaking peoples of the Gold Coast of
       West Africa: their religion, manners, customs, laws,
       language, etc. , with an appendix containing a comparison of
       the Tshi, Ga, Ewe, and Yoruba languages.   Chicago: Benin
       Press, 1964.   402 p.

643   "Establishment of the Institute of African Studies at the Uni-
       versity of Ghana, " Africa, XXXII (July 1962), 288-9.

644   Fadeyi, G. A.   "Impact of differing cultures on towncapes in
       modern West Africa: an attempt at a classificatory analysis, "
       Doctoral Dissertation, University of Birmingham, 1970.

645   Fiawoo, D. K.   "The Influence of contemporary social change
       in the magico-religious concepts and organization of the
       Southern Ewe-speaking peoples of Ghana, " Doctoral Disserta-
       tion, Edinburgh University, 1959.

646   Field, Margaret Joyce.   Akim-Kotoku: an oman of the Gold
       Coast.   London: Crown Agents for Gold Coast Govt. , 1948.
       221 p.

647   _____ .   The Social organization of the Ga people.   London:
       Crown Agents, 1940.   231 p.

648   _____ .   "A Unique Ghana stool, " Man, LXV (Nov. /Dec.
       1965), 195.

649   Ffoulkes, Arthur.   "The Fanti family system, " J. Afr. Soc. ,
       VII (July 1908), 394-409.

650   _____ .   "Fanti marriage customs, " J. Afr. Soc. , VIII
       (Oct. 1908), 31-48.

651 Forde, Daryll. "The Cultural map of West Africa: successive
     adaptations to tropical forests and grasslands," Trans. N. Y.
     Acad. Sci. (Series 2), XV (1953), 206-19.

652 _____ and P. M. Kaberry, eds. West African kingdoms in
     the nineteenth century. London: Oxford University Press,
     1967. 289 p.
          Rev: J. Afr. Hist., IX, No. 2 (1968), 319-20.

653 Fortes, Meyer. "Ashanti survey, 1945-1946: an experiment
     in social research," Geographical Journal, CX (Oct. /Dec.
     1947), 149-79.

654 _____. The dynamics of clanship among the Tallensi; being
     the first part of an analysis of the social structure of a
     trans-Volta tribe. London: Oxford University Press, 1945.
     270 p.
          Rev: Afrikanistische Studien, VI, (June 1947), 57-76.

655 _____. "Kinship and marriage among the Ashanti." In
     A. R. Radcliffe-Brown and Daryll Forde, eds. African
     systems of kinship and marriage. London: Oxford Univer-
     sity Press for the International African Institute, 1950,
     pp. 252-84.

656 _____. "Kinship, incest and exogamy of the Northern terri-
     tories of the Gold Coast." In L. H. Buxton, ed. Custom is
     king; Essays presented to R. R. Marett. London: Hutchinson,
     1935, pp. 239-56.

657 _____, ed. Marriage in tribal societies. Cambridge:
     Cambridge University Press, 1962. 157 p.
          Third in a series of studies published by the Dept. of
     Anthropology, Cambridge University, with an introduction
     by Meyer Fortes. Four essays, each written by one of
     Fortes' former students. Includes "Conjugal separation and
     divorce among the Gonja of Northern Ghana," by E. N.
     Goody.
          Rev: Amer. Anthrop., LXIV (Dec. 1962), 1311.

658 _____. "Ritual and office in tribal societies." In M.
     Gluckman, ed. Essays in the ritual of social relations.
     Manchester: Manchester University Press, 1962, pp. 53-
     88.

659 _____. Social structure: studies presented to A. R. Rad-
     cliffe-Brown. New York: Russell & Russell, 1963. 232 p.
     A reprint of the 1949 edition.

660 _____. Time and social structure; and other essays. New
     York: Humanities Press, 1970. 287 p. (London School of
     Economics. Monographs on social anthropology, no. 40.)

661 _____. The Web of kinship among the Tallensi. London:
Oxford University Press, 1949. 358 p.
Continues Dynamics of clanship among the Tallensi (1945).
Examines the problems of social organization in patriarchal
societies.

662 Frimpong, Kwame. "The Final obsequies of the late Nana Sir
Ofori Atta," Africa, XV (April 1945), 80-6.

663 Gibson, Gordon D. "A Bibliography of anthropological bibliographies: Africa," Current Anthropology, X (Dec. 1969),
527-66.
Annotated entries topically and geographically arranged.
Subjects include ethnology and ethnography, culture history,
historic archaeology, prehistory, linguistics, race and ancient
man. Author and institutions indexes.

664. Gill, J. Withers. The Moshi tribe: a short history. Accra:
Govt. Printer, 1924. 24 p.

665 Gluckman, Max. "An Advance in African sociology," Afrikanistische Studien, VI, (June 1947), 57-76.

665a _____. Custom and conflict in Africa. Oxford: Black-
well, 1955. 173 p.

666 Goody, Esther. "Conjugal separation and divorce among the
Gonja of Northern Ghana." In Meyer Fortes, ed. Marriage
in tribal societies. Cambridge: Cambridge University Press,
1962, pp. 14-54.
The Gonja state is a loose federation of large autonomous
divisions with a population of some 85,000.

667 Goody, John Rankine. "The Akan and the North," Ghana Notes
and Queries, (Nov. 1966), 18-24.

668 _____, ed. Comparative studies in kinship. Stanford,
California: Stanford University Press, 1969. 261 p.
A collection of ten papers dealing primarily with the
social life and customs in Northern Ghana. Goody, a social
anthropologist, is Director of the African Studies Center,
Cambridge University.
Rev: TLS (Nov. 13. 1969), 1302.

669 _____. The Ethnography of the Northern Territories of the
Gold Coast, West of the White Volta. London: Colonial
Office, 1954. 59 p. (Typescript)

670 _____. "Ethnology and the Akan of Ghana," Africa, XIX
(Jan. 1959), 67-81.

671 _____. Death, property and ancestors: a study of the mortuary customs of the La Dagaa of West Africa. Stanford,
California: Stanford University Press, 1962. 452 p.
        Rev: Amer. Anthrop., LXVIII (Aug. 1966), 1039.

672. _____, ed. The developmental cycle in domestic groups.
Cambridge: Cambridge University Press, 1958. 145 p.
(Cambridge papers in social anthropology, no. 1.)

673 _____, ed. Literacy in traditional societies. Cambridge:
Cambridge University Press, 1968. 347 p.
        An important work by different contributors on the cultures
of African societies at different levels of sophistication and
on literacy, with special reference to the importance of
writing in the development of these societies.
        Rev: Amer. Anthrop., LXXII (April 1970), 430.

674 _____. "'Normative,' 'recollected' and 'actual' marriage
payments among the Lowiili of Northern Ghana, 1951-1966,"
Africa, XXXIX (Jan. 1969), 54-61.

675 _____. The Social organization of the Lowiili. 2nd ed.
London: Oxford University Press for the International African
Institute, 1967. 123 p. 1st ed. 1956, by H. M. S. O., London.

675a _____. Succession to high office. Cambridge: Cambridge University Press, 1966. 181 p. (Cambridge papers
in social anthropology, no. 4.)
        Rev: Choice, IV (May 1967), 352.

676 _____ and J. A. Braimah. Salaga: the struggle for power.
London: Longmans, 1967. 222 p.
        Part I: Two Isanwurfos. Part 1: The Struggle for
Salaga.
        Rev: West Africa, No. 2670 (Aug. 3, 1968), 894-5.

677 _____ and Esther Goody. "The Circulation of women and
children in Northern Ghana," Man, (New series), II (Jan.
1967), 226-48.

678 _____. "Cross-cousin marriages in Northern Ghana,"
Man, (New series), I (1966), 343-55.

679 Grottanelli, V. L. "Emblemi totemici fra gli Nzima del
Ghana," Anthropos, LVII, nos. 3-6 (1962), 498-508.

680 Hall, W. M. The Great drama of Kumasi. London: Putnam,
1939. 367 p.

681 Halleran, T. "Krobo marriage customs," Anthropos, XLVI,
(Sept. /Dec. 1951), 996-7.

682 Hannigan, A. St. J. "The Impact of English law upon the existing Gold Coast custom and the possible development of the resulting order," J. Afr. Adm., VIII (July 1956), 126-132.

683 _____. "The Present system of succession among the Akan people of the Gold Coast," J. Afr. Adm., VI (Oct. 1954), 166-71.

684 Harper, Charles H., et al. "Notes on the totemism of the Gold Coast," J. Roy. Anthrop. Inst., XXXVI (1906), 178-88.

685 Hayford, Casely. Gold Coast native institutions; with thoughts upon a healthy imperial policy for the Gold Coast and Ashanti. London: Cass, 1970. 418 p. (Cass Library of African Studies, Africana modern library, no. 11.) A reprint of the 1903 edition, by Sweet & Maxwell, London.

686 Herskovits, Merville and F. S. Herskovits. Dahomean narrative: a cross-cultural analysis. Evanston: Northwestern University Press, 1958. 490 p. (African studies, no. 1.)
A study of the myths of the Dahomean people--exploits of gods, tales of divination, hunter stories, etc.
Rev: TLS, (Jan. 16, 1959), 34.

687 Huber, Hugo. "Adangme purification and pacification rituals," Anthropos, LIII, Nos. 1-2 (1958), 161-91.

688 _____. "Adangme varianten zum Thema: Himmelseil, Himmelmensch," Zeitschrift für Ethnologie, LXXXVIII, No. 2 (1963), 234-42.

689 _____. "Initiation into womanhood among the SE (Ghana)," Nigerian Field, XXIII, No. 3 (1958), 99-119.

690 _____. The Krobo: traditional social and religious life of a West African people. St. Augustin, (Bonn): Anthropos Inst., 1963. 306 p.
A study conducted between 1951 and 1957 on the Krobo of Eastern Ghana.

691 _____. "Representations of figures in the roof decoration of the Krobo and their symbolism," Anthropos, LV, Nos. 3-4 (1960), 578-80.

692 _____. "Ritual oaths as instruments of coercion and self-defence among the Adangme of Ghana," Africa, XXIX, (Jan. 1959), 41-9.

693 Hunter, John M. "The Clans of Nangodi," Africa, XXXVIII (Oct. 1968), 377-412.

694 Irwin, G. "The Origins of the Akan and Akan culture, " Uni-
     versitas, IV (March 1961), 138-41.

695 Jeibeks, K. "Geburt eines Kindes in Ghana, " Afrika Heute,
     XVIII (Sept. 15, 1967), 268.

696 Kelly, Michael. "Personal testament, " New Blackfriars,
     XLVIII (Dec. 1966), 147-51.

697 Kotei, S. I. A. The Akan of Ghana: a select bibliography.
     Accra: Research Library on African Affairs, 1963. 17 p.

698 Kyerematen, A. A. "The Royal stools of Ashanti, " Africa,
     XXXIX (Jan. 1969), 1-10.

699 Labouret, Henri. Les tribus du remeau lobi (Volta noire
     moyenne). Paris: Institut d'Ethnologie, 1931. 510 p.

700 Lantis, Margaret. "Fanti omens, " Africa, XIII, No. 2
     (1940), 150-60.

701 Lystad, Mary H. "Traditional values of Ghanaian children, "
     Amer. Anthrop., LXII (June 1960), 454-64.
        Changes of cultural values demonstrated by tests.

702 Lystad, R. A. The Ashanti: a proud people. New Brunswick,
     New Jersey: Rutgers University Press, 1958. 212 p.
        Description of the culture of the people of the little town
     of Goaso in the southwestern corner of Ashanti--their daily
     life, religion, economy, education and government.
        Rev: Amer. Anthrop., LX (Dec. 1958), 1218.

703 McCall, Daniel F. "The Effect on family structure of changing
     economic activities of women in a Gold Coast town, " Doctoral
     Dissertation, Columbia University, 1956. 125 p.

704 McCowan, A. , et al. Race and power: studies in leadership
     in five British dependencies. London: Bow Group, 1956.
     132 p.
        The countries discussed are British Guiana, the Gold
     Coast, Kenya, Malaya and Northern Rhodesia.

705 McLeod, M. D. "A Survey of the literature on witchcraft in
     Ghana (excluding the Northern territories) with particular
     reference to the Akans, " B. Litt's Thesis, Oxford University,
     1965/66.

706 Manoukian, Madeline. Akan and Ga-Adangme peoples of the
     Gold Coast. London: International African Institute, 1950.
     112 p. (Ethnographic survey of Africa, Western Africa,
     Part I.)

707 _____ . The Ewe-speaking people of Togoland and the Gold
Coast. London: International African Institute, 1952. 63 p.
(Ethnographic survey of Africa, Western Africa, Part 6.)

708 _____ . Tribes of the Northern Territories of the Gold
Coast. London: International African Institute, 1951. 101 p.
(Ethnographic survey of Africa, Western Africa, part 5.)

709 Mead, Margaret. "A Twi relationship system," J. Roy.
Anthrop. Inst., LXVII (July/Dec. 1937), 297-304.

710 Meek, Charles Kingsley, et al. Europe and West Africa:
some problems and adjustments. London: Oxford University Press, 1940. 143 p.
    Dr. Meek is a British anthropologist once attached to
the Nigerian Government and author of Law and authority in
a Nigerian tribe (1937).

711 Mensah-Brown, A. K. "An African chiefdom in modern
Ghana," Présence Africaine, No. 62 (1967), 94-120.

712 Meyerowitz, Eva Lewin. "The Akan and Ghana," Man, (June
1957), 83-8.

713 _____ . Akan traditions of origin. London: Faber &
Faber, 1952. 149 p.
    Examines the historical traditions in the areas south of
the Sudanese Kingdoms of Ghana, Mali and Songhai.

714 _____ . At the court of an African king. London: Faber &
Faber, 1962. 244 p.
    Describes the court life of Bono-Tekyiman.

715 _____ . "A Note on the origins of Ghana," African Affairs,
LI (Oct. 1952), 319-23.

716 Mitchison, N. H. Other people's worlds. London: Secker &
Warburg, 1958. 160 p.
    Impressions of Ghana during Independence celebrations.

717 Mohr, R. "Historische Uberlieferungen und Gesellschaftord-
nung in Kpandu (Ost-Ghana)," Zeitschrift für Ethnologie,
LXXXVIII, No. 2 (1963), 243-65.

718 Nukunya, G. K. Kinship and marriage among the Anlo-Ewe.
New York: Humanities Press, 1969. 217 p. (London
School of Economics. Monographs on social anthropology,
no. 37.)
    Revision of author's doctoral dissertation, London University.

719 Obumselu, Mrs. C. D. "Ritual and authority in a West African
society: the Akan of Ghana," B. Litt's Thesis, Oxford University, 1965/66.

720   Oddoye, D. E. M.   A Select bibliography of folklore, legends
      and traditions of African peoples.   2nd ed.   Accra: Research
      Library on African Affairs, 1964.   41 p.   1st ed. 1963.

721   Offonry, H. K.   "Age grades: their power and influence in
      village life, " W. Afr. Rev. , XIX, No. 255 (1948), 378-9.

722 Opler, M. K.   "Cultural definitions of illness: social psychiatry
      views intercultural and inter-class communication in Ghana. "
      In Arden House Conference on Medicine and Anthropology.
      Man's image in medicine and anthropology.   New York:
      International Universities Press, 1963, pp. 446-73.

723   Opon, Sebastian K.   "Democratic elements in Akan indigenous
      society, " Doctoral Dissertation, University of Chicago, 1954.

724   Page, Roger E.   "The Osu and kindred peoples, " Gold Coast
      Review, I (June/Dec. 1925), 66-70.

725   Parkin, D. J.   "Urban voluntary associations as institutions
      of adaptation, " Man (New series), I (March 1966), 90-5.

726   Parsons, D. St. John.   Legends of Northern Ghana.   London:
      Longmans, Green, 1958.   70 0.

727   _____.   More legends of Northern Ghana.   London: Long-
      mans, 1960.   69 p.

728   Paulme, D.   Classes et associations d'age en Afrique de
      l'Ouest.   Paris: Plon, 1971.   354 p.
         Based upon a colloquium held in Paris in Spring 1969
      with theme, "Age Classes in West Africa. "
         Rev: Africa, XLII (1972), 346-7.

728a   _____.   Organization sociale des Dogon.   Paris: Ed.
      Domatmontchrestien, 1940.   603 p.

729   Polgar, Steven.   "Akan clerks: a study of an intermediate
      non-localized group in situation of culture change, " Doc-
      toral Dissertation, University of Chicago, 1956.

730   Pollack-Eltz, Angelina.   "El Culto de los gemelos en Africa
      occidental; y en las Americas, " America Latina, XII
      (April/June 1969), 66-78.
         Attitudes of the Ashanti, Fanti, Ga, Ewe, Yoruba, Ibo
      and Latin American peoples towards twins.

731   Potehin, I. I.   Stanovlenie novoj Gany (Russian.   The Building
      of New Ghana).   Moskva: Nauka, 1965.   352 p.

732   Puplampu, D. A.   "The National epic of the Adangme, " African
      Affairs, L (July 1951), 236-41.

733 Rapp, Eugen Ludwig. "The African explains witchcraft:
     Adangme," Africa, VIII, No. 4 (1935), 554-5.

734 Rattray, Robert Sutherland. Akan-Ashanti folktales ... illus-
     trated by Africans of the Gold Coast Colony. Oxford:
     Clarendon Press, 1930. 275 p.
     In Twi and English.

735 _____. Ashanti. Oxford: Clarendon Press, 1955. 348 p.
     Reprint of the 1923 edition.

736 _____. Ashanti proverbs: the primitive ethics of a savage
     people; translated from the original with grammatical and
     anthropological notes. London: Oxford University Press,
     1961. 190 p. Reprint of the 1916 edition.

737 _____. "The Tribes of the Ashanti hinterland," J. Afr.
     Soc., XXX (Jan. 1931), 40-57.

738 _____. Tribes of the Ashanti hinterland. Oxford: Claren-
     don Press, 1932. 2 v. 604 p.

739 Redmayne, A. H. "The Concept of feudalism in African eth-
     nology," B. Litt. Thesis, Oxford University, 1961/62.

740 Richards, A. I. "African kings and their royal relatives,"
     J. Roy. Anthrop. Inst., XCI (1961), 135-50.

741 _____. "Social mechanisms for the transfer of political
     rights in some African tribes," J. Roy. Anthrop. Inst.,
     XC (1960), 175-9.

742 Rubin, Leslie. "Chieftaincy and adaptation of customary law
     in Ghana." In J. Butler and A. A. Castagno, eds. Boston
     University Papers on Africa; transition in African politics.
     New York: Praeger, 1967, pp. 115-34.
     Examines how the traditional role of chieftaincy has been
     adapted to the requirements of a modern state.

743 Sarpong, Peter K. "The Sacred stools of the Ashanti,"
     Anthropos, XXVI, Nos. 1-2 (1967), 1-60.

743a Schott, Rudiger. Aus Leben und Dichtung eines westafri-
     kanischen Bauervolkes: Ergebnisse völkerkundlicher
     Forschungen bei den Bulsa in Nord-Ghana 1966/7. Köln:
     Westdeutscher Verlag, 1970. 96 p.
     The Bulsa or Builsa, numbering about 7000 people, are a
     little known tribal group in Northern Ghana, resembling the
     Tallensi and Lo Dagaba in their political and social organiza-
     tion.
     Rev: Africa, XLII (Oct. 1972), 342-3.

744 Sellinow, I.   "Bericht über eine Reise nach Nordghana, "
    Ethnographisch-Archaologische Zeitschrift, VIII, No. 2 (1967),
    169-73.

745 Senayah, Emmanuel.   "African marriage customs: Ewe tradi-
    tions, " W. Afr. Rev. , (March 1953), 277-9.

746 Skinner, Elliott P.   "Labour migration and its relationship to
    socio-cultural change in Mossi society, " Africa, XXX, (Oct.
    1960), 375-99.

747 Somerfelt, Axel.   Political cohesion in a stateless society:
    the Tallensi of the Northern Territories of the Gold Coast.
    Oslo: Broggers, 1958.   215 p.
    In Norwegian, with English summary.

748 Southall, Aidan W.   "The Illusion of tribe, " J. Asian Afr.
    Stud. , V (Jan. /April 1970), 28-50.

749 Tait, David.   The Konkomba of Northern Ghana.   Edited from
    his published and unpublished writings by Jack Goody.   Lon-
    don: Oxford University Press, 1961.   255 p.
    "The first part ... consists of the doctoral dissertation
    ... submitted to the University of London, 1952. "

750 _____ .   "A Sorcery hunt in Dagomiba, " Africa, XXXIII
    (April 1963), 136-47.

751 Tamakloe, E. Forster.   A Brief history of the Dagbamba
    people.   Accra: Govt. Printer, 1931.   76 p.

752 _____ .   "Mythical and traditional history of Dagomba. "
    In Allan Cardinall, ed.   Tales told in Togoland.   London:
    Oxford University Press, 1931, pp. 230-79.

753 Thomas, L. V.   "Acculturation et déplacement de populations
    en Afrique de l'Ouest, " Rev. Psych. Peuples (Le Havre),
    XVI, No. 1 (1961), 49-76.
    Countries treated: Upper Volta, Dahomey, Ghana and
    Guinea.

754 Tufuo, J. W. and C. E. Donkor.   Ashantis of Ghana: people
    with a soul.   Accra: Anowuo Educational Publications,
    1969.   127 p.

755 Uchendu, V. C.   "The Passing of tribal man: a West African
    experience, " J. Asian Afr. Stud. , V (Jan. /April 1970), 51-
    65.

756 _____ .   "Priority issues for social anthropological research
    in Africa in the next two decades. "   In Gwendolen Carter
    and Ann Paden, eds.   Expanding horizons in African studies.

Evanston: Northwestern University Press, 1969, pp. 3-23.
The author is a Nigerian anthropologist teaching at Stanford University, California.

757 Van Dyck, C. "An Analytic study of the folktales of selected peoples of West Africa, " Doctoral Dissertation, Oxford University, 1966/67.

758 _____. "Aspects of traditional Akan society and culture, as represented in Akan sayings, with special reference to oaths and proverbs, " B. Litt's Thesis, Oxford University, 1962/63.

759 Wartemberg, J. Sylvanus. Sao Jorge d'El Mina, premier West African settlement: its tradition and customs. Ilfracombe: Stockwell, 1951. 166 p.

760 Westermann, Diedrich Hermann. Die Glidyi-Ewe in Togo: Züge aus ihren Gesellschaftsleben. Berlin: In Kommission bei W. de Gruyter & Co. , 1935. 332 p.

761 _____. "Texte in der Ge-Mundart des Ewe, " Afrika und Übersee, XXXIX, (Dec. 1954), 1-5; (Sept. 1955), 119-27.

762 Wild, Robert P. "Vestiges of a pre-Ashanti race at Obuasi, " Gold Coast Review, V (Jan. /June 1929), 1-17.

763 Wilks, Ivor. "Akwamu Otublohum: an eighteenth-century marriage arrangement, " Africa, XXIX, (Oct. 1959), 391-403.

764 Witte, A. "Zur Trommelsprache bei den Ewe Leuten, " Anthropos, V, Nos. 1-2 (1910), 50-3.

765 Worsley, P. M. "The Kinship system of the Tallensi: a revaluation, " J. Roy. Anthrop. Inst. , LXXXVI, No. 1 (1956), 37-75.

(2) ARCHAEOLOGY

766 Addison, F. "Jebel Moya" wellcome excavations in the Sudan. London: Oxford University Press, 1949. 2 v.

767 Alimen, H. The Prehistory of Africa. Translated by Alan Houghton Brodrick. London: Hutchinson, 1957. 438 p.

768 Anquandah, J. "Ghana's terracotta cigars, " Ghana Notes & Queries, No. 7 (1965), 25.

769   Arkell, A. J.   "Gold Coast copies of 5th-7th century bronze
      lamps, " Antiquity, XXIV, No. 93 (1950), 38-40.

770   Atherton, John H. and Milan Kalous.   "Nomali, " J. Afr.
      Hist. , XI (1970), 303-17.
            Describes various kinds of nomali, mostly human figures
      or heads, semi-human or semi-animal monsters.   Nomali
      is a name usually applied to some stone sculptures in
      Sierra Leone.

771   Balfour, Henry.   "Modern brass-casting in West Africa, "
      J. Roy. Anthrop. Inst. , XL (1910), 525-8.

772   _____.   "Notes on a collection of ancient stone implements
      from Ejura, Ashanti, " J. Roy. Afr. Soc. , XII (1912), 1-6.

773   Braunholtz, H. J.   "Archaeology in the Gold Coast, " Antiquity,
      X (1936), 469-74.

774   Brill, Robert H. and Harrison Hood.   "A New method for
      dating ancient glass, " Nature (London), CLXXXIX (Jan.
      1961), 12-14.

775   Bristowe, L. W. and H. P. Marriott.   "Stone implements on
      the Gold Coast, " Knowledge, XXII (1900), 241-4.

776   Brückner, W. D.   "The Mantle-rock (laterite) of the Gold
      Coast and its origin, " Geo. Rund. , XLIII (1955), 307-27.

777   _____ and M. M. Anderson.   "A Study of the criteria neces-
      sary for determining the morphological development and the
      young geological history of Ghana, " Quaternaria, V (1962),
      95-108.

778   Bumpus, B. S.   "Biconically pierced stones of the Gold Coast, "
      Nigerian Field, XVIII, No. 2 (1953), 78-86.

779   Burke, Kevin, et al.   "A Dry phase South of the Sahara
      20, 000 years ago, " W. Afr. J. Archaeol. , I (1971), 1-8.
            Discusses late Quaternary geological successions from
      13 localities South of the Sahara, correlating them on the
      basis of continuity of outcrop, lithological similarity and
      about 40 published radiocarbon dates.

780   Calvocoressi, D. S.   "Comments on recommendations and dis-
      cussion on terminology in African archaeology at Fourah Bay,
      June 1966, " W. Afr. Arch. Newsletter, No. 7 (1967), 9-12.

781   _____.   "European traders on the Gold Coast, " W. Afr.
      Arch. Newsletter, No. 10 (1968), 16-19.

782 _____ . "Report on the Third Conference of West African Archaeologists, Accra, 1969," W. Afr. Arch. Newsletter, No. 12 (1970), 53-90.

783 _____ . "Rockshelters in Ghana," W. Afr. Arch. Newsletter, No. 5 (1966), 29-30.

784 _____ . "West Africa," COWA Surveys and Bibliographies, Area 11, No. 4 (1969), 1-15.
A general survey of archaeological activities in individual West African states.

785 _____ and R. N. York. "The state of archaeological re- search in Ghana," W. Afr. J. Archaeol., I (1971), 87-103. pp. 96-103: Bibliography of archaeology in Ghana.

786 Carter, G. F. "Archaeological maize in West Africa; a dis- cussion of Stanton and Willett," Man, LXIV (1964), 85-6.

787 Carter, P. L. and P. J. Carter. "Rock-paintings from Northern Ghana," Trans. Hist. Soc. Ghana, VII (1965), 1-3.

788 Cardinall, A. W. "Stone armlets on the Gold Coast," Man, XXIII, No. 106 (1923), 169.

789 _____ . "Stone implements from Ashanti," Man, XVII, No. 5 (1917), 10-12.

790 _____ . "A West African monolith," Man, XXI, No. 82 (1921), 136-7.

791 Casson, Stanley. The Story of the inquiry into human origins: the discovery of man. London: Readers Union Ltd. with Hamish Hamilton, 1940. 339 p.
An evaluative survey of major archaeological and anthro- pological studies from the ancient times to 1940.

792 Chard, C. S. "Implications of early human migrations from Africa to Europe," Man, LXIII (1963), 124-5.

793 Clark, J. D. "The prehistoric origins of African culture," J. Afr. Hist., V (1964), 161-83.

794 _____ . "Excavation at Dawu," Man, LXII, No. 221 (1961), 140-1.
Review of Thurstan Shaw's Excavation at Dawu (1961).

795 _____ . "A Provisional correlation of prehistoric cultures North and South of the Sahara," South Afr. Arch. Bull., IX (1954), 3-7.

796 _____ . "The Quaternary in the coastlands of Guinea,"
        W. Afr. Arch. Newsletter, No. 9 (1968), 37-40.
        Review of Oliver Davies' The Quaternary in the coast-
        lands of Guinea (1964).

797 _____ . World prehistory; a new outline.   2nd ed. Cam-
        bridge: Cambridge University Press, 1969.   347 p.
        Rev: W. Afr. J. Archaeol., I (1971), 109-110.

798 Clarke, David L.   Analytical archaeology.   London: Methuen,
        1968.   684 p.
        Discusses the significance "of developing models both for
        the archaeologist's procedure and for the process of cultural
        change and development," with emphasis on the latter and
        draws upon some mathematical theories such as Cybernetics,
        Information Theory, the Theory of Games and the more
        fundamental mathematics of Set Theory.
        Rev: W. Afr. J. Archaeol., I (1971), 105-108.

799 Connah, G. and C. Thurstan Shaw. "A West African archae-
        ological journal; the necessity and the possibilities," W. Afr.
        Arch. Newsletter, No. 9 (1968), 63-72.

800 Cornevin, Robert.   Histoire de l'Afrique des origines à nos
        jours.   Paris: Payot, 1956.   404 p.
        Includes a survey of the archaeology of Africa.

801 Coursey, D. G.   Yams: an account of the nature, origins,
        cultivation and utilisation of the useful members of the
        Dioscoreaceae.   London: Longmans, 1967.   230 p.   (Tropi-
        cal agriculture series.)
        A comprehensive account of one of the most important
        crops in West Africa--its agricultural and economic aspects,
        origin, natural distribution and use, early historical refer-
        ences and significance of yam festivals in modern societies.
        Includes 28 pls. and 16 figs.
        Rev: Odu (New series), I (1969), 101-7.

802 Dark, P. J. C. "West African bronzes," Africa South, III
        (1959), 109-16.

803 Davidson, Basil. "Archaeology in Africa," Atlantic Monthly,
        CCIII (April 1959), 40-43.
        A historical survey of archaeological activity in Africa.

804 _____ . The Lost cities of Africa.   Boston: Little, Brown,
        1959.   209 p.
        Surveys the protohistoric civilisations of Africa South of
        the Sahara, covering both traditional history and archaeology,
        and attempts to correct the prevalent misconception that
        Black Africa was an isolated, savage, backward area before
        the European arrival.
        Rev: J. Afr. Hist., I, No. 1 (1960), 149-51.

805   Davies, Oliver. "African Pleistocene pluvials and European
       glaciations," Nature (Lond.), CLXXVIII (Oct. 6, 1956), 757-8.
           Evidence from Ghana, Dahomey and Nigeria supports the
       view that there are three pluvial periods in these areas
       rather than four as found by Leakey in East Africa.

806   _____. "Archaeological exploration in the Volta Basin,"
       Bull. Ghana Geogr. Assoc., IX (July 1964), 28-33.

807   _____. "An Archaeological link with ancient Ghana,"
       Universitas, III (June 1959), 175-6.
           Discusses terracotta head of middle Niger affinities said
       to have come from the Gold Coast.

808   _____. Archaeology in Ghana: papers. Edinburgh: Nelson
       for the University College of Ghana, 1961. 45 p.

809   _____. Archaeology in the Volta Basin; first monograph.
       Legon: Dept. of Archaeology, University of Ghana, 1969.
       100 p.
           Describes the archaeological work in the Basin, especially
       the excavations at Akiso by Africans. The study was moti-
       vated by the need for urgent salvage following the building
       of the dam at Akosombo on the Volta.

810   _____. "The Climatic and cultural sequence in the late
       Pleistocene of the Gold Coast," Proceedings of the Third
       Pan-African Congress on Prehistory, 1955, (1957), 1-5.

811   _____. "Earliest man and how he reached Ghana," Uni-
       versitas, III (March 1958), 35-7.

812   _____. "The Equipment of an Acheulean man in Africa,"
       Archaeology XII (1959), 172-7.

813   _____. Excavations at Sekondi. Accra: Ghana Univer-
       sities Press, 1970. 100 p.
           Report on the excavation of burials and houses at Sekondi
       in Ghana.

814   _____. "Galets perforés du Ghana et des pays voisins,"
       Notes Africaines (Dakar), No. 86 (April 1960), 37-9.

815   _____. "Geological and archaeological evidence for the
       late quartenary climatic sequence in West Africa," Ghana J.
       Sci., I (1961), 69-73.

816   _____. "Gonja painted pottery," Trans. Hist. Soc. Ghana,
       VII (1965), 5-11.

817   _____. "The Invaders of Northern Ghana; what archaeolo-
       gists are teaching the historians," Universitas, IV (March
       1961), 134-6.

818 _____ . "The Invasion of Ghana from the Sahara in the
early Iron Age," Actes du Cinquième Congres Pan-africain
de préhistoire et de l'étude du Quaternaire, Tenerife, 1963,
(1966), 27-42.
Excavations at Ntereso in Northern Ghana indicate that a
number of immigrants may have moved South into Ghana
during Sub-pluvial III.

819 _____ . "Mesoneolithic excavations at Legon and New
Todzi," Bull. IFAN, (B), XXX, No. 3 (1968), 1147-94.

820 _____ . "Native cultures in the Gold Coast at the time of
the Portuguese discoveries," Congresso Internacional de
Historia dos Descobrimentos (Lisbon), III (1960), 97-109.

821 _____ . "Neolithic cultures in Ghana." In J. Nenquin, ed.
Proceedings of the Fourth Panafrican Congress of Prehistory,
Leopoldville, 1959, III (1962), 291-302.

822 _____ . "The Neolithic revolution in Tropical Africa,"
Trans. Hist. Soc. Ghana, IV (1960), 14-20.

823 _____ . "The Old and middle palaeolithic in West Africa,"
Rivista di Scienze Preistoriche, XIX (1965), 1-21.

824 _____ . "The Old Stone Age between the Volta and the
Niger," Bull. IFAN (B), XIX (1957), 592-616.

825 _____ . "Le paléolithique sangoen de Gold Coast et ses
relations avec la forêt equatoriale," Notes Africaines, LXIII
(1954), 65-9.

826 _____ . Quaternary in the coastlands of Guinea.   Glasgow:
Jackson, 1964.   276 p.
Rev: Amer. Anthrop., LXX (Feb. 1968), 156 p.

827 _____ . "The Raised beaches of the Gold Coast and their
associated archaeological material," Quaternaria, II (1956),
91-3.

828 _____ . "Recent archaeological research in the Volta Basin,"
Bull. Inst. Afr. Stud. (Legon), I. No. 2 (1965), 16-19.

829 _____ . "Report on quaternary studies in Ghana," Bull.
IFAN, XXVIII, No. 1 (1966), 406-7.

830 _____ . "Timber construction and wood carving in West
Africa in the second millennium B.C.," Man (New series)
II, No. 1 (1967), 115-8.

831 _____ . West Africa before the Europeans; archaeology and
prehistory.   London: Methuen, 1967.   364 p.   (Methuen

Handbooks of Archaeology.)
With emphasis on Ghana, where the author has done most
of his field work, the book surveys West African archaeology
up to the Portuguese arrival on the Guinea Coast.   Includes
115 figs., 50 pls., bibliography, subject and topographical
indexes.
Rev: Amer. Anthrop., LXX (Aug. 1968), 810.   Choice,
V (June 1968), 540.

832   Fagan, B.M.   "Radiocarbon dates for Sub-Saharan Africa,
v. 1," J. Afr. Hist., X (1969), 149-69.

833   Fage, J.D.   "Ancient Ghana; a review of the evidence," Trans.
Hist. Soc. Ghana, III, Part 2 (1957), 77-98.
An examination of "the Ghana question" based chiefly on
literary evidence.

834   _____.   An Introduction to the history of West Africa.
Cambridge: Cambridge University Press, 1955.   209 p.
Contains some references to the ruined cities of the
former West African Kingdoms and to the bronze castings
and provides also a good historical background for the study
of the remains.

835   _____.   "A New check-list of the forts and castles of
Ghana," Trans. Hist. Soc. Ghana, IV, Part 1 (1955), 57-67.

836   _____.   "Some remarks on beads and trade in lower Guinea
in the sixteenth and seventeenth centuries," J. Afr. Hist.,
III, No. 2 (1962), 343-7.

836a Fagg, Bernard.   "Recent work in West Africa: new light on
the Nok culture," World Archaeology, I (1969), 41-50.

837   Fauconnet, Max.   "Mythology of black Africa," In Larousse
Encyclopedia of Mythology.   Translated by Richard Aldington
and Delano Ames.   London, 1959.   pp. 480-92.

838   Flight, C.R.   "Kintampo 1967," Bull. Inst. Afr. Stud. (Legon),
III, No. 3 (1967), 72-7.   Also in W. Afr. Arch. Newsletter,
No. 8 (1968), 15-20.

839   _____.   "Radiocarbon dates from Ghana: Kintempo series,"
Bull. Inst. Afr. Stud. (Legon), IV, No. 2 (1968), 105-7.

840   _____.   "The Settlement mounds of central Gonja," Bull.
Inst. Afr. Stud. (Legon), IV, No. 3 (1968), 94-107.

841   Field, M.J.   "An Investigation of the ancient settlement of
the Accra plain," Ghana Notes and Queries, No. 4 (Jan. /
June, 1962), 4-6.

842   Goodwin, A. J.   "The Medieval empire of Ghana," South Afr.
      Arch. Bull., XII (Sept. 1957), 47.
          Summary of the history of the medieval kingdom of Ghana
      and its relations with the Arabs of North-West Africa.

843   Gray, R.   "Report on the Third Conference on African History
      and Archaeology," J. Afr. Hist., III (1962), 175-91.

844   Hinderling, P.   "Three human figures from near Kumasi,
      Ghana," Man, LXI, No. 245 (1961), 207-8.

845   Jeffreys, M. D.   "Maize in West Africa," Man, LXIII, No.
      247 (1963), 194-5.

846   _____.   "Who were the aborigines of West Africa?"
      W. Afr. Rev., XXII (May 1951), 466-7.

847   Jones, D. H., ed.   History and archaeology in Africa, Second
      Conference held on July 1957 at the School of Oriental and
      African Studies.   London: School of Oriental and African
      Studies, 1959.   58 p.
          Summarizes the seventy papers presented at the conference,
      and includes a separate section on the archaeology and pro-
      tohistory of West Africa and another on dating techniques.

848   Kennedy, R. A.   "West African prehistory," History Today,
      VIII (Sept. 1958), 646-53.

849   Kitson, A. E.   "The Gold Coast: Some considerations of its
      structure, people, and natural history," Geogr. J., XLVIII
      (1916), 369-92.

850   Kwapong, A. A.   "Africa antiqua," Trans. Gold Coast & Togo-
      land Hist. Soc., II, Part 1 (1956), 1-11.
          A noted Ghanian classical scholar surveys the documentary
      evidence concerning Africa South of the Sahara during the
      classical period and agrees with the contention that Hanno,
      a Carthaginian general, did not sail along the Atlantic Coast
      beyond Morocco.

851   Lawrence, A. W.   "Ghana forts," Arch. Rev., CXXXV (April
      1964), 293-6.

852   _____.   "The National Museum of the Gold Coast,"
      Universitas, I (March 1954), 10-12.

853   _____.   Trade castles and forts of West Africa.   London:
      Cape, 1963.   390 p.

854   London. University. School of Oriental and African Studies. His-
      tory and archaeology in Africa, report of a conference held in
      July 1953 at the School of Oriental and African Studies.
      Edited by R. A. Hamilton, 1955.   99 p.

855 Mathewson, R. D. "Excavations at Jakpasere, 1968," Bull.
     Inst. Afr. Stud., (Legon), IV, No. 3 (1968), 88-93.

856 _____. "The Painted pottery sequence in the Volta Basin,"
     W. Afr. Arch. Newsletter, No. 8 (1968), 24-31.

857 _____. "Report on fieldwork carried out in northern Ghana
     August 1965," Bull. Inst. Afr. Stud. (Legon), II, No. 2
     (1965), 46-8.

858 _____. "Some notes on the settlement mounds of central
     Gonja," Bull. Inst. Afr. Stud. (Legon), IV, No. 2 (1968),
     108-14.

859 _____. "Towards a general chronology of the Ghanaian
     Iron Age," A Seminar Paper, Departments of Archaeology
     and History, Legon, 21, January 1969.

860 Mauny, R. "Bibliographie de la préhistoire et de la proto-
     histoire de l'Ouest africain," Bull. IFAN (B), XXIX (1967),
     879-917.

861 _____. "Contribution à la bibliographie de l'histoire de
     l'Afrique noire des origines à 1850," Bull. IFAN (B),
     XXVIII (1966), 927-65.

862 _____. "The Question of Ghana," Africa (Lond.), XXIV
     (July 1954), 200-13.
     Summarizes the historical evidence on the Ghana Empire,
     derived primarily from the excavations of Koumbi Saleh,
     the probable side of the capital of the Empire. Rejects the
     contention that the Akans are descendants of the Ghana
     people--a fact upon which the subsequent change of the name
     of the Gold Coast to Ghana is based.

863 _____. Tableau géographique de l'Ouest africain au moyen
     age d'après les sources écrites, la tradition et l'archéologie.
     Dakar, 1961, pp. 174-8.

864 Meyerowitz, Eva L. "A Note on the origin of Ghana," African
     Affairs, LI (Oct. 1952), 319-23.
     Presents arguments to support the popular belief among
     the Akans that they descended from the Negroes of the
     medieval Ghana Empire.

865 Migeod, F. W. "Antiquity of man in West Africa," Man, XVII,
     No. 19 (1917), 134.

866 _____. "The Discovery of a presumed palaeolithic in
     Northern Ashanti (Gold Coast)," Man, XVI, No. 36 (1916),
     56-8.

867 _____. "Discovery of palaeoliths and pierced stones,"
Man, XIX, No. 6 (1919), 13-14.

868 Miracle, M. P. "The Introduction and spread of maize in
Africa," J. Afr. Hist., VI, No. 1 (1965), 39-55.

869 Newlands, H. S. "An Archaeological puzzle from West
Africa," J. Roy. Afr. Soc., XIX, No. 73 (1920), 40-4.

870 Nunoo, R. B. "Archaeological survey at the College of Technology," J. Kumasi Coll. Tech., I (1959), 17-19.

871 _____. "Excavations at Asebu in the Gold Coast," J. W.
Afr. Sci. Assoc., III (Feb. 1957), 12-44.
Report on the excavation of a probably 17th century site
in Fanti territory.

872 _____. "A Report on excavations at Nsuta Hill, Gold
Coast," Man, XLVIII (July 1948), 73-6.

873 O'Neil, J. B. N. Report on ancient and historic monuments.
Accra, 1951. 53 p.

874 Ozanne, P. C. "Adwuku: a fortified hilltop village in Shai,"
Ghana Notes & Queries, No. 7 (1964), 4-5.

875 _____. "The Diffusion of smoking in West Africa," Odu
(New series) II (1969), 29-42.

876 _____. "An Early site near Achimota," Ghana Notes &
Queries, No. 8 (1966), 9-10.

877 _____. "An Earthenware oil-lamp from near Nsawam,"
Trans. Hist. Soc. Ghana, V, No. 2 (1961), 75-7.

878 _____. "Excavation at Dawu," Trans. Hist. Soc. Ghana,
VI (1962), 119-23.
Review of Thurstan Shaw's Excavation at Dawu (1961).

878a _____. "Ladoku: an early town near Prampram,"
Ghana Notes & Queries, No. 7 (1964), 6-7.

879 _____. "Notes on the early historic archaeology of Accra,"
Trans. Hist. Soc. Ghana, VI (1962), 51-70.

880 _____. "Report on field work at Banda and Wenchi, 8-16
August, 1964," Bull. Inst. Afr. Stud., (Legon), I, No. 1
(1965), 19-23.

881 Painter, C. "The Guang and West African historical reconstruction," Ghana Notes & Queries, No. 9 (1966), 58-65.

882   Pearce, S. V.   "The Appearance of iron and its use in pre-
      historic Africa," Master's Thesis, London University, 1959/
      60.

883   Posnansky, Merrick.   "Archaeology at the University of Ghana,
      Legon," Afr. Stud. Bull., XI (Dec. 1968), 34-5.

884   _____.   Myth and methodology--the archaeological contribu-
      tion to African history, Accra, 1969.

885   _____.   "Yams and the origins of West African agriculture,"
      Odu (New series) I (1969), 101-7.
      Review of D. G. Coursey's Yams (1967).

886   Shaw, Thurstan.   Archaeology and the Gold Coast.   Accra:
      Dept. of Information, 1945.   16 p.

887   _____.   "Archaeology in the Gold Coast," Afr. Stud., II,
      No. 3 (1943), 139-47.

888   _____.   "Chronology of excavation at Dawu, Ghana," Man,
      LXII, No. 217 (1962), 136-7.

889   _____.   "Early smoking pipes in Africa, Europe and
      America," J. Roy. Anthrop. Inst., XC (July/Dec. 1960),
      272-305.

890   _____.   Excavation at Dawu: report on an excavation in a
      mound at Dawu, Akuapim, Ghana.   London: Nelson for Uni-
      versity College of Ghana, 1961.   124 p. (60 p.)
      History of the discovery and position of the mound; and
      analysis of the finds.   Bibliography and index.
      Rev: Man, LXII, No. 221 (1963), 140-1.   Trans. Hist.
      Soc. Ghana, VI (1962), 119-23.

891   _____.   "Smoking in Africa," South Afr. Arch. Bull., XIX,
      No. 75 (1964), 75-6.

892   _____, et al.   "Radiocarbon chronology of the Iron Age in
      Sub-Saharan Africa," Current Anthropology, X, Nos. 2-3
      (1969), 226-31.

893   Shinnie, P. L., ed.   The African Iron Age.   London: Oxford
      University Press, 1971.   320 p.

894   _____.   "Excavations at Yendi Dabari," Ghana Notes &
      Queries, No. 1 (1961), 10-11.   See also No. 3 (1961), 4-5.

895   _____ and P. C. Ozanne.   "Excavations at Yendi Dabari,"
      Trans. Hist. Soc. Ghana, VI (1962), 87-118.

896 _____ and I. G. Wilks. "A Burial mound near Tamale,
Ghana," J. W. Afr. Sci. Assoc., VI, No. 1 (1960), 47-8.

897 Sordinas, A. "Modern Koli beads in Ghana," Man, LXIV,
No. 90 (1964), 75-6.

898 Tamers, M. A. and F. J. Pearson. "Validity of radiocarbon
dates on bone," Nature (London), CCVIII (1965), 1053-5.

899 "Third Conference on African History and Archaeology; papers
on the history of food crops," J. Afr. Hist., (1962), 195-
267.

900 Wayland, E. J. "African pluvial periods," Nature (Lond.),
CXXIII (1929), 607.

901 Wells, L. B. H., ed. "Symposium on human skeletal remains
from the Cape Coast," South Afr. J. Sci., XXXII (1935),
603-15.

902 Wild, Robert P. "Funerary equipment from Agona-Swedru,
Winnebah district, Gold Coast," J. Roy. Anthrop. Inst.,
XLVII (1937), 67-76.

903 _____. "Inhabitants of Gold Coast and Ashanti before the
Akan invasion," Gold Coast Teachers' Journal, VI, No. 3
(1935), 195-201.

904 _____. "A Method of bead making practiced in the Gold
Coast," Man, XXXVIII (June 1937), 96-7.

905 _____. "Nyame Akuma, or God axes," Gold Coast Rev.,
V, No. 1 (1931), 156-65.

906 _____. "The Pottery of the 'Nyame Akuma people,'" Gold
Coast Teachers J., IX, No. 2 (1937), 94-9.
See also IX, No. 3 (1937), 43-8; X, No. 3 (1938), 249-55.

907 _____. "Stone age pottery from the Gold Coast and Ashanti,"
J. Roy. Anthrop. Inst., LXIV (1934), 203-15.

908 _____. "Stone artifacts of the Gold Coast and Ashanti,"
Gold Coast Rev., III, No. 2 (1927), 157-9.

909 _____. "Stone implements of the palaeolithic type from
the Gold Coast," Gold Coast Rev., V, No. 1 (1931), 174-
80.

910 _____. "An Unusual type of primitive iron-smelting surface
at Abomposu, Ashanti," Gold Coast Rev., V, No. 2 (1931),
184-92.

911 _____. "Vestiges of a pre-Ashanti race at Obuasi (Ashanti),"
Gold Coast Rev., V, No. 1 (Jan./June 1929), 1-17.

912 Wilks, I. G. "The Chronology of the Gonja Kings," Ghana
Notes and Queries, No. 8 (1966), 26-28.

913 _____. "The Growth of the Akwapim state; a study in the
control of evidence." In J. R. Vansina, et al., eds. The
Historian in tropical Africa. London: Oxford University
Press, 1964, pp. 390-41.

914 Willett, Frank. "Archaeology in Africa," In Gwendolen
Carter and Ann Paden, eds. Expanding Horizons in African
Studies--Evanston: Northwestern University Press, 1969,
pp. 91-110.

915 _____. "Pottery classification in African archaeology; a
basis for discussion," W. Afr. Arch. Newsletter, No. 7
(1967), 44-55.

916 _____. "A Survey of recent results in the radiocarbon
chronology of Western and Northern Africa," J. Afr. Hist.,
XII, No. 3 (1971), 339-70.
General summary of African archaeological activities,
including those of individual countries.

917 Wood, W. Raymond. "An Archaeological appraisal of early
European settlements in the Senegambia," J. Afr. Hist.,
VIII (1967), 39-64.

918 York, R. N. "Archaeology and the reconstruction of Ghana's
history," New Era, II, No. 1 (1969), 26-7.

919 _____. "Excavations at Bui: a preliminary report," Bull.
Inst. Afr. Stud., I, No. 2 (1965), 36-9.

920 _____. "Pottery classification: some methods and results
from New Buipe," W. Afr. Arch. Newsletter, No. 7 (1967),
55-61.

921 _____. "Volta Basin Research Project excavations at
New Buipe, 1965-1967," Ghana Notes and Queries, No. 10
(Dec. 1968), 33-5.

922 _____. "The Volta Basin Research Project, Ghana," W.
Afr. Arch. Newsletter, No. 5 (1966), 27-8.

923 _____. Archaeology in the Volta Basin, 1963-1966. Legon,
1967. 45 p.
A survey of some twenty-five sites excavated in the Volta
Basin during the period, 1963-1966, as part of the rescue
operations prompted by the construction of a hydroelectric
dam at Akosombo.

(3)   ART

924   Allison, Philip. African stone sculpture. London: Lund
      Humphries, 1968. 71 p. Bibliog.
           Topics discussed include the status of stone sculpture in
      African art; Yoruba stone sculptures; worked stones of the
      Western Sudan and the Sahara; African stone sculpture, past
      and present. 99 plates, maps and bibliography.
           Rev: West Africa, No. 2693 (Jan. 11, 1969), 33.

925   Antubam, Kofi. "Arts of Ghana," United Asia, IX, No. 1
      (1957), 61-70.

926   _____. Ghana art and crafts. Accra: Govt, Printer,
      1963. 48 p.
           Published in cooperation with the Arts Council, Ghana
      Information Services, and the Ghana Museum and Monuments
      Board. Gives illustrations and notes on more common
      traditional art forms.

927   _____. Ghana's heritage of culture. Leipzig: Koehler &
      Amelang, 1963. 221 p.
           Deals primarily with the traditional conceptions of beauty,
      religion, time and life.

928   Asihene, E. V. Introduction to traditional art of Western
      Africa. London: Constable, 1970. 88 photos.

929   Balfour, Henry. "A Collection of stone implements from
      Ejara, Ashanti. J. Afr. Soc., XII (1912), 1-16.

930   Bascom, William R. and Paul Gebauer. Handbook of West
      African art. Assembled and edited by Robert E. Ritzen-
      thaler. Milwaukee: Bruce Publishing Co., 1954. 83 p.
      (Milwaukee Public Museum popular science handbook series,
      No. 5.)
           Contents: West African art, by W. R. Bascom; Art of the
      British Cameroons, by P. Gebauer.

931   Beier, Horst Ulli. Contemporary art in Africa. New York:
      Praeger, 1968. 173 p.
           Emphasis is on the artists in Nigeria, the Sudan, Mozam-
      bique, Rhodesia and Ethiopia. The author is a German
      artist, poet, and literary critic who has been living in
      Nigeria since 1950.
           Rev: Africa Report, XV (Jan. 1970), 39. TLS (June 20,
      1968), 645.

932   Berry, Jack. Spoken art in West Africa. London: School of
      Oriental and African Studies, 1961. 24 p.
           "An inaugural lecture delivered on 8 December 1960."

933 Biebuyck, Daniel, ed. Tradition and creativity in tribal art.
     Berkeley: University of California Press, 1969. 236 p.
        Collection of papers on primitive art, concerned primarily
     with aspects and sources of stylistic and functional variation
     within specific art areas, and possible role of artists and
     critics in this regard.
        Rev: Choice, VII (April 1970), 222. Library J., XCV
     (Feb. 15, 1970), 653.

934 Bodrogi, Tibor. Art in Africa. New York: McGraw-Hill,
     1968. 131 p. plates.
        Primarily on sculptured pieces and masks in West Africa
     and Central Africa. Bibliography and Index.
        Rev: Library J., XCIII (Dec. 15, 1968), 4642.

935 Bravmann, René A. West African Sculpture. Seattle: Uni-
     versity of Washington Press, for the Henry Art Gallery,
     1970. 80 p. (Index of art in the Pacific Northwest, No. 1.)
        "Catalogue for an exhibition held at the Henry Art Gallery,
     University of Washington, Feb. 8-March 8, 1970."

936 Brinkworth, Ian. "Ashanti art in London: the Wallace Col-
     lection," W. Afr. Rev., (March 1960), 26-30.

937 Carter, P. L. and P. J. Carter. "Rockpaintings from Northern
     Ghana," Trans. Hist. Soc. Ghana, VII (1964), 1-3.

938 Christensen, Erwin Ottoman. Primitive art. New York:
     Viking Press, 1955. 384 p. (A Studio publication.)
        A pictorial and textual survey of the art of black Africa,
     the South Seas, the aborigines of North and South America
     and Australia, and the men of the Stone and Ice Ages.
        Rev: N. Y. Times Bk. Rev., (Dec. 18, 1955), 5. New
     Yorker, XXXI (Dec. 17, 1955), 171.

939 Cockburn, C. "Pattern of change; the training of the architect
     in relation to the needs of the developing countries," Arch.
     Rev., CXXXVII (May 1965), 333-5.

940 Contemporary African art. Catalogue of an Exhibition of
     Contemporary Art held at the Camden Arts Centre, London,
     August 10-September 8, 1969. New York: Africana Pub-
     lishing Corp., 1970. 40 p.
        An attractively illustrated catalogue representing one of
     the first exhibitions of truly contemporary African art drawn
     from various African countries. Includes supplementary
     essays and biographies by prominent African scholars on
     contemporary art scene in Africa.

941 Cordwell, Justine Mayer. "African art." In William Bascom
     and Melville Herskovits, eds. Continuity and change in

African cultures.   Chicago: University of Chicago Press,
1959, pp. 28-48.

942 _____ .   "The problem of process and form in West African
art."   In Proceedings of the Third International West African
Conference, Ibadan, 1949.   Lagos: Nigerian Museum, 1956,
pp. 53-60.

943 Crowley, Daniel J.   "The Contemporary-traditional art market
in Africa," African Arts, IV, No. 1 (1970), 43-9.

944 _____ .   "Traditional and contemporary art in Africa."
In Gwendolen Carter and Ann Paden, eds.   Expanding Hori-
zons in African Studies.   Evanston: Northwestern University
Press, 1969, pp. 111-8.

945 Duerden, Dennis.   "African art and its critics, " Ibadan, No.
6 (June 1959), 14-17.

946 _____ .   African art: the colour library of art.   London:
Hamlyn, 1968.   39 p.   Text.   50 p.   Plates.
Each plate is briefly analyzed.   Includes bibliography and
maps.

947 Ehsanullah, Lilian.   "Ashanti goldweights, " Nigerian Field,
XXIX (April 1964), 82-8.

948 Eicher, Joanne B.   African dress: an annotated bibliography.
East Lansing: African Studies Center, Michigan University,
1970.

949 Elisofon, Eliot.   "African sculpture, " Atlantic Monthly, CCIII
(April 1959), 48-60.
An excellent article on various kinds of art--paintings,
masks, wooden figures.   Examines also foreign influences
on them.   Sixteen plates.

950 _____ and William Fagg.   The Sculpture of Africa; 405
photographs.   Text by William Fagg.   New York: Praeger,
1958.   256 p.   Bibliog.   (Books that matter.)
Rev: Library J. , LXXXIV (Feb. 1, 1959), 510.   TLS
(Feb. 20, 1959), 92.

951 Fagg, William Buller.   The Art of Western Africa; tribal
masks and sculpture.   London: Collins in association with
UNESCO, 1967.   60 p.   (Fontana UNESCO art books.)

952 _____ .   "On the nature of African art. " Memoirs and
Proceedings of the Manchester Literary and Philosophical
Society XCIV (1953), 93-104; Also in Colin Legum, ed.
Africa; a handbook to the continent.   London: Anthony Blond,
1961, pp. 414-24.

953 _____. "The Study of African art," Bulletin of the Allen
Memorial Art Museum, XII (1955-56), 44-61.

954 _____. Tribes and forms in African art. New York:
Tudor Publ. Co., 1965. 19 p. 122 illus.
Based on the exhibition Africa: 100 Stamme, 100 Meister-
werke, sponsored by the Congress for Cultural Freedom at
the Berlin Festival, 1964.
Rev: TLS (July 7, 1966), 588.

955 _____ and Margaret Plass. African sculpture; an anthology.
London: Studio Vista, 1964. 157 p. (A Dutton Vista pic-
ture back, 8.)
Rev: Nigeria Magazine, No. 86 (Sept. 1965), 216-7.

956 Foyle, A. M. "The Development of architecture in West
Africa," Doctoral Dissertation, London University, 1958/59.

956a Fraser, Douglas and Herbert Cole, eds. African art &
leadership. Madison: University of Wisconsin Press, 1972.
332 p.
Comprises fourteen papers, six of which were originally
presented at a symposium entitled, "The Aristocratic
Traditions in African art," held at Columbia University,
May 1965.

957 Frobenius, Leo. Kulturgeschichte Afrikas: prolegomena zur
einer historischen gestaltlehre. Zurich: Phaidon, 1933.
164 p.

958 _____. Das unbekannte Afrika. Munich: Oscar Beck,
1923.

959 Georges, Hardy. L'Art nègre, l'art animiste des noirs
d'Afrique. Paris: Henri Laurens, 1927. 168 p.
Surveys the influence of animism, worship of the dead
and spirits and habits of secret societies on artistic creation,
with specific examples from various African countries.

960 Gerbrands, Adrianus Alexander. Art as an element of culture,
especially in negro Africa. Leiden, Holland: E. J. Brill,
1957. 158 p. Bibliog.
Originally submitted as doctoral dissertation, Leiden University, 1956, and later published in Dutch.

961 Godwin, G. "Monuments to the white man's wars," Arch. Rev.,
(Jan. 1938), 40-2.
Elmina and Shama Castles.

962 Goldwater, Robert. Bambara sculpture from the Western
Sudan. New York: Museum of Primitive Art, 1960. 64 p.

963 _____ . Senufo sculpture from West Africa. Greenwich:
          New York Graphic Society, 1964. 126 p.
          Emphasis is on styles, aesthetic qualities and iconology.
          The bulk of the work is analyzed into 12 classes, each dis-
          cussed in terms of form, meaning and artistic merit.
          Rev: Amer. Anthrop. , LXVII (April 1965), 563.

964 _____ . Traditional art of the African nations. New York:
          Museum of Primitive Art, 1961.

965 Greenaway, F. "Basic science museum; reflections on a mis-
          sion to Ghana; proposal for a national science museum, "
          Museums Journal, LXIV (March 1965), 313-22.

966 Grobel, L. "Ghana's Vincent Kofi, " African Arts, III (Sum-
          mer 1970), 8-11, 68-70.
          A discussion of a Ghanaian artist and his work.

967 Grottanelli, Vinigi L. "Asonu worship among the Nzema: a
          study in Akan art and religion, " Africa, XXXI (Jan. 1961),
          46-60.
          "Describes and discusses a group of earthenware figurines
          made and used for ritual purposes by the Nzema of south-
          western Ghana. The material was collected by me during a
          six week stay in the Nzema village of Ebebaku, near Atuabo,
          in the autumn of 1954. "

968 Grove, David and Luszlo Huszar. Towns of Ghana: the role
          of service centres in regional planning. Accra: Ghana Uni-
          versities Press, 1964. 98 p. (Planning Research Studies,
          No. 2.)
          Rev: Town Planning Review, XXXVII (July 1966), 147-8.

969 Hale, S. "Kente cloth of Ghana, " African Arts, III (Spring
          1970), 26-9.

970 Hinderling, P. "Three human figures from near Kumasi,
          Ghana, Man, LXI (Dec. 1961), 207-8.

971 Huber, Hugo. "Traditional crafts in a Nigo village (Ghana), "
          Anthropos, LIV, No. 3-4 (1959), 574-6.

972 Hull, May. Embroidery for Africa. London: Oxford Univer-
          sity Press, 1967. 70 p.

973 Jeffreys, M. D. "Notes on Ashanti goldweights, " Nigerian
          Field, XXIX (Oct. 1964), 191-92.

974 Jolly, D. "Bibliography and the arts of Africa, " Afr. Stud.
          Bull. , III, No. 1 (1960), 4-9.

975 Kedjanyi, J. "Masquerade societies in Ghana, " Research
          Review (Legon) III, No. 2 (1967), 51-7.

976 Kent, Kate P. West African cloth. Illus. by Arminta Neal.
     Denver, Colorado: Museum of Natural History, 1971. 83 p.

977 Kofi, Vincent. Sculpture in Ghana. Accra: Ghana Informa-
     tion Services, 1964. 58 p. 69 plates.
     A brief survey of wood carving in Ghana by the leading
     Ghanaian sculptor.

978 Krieger, Kurt and Gerdt Kutscher. Westafrikanische Masken.
     Berlin: Museum fur Volkerkunde, 1960.

979 Kyerematen, A. A. Asante Cultural Centre. Accra: Guinea
     Press, 1959. 22 p.
     The Centre located in Kumasi includes a library, museum
     and zoological gardens.

980 _____. Panoply of Ghana: ornamental art in Ghanaian
     tradition and culture. New York: Praeger, 1964. 120 p.
     Rev: Choice, I (Jan. 1965), 511.

981 Lambo, T. Adeoye. "The Place of art in the emotional life
     of the African," Présence Africaine, No. 60 (1966), 8-21.
     Dr. Lambo is the leading Nigerian psychiatrist and
     former Vice-Chancellor of the University of Ibadan, Nigeria.

982 Lawrence, A. W. "Ghana forts and trading stations," Arch.
     Rev., CXXXV (April 1964), 293-6.

983 Leuzinger, Elsy. Africa: the art of the negro peoples. Lon-
     don: Methuen, 1960. 247 p.
     Rev: Library J., LXXXVI (Feb. 1, 1961), 570. New
     Statesman, LX (Dec. 3, 1960, 893.

984 Lippmann, M. "Westafrikanische Bronzen," Phil F., Berlin,
     1940.

985 Lystad, Mary H. "Paintings of Ghanaian children," Africa,
     XXX (July 1960), 238-42.

986 McEwen, Frank. "Return to origins; new directions for
     African arts," African Arts, I, No. 2 (1968), 18-25, 88.

987 Meauze, Pierre. African art: sculpture. New York: World
     Publishing Co., 1968. 219 p.
     "It merely tries to cast light--on the large masks and
     statues inspired by everyday occurrences, and to view them
     with the somewhat fearful and respectful detachment appro-
     priate to objects imbued with magic" (Introduction).

988 Menzel, Brigitte. Goldgewichte aus Ghana (Goldweights from
     Ghana). Berlin: Museum Volkerkunde, 1968. 241 p.
     In German and English. Deals mainly with the goldweights

and accessories for weighing gold kept in the Ethnographical
Museum in Berlin, collected during the period, 1849 to 1967.
Rev: <u>Afr. Stud.</u>, **XXX**, No. 1 (1971), 69.

989   Meyerowitz, Eva Lewin-Richter. <u>The Divine Kinship in
      Ghana and ancient Egypt.</u> London: Faber & Faber, 1960.
      260 p.

990   Monti, Franco. <u>African masks.</u> Translated from the Italian.
      London: Hamlyn, 1969. 159 p. 69 plates. The Italian
      title: <u>Le Muschere africane,</u> published by Fratelli Fabbri
      Editori, Milan, 1966.
      Stresses the importance of masks in traditional African
      societies.

991   Museum of Primitive Art. <u>Art: masterpieces in the Museum
      of the Primitive Art: Africa, Oceania, North America,
      Mexico, Central to South America, Peru.</u> New York, 1965.
      134 p. (New York Museum of Primitive Art. Handbooks,
      No. 1.)

992   Odita, Emmanuel Okechukwu. "Contemporary art in Africa by
      Ulli Beier," <u>Africa Report,</u> XV (Jan. 1970), 39-40.
      A review of Beier's <u>Contemporary art in Africa</u> (1968).

993   _____. "Some observations on contemporary African art,"
      <u>J. New Afr. Lit. Arts,</u> (Fall 1966), 60-3. Also in Joseph
      Okpaku, ed. <u>New African Literature and the Arts,</u> v. 1,
      New York: Crowell, 1970, pp. 326-31.
      A survey of the fundamental influences on and nature of
      contemporary sculpture and paintings of Sub-Saharan Africa,
      reviewing also the conflicting views of the three schools of
      thought on African art. "The first perceives real value only
      in traditional African art, the second despises traditional
      art and favors the classical trends in European art, and
      the last advocates a synthetic blend of both."

994   _____. <u>Traditional African art.</u> Columbus: Ohio State
      University Press, 1971. 76 p. Bibliog.
      An exhibition held on February 14 to 19, 1971 at Ohio
      State University during the Black History Week, designed
      to give the students and the University community the oppor-
      tunity to appreciate specimens of African traditional art
      forms. The introduction discusses the nature and state of
      African art. The main section briefly analyzes different
      artistic works from different countries; with texts and illus-
      trations side by side. Extensive bibliography. The author
      is a noted Nigerian artist and Professor of Art, Ohio
      State University.

995   Plass, Margaret. <u>African miniatures: goldweights of the
      Ashanti.</u> New York: Praeger, 1967. 26 p. text. 96 plates.
      (Books that matter.)

Heavily illustrated and includes bibliography.
Rev: Sci. Amer., CCXVIII (June 1968), 136. TLS,
(Feb. 29, 1968), 209.

996 Plumer, Cheryl. Handicrafted African textiles; a reference
     guide by tribes and geographic origins. East Lansing:
     African Studies Center, Michigan State University, 1970.

997 "Preserving Ashanti culture: Cultural Centre at Kumasi,"
     W. Afr. Rev., XXXI (Oct. 1960), 43-5.

998 Prussin, Labelle. Architecture in Northern Ghana; a study
     of forms and functions. Berkeley: University of California
     Press, 1969. 120 p. Plates, drawings, maps and bibliog.
     Rev: Africa Report, XVI (Feb. 1971), 38-9. TLS,
     (Nov. 27, 1970), 1401.

999 _____. "The Architecture of Islam in West Africa,"
     African Arts, I, No. 2 (1968), 32-5, 70-4.

1000 _____. "The Impact of Islam on architecture in West
     Africa." Paper presented at the Annual Meeting of the
     African Studies Association, New York, November 1967.
     23 p.

1001 Quarcoo, A. K. and R. Sieber. "A Note on tradition and the
     history of art in Western Ghana," Research Review, III,
     No. 3 (1967), 84-90.
     A survey of art since the 17th century.

1002 Rattray, Robert Sutherland. "Arts and crafts of Ashanti,"
     J. Afr. Soc., XXIII (July 1924), 265-70.

1003 _____. Religion and art in Ashanti. With chapters by
     G. T. Bennett, Vernon Blake, H. Dudley Buxton, R. R.
     Marett, C. G. Seligman. New York: Oxford University
     Press, 1959. 432 p. (Oxford reprint series.) Reprint of
     the 1927 edition.
     An excellent study chiefly dealing with pottery and
     aesthetics.

1004 "Republic of Ghana." In Evelyn S. Brown. Africa's con-
     temporary art and artists.... New York: Division of
     Social Research and Experimentation, Harmon Foundation,
     1966, pp. 22-30.
     Reviews various kinds of traditional art; schools for
     art training, art centers, and gives biographies of leading
     Ghanaian artists.

1005 Sadler, Michael, ed. Arts of West Africa (excluding music).
     With an introduction by William Rothenstein. London: Ox-
     ford University Press, for the International Institute of

African Languages and Cultures, 1935. 101 p.
Contents: Significance and vitality of African art, by
Michael Sadler--Educational significance of indigenous
African art, by G. A. Stevens--Teaching wood-carving at
Achimota, by Gabriel Pippet--Arts of West Africa, 32
plates with descriptive notes, by Richard Carline--Bibli-
ography of indigenous art in West Africa, by Michael
Sadler.

1006 Sannes, G. W. African "primitives," function and form in
African masks and figures. Translated from the Dutch by
Margaret King; photographs by Marianne Dommisse. London: Faber & Faber, 1970. 114 p.
An examination of forty masks and figures from West
Africa most of them from Dogon, Bambara, and Senufo
tribal areas in and around Mali, evaluatively outlining
their probable functions and origins. Includes a valuable
appendix, list of museums containing African art and Bibliography.

1007 Schmalenbach, Werner. African art. Translated from the
German by Glyn T. Hughes. New York: Macmillan, 1954.
176 p. 148 figs. (Holbein art series.)
Life in African villages and the place of the artists in
African society.
Rev: TLS (Jan. 21, 1955), 36.

1008 Segy, Ladislas. African sculpture speaks. 3rd ed. New
York: Hill and Wang, 1969. 315 p. 1st ed. 1955.
Describes the artistic works of about 150 tribes with
emphasis on the art of West Africa.
Rev: Choice, VII (May 1970), 377.

1009 _____. "'The Ashanti Akua' ba statues as archtype, and
the Egyptian Ankh; the theory of morphological assumptions," Anthropos, LVIII, Nos. 5-6 (1963), 839-67.

1010 Shaw, Thurstan. "Bead-making with a bow-drill in the Gold
Coast," J. Roy. Anthrop. Inst., LXXV, Nos. 1-2 (1945),
45-50.

1011 Sieber, Roy. "The Arts and their changing social functions,"
Ann. N. Y. Acad. Sci., XCVI (1962), 653-8.

1012 _____. "Masks as agents of social control. " In Douglas
Fraser, comp. The Many faces of primitive art: a critical anthology. Englewood Cliffs, New Jersey: Prentice
Hall, 1966, pp. 257-63. Also in Afr. Stud. Bull., V, No.
2 (1962), 8-13.

1013 Smith, Marian. The Artist in tribal society; proceedings of
a symposium held at the Royal Anthropological Institute.
London: Routledge & Kegan Paul, 1961. 150 p.

1014   Sordinas, A.   "Modern Koli beads in Ghana, " Man, LXIV
       (May/June 1964), 75-6.

1015   Sutherland, Carol Humphrey.   Gold: its beauty, power and
       allure. 2nd ed. London: Thames & Hudson, 1969. 195 p.
       1st. 1959.

1016   Swithenbank, Michael. Ashanti fetish houses. Accra: Ghana
       Universities Press, 1969. 68 p. Bibliog.
            Chiefly concerned with a building style found mostly in
       Kumasi, the principal town of Ashanti, former capital of
       the powerful Ashanti Kingdom.

1017   Sydow, Eckart Von. Handbuch der westafrikanischen Plastik.
       Berlin: Reimer, 1930. Bd. 1. 494 p.

1018   Terrisse, A.   L'Afrique de l'Ouest Berceau de l'art nègre.
       Preface de L. S. Senghor. Paris: Fernand Nathanel, 1965.
       159 p.
            The text and numerous plates describe different paintings,
       masks, and other art forms in West Africa.

1019   Thompson, R. F.   "Esthetics in traditional Africa, " Art News,
       LXVI, No. 9 (1968), 44-5, 63-6.

1020   "The Treasures of Ghana: focus on the greatest artistic
       achievement of the Ashanti nation, " W. Afr. Rev. (March
       1957), 297-302.

1021   Trowell, Kathleen Margaret. African design. 3rd ed. New
       York: Praeger, 1970. 78, (76 p.) 78 plates. Bibliog.
       1st ed. 1960.
            Describes the materials, techniques and motifs employed
       in wall decoration, textile design, bead work, leather work,
       pottery, etc.
            Rev: Amer. Anthrop., LXIII (June 1961), 620. Library
       J., LXXXV (Dec. 1, 1960), 4360.

1022   _____. African tapestry. London: Faber & Faber, 1957.
       164 p.

1023   _____. Classical African Sculpture. 3rd. rev. ed. Lon-
       don: Faber & Faber, 1970. 101 p. Text; 48 p. plates
       1st ed. 1954.
            Contents: The application of African art--The function of
       the craftsman and his art--Geography, history and social
       pattern--A Brief critique of African sculpture. Emphasis
       on Nigeria and limited to West Africa and the Congo.

1024   _____ and Hans Nevermann. African and Oceanic art.
       New York: Abrams, 1968. 263 p. (Panorama of world
       art.)

Contents: Form and content of African art, by Trowell--
The Art of Oceania, by Nevermann, translated from the
German by Robert E. Wolf.

1024a Underwood, Leon. Bronzes of West Africa. London:
Tiranti, 1949. 32 p. 64 plates. Bibliog.

1025 _____. Figures in wood of West Africa. New enl. ed.
London: Tiranti, 1964. Bibliog. 1st ed. 1947.

1026 _____. Masks of West Africa. London: Tiranti, 1948.
49 p.

1027 Wild, R. P. "Stone age pottery from the Gold Coast and
Ashanti, " J. Roy. Anthrop. Inst. , LXIV (1934), 203-16.

1028 Willett, Frank. African art: an introduction. New York:
Praeger, 1971. 288 p. (Praeger world art series.)
Contents: The Development of the study of African
art--Towards a history of African art--African architecture--
Looking at African sculpture--Understanding African sculp-
ture--African art today. Notes, bibliography and index.
Rev: African Arts (Summer 1971), 72-4.

1029 Wingert, Paul Stover. The Sculpture of negro Africa. New
York: Columbia University Press, 1950. 96 p. 115
plates.
Under four broad geographical regions--West Africa,
Cameroon, Central Africa, and East Africa--various major
art areas are analyzed, specifying important tribal styles
characteristic of them.
Rev: N. Y. Times Bk. Rev. , (Dec. 31, 1950), 15.

1030 _____. Primitive art; its traditions and style. New York:
Oxford University Press, 1962. 421 p.
Examines the artistic traditions and styles of black
African, Oceanic and North American primitive art.
Rev: TLS (July 26, 1963), 544.

1031 Zwernemann, Jurgen. "Eine Maske aus mittel-Ghana, "
Tribus, XI (Nov. 1962), 143-8.

(4) BIOGRAPHIES--COLLECTIVE

1032 Ahuma, S. R. Memoirs of West African celebrities. Europe,
etc. (1700-1850). With special reference to the Gold
Coast. Liverpool: Marples, 1905. 260 p.
Includes portraits of Casely-Hayford, Mensah Sarbah and
other important Ghanaians.

1033 Fax, Elton C. West Africa vignettes. New York: American
      Society of African Culture, 1960. 62 p.
          Includes biographies of Evelyn Amarteifo, Philip Gbeho
      and Seth D. Cudjoe.

1034 Fung, Karen. "Index to portrait in West Africa, 1948-1966,"
      African Studies Bulletin, IX (Dec. 1966), 103-20.
          An alphabetical listing of Africans whose portraits have
      appeared in West Africa, 1948-1966. Includes date of the
      issue and page citation.

1035 "Ghana." In Sidney Taylor, ed. The New Africans: a
      Guide to the contemporary history of emergent Africa and
      its leaders. New York: Putnam, 1967. pp. 156-81.
          Biographies of leading Ghanaian personalities, with a
      brief summary of the events leading to the country's inde-
      pendence and the subsequent overthrow of the Nkrumah
      regime.

1036 Johnston, Harry. Pioneers in West Africa. London:
      Blackie & Sons, 1912.

1037 Jones-Quartey, K. A. B. "A Note on J. M. Sarbah and J. E.
      Casely Hayford: Ghanaian leaders, politicians, and
      journalists--1864-1930," Sierra Leone Stud. (New series)
      No. 14 (Dec. 1960), 57-62.

1038 Rogers, J. A. World's great men of color. New York: The
      Author, 1947. 2 v.
          Includes portraits of some noted Ashanti rulers, Osei
      Tutu and King Prempeh.

1039 Sampson, Magnus J. Gold Coast men of affairs; past and
      present. Ilfracombe: Stockwell, 1937. 224 p.
          On early twentieth century personalities, including Dr.
      Aggrey, Casely-Hayford, J. M. Sarbah, etc.

1040 _____. Makers of Modern Ghana. Accra: Anowuo Edu-
      cational Publications, 1969. V. 1, 190 p.

(4) BIOGRAPHIES--INDIVIDUAL

ACQUAYE, SAKA

1041 Hagan, W. B. "Profile: Saka Acquaye blends the arts in
      Ghana," Africa Report, XVI (Jan. 1971), 34-5.
          A musician, playwright and artist.

AGGREY, J. E. K.

1042 Adu, Ammishaddai. "The Real Aggrey," W. Afr. Rev.,
      (April 1953), 381-4.

1043   Chirgwin, A. M. Yarns on Men of Africa. Edinburgh: Edin-
        burgh House Press, 1931. 70 p. Dr. Aggrey. p. 55+.

1044   Macartney, William M. Dr. Aggrey, Ambassador for Africa.
        London: SCM Press, 1949. 106 p. (The torch biographies.)

1045   Musson, M. Aggrey of Achimota. London: Lutterworth,
        1944. 56 p.
            See also Concise dictionary of the Christian World Mis-
        sion, by Stephen Neil. New York: Abingdon Press, 1971,
        p. 10.

1046   Niven, Cecil. "Aggrey the teacher." In Nine great Africans,
        London: Bell, 1965, pp. 149-66.

1047   Obeng-Addae, H. E. Okunini Aggrey. Edinburgh: Nelson,
        1949. 66 p.
            Biography of Aggrey in Twi.

1048   Parr, Jardine. Famous names in Africa. London: Evans,
        1962. 64 p. (Records of achievement series.) Dr.
        Aggrey, pp. 55-60.

1049   Smith, Edwin W. Aggrey the African, being Edwin W.
        Smith's "Aggrey of Africa," edited as a simpler and shorter
        story by C. Kingsley Williams. London: Sheldon Press,
        1933. 144 p.

1050   _____. Aggrey of Africa; a study in black and white. 8th
        ed. London: Student Christian Movement, 1932. 202 p.

                        AKROFI, C. A.

1051   "Dr. C. A. Akrofi, 1901-1967," Research Review, (Legon)
        IV, No. 1 (1967), 3-5.
            A noted Ghanaian linguistic expert and lexicographer.

1052   [entry omitted]

                     AMO, ANTON WILHELM

1053   Lochner, Norbert. "Anton Wilhelm Amo: a Ghana scholar
        in the eighteenth century Germany," Trans. Hist. Soc.
        Ghana, III (1957), 169-79.

                  ARMATTOE, RAPHAEL ERNEST

1054   Kwaku, William A. "Raphael Ernest Glikpo Armattoe (1913-
        1953)," Afrika und Ubersee, XXXVIII (June 1954), 111-2.
            A Ghanaian poet.

AZIKIWE, NNAMDI

1055 Jones-Quartey, Kwatei. A Life of Azikiwe. Baltimore:
        Penguin, 1965. 272 p. (Penguin Africa Series, WA 14.)
        A readable biographical study of a noted Nigerian poli-
        tician, the architect of Nigerian independence, whose con-
        frontation with the British Colonial Administration began
        with his establishment of the newspaper, the African
        Morning Post, in the Gold Coast on his return from the
        United States in 1934 after many years of study. The
        author is a Ghanaian Professor of African Studies at the
        University of Ghana.

BLANKSON, GEORGE K.

1056 Akita, J. M. "Biographical sketch of George Blankson of
        Anomabu, " Trans. Gold Coast & Togoland Hist. Soc., I
        Part V (1955), 215-22.
        The first Ghanaian to be appointed a member of the
        Legislative Council.

BOYLE, D.

1057 Boyle, D. With arduous manifold. London: Hutchinson,
        1959. 339 p.
        The author was District Commissioner in Ashanti and
        Accra, 1914-1917.

BREW, RICHARD

1058 Priestley, Margaret. "Richard Brew: an eighteenth trader
        at Anomabu, " Trans. Hist. Soc. Ghana, IV (1959), 29-46.

BURNS, ALAN

1059 Burns, Alan. Colonial civil servant. London: Allen &
        Unwin, 1950. 324 p.
        Governor of the Gold Coast, 1941-1947.

BUSIA, KOFI ABREFA

1060 "Busia, Kofi Abrefa. " In Sidney Taylor, ed. The New
        Africans: a guide to the contemporary history of emergent
        Africa and its leaders. New York: Putnam, 1967. pp.
        172-3.

1061 "The Story of 'Prof' " West Africa, No. 2728 (Sept. 13, 1969),
        1085.
        A portrait of Dr. K. A. Busia, former Professor of
        Sociology at the University of Ghana, the Ghanaian Prime
        Minister from October 1969 to January 12, 1972, when his
        government was overthrown in a military coup.

1062   Time, XCIV (Sept. 12, 1969), 39.

CARSTENSEN, EDWARD

1063   Carstensen, Edward. Governor Carstensen's diary, 1842-
       1850. Legon: University of Ghana, 1965. 60 p.

DANQUAH, JOSEPH BOAKYE, 1895-1965

1064   Akyeampong, Henry Kwasi. The undying memories of a gal-
       lant man: tributes to the late Dr. Joseph Boakye Danquah,
       the doyen of Ghana politicians. Accra: State Publishing
       Corp., 1967. 48 p.

1065   Danquah, Joseph Boakye. Liberty: a page from the life of
       J. B. Accra: H. K. Akyeampong, 1960. 34 p.

1066   Illus. Lond. News, CCXLVI (Feb. 13, 1965), 27.

1067   N. Y. Times, Feb. 5, 1965, p. 31.

DU BOIS, W. E. B.

1068   Du Bois, W. E. B. The autobiography of W. E. B. Du Bois: a
       soliloquy on viewing my life from the last decade of its
       first century. Edited by Herbert Aptheker. New York:
       International Publishers, 1968. 448 p.
          Rev: Nation, CCVI (April 29, 1968), 574. Sat. Rev.,
       LI (Feb. 24, 1968), 42.

1069   Kotei, S. I. A. Dr. W. E. B. Du Bois, 1868-1963: a bibli-
       ography. Accra: Research Library on African Affairs,
       1964. 39 p.

1070   Lacy, Leslie Alexander. Cheer the lonesome traveler; the
       life of W. E. B. Du Bois. Illus. by James Barkeley. New
       York: Dial Press, 1970. 183 p.
          The career of the black sociologist who devoted his life
       to gaining equality for the blacks in America. Gives also
       an outline of the evolution of black protest in post-recon-
       struction America.
          Rev: Library J., XCVI (June 1970), 2541. N. Y.
       Times Bk. Rev., (Aug. 16, 1970), 22.

FERGUSON, GEORGE EKEM

1071   Sampson, Magnus J. "George Ekem Ferguson of Anomabu,"
       Trans. Gold Coast & Togoland Hist. Soc., II Part I (1956),
       30-45.
          Born in Anomabu in 1864 and dead at the young age of
       33, Ferguson was a surveyor and British agent in Northern
       Territories. Includes some of his correspondences.

FRASER, ALEXANDER GARDEN

1072   Ward, W. E. F.   A. G. F. , 1873-1962.   Accra: Govt. Printer,
       1962.   57 p.
       A. G. Fraser was the first Principal of Achimota school.

1073   _____ .   Fraser of Trinity and Achimota.   Accra: Ghana
       Universities Press, 1965.   328 p.
       "W. E. F. Ward, already established as a historian in
       Ghana, now combines scholarship and affection to produce
       a convincing and compelling biography of one of the great
       figures in the history of Ghanaian education. "--Africa Re-
       port, XI (June 1966),   70.

FREEMAN, THOMAS BIRCH

1074   Beetham, T. A.   "Freeman, Thomas Birch (1806-1890)."   In
       Stephen Neil, et al, eds.   Concise dictionary of the Chris-
       tian World Mission.   New York: Abingdom Press, 1971,
       pp. 218-9.
       Biographical account of a Wesleyan Methodist, son of a
       freed African slave with an English mother.   Describes
       also the consolidation of Methodist societies in Ghana.

1075   Birtwistle, Allen.   "Missionary administrator: the story of
       Thomas Birch Freeman, " W. Afr. Rev. , (Dec. 1951),
       1392-5.

1076   _____ .   Thomas Birch Freeman: West African pioneer.
       London: Cargate Press, 1950.   112 p.
       One of the early African clergymen.

1077   Walker, F. Deaville.   Thomas Birch Freeman: the son of
       an American.   London: S. C. M. Press, 1929?   221 p.

1078   Wright, Harrison.   "Thomas Birch Freeman: the techniques
       of a missionary. "   In D. F. McCall, ed.   West African
       history.   New York: Praeger for the African Studies
       Center, Boston University, 1969, pp. 182-203.
       The missionary activities of a Wesleyan Methodist be-
       tween 1838 and 1857.

GRIFFITH, WILLIAM BRANDFORD

1079   Griffith, William Brandford.   The far horizon: portrait of a
       colonial judge.   Ilfracombe: Stockwell, 1951.   319 p.

GUGGISBERG, FREDERICK GORDON

1080   "Sir Frederick Gordon Guggisberg" (an obituary), Royal
       Engineers Journal, (Mar. 1931),   135-40.

1081 Wraith, R. E. Guggisberg. London: Oxford University
      Press, 1967. 342 p.
         Biography of the governor of the Gold Coast after the
      World War I, responsible for "the creation of Achimota as
      an educational establishment--the construction of a deep
      water harbour at Takoradi and the Korle Bu Hospital at
      Accra. He is remembered today by the people of Ghana
      as the best governor of the colonial days."
         Rev: Amer. Hist. Rev, LXXIII (Feb. 1968), 873.
      TLS (July 6, 1967), 597.

                        HALL, PETER

1082 Hall, Peter. Autobiography of Rev. Peter Hall. Accra:
      Waterville, 1965. 74 p.

                      HAYFORD, CASELY

1083 "An outstanding nationalist," West Africa, No. 2764, (May
      30, 1970), 585.
         Biography of Casely Hayford, author of Ethiopia Unbound.
      "His main concern always was to assert the value of
      African tradition and culture."

                        HOLT, JOHN

1084 Holt, C. R. , ed. The Diary of John Holt, 1862-72. Liver-
      pool: Young, 1948. 278 p.
         John Holt was the founder of the merchant shipping line
      in West Africa; and the Holt Companies are found today
      in various West African countries.

                HOWARD-BENNETT, ROSEMARY

1085 Howard-Bennett, Rosemary. I Choose the Cloister. London:
      Hodder & Stoughton, 1956. 125 p.
         Anglican sister at Mampong.

                 KOTOKA, EMMANUEL KWASI

1086 Agyeman-Dickson, Yan Duah. "Dedicated to memory of
      Ghana's most illustrious soldier, leader, patriot, Lt. Gen-
      eral Emmanuel Kwasi Kotoka," Insight (Cape Coast), II
      (Sept. 1967), 63-4.
         Lt. General Kotoka led the Ghanaian Armed Forces that
      ousted Nkrumah from office.

1087 Ghanatta, Y. Boakye. Price of freedom: Life of Kotoka
      from birth to death. Accra: State Publishing Corp. , 1967.
      40 p.

KOTOKO (ASHANTI)

1088   Awuah, Baafour.   The Fabulous Ashanti Kotoko: thirty years
       of dedication, 1935-1965.   Kumasi: Asante Kotoko Sporting
       Club, 1965.   64 p.

KWABENA BONNE III, NII

1089   Nii Kwabena Bonne III.   Milestones in the history of the Gold
       Coast: Autobiography of Nii Kwabena Bonne III Osu Alata
       Mantse, also Nana Owusu Akenten III Oyokohene of Techi-
       man Ashanti.   London: Diplomatist Publications, 1954.
       92 p.

KWAPONG, ALEXANDER

1090   "Kwapong, Alexander A."   In Sidney Taylor, ed.   The New
       Africans.   New York: Putnam, 1967, p. 176.
          One of the leading African classical scholars and Vice-
       Chancellor (Head) of the University of Ghana.

MACLEAN, GEORGE

1091   Metcalfe, George E.   Maclean of the Gold Coast; the life and
       times of George Maclean, 1801-1847.   New York: Oxford
       University Press, 1962.   344 p.
          A political biography of former President of the Council
       of British Merchants who assumed the administration of the
       Gold Coast from 1830 to 1843.
          Rev: Amer. Hist. Rev., LXIX (Oct. 1963), 224.   TLS
       (July 20, 1962), 522.

1092   Moseley, Maboth.   "Maclean of the Gold Coast," W. Afr. Rev.,
       (Mar-Aug. 1952), 234+.

MENSAH, JOHN

1093   De Wilson, George.   The biography of Prophet John Mensah.
       Cape Coast: The author, 1960?   42 p.
          On the founder of the Independent Church of Christ, in
       1959, at Cape Coast.

NEAL, JAMES

1094   Neal, James.   Ju-ju in my life.   London: Harrap, 1966.
       191 p.
          The autobiography of a former Chief Investigations
       Officer for the Ghanaian Government.

NKETIA, JOSEPH HANSON

1095   "Nketia, Joseph Hanson Kwabena," Contemporary authors,

V. 11-12. Detroit, Michigan: Gale, 1965. p. 297.
   Biographical sketch of a noted Ghanaian musician and
poet, currently Professor of Music at the University of
Ghana. Author of numerous works in English and Twi.

NKRUMAH, KWAME

1096   "Dr. Kwame Nkrumah--pioneer for African independence."
       In Thomas Melady. Profiles of African leaders. New
       York: Macmillan, 1961, pp. 125-39.

1097   Garrison, Lloyd. "Exit Nkrumah, an old dreamer; enter
       Ankrah, a new realist," N.Y. Times Mag., (April 3,
       1966), 32-3+.
          The Nkrumah government was overthrown by the Ghanaian
       Armed Forces led by Lt. Gen. Kotoka.

1098   Gunther, John. Procession. New York: Harper & Row,
       1965., pp. 388-402.
          Biography of Kwame Nkrumah.

1099   Lacy, Leslie Alexander. The Rise and fall of a proper
       negro: an autobiography. New York: Macmillan, 1970.
       244 p.
          Records how an American black from a proper Southern
       family in the U.S.A. eventually settled in Ghana--a non-
       violent activist, a militant nationalist, admired by the
       Afro-American community and Nkrumah. The fall of the
       Nkrumah ended his African life; he now teaches and writes
       at Howard University in the United States.
          Rev: New Republic, CLXIII (Oct. 3, 1970), 24. N.Y.
       Times Bk. Rev., (Oct. 18, 1970), 26.

1100   Nkrumah, Kwame. Ghana: the autobiography of Kwame
       Nkrumah. New York: Nelson, 1957. 320 p.
          The French edition translated from the English by
       Charles L. Patterson, published in Paris, by Présence
       Africaine, 1960. (Coll. Leaders Politiques Africaines.)
          Rev: New Republic, CXXXVI (April 8, 1957), 16.
       TLS, (Mar. 8, 1957), 139.

1101   "Nkrumah, Kwame." In Sidney Taylor, ed. The New
       Africans: a guide to contemporary history of emergent
       Africa and its leaders. New York: Putnam, 1967, pp.
       177-80.
          See also Current biography yearbook, 1953 (New York),
       pp. 458-60; Ebony, XXI (Sept. 1966), 138-40+.

1102   "The Osagyefo and others," Economist (Dec. 31, 1960), 1366-
       8.

1103   Padmore, George. "Ghana: L'autobiographie de Kwame

Nkrumah, " Présence Africaine, No. 12 (1957), 27-31.
A review of Nkrumah's autobiography.

1104 Philips, John Frederick. Kwame Nkrumah and the future of
Africa. London: Faber & Faber, 1960. 272 p.
Considers Nkrumah as one of the best known but con-
troversial leaders that shaped African politics.
Rev: New Statesman, LXI (Jan. 13, 1969), 59. N. Y.
Times Bk. Rev., (Feb. 12, 1969), 3.

1105 Segal, Ronald. "Kwame Nkrumah of Ghana." In Ronald
Segal. African profiles, rev. ed. Baltimore: Penguin,
1963. pp. 253-71.

1106 Timothy, Bankole. Kwame Nkrumah: his rise to power.
With a foreword by Kojo Botsio. London: Allen & Unwin,
1955. 201 p.
A political but friendly biography of the first African
Constitutional Head of Ghana, by a Ghanaian journalist.
Rev: Christian Cent., LXXIII (Nov. 7, 1956), 1299.
TLS, (Jan. 6, 1956), 4.

PADMORE, GEORGE

1107 Kotei, S. I. A. "George Padmore, black revolutionary: a
portrait, " Legon Observer, II, No. 21 (1967), 18-21.

QUAQUE, PHILIP

1108 Bartels, F. L. "Philip Quaque, 1741-1816," Trans. Gold
Coast & Togoland Hist. Soc., I (1955), 153-77.
Biography of the first African chaplain at Cape Coast.

QUAISON-SACKEY, ALEXANDER

1109 "Ambassador from Ghana Alexander Quaison-Sackey, " New
Yorker, XXXIX (Aug. 3, 1963), 20-2.
The career of Ghana's Permanent Representative to the
United Nations and later President of the UN General
Assembly. Includes an extract from and comment on his
book, Africa Unbound; Reflections of an African Statesman
(1963).

(5) ECONOMICS--GENERAL

1110 Adams, J. G. U. "The Spatial structure of the economy of
West Africa, 1967," Doctoral Dissertation, London University, 1970.

1111   Affrifah, S. F.   "Some aspects of Hausa economy, 1817-1857, "
       Master's Thesis, University of Ghana, 1965.   124 p.

1112   Agama, C. K.   "Structural changes in the economy of Ghana,
       1891-1911, " Nigerian J. Econ. Soc. Stud., VIII (Nov. 1966),
       491-500.

1113   Amin, Samir.   Trois expériènces africaines de développment:
       Le Mali, La Guinée and le Ghana.   Paris: Presses Uni-
       versitaires de France, 1965.   233 p.

1114   Amoa, R. K.   "Ghana: the new republic; special survey;
       Ghana's economic challenge, " New Commonwealth, XXXVIII
       (Aug. 1960), 503-10.

1115   Appeadu, K. K.   Notes on the history of the Gold Coast co-
       operative movement.   Accra: Dept. of Agriculture, 1956.

1116   Apter, David Ernest.   "Economic factors in the political
       development of the Gold Coast, " J. Econ. Hist., XIV
       (1954), 409-27.
           The feasibility of an under-developed country attaining
       a truly democratic government pari passu with the pursuit
       of rapid economic development.

1117   Awunyo-Akaba, S. K.   "Development priorities in a stage
       development plan of the Central Region, 1970-75, " Master's
       Thesis, University of Science and Technology, 1968.   167 p.

1118   Background to agricultural policy in Ghana; proceedings of a
       seminar organized by the Faculty of Agriculture, University
       of Ghana.   Legon: Faculty of Agriculture, University of
       Ghana, 1969.   167 p.

1119   Barclays Bank, D. C. O.   Ghana: an economic survey.   Lon-
       don, 1964.

1120   Bartlett, Vernon.   Struggle for Africa.   London: Muller,
       1953.   251 p.
           Includes a political survey of the Gold Coast and its
       economic potentialities.

1121   Berry, B. J.   "Urban growth and the economic development
       of Ashanti. "   In Forest R. Pitts, ed.   Urban System and
       economic development.   Eugene: School of Business Ad-
       ministration, University of Oregon, 1962, pp. 53-64.

1122   Bevin, H. J.   "The Gold Coast economy about 1880, " Trans.
       Gold Coast & Togoland Hist. Soc., II (1956), 73-86.
           Based chiefly on records preserved in the Government
       Archivist's Office, Accra, dealing with the period just be-
       fore the country's rapid economic development.

1123 Birmingham, W. B. "The Economic development of Ghana."
      In Walter Birmingham and A. G. Ford, eds. Planning and
      growth in rich and poor countries. New York: Praeger,
      1965, pp. 172-94.

1124 _____, et al., eds. A Study of contemporary Ghana; v. 1.
      The economy of Ghana. London: Allen & Unwin for the
      Ghana Academy of Sciences, 1966. 472 p.
          Arranged in 5 sections with 18 chapters by 4 contribu-
      tors, it includes bibliographical notes, running commentary
      and index.
          Rev: Amer. Econ. Rev., LVII (June 1967), 615.
      Choice, IV (June 1967), 454.

1125 Bissue, Isaac. "Ghana's Seven-Year Development Plan in
      Retrospect," Econ. Bull. Ghana, XI, No. 1 (1967), 21-44.

1126 Booker, W. L. "The Development of official statistics in
      Ghana," Econ. Bull. Ghana, III (Oct. 1959), 1-15.

1127 _____. "Economic investigations in rural areas," Econ.
      Bull. Ghana, III, No. 1 (1959), 3-6.

1128 Bridier, M. La politique economie du Ghana. Paris:
      Centre d'Etudes Financières, Economiques et Bancaires,
      1965. 64 p.

1129 Brokensha, David, ed. Ecology and economic development
      in tropical Africa. Berkeley: Institute of International
      Studies, University of California, 1965. 265 p. (Institute
      of International Studies Research series, no. 9.)

1130 Butterworth, E. G. "Economic self-rule in the Gold Coast,"
      New Commonwealth (Jan. 9, 1956), 22-6.

1131 Byl, Adhemar. "Ghana's struggle for economic independence,"
      Current History, XLIII (Dec. 1962), 359-65.

1132 Caldwell, J. C. "Fertility attitudes in three economically
      contrasting rural regions of Ghana," Econ. Dev. Cult.
      Change, XV (Jan. 1967), 217-38.

1133 _____. "Population change and rural transformation in
      Ghana." Paper presented at a Seminar on Economics of
      East and West African Agricultural Development, East
      Lansing, Michigan State University, June 1968.

1134 Carney, David Edward. Government and economy in British
      West Africa: a study of the role of public agencies in the
      economic development of British West Africa in the period
      1947-1955. New York: Bookman Associates, 1961. 207 p.
          Revision of author's doctoral dissertation, University of

Pennsylvania, 1958.
Rev: Library J., LXXXVI (June 15, 1961), 2310.

1135   Chambers, Robert.   "The Organization of settlement schemes."
       Doctoral Dissertation, Manchester University, 1967.

1136   Church, R. J. H.   "Urban problems and economic development
       in West Africa," J. Mod. Afr. Stud., V (Dec. 1967), 511-
       20.

1137   Cissé, D.   "Le problème de la formation de l'epargne interne
       en Afrique occidentale," Thèse, Faculté de Droit et des
       Sciences Economiques de Paris, 1967.   150 p.
            Economic stability of a country depends primarily on
       its ability to stand on its feet by its own resources.   Ex-
       ternal aid should only be supplementary.

1138   Dadson, John Alfred.   Socialized agriculture in Ghana.   Cam-
       bridge: Harvard University Press, 1970.   312 p. maps,
       tables, bibliog.
            Doctoral dissertation, Harvard University.

1139   Dalton, John H.   "Gold Coast economic development: prob-
       lems and policies."   Doctoral Dissertation, University of
       California, Berkeley, 1955.   300 p.

1140   Davey, P. L. P.   A "Nutrition survey of Ghana," Econ. Bull.
       Ghana, VI, No. 1 (1962), 15-20.

1141   De Graft-Johnson, John Coleman.   An Introduction to the
       African economy.   Delhi: Asia Publishing House, 1959.
       115 p.   (Delhi University School of Economics.   Occa-
       sional papers, No. 12.)

1142   _____.   "The Population of Ghana, 1846-1967," Trans.
       Hist. Soc. Ghana, X (1969), 1-12.

1143   "The Demographic situations in Western Africa," Econ. Bull.
       Afr., VI (July 1966), 89-102.
            Based upon the papers presented by the Economic Com-
       mission for Africa at the Sub-Regional Meeting on Economic
       Cooperation in West Africa, Niamey, October 1966, it
       examines the present demographic structures in West Africa
       and notes the recent population trends and the future pro-
       spects.

1144   Dickson, K. B.   "Background to the problem of economic
       development in Northern Ghana," Ann. Assoc. Amer. Geogr.,
       LVIII, No. 4 (1968), 686-96.

1145   _____.   "Ghana: the cost of power," Economist, CCXXXI,
       No. 6555 (1969), 40.

1146   Dorjahn, V. R.   "The Demographic aspects of African poly-
       gyny," Doctoral Dissertation, Northwestern University,
       1954.

1147   Dowse, Robert E.   Modernization in Ghana and the U. S. S. R. :
       a comparative study.   New York: Humanities Press, 1969.
       107 p.
           Rev: Choice, VI (Jan 1970), 1656.   TLS, (Sept. 4,
       1969), 972.

1148   Due, J. M.   "Agricultural development in the Ivory Coast and
       Ghana," J. Mod. Afr. Stud., VII (Dec. 1969), 637-60.

1149   "Economics of independence," West Africa, No. 2337 (March
       17, 1962), 293.

1150   Eicher, Carl K.   Research on agricultural development in
       five English-speaking countries in West Africa.   New York:
       Agricultural Development Council, 1970.   152 p.
           The sixth monograph in a series sponsored by the Ameri-
       can Universities Research Program of the Agricultural De-
       velopment Council.   Discusses agricultural development in
       Gambia, Ghana, Liberia, Nigeria and Sierra Leone providing
       "an inventory, classification and evaluation of recent and
       current research on agricultural development, a discussion
       of major rural development problems in West Africa in the
       1970's and a discussion of priority areas of research needing
       attention in the 1970's."   There is an extensive bibliography
       classified by form under the country; including doctoral dis-
       sertations and research in progress.   No index.   The author
       who has worked in West Africa since 1963 is Associate
       Professor of Agricultural Economics and African Studies at
       Michigan State University.

1151   [No entry]

1152   Engel, Lothar.   "Eindrücke nach einem Studienaufenthalt in
       Ghana," Oekumenische Rundschau (Stuttgart), No. 4 (Jan.
       17, 1968), 396-403.

1153   Eshag, E. and P. J. Richards.   "A Comparison of economic
       developments in Ghana and the Ivory Coast since 1960,"
       Oxford Univ. Inst. Econ. Stat. Bull., XXIX (Nov. 1967),
       353-72.

1154   Esseks, John D.   "Economic independence in a new African
       state."   Doctoral Dissertation, Harvard University, 1967.
           A study of Nkrumah's efforts 1957-1965, to Africanize
       Ghana's economy, indicating the methods adopted to create
       viable domestic enterprises, the devices used to restrict
       foreign firms and the measure of his achievement in the
       eight year period.

1155 _____ . "Political independence and economic decoloniza-
     tion: the case of Ghana under Nkrumah," Western Pol. Q.,
     XXIV (March 1971), 59-64.

1156 Firth, Raymond. "Social problems and research in British
     West Africa," Africa, XVII (April/July 1947), 77-92, 170-
     80.
          Suggests that scientists are needed to help solve the
     problem of economic insufficiency due to disease, inade-
     quate technical training and research, etc.

1157 "General economic survey of Ghana," Afro-Asian Econ. Rev.,
     (Cairo), III (July 1961), 6-16.

1158 Gevoud, R. G. Nationalism and economic development in
     Ghana. New York: Praeger, 1969. 244 p.
          The process of decolonization Ghana experienced under
     Kwame Nkrumah between 1951 and 1966. Part I: Assess-
     ment of the Gold Coast in the 1950's in terms of its socio-
     economic structures on which economic development is
     based. Part II: Examination of the economic and political
     problems the country faced in trying to implement its
     Development Plan.

1159 Ghana. Central Bureau of Statistics. Directory of Industrial
     enterprises and establishments, mining and quarrying,
     manufacturing, construction, electricity, gas and steam.
     Accra, 1964. 313 p.

1160 _____ . Ghana: Economic Survey, 1962. Accra: Govt.
     Printer, 1963. 130 p. The 1964 survey, 151 p.

1161 _____ . Ghana: Economic Survey, 1968. Accra: The
     Principal Secretary, Ministry of Information, Central
     States Division, 1968.

1162 Ghana. Information Services. Golden harvest: the story of
     the Gold Coast cocoa industry. Accra, 1963. 53 p.

1162a Ghana. Ministry of Information. Ghana's economy and aid
     requirements in 1967. Accra, 1967. 43 p.

1163 Ghana. Official Planning Commission. Seven-year Plan for
     National Reconstruction and Development. Accra, 1964.
     305 p.

1164 "Ghana: the poor little rich land," Sepia, XV (Oct. 1966),
     66-70.

1165 "Ghana's new elective government aims to direct resources
     toward expanded economic growth rate," Int. Commerce,
     LXXVI (Feb. 16, 1970), 22-4.

1166 "Ghana's land revolution," New Commonwealth, XLII (Feb.

1964), 82-5.

1167 Gildea, Ray Y. "Culture and land tenure in Ghana," Land
      Econ., XL (Feb. 1964), 102-4.

1168 Godfrey, E. M. "West Africa: the economics of military
      rule," Banker (Lond.) CXVII (April 1967), 328-31.

1169 Gordon, Sara Lee. "Aspects of economic development in
      Ghana." Doctoral Dissertation, Stanford University, 1971.
      419 p.

1170 Gorst, Sheila. Cooperative organization in tropical countries:
      a study of cooperative development in non-self-governing
      territories under United Kingdom Administration, 1945-1955.
      Oxford: Blackwell, 1959. 343 p.

1171 Great Britain. Board of Trade. British West Africa;
      economic and commercial conditions in the territories of
      Nigeria, Gold Coast, Sierra Leone and the Gambia by
      Aubrey R. Starck. London: H. M. S. O., 1949. 51 p.
      (Overseas economic survey.)
      Covers finance, production, trade and communications.

1172 Green, Reginald H. "Economic research in the Ghanaian
      context: a forward stride," Econ. Bull. Ghana, VIII,
      No. 2 (1964), 26-31.

1173 _____. "Four African development plans: Ghana, Kenya,
      Nigeria and Tanzania," J. Mod. Afr. Stud., III (Aug. 1965),
      249-79.
      Includes extensive bibliography.

1174 Greenstreet, D. K. "The Development of the Ghanaian public
      service," J. Management Stud., II, No. 2 (1963), 23-9.

1175 Grove, D. Population patterns: their impact on regional
      planning; a preliminary analysis of the 1960 census of
      Ghana. Kumasi: Building Research Group, University of
      Science and Technology, 1963. 43 p.

1176 Grundy, Kenneth W. "Nkrumah's theory of underdevelopment,"
      World Politics, XV (April 1963), 438-54.

1177 Hallett, Robin. People and progress in West Africa: an in-
      troduction to the problems of development. Oxford: Perga-
      mon Press, 1966. 161 p.

1178 Hance, W. A. African economic development. London: Ox-
      ford University Press, 1958. 307 p. (Council on Foreign
      Relations Publications.)
      On the Volta River Project.
      Rev: Amer. Econ. Rev., XLIX (March 1959), 175.

1179   Harris, R. L.   "Effects of political change on the role set of
       the senior bureaucrats in Ghana and Nigeria," Adm. Sci. Q.,
       XIII (Dec. 1968), 386-401.

1180   Hopkins, Antony Gerald.   "Economic aspects of political
       movement in Nigeria and in the Gold Coast, 1918-1939,"
       J. Afr. Hist., VII, No. 1 (1966), 133-52.

1181   _____. An Economic history of West Africa.   London:
       Longmans, 1971?

1182   Hunter, Guy.   The Best of both worlds?   A challenge on
       development policy in Africa.   London: Oxford University
       Press, 1967.   132 p.
           Rev: TLS, (Sept. 14, 1967), 814.

1183   _____. The New societies of tropical Africa: a selective
       study. London: Oxford University Press for the Institute
       of Race Relations, 1962.   376 p.
           Designed primarily for foreign managers of firms in
       Africa, it gives a readable description of the economic,
       political and social problems of independent African
       states.
           Rev: Africa, XXXIII (1963), 75. Canadian Forum,
       XLIII (July 1963), 91.

1184   Hymer, Stephen H.   "Economic forms in pre-colonial Ghana,"
       J. Econ. Hist., XXX (March 1970), 33-50.

1185   _____. The Political economy of the Gold Coast and
       Ghana. New Haven: Yale University Press, 1970.
           Historical and theoretical implications of the govern-
       ment's policies for the economic development of the
       country.

1186   Inter-African Labour Institute.   The Human factors of produc-
       tivity.   2nd ed.   London, 1960.   159 p.

1187   Irvine, Frederick.   Wood plants of Ghana, with special
       reference to their uses.   London: Oxford University Press,
       1961.   868 p.

1188   Johnson, Omotunde E.   "A Note on the economics of frag-
       mentation," Nigerian J. Econ. Soc. Stud., XII (July 1970),
       175-84.
           A micro-theoretic examination of some aspects of the
       fragmentation issue, beginning with the gains from consoli-
       dation, and then the relationship between specialization and
       fragmentation, indicating some empirical and policy impli-
       cations of the analysis.

1189   Johnston, Bruce F.   "Agriculture and economic development
       in Ghana: the relevance of Japan's experience," Econ.
       Bull. Ghana, XI, No. 4 (1967), 34-40.

1190 _____. The Staple food economics of western tropical
Africa. Stanford: Stanford University Press, 1958. 305 p.

1191 Kalitsi, F. N. An Economic history of Ghana. Accra: State
Publishing Corp., 1970.

1192 _____. Visages du Ghana. Lille, France: Institut Su-
périor de Culture Française Contemporaine, 1969? 60 p.
Historical survey of Ghana, emphasizing its economic
condition.

1193 Kamarck, Andrew M. "African economic development:
problems and prospects," Africa Report, XIV (Jan. 1969),
16-20, 37.
Includes 4 valuable tables on gross domestic product;
economic indicators for selected developing and industri-
alized nations; value of exports from developing and indus-
trialized nations; value of exports from developing countries.

1194 _____. The Economics of African development. Preface
by Pierre Moussa. New York: Praeger, 1967. 294 p.
Bibliog.
Attempts to provide historical reasons for Africa's
underdevelopment and its legacy of slavery and describes
economic theories and practices in Africa.
Rev: Amer. Econ. Rev., LVII (Dec. 1967), 1339.
TLS, (Oct. 19, 1967), 978.

1195 Kerstiens, Thom. The New elite in Asia and Africa: a
comparative study of Indonesia and Ghana. New York:
Praeger, 1966. 282 p. (Special studies. International
economics and development.)
Rev: Choice, III (Nov. 1966), 821.

1196 Kowal, J. M. L. "The Agricultural development of the black
clay soils of the Accra plains," Doctoral Dissertation,
London University, 1963.

1197 La-Anyane, S. Ghana agriculture: its economic development from early times to the middle of the twentieth
century. London: Oxford University Press, 1963. 228 p.
The first authoritative study on the subject by the Chief
Agricultural Economist in Ghana's Ministry of Agriculture.

1198 Lawson, R. M. "The Distributive system in Ghana: a review
article," J. Dev. Stud., III (Jan. 1970), 195-205.

1199 _____. "Engel's law and its application to Ghana," Econ.
Bull. Ghana, VI, No. 4 (1963), 34-46.

1200 _____. "Ghana in economic transition," South Afr. J.
Econ., XXV (June 1957), 103-14.

1201 Macphee, Allan. The Economic revolution in British West
      Africa. London: Routledge, 1926. 322 p. (Studies in
      economics and political science, No. 89.)

1202 Manshard, Walther. Die geographischen Grundlagen der
      Wirtschaft Ghanas, unter besonderer Berücksichtigung der
      agrarischen Entwicklung. Wiesbaden: F. Steiner, 1961.
      308 p. (Beitrage zur Landerkunde Afrikas, Heft 1.)

1203 Merklinghaus, S. "Die Wirtschaftraum Westafrikas und seine
      Verkehrsbeziehungen unter bes. Berücks. der Woermann-
      Linie," Phil. F., Greifswald, 1933.

1204 Nitsche, K. "Die Eigeborenwirtschaft in Britisch-Westafrika,"
      Rechts. u. Staatswiss. F., Hamburg, 1942.

1205 Obeng, H. B. The Development of Ghana's natural resources:
      twenty years of soil survey and classification in Ghana.
      Kumasi: Soil Research Institute, Ghana Academy of Sciences,
      1965.

1206 Okigbo, Pius. "Social consequences of economic development
      in West Africa," Ann. Amer. Acad. Pol. Soc. Sci., CCCV
      (May 1956), 126-33.

1207 Oluwasanmi, H. A. "Agriculture and economic development
      in tropical Africa," Nigerian J. Econ. Soc. Stud., I, No. 1
      (1959), 41-50.

1208 Ord, H. W. and Ian Livingstone. An Introduction to West
      African economics. London: Heinemann Educational,
      1969. 457 p.

1209 Oyebola, Areyo. A Modern Approach to economics of West
      Africa. Ibadan: Education Research Institute, 1970.
      282 p.

1210 Petch, George Allan. Economic development and modern
      West Africa. London: University of London Press, 1961.
      224 p.

1211 Plessz, Nicolas G. Problems and prospects of economic
      integration in West Africa. Montreal: McGill University
      Press for Centre for Developing Area Studies, 1968. 91 p.
      (Centre for Developing-Area Studies, McGill University.
      Keith Callard Lectures, series 21.)

1212 Raeburn, J. R. Report on a preliminary economic survey of
      the Northern Territories of the Gold Coast. London:
      H. M. S. O., 1950. 47 p.

1213 Rake, Alan. "Ghana's economic crisis," Africa Report, X
      (March 1965), 47-8.
      The Government's acute economic problem is revealed
      in the announced budget for 1965 financial year.

1214 Rimmer, Douglas. "The Crisis in the Ghana economy,"
      J. Mod. Afr. Stud., IV (May 1966), 17-32.

1215 Robson, Peter and D. A. Lury. The Economies of Africa.
      London: Allen & Unwin, 1969. 528 p.
      A series of essays, varying from 30 to 70 pages each
      on the economies of Ghana, Nigeria, the Ivory Coast,
      Cameroun, Liberia, East Africa, Central Africa, the
      Sudan and Algeria.
      Rev: African Affairs, LXX (Jan. 1971), 86.

1216 Rose, L. N. Impact of information services in Ghana.
      Kumasi: University of Science and Technology, 1970.

1217 Royal Institute of International Affairs. Information Dept.
      Ghana: a brief political and economic survey. London,
      1957. 62 p.
      Provides brief historical, social, political and economic
      information on Ghana immediately before its independence
      on March 6, 1957.

1218 Scott, Douglas A. "Growth and crisis: economic policy
      in Ghana, 1946-1965." Doctoral Dissertation, Harvard
      University, 1967.

1219 Seidman, Ann. "The Economics of new-colonialism in West
      Africa," Econ. Bull. Ghana, VIII, No. 3 (1964), 3-14.

1220 _____. "Ghana's development experience, 1951-1965."
      Doctoral Dissertation, University of Wisconsin, 1968.
      502 p.

1221 Sey, S. "The Role of agricultural policy in the economic
      development of Ghana." Master's Thesis, London Univer-
      sity, 1963/64.

1222 Stein, J. L. "The Pattern of economic development in se-
      lected British territories in Africa since 1940." Doctoral
      Dissertation, Yale University, 1953.

1223 Stockdale, F. A. Report on a visit to Nigeria, Gold Coast,
      and Sierra Leone, 1935-6. London: H. M. S. O., 1936.
      125 p.

1224 Strong, T. H. "Agricultural economics in Ghana: the need,
      scope and function," Econ. Bull. Ghana, III (April 1958),
      16-17.

1225 _____. "Agriculture in relation to economic development,"
Ghana Geogr. Assoc. Bull., VI (July 1961), 13-21.

1226 Szereszewski, R. "The Inter-sectoral structure of the
economy of Ghana," Econ. Bull. Ghana, VII, No. 2 (1963),
12-29.

1227 _____. "The Process of growth in Ghana, 1891-1911,"
J. Dev. Stud., I (Jan. 1965), 123-41.

1228 _____. Structural changes in the economy of Ghana, 1891-
1911. London: Weidenfeld and Nicolson, 1965. 161 p.
Originally submitted as doctoral dissertation, London
University, 1963/64.

1229 United Nations. Economic Commission for Africa. A Survey
of economic conditions in Africa, 1960-1964. New York,
1968. 269 p.

1230 United Nations. Housing in Ghana. Prepared for the Government of Ghana by the U.N. Technical Assistance Housing
Mission to Ghana. New York, 1957. 220 p.
Reprint of the U.N. Mission to Ghana, 1954-55 and
that of Dr. Koenigsberger who returned to Ghana in 1956
as Housing Coordinator.

1231 U.S. Dept. of Commerce. Bureau of International Programs.
Basic data on economy of Ghana. Prepared by Gary L.
Lent. Washington, D.C.: Govt. Printing Office, 1962.

1232 West African Institute of Social and Economic Research.
Annual Conference, Economics Section, Achimota, April,
1953, proceedings. Ibadan: University College, 1953.
176 p.

1233 Whetham, E.H. Cooperation, land reform and land settlement: report on a survey in Kenya, Uganda, Sudan,
Ghana, Nigeria and Iran. London: Plunkett Foundation
for Cooperative Studies, 1968. 79 p.

1234 Williams, David. "The Ghana economy," World Today, XXII
(Nov. 1966), 475-81.
Criticizes the extravagance of the Nkrumah regime which
has brought the nation to the brink of bankruptcy and calls
for immediate economic improvement to avert a national
economic disaster.

1235 Wills, John Brian, ed. Agriculture and land use in Ghana.
London: Oxford University Press for the Ghana Ministry
of Food and Agriculture, 1962. 504 p.
A collection of technical reports by University teachers,
senior civil servants and research scientists in Ghana.

1236 Worthington, E. B. Science in the development of Africa: a
      review of the contribution of physical and biological knowl-
      edge south of the Sahara. London: C. C. T. A., 1958.
      462 p.

(5) ECONOMICS--INDUSTRY AND LABOR

1237 Adamu, G. M. "A Study of the Ghana diamond industry,"
      Doctoral Dissertation, Birmingham University, 1969.
      A study of economic dualism in the Ghana industry.

1238 Adomako-Sarfo, J. "The Development of Cocoa farming in
      Brong-Ahafo South (with special reference to the migration
      of farmers,) Master's Thesis, University of Ghana, 1965,
      96 p.

1239 Ady, Peter. "Supply functions in tropical agriculture,"
      Oxford Univ. Inst. Econ. Stat. Bull., XXX (May 1968),
      157-88.

1240 _____. "Trends in cocoa production, British West Africa,"
      Oxford Univ. Inst. Econ. Stat. Bull., XI (Dec. 1949), 389-
      404.

1241 Akuamoa, R. I. L. O. and African women workers; with
      particular reference to Ghanaian women workers. Geneva:
      Graduate Institute of International Studies, 1969. 150 p.
      Originally submitted as doctoral dissertation at the Insti-
      tute, 1969, it deals with conventions and recommendations
      of the International Labour Organization on women workers
      in the African member states.

1242 Akwawuah, K. A. Prelude to Ghana's industrialisation. London:
      Mitre Press, 1959. 96 p.

1243 Amegashie, R. S. "Ghana's mineral wealth," New Common-
      wealth, XLVII (Oct. 1968), 20-1.

1244 Ampah, Sampson Kofi. "Food processing industry as a
      factor in comprehensive regional planning," Master's
      Thesis, University of Science and Technology, Kumasi,
      1967. 133 p.

1245 Balogh, T. "Ghana: failure on the Volta." In T. Balogh,
      ed. The economics of poverty. New York: Macmillan,
      1966, pp. 283-92.

1246 Bareau, P. Cocoa: a crop with a future. Bournville:
      Cadbury Press, 1953. 39 p.

1247 Bateman, Merrill J.   "Aggregate and regional supply func-
      tions of Ghanaian cocoa, 1946-62," J. Farm Econ., XLVII
      (May 1965), 384-401.

1248 _____. "Cocoa in the Ghanaian economy," Doctoral Dis-
      sertation, Massachusetts Institute of Technology, 1965.

1249 _____. "The Supply function for Ghanaian cocoa: regional
      supply," J. Farm Econ., XLVIII (Nov. 1966), 1032-4.

1250 Beal, R. E., et al.   "Rationality and migration in Ghana,"
      Rev. Econ. Stat., XLIX (Nov. 1967), 480-6.

1251 Beer consumption in Ghana: survey directed and reported
      prepared by F. A. Nzeribe.   Accra: Jeafan Ltd., 1968.
      67 p.

1252 Berg, E. J.   "The Recruitment of a labor force in tropical
      Africa," Doctoral Dissertation, Harvard University, 1960.

1253 Birmingham, W. B.   "Standards of living in the Gold Coast."
      In Proceedings of the Third Conference of West African
      Institute for Social and Economic Research, 1956, pp. 25-
      32.

1254 Cantor, David.   "Import-replacing industrialization and
      economic development in Ghana," Doctoral Dissertation,
      Harvard University, 1966.
         Observes that the dualistic structure of Ghana's economy
      has made prospects for import-replacing industry appear
      problematical and examines low income in the traditional
      sector, low level of demand for home manufacture, and
      the lack of skilled labor.

1255 Clottey, St. John Atukwei.   "An approach to the development
      of meat technological research in developing countries,"
      Master's Thesis, Cornell University, 1966.   99 p.

1256 Collins, W. B.   "The Sea is their hunting ground: the ro-
      mance of the Gold Coast fishing industry," W. Afr. Rev.,
      (July 1955), 589-94.

1257 Danmolé, Mashood B.   "The Supply of labor in the economic
      growth of Ghana," Master's Thesis, University of Cali-
      fornia, Berkeley, 1959.   100 p.

1258 Darkoh, Michael B.   "The Distribution of manufacturing in
      Ghana; a case study of industrial location in a developing
      country," Scottish Geogr. Mag., LXXXVII (April 1971),
      38-57.

1259   Davison, R. B.   "Labour relations and trade unions in the
       Gold Coast," Industrial and Labour Rel. Rev., VII (July
       1954), 592-604.
       The industrial relations legislation passed by the British
       colonial Administration to control formation of trade
       unions and to arbitrate in trade disputes in the Gold Coast.

1260   _____ .   "Labor relations in Ghana," Ann. Amer. Acad.
       Pol. Soc. Sci., CCCX (March 1957), 133-41.

1261   _____ .   A Pilot survey of migrant labour in the Gold
       Coast.   Achimota: University College of the Gold Coast,
       1954.   44 p.

1262   _____ .   "The Study of industrial relations in West Africa."
       Paper presented at the Annual Conference of the West
       African Institute of Social and Economic Research, Ibadan,
       1953.

1263   Dickson, K. B.   "Cocoa in Ghana," Doctoral Dissertation,
       London University, 1959.

1264   _____ .   "Origin of Ghana's cocoa industry," Ghana Notes
       and Queries, No. 5 (April 1963), 4-9.

1265   "Education, manpower, and employment in Ghana," Oversea
       Educ., IV (Dec. 1964), 108-9.

1266   Engmann, E. V. T.   "Population movements in Ghana: a study
       of internal migration and its implications for the planners,"
       Bull. Ghana Geogr. Assoc., X, No. 1 (1965), 41-65.

1267   Erlichman, Samuel.   "The Attitude of trade unions towards
       productivity; the cases of Norway, Israel and Ghana,"
       Doctoral Dissertation, New School for Social Research,
       New York, 1966.

1268   Futa, A. B.   "The Volta River Project," Econ. Bull. Ghana,
       V (May 1961), 1-15.

1269   Garaj, V.   "A note on the state of cocoa processing industry
       in Ghana," Econ. Bull. Ghana, XI, No. 4 (1967), 41-7.

1270   Gazekpo, H. S.   "The Oil industry in Southeast Ghana: a
       deductive study of the changes that may take place when
       crude oil is found in commercial quantity," Master's
       Thesis, University of Science and Technology, Kumasi,
       1967.   115 p.

1270a Ghana.   Mineworkers Union.   Brief history: 3rd Miners'
       day celebrations, 20th Nov. 1963.   Accra: Secretariat,
       1963.   52 p.

1271   Ghana. Survey of cocoa producing families, 1956-57.
       Accra, 1960. 112 p. (Statistical and economic papers,
       No. 7.)

1272   Ghana. Trades Union Congress. Comparative collective
       agreements negotiated to date by National Unions of the
       Trades Union Congress. Berlin: Verlag Tribune, 1961.
       390 p.
            Gives the text of the Industrial Relations Act of 1958,
       and different collective agreements between Trades Union
       Congress affiliates and employers.

1273   Ghana. The Volta Project: statement by the Government
       of Ghana, 20th February 1961. Accra, 1961. 99 p.
            Describes the history, scope and agreements with the
       Volta Aluminum Company.

1274   "Ghana may join offshore oil producers," Oil and Gas J.,
       LXVIII (July 13, 1970), 38.

1275   "Ghana's industrial future brightens as the Volta opens,"
       Illus. Lond. News, CCXLVIII (Feb. 5, 1966), 22-3.

1276   "Ghana's road to socialism, industry and mining," West
       Africa, No. 2395   (April 27, 1963), 459-60.

1277   Godfrey, E. M. "Unemployment, rural-urban migration,
       food supply and price legislation--a model for Ghana,"
       Doctoral Dissertation, Manchester University, 1970.

1278   Gold Coast. Forestry Dept. Gold Coast timber industry:
       report of a fact finding committee. Accra: Govt.
       Printer, 1951. 69 p.

1279   Gold Coast. Public Relations Dept. Wealth in wood: a
       brief description of forestry and the timber industry in
       the Gold Coast. Accra: Govt. Printer, 1950. 24 p.

1280   Gold Coast. Report of the Gold Coast Mines Board of
       Inquiry 1956. Accra: Govt. Printer, 1956. 139 p.
            Traces the history of a wage dispute from 1953 to the
       1955 strike; and examines various aspects of mines' opera-
       tion--employment condition, cost of living, labor relations,
       labor force, etc. Includes 13 schedules of general sta-
       tistics and 8 statements of financial accounts by mining
       firms.

1281   Gordon, J. "The Cocoa industry and economic development,"
       Econ. Bull. Ghana, IV (March 1960), 17-18.

1282   Green, R. H. "The Ghana cocoa industry: an examination of
       some current problems," Econ. Bull. Ghana, (May 1961),

16-32.
Stresses the importance of cocoa in the Ghana economy
and suggests ways to counteract threats to the industry.

1283 _____ and S. H. Hymer. "Cocoa in the Gold Coast: a
study in relations between African farmers and agricultural
experts," J. Econ. Hist., XXVI, No. 3 (1966), 299-319.

1284 Greenstreet, M. "Employment of women in Ghana," Int.
Labour Rev., CIII (Feb. 1971), 117-29.

1285 Gyasi, E. M. "Economic organization of the poultry industry
of Ghana," Master's Thesis, University of Ghana, 1970.

1286 Gyasi-Twum, K. "The Role of government and other public
bodies in the development of Ghana and Nigeria," Master's
Thesis, Durham University, 1960/61.

1287 Hauser, A. "A Note on some labour problems in Ghana,"
Inter-African Labour Inst. Bull., IV (Nov. 1957), 76-83.

1288 Heath, R. G. Crop production possibilities under conditions
of irrigation in the Volta Flood plain area. Rome: FAO,
1961.

1289 Heigham, J. B. "Industrial relations in the Gold Coast,"
Inter-African Labour Inst. Bull. (Nov. 1955), 8-24.

1290 Hill, Polly. The Gold Coast cocoa farmer: a preliminary
survey. London: Oxford University Press, 1956. 139 p.
The effect of cash economy on the people. Includes
discussion of the employment of laborers, the pledging
of cocoa farms, and cocoa farmers' income and expenditure.

1291 _____. "How large are Ghana farms (and farmers)?"
Econ. Bull. Ghana, IV, No. 5 (1961), 2-6.

1292 _____. The Migrant cocoa farmers of Southern Ghana:
a study in rural capitalism. Cambridge: Cambridge
University Press, 1963. 265 p.
Covers the period, 1890-1930.
Rev: Econ. Geogr., XLI (July 1965), 279. Econ.
Journal, LXXIV (Sept. 1964), 683-5.

1293 _____. "The migrant cocoa farmers of Southern Ghana,"
Africa, XXXI (July 1961), 209-30.

1294 _____. The Occupation of migrants in Ghana. Ann
Arbor: University of Michigan, 1970. 76 p. (University
of Michigan Museum of Anthropology. Anthropological
papers No. 42.)

1295 _____. "Three types of Southern Ghanaian cocoa farmer."
      In Daniel Biebuyck, ed. African agrarian systems. Lon-
      don: Oxford University Press, 1963, pp. 203-23.

1296 Hilton, Thomas Eric. "The Fisheries of the Volta System
      of Ghana," Oriental Geogr., V, No. 1 (1961), 21-34.

1297 Hollander, E. D. "Observation on the political economy of
      manpower in Ghana," Econ. Bull. Ghana, IV (June 1960),
      9-18.

1298 Hunter, John M. "Cocoa migration and patterns of land
      ownership in the Densu, Valley near Suhum, Ghana,"
      Inst. Brit. Geogr., Papers Trans., XXXIII (1963), 61-
      87.

1299 Hymer, Stephen. "Cocoa and Ghanaian growth." Paper
      presented at the 9th Annual Meeting of the African Studies
      Association, 26-29 October 1966, Bloomington, Indiana.
      A survey of principal economic trends since 1900.

1300 International Labour Office. African labour survey. Geneva,
      1958. 712 p.

1301 _____. Report of the Government of Ghana on the Develop-
      ment of the Employment and Manpower Information Pro-
      gramme. Geneva, 1963. 138 p.

1302 Irvine, Frederick. The Fishes and fisheries of the Gold
      Coast. London: Crown Agents, 1947. 352 p.

1303 Jeroch, Michael. Voraussetzungen und Moglichkeiten einer
      industriellen Entwicklung in Ghana. Hamburg: Afrika-
      Verein e. V., Technisch-Wirtschaftlicher Dienst, 1967.
      148 p.

1304 Kaiser Engineers and Constructors. Tema aluminum smelter
      site investigation and port facilities, prepared by K. Nicolls.
      Oakland, 1960. 28 p.

1305 _____. Volta River Project: Akosombo Development
      Foundation report. Oakland, 1966. 2 v.

1306 Lacy, Leslie. "A History of railway unionism in Ghana,"
      Master's Thesis, University of Ghana, 1965.

1307 Lawson, Rowena M. "The Economics of village life on the
      lower Volta," Master's Thesis, University of South Africa,
      1958. 122 p.

1308 _____. An Interim appraisal of the Volta Resettlement
      Scheme. Legon: Ghana Universities Press, 1970.

1309 _____. "The Nutritional status of a rural community on the Lower Volta, Gold Coast," J. West Afr. Sci. Assoc., III (Feb. 1957), 123-9.
A five-month investigation into the diets of five households.

1310 _____. "The Structure, migration and resettlement of Ewe fishing units," Afr. Stud., XVII, No. 1 (1958), 21-7.
The Ewe fishermen are traditionally migratory and the introduction of the modern crafts and fishing techniques may lead to more inland fishing, especially if a lake is created in the Volta River by damming.

1311 Leonard, J. D. "Nkrumah seeks to industrialize Ghana, diversify country's economy," Foreign Comm. Wkly., LXVI (Dec. 25, 1961), 7-8+.

1312 Levy, Mildred B. "Interregional labor migration in Ghana," Doctoral Dissertation, Northwestern University, 1966.

1313 Lewis, William Arthur. "Industrialization and the Gold Coast," Colonial Rev., (March 1954), 140-1.

1314 _____. Report on industrialization and the Gold Coast. Accra: Govt. Printer, 1953. 24 p.

1315 MacDonald, G. Report on conditions of mining labour in the Northern Territories of the Gold Coast. The Ross Institute, 1952.

1316 Mai, Erwin. "Die Kakaokultur an der Goldküste und ihre sozialgeographischen Wirkungen," Phil. F. Diss., Berlin, 1934.

1317 Mensah, Isaac Ackom. "Some implications of the assumption of the role of management by Trade Union in Ghana," J. Management Stud., IV (1967), 26-42.

1318 Menezes, Carmen F. "Agricultural migration and rural development in Ghana," Doctoral Dissertation, Northwestern University, 1966.

1319 Milne, E. M. "Ghana's giant printing press," Bookseller (Oct. 10, 1964), 1682.

1320 Nez, George. "National physical development plan--a pioneering effort in Ghana," Econ. Bull. Ghana, VI, No. 3 (1962), 1-8.

1321 Nicholson, Marjorie. "How trade union failed in West Africa," W. Afr. Rev. (June 1960), 6-9.
Contends that trade unions have some achievements fre-

quently obscured in the persistent political conflicts in the
West African societies.

1322   Nsiah, M. E. R.   "Suitable areas for location of small-scale
       manufacturing: Ashanti-Brong-Ahafo. " Master's thesis,
       University of Science and Technology, Kumasi, 1965. 112 p.

1323   Panofsky, Hans. "The Significance of labour migration for
       the economic growth of Ghana, " Master's Thesis, Cornell
       University, New York, 1958. 138 p.

1324   _____. "The Significance of labour migration for the
       economic welfare of Ghana and the Voltaic Republic, "
       Inter-African Labour Inst. Bull. , VII (July 1960), 30-45.

1325   Peil, M.   Ghanaian factory workers: industrial men in
       Africa.   Washington, D. C: National Institute of Mental
       Health, 1970.

1326   Piault, M. P.   "The Migration of workers in West Africa, "
       Inter-African Labour Inst. Bull. , (Feb. 1961), 98-123.

1327   Poleman, Thomas T.   The Food economies of urban middle
       Africa; the case of Ghana.   Stanford: Food Research
       Institute, Stanford University, 1961.   175 p.

1328   _____. "The Food economies of urban middle Africa:
       the case of Ghana, " Food Res. Inst. Stud. , II (May
       1961), 121-74.

1329   "Power and bauxite benefit Ghana, " Steel, CXLVIII (March 6,
       1961), 35-6.

1330   Rado, E. R.   "The Volta River Project; retrospect and pro-
       spect, " Econ. Bull. Ghana (Feb. 1960), 11-20.
              Summarizes the history of the project, outlining the
       problems of financing the dam.

1331   Rawson, G. C. and J. N. Adjetey. "The Development of
       fishery resources in Ghana, " Ghana J. Sci. , II (Oct. 1,
       1962), 138-41.

1332   "Resettlement on the Volta, " West Africa, Nos. 2347-2349
       (May/June 1962).
              A series of three articles.

1333   Rimmer, Douglas. "The Industrial Relations Act, 1958, "
       Econ. Bull. Ghana, III (April 1959), 6-15.

1334   _____. "New industrial relations in Ghana, " Industrial
       Labor Rel. Rev. , XIV (Jan. 1961), 206-26.

1335   Roper, J. I. Labour problems in West Africa. London:
       Penguin, 1958. 112 p.

1336   Rosen, Stanley. "The Ghana Labor movement: a study of
       trade union nationalism," Master's Thesis, Rutgers Uni-
       versity, 1961.

1337   Roth, Y. and Y. S. Brenner. "Mechanization of agriculture
       in West Africa," Africa Quarterly, VI (July/Sept. 1966),
       147-54.

1338   Saadia, Y. Droit du travail comparé francophone et anglo-
       phone en Afrique occidentale. Tel Aviv: Institut Afro-
       Asiatique d'Etudes Cooperatives et du Travail, 1967.
       215 p.

1339   Schwarz, Walter. "Crisis in Ghana's gold mines: uncer-
       tainty in mining, industry resolved by Government action,"
       W. Afr. Rev., XXXII, No. 402 (1961), 6-9.

1340   Seers, Dudley. "The Stages of economic development of a
       primary producer in the middle of the twentieth century,"
       Econ. Bull. Ghana, VII, No. 4 (1963), 57-69.

1341   Sellier, R. Twin-brother hell. London: Hutchinson, 1960.
       208 p.
           Describes saw-milling operations in Ghana.

1342   Symposium on Farm Mechanization, University of Ghana,
       Legon, 1969. Proceedings. Legon: Faculty of Agricul-
       ture, University of Ghana, 1969. 128 p.
           The conference was sponsored by the Ministry of Agri-
       culture, Council for Scientific and Industrial Research,
       the University of Ghana, Legon, and the University of
       Science and Technology, Kumasi.

1343   Tanburn, E. Intensive survey of the cocoa-producing areas
       of the Gold Coast and trends in potential production.
       Accra: Dept. of Agriculture, 1955. 63 p.

1344   Tettegah, J. K. A New chapter for Ghana labour. Accra:
       Ghana Trades Union Congress, 1958. 51 p.

1345   "The Textile industry in the Western African sub-region,"
       Econ. Bull. Africa, VII (Nov. 1968), 103-25.
           The current market structure and consumption patterns
       of textiles in the fourteen Western African countries from
       1951-1966.

1346   Tiger, L. S. "Bureaucracy in Ghana: the civil service,"
       Doctoral Dissertation, London University, 1962/63.

1347   Trachtman, Lester. "Ghanaian labor legislation since inde-
       pendence, " Labor Law J. , XII (June 1961), 547-56.
            Indicates the advantages of the Industrial Relations Act
       of 1958.

1348   _____. "The Labor movement of Ghana: a study in
       political unionism, " Master's Thesis, Cornell University,
       1960.   230 p.
            The influence of the International Labour Organization
       and British labor policy on Ghana's trade union organiza-
       tion and the 1958 Industrial Relations Act.   Includes also
       the history of the Government labor policy.

1349   _____. "The labor movement of Ghana: a study in
       political unionism, " Econ. Dev. Cult. Change, X (Jan.
       1962), 183-200.

1350   Traore, Diawa-Mory. "Industry growth and foreign trade in
       four West African countries: Ghana, Nigeria, The Ivory
       Coast, and Senegal, " Doctoral Dissertation, University of
       Pittsburgh, 1969.   205 p.

1351   Turton-Hart, F. "Growth of West African industry, "
       African Affairs, LXV (Oct. 1966), 281-8.

1352   United Africa Company.   "What cocoa means to the economy
       of the Gold Coast, " Statistical & Econ. Rev. (U. A. C.), II
       (Sept. 1948), 1-28.

1353   United Nations.   Economic Commission for Africa.   "Indus-
       trial development in West Africa: integration and develop-
       ments. "   Paper presented at the Sub-Regional Meeting on
       Economic Cooperation, Niamey, October 1966.

1354   U. S. Dept. of the Army. Special warfare area handbook for
       Ghana. Washington, D. C. 1962.   533 p.
            Chapter 20, pp. 369-90 deals with the labor force,
       wages and working conditions, history, structure and
       organization of labor union, etc.

1355   U. S. Dept. of Labor.   Labor Statistics Bureau. Bibliography
       on labor in Ghana.   Prepared by Division of Foreign
       Labor Conditions, Washington, D. C. , 1962.

1356   Urquhart, Duncan Hector.   Report on the cocoa industry in
       Sierra Leone and notes on the cocoa industry of the Gold
       Coast.   Bournville: Cadbury Bros. , 1955.   43 p.

1357   _____.   Cocoa. 2nd ed. London: Longmans, 1961.
       293 p.   (Tropical Agriculture series.)

1358   Volta River Authority. <u>Volta Resettlement Symposium papers</u>
       <u>--Kumasi, 23-27 March 1965.</u>   Kumasi, Ghana: Univer-
       sity of Science and Technology, 1965.

1359   Wallenberg, Erik.   <u>Food packaging in Ghana.</u>   Accra: Food
       Research Institute,   1967.   73 p.

1360   Wright, Giles Robert.   "Pan-Africanism and the Ghana Trades
       Union Congress; the international policy of an African Trade
       Union Federation," Master's Thesis, Howard University,
       1962.
          Ghana Trades Union's role in leading African trade
       unions to sever connections with non-African international
       trade union bodies, such as the International Confederation
       of Free Trade Union, in order to create an indigenous
       internal African trade union.

1361   Yankey, David Beikwaw.   "The Industrial relations system
       in Sweden with suggestions concerning its relevance to an
       African nation, Ghana," Doctoral Dissertation, University
       of Southern California, 1969.   271 p.

1362   Younger, Kenneth.   <u>Public service in new states: a study</u>
       <u>in some trained manpower problems.</u>   London: Oxford
       University Press, 1960.   113 p.
          With a brief examination of the typical problems of
       civil service in newly independent African states, the
       Director-General of the Royal Institute of International
       Affairs focuses on the federal and regional services of
       Nigeria, comparing them with those of Ghana, Malaya and
       the Sudan.
          Rev: <u>Amer. Pol. Sci. Rev.</u>, LIV (Dec. 1960), 995.
       <u>Ann. Amer. Acad. Pol. Soc. Sci.</u>, CCCXXXIII (Jan. 1961),
       <u>200.</u>

(5)   ECONOMICS--INVESTMENTS (Domestic and Foreign)

1363   Adjei, Kwame Efah.   "Occupational choice and organizational
       selection: a study of Ghanaian executives in the civil
       service, state enterprises and private foreign-owned cor-
       porations in Ghana," Doctoral Dissertation, New York
       University, 1967.   636 p.

1364   Amegashie, R. S.   "My country wants foreign investment,"
       <u>FAO Rev.</u>, I (Jan. /Feb. 1968), 47-50.

1365   Blunt, M. E.   "State enterprise in Nigeria and Ghana: the
       end of an era?"   <u>African Affairs,</u> LXIX (Jan. 1970), 27-
       43.

1366   Breuer, Helmut.   Estimation of foreign capital requirements
       as a guide to economic policy; the case of Ghana for 1968-
       1972.   Berlin: Verlag Bruno Hessling, 1969.   92 p.
          Based on the information gathered during a field trip to
       Ghana, October to December 1967, under the auspices of
       the German Development Institute, it is designed "to apply
       empirically some new methods of economic analysis---It
       permits independent estimations of the capital import re-
       quirements by the investment savings gap and the import-
       export gap, and their use for shaping economic policy. "
       Preface).   Includes bibliography.

1367   "British stake: what price Volta?"   Economist, CXCVII
       (Oct. 15, 1969), 212.

1368   De Freitas, Geoffrey.   "Britain and Ghana's economy, "
       African Affairs, LXII (Oct. 1963), 290-9.

1369   Deku, A. K.   "Prospects for investment in tourism, " New
       Commonwealth, XLVII (Oct. 1968), 18.

1370   Dixon-Fyle, S. R.   "Economic inducements to private foreign
       investment in Africa, " J. Dev. Stud. , IV (Oct. 1967),
       109-37.

1371   Earle, F. M.   "Geographic influences upon British economic
       policy in West Africa, " Doctoral Dissertation, George
       Washington University, 1929.

1372   Easmon, Aarku.   Direct foreign investment in Ghana.
       Accra: Gasarm Partners, 1970.

1373   Esseks, J. D.   "Government and indigenous private enter-
       prise in Ghana, " J. Mod. Afr. Stud. , IX (May 1971), 11-
       29.

1374   Frankel, Sally Herbert.   Capital investment in Africa: its
       course and its effects.   New York: H. Fertig, 1969.
       487 p.
          Reprint of the 1938 edition.   Issued by the Committee
       of the African Research Survey under the auspices of the
       Royal Institute of International Affairs.   Covers capital
       investment, trade and public finance.
          Rev: J. Pol. Econ. , XLVII (Dec. 1939), 906.

1375   _____ .   The Economic impact on under-developed societies;
       essays on international investment and social change.   Ox-
       ford: Blackwell, 1953.   179 p.

1376   Gardiner, Robert Kweku Atta.   United Nations regional com-
       missions and international cooperation: the twenty-third
       Montague Burton lecture on international relations delivered

in the University of Leeds on March 1965.   Leeds: Leeds
University Press, 1967.   25 p.   (Montague Burton lecture
on international relations, 23.)

1377   Garlick, Peter Cyril.   "Africal-owned private-enterprise
company formation in Ghana," Econ. Bull. Ghana, IV
(Feb. 1960), 1-10.
A historical analysis of Ghanaian companies.   Part I:
1906-1947.   Part II: 1948-1959.

1378   _____.   "Development of Kwahu business enterprise in
Ghana since 1874--an essay in recent oral tradition,"
J. Afr. Hist., VIII, No. 3 (1967), 463-80.

1379   Ghana.   Capital Investments Board.   Investor's manual.
Accra, 1967.   35 p.

1380   "Ghana and Eastern Europe; Business as usual," Economist,
CCXXIV (1967), 1384.

1381   "Ghana deserves a square deal--European companies share
debts guilt," (an editorial) Afr. Dev. (London) (Nov. 1969),
3.
Dr. Kofi Busia's tour of European countries for economic aid.

1382   "Ghana defreezes an asset," Economist, CCXXII (Feb. 25,
1967), 742-3.
The civilian Government's drastic cut in the expansion
plans of the Ghana Fishing Corporation, strongly supported
with Japanese and Russian technological skill under the
Nkrumah regime.   The Russian asset is also frozen.

1383   "Ghana issues manual for foreign investors," Int. Commerce,
LXXIII (Dec. 11, 1967), 5.

1384   "Ghana--new moves against 'foreign' ownership of business,"
East Afr. Trade and Industry, IX (Sept. 1962), 26-8.

1385   "Ghana's Soviet debts," West Africa (April 1967), 431-2.

1386   Hart, Keith.   "Small-scale entrepreneurs in Ghana and
development planning," J. Dev. Stud., VI (July 1970),
104-20.

1387   Kloman, Erasmus H.   "The Climate for private investment
in three countries of West Africa: Liberia, Ghana, and
the Ivory Coast," Doctoral Dissertation, University of
Pennsylvania, 1962.
A study based on government publications and interviews
with representatives of private companies and government
officials.

1388   Kons, Enoch D. Family lands in Ghana. Legon: Ghana
       Universities Press, 1970.

1389   Krassowski, A. External resources in Ghana's development.
       Accra: Essiebon Trading Co. , 1970.

1390   "Make it in Ghana, please, " Economist, CCXX (Aug. 6,
       1966), 563-4.
       The prospects for foreign investments in Ghana.

1391   Miracle, Marvin P.   "The Small holder in agricultural policy
       and planning: Ghana and the Ivory Coast, 1960 to 1966, "
       J. Dev. Areas, IV (April 1970), 321-32.

1392   Moxon, James. Volta: man's greatest lake.   New York:
       Praeger, 1969.   256 p.   Bibliog.
       The study of the building of the great Volta Dam in
       Ghana under Knrumah's leadership.   The success of this
       technological enterprise backed by the United States, Britain
       and the World Bank caused a displacement of some 80, 000
       Ghanaians.   The author, District Commissioner of the
       Volta River District, later joined Ghana's Information Ser-
       vice before his retirement.
       Rev: Ann. Amer. Acad. Pol. Soc. Sci. , CCCXCI
       (Sept. 1970), 223.   Library J. , XCV (June 15, 1970), 156.

1393   "New provident fund scheme in Ghana, " Int. Labour Rev. ,
       XCIII (March 1966), 305-6.

1394   Nicholson, Stanley A.   "The Economy of Ghana, with special
       reference to government strategy for economic development, "
       Doctoral Dissertation, Duke University, Durham, 1965.
       Emphasis is on state investments in communal schemes.

1395   Radix, A.   "Foreign participation in state enterprises: the
       case of Abbot Laboratories (Ghana) Ltd. , " Legon Observer,
       II, No. 23 (1967), 2-7.

1396   Siekman, P.   "Edgar Kaiser's gamble in Africa, " Fortune,
       LXIV (Nov. 1961), 128-31.
       The Volta River Project.

1397   Smith, Hadley E. , ed.   Problems of foreign aid; proceedings
       of the Conference on Public Policy sponsored by the Univer-
       sity of East Africa at the University College, Dar es
       Salaam, Tanzania, November, 1964.   Nairobi: Oxford
       University Press, 1966.   296 p.   (Institute of Public Ad-
       ministration, No. 3.)

1398   Smith, J. I.   External assistance and industrialization; a case
       study of medium-term finance to Ghana, 1951-1966.   New
       York: Praeger, 1969.

1399 Streeten, Paul. Aid to Africa: a policy outline for the
      1970's. New York: Praeger, 1971. 190 p. (Praeger
      special studies. International economics and development.)
          Analyzes the quantity and quality of aid given to African
      nations by both Communist and non-Communist powers, in-
      dicating the donors' policies and attitudes. Two forms of
      estimating aid requirements--the resources or investment-
      saving gap and absorptive capacity--are also examined. The
      author, former U.N. Consultant on development economics,
      is Director of the Institute of Commonwealth Studies and
      Fellow of Balliol College, Oxford University.

1400 "Transition to civilian rule may affect Ghana's economic
      patterns: foreign investors seen welcome," Int. Com-
      merce, LXXV (June 30, 1969), 38-9.

1401 U.S. Dept. of Agriculture. Ghana--projected level of de-
      mand, supply and imports of agricultural products in 1965,
      1970, 1975. Washington, D.C. 1965. 120 p.

1402 Volta River Preparatory Commission. The Volta River Pro-
      ject. London: H.M.S.O. for the Governors of the United
      Kingdom and the Gold Coast, 1956. 3 v.

1403 Wittman, G.H., Inc. The Ghana report: economic develop-
      ment and investment opportunities, legal problems relative
      to investment, sociological factors relative to general
      economic development. New York, 1959. 236 p.

1404 Woodman, G.R. "The Acquisition of family land in Ghana,"
      J. Afr. Law, VII, No. 3 (1963), 136-51.

(5) ECONOMICS--TRADE AND FINANCE

1405 Ahmad, N. Deficit financing in Ghana, 1957-1965. Legon:
      Dept. of Economics, University of Ghana, 1967. 100 p.

1406 Anderson, Gerald H. "The Feasibility of the use of the
      Bauer-Paish income stabilization proposal by the Ghana
      Cocoa Marketing Board," Doctoral Dissertation, Indiana
      University, 1965.
          Examines some aspects of the operation of the 1952
      proposal by P.T. Bauer and F.W. Paish for stabilizing
      the cash receipts of many small cocoa producers in Ghana.

1407 Andic, Fuat and Suphan Andic. "A Survey of Ghana's tax
      system and finances," Public Finance, XVIII, No. 1 (1963),
      5-41.

1408 Ansere, J.K. "Financial problems of the Accra-Tema City
      Council," Master's Thesis, University of Ghana, 1968.
      179 p.

1409   Ayatey, Siegfried B. Central banking, international law and
       economic development: Studies on West Africa. Dubuque,
       Iowa: W. C. Brown Book Co. , 1968. 101 p.
              Includes a discussion of the strategic role of the Central
       Bank in economic development with specific reference to
       Ghana.

1410   Bank of Ghana. Board of Directors. Report for the financial
       year ended, 30th June, 1970. Accra (P. O. B. 2674, Accra,
       Ghana), 1971. 75 p.

1411   Behrman, J. R. "Monopolistic pricing in international com-
       modity agreements: a case study of cocoa." Paper pre-
       sented at the Wharton School of Economics, University of
       Pennsylvania, 1966. (Discussion paper No. 40.)

1412   Birmingham, W. "An Index of real wages of the unskilled
       labourer in Accra, 1939-1959," Econ. Bull. Ghana, IV
       (March 1960), 2-6.

1413   Brooks, G. E. Yankee traders, old coasters and African
       middlemen: a history of American legitimate trade with
       West Africa in the nineteenth century. Boston: Boston
       University Press, 1970. 370 p.

1414   Bwasty-Semme, A. Ghana and the decimal currency. Accra:
       Research Africana Press, 1965. 48 p.

1415   Carbon Ferrière, Jacques de. La Gold Coast: Administra-
       tion, finances, économie. Paris: Librairie Technique et
       Economique, 1937. 246 p.

1416   _____ . L'Organisation politique administrative et finan-
       cière de la colonie britannique de la Gold Coast. Paris:
       Librarie Technique et Economique, 1936. 207 p.
              Originally submitted as Doctoral Dissertation, University
       of Paris, 1936.

1417   Christensen, James Boyd. "Marketing and exchange in a
       West African tribe," Southwestern J. Anthrop. , XVII
       (Summer 1961), 124-39.

1418   "Controlling Ghana's imports," West Africa (Dec. 9, 1961),
       1351.

1419   Cousins, A. M. "The Dutch West India Company on the West
       Coast of Africa up to 1660," Master's Thesis, University
       of Belfast, 1953/54.

1420   Cowan, E. A. Evolution of trade unionism in Ghana. Accra:
       Trades Union Congress, 1963. 202 p.

1421 Cox-George, Noah A. Finance and development in West
      Africa: the Sierra Leone experience. London: Dobson,
      1961. 333 p.
      Originally submitted as doctoral dissertation, London
      University.

1422 _____. "Studies in finance and development in the Gold
      Coast experience, 1914-1918," Public Finance, XIII, No.
      2 (1958), 146-77.
      Discusses the position of the export economy at war,
      and finance and development in war time.

1423 Crossley, M. "Some puzzling spending habits in Ghana: a
      comment," Econ. Bull. Ghana, II, No. 3 (1958), 12-16.

1424 Cugoano, Ottobah. Thoughts and sentiments--on the evil
      and wicked traffic of the slavery and commerce of the
      human species. Legon: Institute of African Studies, Uni-
      versity of Ghana, 1970.

1425 Daaku, Kwame Yeboa. Trade and politics on the Gold Coast,
      1600-1720; a study of the African reaction to European
      trade. Oxford: Clarendon Press, 1970. 219 p.

1426 Davey, P. L. P. "Household budgets in rural areas," Econ.
      Bull. Ghana, VII, No. 1 (1963), 17-28.

1427 De Graft-Johnson, J. C. African experiment: cooperative
      agriculture and banking in British West Africa. London:
      Watts, 1958. 198 p.
      Dealing with the colonial economic policy, it attempts
      to relate the cooperative movement to agricultural credit.

1428 _____. "Cooperation in agriculture and banking in British
      West Africa," Doctoral Dissertation, Edinburgh University,
      1946/47.

1429 _____. "Some historical observations on money and the
      West African Currency Board," Econ. Bull. Ghana, XI,
      No. 2 (1967), 3-19.

1430 Dibbs, J. L. Fish marketing in Ghana. Rome: FAO, 1961.

1431 Dickson, K. B. "Trade patterns in Ghana at the beginning of
      the eighteenth century," Geogr. Rev., LVI (July 1966),
      417-31.

1432 Dinour, D. "Problems in budgetary techniques," Econ. Bull.
      Ghana (Dec. 1959), 1-13.
      Discussion of general problem and procedure in budgeting
      in Ghana, by a UN expert attached to the Ghana Ministry
      of Finance.

1433   Due, John Fitzgerald. Indirect taxation in developing econo-
       mies; the role and structure of customs duties, excises
       and sales taxes. Baltimore: Johns Hopkins Press, 1970.
       201 p.
            Based on a series of lectures given 3-7 December 1962,
       at Massachusetts Institute of Technology under the auspices
       of the Harvard Law School International program in taxation
       and the M. I. T. School of Industrial Management. The
       emphasis is on sales taxes.
            Rev: Ann. Amer. Acad. Pol. Soc. Sci., CCCXCV
       (May 1971), 237. Choice, VIII (May 1971), 440.

1434   _____. Taxation and economic development in tropical
       Africa. Cambridge: Massachusetts Institute of Technology
       Press, 1963. 172 p.
            A study of taxing in eight African states including Ghana
       and Nigeria, noting its relation to the country's economic
       development. Based on a series of lectures delivered in
       December 1962 under the auspices of the Harvard Law
       School's International Program in Taxation.
            Rev: Amer. Econ. Rev., LIV (Sept. 1964), 819.
       Library J., LXXXIX (Feb. 15, 1964), 860.

1435   _____. "Taxation of property in developing economies:
       the African experience," Land Econ., XXXIX (Feb. 1963),
       1-14.

1436   Dutta-Roy, D. K. and S. J. Mabey. Household budget survey
       in Ghana. Legon: Institute of Statistics, University of
       Ghana, 1968. 108 p. (Technical publication series No. 2.)

1437   Fagerlund, Vernon G. and Robert T. Smith. "A Preliminary
       map of market periodicities in Ghana," J. Dev. Areas, IV
       (April 1970), 333+.

1438   Gandhi, Ved P. "Are there economies of size in government
       current expenditures in developing countries?" Nigerian J.
       Econ. Soc. Stud., XII (July 1970), 157-73.
            The author is an economic expert with the International
       Bank for Reconstruction and Development.

1439   Gardiner, Robert Kweku. "Development and trade in Ghana,"
       African Affairs, LXV (Jan. 1966), 1-14.

1440   Garlick, Peter Cyril. "African and Levantine trading firms
       in Ghana." In Proceedings of the Nigerian Institute of
       Social and Economic Research Conference, Ibadan, Decem-
       ber 1960, pp. 119-31.

1441   _____. African business enterprise: a study of a group
       of traders in Kumasi. Achimota: University College of
       Ghana, 1958. 68 p. (Economic Research Division, mono-
       graph No. 1.)

1442 _____. African traders in Kumasi. Accra: Economic
Research Division, University College of Ghana, 1960.
115 p. (African business series, No. 1.)
Limited to those traders with permanent premises.

1443 Ghana. Cocoa Marketing Board. The Ghana Cocoa Marketing Board at work. 3rd ed. Accra, 1959. 20 p.

1444 _____. Hints to cocoa farmers. Accra, 1959. 40 p.
In English, Ashanti-Twi, Akwapim-Twi, Fante and Ewe.

1445 _____. Central Bureau of Statistics. Directory of distributive trade establishments. Accra, 1968. 363 p.

1446 _____. Government. Report of the Commission of Inquiry
into Alleged Irregularities and Malpractices in Connection
with the issue of Import Licenses. Accra: Govt. Printer,
1964. 39 p.

1447 _____. Ministry of Trade. Handbook of commerce and
trade. Accra, 1968. 321 p.

1448 "Ghana after Nkrumah," Economist, CCXX (Aug. 6, 1966),
549-64.
On the poor state of Ghana's economy.

1449 "Ghana goes for broke; economy nears a crisis as President
Nkrumah rushes African nation toward industrialization
and socialism," Business Week (May 1, 1965), 41-2.

1450 Gold Coast. Laws, Statutes, etc. The Trade Unions
Ordinance, 1941. Accra, 1941. 28 p. (Its No. 13 of
1941.)

1451 Great Britain. Board of Trade. Report of the United Kingdom Trade and industrial Mission to Ghana. London:
H.M.S.O., 1959. 60 p.

1452 Green, R.H. "The West African shipping conferences and
Ghana: some aspects of colonial oligopoly and national
policy," Econ. Bull. Ghana, VIII, No. 3 (1964), 39-45.

1453 Hawkins, E.K. "Capital formation in Nigeria and Ghana,
1946-1955," Oxford Univ. Inst. Econ. Stat. Bull., XXI
(Feb. 1959), 39-46.

1454 _____. "The Growth of a money economy in Nigeria and
Ghana," Oxford Econ. Papers, X (Oct. 1958), 339-54.

1455 _____. "Marketing boards and economic development in

Nigeria and Ghana, " Rev. Econ. Stud. , XXVI (Oct. 1958),
51-62.

1456   Hazlewood, Arthur D. "Ghana's finances, " Banker's Magazine (April 1957), 311-30.
Surveys Ghana's finances over the past few years and
assesses her financial situation at the outset of her independence career.

1457   _____. "How poor is Ghana?" West Africa (March 30,
1957), 295-6.

1458   Hicks, Ursula Kathleen. Development from below: local
government and finance in developing countries of the
Commonwealth. Oxford: Clarendon Press, 1961. 549 p.
Investigates efforts made by the British Government to
build up local government in preparation for independence
in former colonial territories of the Commonwealth, cover-
ing East and West Africa, the West Indies, India and
Ceylon.
Rev: Amer. Econ. Rev., LI (Dec. 1961), 1103. TLS
(May 26, 1961), 319.

1459   [No entry]

1460   Hill, Polly. "The Case against double taxation of cocoa
farmers, " Econ. Bull. Ghana, II (Sept. 1958), 15-18.

1461   _____. "Jottings on Ghana's external trade in merchandise, "
Econ. Bull. Ghana, III (May 1959), 19-22.

1462   _____. "Landlords and brokers: a West African trading
system (with a note Kumasi butchers), " Cahiers Etud. Afr. ,
VI (1966), 349-66.

1463   _____. "The Northern Ghanaian trade. " In Markets and
Marketing in West Africa; proceedings of a seminar in
Edinburgh, 1966, pp. 65-80.

1464   _____. Studies in rural capitalism in West Africa. Cam-
bridge: Cambridge University Press, 1970. 173 p.
(African Studies series, 2.)
Much of the book deals with cattle raising and trading on
the Accra plains in Northern Ghana.
Rev: Africa, XLI (April 1971), 170-1. Choice, VII
(Sept. 1970), 892. West Africa No. 2758 (April 18, 1970),
427-9.

1465   Hilling, D. Development of the Ghanaian port system. Legon:
Pioneer Book Co. , 1970.

1466   Howe, R. W. "Ivory Coast and Ghana compare balance
sheets, " Atlas, XIX (Oct. 1970), 44.

1467 Islam, Nasir. "Pay in the public service: a comparative
      study of Ghana, Nigeria, India and Pakistan," Doctoral
      Dissertation, University of Southern California, 1966.
      453 p.

1468 Italy. Istituto per Il Commercio Estero. Ghana. Roma,
      1960. 184 p.

1469 Jucker-Fleetwood, Erin Elver. Money and finance in Africa:
      the experience of Ghana, Morocco, Nigeria, the Rhodesias,
      and Nyasaland, the Sudan, and Tunisia from the establish-
      ment of their central banks until 1962. New York:
      Praeger, 1964. 332 p. Bibliog.
      Rev: Amer. Econ. Rev., LV (June 1965), 599-601.
      Econ. Journal, LXXV (Sept. 1965), 591-3.

1470 Killick, T. "Ghana's balance of payments since 1950,"
      Econ. Bull. Ghana, III (1962), 3-18.

1471 Klein, H. "Die Finanzwirtschaft westafrikanischer Koni-
      greiche," Wirtsch. u. Sozialwiss. F., Frankfurt, 1946.

1472 Lawson, Rowena M. Elements of Commerce in West Africa.
      Rev. ed. London: Longmans, 1961. 136 p. 1st ed.
      1957.

1473 McCall, Daniel F. "The Koforidua market." In Paul Bohan-
      nan and G. Dalton, eds. Markets in Africa. Evanston:
      Northwestern University Press, 1962. pp. 667-97.
      Designed "to present the facts about economic activities
      of traders, the organization of Koforidua market in what
      is the new Ghana, and to analyze the complex of marketing
      in the area which has its center in the town of Koforidua."

1474 Naseem, Ahamad. "Some aspects of budgetary policy in
      Ghana," Econ. Bull. Ghana, X, No. 1 (1966), 3-22.

1475 Niculescu, B.M. "The Growth of banking in Ghana," Bankers'
      Magazine, CXCII (Dec. 1961), 403-12.

1476 Nypan, Astrid. Market trade: a sample survey of market
      traders in Accra. Accra: Economic Research Division,
      University College of Ghana, 1960. 78 p.
      A study of the markets and marketing in Ghana's princi-
      pal city.

1477 _____. "Market trade in Accra," Econ. Bull. Ghana, IV
      (March 1960), 7-16.

1478 Olakanpo, Joshua O. Central banking in the Commonwealth;
      a comparative study of monetary problems and techniques.
      Calcutta: Bookland Private Ltd., 163. 331 p.

Based on his doctoral dissertation, London University, under title: "Central banking problems in Commonwealth countries: a review of experiences since 1945."

1479 Omaboe, E. N. "Ghana's national income in 1930," Econ. Bull. Ghana (Aug. /Sept. 1960), 6-11.
Intended to correct some errors the author claims to have found in A. W. Cardinall's 1930 national income estimate.

1480 _____. "Some problems of national income accounting in Ghana," Econ. Bull. Ghana, II (May 1958), 14-17.

1481 Osmond, Kevin F. "Getting your goods into Ghana; here's a market of nearly seven million people, who import about $395 million worth of goods a year," Foreign Trade (Canada) CXIX (May 18, 1963), 3-6.

1482 _____. "Ghana: Ghana's economy still rests solidly on cocoa, and production and export are rising," Foreign Trade (Canada), CXIII (May 7, 1960), 3-5.

1483 Priestley, Margaret. West African trade and coast society: a family study. London: Oxford University Press, 1969. 207 p.
A Ghanaian family of mixed descent, the Brews.

1484 Prindl, Andreas R. "The West African Currency Board: an analysis of a colonial monetary system," Doctoral Dissertation, University of Kentucky, 1964.

1485 "Report describes Ghana's market for U. S. products, which now make up 20% of total imports," Int. Commerce, LXX (June 1, 1970), 30-1.

1486 Report of the Commission of Enquiry into Trade Malpractices in Ghana. Accra: Govt. Printer, 1966.

1487 Reusse, Eberhard. "Marketing operations of the Ghana State Fishing Corporation," FRI Res. Bull. (Accra), I (Jan. 1968), 48-60.

1488 _____ and Rowena Lawson. "The Effect of economic development on metropolitan food marketing--a case study of food retail trade in Ghana," East J. Rural Dev., II, No. 1 (1969), 33-55.
Discusses the structure of retail trade in local and imported food stuffs in Accra and the means of meeting the demands of the fast growing city.

1489 Rimmer, Douglas. "Income tax and cocoa farmers," Econ. Bull. Ghana, II (Aug. 1958), 3-13.

1490 _____. "Stabilization of the price of cocoa, " Econ. Bull.
      Ghana, II (April 1958), 3-7.

1491 Röper, B. "Das Geldwesen in Westafrika, " Rechts. u.
      Staatswiss. F. , Hamburg, 1946.

1492 Rudd, Anthony. "Ghana and the sterling area, " The Banker
      (March 1957), 166-71.
      A brief outline of Ghana's economy with emphasis on the
      effect of the national independence on the sterling area.

1493 Seers, Dudley and C. R. Ross. Report on financial and
      physical problems of development in the Gold Coast. Accra:
      Office of the Govt. Statistician, 1952. 172 p.
      The essential elements of economic structure and recent
      economic history of the Gold are examined, including an
      analysis of problems of inflation, finance and physical
      limitation to development; technique of planning and the
      Development plan. Appendices contain vital statistical
      information such as estimates of national income.

1494 "Settling Nkrumah's debts, " West Africa, No. 2682 (Oct. 26,
      1968), 1245-6.

1495 Seven-Year Plan for National Reconstruction and Development:
      Financial Years, 1963/64-1969/70. Accra: Office of the
      Planning Commission, 1964.

1496 Skinner, Snider. Ghana's agriculture and trade in farm
      products. Washington, D. C. : U. S. Dept. of Agriculture,
      1958.

1497 Strasburg, P. A. "West African trade with special reference
      to the exports of Sierra Leone, " Master's Thesis, London
      University, 1964.

1498 Swanzy, H. "A Trading family in the nineteenth century
      Gold Coast, " Trans. Gold Coast & Togoland Hist. Soc.,
      II, Part 2 (1956), 87-120.
      History of the firm of F. and A. Swanzy and earlier
      members of the trading family.

1499 Théberge, P. A. "Trade prospects: Ghana, " Foreign Trade
      (Canada), CXX (Aug. 10, 1963), 17-18.

1500 U. S. Dept. of Commerce. Bureau of International Programs.
      Import tariff system of Ghana. Washington, D. C. : Govt.
      Printing Office, 1962.

1501 United Africa Company. "Merchandise trading in British
      West Africa, " Statistical & Econ. Rev. , (U. A. C.) (March
      1950), 1-36.

1502   Wanner, Gustaf Adolf. <u>Die Basler Handels-Gesellschaft, A. G.</u>,
       <u>1859-1959.</u> Basel: Basler Handels-Gesellschaft, A. G. ,
       1959. 677 p.
       History of the commercial enterprise of the Basel
       Trading Company in Ghana.

1503   Wehner, Harrison. "The Cocoa Marketing Board and economic
       development in Ghana: a case study," Doctoral Dissertation,
       University of Michigan, 1963.
       Analysis of the Ghana Cocoa Marketing Board's perform-
       ance during 1947-48 to 1960-61 period in order to deter-
       mine and evaluate its policy objectives.

1504   Williams, J. W. "State banking in the Gold Coast," <u>Banker</u>,
       CVII (March 1957), 171-5.
       Surveys the operations of the government's Commercial
       Bank established in 1953.

1505   Wolfson, Freda. "A Price agreement on the Gold Coast--
       the Krobo oil boycott, 1858-1866," <u>Econ. Hist. Rev.</u>, VI
       (Aug. 1953), 68-77.
       The boycott is compared with the Gold Coast cocoa
       hold-up of 1937-38.

1506   Wood, R. , et al. <u>Report on trade and investment oppor-</u>
       <u>tunities in the Gold Coast.</u> Rev. ed. Accra: Ministry
       of Trade and Labour, 1956. 105 p.

1507   Yannoulis, Y. and M. Bostock. "Urban household income
       and expenditure patterns in Ghana," <u>Econ. Bull. Ghana</u>,
       VII, No. 3 (1963), 12-18.

(6)   EDUCATION

1508   Abbiw, Daniel K. "The Aim and the need for the training of the
       mother tongue in the primary school," <u>Ghana Teachers'</u>
       <u>J.</u>, No. 56 (Oct. 1967), 24-9.

1509   _____ . "The Teaching of English in the primary schools
       of Ghana," <u>Ghana Teachers' J.</u>, No. 50 (April 1966), 12-
       22.

1510   _____ . "Story-telling in the primary school," <u>Ghana</u>
       <u>Teachers' J.</u> , No. 54 (April 1967), 1-9.

1511   Abedi-Boafo, J. <u>Modern problems in Gold Coast elementary</u>
       <u>schools.</u> Mampong Akwapim: The Author, 1951. 53 p.

1512   Achimota College.   Achimota in 1932; report on Achimota
       College.   Achimota: College Press, 1933.

1513   Adam, Roy.   "Education and politics in developing countries,"
       Teachers Coll. Rec., LXX (March 1969), 495-502.

1514   Adams, Cynthia.   A Study guide for Ghana.   Boston: African
       Studies Center, Boston University, 1967.   95 p.

1515   Addi-Mortty, Geormbeeyi.   "Adult education and international
       understanding," Adult. Educ., XXVIII, No. 1 (1955), 29-37.

1516   Addo, S. and E.O. Koranteng.   A Practical English course.
       London: Macmillan, 1966.   75 p.   Reader 2.

1517   _____.   Work book for second year.   London: Macmillan,
       1966.   65 p.

1518   Adjei, Ako.   "Imperialism and spiritual freedom: an African
       view," Amer. J. Soc., L (Nov. 1944), 189-98.
            Condemns the Christian mission educational philosophy
       that has trampled upon traditional culture, religion and
       morality and urges expansion of technical education to meet
       African needs.

1519   Afari, Nathan M.   "Education for freedom and authority in
       Ghana, including an investigation of the attitudes of her
       teachers," Doctoral Dissertation, Clark University, 1964.
            Analysis of the attitudes of 914 teachers in Ghana on
       a 68-item questionnaire.

1520   "African elites," Int. Soc. Sci. Bull., VIII, No. 3 (1956),
       424-88.
            Seven articles on the elites in Ghana, South Africa,
       Senegal, the Congo, Nigeria and the Portuguese territories.

1521   Agyemang, Fred M.   A Century with boys: the story of
       middle boarding schools in Ghana, 1867/1967.   Accra:
       Waterville, 1967.   103 p.

1522   _____.   School and career (some thoughts on education
       in Ghana).   Accra: Waterville, 1968.   85 p.

1523   Agyeman-Dickson, Y.D., et al.   "The Ibadan workshop on
       teaching African history," W. Afr. J. Educ., IX (June
       1965), 89-92.

1524   Akpropong Presbyterian Boys Middle School.   Century cele-
       bration 1867-1967:   history and programme.   Accra:
       Presbyterian Press, 1967.   16 p.

1525 Amissah, S. H. "The Future of teacher education in Ghana,"
      W. Afr. J. Educ., VII (June 1963), 85-6.

1526 Anene, F. K. Kofi Mensah. Illustrated by Kofi Banahene.
      Accra: Ghana Publishing House, 1968. 60 p.

1527 Asamoa, E. A. "The Problems of language in education in
      the Gold Coast," Africa, XXV (Jan. 1955), 60-78.

1528 Ashby, Eric. African universities and western tradition.
      Cambridge: Harvard University Press, 1964. 124 p.
      (The Godkin lectures at Harvard University, 1964.)
          The impact of African nationalism upon modern African
      universities, as shown by Ghanaian and Nigerian universi-
      ties. "Based on the Godkin lectures delivered at Harvard
      University on April 7, 8 and 9, 1964."
      Rev: Univ. Quarterly, XIX (Sept. 1965), 396-408.

1529 _____. Universities; British, Indian, African: a study in
      the ecology of higher education. Cambridge: Harvard
      University Press, 1966. 558 p.

1530 Auger, G. A. "Expansion of primary and mass education in
      Africa," World Year Bk. Educ., (1965), 435-45.

1531 Ayi-Bonte, S. G. Physical education for elementary schools:
      a handbook for teachers. London: Macmillan, 1966. 88 p.

1532 Balme, D. M. "University aims in the Gold Coast, " Uni-
      versitas, I, No. 3 (1954), 13-15.

1533 _____. The University College of the Gold Coast, 1948-
      1952. Legon: University College, 1954. 71 p.

1534 Bernard, Laureat J. "The Impact on teacher training of
      American educational philosophies," Ghana Teachers' J.,
      IV (Oct. 1968), 1-18.

1535 Banfield, B. "Ghana: an emerging nation that lit the fuse,"
      Grade Teacher, LXXXVI (Oct. 1968), 54-5+.

1536 Bannerman, R. H. O. "The Education of medical students in
      the social aspects of obstetrics and gynaecology," Ghana
      Med. J., V (Dec. 1966), 144-7.

1537 Barker, W. H. "Early days of the Accra Training Institution,"
      Gold Coast Teachers' J., I (1929), 136-40.

1538 Bartels, F. L. "Education in the Gold Coast," African
      Affairs, XLVIII (Oct. 1949), 300-9.

1539 _____ . "The Gold Coast: educational problems," World
     Year Bk. Educ., (1949), 348-58.

1540 Barton, T. Education in the Gold Coast. London: Nelson,
     1954.

1541 Bassa-Quansah, Y. "The Double-shift system in Ghanaian
     primary schools," Teacher Educ. New Countries, XI
     (Nov. 1970), 134-42.
        A survey of teachers indicates that the majority prefer
     regular school schedule to double sessions.

1542 Beeby, C. E. The Quality of education in developing countries.
     Cambridge: Harvard University Press, 1966. 139 p.
        The need for the developing nations to develop their own
     educational policies and methods to meet their needs. In-
     cludes discussion of teacher training and the balance be-
     tween educational and economic theories.
        Rev: Library J., XCI (March 1, 1966), 1219.

1543 Belshaw, H. "Religious education in the Gold Coast," Int.
     Rev. Missions, XXXIV (July 1945), 267-72.

1544 Bending, H. B. "Problems of discipline among training col-
     lege staff and students in Ghana," Teacher Educ., III (Feb.
     1963), 188-95.

1544a Bibby, John and Paul Johnson. An Annotated bibliography
     of education in Ghana. St. Andrews, Fife: Dept. of Sta-
     tistics, University of St. Andrews (In progress).
        Aided by the grant made by the British Social Science
     Research Council, it covers material, published and un-
     published, written since 1957. Excludes material dealing
     with teaching methods.

1545 Biobaku, Saburi O. "Africa's needs and Africa's univer-
     sities," W. Afr. J. Educ., VII (June 1963), 61-3.
        The author, a Nigerian, is former Vice-Chancellor
     of the University of Lagos, Nigeria.

1546 Birthwhistle, Norman Allen. Putting it over; a handbook
     of suggestion for all who are engaged in missionary educa-
     tion. London: Cargate Press, 1950. 60 p.

1547 Blumer, B. C. The Case for Achimota. Achimota: Achimota
     Press, 1933. 19 p.

1548 Bodine, R. "Ghanaian freighter; key to learning," Penn.
     Sch. J., CXVII (Feb. 1969), 367-8.

1549 Botsio, Kojo. Plan for mass literacy and mass education.
     Accra: Dept. of Social Welfare, 1951. 44 p.

1550   Bowden, B. V.   "Universities and technical education in
       Ghana," Oversea Q., II (June 1960), 40-2.

1551   Bradshaw, D. C.   "The History of teacher training in Ghana:
       its relation to the development of education within the con-
       text of the country's development," Master's Thesis, Shef-
       field University, 1965/66.

1551a Brokensha, David.   "The Peace Corps and Ghana," New
       African, II (Sept. 1963), 167-8.

1552   Brown, Godfrey N.   "British educational policy in West and
       Central Africa," J. Mod. Afr. Stud., II, No. 3 (1964),
       365-77.
           Inter-War policy stressed leadership for West Africa,
       and mass education for Central Africa.   After World War
       II, efforts are made towards a more balanced educational
       policy in both areas.

1553   _____.   "Education in the Ghana-Guinea Union: a com-
       parative sketch of educational development," Teacher Educ.,
       II (May 1961), 45-51.
           Ghana seems to have continued with colonial educational
       system, while Guinea is quickly restructuring its curricula
       to meet its needs.

1554   _____.   "The Meaning of African education," New Era,
       XLIV (1963), 155-8.

1555   Bureau of Modern Publications and Distributors, Whitehall.
       Games and sports.   Physical education in the elementary
       schools: a handbook for teachers.   Accra, 1968.   67 p.

1556   Burns, Donald G.   African education: an introductory survey
       of education in Commonwealth countries.   London: Oxford
       University Press, 1965.   215 p.
           Discusses various aspects of education--elementary,
       secondary and university--in the Commonwealth nations.
           Rev: Choice, III (Jan. 1967), 1057.

1557   Busia, Kofi Abrefa.   The Challenge of Africa.   New York:
       Praeger, 1962.   150 p.
           Examines traditional education and the limitations of
       the colonial educational system, and suggests a modifica-
       tion and improvement of curricula and teaching methods.

1558   _____.   Purposeful education for Africa.   The Hague:
       Mouton, 1964.   107 p.
           Analysis of the traditional and western education and the
       role of the relevant education in the social and political
       development of Africa.

1559   Caldwell, J. C.   "Extended family obligations and education:
       a study of an aspect of demographic transition amongst
       Ghanaian university students," Pop. Stud., XIX (Nov. 1965),
       183-99.

1560   Cerych, Ladislav.   Problems of aid to education in developing
       countries.   Translated from the French by Nod Lindsay,
       et al.   New York: Praeger for the Atlantic Institute, 1965.
       213 p.   (Praeger special studies in international economics
       and development.)
           Rev: Choice, III (Oct. 1966),   694.

1561   Chaplin, B. H.   "Investigation and experience of curriculum
       planning for science education in Ghana," Teacher Educ.,
       III (Feb. 1963), 204-10.

1562   _____.   "Teaching science in Ghana," Ghana Teachers J.,
       (Jan. 1962), 38-42.

1563   Chapman, Daniel.   "Achimota College, Gold Coast," Scottish
       Geogr. Mag., LX (June 1944), 12-14.

1564   Chasin, Doris H.   "Current practices in selected teacher
       training colleges in Ghana," Doctoral Dissertation, Univer-
       sity of California, Los Angeles, 1969.   134 p.
           Course content, curriculum and teaching materials in
       use; methods of teaching; characteristics of the campuses;
       their physical plants, etc.

1565   Clark, Violet E.   "Cross-cultural academic experience of
       Ghanaian students in the United States, 1959-1960,"
       Doctoral Dissertation, University of Michigan, 1963.

1566   Clignet, Remi.   "Inadequacies of the notion of assimilation
       in African education," J. Mod. Afr. Stud., VIII, No. 3
       (1970), 425-44.
           Attempts to define the concepts of "assimilation" and
       "accommodation" and indicate the ways they have been
       used by both colonial powers and Africans themselves.

1567   Cobb, F. W.   "Achimota: an experiment in African education,"
       Landmark (Lond.), IX (1927), 502-4.

1568   Combes, Peter and John Tiffin.   "Report on Ghana schools
       television," Educ. Television Int., IV (March 1970), 76-
       85.

1569   Committee on Pre-University Education.   Report of the Com-
       mittee on Pre-University Education.   Accra, 1963.   44 p.
           Reviews the structure and content of pre-university edu-
       cation, with recommendations for improvement.

1570 "Conference of African States of the Development of Education
      in Africa," Ghana Teachers' J., No. 36 (Oct. 1962), 38-41.

1571 Cowan, L. Gray. "British and French education in Africa:
      a critical appraisal." In Don C. Piper and Taylor Cole,
      eds. Post-primary education and political and economic
      development. Durham: Duke University Press, 1964,
      pp. 178-99.

1572 Cox, Christopher. "The Impact of British education on the
      indigenous peoples of overseas territories," Adv. Sci.,
      XIII (Sept. 1956), 125-36.
          The basic factor in colonial education is attitudes of
      the governed.

1573 Crookall, R. E. Handbook for history teachers in West Africa.
      London: Evans, 1960. 270 p.

1574 Cruise O'Brien, Conor. "Address by the Vice-Chancellor,
      Dr. Conor Cruise O'Brien, to the Congregation of the Uni-
      versity of Ghana," Minerva, II (Summer 1964), 484-91;
      III (Spring 1965), 343-55.

1575 Curle, Adam. Educational problems of developing societies;
      with case studies of Ghana and Pakistan. New York:
      Praeger, 1969. 150 p. (Special studies in international
      economics and development.)

1576 _____. "Nationalism and higher education in Ghana,"
      Univ. Quarterly, XVI (June 1962), 229-42.

1577 Dake, J. Mawuse. "The Role of our universities in building
      a new Ghana," Insight, II, (Sept. 1967), 15-22.

1578 Dako, H. T. "The Presbyterian Training College, Akropong-
      Akwapim," Ghana Teachers' J., No. 56 (Oct. 1967), 30-43.

1579 Darkwa, K. A. "Education for cultural integrity: the
      Ghanaian case," Teachers Coll. Rec., LXIV (Nov. 1962),
      106-11.
          Dangers in educational expansion not geared to economic
      and social development of the country and the difficulties
      encountered in selecting languages of instruction.

1580 Davidson, J. R. " African textbook problems," Ghana Teachers'
      J., No. 36 (Oct. 1962), 21-6.

1581 De Graft Johnson, J. C. "African traditional education,"
      Présence Africaine, No. 7, (avr.-mai 1956), 51-5.

1582 Dodd, W. A. Primary school inspection in new countries.
      London: Oxford University Press, 1968. 110 p. (A
      Teachers' Library)

1582a du Sautoy, Peter. The Planning and organisation of adult
       literacy programmes in Africa. Paris: UNESCO, 1966.
       (Manuals on adult and youth education, no. 4.)

1583   Edu, John E. "Plan for mass literacy and mass education,
       Gold Coast: report on the 1952 literacy drive," Community
       Dev. Bull., IV (Dec. 1952), 13-14.

1584   Ekuban, E. E. "Cape Coast," World Year Bk. Educ., (1970),
       95-109.

1585   Emerson, R. "Crucial problems involved in nation-building
       in Africa," J. Negro Educ., XXX (Summer 1961), 193-205.

1586   Ezekiel, R. S. "Authoritarianism, acquiescence and field be-
       haviour," J. Personality, XXXVIII (March 1970), 31-42.

1587   _____. "Differentiation, demand and agency in projections
       of the personal future: predictive study of the performance
       of Peace Corps teachers," Doctoral Dissertation, Univer-
       sity of California, Berkeley, 1964.

1588   _____. "Setting and the emergence of competence during
       adult socialization: working at home vs. working out
       there," Merrill-Palmer Q. Beh. Dev., XV (Oct. 1969),
       389-96.

1589   Fafunwa, Alliu Babatunde. "African education and social
       dynamics," W. Afr. J. Educ., VII (June 1963), 66-70.
       Former Dean of the Faculty of Education, University of
       Nigeria, Nsukka.

1590   Fiaxer, Samuel. "A School for the deaf in Ghana," Educ.
       Panorama, VII, No. 2 (1962), 14.

1591   Finlay, David J. "Students and politics in Ghana," Daedalus,
       XCVII (Winter 1968), 51-69.

1592   Fishell, Murray. "Attitudes towards the curriculum of the
       African university," W. Afr. J. Educ., XIII (Feb. 1969);
       (June 1969), 90-2; (Oct. 1969), 137-9.
       Three articles in a series.

1593   Fortes, Meyer. Social and psychological aspects of education
       in Taleland. London: Oxford University Press for the
       International African Institute, 1938. 64 p. (International
       Institute of African Languages and Cultures. Memorandum
       XVIII.)

1594   Foster, P. J. Education and social change in Ghana. Lon-
       don: Routledge and Kegan Paul, 1963. 322 p.
       Principal factors that influence Ghana's education. Part

I: Historical background. Part II: Popular misconceptions
about African educational system.

1595 _____. "Educational development in Ghana and the Ivory
Coast." Paper presented at the Annual Meeting of the
African Studies Association, New York, November 1969.
19 p.

1596 _____. "Ethnicity and the schools in Ghana," Comp.
Educ. Rev., VI (Oct. 1962), 127-35.
Ethnic loyalty in Ghanaian schools is aggravated by an
unequal distribution of schools in the country.

1597 _____. "Secondary school leavers in Ghana: expectations
and reality," Harvard Educ. Rev., XXXIV (Fall 1964),
537-58.

1598 Fraser, Alexander G. Achimota: comments on the in-
spectors' report. Achimota: Prince of Wales School
Press, 1932. (Achimota pamphlet, No. 8.)

1599 _____. "My education policy," Oversea Educ., XXIX,
No. 4 (1958), 145-51.

1600 Frazier, E. Franklin. "The Impact of colonialism on African
social forms and personality." In C. W. Stillman, ed.
Africa in modern world. Chicago: University of Chicago
Press, 1955, pp. 70-96.
School considered as a chief agent of culture change
and conflict.

1601 Gamlin, John F. "Education and economic development in
Ghana," W. Afr. J. Educ., XIV (Oct. 1970), 183-7.

1602 Gardiner, R. K. "The Structure of education in rural areas,"
Legon Observer, V, No. 13 (1970), 6-14.

1603 Ghana. Centre for Civic Education. Your rights and respon-
sibilities as a Ghanaian citizen: a current affairs and
civic education casebook. Accra: Anowuo Educational
Publications, 1968. 102 p. (Its civic education series,
No. 1.)
"Adapted from the book by Charles N. Quigley."

1604 Ghana. Commission on University Education. Report of the
Commission on University Education. Accra: Govt. Printer,
1961.

1605 Ghana. Ministry of Education. Education in Ghana: text of
speech given in the Ghana Parliament June 13, 1957. Washington, D. C.: Information Office, Embassy of Ghana, 1957.
10 p.

The speech was given by C. T. Nylander.

1606   _____. First Seminar on Writing of School Textbooks for
        Ghana: the background papers. Accra: Bureau of Ghana
        Languages, 1959. 64 p.

1607   Ghana. Ministry of Information and Broadcasting. Statement
        by the Government on the report of the Commission on
        University Education, December 1960-January 1961. Accra,
        1961.

1608   Ghana. University Advisory Committee (Faculties of Arts,
        Social Studies and Law). Report on secondary and higher
        education systems and national research in Ghana and the
        internal problems of the University of Ghana, 1967. Legon,
        1967. (Variously paged.)

1609   Ghana. Govt. Education report for the years 1958-1960 (Jan.
        1958 to Aug. 1960). Accra: Ministry of Information and
        Broadcasting, 1962. 68 p.

1610   Ghana National Association of Teachers. Constitution and
        rules. Accra, 1966. 18 p.

1611   "Ghana plans for progress: scheme for more universities,"
        W. Afr. Rev., (Sept. 1961), 27-31.

1612   "Ghana's teaching crisis," West Africa, No. 2682 (Oct. 26,
        1968), 1261-2; No. 2683 (Nov. 2, 1968), 1284-5.
        Two articles in a series.

1613   "Ghana's two universities," New Commonwealth (July 1961),
        467-8.

1614   Gold Coast. Dept. of Social Welfare and Community Develop-
        ment. Literacy campaign. Accra: West African Graphic
        Co., 1952. 52 p.

1615   Gold Coast. University College. The University College of
        the Gold Coast, 1948-52; report by the Principal (D. M.
        Balme). London: Nelson, 1953. 71 p.

1616   Gold Coast. Govt. Report of the Committee appointed in 1932
        by the Governor of the Gold Coast Colony to inspect the
        Prince of Wale's College and School, Achimota. London:
        Crown agents, 1932. 82 p.

1617   Goody, John Rankine, ed. Literacy in traditional societies.
        Cambridge: Cambridge University Press, 1968. 349 p.
        Rev: Amer. Anthrop., LXXII (April 1970), 430.

1618   Graham, C. K.   The History of education in Ghana from the
       earliest times to the declaration of independence.   London:
       Cass, 1971.   232 p.
           The first comprehensive study of Ghana's educational
       growth and development, noting the role of government,
       the missionary bodies, private and commercial companies
       and individuals.

1619   Great Britain.   Colonial Office.   Report of the Commission
       on Higher Education in West Africa.   London: H. M. S. O.,
       1945.   (W. E. Elliot, Chairman.)

1620   _____.   Report of the Commission on Higher Education in
       the Colonies.   London: H. M. S. O., 1945.   (C. Asquith,
       Chairman.)

1621   Greenough, Richard.   Perspectives africaines, le progrès de
       l'éducation   Paris: UNESCO, 1966.   117 p.

1622   Griffin, Ella.   "Popular reading materials for Ghana," Int.
       J. Adult Youth Educ., XV, No. 3 (1963), 125-32.

1623   _____.   Reading habits of adults in Ashanti and Togoland.
       Accra: Govt. Publications Bureau, 1970.

1624   _____.   A Study of the reading habits of adults in Ashanti,
       Southern Ghana and Trans-Volta Togoland.   Accra: Bureau
       of Ghana Languages, 1958?   98 p.

1624a Grindal, Bruce T.   Growing up in two worlds.   Education and
       transition among the Sisala of Northern Ghana.   New York:
       Holt, Rinehart & Winston, 1972.   114 p.   (Case studies in
       education and culture.)

1625   Guggisberg, Frederick Gordon.   "The Goal of the Gold Coast,"
       J. Afr. Soc., XXI (Jan. 1922), 81-91.
           The address delivered by the author, a Brigadier-Gen-
       eral and Governor-General of the Gold Coast, at a Luncheon
       Meeting of the Royal African Society, London, on November
       19, 1921.

1626   _____.   The Keystone: education is the keystone of pro-
       gress.   London: Simpkin, Marshall, Hamilton, Kent, 1924.
       59 p.

1627   _____ and Alexander G. Fraser.   The Future of the negro:
       some chapters in the development of a race.   London:
       S. C. M., 1929.   152 p.

1628   Hart, Thomas A.   "Ghana, West Africa as I saw it," J.
       Negro Educ., XXXI (Winter 1962), 92-6.
           Experiences of a Howard University Professor of Physical
       Education.

1629 Hayward, Fred M. "Ghana experiments with civic education:
      Center for Civic Education aims to inculcate democratic
      values," Africa Report, XVI (May 1971), 24-7.

1630 Herbert, A. "Co-operation in West Africa's universities,"
      W. Afr. Rev., XXXIII (March 1962), 12-13.

1631 Hilliard, F. H. A Short history of education in British West
      Africa. London: Nelson, 1957. 186 p.
            Deals primarily with formal education on the European
      pattern up to 1955 in Sierra Leone, Gambia, the Gold
      Coast and Nigeria.

1632 Hinchliffe, J. Keith. "A Comparative analysis of educational
      development in Ghana and the Western Region of Nigeria,"
      Nigerian J. Econ. Soc. Stud., XII (March 1970), 103-13.
            The author works with the Higher Education Research
      Unit, London School of Economics.

1633 Hodge, Peter. "Work with youth in the towns of Ghana,"
      W. Afr. J. Educ., II, No. 3 (1958), 96-100.

1634 Hoon, N. M. and R. P. Abell. "Classroom potential of West
      African literature," Soc. Educ., XXXIII (April 1969), 418-
      24+.

1635 Hurd, G. E. and J. J. Johnson. "Education and social mo-
      bility in Ghana," Sociol. Educ., XLI (Winter 1968), 111-21.

1636 Huxley, Julian. Aggrey-Fraser-Guggisberg memorial lectures
      1961. Accra: University of Ghana, 1961. 47 p.

1637 Ifaturoti, M. A. "Patterns of education in the West," W. Afr.
      Rev., XXXII (June 1961), 43-7.

1638 Ipaye, B. "Philosophies of education in colonial West Africa:
      a comparative study of the British and French systems,"
      W. Afr. J. Educ., XIII (June 1969), 93-7. Reply: XIV
      (Feb. 1970), 80.

1639 Jahoda, Gustav. "Aspects of westernization: a study of
      adult-class students in Ghana," Brit. J. Soc., XII (Dec.
      1961), 375-86.

1640 _____. "The Social background of a West African student
      population," Brit. J. Soc., V (Dec. 1954), 355-65.
            The relationship of the West African educated elite with
      their home and village.

1640a Jeffries, Charles. Illiteracy: a world problem. New York:
      Praeger, 1967. 204 p.
            World-wide examination of illiteracy, comparing its

problems in developed countries with those of the developing
countries, noting various methods of combatting them. Includes maps of illiteracy, bibliography and index. The
author is former Deputy Under-Secretary of State in the
British Colonial Office.
    Rev: Economist, CCXXVI (Feb. 10, 1968), 44. Library
J. , XCIII (May 15, 1968), 2001.

1641   Jigge, Annie. "Education and the task of nation building, "
        Insight, I (Nov. 1966), 49-51.

1642   Johnson, Adolph. "The Evolution of Ghanaian education, "
        Master's Thesis, University of Southern California, 1971.
        115 p.

1643   Jones-Quartey, K. A. B. "L'éducation des adults et la révolu-
        tion africaine, 1961, " Rev. Int. Educ. Adult Jeunesse
        (Paris), XIII, No. 4 (1962), 206-12.

1644   Judges, A. V. "Gold Coast independence and education, "
        Brit. J. Educ. Stud. , V (May 1957), 167-8.

1645   Karikari, K. A. "Adult education: a means to modernization
        and national development, " Insight & Opinion, III, No. 4
        (1968), 90-4+.

1646   Kaye, Barrington. Bringing up children in Ghana: an impres-
        sionist survey. London: Allen & Unwin, 1962. 244 p.
            Rev: Anthropos, LIX, Nos. 1-2 (1964), 313-6.

1647   _____ . Child training in Ghana: an impressionistic sur-
        vey. Legon: Institute of Education, University of Ghana,
        1960. 686 p. (Institute of Education child development
        monographs, No. 1.) (Typescript)

1648   Kelley, Gail Margaret. "The Ghanaian intelligentsia, "
        Doctoral Dissertation, University of Chicago, 1959.

1649   Kimble, David. Progress in adult education. Accra: Uni-
        versity College of the Gold Coast, 1950.

1650   Kinross, F. Teaching English by radio in primary schools.
        Accra: Govt. Publications Bureau, 1970.

1651   Kirkham, W. R. "Academic freedom in Ghana: slow re-
        covery, " Times Educ. Supp. (Nov. 24, 1967), 1200.

1651a   Kissack, I. J. "Language inadequacy and intellectual potential;
        an educational priority in Ghana, " Comparative Education,
        VII (Nov. 1971), 69-71.

1652   Klime, P. "Extraversion, neuroticism and academic per-
        formance among Ghanaian university students," Brit. J.
        Educ. Psych., XXXVI (Feb. 1966), 92-4.

1653   Klitgaard, S. A. Educational books in West, Central and East
        Africa. Copenhagen: Danish National Commission for
        UNESCO, 1966. 74 p.

1654   Koehl, Robert. "The Uses of the University: Past and
        present in Nigerian educational culture," Comp. Educ. Rev.,
        XV (June 1971), 116-31.
             Points raised are also relevant to Ghana and includes a
        discussion of the Achimota College. Extensive bibliography.

1655   Koplin, Roberta Ellen. "Education and national integration in
        Ghana and Kenya," Doctoral Dissertation, University of
        Oregon, 1968.

1656   Kumasi. University of Science and Technology. Dept. of
        Art Education. Experiments in art education. Kumasi,
        1966. 101 p.

1657   Kwapong, Alexander A. "Address by the Vice-Chancellor,"
        Minerva, IV (Summer 1966), 542-54.
             Dr. Kwapong is the Vice-Chancellor of the University of
        Ghana.

1658   _____. The Role of classical studies in Africa today: a
        lecture delivered at the University of Lagos on April 25,
        1969. Lagos: University of Lagos, 1969. 16 p. (Annual
        lectures, 2.)

1659   _____. "University of Ghana: Address by the Vice-
        Chancellor, Dr. Alexander Kwapong, to Congregation,"
        Minerva, VI (Autumn 1967), 87-98.

1660   _____. "Vice-Chancellor's address to the students of the
        University of Ghana on 16th Nov. 1968," Univ. Ghana
        Reporter, VIII, No. 4 (1968), 72-80.

1661   Learoyd, F. G. "The Teaching of English as a national
        second language," Ghana Teachers J., No. 52 (Oct. 1966),
        13-20.

1662   Lewis, Leonard John. Education and political independence in
        Africa, and other essays. Edinburgh: Nelson, 1962. 128 p.

1663   _____. Education and social growth. Edinburgh: Nelson
        for the University College of the Gold Coast, 1957. 18 p.

1664   _____. Educational policy and practice in British tropical
        areas. Edinburgh: Nelson, 1954. 141 p.

1665   _____. "Ghana teacher training: a scheme of directed
          studies for tutors," Oversea Educ., XXX (Jan. 1959), 170-3.

1666   _____. "Higher education in Ghana," Inst. Int. Educ.
          News Bull., XXXIII (Sept. 1957), 6-11.

1667   _____. An Outline chronological table of the development
          of education in British West Africa. Edinburgh: Nelson,
          1953.   21 p.

1668   _____. Phelps-Stokes reports on education in Africa.
          London: Oxford University Press, 1962.   220 p.
              One of the objects of the Phelps-Stokes Fund established
          in 1911 is to aid research on African education.   These
          reports originally made in 1922 and 1924, were reprinted
          for the jubilee of the Fund.

1669   _____. Perspectives in mass education and community
          development. London: Nelson, 1955.   101 p.

1670   _____. "Technological change and the curriculum in
          Ghana," World Year Bk. Educ. (1958), 421-5.

1671   _____   and A. J. Loveridge.   The Management of education:
          a guide for teachers to the problems in new and developing
          systems.   New York: Praeger, 1965.   124 p.

1672   Liveright, A. A.   "Layman's view of adult education in West
          Africa," Adult Educ., XIII (Winter 1963), 67-79.

1673   Lugard, Frederick.   "Education in tropical Africa," Edinburgh
          Rev., CCXLII (July 1925), 1-19.
              The former Governor-General of Nigeria gives what he
          considers the basic goals of African education.

1674   McElligott, Theresa Elizabeth.   "Education in the Gold Coast
          Colony, 1920-1949," Doctoral Dissertation, Stanford Univer-
          sity, 1950.   233 p.
              Historical development of education in the country with
          special attention to the progressive steps in the formulation
          of educational policies and the relationship between the
          educational expansion and economic and political advance-
          ment.

1675   McEvoy, Catherine.   "Teaching drama in a Ghanaian secondary
          school," W. Afr. J. Educ., IX (Feb. 1965), 25-8.

1676   McWilliam, Henry.   The Development of education in Ghana:
          an outline. London: Longmans, Green, 1959.   114 p.
              Historical development of education from the first Euro-
          pean settlements up to 1957.

1677   Maas, J. Van Lutsenburg.   "Educational change in pre-
       colonial societies: the cases of Bugunda and Ashanti, "
       Comp. Educ. Rev. , XIV (June 1970) 174-85.
            Reply with rejoinder by P. J. Foster in Comp. Educ.
       Rev. , XIV (Oct. 1970), 377-84.

1678   "Mass literacy, " Advance, No. 40 (Oct. 1963).
            Entire issue devoted to mass literacy campaigns in Ghana.
       Presents the history of previous literacy campaigns and
       problems faced; the nature of the 1963 campaign, and the
       training of literacy teachers.

1679   Mensah, Godwin.   "Adisadel: a vivacious educational establish-
       ment, " W. Afr. Rev. (Dec. 1951), 1435-7.

1680   Miller, Andrew and John Bibby.   "Aspirations and expecta-
       tions of fifth form pupils: some implications for policy
       and research, " Ghana J. Educ. , I (Sept. 1969), 17-27.
            Examination of the job preferences of 599 Form V
       secondary schools in the Accra area.
            See also W. Afr. J. Educ. , XII (Oct. 1968), 170-4.

1681   Mitchison, Naomi.   Other peoples' worlds: impressions of
       Ghana and Nigeria.   London: Secker & Warburg, 1958.
       160 p.
            Includes a discussion of countries' desires to restructure
       and Africanize their educational curricula.

1682   Morrison, Gresham.   "Education for nationhood: a study in
       African national education among the negro tribes of the
       Gold Coast, " Doctoral Dissertation, Hartford Theological
       Seminary, 1923.   2 v.

1683   Mortimer, C. T.   "University education in Ghana, " Nature,
       CXCII (Oct. 7, 1961), 14-16.

1684   Morton, G.   "Pre-school education in Ghana and Nigeria, "
       J. Nursing Educ. , XVII (Summer 1962), 191.

1685   Mumford, W. Bryant.   "Educational and social adjustment of
       the primitive peoples of Africa to European culture, "
       Africa, II (April 1929), 138-61.

1686   Mundy-Castle, A. C.   "Pictorial depth perception in Ghanaian
       children, " Int. J. Psych. , I, No. 4 (1966), 289-300.

1687   Munger, Edwin S.   "Education for responsibility in the Gold
       Coast, " Inst. Int. Educ. News Bull. , XXIX (March 1959),
       25-8.

1688   Munier, H.   Ghana: literacy planning mission, October-
       November 1967.   Paris: UNESCO, 1968.   69 p.

1689   "The National Apprenticeship in Ghana," Int. Labour Rev.,
       (June 1962), 612-21.

1690   Niculescu, B. M.   "Some economic implications of higher
       education in Ghana," Econ. Bull. Ghana, IV (Oct. /Dec.
       1960), 1-11.

1691   Nketia, Joseph Hanson K.   "Progress in Gold Coast educa-
       tion," Trans. Gold Coast & Togoland Hist. Soc., I (1953),
       63-71.

1692   Nkrumah, Kwame. Flower of learning: some reflections on
       African learning, ancient and modern, contained in two
       speeches on his installation as Chancellor of the University
       of Ghana, Legon, and of the University of Science and
       Technology at Kumasi.   Accra: Govt. Printer, 1962.
       16 p.

1693   _____ . The Role of our universities: speech delivered
       by Kwame Nkrumah at University dinner on Sunday, 24th
       February, 1963.   Accra: Ministry of Information and
       Broadcasting, 1963.

1694   Norman, Leys.   "Achimota College," New Statesman (April
       22, 1933), 499-500.

1695   Nwosu, S. N.   "Mission schools in Africa," World Year Bk.
       Educ. (1966), 186-99.

1696   Odoi, N. A.   Facts to remember.   Accra: Presbyterian Book
       Depot, 1962. 151 p.
           Outlines the essential facts in hygiene, geography, his-
       tory, and nature study.

1697   Ofosu-Appiah, L. H.   "African universities and the western
       tradition," Legon Observer, II, No. 22 (1967), 7-9.
       See also No. 23 (1967), 11-14.

1698   _____ . "The Liberal arts in the University of Ghana,"
       Legon Observer, I, No. 12 (1966), 5-7.

1699   _____ . "The Physical sciences in the University of
       Ghana," Legon Observer, I, No. 10 (1966), 9-12.

1700   _____ . "Science in the University of Ghana," Legon Ob-
       server, I, No. 7 (1966), 8-10.

1701   Okina, A.   "The Fraser School project in Ghana," W. Afr.
       J. Educ., X (June 1966), 82-3.

1702   Okyne, Robert R.   "Komenda College," Ghana Teachers' J.,
       No. 54 (April 1967), 49-61.

1703 Oldham, J.J. "The Educational work of Missionary Societies,"
      Africa, VII (Jan. 1934), 47-59.

1704 Onyewu, N.D. Ukachi. "European scholars and the teaching
      of African studies," Black Acad. Rev., I, No. 3 (1970),
      55-62.
      Critical of the methods used by western scholars in
      teaching African subjects that have made it difficult for
      European students to appreciate African values.

1705 Opoku, T.C. "Backwardness in pupils in rural areas,"
      Ghana Teachers' J., No. 54 (April 1967), 27-32.

1706 Oppong, C. "The Dagomba response to the introduction of
      state schools," Ghana J. Soc., II (Feb. 1966), 17-25.
      Reasons for the strong opposition of the parents to
      state schools.

1707 Ormsby-Gore, W. "Educational problems of the colonial
      Empire," J. Roy. Afr. Soc., XXXVI (April 1937), 162-9.
      Three objectives of British colonial education--providing
      the benefits of British experience; training the individual
      to serve his community; and preserving and enhancing
      local traditions and culture.

1708 Oshin, N.R.O. Education in West Africa: a bibliography.
      Lagos: West African Examinations Council, 1969. 55 p.

1709 Owusu, C.A. "Nursery schools in tropical countries--
      Ghana," African Women, III (June 1959), 26-8.

1710 Partos, Elizabeth. "The Place of western music in the
      music education of Africa," Research Rev., II, No. 3
      (1966), 54-60.

1710a Pedler, Frederick. "Universities and polytechnics in Africa;
      the twelfth Lugard Memorial Lecture," Africa, XLII (Oct.
      1972), 263-74.
      The lecture was delivered at University College, London,
      27 June 1972 during the annual meeting of the Executive
      Council of the International African Institute, by Chairman
      of the Council for Technical Education and Training for
      Overseas Countries (TETOC).

1711 Peil, M. "Ghanaian university students: the broadening
      base," Brit. J. Soc., XVI (March 1965), 19-28.

1712 Penrose, Kwafo. Notes on school administration, organiza-
      tion and methods for students and teachers. Accra:
      Waterville, 1965. 101 p.

1713   Peshkin, Alan. "Educational reform in colonial and inde-
       pendent Africa," African Affairs, LXIV (July 1965), 210-6.
              Comparing the 1952 and 1961 Addis Ababa education con-
       ferences, he argues that schools and educational problems
       in Africa have not changed, quantitatively speaking, despite
       Africans' efforts to create a truly African educational
       system.

1714   Pickard-Cambridge, A. W.   "The Place of Achimota in West
       African education," J. Roy. Afr. Soc., XXXIX (April 1940),
       143-53.
              The author was the Chairman of the Achimota Commission.

1715   Powell, T. T.   "The Adaptability of Ghanaian student teachers,"
       Teacher Educ. New Countries, XI (May 1970), 22-6.

1716   Pwamang, R. L.   A Guide for primary and middle school
       teachers.   Accra: Catholic Press, 1960.   58 p.

1717   Read, Margaret.   "Education in Africa: its pattern and role
       in social change," Ann. Amer. Acad. Pol. Sci., CCXLVIII
       (March 1955), 170-7.
              Criticizes the colonial education for its lack of vital
       elements and for creating situations that have made equal
       educational opportunities virtually impossible.

1718   "Republic of Ghana." In Martena Sasnett and Inez Sepmeyer.
       Educational systems of Africa.   Berkeley: University of
       California Press, 1966, pp. 385-428.
              Historical, sociological and cultural background; char-
       acteristics of elementary and secondary schools, univer-
       sities and colleges, etc.

1719   Rhodes, K.   "Development in Ghana of higher education in
       Home Economics," J. Home Econ., LIX (April 1967),
       265-70.

1720   Rotimi, B. O.   "Education: early European attempts in West
       Africa," W. Afr. J. Educ., IV, No. 3 (1960), 116-28.

1721   Ruete, T.   "Achimota: Britain's black university," United
       Empire, XX (1929), 630-3.

1722   Rukare, E. H.   "Aspirations for education in the new and
       free nations of Africa," Educ. Leadership, XXVII (Nov.
       1969), 124-8.

1723   Sangster, Ellen Geer.   "Creative writing in schools and
       colleges," Ghana Teachers' J., No. 51 (July 1966), 6-14.

1724   Sarpong, Peter Kwasi.   "What the nation expects from the
       university student," Insight, II (Sept. 1967), 6-14.

1725 Sawyerr, H. "The University in contemporary independent
      West Africa. 1. Its climate--cloister or market place.
      2. Caveats." W. Afr. J. Educ., XII, (Oct. 1968), 191-5;
      XIII (Feb. 1969), 28-32.
      The universities are putting emphasis on the functional
      role of the curricula to enable young graduates to contribute
      to their community.

1726 Scanlon, David G. Church, state and education in Africa.
      New York: Teachers College Press, Columbia University,
      1966. 313 p.

1727 Smith, D. A. "Progress and problems in secondary education
      in Ghana," W. Afr. J. Educ., I (Oct. 1957), 72-3.

1728 Smith, M. Brewster. "An Analysis of two measures of
      'authoritarianism' among Peace Corps teachers," J. Per-
      sonality, XXXIII (1965), 513-35.

1729 _____. "Exploration in competence: a study of Peace
      Corps teachers in Ghana," Amer. Psych., XXI (June 1966),
      555-66.

1730 _____. Peace Corps teachers in Ghana. Final report of
      evaluation of Peace Corps project in Ghana. Berkeley:
      Institute of Human Development, University of California,
      1964. (mimeographed)

1731 _____, et al. "Factorial study of morale among Peace
      Corps teachers in Ghana," J. Soc. Issues, XIX (July 1963),
      10-32.

1732 Stamford-Bewlay, P. "The Role of government technical
      institutes in Ghana," Ghana Teachers' J., (Jan. 1958),
      30-5.

1733 Stejskal, Vaclau. "Children's literature and education,"
      Ghana Teachers' J., No. 52 (Oct. 1966), 47-54.

1734 Strain, W. H. "Problems of educational exchange with English-
      speaking countries of West and East Africa," Coll. Univ.,
      XLI (Winter 1966), 145-61.

1735 Stratmon, David L. "The Ghana educational system," J.
      Negro Educ., XXVIII (Fall 1959), 394-404.

1736 Sullivan, George Edward. The Story of the Peace Corps.
      New York: Fleet Publishing Co., 1964. 160 p.
      The activities of the Peace Corps volunteers in developing
      countries.

1737   Sulton, Francis. "Education and the making of modern na-
       tions, " In James S. Coleman, ed. Education and political
       development. Princeton: Princeton University Press, 1965.
       pp. 51-74.

1738   Taylor, A. "Development of personnel selection in the Insti-
       tute of Education, University of Ghana, " Teacher Educ. , I
       (Feb. 1961), 7-15.

1739   _____, ed. Educational and occupation selection in West
       Africa. London: Oxford University Press, 1962. 232 p.
       The report of a conference at which the process of
       selection in English-speaking countries of West Africa was
       examined by both foreign consultants and West African
       educators.

1740   Tetteh-Lartey, A. C. The Schooldays of Shango Solomon.
       Cambridge: Cambridge University Press, 1965. 79 p.

1741   Textor, Robert. Cultural frontiers of the Peace Corps.
       With a forward by Margaret Mead. Cambridge, Mass. :
       M. I. T. Press, 1966. 363 p.
       American Peace Corps work in thirteen countries
       described by different contributors, each account by an
       authority who has either observed the activities of the
       Peace Corps volunteers in that country or has been in-
       volved in their programs. Contributors include anthro-
       pologists, psychologists, political scientists, and a soci-
       ologist.
            Rev: Amer. Soc. Rev. , XXXI (Dec. 1966), 880.
       Library Quarterly, XXXVI (Oct. 1966), 365.

1742   Theobald, Robert, ed. The New nations of West Africa.
       New York: H. W. Wilson, 1960. 179 p.

1743   The Tradition of Islamic learning in Ghana--checklist of
       Arabic works from Ghana. Legon: Institute of African
       Studies, University of Ghana, 1970.

1744   Trent, Richard D. "Development of psychological tests in
       Ghana: the number sequences and vocabulary tests, "
       Ghana J. Sci. , V (July 1965), 173-80.

1745   _____. "A Study of the self-concepts of Ghanaian children
       utilizing the who-are-you-technique, " Ghana J. Sci. , V
       (April 1965), 78-91.

1745a UNESCO. Final report of the Regional Conference on the
       Planning and Organization of Literacy Programmes in
       Africa. Paris: UNESCO, 1964. (Conference documents
       and reports, ED/203.)

1746   University, college and day nursery finder: list of all uni-
        versities, colleges, and day nurseries in Ghana.   Accra:
        Advancing, Co. , 1967.   40 p.

1747   "The University of Ghana, " Univ. Rev. , XXXIV (Feb. 1962),
        52-8.
            Historical development of the university; political impact
        upon it; the relationships between educated elites and the
        politicians, etc.

1748   Vlach, John M. "Father Bacchus and other vandals: folklore
        at the University of Ghana, " Western Folklore, XXX, No. 1
        (1971), 33-44.
            Description of the folklore and rituals of Commonwealth
        Hall at the University of Ghana, the history of this tradition
        dating back to 1958 when the young male students assigned
        to the Hall began referring to themselves as "vandals. "

1749   Wakely, Patrick I. Development of a primary school building
        system for Ghana.   Kumasi: Faculty of Architecture,
        University of Science and Technology, 1968.   1 v. (Occa-
        sional report, No. 11.)

1750   Wallbank, T. W. "Achimota College and Educational objectives
        in Africa. " J. Negro Educ. , IV (1935), 230-45.

1751   Ward, Barbara. Five ideas that changed the world.   London:
        Hamilton for the University College of Ghana, 1959.   143 p.
        (Aggrey-Fraser-Guggisberg lectures.)

1752   Ward, William Ernest. "The Early days of Achimota, " W.
        Afr. J. Educ. , IX (Oct. 1965), 125-8.

1753   _____ . Educating young nations.   London: Allen and
        Unwin, 1959.   194 p.

1754   _____ . Fraser of Trinity and Achimota.   Legon: Ghana
        Universities Press, 1965.   328 p.

1755   Watts, Margaret. The New generation.   Accra: Ghana
        Association of Teachers of English, 1970.

1756   Weaver, H. D. "Black African educational needs and the
        Soviet response, " The Record (New York), LXXI (May 1970),
        613-28.

1757   West African Journal of Education, VIII (June 1964).
            The entire issue is devoted to discussion of school
        examinations and syllabuses in English-speaking West Africa.

1758   Widstrand, C. G. , ed. Development and adult education in
        Africa.   Uppsala: Scandinavian Institute of African Studies,
        1965.   97 p.

1758a Wilks, Ivor. "The Transmission of Islamic learning in the
       Western Sudan." In John Rankine Goody, ed. Literacy in
       traditional societies. Cambridge: Cambridge University
       Press, 1968, pp. 161-97.
             The Western Sudan comprises Mali, Guinea, the Upper
       Volta, the Ivory Coast and Ghana. The article is based
       upon a fieldwork conducted between 1959 and 1966, largely
       sponsored by the Institute of African Studies, University of
       Ghana.

1759   Williams, Chancellor. "Educational obstacles to Africaniza-
       tion in Ghana, Nigeria, and Sierra Leone," J. Negro Educ.,
       XXX, No. 3 (1961), 261-5.

1760   Williams, Charles Kingsley. Achimota: the early years,
       1924-1948. Accra: Longmans, 1962. 158 p.

1761   Williams, T. D. "Educational development in Ghana and
       Guatemala: some problems in estimating levels of educa-
       tional growth," Comp. Educ. Rev., X (Oct. 1966), 462-9.

1762   _____. "Sir Gordon Guggisberg and educational reform
       in the Gold Coast, 1919-1927," Comp. Educ. Rev., VIII
       (Dec. 1964), 290-306.

1763   _____. "Some economic implications of the education
       explosion in Ghana," World Year Bk. Educ. (1965), 479-
       94.

1764   Williamson, S. G. "Missions and education in the Gold
       Coast," Int. Rev. Missions, XLI (July 1952), 364-73.

1765   Wilson, John. Education and changing West African culture.
       London: Oxford University Press, 1966. 130 p.
             History of education in English-speaking West Africa,
       1923-1960, emphasizing the need for qualified teachers to
       help create a truly African educational system.

1766   Wise, Colin G. History of education in British West Africa.
       London: Longmans, 1956. 134 p.

1767   Wolf, W. Untersuchung über Schüler und Unterrichtsmittel
       in Ghana. Berlin, 1966. 137 p.

1768   Wyllie, R. W. "Ghanaian university students: a research
       note," Brit. J. Soc., XVII (Sept. 1966), 306-11.

1769   _____. "The New Ghanaian teacher and his profession,"
       W. Afr. J. Educ., VIII, No. 3 (1964), 171-6.

1770   Yankah, J. T. N. "The Gold Coast Teachers' Union," Gold
       Coast Teachers' J., III (Dec. 1955), 18-23.

1771 Zeitlin, Arnold. To the Peace Corps with love. Garden
      City, New York: Doubleday, 1965. 351 p.
      Recounts the experiences of an American Peace Corps
      teacher in Ghana.

(7) GEOGRAPHY AND TRAVEL--GEOGRAPHY

1772 Abell, Hellen C. Farm radio forum project--Ghana, 1964-5.
      Waterloo, Ontario: Dept. of Geography, University of Water-
      loo, 1965. 179 p.

1773 Ackah, C. A. West Africa: a general certificate geography.
      2nd ed. London: University of London Press, 1966. 224 p.
      1st ed. 1958.

1774 Adams, David Thickens. An Elementary geography of the
      Gold Coast. 3rd ed. London: University of London Press,
      1941. 240 p.
      Written for elementary and secondary schools, it surveys
      physical, sociological and economic aspects of the Gold
      Coast.

1775 _____. A Ghana geography. New ed. London: University
      of London Press, 1960. 192 p.
      A revision of A Gold Coast geography (1951).

1776 Affran, Dan Kojo. "Cassava and its economic importance,"
      Ghana Farmer, XII (Nov. 1968), 172-8.

1777 Amoah, F. E. "Accra: a study of the development of a West Afri-
      can city," Master's Thesis, University of Ghana, 1964. 197 p.

1778 Anang, J. L. New era geographies for Ghana, Book 3. Lon-
      don: Macmillan, 1966. 143 p.

1779 _____ and J. B. Hampshire. Ghana for middle schools.
      London: Evans, 1960. 106 p. (Geography for Ghanaian
      Schools series.)

1780 Andah, E. "The Need for agricultural marketing training in
      Ghana," Paper presented at the Seminar on Training in
      Agricultural Marketing, Berlin, Germany, 22 Jan. - 3 Feb.,
      1968. 15 p.

1781 Anipa, Seth Emmanuel. "Settlement pattern in regional
      planning," Master's Thesis, University of Science and
      Technology, Kumasi, 1967. 76 p.

1782 Baiden-Amissah, J.   "The Volta River Project and Tamale:
      a study of the implications for Tamale and its environs,"
      Master's Thesis, University of Science and Technology,
      1967.   33 p.

1783 Bannerman, Joseph Ebao.   "Problems of transportation in
      regional planning in Ghana: Central Region," Master's
      Thesis, University of Science and Technology, Kumasi,
      1967.   135 p.

1784 Barbour, K. M.   Population in Africa; a geographical approach:
      an inaugural lecture delivered at the University of Ibadan
      on 12 March 1963.   Ibadan: Ibadan University Press, 1966.
      40 p.
      The author is former Head of the Geography Dept.,
      University of Ibadan.

1785 Benneh, George.   "Land tenure and farming system in
      Nkrankwanta," Bull. Ghana Geogr. Assoc., X (July 1965),
      6-15.

1786 _____.   "The Role of agricultural geography in the economic
      development of Ghana," Bull. Ghana Geogr. Assoc., XII
      (1967),   51-64.

1787 Biaku, C. Y.   "Kpandu district: a study of settlements and
      land use," Master's Thesis, University of Science and
      Technology, Kumasi, 1966.   114 p.

1788 Boaten, K.   "A Historical geography of Northern Asante,"
      Master's Thesis, University of Ghana, 1969.

1789 Boateng, E. A.   "The Evolution of the political map of the
      Gold Coast," Bull. Ghana Geogr. Assoc., I (July 1956),
      16-19.

1790 _____.   A Geography of Ghana.   2nd ed.   Cambridge:
      Cambridge University Press, 1966.   212 p.   1st ed. 1959.
      Designed for School Certificate and University students.
      Rev: Geogr. J., CXXXIII (June 1967), 233.

1791 _____.   "Ghana Geographical Association: a review of the
      first seven years," Bull. Ghana Geogr. Assoc., VIII (Jan.
      1963), 3-10.

1792 _____.   Ghana junior atlas.   London: Nelson, 1966.   33 p.

1793 _____.   "The Growth and functions of Accra," Bull.
      Ghana Geogr. Assoc., IV (July 1959), 4-15.

1794 _____.   "Land use and population in the first zone of Ghana,"
      Bull. Ghana Geogr. Assoc., VII (Jan. /July 1962), 14-20.

1795 _____ . "Problems of settlement study in the Gold Coast,"
Bull. Ghana Geogr. Assoc., I, No. 1 (1956), 10-12.

1796 _____ . "Recent changes in settlement in Southeast Gold
Coast," Trans. Inst. Brit. Geogr., XXI (1955), 157-69.

1797 _____ . "Some geographical aspects of the 1960 population census of Ghana," Bull. Ghana Geogr. Assoc., V
(July 1960), 2-8.

1798 _____ . "The Volta River Project: report of the Preparatory Commission," Bull. Ghana Geogr. Assoc., II (Jan.
1957), 27-9.

1798a Brand, R. R. A Selected bibliography of Accra, Ghana, a
West African colonial city (1877-1960). Monticello, Ill.:
Council of Planning Librarians, 1970. 27 p.

1799 British West African Meteorological Services. Frequencies
of temperature and dew point on specific ranges at airports
in Nigeria, Gold Coast and Sierra Leone. Lagos: Survey
Dept., 1953.

1800 Buchanan, Keith. "Review of West Africa by R. J. R. Church,"
Econ. Geogr., XXXIV (July 1958), 277-8.
The 6th edition of the book was published in 1968.

1801 _____ . "The Towns of West Africa," Geogr. Rev., XLII
(Jan. 1952), 141-3.

1802 Caldwell, John C. African rural-urban migration: the move-
ment to Ghana's towns. New York: Columbia University
Press, 1969. 257 p.
Examines the kinds of people migrating to towns or
rural areas; the effects of such migration; methods of
travel; their reasons for doing so.
Rev: Ann. Amer. Acad. Pol. Soc. Sci., CCCXCI
(Sept. 1970), 222.

1803 _____ . "Determinants of rural-urban migration in Ghana,"
Pop. Stud., XXII, No. 3 (1968), 361-77.

1804 _____ and Chukuka Okonjo, eds. The Population of tropical
Africa. New York: Columbia University Press, 1968.
457 p.
Rev: Amer. Anthrop., LXXI (April 1969), 377. Amer.
Soc. Rev., XXXIV (April 1969), 298.

1805 Cann, G. L. "Some problems of geographical research for
regional planning in Ghana: a case of Central Region,"
Master's Thesis, University of Science and Technology,
Kumasi, 1967. 102 p.

1806   Chorley, R. J. and P. Haggett, eds. Frontiers in geograph-
       ical teaching. London: Methuen, 1965. 378 p.
             Rev: Nigerian Geogr. J., IX (Dec. 1966), 175-6.

1807   Church, Ronald James. "The Case for colonial geography,"
       Trans. Inst. Brit. Geogr., XIV (1948), 15-25.

1808   _____. "A Geographical agenda for Ghana," Bull. Ghana
       Geogr. Assoc., IV (Jan. 1959), 9-13.

1809   _____. Some geographical aspects of West African de-
       velopment: an inaugural lecture. London: Bell, 1966.
       40 p.
             The author, long associated with West Africa, is a
       Professor of Geography at the London School of Economics.
             Rev: Nigerian Geogr. J., IX (Dec. 1966), 170-1.

1810   _____. West Africa: a study of the environment and of
       man's use of it. 6th ed. New York: Longmans, 1968.
       543 p. (Geographies for advanced study.)
             Rev: Econ. Geogr., XXXIV (July 1958), 277-8.

1811   Cochraine, T. W. Preliminary bibliography of the Volta River
       Authority Programme. Accra: Volta River Authority, 1968.
       36 p. (mimeographed)

1812   Cofie, J. "The Desert of Gofan: was it ever densely in-
       habited?" Ghana Notes and Queries, No. 5 (1963), 10-15.

1813   Collins-Longmans Pathfinder atlas for West Africa. Edited
       by K. H. Huggins, et al. 6th ed. rev. and enl. Glasgow:
       Collins, 1956. 56 p.
             Physical, climatological, vegetation, economic, popula-
       tion, etc.

1814   Crosbie, A. J. "The Soils of the closed forest zone of
       Ghana," Doctoral Dissertation, Edinburgh University, 1965/
       66.

1815   Curnow, I. J. "Progress of topographic mapping in the Gold
       Coast," Scottish Geogr. Mag. (March 1927), 91-7.

1816   Dallimore, H. A Geography of West Africa, with special
       reference to the colonies of British West Africa as re-
       quired by the educational codes of the colonies of West
       Africa. 3rd ed. rev. London: United Society for
       Christian Literature, 1949. 113 p.

1817   Darkoh, M. B. "A Historical geography of the Ho-Kpando-
       Buem area of the Volta Region," Master's Thesis, Univer-
       sity of Ghana, 1966.

1818 _____. "Togoland under the Germans: thirty years of economic development (1884-1914), Part 1," Nigerian Geogr. J., X (Dec. 1967), 107-22.

1819 Darko, S. A. "The Changing patterns of settlement in the mining areas of Ghana," Master's Thesis, London University, 1962/63.

1820 _____. "The Effects of modern mining on settlements in the mining areas of Ghana," Bull. Ghana Geogr. Assoc., VIII (Jan. 1963), 21-31.

1821 Dickson, Kwamina B. "Ashanti and the evolution of human geography of Ghana," Bull. Ghana Geogr. Assoc., XII (1967), 23-24.

1822 _____. "Development of the copra industry in Ghana," J. Trop. Geogr., XIX (Dec. 1964), 27-34.

1823 _____. "Evolution of seaports in Ghana, 1800-1928," Ann. Assoc. Amer. Geogr., LV (March 1964), 98-111.

1824 _____. A Historical geography of Ghana. Cambridge: Cambridge University Press, 1969. 379 p.
One of the few books on the subject by a Ghanaian geographer.
Rev: Africa, XLI (Jan. 1971), 78. Nigerian Geogr. J., XIII (June 1970), 99-100.

1825 _____. "Historical geography in West Africa," Bull. Ghana Geogr. Assoc., VIII (Jan. 1963), 11-20.

1826 Duru, R. C. "The Scale factor in the population mapping of West Africa," Nigerian Geogr. J., VII (June 1964), 16-23.

1827 Effah, E. "Pedestrians in Kumasi city centre," Master's Thesis, University of Science and Technology, Kumasi, 1967. 73 p.

1828 Engmann, E. V. "Population movements in Ghana: a study of internal migration and its implication for the planner," Bull. Ghana Geogr. Assoc., X (Jan. 1965), 41-65.

1829 Fagerlund, V. G. and R. H. Smith. "A Preliminary map of market periodicities in Ghana," J. Dev. Areas (April 1970), 333-47.

1830 Forde, Daryll. "The Cultural map of West Africa: successive adaptations to tropical forests and grasslands," Trans. N. Y. Acad. Sci., XV (April 1953), 206-19.

1831   Forde, Enid Rosamund. The Populations of Ghana: a study
        of the spatial relationship of its socio-cultural and economic
        characteristics. Evanston: Dept. of Geography, North-
        western University, 1968. 154 p. (Studies in geography,
        No. 15.)
            Originally submitted as doctoral dissertation, North-
        western University, 1967.

1832   Fortes, Meyer. "Human ecology in West Africa, " African
        Affairs, XLIV (Jan. 1945), 27-31.

1833   _____, et al. "Ashanti survey: 1945-46; an experiment
        in social research, " Geogr. J. , CX (Oct. /Dec. 1947),
        149-79.

1834   Gaisie, S. K. "An Analysis of fertility levels and differentials
        in contemporary Ghana, " Master's Thesis, London Univer-
        sity, 1963 /64.

1835   _____. Dynamics of population growth in Ghana. Legon:
        Ghana Universities Press, 1969. 118 p.

1836   _____. "Estimation of vital rates for Ghana, " Pop. Stud. ,
        XXIII (March 1969), 21-42.
            Ghana's fertility rate considered one of the highest in
        the world.

1837   _____. "Some aspects of fertility studies in Ghana, "
        In J. C. Caldwell and C. Okonjo, eds. The Population of
        tropical Africa. London, 1969, pp. 238-46.

1838   Gamble, D. P. "Urbanization in West Africa, " The Bulletin
        (Freetown, Sierra Leone), Nos. 7-8 (1964), 7-8.

1839   Garnier, B. J. "Maps of water balance in West Africa, "
        Bull. IFAN (A), XII (1960), 709-22.

1840   Gautier, E. F. L'Afrique noire occidentale: esquisse des
        cadres géographiques. 2nd éd. Paris: Larose, 1943.
        188 p.

1841   Gbeckor-Kove, N. A. "Soil temperatures and weather con-
        ditions in Accra, " Ghana J. Sci. , V (Oct. 1965), 191-220.

1842   Ghana. Information Services. Ghana at a glance. 4th ed.
        Accra: State Publishing Corp. , 1967. 90 p.

1843   _____. Ghana main towns and cities. Accra, 1965. 64 p.

1844   _____. Ghana's new town and harbour: Tema. Accra,
        1961. 52 p.
            Describes the chief features of the new harbour town.

1845   . A Guide to Accra. Accra, 1962. 59 p.

1846 Ghana. People and Cities Workshop. Description of Accra
     Metropolitan area of Ghana. Accra, 1967. 6 p. (Type-
     script)

1847 Ghana atlas, specially compiled and produced for use in
     Ghanaian schools with 19 maps of Ghana. Glasgow: Col-
     lins-Longmans, 1963.

1848 Gilbert, D. A. The Teshi settlement of Accra plains. Legon:
     Institute of African Studies, University of Ghana, 1970.

1849 Gleave, M. B. and H. P. White. "Population density and
     agricultural systems in West Africa." In M. F. Thomas
     and G. W. Whittington, eds. Environment and land-use in
     Africa. London: Methuen, 1969, pp. 273-300.

1850 Glover, B. K. "The Savanna landforms of the Accra plains,"
     Master's Thesis, University of Ghana, 1966.

1851 Goble, P. L. "A Geographical study of the development of
     British West Africa in relation to modern economic needs,"
     Master's Thesis, University of Wales, 1953/54.

1852 Gold Coast. Survey Dept. Atlas of the Gold Coast. Accra,
     1949.
          No text. Colored maps indicating various administrative
     areas, population and tribal distribution, languages, min-
     eral deposits, rainfall, agricultural products, etc.

1853 Goodall, George, ed. The Pictorial atlas for West Africa.
     Lagos: C. M. S. Bookshop, 1951.
          Physical, climatological, vegetation, population, agri-
     cultural, tribal, etc.

1854   , ed. The West African atlas. Port Harcourt,
     Nigeria: C. M. S. Bookshop, 1950. 24 p.

1855 Gould, Peter R. The Development of the transportation pat-
     tern in Ghana. Evanston: Dept. of Geography, North-
     western University, 1960. 163 p. (Studies in geography,
     No. 5.)
          Doctoral dissertation, 1960.

1856   . "Man against his environment: a game theoretic
     framework," Ann. Assoc. Amer. Geogr., LIII (Sept. 1963),
     290-7.

1857 Great Britain. Admiralty. Hydrographic Dept. Africa
     pilot. Vol. I: West Coast of Africa. 11th ed. London:
     H. M. S. O., 1953. 515 p.

1858   Great Britain.   Meteorological Office.   A Pilot's primer of
       the West African weather.   London, 1944.

1859   _____ .   Weather on the West Coast of tropical Africa.
       London: H. M. S. O. , 1949.   281 p.

1860   Grove, David.   Population patterns: their impact on re-
       gional planning.   A preliminary analysis of the 1960 census
       of Ghana.   Kumasi: K. N. U. S. T. , 1963.   48 p.

1861   _____ and Laszlo Huszar.   The Towns of Ghana: the role
       of service centres in regional planning.   London: Oxford
       University Press, 1965.   128 p.   (Planning research
       studies, No. 2.)
       Rev: Geogr. J. , CXXXII (March 1966),   111.

1862   Grove, J. M.   "Some aspects of the economy of the Volta
       Delta, "   Bull. IFAN (B),   XXVIII (1966),   381-432.

1863   Gwasi-Twum, K.   "Ghana, Gold Coast or Cocoa Coast, "
       The Bulletin (Freetown, Sierra Leone), No. 3 (1959), 6-
       15.

1864   Hamdan, G.   "Capitals of the new Africa, "   Econ. Geogr. ,
       XL (July 1964),   239-53.

1865   Havinden, M. A.   The History of crop cultivation in West
       Africa: a bibliographical guide.   Exeter: Dept. of
       Economic History, University of Exeter, 1970.   20 p.
       Surveys the published literature in English and French
       dealing with the history of crop cultivation in West Africa.
       Divided into 3 periods.   (1) Origins of the crops.
       (2) Diffusion of the crops from Malaysia and America be-
       fore 1800.   (3) Rise of export staples from about 1800 to
       the present day.

1866   Hayward, D. H.   "On the pattern of the Weija gap, "   Bull.
       Ghana Geogr. Assoc. ,   XII (1967),   35-50.

1867   Higson, F. G.   A Certificate geography of West Africa.   Lon-
       don: Longmans, 1961.   223 p.

1868   Hilling, D.   Development of the Ghanaian post system.   Lon-
       don: Dept. of Geography, University of London, 1969?
       350 p.
       Evolution of the postal system studied as an important
       factor in the development of Ghana's economy and trans-
       portation system.

1869   _____ and B. S. Hoyle, eds.   Seaports and development in
       tropical Africa.   London: Macmillan, 1970.   272 p.

1870 Hilton, Thomas E. "The Coastal fisheries of Ghana,"
      Bull. Ghana Geogr. Assoc., IX (July 1964), 34-51. Also
      in Oriental Geogr. (Dacca), VIII (Jan. 1964), 61-78.

1871 _____. Demographic maps of West Africa. Dakar:
      IFAN, 1967.
      Maps of population density and urban distribution.

1872 _____. The Distribution and density of population in
      Ghana. Legon: Ghana Universities Press, 1968. 60 p.

1873 _____. Ghana population atlas: the distribution and
      density of population in the Gold Coast and Togoland under
      United Kingdom. Edinburgh: Nelson, 1960. 40 p.
      Text accompanied by detailed map of population distribu-
      tions and densities, birthplaces, migration, occupations,
      etc.

1874 _____. "Land planning and resettlement in Northern
      Ghana," Geography, XLIV (1959), 227-40.

1875 _____. "Landforms in North-eastern Ghana," Geogr. J.,
      CXXVII (Dec. 1961), 560-2.

1876 _____. "Population mapping in Ghana." In K. M. Bar-
      bour and R. M. Prothero, eds. Essays on African popula-
      tion. New York: Praeger, 1961, pp. 83-98.

1877 _____. Practical geography in Africa. 2nd ed. London:
      Longmans, 1964. 352 p. 1st ed. 1961.

1878 _____. "River captures in Ghana," Bull. Ghana Geogr.
      Assoc., IX (Jan. 1964), 13-24.

1879 _____. "The Settlement pattern of the Accra plains,"
      Geography, LV (July 1970), 289-306.

1880 Holzer, Jerry. "The Seasonality of vital events in selected
      cities of Ghana: an analysis of registration data relating
      to the period, 1956-1960." In John C. Caldwell and
      Chukuka Okonjo, eds. The Population of tropical Africa.
      New York: Columbia University Press, 1968, pp. 225-33.

1881 Hulman, Diana. Ghana (Avec 36 dispositives). Lausanne:
      Editions rencontre. 1964. 103 p. (Coll. Bibliovision
      rencontres Sér. Le livre d'images du monde, 9.)

1882 Hunter, John M. "Akotuakrom: a case study of a devastated
      cocoa village in Ghana," Trans. Inst. Brit. Geogr., No.
      29 (1961), 161-86.

1883 _____ . "Cocoa migration and patterns of land ownership in the Densu Valley, near Suhum, Ghana," Trans. Inst. Brit. Geogr., No. 33 (Dec. 1963), 61-87.

1884 _____ . "An Exercise in applied geography, geographical planning in urban areas for the 1960 census of Ghana," Geography, XLVI (Jan. 1961), 1-8.

1885 _____ . "Geography and development planning in elementary education in Ghana," Bull. Ghana Geogr. Assoc., IX (Jan. 1964), 55-64.

1886 _____ . "Morphology of a bauxite summit in Ghana," Geogr. J., CXXVII (Dec. 1961), 469-76.

1887 _____ . "A Note on the post-enumeration uses of the 1960 population census enumeration area maps of Ghana," Bull. Ghana Geogr. Assoc., VIII (July 1963), 27-32.

1888 _____ . "Population pressure in a part of the West African savanna: a study of Nangodi, Northeast Ghana," Ann. Assoc. Amer. Geogr., LVII, No. 1 (1967), 101-14.

1889 _____ . "The Social roots of dispersed settlement in Northern Ghana," Ann. Assoc. Amer. Geogr., LVII, No. 2 (1967), 338-49.

1890 _____ . "Transformation of rural communities in Africa," Geogr. Rev., LVII (Oct. 1967), 565-7.

1891 _____ and D. F. Hayward. "Towards a model of scarp retreat and drainage evolution: evidence from Ghana," Geogr. J., CXXXVII (March 1971), 51-68.

1892 Hutchinson, J. "Land and human populations," Adv. Sci., CXXIII (1966), 241-54.

1892a Iloeje, Nwadilibe P. A New geography of West Africa. Harlow, Eng.: Longmans, 1972. 176 p.

1893 Jarrett, Harold Reginald. A Geography of West Africa, including the French territories, Portuguese Guinea and Liberia. New ed. London: Dent, 1957. 173 p. 1st ed. 1956.

1894 _____ . Physical geography for West Africa. London: Longmans, 1958. 146 p.

1895 Jennings, J. H. Elementary map interpretations based on maps of Nigeria, Ghana and Sierra Leone. Cambridge: Cambridge University Press, 1960. 62 p.

1896 Jopp, Keith. Tema: Ghana's new town and harbour. Accra:
      Ministry of Information and Broadcasting, 1961. 52 p.

1897 Kimble, George. Ghana. Prepared with the cooperation of
      the American Geographical Society. Garden City, New
      York: Doubleday, 1965. 64 p.

1898 Kirchherr, E. C. "Some notes on the study of settlement
      geography in Ghana," Bull. Ghana Geogr. Assoc., VIII
      (July 1963), 12-16.

1899 Kpedepko, G. M. K. "Working life tables for males in Ghana,"
      J. Amer. Stat. Assoc., LXIV (March 1969), 102-10.

1900 Kuczynski, R. R. A Demographic survey of the British
      colonial Empire. Vol. 1: West Africa. London: Oxford
      University Press, 1948. 821 p.

1901 Kuivi, P. Y. "Coastal morphology of Accra to Ada," Master's
      Thesis, University of Ghana, 1968.

1902 La-Anyane, S. "Distribution of the oil palm in West Africa,"
      Legon J. Agric., I (March 1968), 47-56.

1903 Lawson, Rowena M. "The Transition of Ghana's fishing from
      a primitive to a mechanized industry," Trans. Hist. Soc.
      Ghana, IX (1968), 90-104.

1904 Lee, Douglas Harry. Climate and economic development in
      the tropics. New York: Harper for the Council on Foreign
      Relations, 1957. 182 p.
      Rev: Nigerian Geogr. J., V (June 1962), 65.

1905 McCall, D. F. "The Koforidua market." In Paul Bohannan
      and G. Dalton, eds. Markets in Africa. Evanston: North-
      western University Press, 1962, pp. 667-97.

1906 McNulty, Michael L. "Urban centers and spatial patterns of
      development in Ghana," Doctoral Dissertation, Northwestern
      University, 1966.

1907 _____. "Urban structure and development: the urban system
      of Ghana," Paper presented at the Second International
      Congress of Africanists on Scientific Research in Aid to
      Africa, University of Dakar, Senegal, December 1967.
      38 p.

1908 Manshard, W. Die geographischen Grundlagen der Wirtschaft
      Ghanas. Wiesbaden: Steiner, 1961. 308 p. (Beiträge zur
      Landerkunde Afrikas, H. 1.)

1909 _____. "Die Stadt Kumasi. Stadt und Umland in ihren

funktionalen Beziehungen," Erdkunde (Bonn), XV (Sept.
1961), 161-79.

1910   Mante, E. F. G. and E. J. Khan.   "Preliminary studies of
the irrigation requirement for cotton in the Northern Accra
plains," Legon J. Agric., I (March 1968), 24-35.

1911   Mellor, M.   A Practical modern geography.   Book 3:   West
Africa.   4th ed.   London: Oxford University Press, 1957.
120 p.

1912   Mensah, P. J.   "The Population and settlement in the Ada
District of Ghana," Master's Thesis, University of Ghana,
1966.

1913   Migeod, Frederick.   "The Gold Coast: its physical features,
flora, fauna and ethnology," J. Afr. Soc., XIII (July 1914),
369-84.

1914   Morgan, W. B.   "Food imports of West Africa," Econ. Geogr.,
XXXIX (Oct. 1963), 351-62.

1915   _____.   "The Forest and agriculture in West Africa,"
J. Afr. Hist., III (1962), 235-9.

1916   Munger, E. S.   "Social problems in the Gold Coast," Geogr.
Rev., XLII (Dec. 1952), 658-9.

1917   Musgrove, F.   "The Place of geography in African education,"
Geography, XXXVII (1952), 71-8.

1918   Niven, Cecil R.   The Land and people of West Africa.
London: Black, 1958.   84 p.

1919   Nsiah, M. E. K.   "Suitable areas for location of mail-scale
manufacturing industries: Ashanti/Brong Ahafo," Master's
Thesis, University of Science and Technology, Kumasi,
1965.   112 p.

1920   Nyarko, K. A.   "The Development of Kumasi," Bull. Ghana
Geogr. Assoc., IV (Jan. 1959), 3-8.

1921   Oboli, Herbert Oguejiofo.   An Outline geography of West
Africa.   With editorial assistance from R. J. Harrison
Church.   6th ed. rev.   London: Harrap, 1969.   224 p.
1st ed. 1957.

1922   O'Connor, Anthony Michael.   The Changing geography of
tropical Africa.   Oxford: Pergamon Press, 1969.
Examines the principal changes in the geography of
tropical Africa in the period, 1956-1968, with particular
attention to the geographical pattern of recent and current
economic development.

1923 _____ . A Geography of tropical African development.
Oxford: Pergamon Press, 1971. 207 p. (Pergamon Oxford geographies.)

1924 Ogunsheye, F. A. "Maps of Africa--1500-1800: a bibliographic essay," Nigerian Geogr. J., VII (June 1964), 34-
42.
"Intended to cover sources for all maps, charts, plans
and sketches of Africa and of its parts, that are in single
sheets or sketches used to illustrate travel and exploration
accounts." The author is Professor of Librarianship,
University of Ibadan, Nigeria.

1925 Ojo, Gabriel Jimoh. "Geographical problems of land use in
West Africa," Master's Thesis, National University of
Ireland, 1957/58.

1926 _____ . Geography--Book two: objective questions in
School Certificate and G. C. E. Ordinary Level. Lagos:
Macmillan, 1969. 182 p.

1927 _____ . "The New West African School Certificate geography syllabus," Nigerian Geogr. J., VII (June 1964), 47-
53.

1928 Okorafor, Apia Ekpe. "Africa's population problems," Africa
Report, XV (June 1970), 22-3.

1929 _____ . "Demographic characteristics of Ghana and Uganda,"
Doctoral Dissertation, University of Chicago, 1969. 194 p.

1930 Omaboe, E. N. "Estimating the population in Ghana." Econ.
Bull. Ghana, III, No. 3 (1959), 3-12.

1931 Opoku-Afriyie, Yaw. "Rural-urban migration as a problem of
regional planning," Master's Thesis, University of Science
and Technology, Kumasi, 1969. 179 p.

1932 Pedler, F. J. Economic geography of West Africa. London:
Longmans, 1955. 232 p.

1933 _____ . West Africa. 2nd ed. London: Methuen, 1959.
233 p.

1934 Philip's new age atlas for West Africa. Edited by Harold
Eullard. 4th ed. London: George Philip, 1960. 32 p.

1935 Pool, D. I. "A Note on a demographic sample survey for
the study of factors affecting fertility in Ghana," Africa,
XXXVII (July 1967), 327-34.

1936   Prothero, R. M.   "Population movement in West Africa, "
       Geogr. Rev. , XLVII (July 1957), 434-7.

1937   _____.   "Post-war West African censuses. "   In K. M. Bar-
       bour and R. M. Prothero, eds.   Essays on African popula-
       tion.   London: Routledge & Kegan Paul, 1961, pp. 7-16.

1938   Pugh, J. C. and A. E.   Perry.   A Shorter geography of West
       Africa.   London: University of London Press, 1961.   288 p.

1939   Quinn-Young, Charles T.   Handbook for geography teachers
       in West Africa.   London: Evans, 1960.   272 p.

1940   Republic of Ghana.   Population planning for national pro-
       gress and prosperity.   Ghana population policy.   Accra-
       Tema: Ghana Publishing Corp. , 1969.

1941   Riley, Bernard W.   "Human ecology and geographic viability:
       two case studies from Africa: Ghana and Zambia, " Doc-
       toral Dissertation, Indiana University, 1967.   351 p.

1942   The Shell Company of Ghana Ltd.   Road map of Ghana.
       Accra, 1962.

1943   Simms, Ruth.   Urbanization in West Africa: a review of
       the literature.   Evanston: Northwestern University Press,
       1965.   109 p.
       A revision of the author's master's thesis.

1944   Sircar, P. K.   "Ghana and the Volta Project, " Geogr. Rev.
       India, XXIII (June 1961), 9-18.

1945   Smith, Stanton R.   "Outline programme for hydro-electric
       development in West Africa to 1980. "   In W. M.   Warren and
       N. Rubin, eds.   Dams in Africa: an interdisciplinary study
       of man-made lakes in Africa.   London: Cass, 1968, pp.
       158-88.

1946   Steel, R. W.   "The Population of Ashanti: a geographic
       analysis, " Geog. J. , CXII (July/Sept. 1948), 64-77.

1947   Sterling Editors.   Ghana in pictures.   New York: Sterling,
       1965.   (Visual geography series.)

1948   Taaffe, E. J. , et al.   "Transport expansion in underdeveloped
       countries: a comparative analysis, " Geogr. Rev. , LIII
       (Oct. 1963), 503-29.

1949   Tamakloe, Alexander A.   "Population and land use in the
       Southeastern sandbar, " Master's Thesis, University of
       Science and Technology, Kumasi, 1967.   70 p.

1950   Thomas, Benjamin E.   "The Location of West African cities, "
       In Hilda Kuper, ed.   Urbanization and migration in West
       Africa.   Berkeley: University of California Press, 1963,
       pp. 23-38.

1951   Turton-Hart, Francis.   "The Growth of West African in-
       dustry, " African Affairs, LXV, No. 261 (1966), 281-8.
       Chiefly on Nigeria and Ghana.

1952   U. S. Board on Geographic Names.   Ghana: Official standard
       names approved by the U. S. Board on Geographic Names.
       Washington, D. C.:   U. S. Govt. Printing Office, 1967.
       282 p.

1953   Varley, William and H. P. White.   The Geography of Ghana.
       London: Longmans, 1958.   313 p.

1954   Weigend, Guido Gustav.   "Some elements in the study of
       port geography, " Geog. Rev. , XLVIII (April 1958), 185-
       200.

1955   Whetham, Edith H. and Jean Currie, eds.   Readings in the
       applied economics of Africa: I: microeconomics.   Cam-
       bridge: Cambridge University Press, 1967.   216 p.
       A collection of 18 papers on the use of resources in
       agriculture and industry, prices and markets.   Includes
       "The Markets for foods in Ghana, " by R. M. Lawson.

1956   White, H. P.   "Mechanised cultivation of present holdings in
       West Africa, " Geography, XLIII (1958), 269-70.

1957   _____ .   "Port development on the Gold Coast, " Scottish
       Geogr. Mag. , LXXI (Dec. 1955), 170-3.

1958   _____ .   "Provisional agricultural regions of Ghana, "
       Malayan J. Trop. Geogr. , II (1958), 90-0.

1959   _____ and M. B. Gleave.   An Economic geography of West
       Africa.   London: Bell, 1971.   322 p.

1960   Wise, C. G.   "Climatic anomalities on the Accra plain--a
       summary, " Geography, XXIX (1944), 35-8.

(7)   GEOGRAPHY--TRAVELS AND EXPLORATIONS

1961   Anderson, Rosa Claudette.   River, face homeward (Sutan dan
       wani hwe fie): an Afro-American in Ghana.   New York:
       Exposition Press, 1966.   120 p.

1962   Bowdich, Thomas Edward.   Mission from Cape Coast Castle
       to Ashantee.   Edited with notes and an introduction by

William E. Ward. London: Cape, 1966. 512 p.

1963 Bradley, Kenneth. Once a District Officer. London: Macmillan, 1966. 210 p.
Experiences of a British colonial official in various
African countries, including the Gold Coast, where he
served for two years as Under-Secretary.
Rev: Listener (June 16, 1966), 879. TLS (April 28,
1966), 363.

1964 Cadbury, L. J. "Romance of the Gold Coast, " Geogr.
Magazine (July 1937), 153-68.

1965 Campbell, Alexander. The Heart of Africa. London: Long-
mans, Green, 1954. 470 p.
Describes his visits to the Gold Coast, Nigeria, the
Belgian Congo, Portuguese Africa, Kenya, etc.

1966 Cardinall, Allan Wolsey. In Ashanti and beyond: a record
of a resident magistrate's many years in tropical Africa,
his arduous and dangerous treks both in the course of his
duty and in pursuit of big game, with descriptions of the
people, their manner of living and the wonderful ways of
beasts and insects. London: Seeley, 1927. 288 p.
A leisured but anecdotal description of life in the Gold
Coast by the Resident District Commissioner.
Rev: Nation and Athenaeum, XL (Feb. 26, 1927), 734.
Nature, CXX (Dec. 10, 1927), 837.

1967 Chapman, Eddie. Free Agent: being the further adventures
of Eddie Chapman. London: Wingate, 1955. 223 p.

1968 Clarke, John Heinrik. "Third class on the blue train to
Kumasi, " Phylon, XXIII (Fall 1962), 294-301.
A fascinating story of the author's travel from James-
town, the Ga community in Ghana to the Ashanti town of
Kumasi. Traditional enmity between the Ga and the
Ashanti, the history, religion and folklore of the Akan
people are all vividly portrayed by the author's traveling
companion, an affable, loquacious Ghanaian.

1969 Cloete, Stuart. The African giant: the story of a journey.
Boston: Houghton-Mifflin, 1955. 400 p.
An account of his trip to various African states under-
taken partly for adventure and partly to "clarify our minds
about the racial ferment in Africa." Countries visited
include Rhodesia, Nigeria, the Gold Coast, Liberia, the
Congo, Uganda, Kenya and South Africa.

1970 Cone, Virginia. Africa--a world in progress: an American
family in West Africa. Jericho, New York: Exposition
Press, 1960. 99 p.

1971 Cruickshank, Brodie. Eighteen years on the Gold Coast of
       Africa: including the account of the native tribes and their
       intercourse with Europeans. 2nd ed. London: Cass,
       1966. 2 v.
            Rev: Choice, IV (Oct. 1967), 888.

1972 Cudjoe, Robert. "Some reminiscences of a senior inter-
       preter," Nigerian Field, XVIII (Oct. 1953), 148-64.
            The experiences of a Ghanaian in Eastern Nigeria.

1973 Dupuis, Joseph. Journal of a residence in Ashantee.   Edited
       with notes and an introduction by William E. Ward.   Lon-
       don: Cass, 1966. 520 p.

1974 Eskelund, Karl. Black man's country: a journey through
       Ghana. London: Alvin Redman, 1958. 164 p.

1975 Freeman, Richard Austin. Travels and life in Ashanti and
       Jaman; with about one hundred illustrations by the author
       and from photographs. London: Cass, 1967. 559 p.
       (Cass Library of African Studies. Travels and narratives,
       No. 17.) Reprint of the 1898 edition.

1976 Green, L. G. White man's grave: the story of the West
       African coast, the cities, seaports and castles, white
       exiles and black magic. London: Paul, 1954. 249 p.

1977 Gunther, John. Inside Africa. New York: Harper, 1953.
       952 p.
            Chapter 40: "Prime Minister Nkrumah of the Gold
       Coast." Chapter 42: "The Gold Coast and the Gold
       Stool." Gunther is a well-known author of many travel
       books.

1978 Hallett, Robin. The Penetration of Africa, European enter-
       prise and exploration principally in Northern and Western
       Africa up to 1830. London: Routledge & Kegan Paul,
       1965. 458 p.

1979 Howard, C., ed. West African explorers: selections.   Lon-
       don: Oxford University Press, 1951. 598 p. (World
       classics, 523.)

1980 Howe, R. W. Black star rising: a journey through West
       Africa in transition. London: Jenkins, 1958. 254 p.

1981 Hutchinson, Alfred. Road to Ghana. London: Gollancz,
       1960. 190 p.
            The story of the escape of a colored South African
       politician to Ghana.
            Rev: New Statesman, LIX (April 2, 1960), 492. Sat.
       Rev., XLIII (Nov. 26, 1960), 20.

1982 Huxley, Elspeth. Four guineas: a journey through West
      Africa. London: Chatto & Windus, 1953. 303 p.

1983 Ingrams, William Harold. Seven across the Sahara from
      Ash to Accra. London: Murray, 1950. 231 p.
      The author was the Northern Territories' Chief Commis-
      sioner, 1947-48.

1984 Jahn, Janheinz. Through African doors; experiences and en-
      counters in West Africa. Translated from the German by
      Oliver Coburn. London: Faber & Faber, 1962. 232 p.
      A vivid description of daily life in Nigeria and Ghana
      by German Africanist, critic and bibliographer.
      Rev: Library J., LXXXVII (Oct. 15, 1962), 3666.
      N. Y. Times Bk. Rev. (Oct. 7, 1962), 3.

1985 Killmer, Lothar. Die Freiheitstrommel von Accra: Reise-
      notizen aus Ghana. Berlin: Neues Leben, 1962. 168 p.

1986 Kingsley, Mary Henrietta. Travels in West Africa: Congo
      français, Corisco and Cameroons. With an introduction by
      John E. Flint. 3rd ed. London: Cass, 1965. 743 p.

1987 _____. West African studies. With an introduction by
      John E. Flint. 3rd ed. New York: Barnes & Noble,
      1964. 507 p.

1988 Klager, Jürg. Navrongo: ein Afrikabuch mit 108 aufnahmen.
      Zürich: Rotapfel, 1953. Unpaged.

1989 Meredith, Henry. An Account of the Gold Coast of Africa,
      with a brief history of the African Company. London: Cass,
      1967. 264 p. (Cass Library of African studies. Travels
      and narratives, No. 20.) Reprint of the Longmans 1812
      edition.
      Includes the history of the Royal African Company of
      England.

1990 Mitchison, Naomi. Other people's worlds. London: Secker &
      Warburg, 1958. 160 p.
      One of the truest and most readable descriptions of life
      in Ghana and Nigeria.

1991 Mosley, Nicholas. African switchback. London: Weidenfeld &
      Nicholson, 1958. 244 p.
      A journey from Dakar, Senegal, to Lagos, Nigeria.

1992 Nassau, Robert Hamill. In an elephant corral, and other
      tales of West African experiences. New York: Negro
      Universities Press, 1969. 180 p. A reprint of the 1912
      edition.

1993 Reynolds, Alexander Jacob. African passage. London:
Muller, 1935. 303 p.

1994 _____. From the Ivory Coast to the Cameroons. London:
Knopf, 1929. 298 p.

1995 Rouch, Jane. Ghana. Photos de Marc Riboud. Lausanne:
Editions Rencontre, 1964. 205 p. (Coll. L'atlas des
voyages, 27.)

1996 _____. Le rire n'a pas de couleur. Paris: Gallimard,
1956. 267 p.
The Gold Coast before independence.

1997 Ryan, Isobel. Black man's town. London: Cape, 1953.
249 p.
On Takoradi.

1998 Schabowski, Günter. Visiting friends in free Africa: with the
F. D. G. B. delegation in Guinea and Ghana. Berlin: Verlag
Tribune, 1960. 78 p.

1999 Schmidt-Dannert, Christa. Birgit im Busch: Erzählung von
der Goldküste. Stuttgart: Evang. Missionsverlag, 1955.
112 p.

2000 Sutherland, Efua. Roadmakers: a picture of Ghana. Photos
by Willis E. Bell. Accra: Ghana Information Services,
1961. 63 p.
Chiefly illustrated.

2001 Vane, M. Black magic and white medicine: a mine medical
officer's experiences in South Africa, the Belgian Congo,
Sierra Leone and the Gold Coast. London: Chambers,
1957. 254 p.

2002 Warner, D. Ghana and the new Africa. London: Muller,
1960. 181 p.

2003 Wills, Colin. White traveler in black Africa. London: Dobson, 1951. 207 p.
Chiefly on West Africa.

2004 Wright, Richard. Black power: a record of reactions in a
land of pathos. New York: Harper, 1954. 358 p.
This noted American black novelist describes his visit
to the Gold Coast (Ghana), expressing his admiration for
Kwame Nkrumah and his opposition to any western inter-
ference in African economic and political policies.
Rev: Nation, CLXX (Oct. 16, 1954), 332. Sat. Rev.,
XXXVII (Oct. 23, 1954), 19.

2005 _____. Puissance noire. Traduit de l'Americain par
Roger Giroux. Paris: Chastel, 1955. 400 p.

(8) HISTORY--GENERAL

2006 Ackah, J. Y. "Kaku Ackah and the split of Nzema," Master's
Thesis, University of Ghana, 1965.

2007 Aderibigbe, A. A. B. "West African integration: an historical
perspective," Nigerian J. Econ. Soc. Stud., V (1963), 9-
14.

2008 Agbodeka, F. African politics and British policy in the Gold
Coast, 1868-1900; a study in the forms and force of protest. Evanston, Ill.: Northwestern University Press, 1971.
206 p.
Revision of author's doctoral dissertation, 1968.

2008a _____. "The African protest movement and its effects on
British policy on the Gold Coast, 1868-1900," Doctoral Dissertation, University of Ghana, 1968.

2009 _____. The Rise of the nation states: a history of the
West African peoples, 1800-1964. London: Nelson, 1965.
182 p.

2010 Agyeman, Nana Yaw Twum Duah. West Africa on the march:
an intimate survey of problems and potentialities. New
York: William-Frederick Press, 1952. 73 p.

2011 Ajayi, J. F. A. "The Continuity of African institutions under
colonialism." In T. O. Ranger, ed. Emerging themes of
African history. Nairobi: East African Publishing House,
1968, pp. 189-200.
Historical view of the African past and the impact of
colonialism upon African societies.

2012 _____. "Place of African history and culture in the process of nation-building in Africa South of the Sahara,"
J. Negro Educ., XXX (Summer 1961), 206-13.

2013 _____ and Ian Espie, eds. A Thousand years of West
African history: a handbook for teachers and students.
With a foreword by K. O. Dike. Ibadan: Ibadan University
Press, 1965. 543 p.
Rev: TLS (June 2, 1966), 490.

2014   Akinjogbin, Isaac A.   Dahomey and its neighbours, 1708-1818.
        Cambridge: Cambridge University Press, 1967. 233 p.
        Originally submitted as doctoral dissertation, London
        University, 1963, it examines the growth of political insti-
        tutions in Dahomey during the period and the relationship
        between its kings and the Yoruba Empire of neighboring
        Oyo.
        Rev: Nigeria Magazine, No. 97 (1968), 134-5; 141-2.
        TLS (Feb. 15, 1968), 158.

2015   Akinola, G. A.   "The Lindi coast in the 18th century; some
        new light from unpublished French documents," Master's
        Thesis, University of Ghana, 1966. 157 p.

2016   Akita, J. M.   "Documentary material available for historical
        research in the Gold Coast," Trans. Gold Coast & Togo-
        land Hist. Soc., I (1952), 21-3.

2017   Amenumey, D. E.   "The Ewe people and the coming of
        European rule, 1850-1914," Master's Thesis, London Uni-
        versity, 1963/64.

2018   _____ .   "The Extension of British rule to Anlo (South-
        east Ghana), 1850-1890," J. Afr. Hist., IX, No. 1 (1968),
        99-117.

2019   _____ .   "The Pre-1947 background to the Ewe unification
        question: a preliminary sketch," Trans. Hist. Soc. Ghana,
        X (1969), 65-85.
        Includes a map of the Ewe-speaking area of French and
        British Togoland, and of the Gold Coast.

2019a   Anderson, John D. and Obaro Ikime.   West Africa and East
        Africa in the nineteenth and twentieth centuries.   Book 1:
        West Africa.   Book 2: East Africa.   London: Heinemann
        Educational, 1972. 232 p. ; 378 p.   (Histories of the
        people of Africa.)

2020   Anstey, R. T.   "British trade and policy in west central
        Africa between 1816 and the early 1880's," Trans. Hist.
        Soc. Ghana, III (1957), 47-71.

2021   Arhin, Kwame.   "Status differentiation in the nineteenth
        century: a preliminary study," Research Review (Legon),
        IV, No. 3 (1968), 34-52.

2022   Armstrong, R. G.   "State formation in negro Africa," Doc-
        toral Dissertation, University of Chicago, 1952.

2023   Asiegbu, Johnson U.   Slavery and the politics of liberation,
        1787-1861; a study of liberated African emigration and
        British anti-slavery policy.   New York: Africana Publishing

Corp., 1969.   231 p.
Based on author's doctoral dissertation, Cambridge University, it examines British policy towards liberated Africans considered in the light of emigration from West Africa to the West Indies.

2024   Attafua, A.B.   "Traditional history," Trans. Gold Coast & Togoland Hist. Soc., I (1952), 18-20.

2025   Bains, I.   "British policy in relation to Portuguese claims in West Africa, 1876-84," Master's Thesis, London University, 1940.

2026   Berge, François.   "Le Sous-secrétariat et les Sous-secrétaires d'Etat aux colonies: histoire de l'émancipation de l'administration coloniale," Rev. Fr. Hist. d'Outre-Mer, XLVII (1960), 301-86.

2027   Bevin, H.J.   "The Gold Coast economy about 1880," Trans. Gold Coast & Togoland Hist. Soc., II (1956), 73-86.

2028   Bing, Geoffrey.   Reap the whirlwind: an account of Kwame Nkrumah's Ghana from 1950-1966.   London: MacGibbon & Kee, 1968.   519 p.
Rev: Listener, LXXX (July 11, 1968), 52.   TLS (June 6, 1968), 568.

2029   Birmingham, David.   "A Note on the kingdom of Fetu," Ghana Notes & Queries, No. 9 (1966), 30-3.

2030   Blake, John W.   European beginnings in West Africa, 1454-1578; a survey of the first century of white enterprise in West Africa, with special emphasis upon the rivalry of the great powers.   London: Longmans for the Royal Empire Society, 1937.   (Royal Empire Society Imperial Studies.)   212 p.
Portuguese discoveries on the West African coast; Spanish efforts to establish an empire; British and French competition for the Guinea trade--ivory, oil and slaves.
Rev: Amer. Hist. Rev., XLIV (Jan. 1939), 339.   TLS (Jan. 1, 1938), 1.

2031   _____.   Europeans in West Africa, 1450-1560.   London: Hakluyt Society, 1942.   2 v.
v. 1: Portuguese discoveries and enterprise on the West Coast.   v. 2: English voyages to Barbary and Guinea before the John Hawkins slave transportation to America.

2032   _____.   "International rivalry in West Africa, 1454-1559," Master's Thesis, London University, 1936.

2033 Boahen, Albert Adu. Britain, the Sahara and the Western
      Sudan, 1788-1861. New York: Oxford University Press,
      1964. 268 p.
          This revision of author's doctoral dissertation attempts
      to account for British exploration in the areas and their
      diplomatic activity up to Heinrich Barth's missions of the
      1850's.
          Rev: Amer. Hist. Rev., LXX (July 1965), 1211.
      English Hist. Rev., LXXX (July 1965), 617.

2034 _____. "British penetration of the Sahara and Western
      Sudan, 1788-1861," Doctoral Dissertation, London Univer-
      sity, 1959.

2035 _____. "The Caravan trade in the nineteenth century,"
      J. Afr. Hist., III, No. 2 (1962), 349-59.

2036 _____. "A New Look at the history of Ghana," African
      Affairs, LXV (July 1966), 212-22.

2037 _____. "The Roots of Ghanaian nationalism," J. Afr. Hist.,
      127-32.

2038 _____. Topics in West African history. London: Long-
      mans, 1966. 174 p.

2039 Bourret, F. M. Ghana: the road to independence, 1919-1957.
      Rev. ed. London: Oxford University Press, 1960. 246 p.
          First published in 1949 under title: The Gold Coast,
      1919-1951.

2040 _____. The Gold Coast: a survey of the Gold Coast and
      British Togoland, 1919-1946. Stanford, California: Stan-
      ford University Press, 1949. 231 p. (The Hoover Library
      on War, Revolution and Peace. Publication, No. 23.)
          A revision of the author's doctoral dissertation, Stanford
      University, 1947 under title: "The Gold Coast and the
      British mandate of Togoland, 1919-1939."

2041 Bousquet, Georges Henri. Les Berbères: histoire et insti-
      tutions. Paris: Presses Universitaires de France, 1957.
      116 p.

2042 Bovill, E. W. "The Moorish invasion of the Sudan," J. Roy.
      Afr. Soc., XXVI (1926), 245-62; 380-7, XXVIII (1927),
      47-56.

2043 Brady, Thomas F. "Gold Coast: laughter, wealth, freedom,"
      N. Y. Times Magazine (Oct. 7, 1956), 14-16+.
          Background account of the Gold Coast and its prospects
      following the announcement of independence for the country.

2044   Braimah, J. A. and J. R. Goody.   Salaga: the struggle for
       power.   London: Longmans, 1967.   222 p.
              Chiefly concerned with Salaga's place in the Gonja his-
       tory and especially the civil war of the early 1890's and
       its repercussions.
              Rev: J. Asian Afr. Stud. , V (Jan. /April 1970), 144-5.
       Trans. Hist. Soc. Ghana, X (1969), 129-31.

2045   Brooks, George E.   Yankee traders, old coasters and African
       middlemen: a history of American legitimate trade with
       West Africa in the nineteenth century.   Boston: Boston
       University Press, 1970.   370 p.   (Boston Univ. African
       res. studies, No. 11.)
              Rev: Amer. Hist. Rev. , LXXVI (Oct. 1971), 1131.
       Choice, VIII (March 1971), 108.

2046   _____.   "The Letter book of Captain Edward Harrington, "
       Trans. Hist. Soc. Ghana, VI (1962), 71-8.

2047   Brooks, H.   "The Gold Coast Historical Society, " W. Afr. Rev. ,
       XVII (Aug. 1946), 935.

2048   Brown, Godfrey.   An Active history of Ghana.   London:
       Allen & Unwin, 1961.   2 v.
              v. 1: From the earliest times to 1844.   v. 2: Since
       1845.

2049   Brunschwig, Henri.   "Les Origines du partage de l'Afrique
       occidentale, " J. Afr. Hist. , V (1964), 121-5.
              Review of Prelude to the partition of West Africa
       (1963), by John D. Hargreaves.

2050   Buah, F. K.   An Elementary history for schools.   London:
       Macmillan, 1967.   94 p.

2051   _____.   A New history for schools and colleges.   London:
       Longmans, 1967.   2 v.
              Contents: Book I. The Ancient World. 183 p.   Book
       II. West Africa and Europe.   246 p.

2052   Cartland, G. B.   "The Gold Coast: a historical approach, "
       African Affairs, XLVI (April 1947), 89-97.

2053   Cary, Joyce.   Britain and West Africa.   Rev. ed.   London:
       Longmans, Green, 1947.   79 p.
              An outline history of the West African colonies by a
       British novelist.

2054   Cave, R. M.   Gold Coast forts.   London: Nelson, 1957.
       60 p.
              (Background to modern Africa Series.)

2055   Chantler, C. The Ghana story. London: Linden Press,
       1971. 214 p.

2056   Clarke, John H. "New Ghana," Negro Hist. Bull. , XXIII
       (Feb. 1960), 117-8.

2057   _____. "Old Ghana," Negro Hist. Bull. , XXIII (Feb.
       1960), 116-7.

2058   Clausen, Wolfgang. Die Staatwerdung Ghanas. Studie über
       die Verfassungsentwicklung kolonialer Gebiete zum
       unabhangigen Staat. Hamburg: Hansischer Gildenverl,
       1966. 196 p.

2059   Coleman, James S. Togoland. New York: Carnegie
       Endowment for International Peace, 1956. 51 p. (Inter-
       national Conciliation, no. 509.)
       A study of "the divided trust territory as an infinitely
       complex admixture of political, economic, and tribal as-
       pirations--further complicated by the aftermath of nine-
       teenth century imperialism." Special emphasis on the
       plebiscite in British Togoland in May 1956 resulting in its
       union with the Gold Coast.

2060   Commisariat de la Republic Française au Togo. Guide de la
       colonisation au Togo. Paris: Larose, 1926. 198 p.

2061   Constantine, J. R. "The African slave trade: a study of
       eighteenth century propaganda and public controversy,"
       Doctoral Dissertation, Indiana University, 1953.

2062   Cookey, S. J. S. "West African immigrants in the Congo,
       1885-1896," J. Hist. Soc. Nigeria, III (1965), 261-70.

2063   Coombs, Douglas. The Gold Coast, Britain and the Nether-
       lands, 1850-1874. London: Oxford University Press,
       1963. 160 p. (West African history series.)
       The competition among the imperial powers for the pos-
       session of important trading positions.
       Rev: English Hist. Rev. , LXXX (April 1965), 424.
       International Affairs (April 1964), 342.

2064   Cousins, A. N. "The Dutch West India Company on the West
       coast of Africa up to 1660," Master's Thesis, University
       of Belfast, 1953.

2065   Crookall, R. E. Handbook for history teachers in West
       Africa. London: Evans, 1960. 270 p.

2066   Crowder, Michael. "Colonial rule and West Africa: factor
       for division or unity?" Civilisations, XIV, Nos. 3-4
       (1964), 167-78.

Professor Crowder is former Director of the Institute of African Studies, University of Ife, Nigeria.

2067 _____. "Indirect rule, French and British style," Africa, XXXIV (1964), 197-205.

2068 _____, ed. West African resistance; the military response to colonial occupation. New York: Africana Publishing Corp., 1971. 314 p.
Specialists in West African history discuss nine examples of military confrontation between European and African armies, considering also the Islamic influence on the area.
Rev: Economist, CCXXXIX (April 3, 1971), p. xiii. Library J., XCV (Dec. 1, 1971), 4170.

2069 _____. West Africa under colonial rule. London: Hutchinson, 1968. 540 p.
Evaluates the benefits of colonial rule and contends that it was not necessary for integration of African peoples into the modern world.
Rev: Amer. Hist. Rev., LXXIV (June 1969), 1679. West Africa, No. 2674 (Aug. 31, 1968), 1013-5.

2070 _____ and Obaro Ikime, eds. West African chiefs; the changing status under colonial rule and independence. Translated from the French by Brenda Packman. New York: Africana Publishing Corp., 1970. 453 p.
Selected papers of an international seminar held by the Institute of African Studies, University of Ife, Dec. 17-21, 1968. The 21 contributors that survey chieftaincies in English and French West Africa analyze the position of individual chiefs within the political structure of their countries before and after independence.
Rev: Choice, VIII (Sept. 1971), 888. TLS (April 30, 1971), 506.

2071 Crowe, S. E. The Berlin West African Conference, 1884-1885. London: Longmans, 1942. 249 p. (Royal Empire Soc. Imperial studies.)
Originally submitted as doctoral dissertation, Cambridge, 1939.
Rev: Amer. Hist. Rev., XLVIII (July 1943), 787. Pol. Sci. Q., LVIII (Sept. 1943), 474.

2072 Cunard, Nancy and George Padmore. The white man's duty: an analysis of the colonial question in the light of the Atlantic Charter. London: W. H. Allen, 1943. 48 p.

2073 Curtin, Philip, et al., eds. Africa remembered; narratives by West Africans from the era of the slave trade. Ibadan: Ibadan University Press, 1967. 363 p.
Rev: African Affairs, LXVI (Oct. 1967), 372-3.

2074 _____ and Jan Vansina. "Sources of the nineteenth century Atlantic slave trade," J. Afr. Hist., V, No. 2 (1964),
184-208.

2075 Daaku, Kwame Yeboa. "The Slave trade and Africa society."
In T. O. Ranger, ed. Emergency themes in African history. Nairobi: East African Publishing House, 1968, pp.
134-40.
Limited to West Africa.

2076 _____. Trade and politics on the Gold Coast, 1600-1720:
a study of the African reaction to European trade. Oxford:
Clarendon Press, 1970. 219 p. Bibliog.
Originally submitted as doctoral dissertation, London,
1964. 385 p.
Rev: J. Afr. Hist., XII, No. 2 (1971), 330-1.

2077 Dalton, Heather. "The Development of the Gold Coast under
British administration, 1874-1901," Master's Thesis,
University of Ghana, 1957. 322 p.

2078 Dalton, John H. "Colony and metropolis: some aspects of
British rule in Gold Coast and their implications for an
understanding of Ghana today," J. Econ. Hist., XXI (Dec.
1961), 552-65.

2079 Danquah, Joseph Boakye. Historic speeches and writings on
Ghana. Compiled by H. K. Akyeampong. Accra: G.
Boakie, 1966. 177 p.

2080 _____. "The Historical significance of the Bond of 1844,"
Trans. Hist. Soc. Ghana, III (1957), 3-29.

2081 Davidson, Basil and F. K. Buah. History of West Africa to
the nineteenth century. Rev. ed. Garden City, New York:
Anchor Books, 1966. 342 p.
First published in 1945 under titles: The Growth of
African civilization.
Rev: Choice, IV (April 1967), 205.

2082 Davies, K. G. The Royal African Company. London: Longmans, 1956. 396 p.

2083 Davies, Oliver. West Africa before the Europeans: archae-
ology and prehistory. London: Methuen, 1967. 364 p.
Bibliog.
Rev: Amer. Anthrop., LXX (Aug. 1968), 810. Choice,
V (June 1968), 540.

2084 De Graft Johnson, John C. "African empires of the past,"
Présence Africaine (avr.-mai 1957), 58-64.

2085 _____. African glory: the story of vanished negro
       civilizations. New York: Walker, 1966. 211 p.
              Reprint of the 1954 edition of Praeger. A study of the
       ancient empires of West Africa, Mali, Songhai and Ghana.
              Rev: TLS (Jan. 14, 1955), 19. Wilson Lib. Bull.,
       LI (Sept. 1955), 9.

2086 Dennett, Richard Edward. At the back of the black man's
       mind, or, notes on the kingly office in West Africa. Lon-
       don: Macmillan, 1906. 288 p.
              Rev: Nature, LXXV (Feb. 10, 1907), 248. Sat. Rev.,
       CIII (May 18, 1907), 622.

2087 Denzer, La Ray E. "The National Congress of British West
       Africa; Gold Coast section," Master's Thesis, University of
       Ghana, 1965. 92 p.

2088 Du Bois, Shirley Graham. What happened in Ghana? The
       inside story. Sketches by Tom Feelings. New York:
       Freedomways Associates, 1966. 223 p.

2089 _____. "What happened in Ghana? The inside story,"
       Freedomways, VI (Summer 1966), 200-23.

2090 Dumett, R. E. "British official attitudes in relation to
       economic development in the Gold Coast, 1874-1905,"
       Doctoral Dissertation, London University, 1965/66.

2091 Edmonds, W. D. "The Newspaper press in British West
       Africa, 1918-1939," Master's Thesis, Bristol University,
       1951/62.

2092 Edokpayi, S. I. "The External trade of the Gold Coast and
       Nigeria, 1885-1945," Master's Thesis, London University,
       1957/58.

2093 Ekomode, G. S. "The Kilindi Kingdom of Vuga, 1725-1890,"
       Master's Thesis, University of Ghana, 1966. 177 p.

2094 Eluwa, Gabriel I. "The Colonial Office and the emergence of
       the National Congress of British West Africa," Doctoral
       Dissertation, Michigan State University, 1967.

2095 Fage, J. D. "The Administration of George Maclean on the
       Gold Coast, 1830-44," Trans. Gold Coast & Togoland Hist.
       Soc., I, Part IV (1954), 104-20.

2096 _____. An Atlas of African history. London: E. Arnold,
       1958. 64 p.

2097 _____. Ghana: a historical interpretation. Madison:
       University of Wisconsin Press, 1959. 122 p.

2098 _____. A History of West Africa: an introductory survey.
4th ed. London: Cambridge University Press, 1969.
239 p. 1st ed. 1955.
Intended for use in secondary schools. The author is
former Professor of History, University College of Ghana.
Rev: J. Hist. Soc. Nigeria, V (June 1971), 598.

2099 _____, ed. "A New check list of the forts and castles
of Ghana," Trans. Hist. Soc. Ghana, IV, Part 1 (1959),
57-66.

2100 _____. "On the reproductions and editing of classics of
African history," J. Afr. Hist., VIII, No. 1 (1967), 157-
61.

2101 _____. "Some general considerations relevant to historical
research in the Gold Coast," Trans. Gold Coast & Togoland
Hist. Soc., I (1952), 24-9.

2102 _____. "Some notes on a scheme for investigation of
oral tradition in the northern territories of the Gold Coast,"
J. Hist. Soc. Nigeria, I (Dec. 1956), 15-19.

2103 _____. "Some remarks on beads and trade in lower Guinea
in the sixteenth and seventeenth centuries," J. Afr. Hist.,
III, No. 2 (1962), 343-7.

2104 _____ and R. A. Oliver, eds. Papers in African prehistory. Cambridge: Cambridge University Press, 1970.
331 p.
Rev: J. Hist. Soc. Nigeria, V (June 1971), 583-5.

2105 Fitch, Robert B. "Opposition movements in Ghana, 1954-
1958," Master's Thesis, University of California, Berkeley,
1966. 145 p.

2106 Flint, John E. Nigeria and Ghana. Englewood Cliffs, N. J.:
Prentice-Hall, 1966. 176 p. (A spectrum book. The
modern nations in historical perspective, S-618.)
A comparative study of the two former British colonies--
their pre-colonial past; cultural differences; political
organization; the effects of slave trade; the impact of
Christianity and Islam.
Rev: Amer. Hist. Rev., LXXII (April 1967), 1046.
J. Afr. Hist., VIII, No. 3 (1967), 541.

2107 Forde, Cyril Daryll and P. M. Kaberry, eds. West African
kingdoms in the nineteenth century. London: Oxford University Press for the International African Institute, 1967.
289 p.
A collection of studies on the later development and
organization of larger states that played much part in the

earlier economic, political and cultural life of West Africa.
Useful introductory essay by the editors, notes and sources
grouped by chapter and a general index.
Rev: Amer. Hist. Rev., LXXIII (Feb. 1968), 872.
J. Negro Hist., LIII (Jan. 1968), 93.

2108   Fortes, Meyer.   "The Impact of the war on British West
Africa, " Int. Affairs, XXI (April 1945), 206-19.

2109   Fraser, Jan J.   "What happened to the Dutch?" W. Afr. Rev.
(Feb. 1960), 65-8.
The Dutch departure from the Gold Coast.

2110   Friedlaender, Marianne.   "Zur Frage der Klassenverhättnisse
der Ewe unter dem Einfluss der Kolonisation, " Ethnog-
Archaöl. Z., IV, No. 2 (1963), 147-52.

2111   Furley, John T.   "Notes on some Portuguese Governors of
the Captaincy Da Mina, " Trans. Hist. Soc. Ghana, III
(1957), 194-214.

2112   _____.   "Provisional list of some Portuguese Governors of
the Captaincy Da Mina, " Trans. Gold Coast & Togoland
Hist. Soc., II, Part II (1956), 53-62.
Chronological listing with notes on the Governors.

2113   Gavin, R. J.   "Palmerston's policy towards East and West
Africa, 1830-1865, " Doctoral Dissertation, Cambridge University, 1959/60.

2114   George, Claude.   The Rise of British West Africa, comprising
the early history of the colony of Sierra Leone, the Gambia,
Lagos, Gold Coast, etc. with a brief account of climate,
the growth of education, commerce and religion and a comprehensive history of the Bananas and Bance Islands and
sketches of constitution.   London: Cass, 1968.   468 p.

2115   Gertzel, Cherry J.   "Imperial policy towards the British
settlements in West Africa, 1860-1875, " B. Litt's Thesis,
Oxford University, 1953/54.

2116   _____.   "John Holt: a British merchant in West Africa in
the era of 'imperialism,'" Doctoral Dissertation, Oxford
University, 1959/60.

2117   Ghana.   Government.   Ghana, ten great years, 1951-1960,
[by Keith Jopp].   Accra, 1960.

2118   "The Ghana question: where the experts disagree, " W. Afr.
Rev. (March 1957), 267-72.

2119 Gillespie, W. H. The Gold Coast policy, 1844-1938. Accra:
      Govt. Printer, 1955. 89 p.

2120 Gold Coast. Government. Correspondence relating to the
      change of title of the West African Frontier Force to that
      of Royal West African Frontier Force. Accra, 1928. 5 p.
      (Sessional paper, No. 17 of 1928/29.)

2121 _____. Gold Coast and its dependencies. Accra, 1917.
      72 p. (Sessional paper, No. 2 of 1917/18.)

2122 Goody, John Rankine. "The Myth of a state," J. Mod. Afr.
      Stud., VI (Dec. 1968), 461-73.

2123 _____. "Salaga in 1876," Ghana Notes & Queries, No. 8
      (1966), 1-5.

2124 Gray, Richard and David Sanderson Chambers. Materials for
      West African history in Italian archives. London: Athlone
      Press, 1965. 164 p. (Guides to materials for West
      African history in European archives, No. 3.)

2125 Great Britain. Central Office of Information. The Making
      of Ghana. London, 1957. 46 p.

2126 Great Britain. Colonial Office. Introducing West Africa.
      3rd ed. London, 1956. 79 p.

2127 _____. Native administration and political development in
      British tropical Africa: report, by Lord Hailey. London,
      1940-42. 293 p.

2128 _____. Native administration in the British African terri-
      tories. Part III. West Africa, by Lord Hailey. London:
      H. M. S. O., 1951. 350 p.

2129 _____. Report to the General Assembly of the United
      Nations on Togoland under United Kingdom administration
      for the year 1955. London, 1956. 198 p.

2130 Great Britain. War Office. Military report on the Gold
      Coast, Ashanti, the Northern territories and mandated
      Togoland. Vol. 1: General. London: H. M. S. O., 1931.

2131 Guggisberg, Frederick Gordon. The Gold Coast; a review
      of events of 1920-1926 and the prospects of 1927-1928.
      Accra: Govt. Printer, 1927.

2132 _____. Post-war Gold Coast: a review of the events of
      1923, with a statement showing the policy adopted by the
      government for the progress of the people. 1924. 180 p.

A useful sourcebook for political history and social
development.

2133   Haliburton, G. M.   "The Prophet Harris and his work in the
        Ivory Coast and Western Ghana, " Doctoral Dissertation,
        London University, 1965/66.

2134   Hargreaves, John D.   Prelude to the partition of West
        Africa.   London: Macmillan, 1963.   383 p.
            European interests and imperialism along the West
        African coasts, 1860-1885 and their expansion after the
        1884-85 Berlin Conference.
            Rev: J. Afr. Hist., V (1964), 121-5.   English Hist.
        Rev., LXXX (July 1965), 630.

2135   Hayford, Casely.   Collected papers.   Edited by E. U. Essien-
        Udom.   London: Cass.   (forthcoming)
            A significant collection of papers and documents previ-
        ously unpublished throwing new light on Hayford's life and
        work.

2136   .   The Truth about the West African land question.
        New York: Negro Universities Press, 1969.   203 p.
            Reprint of the 1913 edition.

2137   Haywood, A. and F. A. Clarke.   History of the Royal West
        African Frontier Force.   Aldershot: Gole & Polden, 1964.
        540 p.
            Describes the origin of the force largely Nigerian since
        its creation in 1897 and its military campaigns in Africa
        during World War I and in Asia and Africa during the
        World War II.

2138   Helly, D. O.   "British attitudes towards tropical Africa, 1860-
        1890, " Doctoral Dissertation, Radcliffe College, 1960.

2139   Hodson, Arnold E.   "The G. C. B. in the East African campaign,
        1940-41; 2. Italian Somaliland, " J. Roy. Afr. Soc. (Jan.
        1942), 14-28.
            G. C. B. is the Gold Coast Brigade.

2140   Holden, J. J.   "The Zabarima conquest of North-West Ghana,
        Part I, " Trans. Hist. Soc. Ghana, Part I, VIII (1965),
        60-86.

2141   Hooper, Everett E.   "Boundaries and frontiers of Ghana, "
        Master's Thesis, American University, Washington, D. C.,
        1964.   108 p.
            Critical of colonial boundaries in Africa in general, that
        have caused much friction among African states, it analyzes
        the Ghanaian boundaries and frontiers with special reference
        to the Ewe people and presents some of the factors likely

to affect contemporary African states.

2142   Hopkins, A. G.   "Economic aspects of political movements in
       Nigeria and in the Gold Coast, 1918-1939," J. Afr. Hist.,
       VII (1966), 132-52.

2143   Howitt, William.   Colonization and Christianity; a popular
       history of the treatment of the natives by the Europeans
       in all their colonies.   New York: Negro Universities
       Press, 1969.   508 p.
       First published in 1838.

2144   James, P. G.   "British policy in relation to the Gold Coast,"
       Master's Thesis, London University, 1953.

2145   Johnson, Marion.   "The Ounce in eighteenth century West
       Africa trade," J. Afr. Hist., VII, No. 2 (1966), 197-214.

2146   _____ .   "Salaga, 1875-1900," Research Rev., (Legon),   II
       (Nov./Dec. 1965), 72-3.

2147   _____ .   "The Wider background of Salaga civil war,"
       Research Rev., (Legon), II, No. 2 (1966), 31-9.

2148   Jones-Quartey, K. A. B.   "Anglo-African journals and
       journalists in the nineteenth and early twentieth century,"
       Trans. Hist. Soc. Ghana, IV, Part 1 (1959), 47-56.
       Examines the characteristics of anti-slavery and pro-
       emancipation journals which helped to expose the evils
       of slave trade and hasten its end.   Includes a list of
       periodicals and newspapers published in Britain from 1875
       to 1930 directly concerned with Gold Coast affairs.

2149   _____ .   "Sierra Leone's role in the development of Ghana,
       1820-1930," Sierra Leone Stud. (New series), No. 10
       (1958), 73-84.

2150   July, Robert W.   The Origin of West African thought: its
       development in West Africa during the nineteenth and
       twentieth centuries.   New York: Praeger, 1967.   512 p.
       Rev: Amer. Hist. Rev., (Dec. 1968), 683.   Library J.,
       XCII (Dec. 1, 1967), 4411.

2151   Kafe, Joseph Kofi T.   European contacts with West Africa in
       the fifteenth and sixteenth centuries: a select bibliography
       submitted in part requirement for University of London
       Diploma in Librarianship.   Legon: Balme Library, 1964.
       85 p.

2152   Kalous, M.   "A contribution to the problem of the hypothetical
       connection between Ife and the Gold Coast before the 15th
       century," Archiv Orientalni, XXXV, No. 4 (1967), 549-55.

2152a Kay, G. B., ed. The Political economy of colonialism in
       Ghana: a collection of documents and statistics, 1900-1960.
       New York: Cambridge University Press, 1972. 431 p.

2153   Kea, R. A. "Firearms and warfare on the Gold and Slave
       Coasts from the sixteenth to the nineteenth centuries,"
       J. Afr. Hist., XII, No. 2 (1971), 185-213.

2154   Kible, G. H. "The Mapping of West Africa in the 14th and
       15th centuries, as illustrative of the development of geo-
       graphical ideas," Master's Thesis, London University,
       1931.

2155   Kimble, David. A Political history of Ghana: the rise of
       Gold Coast nationalism, 1850-1928. Oxford: Clarendon
       Press, 1963. 587 p. Bibliog.
           A revision of author's doctoral dissertation, London
       University.
           Rev: Amer. Hist. Rev., LXIX (1964), 462-3. J. Afr.
       Hist., V (1964), 127-32.

2156   Klingberg, F. J. "The Parliamentary history of the abolition
       of slavery and the slave trade in the British colonies,"
       Doctoral Dissertation, Yale University, 1911.

2157   Knoll, Arthur J. "Togo under imperial Germany, 1884-1910,"
       Doctoral Dissertation, Yale University, 1963.

2158   Kwapong, Alexander A. "Africa antiqua," Trans. Gold Coast
       & Togoland Hist. Soc., II, Part I (1956), 1-12.
           A critical examination of some aspects of African his-
       tory within the Graeco-Roman era by one of Africa's most
       distinguished classical scholars.

2159   Kwaw-Swanzy, B. E. "The Constitutional development of the
       Gold Coast, 1901-25," M. Litt.'s Thesis, Cambridge Univer-
       sity, 1955.

2160   Lacy, Leslie. "A History of railway unionism in Ghana,"
       Master's Thesis, University of Ghana, 1965.

2161   Latham, Norah. A Sketch-map history of West Africa. Lon-
       don: Hulton Educational Publications, 1959. 80 p.
           Historical, political, economic and religious.

2162   Lawrence, Arnold W. Fortified trade-ports; the English in
       West Africa, 1645-1822. New ed. London: Cape, 1969.
       237 p.

2163   _____. "Some source books for West African history,"
       J. Afr. Hist., II, No. 2 (1961), 227-34.

2164 Lever, A. W.   "The British Empire and the German colonies, 1914-1919," Doctoral Dissertation, University of Wisconsin, 1963.

2165 Levtzion, Nehemia.   Muslims and chiefs in West Africa. Accra: Oxford University Press, 1970.

2166 _____.   "Salaga: a nineteenth century trading town in Ghana," Asian Afr. Stud. (Jerusalem), No. 2 (1966), 207-44.

2167 McCall, D. F.   Africa in time-perspective: a discussion of historical reconstruction from unwritten sources.   A series of lectures given at the University College of Ghana, 1961. Boston: Boston University Press, 1964.   172 p.

2168 _____.   Western African history.   London: Pall Mall, 1969.   258 p.

2169 McIntyre, William David.   "British policy in West Africa, the Malay Peninsula and the South Pacific during the colonial secretaryship of Lord Kimberly and Carnovon, 1870-1876," Doctoral Dissertation, London University, 1959.

2170 _____.   The Imperial frontier in the tropics, 1865-75; a study of British colonial policy in West Africa, Malaya and the South Pacific in the age of Gladstone and Disraeli. London: Macmillan, 1967.   421 p.
      Primarily concerned with the manner the British made their decisions at the peak of their imperialism in the area.   Extensive bibliography.
      Rev: New Statesman, LXXV (March 1, 1968), 271. TLS (Feb. 15, 1968), 147.

2170a Mckee, M.   "Recent British publications on Commonwealth West African history," British Book News (Nov. 1971), 855-62.

2171 Maroix, Jean Eugene.   Le Togo, pays d'influence francaise, etc.   Paris: Larose, 1938.   136 p.

2172 Martin, Eveline Christiana.   The British West African settlements, 1750-1821; a study in local administration.   London: Longmans for the Royal Colonial Institute, 1927. 186 p.   (Imperial studies, No. 2.)

2173 _____.   "The English establishments on the Gold Coast in the second half of the 18th century," Trans. Royal Hist. Soc., IV, Series 5 (1922), 167-208.

2174 Martin, G. B.   "Arabic materials for Ghanaian history," Research Rev., II, No. 1 (1964), 74-83.

2175 Marvill, R. O. G. "The Formation of the protectorates of
      Northern Ghana," Master's Thesis, University of Ghana,
      1967. 79 p.

2176 Mauny, Raymond. "The Question of Ghana," Africa, XXIV
      (July 1954), 200-13.

2177 Mayer, Emerico Samassa. Ghana: past and present. New
      York: Arco Publishing Co., 1968. 112 p.
      Rev: Library J., XCIII (May 15, 1968), 2003.

2178 Mbaeyi, Paul Mmegha. "Military and naval factors in
      British West African history, 1823-74; being an examina-
      tion of the organization of British naval and military forces
      in West Africa, and their role in the struggles for the
      coast and the principal rivers," Doctoral Dissertation,
      Oxford University, 1965/66.

2179 Metcalfe, George E. "After Maclean, some aspects of
      British Gold Coast policy in the mid-19th century," Trans.
      Gold Coast & Togoland Hist. Soc., I (1955), 178-92.
           George Maclean (1801-1847), British military captain,
      administered the Gold Coast from 1830 to 1844.

2180 _____ . Great Britain and Ghana: documents of Ghana
      history, 1807-1957. London: Nelson, 1964. 779 p.
      Rev: New Statesman, LXX (July 30, 1965), 160.

2181 _____ . Maclean of the Gold Coast, the life and times of
      George Maclean, 1801-1847. London: Oxford University
      Press, 1962. 344 p.
           Life of the British administrator and the difficult prob-
      lems he encountered in the early British settlement on the
      Gold Coast.
      Rev: African Affairs, LXI (1962), 348-50.

2182 Moberly, F. J. History of the Great War. Military opera-
      tions in Togo and the Cameroons, 1914-18. London:
      H. M. S. O., 1931.

2183 Montmard, André. La Gold Coast: études, enquêtes, con-
      férences. Dakar: Guv. Gén. de l'A. O. F., Serv. de
      l'Inform., 1949. 76 p.

2184 Morel, Edmund Dene. Affairs of West Africa. With a new
      introduction by Kenneth Dike Nworah. 2nd ed. London:
      Cass, 1968. 328 p. (Cass Library of African Studies,
      General studies, No. 62.) 1st ed. 1902, by Heinemann.

2185 _____ . The Black man's burden: the white man in Africa
      from the fifteenth century to World War I. New York:
      Monthly Review Press, 1969. 241 p.

Reprint of the 1920 edition.

2186   Nathan, Matthew. "The Dutch and English on the Gold Coast
       in eighteenth century," J. Afr. Soc., III (1904), 325-51.

2187   _____. "The Gold Coast at the end of the seventeenth
       century under the Danes and Dutch," J. Afr. Soc., IV
       (Oct. 1904), 1-32.
       The author was then Governor of the Gold Coast Colony.

2188   Newbury, Colin W., ed. British policy towards West
       Africa: select documents, 1786-1874. Oxford: Claren-
       don Press, 1965. v. 1. 656 p.
       Rev: J. Afr. Hist., VI (1965), 423-5.

2189   _____. British policy towards West Africa: select docu-
       ments, 1875-1914 with statistical appendices, 1800-1914.
       London: Oxford University Press, 1971, v. 2. 680 p.
       Documents British relations with West Africa from the
       period of Ashanti War to the amalgamation of Nigeria.
       The statistical appendices cover the period of both volumes
       1 and 2, illustrating the values of British trade with West
       Africa as a whole and the trade revenues and expanditures
       of the four British possessions: Gambia, the Gold Coast,
       Nigeria and Sierra Leone.

2190   _____. "Victorians, Republicans, and the partition of
       West Africa," J. Afr. Hist., III, No. 2 (1962), 493-501.

2191   _____. The Western slave coast and its rulers: European
       trade and administration among the Yoruba and adja-speaking
       peoples of South-Western Nigeria, Southern Dahomey and
       Togo. Oxford: Clarendon Press, 1961. 224 p.
       Rev: J. Afr. Hist., III (1962), 519-21. TLS (April 27,
       1962), 286.

2192   Nikoi, Amon. "Indirect rule and government in Gold Coast
       Colony, 1844-1954; a study in the history, ecology and
       politics of administration in a changing society," Doctoral
       Dissertation, Harvard University, 1956.

2193   Nkrumah, Kwame. "Recovery of African history," Negro
       Digest, XII (April 1963), 89-97.
       Excerpted from his welcome address to the First Inter-
       national Conference of Africanists, Accra, December 1962.

2194   Nwafor, M.O.E. "Anglo-French relations, with special
       reference to West Africa, 1898-1904," Master's Thesis,
       London University, 1958/59.

2195   Nworah, Kenneth Dike. "Humanitarian pressure-groups and
       British attitudes to West Africa, 1895-1915," Doctoral
       Dissertation, London University, 1965/66.

2196 Obichere, Boniface I. West African states and European
      expansion: the Dahomey-Niger hinterland, 1885-1898. New
      Haven, Conn. : Yale University Press, 1971. 400 p.
            The author, Professor of African History at the Univer-
      sity of California, Los Angeles, is a Nigerian historian.

2197 Omosini, Olufemi. "Railway projects and British attitude
      towards the development of West Africa, 1872-1903, " J.
      Hist. Soc. Nigeria, V (June 1971), 491-507.

2198 Omu, Fred I. "The Dilemma of press freedom in colonial
      Africa: the West African example, " J. Afr. Hist., IX,
      No. 2 (1968), 279-98.

2199 Osae, T. A. and S. N. Nwabara. A Short history of West
      Africa, Book one, A. D. 1000 to 1800. London: University
      of London Press, 1968. 191 p.

2200 Osei, Gabriel Kingsley. The African: his antecedents, his
      genius, and his destiny. London: African Publication
      Society, 1967. 210 p.
            In tracing the history of Afamba state in Ghana, the
      author, an Ashanti from Ghana, contends that the recon-
      struction of Africa's glorious past could help in understand-
      ing of the African future.

2201 _____ . Europe's gift to Africa. London: African Publica-
      tion Society, 1968. 120 p.

2202 Owusu-Ansah, R. K. Oral traditions of Badu people. Legon:
      Institute of African Studies, University of Ghana, 1967.
      63 p.

2203 Pachai, B. "The Outline of the history of municipal govern-
      ment at Cape Coast, " Trans. Hist. Soc. Ghana, VIII (1965),
      130-60.

2204 Padmore, George. Africa and world peace, etc. London:
      Secker & Warburg, 1937. 285 p.

2205 _____ . Africa: Britain's third empire. London: Dobson,
      1949. 266 p.

2206 _____ . How Britain rules Africa. London: Wishart
      Books, 1936. 402 p.
            Deals with the political, economic and legal aspects of
      the British administration of their African colonies. Highly
      critical.
            Rev: Economist, CXXIV (Sept. 26, 1936), 564. TLS
      (June 27, 1936), 546.

2207 _____ . How Russia transformed her colonial empire: a
      challenge to imperialist powers.   London: Dobson, 1946.
      178 p.

2208 Page, John. "Some problems of Gold Coast history," Uni-
      versitas, I, No. 6 (1955), 5-9.

2209 Painter, C.   "The Guang and West African historical recon-
      struction," Ghana Notes & Queries, No. 9 (1966), 58-66.
          A linguistic reconstruction of the Guang people living
      mainly in Ghana although there are very few speakers of
      the Guang language in Togo, Dahomey, and the Ivory Coast.

2210 Panikkar, K. M.   The Serpent and the crescent history of
      negro empires of Western Sudan.   London: Asia Publishing
      House, 1963.   386 p.

2211 Papers concerning the Gold Coast and surrounding districts,
      1850-73.   Shannon: Irish University Press, 1971.   634 p.
      (British parliamentary papers, colonies, Africa, 57.)
          Reprint of the first editions by H. M. S. O., London,
      1850-1873.

2212 Payton, Benjamin F.   "The Ethics of decolonization and de-
      velopment in British West Africa; a study of the nature and
      role of moral decision in area of rapid social change,
      1941-1961," Doctoral Dissertation, Yale University, 1963.

2212a Pinkney, R.   Ghana under military rule, 1966-1969.   Lon-
      don: Methuen, 1972.   192 p.   (Studies in African history.)

2213 "Problems of British West Africa," Round Table (March 1939),
      291-308.

2214 Rathbone, Richard.   "The Government of the Gold Coast after
      the Second World War," African Affairs, LXVII (July 1968),
      209-18.

2215 Rohdie, Samuel.   "The Gold Coast aborigines abroad," J.
      Afr. Hist., VI, No. 3 (1965), 389-411.

2216 _____ .   "The Gold Coast hold-up of 1930-31," Trans. Hist.
      Soc. Ghana, IX (1968), 105-27.

2217 Rodney, Walter.   "Gold and slaves on the Gold Coast," Trans.
      Hist. Soc. Ghana, X (1969), 13-28.

2218 Rogers, R. S.   A History of the Ghana Army.   Vol. 1.   Accra:
      Govt. Printer, 1959.   87 p.

2219 Rumpf, Helmut.   Westafrika: Geschichte einer Küste.   Berlin:
      Junker & Dunnhaupt, 1943.   121 p.

2220 Sampson, Magnus J. West African leadership. Edited by
      Dr. E. U. Essien-Udom. London: Cass, 1969. 160 p.
      (African modern library, No. 10.)
           Reprint of the 1951 edition by Stockwell, London. A
      collection of public speeches of Casely Hayford, princi-
      pally his addresses to the National Congress of British
      West Africa which he founded and the Gold Coast Legisla-
      tive Council. They not only throw much light on the life
      of Hayford but also portray the contemporary political
      scene in the Gold Coast.
           Rev: J. Hist. Soc. Nigeria, V (June 1970), 449.

2221 Scott, David. Epidemic disease in Ghana, 1901-1960. Lon-
      don: Oxford University Press, 1965. 226 p. (Oxford med.
      Pub.)

2221a Shaloff, Stanley. "Press controls and sedition proceedings
      in the Gold Coast, 1933-39, " African Affairs, LXXI (July
      1972), 241-63.

2222 Shaw, Thurstan. "Further difficulties of indirect rule in the
      Gold Coast, " Man, XLV (March/April 1945), 27-30.

2223 Shepperson, George. "Notes on negro American influences
      on the emergence of African nationalism, " J. Afr. Hist.,
      I, No. 2 (1960), 299-312.

2224 Sorkpor, Gershon. "Geraldo de Lima and the Awunas, 1862-
      1904, " Master's Thesis, University of Ghana, 1966. 182 p.

2225 Sprigge, R. G. S. "Eweland's Adangbe: an enquiry into an
      oral tradition, " Trans. Hist. Soc. Ghana, X (1969), 87-
      128.

2226 _____. "A Note on the ethno-historical background to the
      Ewe-speaking villages of the Achimota-Legon area, " Ghana
      Notes & Queries, No. 11 (1970), 13-16.

2227 Stengers, Jean. "L'Impérialisme colonial de la fin du XIXe
      siècle: mythe or réalité, " J. Afr. Hist., III, No. 3 (1962),
      469-91.

2228 Stewart, Charles C. "The Tijaniya in Ghana: an historical
      study, " Master's Thesis, University of Ghana, 1965. 85 p.

2229 Stride, G. T. and Caroline Ifeka. Peoples and empires of
      West Africa: West Africa in history, 1000-1800. With
      advice from J. F. Ade Ajayi. New York: Africana Pub-
      lishing Corp., 1971. 356 p.
           An introductory history primarily designed for beginning
      college and secondary school students. Social and economic
      structure, politics and culture of individual states are

analyzed, noting the role of folk tradition in reconstructing
the West African history.

2230 Struchen, P. "Ghana-colony to republic," Canadian Geogr. J.,
      LXI (Nov. 1960), 176-89.

2231 Tenkorang, S. "British slave trading activities on the gold
      and slave coasts in the eighteenth century and their effect
      on African society," Master's Thesis, London University,
      1963/64.

2232 Tranakides, G. "Observations on the history of some Gold
      Coast peoples," Trans. Gold Coast & Togoland Hist. Soc.,
      I, No. 2 (1953), 33-44.

2233 Udoma, E. Udo. The Lion and the oil palm, and the clash
      of cultures. Dublin: University Press, 1943. 36 p.
      A brief analysis of the British rule in West Africa by
      a Nigerian law student now the Chief justice of the
      East African Court of Appeal.

2234 Ukpabi, S.C. "A Critique of official documents as source
      material for West African history," Geneva-Africa, IX
      (1970), 104-28.

2235 _____. "The West African Frontier Force," Master's
      Thesis, Birmingham University, 1964/65.

2236 United Nations. Trusteeship Council. Report of the
      plebiscite administration held in Togoland under United
      Kingdom administration in May 1956. New York, 1956.
      24 p. (T/1269. 18th session. Agenda 12a.)
      Gives the details of the plebiscite.

2237 Varley, W.J. "The Castles and forts of the Gold Coast,"
      Trans. Gold Coast & Togoland Hist. Soc., I (1952), 1-17.

2238 Wallerstein, Immanuel. "The Emergence of two West
      African nations, Ghana and the Ivory Coast," Doctoral
      Dissertation, Columbia University, 1959. 360 p.

2239 _____ and Michael Hechter. "Social rank and nationalism:
      some African data," Public Opinion Q., XXXIV, No. 3
      (1970), 360-70.
      Based on the data obtained in a survey conducted in
      Ghana, April-June 1957, it attempts to explain the impact
      of social rank and ethno-regional factors on the nature of
      support for nationalist movement.

2240 Ward, William Ernest Frank. A History of Ghana. Rev. 3rd
      ed. London: Allen & Unwin, 1966. 452 p.
      First published in 1948 under title: A History of the

Gold Coast.   General description of Ghana and its historical
and political development from even before the first European arrival in the seventeenth century.   Well documented.

2241 _____.   A Short history of Ghana.   London: Longmans,
1966.   275 p.
First published in 1935 under title: A Short History of
the Gold Coast.   Emphasis is on the British acquisition of
the Gold Coast during the 19th and 20th centuries.

2242 Webster, James Bertin and A. A. Boahen.   History of West
Africa: the revolutionary years--1815 to independence.
New York: Praeger, 1970.   333 p.
Published in London by Longmans under title: The Revo-
lutionary years: West Africa since 1800.
Rev: Choice, VII (Nov. 1970), 1282.   Library J., XCV
(Aug. 1970), 2676.

2243 Welman, Charles Wellesley.   The Natives of the Gold Coast:
history and constitution.   London: Dawson, 1969, 2 v.
(The colonial history series.)
v. 1: Peki, 46 p.   v. 2: Ahanta, 88 p.   Reprints of
1925 (v. 1) and 1930 (v. 2) editions.
Rev: West Africa, No. 2744 (Jan. 3, 1970), 13.

2244 Wilks, Ivor.   "A Note on the chronology, and origins of the
Gonja kings," Ghana Notes & Queries, No. 8 (1966), 26-8.

2245 _____.   "A Note on the early spread of Islam in Dagomba,"
Trans. Hist. Soc. Ghana, VIII (1965), 87-98.

2246 _____.   "Tribal history and myth," Universitas, II, No. 3
(1956), 84-6.

2247 Williams, Joseph.   Hebrewisms of West Africa, from Nile
to Niger with the Jews.   New York: Biblo Tannen, 1967.
443 p.
Attempts to establish the historical and cultural connec-
tions between the Ashanti of Ghana and the people of
Jamaica.   Extensive bibliography and index.

2248 Wilson, Henry S.   Origins of West African nationalism.
London: Macmillan, 1969.   391 p.

2249 Wiltgen, Ralph.   Gold Coast mission history, 1471-1880.
Techny, Illinois: Divine World, 1956.   181 p.
Rev: Amer. Hist. Rev., LXIII, No. 2 (1956), 457-8.

2250 Wingfield, R. J.   The Story of old Ghana, Melle and Songhai.
London: Oxford University Press, 1957.   60 p.

2251 Wolfson, Freda. "British relations with the Gold Coast,
      1843-1880, " Doctoral Dissertation, London University,
      1951/52.

2252 _____. "Early English traders in Ghana, " West Africa,
      No. 2079 (1957), 155-6.

2253 _____. "Historical records on the Gold Coast, " Bull.
      Inst. Hist. Res., XXIV, No. 70 (1951), 182-6.

2254 _____. Pageant of Ghana. London: Oxford University
      Press, 1958. 266 p. (West African history series.)
         An anthology of writings on the history of the Gold
      Coast from 1471 to the emergence of Ghana as an inde-
      pendent nation.
         Rev: Amer. Hist. Rev., LXIV (Oct. 1958), 79. TLS
      (April 25, 1958), 228.

2255 Wyndham, Hugh Archibald. The Atlantic and emancipation.
      London: Oxford University Press, 1937. 300 p. (Prob-
      lems of imperial trusteeship.)

2256 _____. The Atlantic and slavery. London: Oxford Uni-
      versity Press, 1935. 310 p. (Problems of imperial
      trusteeship.)

2257 Yegbe, J.B. "The Anlo and their neighbours, 1850-1890, "
      Master's Thesis, University of Ghana, 1966. 190 p.

2258 _____. "Research materials in the Ghana National
      Archives, Accra, on the history of Anlo, 1850-1890, "
      Research Rev., II, No. 3 (1966), 23-26.

(8) HISTORY--Akan (Ashanti, Fanti, et al.)

2258 Agyeman, E.A. "Gyaman--its relations with Ashanti (1720-
      1820), " Master's Thesis, University of Ghana, 1965. 124 p.

2259 Agyeman-Duah, J. "Mampong, Ashanti: a traditional history
      to the reign of Nan Safo Kantanka, " Trans. Hist. Soc.
      Ghana, IV, Part II (1960), 21-5.

2260 Ameyaw, Kwabena. "Kwahu--an early forest state, " Ghana
      Notes & Queries, No. 9 (1966), 39-45.
         A former province of the Ashanti Kingdom.

2261 Ansah, M.P. "Akwamu: a cultural history, " Master's
      Thesis, University of Ghana, 1965. 202 p.

2261a Anti, A.A. Akwamu Denkyira Akuapem and Ashanti in the
      lives of Osei Tutu and Okomfo Anokye. Accra: Ghana

Publishing Corp., 1971. 100 p.
   Anokye lived c. 1635-c. 1719; Tutu, 1645-1717. Both
were legendary and historical founders of Kumasi Kingdom
of the Ashanti.

2262 Appleton, Leslie. "Elmina: most ancient of all the Gold
      Coast castles," W. Afr. Rev. (Jan. 1953), 16-17.

2263 Arhin, Kwame. "Diffuse authority among the coastal Fanti,"
      Ghana Notes & Queries, No. 9 (1966), 66-70.

2264 _____. "The Financing of the Ashanti expansion (1700-
      1820)," Africa, XXXVII (July 1967), 283-91.

2265 _____. "The Missionary role on the Gold Coast and in
      Ashanti: Reverend F. A. Ramseyer and the British take-
      over of Ashanti, 1869-1894," Research Rev. (Legon), IV,
      No. 2 (1968), 1-12.

2266 _____. "The Structure of Greater Ashanti (1700-1824),"
      J. Afr. Hist., VIII, No. 1 (1968), 65-85.

2267 Aryee, R. T. A Short history of Okomfo Anokye, 1660-1740.
      Accra: Catholic Press, 1962. 8 p.

2268 Balmer, William Turnbull. A History of the Akan peoples
      of the Gold Coast. With a foreword by the Hon. C. W.
      Welman. London: Atlantis Press, 1925. 208 p.

2269 Beecham, John. Ashantee and the Gold Coast: being a
      sketch of the history, social state and superstitions of the
      inhabitants--. With an introduction by G. E. Metcalfe. Lon-
      don: Dawson, 1968. 376 p.
         Reprint of the Mason 1841 edition, London.

2270 Boahen, A. Adu. "The Origin of the Akan," Ghana Notes &
      Queries, No. 9 (1966), 3-10.
         After examining various speculations on their origin--
      archaeological, historical and geographical--the author
      tends to believe that "the Akan are an integral part of the
      negroes of West Africa, that their ancestors originated
      somewhere in the Benue-Chad region and moved south-
      westwards, westwards and finally southwards into the region
      of Asante where they developed these institutions and cul-
      tural traits with which they are now so exclusively
      identified."

2271 Brackenbury, Henry. The Ashanti war: a narrative. Edin-
      burgh: Blackwood, 1968. 2 v. 428 p.
         First published in 1874.

2272 Bravmann, René A. "The State sword, a pre-Ashanti tradi-
      tion, " Ghana Notes & Queries, No. 10 (1968), 1-4.

2273 Breffit, G. V. "Ashanti's living legend: the history of the
      sacred stool of Ashanti, " W. Afr. Rev. (Nov. 1960), 40-3.

2274 Brown, Godfrey N. "Asante and Fante in the nineteenth
      century. " In Joseph Anene and Godfrey Brown, eds.
      Africa in the nineteenth and twentieth centuries: a hand-
      book for teachers and students. London: Nelson, 1966,
      pp. 245-54.

2275 Canham, Peter. "An Ashanti case-history, " Africa, XVII
      (Jan. 1947), 35-40.

2276 Claridge, William W. A History of the Gold Coast and
      Ashanti from ancient times to the commencement of the
      twentieth century. 2nd ed. New York: Barnes & Noble,
      1964, 2 v. 1st ed. 1915 by John Murray, London.

2277 Collins, Edmund. "The Panic element in nineteenth century
      British relations with Ashanti, " Trans. Hist. Soc. Ghana,
      V, No. 2 (1962), 79-138.

2278 Correspondence on Ashanti affairs, 1874-1883. Shannon:
      Irish University Press, 1971. 719 p. (British Parlia-
      mentary papers, colonies, Africa, 60.)
      Reprint of the 1883 edition by H. M. S. O. , London.

2279 Daaku, Kwame Yeboa. "The Basis of Dutch relations with
      Axim, " Ghana Notes & Queries, No. 8 (1966), 19-20.

2280 _____. "The European traders and the coastal states,
      1630-1720, " Trans. Hist. Soc. Ghana, VIII (1965), 11-23.

2281 _____. "A Note on the fall of Ahwene Koko and its sig-
      nificance in Asante history, " Ghana Notes & Queries, No.
      10 (1968), 40-4.

2282 _____. "Pre-Ashanti state, " Ghana Notes & Queries, No.
      9 (1966), 10-13.

2283 Danquah, Joseph Boakye. "The Akan claim to origin from
      Ghana, " W. Afr. Rev. (Nov. 1955), 968-70; (Dec. 1955),
      1107-11.

2284 Datta, Ansu K. and R. Porter. "The Asofo system in his-
      torical perspective: an inquiry into the origins and develop-
      ment of a Ghanaian institution, " J. Afr. Hist. , XII (1971),
      279-97.

2285   Dretke, J. P.   "The Muslim community in Accra; a histor-
       ical survey," Master's Thesis, University of Ghana, 1968.
       187 p.

2286   Dumett, Raymond E.   "The Rubber trade of the Gold Coast
       and Asante in the nineteenth century: African innovation
       and market responsiveness," J. Afr. Hist., XII, No. 1
       (1971), 79-101.

2287   Eldridge, C. C.   "Newcastle and the Ashanti War of 1863-64:
       a failure of the policy of anti-imperialism," Renaissance
       and Mod. Stud., XII (1968), 68-90.

2288   Feinberg, Harvey Michael.   "Elmina, Ghana: a history of
       its development and relationship with the Dutch in the
       eighteenth century," Doctoral Dissertation, Boston Univer-
       sity, 1969.   289 p.
              An analysis of Elmina's political development, growth
       and daily life based primarily upon the manuscript re-
       sources of the Archives of the Netherlands Settlements on
       the Guinea Coast and the Archives of the Second West
       India Company.

2289   _____ .   "Who are the Elmina?"   Ghana Notes & Queries,
       No. 11 (1970), 20-6.
              A vexing question to historians and anthropologists, as
       the Elmina people deny that they are Fanti, while acknowl-
       edging an ancient relationship with the Kingdom of Eguafo.
       The author attempts to answer the question by discussing
       Elmina's political structure, historical relations with her
       African neighbors and her relations with the Dutch.

2290   Flight, Colin.   "Chronology of the kings and queen mothers
       of Bono-Manso: a re-evaluation of the evidence," J. Afr.
       Hist., XI, No. 2 (1970), 259-68.

2291   Freestone, Basil.   Osei Tutu: the legend owns the land.
       London: Dobson, 1968.   183 p.

2292   Fuller, Francis.   A Vanished dynasty--Ashanti.   With a new
       introduction by W. E. F. Ward.   2nd ed.   London: Cass,
       1967.   241 p.   1st ed. 1921.
              Rev: West Africa, No. 2671 (Aug. 10, 1968), 925.

2293   Fynn, John K.   Asante and its neighbours, 1700-1807.   Lon-
       don: Longmans, 1972.   175 p.

2293a _____ .   "Ashanti and her neighbours, c. 1700-1807,"
       Doctoral Dissertation, London University, 1963/64.

2294   _____ .   "The Reign and times of Kusi Obodum, 1750-64,"
       Trans. Hist. Soc. Ghana, VIII (1965), 24-32.

2295 _____ . "The Rise of Ashanti," Ghana Notes & Queries,
     No. 9 (1966), 24-30.

2296 Ghana. University. Institute of African Studies. Ashanti
     and the Northwest. Edited by John Rankine Goody and
     Kwame Arhin. Legon, 1964. 185 p. (Ashanti Research
     Project No. 1.)

2297 _____ . Ashanti Research Project: progress report No. 1,
     1963-66. Legon, 1966. 81 p.

2298 Goody, John Rankine. "Ethno-history and the Akan of Ghana,"
     Africa, XXIX, No. 1 (1959), 67-81.

2299 Gordon, J. "Some oral traditions of Denkyira," Trans. Gold
     Coast & Togoland Hist. Soc. , I, No. 3 (1953), 27-33.

2300 Great Britain. Colonial Office. Correspondence relating to
     the Ashanti War, 1900 (and) correspondence relating to
     Ashanti, 1901. London: H. M. S. O. , 1901.

2301 Hayford, Casely. Gold Coast institutions, with thoughts upon
     a healthy imperial policy for the Gold Coast and Ashanti.
     London: Cass, 1970. 418 p. (Cass Library of African
     Studies. Africana modern library, No. 11.)
         First published 1913 by Sweet & Maxwell, London. "Con-
     stitution of the New Fantee Confederacy," pp. 327-40.

2302 Horton, James Africanus. Letters on the political condition
     of the Gold Coast since the exchange of territory between
     the English and Dutch Governments, on January 1, 1868,
     together with a short account of the Ashanti War, 1862-64,
     and the Awoonah War, 1886. 2nd ed. With a new intro-
     duction by E. A. Ayandele. London: Cass, 1970. 179 p.
     (Cass Library of African Studies, Africana modern library,
     No. 12.)

2303 Johnson, Marion. "Ashanti, east of the Volta," Trans. Hist.
     Soc. Ghana, VIII (1964), 33-59.

2304 Kea, R. A. "Akwamu-Anlo relations, c. 1750-1813," Trans.
     Hist. Soc. Ghana, X (1969), 29-63.

2305 _____ . "Ashanti-Danish relations, 1780-1831," Master's
     Thesis, University of Ghana, 1967. 585 p.

2306 _____ . "Four Asante officials in the South-east Gold
     Coast (1808)," Ghana Notes & Queries, No. 11 (1970),
     42-7.

2307 _____ . "Osei Kwame's interdiction on Danish trade, 1783-
     89," Ghana Notes & Queries, No. 11 (1970), 36-41.

2308   Kullas, H. and G. A. Ayer. What the elders of Ashanti say.
       Kumasi: University Press, 1967. 104 p.

2309   Kumah, John Kweku. "Denkyira: 1600-1730 A. D." Master's
       Thesis, University of Ghana, 1965. 171 p.

2310   _____. "The Rise and fall of the Kingdom of Denkyira,"
       Ghana Notes & Queries, No. 9 (1966), 33-5.

2311   Kwamena-Poh, M. A. "The Emergence of Akuapem state,
       1730-1850," Ghana Notes & Queries, No. 11 (1970), 26-36.

2311a _____. Government and politics in the Akuapem State,
       1730-1850. Evanston: Northwestern University Press, 1971.
       172 p. (Legon history series.)

2311b Kyerematen, A. A. Interstate boundary litigation in Ashanti.
       Cambridge: African Studies Centre, Cambridge University,
       1972. 139 p.

2312   Legassick, Martin. "Accra: an informal profile of Ghana's
       capital," Africa Today, XI (Nov. 1964), 4-6.

2313   _____. "Firearms, horses and Samorian Army organiza-
       tion, 1870-1898," J. Afr. Hist., VII (1966), 95-115.

2314   Levtzion, Nehemia. "Early nineteenth century arabic manu-
       scripts from Jamasi," Trans. Hist. Soc. Ghana, VIII (1965),
       99-119.

2315   Lloyd, Alan. The Drums of Kumasi: the story of the
       Ashanti wars. London: Longmans, 1964. 209 p.

2316   Matson, J. N. A Digest of the minutes of the Ashanti Con-
       federacy Council, 1935-49, and a revised edition of War-
       rington's notes on Ashanti custom, prepared for the use of
       District Commissioners. Cape Coast: Prospect Printing
       Press, 1951. 76 p.

2317   Mate-Kole, Azzu. "The Historical background of Krobo cus-
       tom," Trans. Gold Coast & Togoland Hist. Soc., I, Part
       VI (1955), 133-40.
          It is traditionally believed that the Krobos originally
       migrated from North-Eastern Nigeria.

2318   Meyerowitz, Eva L. "The Akan and Ghana," Man, LVII
       (June 1957), 83-8.

2319   _____. Akan traditions of origin. London: Faber &
       Faber, 1952. 149 p.
          Early history of the Gold Coast.
          Rev: African Affairs, LI (1952), 344-5.

2320 _____ . At the court of an African king. London: Faber
& Faber, 1962.
The King of Bono in Ghana regains, on the intercession
of the author, his villages lost to the Ashanti.
Rev: TLS (Dec. 28, 1962), 933-4.

2321 _____ . "A Note on the early history of the Jamasi people,"
Trans. Gold Coast & Togoland Hist. Soc., I (1954), 141-3.

2322 _____ . "A Note on the origin of Ghana," African Affairs,
LI (Oct. 1952), 319-23.

2323 Moseley, Maboth. "Soldiers of the Queen in Ashanti" [1873]
W. Afr. Rev. (Dec. 1952), 1236-9.

2324 Myatt, Frederick. The Golden stool: an account of the
Ashanti War of 1900. London: Kimber, 1966. 192 p.

2325 Nathan, Matthew. "Historical chart of the Gold Coast and
Ashanti, compiled from various sources," J. Afr. Soc.,
IV (Oct. 1904), 33-43.

2326 Padmore, George. The Gold Coast revolution, the struggle
of an African people from slavery to freedom. London:
Nisbet, 1953. 272 p.
Account of the Gold Coast from the foundation of the
Ashanti Confederacy to the Nkrumah regime.
Rev: Library J., LXXVIII (Sept. 1, 1953), 1429. TLS
(May 29, 1953), 346.

2327 Papers concerning Gold Coast and Ashanti affairs, 1890-96.
Shannon: Irish University Press, 1971. 642 p. (British
parliamentary papers, colonies, Africa, 62.) Reprint of
the first editions by H. M. S. O., London, 1890-96.

2328 Potekhin, I. I. "On feudalism of the Ashanti." Paper presented at the International Congress of Orientalists, Moscow, 1960.

2329 Priestley, Margaret. "The Ashanti question and the British:
eighteenth century origins," J. Afr. Hist., II, No. 1 (1961),
35-49.

2330 _____ and Ivor Wilks. "The Ashanti kings in the eighteenth
century: a revised chronology," J. Afr. Hist., I, No. 1
(1960), 83-96.

2331 Reindorf, Carl Christian. The History of the Gold Coast and
Asante, 1500-1860. With a biographical sketch. 2nd ed.
Basel: Basel Mission Book Depot, 1951. 351 p. 1st ed.
1895.
An important sourcebook by one of the first Africans to

be ordained by the Basel missionaries. The introductory
biography of the author by his son contains many translations of Ga anecdotes, sayings and songs.

2332   Saffell, John Edgar. "The Ashanti War of 1873-1874, " Doctoral Dissertation, Case Western Reserve University, 1965.
401 p.

2333   Stewart, J.M. "Akan history: some linguistic evidence, "
Ghana Notes & Queries, No. 9 (1966), 54-8.
Designed "to give the genetic and acculturational relationships of the Akan (Twi-Fante) language and its neighbours as they appear in the light of the most recent
research and to suggest historical interpretations. "

2334   Tenkorang, S. "The importance of firearms in the struggle
between Ashanti and the Coastal states, 1708-1807, " Trans.
Hist. Soc. Ghana, IX (1968), 1-16.

2334a Tordoff, William. "The Ashanti Confederacy, " J. Afr. Hist. ,
III, No. 3 (1962), 399-417.

2335   . "The Exile and repatriation of Nana Prempeh I of
Ashanti (1896-1924), " Trans. Hist. Soc. Ghana, IV, No. 2
(1960), 33-58.

2336   . "The Political history of Ashanti, 1888-1935, "
Doctoral Dissertation, London University, 1961.

2337   Van Dantzig, Albert. "The Dutch military recruitment agency
in Kumasi, " Ghana Notes & Queries, No. 8 (1966), 21-4.

2338   Wasserman, B. "The Ashanti War of 1900: a study in cultural conflict, " Africa, XXXI (April 1961), 167-78.

2339   Wild, Robert P. "The Inhabitants of the Gold Coast and
Ashanti before the Akan invasion, " Gold Coast Teachers' J. ,
VI, No. 3 (1935), 195-201.

2340   Wilks, Ivor. "Akwamu and Otublohum, an 18th century marriage arrangement, " Africa, XXIX, No. 4 (1959), 391-404.

2341   . "Akwamu, 1650-1750, " Master's Thesis, University College, Cardiff, 1958.

2342   . "Aspects of bureaucratization in Ashanti in the
nineteenth century, " J. Afr. Hist. , VII (1966), 215-32.

2343   . "The Growth of the Akwapim state. " In J. Vansina, et al. , eds. The historian in tropical Africa. London: Oxford University Press, 1964, pp. 390-409.

2344   .   The Northern factor in Ashanti history.   Legon:
          Institute of African Studies, University of Ghana, 1961.
          46 p.
                    Rev: J. Afr. Hist., III (1962), 518-9.

2345   .   "The Northern factor in Ashanti history: Begho
          and the Mande," J. Afr. Hist., II, No. 1 (1961), 25-34.

2346   .   "The Rise of the Akwamu Empire, 1650-1710,"
          Trans. Hist. Soc. Ghana, III, No. 2 (1957), 99-136.

2347   Wolfson, Freda. "A Price agreement on the Gold Coast:
          the Krobo oil boycott," Econ. Hist. Rev., VI (1953), 68-
          77.

(9) LAW

2348   Acquaye, E. "Administration and development of stool land
          in Ghana," Rev. Ghana Law, I (Dec. 1969), 174-82; II
          (April 1970), 22+.

2349   Adjetey, Peter. "Some legal consequences of polygamous
          marriage in Ghana," Universitas, IV, No. 6 (1961), 168-71.

2350   Afreh, D. Kwame. "Ghana." In Antony Allott, ed. Judicial
          and legal systems in Africa, 2nd ed. London: Butter-
          worths, 1970, pp. 25-39.
                    Analysis of Ghanaian courts with specifications as to
          their date of establishment, composition, jurisdiction, etc.

2351   .   "Ghana's legal muddles--1," West Africa, No.
          2659 (May 18, 1968), 572-3.
                    Contends that the confused state of the Ghana law stems
          from "the Supreme Court Ordinance, 1876, which estab-
          lished a typical British colonial dual legal system."

2352   .   "Ghana's legal muddle--2," West Africa, No.
          2660 (May 25, 1968), 604-5.
                    Ghana law on marriage, property and inheritance. The
          author is former Dean of the Faculty of Law, University
          of Ghana.

2353   African Conference on the Rule of Law, Lagos, Nigeria, Jan.
          3-7, 1961. A Report on the proceedings of a conference.
          Geneva: International Commission of Jurists, 1961. 181 p.
                    General theme of the conference: "Government action,
          state security and human rights."

2354 Afrika Instituut, Leiden. Future of customary law in Africa.
      Leiden: University Press, 1956. 323 p.

2355 Aidoo, J. E. "Ghana law of succession." B. Litt's Thesis,
      Oxford University, 1963/64.

2356 Akyempim, Owusu. The Native court and its functions.
      Kumasi: Adom Press, 1955. 30 p.

2357 Allott, Antony Nicolas. "The Akan law of property," Doc-
      toral Dissertation, London University, 1953/54.

2358 _____. "The Changing law in changing Africa," Sociologus,
      XI, No. 2 (1961), 115-31.

2359 _____. "The Development of the law of Ghana," Ann.
      Fac. Droit Istanbul, (1962), 210-7.

2360 _____. "The Effect of marriage on property in the Gold
      Coast," Int. Comp. Law Q., V (Oct. 1956), 519-33.

2361 _____. "Family in West Africa; its juristic basis, con-
      trol and enjoyment." In J. N. D. Anderson, ed. Family
      law in Asia and Africa. New York: Praeger, 1968, pp.
      121-42.

2362 _____, ed. The Future of law in Africa; record of pro-
      ceedings of the London Conference, 28 December 1959-
      8 January 1960. London: Butterworths, 1960. 58 p.

2363 _____, ed. Judicial and legal systems in Africa. 2nd ed.
      London: Butterworths, 1970. 314 p. (African law series,
      No. 4.) 1st edition, 1962.

2364 _____. "Judicial precedent in Africa revisited," J. Afr.
      Law, XII, No. 1 (1968), 3-31.

2365 _____. "Legal development and economic growth in
      Africa." In J. N. D. Anderson, ed. Changing law in
      developing countries. New York: Praeger, 1963, pp.
      194-209.

2366 _____. "Local and customary courts in the former British
      Territories in Africa." In John Gilissen, ed. L'Organisa-
      tion judiciaire en Afrique noire. Bruxelles: Editions de
      l'Institut de Sociologie, Université Libre de Bruxelles, 1969,
      pp. 247-58.

2367 _____. "Marriage and internal conflict of laws in Ghana,"
      J. Afr. Law, II (Autumn 1958), 164-84.

2368 _____ . "Native tribunals in the Gold Coast, 1844-1927: prolegomena to a study of native courts in Ghana," J. Afr. Law, I, No. 3 (1957), 165-71.

2369 _____ , ed. New essays in Africa law. London: Butterworths, 1970. 348 p. (African law series, No. 13.)
Essays on various aspects of African law with special reference to statutory law. Part I. Reception of extraneous law. Part II. Internal conflicts and the application of customary law. Tables of cases, statutes and orders; subject and geographic index. See also Allott's Essays in African law, with special reference to the law of Ghana (1960).
Rev: J. Afr. Law, XIV (Summer 1970), 130-1.

2370 _____ and J. Read. "Practice procedure and evidence in the Africa local or customary courts," J. Afr. Law, V (1961), 131+.
Colloquium on African law, London, June 1961.

2371 Amissah, A. N. E. "The Machinery of criminal justice in Ghana," Univ. Ghana Law J., I (1964), 80+.

2372 _____ . "Police and the courts," Rev. Ghana Law, I (May 1969), 31+.

2373 Anderson, James Norman. Changing law in developing countries. London: Allen & Unwin, 1963. 292 p. (Studies on modern Asia and Africa, No. 2.)
A collection of fourteen lectures read during 1961-62 at the School of Oriental and African Studies, University of London, on selected legal problems in British or former British colonies.
Rev: Amer. Pol. Sci. Rev., LVIII (March 1964), 152. Ann. Amer. Acad. Pol. Soc. Sci., CCCLII (March 1964), 208.

2374 _____ , ed. Family law in Asia and Africa. New York: Praeger, 1967. 301 p. (Studies on modern Asia and Africa, No. 6.)

2375 _____ . Islamic law in Africa. 2nd ed. London: Cass, 1970. 409 p. (Cass library of African law.) 1st edition 1955.
Application of Islamic law in the former British Territories and in the Colony and Protectorate of Aden.

2376 Anti, K. "The Legal institutions of the Gold Coast," Master's Thesis, University of Leeds, 1956/57.

2377 Asamoah, Obed Y. The Legal significance of the declarations of the General Assembly of the United Nations. The Hague: Martinus Nijhoff, 1966. 274 p.

2378 _____. "Problems of law reform in Ghana," Legon Observer, I (July 22, 1966), 9-10.

2379 Asante, S. K. B. "Fiduciary principles in Anglo-American law and the customary law of Ghana--a comparative study," Int. Comp. Law Q., XIV (Oct. 1965), 1144+.

2380 _____. "Interests in land in the customary law of Ghana-- a new apparisal," Yale Law J., LXXIV (April 1965), 848+. Also in Univ. Ghana Law J., VI (1969), 99+.

2381 _____. "Law and society in Ghana," Wis. Law Rev., (Fall 1966), 1113-24.

2382 _____. "Stare decisis in the Supreme Court of Ghana," Univ. Ghana Law J., I (1964), 52+.

2383 Atiyah, P. S. "Commercial law in Ghana," J. Business Law, (Oct. 1960), 430+.

2384 Austin, D. G. "Constitutional development of Ghana," United Asia, IX (1957), 84-90.

2385 Bailey, Sidney D. "Constitutions of the British Colonies, II: Africa," Parl. Affairs, II (Autumn 1949), 399-412.
    Summarizes the constitutional situation in British Colonies in 1949.

2386 Baty, Thomas. The Canons of international law. London: John Murray, 1930. 518 p.

2387 Bennion, Francis A. The Constitutional law of Ghana. London: Butterworths, 1962. 527 p. (African law series, No. 5.)
    Analyzes Ghana's constitutional development up to the end of 1961.

2388 Bentsi-Enchill, Kwamena. "Do African systems of land tenure require a special terminology?" J. Afr. Law, IX (Summer 1965), 114-39.

2389 _____. Ghana land law: an exposition, analysis and critique. London: Sweet & Maxwell, 1964. 408 p. (Law in Africa, No. 10.)
    A critical study of the Ghana land law based on the assumption that "the indigenous law relating to land is essentially viable and worthy to be retained as the foundation of the system of land law in Ghana."
    Rev: Int. Labour Rev., XCI (April 1965), 353.

2390 _____. "Problems in the construction of viable constitutional structures in Africa." In Gwendolen Carter and

Ann Paden, eds. Expanding horizons in African studies. Evanston: Northwestern University Press, 1969, pp. 173-80.

A critical examination of institutional factors conducive to a workable constitutional structure, with special reference to Ghana and Nigeria.

2391 Bevans, Charles I. "Ghana and United States--United Kingdom agreements," Amer. J. Int. Law, LIX (Jan. 1965), 93-7.

2392 Bibliography of African law, 1947-1966. Bibliographie de droit africain, 1947-66. Addis Ababa: Faculty of Law, Haile Selassie University, n. d.

Published as: African law bibliography/bibliographie de droit africain, 1947-1966. Bruxelles: Presses Universitaires de Bruxelles, 1972. 480 p.

2393 Birmingham, R. L. and C. S. Birmingham. "Legal remedies for overurbanization: the Ghanaian experience," UCLA Law Review, XVIII (Dec. 1970), 252+.

2394 Borchard, E. M. The Diplomatic protection of citizens abroad; or the law of international claims. New York: Banks Law Publishing Co., 1915. 988 p.

2395 Brehme, G. "Ortliche Organe der Staatsmacht in Ghana," Staat und Recht, XIII (May 1964), 907+.

2396 _____. "Zerschlagung des alten kolonialen Unterdrükungs-apparates-Grundzug der Entwicklung zum Staat der nationalen Demokratie," Staat und Recht, XI (Dec. 1962), 2188+.

Summary in English and Russian.

2397 Brobbey, S. A. "Selling by installments," Rev. Ghana Law, II (April 1970), 13+; II (Aug. 1970), 104+; II (Dec. 1970), 207+.

A series of three articles.

2398 Bushoven, C. "The Judicial process in a developing nation: the courts of Ghana," Doctoral Dissertation, Duke University, Durham, 1969.

2399 Christian, A. "Situation et statut juridique de la femme ghaneene," Vivante Africaine, No. 243 (1966), 19-21.

2400 Chukura, Olisa. Privy Council digest: a digest of decisions of Her Majesty's Privy Council in appeals from West Africa, 1841 to 1964. Ibadan: Gillford, 1969. 65 p.

2401   Cotran, Eugene and N. N. Rubin, eds.   Readings in African
       law.   New York: Africana Publishing Corp., 1970.   2 v.

2402   Cowen, Denis W.   "African studies--a survey of the field
       and the role of the U. S.," Law Cont. Problems, XXVII
       (Autumn 1962), 545-75.

2403   Daniels, Janet.   Current cases: being a digest of selected
       judgments: ten year case citator, 1959-68.   Accra:
       Ghana Law Reports, 1968.   96 p.

2404   Daniels, W. C. E.   "English law in West Africa: the limits
       of its application," Doctoral Dissertation, London Univer-
       sity, 1962.

2405   _____.   "The Place of equity in West African law,"
       Master's Thesis, London University, 1960/61.

2406   _____.   "Towards the integration of the laws relating
       to husband and wife in Ghana," Univ. Ghana Law J., II
       (1965), 20+.

2407   Danquah, Joseph B.   Akan laws and customs and the Akim
       Abuakwa constitution.   London: Routledge, 1928.   272 p.
            Rev: J. Soc. Pub. Teachers Law (1929), 41-3.

2408   _____.   Cases in Akan law: decisions delivered by the
       Hon. Nana Sir Ofori Atta, K. B. E.   London: Routledge,
       1928.   288 p.
            Rev: J. Soc. Pub. Teachers Law (1929), 41-3.

2409   Date-Bah, S. K.   "Article fifteen of the constitution and the
       tort of false imprisonment," Univ. Ghana Law J., VII
       (1970), 66+.

2410   Davies, S. G.   "Ghana: the criminal procedure code, 1960,"
       Int. Comp. Law Q., XI (April 1962), 588+.

2411   _____.   "The Growth of law in the Gold Coast," Univer-
       sitas, II (Dec. 1955), 4-6.

2412   _____.   The West African law reports, vol. 1.   Achimota:
       West African Law Publishing Co., 1956.   288 p.

2413   De Graft-Johnson, E. V. C.   "The Evolution of the Executive
       in the constitutional development of the Gold Coast," Doc-
       toral Dissertation, University of Leeds, 1958/59.

2414   _____.   "The Marriage laws of the Akan of the Gold Coast,"
       Master's Thesis, University of Leeds, 1953/54.

2415 Dei-Anang, K. K. "Caveat venditor Ghanaiensis," Univ. Ghana
      Law J., VI (1967), 90+.

2416 _____. "Pre-incorporation contract and section 13 of
      the companies code," Univ. Ghana Law J., VI (1969), 1+.

2417 Derrett, J. "Fiduciary principles, the African family and
      the Hindu law," Int. Comp. Law Q., XV (Oct. 1966),
      1205-16.

2418 De Smith, S. A. The Commonwealth and its constitutions.
      London: Stevens, 1964. 312 p.
         Rev: Amer. J. Comp. Law, XIV (1965/66), 702+.

2419 _____. "The Independence of Ghana," Mod. Law Rev.,
      XX (July 1957), 347-63.

2420 _____. "Westminster export models: the legal frame-
      work of responsible government," J. Commonwealth Pol.
      Stud., I (Nov. 1961), 1-14.

2421 "Double and deadly jeopardy: judiciary system overruled
      by Nkrumah," Time, LXXXV (Feb. 19, 1965), 34-5.
         Comments on Nkrumah's expulsion of Ghana's Chief
      Justice from office for failing to convict some Ghanaians
      who allegedly plotted against Nkrumah's life.

2422 Eagleton, Clyde. The Responsibility of states in interna-
      tional law. New York: New York University Press, 1928.
      291 p.

2423 Elias, Taslim Olawale. British colonial law: a comparative
      study of the interaction between English and local laws in
      British Dependencies. London: Stevens, 1962. 323 p.
         The author, a Nigerian, and most distinguished African
      legal scholar, is former Dean of the Faculty of Law, Uni-
      versity of Lagos and for many years Nigeria's Federal
      Attorney-General.
         Rev: Mod. Law Rev., XXV (Sept. 1962), 619. Malayan
      Law Rev., IV (July 1962), 176.

2424 _____. "The Form and content of colonial law," Int.
      Comp. Law Q., III (1954), 645-50.

2425 _____. Ghana and Sierra Leone: the development of
      their laws and constitutions. London: Stevens, 1962.
      334 p. (The British Commonwealth: the development of
      its laws and constitutions, v. 10.)
         "The first comprehensive account of the constitutional
      evolution of either Ghana or Sierra Leone to be written by
      a lawyer, and the description of the entire legal system,
      land law, family law, and criminal law also represents

the only coherent study of each topic in existence" (Fore-word).

2426 _____. The Nature of African customary law. Man-chester: Manchester University Press, 1956. 318 p.
Rev: Rechts. Weekblad, XXV (Dec. 1961), 777.
Law Q. Rev., LXXIII (Jan. 1957), 106.

2427 Erzuah, J. B. "Comparative study of constitutional and ad-ministrative structure in Ghana," Civilisations, XIV, Nos. 1-2 (1964), 85-91.

2428 Fiadjoe, A. "Company returns--some random thoughts on the annual return," Rev. Ghana Law, II (Aug. 1970), 97+.

2429 "Final report of the Commission of Inquiry into the Working and Administration of Present Company Law of Ghana," Mod. Law Rev., XXV (Jan. 1962), 78+.

2430 Fleming, Harold Manchester. States, contracts and progress: dynamics of international wealth. New York: Oceana, 1960. 128 p.

2431 Foighel, I. Nationalization: a study in the protection of alien property in international law. London: Stevens, 1957. 136 p.

2432 Freides, Thelma. "The New nations: bibliography of con-stitutions, 1956-64," Ref. Q., IV (March 1965), 9-15.

2432a Ghana. National Archives. Exhibition of documents on Ghana's constitutional development: Catalogue. Accra, 1957.
Background list of documents on constitutional develop-ment of the Gold Coast from Mid-19th century to 1957.

2433 The Ghana law reports: cases determined by the High Court of Justice and on appeal therefrom in the court of appeal. Accra: General Legal Council, 1959. 3 parts.

2434 The Ghana law reports 1961: cases determined by the Su-preme Court and High Court of the Republic of Ghana. Accra: General Legal Council, 1967. 2 parts. 839 p.

2435 "Ghana's Preventive Detention Act," J. Int. Comm. Jurists, III (Winter 1962), 65-99.
Includes the text of the 1958 Act.

2436 Gilissen, John ed. L'Organisation judiciaire en Afrique Noire: études d'histoire et d'ethnologie juridiques. Bruxelles: Editions de l'Institut de Sociologie, Université Libre de Bruxelles, 1969. 290 p.

Examination of judicial processes and legal systems of
various African states by different authorities.   Detailed
table of contents put at the back; extensive bibliography
and no index.

2437   Gillespie, W. H.   The Gold Coast police, 1844-1938.   Accra:
Govt. Printer, 1955.   91 p.

2438   Gluckman, M., ed.   Ideas and procedures in African customary law.   London: Oxford University Press for International African Institute, 1969.   361 p.
Rev: African Affairs, LXX (Jan. 1971), 89-90.

2439   Gold Coast.   Handbook for native courts in Ashanti.   Accra:
Govt. Printer, 1953.   63 p.

2440   Gollo, F. K.   "The Rights of the citizen within the frame-
work of law," Insight (Cape Coast), II (Feb. 1967), 36-41.

2441   Gower, L. C. B.   Independent Africa--the challenge to the
legal profession.   London: Oxford University Press, 1968.
166 p.
Deals with Nigeria, Ghana, Sierra Leone, the Gambia,
Kenya, Uganda and Tanzania.
Rev: West Africa, No. 2686 (Nov. 23, 1968), 1377-8.

2442   Great Britain.   Colonial Office.   Bibliography of published
sources relating to African land tenure.   London:
H. M. S. O., 1950.   156 p.
Annotated entries, dealing chiefly with native forms of
land tenure, are arranged by country and then by form of
material and publication date.   Though dated, it is of
great historical value.

2443   "The Growth of Executive Power in Ghana," Int. Comm.
Jurists Bull., (May 1962), 21-9.

2444   Griffith, William Brandford.   A Digest of and index to the
reports of cases decided in the Supreme Court of the Gold
Coast Colony.   Accra: Govt. Printer, 1953.

2445   _____ .   A Note on the history of British courts in the
Gold Coast Colony, with a brief account of the changes in
the constitution of the Colony.   Accra: Govt. Printer, 1936.

2446   Gyando, S. O.   "Principles of judicial interpretation of the
republican constitution of Ghana," Univ. Ghana Law J.,
III (1966), 37+.

2447   _____ .   "Role of the judiciary under the constitutional
proposals for Ghana," Univ. Ghana Law J., V (1968),
133+.

2448   Hagan, G. P.   The Judicial process among the Ashanti of
       Ghana.   Accra: Institute of African Studies, University of
       Ghana, 1969.   120 p.

2449   Hannigan, A. St. J.   "Equity and the law in Ghana," Univ.
       Ghana Law J., IV (1967), 28+.

2450   _____.   "The Impact of English law upon the existing
       Gold Coast custom and the possible development of the
       resulting systems," J. Afr. Adm., VIII (July 1956),
       126-32.

2451   _____.   "The Imposition of western law forms upon primi-
       tive societies," Comp. Stud. Soc. Hist., IV (1961), 1-9.

2452   _____.   "Introduction of registration of title to land,"
       Universitas, II (March 1956), 41-3.

2453   _____.   "Native custom, its similarity to English conven-
       tional custom and its mode of proof," J. Afr. Law, II
       (Summer 1958), 101-15.

2454   _____.   "Question of notice under the Ghanaian system
       of the registration of deeds," Univ. Ghana Law J., III
       (1966), 27+.

2455   Harvey, William Burnett.   "Evolution of Ghana law since
       independence," Law Cont. Problems, XXVII (Autumn 1962),
       581-604.

2456   _____.   Law and social change in Ghana.   Princeton,
       New Jersey: Princeton University Press, 1966.   453 p.
           A study of the evolution of the legal order in Ghana by
       a former Professor and Dean of the Law Faculty, Univer-
       sity of Ghana, 1962-64.   Basic data of the study include
       constitutions, statutes, judicial decisions, delegated legisla-
       tion and executive actions.
           Rev: Amer. Soc. Rev., XXXI (Aug. 1966), 562-3.

2457   _____.   "Post-Nkrumah Ghana: the legal profile of a
       coup," Wis. Law Rev., (Fall 1966), 1096-112.

2458   _____.   "Value analysis of Ghanaian legal development
       since independence," Univ. Ghana Law J., I (1964), 4+.

2459   _____   and Conor Cruise O'Brien.   "The Judiciary in
       Ghana," Assoc. Bar City N. Y. Rec., XXI (April 1966),
       222-35.
           Based on authors' addresses.   Dr. O'Brien, an Irish
       historian, is former Vice-Chancellor of the University
       of Ghana.

2460   Hayford, Joseph Ephraim Casely. Gold Coast land tenure
       and the forest bill: a review of the situation. Second
       notice. London: Philips, 1912. 41 p.

2461   Head, L. L. "International standards of civil procedure:
       the alien in the courts of Ghana, " St. Louis Univ. Law J.,
       XII (Spring 1968), 392+.

2462   Hedges, R. Y. "Legal education in West Africa, " J. Soc.
       Pub. Teachers Law, VI (1961), 75-9.

2463   Heidelberg, W. "Rollt in Afrika die Nationalisierungswelle?"
       Ver. Recht Ubersee (West Germany), III (1970), 377+.

2464   Hellawell, R. "Taxation and economic development, " Univ.
       Ghana Law J., VI (1969), 89+.

2465   Heydon, J. D. "Gratuitous options: section 8 (1) of the
       Contracts Act, " Univ. Ghana Law J., VI (1969), 40+.

2466   Hoebel, E. Adamson. "Fundamental legal concepts as
       applied in the study of primitive law, " Yale Law J., LI
       (1942), 951-66.

2467   _____. The Law of primitive man: a study in primitive
       legal dynamics. Cambridge: Harvard University Press,
       1954. 357 p.
       Outlines ideas and methods for the study of law in
       primitive societies, including the ways in which their jural
       postulates are translated into legal forms and actions.
       Rev: Amer. Bar Assoc. J., XLI (March 1955), 255-6.
       Univ. Kansas Law Rev., III (May 1955), 382-4.

2468   Holland, D. C. "Constitutional experiments in British West
       Africa, " Public Law (London), (Spring 1957), 42-57.

2469   Hone, Ralph. "The Legislation providing for the grant of
       independence to Ghana, " J. Afr. Law, I (Summer 1957),
       99-112.
       Analyzes Independence Act of 1957 and the Ghana (Con-
       stitution) Order in Council of 1957.

2470   Hutchison, Thomas W., ed. Africa and law; developing
       legal systems in African Commonwealth nations. With an
       introduction by A. Arthur Schiller. Madison: University
       of Wisconsin Press, 1968. 181 p.
       "Substantially the fall 1966 issue of the Wisconsin Law
       Review with substitutions and additions including a new in-
       troduction by A. Arthur Schiller. " Contents include "Post
       Nkrumah Ghana: the legal profile of a coup, " by W. B.
       Harvey, and "Law and Society in Ghana, " by S. K. B.
       Asante.

2471   Idenburg, P. J.   "Les nouveaux états africains et les normes
       démocratiques occidentales, " Rev. Jur. Pol., XV, No. 2
       (1961), 195-203.
          Justifies one party-systems of government in Africa.

2472   International Institute of Differing Civilizations.   The Consti-
       tutions and administrative institutions of the new states.
       Report of the 33rd session held in Palermo, Sicily, Sep-
       tember 1963.   Brussels, 1965.   888 p.
          In English and French.   Studies of specific constitutional
       and administrative problems of the new states by 160 par-
       ticipants from 34 states.   (Available from INCIDI, 11 Boule-
       vard de Waterloo, Brussels.)

2473   Jearey, J. H.   "Structure, composition of jurisdiction of courts
       and authorities enforcing the criminal law in British African
       Territories, " Int. Comp. Law Q., IX (July 1960), 396+.

2474   _____.   "Trial by jury and trial with the aid of assessors
       in the Superior Courts of British African Territories, " J.
       Afr. Law, V (1961), 82+.

2475   Jennings, William Ivor.   Constitutional laws of the Common-
       wealth.   V. 1.   3rd ed.   Oxford: Clarendon Press, 1957.
       1st ed. 1938 under title: Constitutional laws of the British
       Empire.

2476   Jeol, M.   La réforme de la justice en Afrique noire.   Paris:
       Pedone, 1963.   183 p.   (Collection du Centre de Recherches,
       d'Etudes et de Documentation sur les Institutions et la
       Legislation Africaines, 3.)

2477   Juergensmeyer, J. C.   "African presidentialism: a comparison
       of the Executive under the constitutions of the Federation of
       Nigeria, the Federal Republics of the Congo and Cameroon,
       and the Republics of Ghana, Chad, and the entente, " J. Afr.
       Law, VIII, No. 3 (1964), 157-77.

2478   "Justice in Ghana defied by Nkrumah, " America (National
       Catholic), LXVI (Nov. 1, 1965), 302-3.

2479   Kom, E. D.   "Declaration of title to land, " Univ. Ghana Law
       J., VI (1969), 18+.

2480   _____.   "Nature of a member's interest in family land in
       Nigeria and Ghana, " Univ. Ghana Law J., III (1966), 122+.

2481   _____.   "Unlawful disposition of family land--void or
       voidable?"   Univ. Ghana Law J., IV (1967), 111+.

2482   Korsah, Arku.   Law in the Republic of Ghana: being a
       series of addresses in July and November 1960.   Accra:

Ministry of Information, 1961. 29 p.

2483   Kyermaten, A. A.   "A Study of the inter-state boundary liti-
       gation in Ashanti, " B. Litt.'s Thesis, Oxford University,
       1950/51.

2484   Lavroff, D. G. and G. Peiser, eds. Les constitutions
       africaines. Tome 2: Etats anglophones. Paris: Pedone,
       1964. 391 p. (Collection du Centre de Recherches,
       d'Etudes sur les Institutions et la Legislation Africaines,
       No. 2.)

2485   Lee, J. M.   "Parliament in republican Ghana, " Parl. Affairs,
       XVI (Autumn 1963), 376-95.
       Examines the role of the Ghana National Assembly in
       national politics.

2486   Legal bibliography of the British Commonwealth of Nations.
       2nd ed. London: Sweet & Maxwell, 1955-64. 7 v.
       V. 7 (1964): British Commonwealth, excluding the
       United Kingdom, Australia, New Zealand, Canada, India
       and Pakistan. Entries are arranged alphabetically by
       author or title with a subject index.

2487   Lieck, A.   The Trial of Benjamin Knowles.   London: Hodge,
       1933. 215 p.
       The publicized murder trial of the District Commissioner
       of Bekwai.

2488   Lovens, M.   "Les constitutions du Ghana et de la Guinée:
       étude comparative, " Cahiers Econ. Soc., IV (Juin 1963),
       38-78.

2489   Loveridge, A. J.   "Note on the development of land tenures
       in the Gold Coast, " J. Roy. Afr. Soc., XLII (Jan. 1943),
       31-3.

2490   Lynes, J. and A. Quaison-Sackey.   "Constitution and land, "
       Rev. Ghana Law, II (April 1970), 59-64.

2491   Macaulay, B.   "Assessors in criminal trials in Ghana--a
       study from without, " J. Afr. Law, VII (1963), 18-48.

2492   McClain, W. T.   "Recent changes in African local courts
       and customary law, " Howard Law J., X (Fall 1964), 187+.

2493   Mair, Lucy P.   "Land tenure in the Gold Coast, " Civilisa-
       tions, II, No. 2 (1952), 183-8.

2494   Mardeck, H.   "Rolle der Traditionen in den staatstheoretischen
       Konzeptionen Nkrumahs und Busias und ihre Widerspiegelung
       in Herrschaftsmechanismus der 1. und 2. Republik Ghanas, "
       Staat und Recht (East Germany), XIX (June 1970), 980+.

2495   Matson, J. N.   "Internal conflicts of laws in the Gold Coast,"
       Mod. Law Rev., (1953), 469+.

2496   _____.   "The Supreme Court and the customary judicial
       process in the Gold Coast," Int. Comp. Law Q., II (Jan.
       1953), 47-59.

2497   Maxwell, Leslie F.   A Bibliography of the law of the British
       colonies, protectorates and mandated territories: being
       vol. III of Sweet and Maxwell's legal bibliography.   London:
       Sweet & Maxwell, 1949.

2498   Meek, Charles Kingsley.   Colonial law: a bibliography with
       special reference to native African systems of law and
       land tenure.   London: Oxford University Press, 1948.
       58 p.
            Topically arranged entries, some briefly annotated.
       Chapters on "Native law and procedure," and on "land
       tenure" are subdivided by country.   Author and govern-
       ment publication indexes.

2499   _____.   Land law and custom in the colonies.   With an
       introduction by Lord Hailey.   2nd ed.   London: Cass,
       1968.   337 p.   (Cass Library of African Studies.   Gen-
       eral studies, No. 75.)   A reprint of the 1949 edition.

2500   Mensah, I. Ackom.   Questions and answers based on the
       Companies Code, 1963 (Act 179) of Ghana.   Legon: School
       of Administration, University of Ghana, 1965.   263 p.

2501   Mensah-Brown, A. Kodwo.   "Chiefs and the law in Ghana,"
       J. Afr. Law, XIII (Summer 1969), 57-63.
            The effect of the National Liberation Council Decree
       of 1966 on traditional chiefs--some reduced in rank,
       others dismissed.

2502   _____.   "Marriage in Sefwi-Akan customary law: a com-
       parative study in ethno-jurisprudence," Présence Africaine,
       No. 68 (1968), 61-87; Also in Sociologus, XIX, No. 1
       (1969), 39-65.

2503   _____.   The Supplementary law in canonical jurisprudence:
       a doctoral dissertation in Canon law 1962.   Obuasi: The
       Ashanti Times Press for the author, 1965.   66 p.

2504   Mettle, M. A.   "Police and crime," Rev. Ghana Law, II
       (April 1970), 30-3.

2505   Milner, Alan, ed.   African penal systems.   With an intro-
       duction by Alan Milner.   London: Routledge & Kegan Paul,
       1969.   501 p.
            Part I: Penal systems in specific African countries.

Part II: Special problems encountered. For Ghana, pp. 59-87; 429-62.
Rev: African Affairs, LXX (Jan. 1971), 89-90.

2506 Misfud, F. M. Customary land law in Africa. Rome, 1967. 96 p. (FAO legislative series, No. 7.)

2507 Namasivayam, S. The Drafting of legislation. Accra: Ghana Universities Press, 1967. 158 p.

2508 Nantwi, Emmanuel Kwaku. The Enforcement of international judicial decisions and arbitral awards in public international law. Leyden: A.W. Sijthoff, 1966. 209 p. Bibliog.

2509 "New Company law proposals," Economist, CXCIX (May 6, 1961), 581-2.

2510 Nkrumah, Kwame. "Law in Africa," J. Afr. Law, VI (1962), 103+.

2511 Northrop, F. S. C. "Jurisprudence in the Law School curriculum," J. Legal Educ., I (1949), 482-94.

2512 Ofori-Amankwah, E. H. "Scope and legal basis of the criminal jurisdiction of Ghana," Univ. Ghana Law J., VII (1970), 48+.

2513 Ofori-Boateng, J. "Ejection orders and procedure under the Rent Act, 1963," Rev. Ghana Law, I (Aug. 1969), 87+.

2514 Ocran, Modibo T. "Law and economic development," Legon Observer, V (July 3, 1970), 8-11.

2515 Ogwurike, C. "Functional analysis of Ghanaian legal sources," Univ. Ghana Law J., IV (1967), 122+.
The author is a Nigerian lawyer.

2516 Ollenu, N. A. "Case for traditional courts under the constitution," Univ. Ghana Law J., VII (1970), 82+.

2517 _____. "The Influence of English law on West Africa," J. Afr. Law, V (Spring 1961), 21-35.

2518 _____. "Judicial precedent in Ghana," Univ. Ghana Law J., III (1966), 139+.

2519 _____. The Law in testate and intestate succession in Ghana. London: Sweet & Maxwell, 1966. 332 p. (Law in Africa series, No. 16.)

2520 _____. The Law of succession in Ghana. Accra: Presbyterian Book Depot, 1960. 53 p.

Analysis of various aspects of the succession law among Ghana's disparate tribes.

2521 _____. "Law reform in Ghana in the 1970's," <u>Univ. Ghana Law J.</u>, VII (1970), 1+.

2522 _____. <u>Principles of customary land law in Ghana.</u> London: Sweet & Maxwell, 1962. 272 p. (Law in Africa series, No. 2.)
One of the few works on the subject by a specialist in Customary Law, a Judge of Ghana's Supreme Court and Lecturer at the University of Ghana.
Rev: <u>Int. Comp. Law Q.</u>, XIV (April 1965), 713. <u>Law Q. Rev.</u>, LXXX (July 1964), 443.

2523 Osew, E. A. "Role of a parliamentary commissioner (alias ombudsman)," <u>Rev. Ghana Law</u>, I (May 1969), 45+.

2524 Pennington, R. R. "Company law in Ghana," <u>Solicitors' J.</u>, CV (Aug. 18–Sept. 1, 1961), 693+.

2525 Philips, A. "Marriage laws in Africa," Doctoral Dissertation, London University, 1952/53.

2526 Pogucki, R. J. H. "Customary law of a society in transition," <u>Universitas</u>, II, No. 4 (1956), 119-21.

2527 _____. "A Note on the codification of customary land law on the Gold Coast," <u>J. Afr. Adm.</u>, VIII, No. 4 (1956), 192-6.

2528 _____. <u>Report on land tenure in Adangme customary law.</u> Accra: Govt. Printer, 1955. 58 p.

2529 "Police and Crime," <u>Rev. Ghana Law</u>, I (Aug. 1969), 122-5; (Dec. 1969), 185-7.

2530 "Police and crime. Wrongful imprisonment for debt," <u>Rev. Ghana Law</u>, I (Aug. 1969), 122+.

2531 Pound, Roscoe. <u>Interpretations of legal history.</u> Cambridge: Cambridge University Press, 1923. 171 p.

2532 Quist, C. C. "Problems of law and practice governing statutory corporations," <u>Univ. Ghana Law J.</u>, IV (1967), 82+.

2533 Radix, A. "The Three constitutional decrees," <u>Legon Observer</u>, III, No. 4 (1968), 5-11.

2534 Rattray, Robert Sutherland. <u>Ashanti law and constitution.</u> London: Oxford University Press, 1956. 420 p. First published 1929.

2535   Read, J. S.   "Ghana: the criminal code, 1960, " Int. Comp.
       Law Q. , XI (Jan. 1962), 272+.

2536   "Recent developments in Ghana, " Int. Comm. Jurists Bull. ,
       No. 24 (Dec. 1965), 20-7.
           Criticizes the referendum and constitutional amendment
       on the one-party state of February 1964; the constitutional
       amendment of 1965 on presidential candidates and elections;
       electoral Provisions Acts of May 1965 and elections of June
       1965.

2537   Redwar, H. W.   Comments on some Ordinances of the Gold
       Coast Colony; with notes on a few decided cases.   Preface
       by J. M. Sarbah.   London: Sweet & Maxwell, 1909.   296 p.

2538   Renner, P. A.   Reports, notes of cases and proceedings and
       judgments in appeals, etc. ... relating to the Gold Coast
       Colony and the Colony of Nigeria, from 1861 to 1914.
       London: Sweet & Maxwell, 1915.

2539   Riesman, David.   "Towards an anthropological science of law
       and the legal profession, " Amer. J. Soc. , LVII (1951),
       121-35.

2540   Roberts, Thomas L.   Judicial organization and institutions
       of contemporary West Africa: a profile.   New York:
       Institution of Public Administration, 1966.   137 p.

2541   Roberts-Wray, K.   "The Adaption of imported law in Africa, "
       J. Afr. Law, IV, No. 2 (1960), 66-78.

2542   Robinson, Kenneth.   "Constitutional autochthony in Ghana, "
       J. Commonwealth Pol. Stud. , I (Nov. 1961), 41-55.

2543   Rubin, Leslie.   "Chieftaincy and the adaptation of customary
       law in Ghana. " In J. Butler and A. A. Castagno, eds.
       Boston University papers on Africa: transition in African
       politics.   New York: Praeger, 1967, pp. 115-35.

2544   _____ and Paul Murray.   The Constitution and government
       of Ghana.   2nd ed.   London: Sweet & Maxwell, 1964.
       324 p.   1st ed. 1961.   (Law in Africa series, No. 1.)
           An historical analysis of Ghana's constitutional system.
       The appendices contain the text of Ghana's constitution
       and the Charter of the Organization of African Unity.
           Rev: Law Q. Rev. , LXXX (July 1964), 443.

2545   Rubin, N. N. and Eugene Cotran, eds.   Annual survey of
       African law, v. 1. 1967.   London: Cass, 1970.   426 p.

2546   Sarbah, John Mensah.   Fanti customary laws: a brief in-
       troduction to the principles of the native laws and customs

of the Fanti and Akan districts of the Gold Coast, with a
report of some cases thereon decided in the law courts.   2nd
ed.   London: W. Clowes, 1904.   317 p.
    Photo-offset publication, by Human Relations Area Files,
New Haven, 1959.   13 cm x 20 cm.   1st ed. 1897.

2547   _____.   Fanti national constitution and Fanti law report.
     London: Clowes, 1906.   189 p.

2548   Schwelb, E.   "The Republican constitution of Ghana," Amer.
     J. Comp. Law, IX (Autumn, 1960), 634-56.

2549   Seidman, Robert S.   "Ghana prison system: an historical
     perspective," Univ. Ghana Law J., III (1966), 89+.

2550   _____.   "Insanity as a defence under the Criminal Code,
     1960," Univ. Ghana Law J., I (1964), 42+.

2551   _____.   "Note on the construction of the Gold Coast Re-
     ception Statute," J. Afr. Law, XIII (1969), 45+.

2552   _____.   A Sourcebook of the original law of Africa: cases,
     statutes and materials.   London: Sweet & Maxwell, 1966.
     647 p.   (Law in Africa, No. 21.)

2553   Steel, D.   No entry;   Commonwealth immigration Act, 1968.
     London: Hurst, 1969.   263 p.

2554   Thomas, H. B.   "Native tribunals in the Gold Coast Colony,"
     J. Soc. Comp. Leg., XXVI (Nov. 1944), 30-5.

2555   Thoyer, J. R.   "Use of Ghana statutory materials including
     a bibliography of Ghanaian law," Univ. Ghana Law J., I
     (1964), 125+.

2556   Tixier, Gilbert.   Le Ghana.   Paris: Librairie Générale
     de Droit et de Jurisprudence, 1965.   194 p.   (Coll. Com-
     ment ils sont gouvernés, 10.)

2557   Trachtman, L. N.   "Ghanaian labor legislation since inde-
     pendence," Labor Law J., XII (June 1961), 547+.

2558   Turkson, R. B.   "The Legal statutes of public corporations,"
     Rev. Ghana Law, II (April 1970), 64-73.

2559   Uche, U. U.   "Changes in Ghana law since the military take-
     over," J. Afr. Law, X (Summer 1966), 106-11.

2560   _____.   Contractual obligations in Ghana and Nigeria.
     London: Cass, 1971.   300 p.
     A comparative examination of the law of civil responsi-
     bilities in the West African states and Great Britain.

2561 University of Ife. Institute of African Studies. Integration
      of customary and modern legal systems in Africa. New
      York: Africana Publishing Corp., 1971. 461 p.
      Chiefly devoted to integration of laws in four specific
      areas: civil wrongs and contracts; Land law; Law of suc-
      cession; marriage and divorce. Useful introductory back-
      ground papers.

2562 Wheare, Kenneth C. Constitutional structure of the Common-
      wealth. Oxford: Clarendon Press, 1960. 201 p.
      Assesses the constitutional and legal relationships among
      Commonwealth countries, examining also their problems of
      federalism.

2563 White, G. Nationalization of foreign property. London:
      Stevens, 1961. 283 p. (The Library of world affairs,
      No. 57.)

2564 Wight, Martin, ed. British colonial constitutions, 1947.
      Oxford: Clarendon Press, 1952. 571 p.
      Constitution of Gambia, the Gold Coast, Kenya, Nigeria
      and Sierra Leone.

2565 _____. The Gold Coast Legislative Council. Edited by
      Margery Perham. London: Faber and Faber for Nuffield
      College, 1947. 285 p. (Studies in colonial legislature,
      v. 2.)

2566 Woodman, Gordon R. "The Acquisitions of family land in
      Ghana," J. Afr. Law, VII (1963), 136-51.

2567 _____. "Alienation of family land in Ghana," Univ.
      Ghana Law J., I (1964), 23+.

2568 _____. "Allodial title to land," Univ. Ghana Law J.,
      V (1968), 79+.

2569 _____. "Common customs of Ghana: common law or
      customary law?" Univ. Ghana Law J., V (1968), 1+.

2570 _____. "The Development of customary land law in
      Ghana," Doctoral Dissertation, Cambridge University,
      1965/66.

2571 _____. "Developments in pledges of land in Ghanaian
      customary law," J. Afr. Law, XI, No. 1 (1967), 8-26.

2572 _____. "Formalities and incidents of conveyances in
      Ghana," Univ. Ghana Law J., IV (1967), 1+.

2573 _____. "Palliatives for uncertainty of title: the land
      Development (protection of purchases) Act 1960 and the

Farm Lands (protection) Act 1962," Univ. Ghana Law J.,
VI (1969), 146+.

2574   . "The Scheme of subordinate tenures of land in
Ghana," Amer. J. Comp. Law, XV, No. 3 (1966/67),
457. 77.

2575   . "Some realism about customary law--the West
African experience," Wis. Law Rev., No. 1 (1969), 129-
52.
On Ghana and Nigeria.

2576 Zabel, Shirley. "The Legislative history of the Gold Coast
and Nigerian marriage ordinances," J. Afr. Law, XIV
(Summer 1969), 64-79; (Autumn 1969), 158-78.
Two articles in a series.

(10) LIBRARIANSHIP--GENERAL

2577 Aguolu, Christian Chukwunedu. "Classification of Africana
Collections," Soundings (Santa Barbara, California), II
(May 1970), 36-8.
Reviews the problems of classifying African materials
and suggests a modification of the existing classification
schemes so as to meet the challenge posed by the steady
growth of African literature, especially in the Humanities
and Social Sciences. The author, a Nigerian, is former
Reference Librarian at the University of California, Santa
Barbara.

2578 Akita, J. M. and E. K. Koranteng. "Ghana," Bibliography,
Documentation, Terminology, VI (Jan. 1966), 5-7.
Report on the bibliographical services and archival
organization by Akita, Ghana's Chief Archivist and Koran-
teng, Assistant Director of the Cape Coast University
College of Science Education.

2579 Amedekey, E. Y. The Culture of Ghana: a Bibliography.
London: The Library Association, 1966. 634 p.
Originally submitted as thesis for the Fellowship of
Library Association, Great Britain.
Rev: Ghana Library J., IV, No. 1 (1970), 49-50.

2580 Asheim, Lester, ed. The Core of Education for librarian-
ship: a report of a workshop held under the auspices of
the Graduate Library School of the University of Chicago,
Aug. 10-15, 1953. Chicago: Amer. Lib. Assn., 1954. 68 p.
Rev: Coll. & Res. Lib., XV (July 1954), 148-52.
Reply, XV (Oct. 1954), 467.

2581   _____ . "Distinctive value of books," Library J. , LXXXII
        (July 1957), 1717-21.

2582   _____ , ed. The Future of the book; implications of the
        newer developments in communications; papers presented
        before the Twentieth Annual Conference of the Graduate
        Library School of the University of Chicago, June 20-24,
        1955. Chicago: University of Chicago Graduate Library
        School, 1955. 105 p.
              Dr. Asheim is former Dean of the Graduate Library
        School, University of Chicago.
              Rev: Coll. & Res. Lib. , XVII (Sept. 1956), 444-6.
        Library J. , LXXXI (June 1, 1956), 1418-20.

2583   _____ , et al. The Humanities and the Library: problems
        in the interpretation evaluation and use of library materials.
        Chicago: American Library Association, 1957. 278 p.
              Rev: J. Doc. , XIV (June 1958), 77-8. Library Quarter-
        ly, XXVIII (Jan. 1958), 59-61.

2584   _____ . Librarianship in the developing countries. Urbana.
        Illinois: University of Illinois Press, 1966. 95 p.
        (Phineas L. Windsor series in librarianship.)
              A generalized but readable survey of the library situation
        in developing countries, pervaded with flashes of humor.
        Observes also the role of the American librarianship in
        the development of library systems in those areas.
              Rev: Library Assoc. Rec. , LXIX (Aug. 1967), 295-6.
        UNESCO Bull. Lib. , XXII (March 1968), 90-2.

2585   Avicenne, Paul. Bibliographical services throughout the
        world, 1960-1964. Paris: UNESCO, 1969. 228 p.
              First part describes the development of bibliographical
        services during the period, 1960-1964. Second part, ar-
        ranged by country, surveys the bibliographical achieve-
        ments in 196 countries or territories. No index.
              Rev: Library Assoc. Rec. , LXXII (April 1970), 177.

2586   _____ . Les Services bibliographiques dans le monde,
        1960-1964. Paris: UNESCO, 1967. 233 p.
              See the English edition above.
              Rev: Bull. Doc. Bibliog. , XIII (Sept. /Oct. 1968), 738-9.

2587   Benge, R. C. "Foundations for a library school," Nigerian
        Libraries, I, No. 2 (1964), 81-5.
              Paper presented at the Inaugural Conference of the
        Nigerian Library Association, December 1963, by then
        Head of the University of Ghana Library School.

2587a   _____ . "Library education in Ghana, 1961-67," Library
        Assoc. Rec. , LXIX (July 1967), 225-9.
              Historical development of library education in Ghana

justifying the present educational curricula of the Dept. of
Library Studies, University of Ghana.

2587b _____. "Some notes on reading in Ghana," Library
World, LXIV (Feb. 1963), 210-2.

2588 Berman, Sanford. "African magazines for American libraries,"
Library J., XCV (April 1, 1970), 1289-93.
Analysis of eleven current literary and political periodicals in English published by Africans, with address of the
editorial office. Seven of the periodicals are published by
East Africans; one by South Africans. The three published
by West Africans include African Literature Today, a literary periodical edited by Professor Eldred Jones of the
University of Sierra Leone; Bulletin of the Association for
the African Literature in English superseded by the African
Literature Today; and Legon Observer, a Ghanaian periodical
sponsored by the Legon Society on National Affairs, carrying
articles on political, educational, social and economic topics.

2589 _____. Prejudices and antipathies: a tract on the LC
Subject heads concerning people. Metuchen, New Jersey:
Scarecrow Press, 1971. 249 p.
Rev: Library J., XCVII (Feb. 15, 1972), 658-9.

2590 Bloomfield, Valerie. "African ephemera." In J.D. Pearson
and Ruth Jones, eds. The Bibliography of Africa. London:
Cass, 1970, pp. 223-39.
The author is Librarian of the Institute of Commonwealth
Studies, University of London.

2591 "Blueprint for a library service in developing nations,"
Bookseller, (Aug. 29, 1964), 1194-1200.

2592 Brierley, L. "The Indexing and classification of African
tribal names," Library Mat. Afr., V (March 1968), 76-8.

2592a Chantal, J. de. "Cooperative internationale: donner ou
recevoir?" Canadian Library, XXII, No. 3 (1965), 141-5.
Chiefly on West Africa, it surveys professional training
in the area and assistance obtained from developed nations.

2592b Clark, Alden H. "Publishing in sub-Sahara Africa,"
Scholarly Publishing, II (Oct. 1970), 67-74.

2592c Collings, Dorothy G. "Comparative librarianship." In
Allen Kent and Harold Lancour, eds. Encyclopedia of
library and information sciences. Vol. 5. New York:
Marcel Dekker, 1971, pp. 492-502.
Attempts to define the phrase "comparative librarianship,"
indicating its relationship with comparative education and
reviews the literature in the field. Includes extensive bibliography.

2593 Collison, Robert Lewis. <u>Bibliographical services throughout</u>
      <u>the world, 1950-1959.</u> Paris: UNESCO, 1961. 240 p.
      (UNESCO bibliographical handbooks, No. 9.)
          The cumulated volume of reports covering material pub-
      lished 1951-1959. The first part, arranged by country,
      describes bibliographical activities in over 100 countries
      or territories, noting their progress in national bibliography,
      library cooperation, current special bibliography and retro-
      spective bibliography. The second part summarizes the
      bibliographical activities in more than 80 international
      organizations. No index; updated by UNESCO's <u>Bibliography,</u>
      <u>Documentation, Terminology,</u> V. 1+, 1961+, Bimonthly.

2594 _____. <u>Bibliographies, subject and national; a guide to</u>
      <u>their contents, arrangement and use.</u> 3rd rev. ed. enl.
      London: Crosby Lockwood, 1968. 203 p. 1st ed. 1951.
          Part 1: Subject bibliographies. Part 2: Universal and
      national bibliographies. Many of about 800 items listed
      are annotated. Subject and personal name index, thus ex-
      cluding title entries and almost all organizations.
          Rev: <u>Library World,</u> LXX (Nov. 1968), 146.

2595 _____. <u>Indexes and indexing; guide to the indexing of books,</u>
      <u>and collections of books, periodicals, music recordings,</u>
      <u>films, other materials.</u> Benn: De Graff, 1969. 223 p.
      Bibliog.
          Rev: <u>Library Assoc. Rec.,</u> LXXI (Oct. 1969), 316.
      <u>Library Rev.,</u> XXII (Autumn 1969), 143-4.

2596 _____. <u>SCOLMA directory of libraries and special col-</u>
      <u>lections on Africa.</u> 2nd ed. London: Lockwood, 1967.
      92 p. 1st ed. 1963.
          SCOLMA is Standing Conference on library materials on
      Africa.
          Rev: <u>Choice,</u> IV (Dec. 1967), 1104. <u>Library Assoc.</u>
      <u>Rec.,</u> LXIX (April 1967), 145.

2597 Crossey, J. M. "Building a working collection on Africa:
      notes on bibliographic aids and dealers," <u>Africana Library</u>
      <u>J.,</u> I (Summer 1970), 18-22.

2598 "Current trends in newly developing countries," <u>Library</u>
      <u>Trends,</u> VIII (Oct. 1959). Entire issue.
          Contents: Patterns of library service in Africa. --Educa-
      tion and training of librarians in newly developing British
      Commonwealth countries. --Library buildings in newly
      developing countries. --Preservation of library materials in
      tropical countries. --Provision of vernacular literature.
      Wilfred Plumbe, editor of the whole issue devoted to the
      topic, is Librarian of the University of Malaya, Kuala
      Lumpur.

2599 Dadzie, E. W. and J. T. Strickland. Directory of archives,
      libraries and schools of librarianship in Africa. Paris:
      UNESCO, 1965. 112 p. (UNESCO bibliographical hand-
      books, 10.)
          In English and French. Grouped by country, the 508
      entries are under such headings as archives, schools and
      courses in librarianship; libraries and documentation cen-
      tres, etc. Data for each institution include date of
      founding, qualifications of staff or students; number of
      books and serials; kind of catalog and classification scheme
      used, opening hours, etc.
          Rev: Amer. Arch. , XXX (April 1967), 362-3.

2600 Dalby, David. "A Note on African language bibliography. "
      In J. D. Pearson and Ruth Jones, eds. The Bibliography
      of Africa. London: Cass, 1970, p. 193.
          Linguistic problems in classifying African publications.

2601 Dean, John. "Comparative advantages and disadvantages of
      overseas training as opposed to home training for library
      staff in the developing countries, " UNESCO Bull. Lib. ,
      XXII (July 1968), 192-8.

2602 _____ . "Librarianship in the developing countries, "
      UNESCO Bull. Lib. , XXII (March 1968), 90-2.
          Review of Lester E. Asheim's Librarianship in the
      developing countries (1966).

2603 _____ . "The Nature, development and application of
      standards in libraries in West Africa. " In John Dean,
      ed. Standards of practice for West African libraries....
      Ibadan: Institute of Librarianship, University of Ibadan,
      1969, pp. 17-27.

2604 _____ , ed. Standards of practice for West African li-
      braries: proceedings of a seminar held at the Institute
      of Librarianship, University of Ibadan, 15-16 April 1967.
      Ibadan: Institute of Librarianship, University of Ibadan,
      1969, 116 p. (Occasional paper 1.)
          "The object of the seminar was to discuss the nature,
      development and application of standards generally, and to
      examine specific problems associated with the creation of
      standards for each type of library--university, public,
      school and special, with particular reference to the require-
      ments of West Africa" (Editor). Includes six papers gen-
      erally followed by a discussion; an opening address by
      John Harris, then Acting Vice-Chancellor and Librarian
      of the University of Ibadan, Nigeria. Extensive bibliography.

2605 Drysdale, J. "A possible solution to the problem of col-
      lecting library material from Ghana, " Library Mat. Afr.
      IV (July 1966), 9-15.

An important study conducted in October 1965 by a representative of the Agency for International Publications, New York.

2606 Duignan, Peter. "Bibliographical control of African manuscripts and archives collections." In J. D. Pearson and Ruth Jones, eds. The Bibliography of Africa. London: Cass, 1970, pp. 194-213.
Dr. Duignan is Curator of African Collection, Hoover Institution, Stanford University.

2607 Evans, Evelyn J. "The Ghana Library Board," Library World, LXIV, No. 752 (1963), 205-9.

2607a _____. "Ghana library service," Libn. & Bk World, XLVI (July 1957), 125-7.

2608 _____. Library legislation in the developing territories of Africa," Libri, XVIII, No. 1 (1968), 51-78.
The bulk of the article comprises excerpts from library laws from different African countries. Notes that much more attention is given to library legislation in the English-speaking nations than in the French-speaking countries.

2608a _____. "Library resources in English-speaking countries of West Africa," Unesco Bull. Lib., XV (Sept./Oct. 1961), 227-31.

2609 _____. "Library service in British West Africa," Fund. Educ., III (Jan. 1951), 28-33.

2510 _____. "Presidential address," WALA News, III (May 1960), 211-8.
As President of the West African Library Association.

2611 _____. "Training for librarianship," WALA News, II, No. 3 (1956), 67-72.
Stresses the need for a West African Library School.

2612 _____. A Tropical library service: the story of Ghana's libraries. With a foreword by Dr. Kwame Nkrumah. London: Deutsch, 1964. 174 p. (A Grafton book.)
The first comprehensive study of the library development in Ghana by the first director of the Ghana Library Board. "This account of the preliminary pioneering, the inception and the development of the Gold Coast, later Ghana, public library service up to 1961-2, constitutes both a justification and an endorsement of those ideals, ideas, and administrative practices for which public libraries in the West have struggled for so long. They have stood the test" (Introduction). Part I. The days before the Library Board. Part II. The Ghana Library Board. Part III. The Board's services.

Includes discussion of library education and professional
training.   Three useful appendices and index.
Rev: Library J., XCI (Jan. 15, 1966), 228-30.
Library World, LXVI (Dec. 1964), 157-8.

2613   Fischer, Herta D.   "Science library services in Ghana,"
Unesco Bull. Lib., XXII (Nov. /Dec. 1968), 300-1, 304.
Describes the establishment of a central science library
for the Ghana Academy of Science.

2614   Foskett, Antony Charles.   The Subject approach to information.
Hamden, Connecticut: Archon Books, 1969.   310 p.
The author is Librarian of the Institute of Education,
University of London.
Rev: J. Doc., XXVI (March 1970), 76-8.   Library J.,
XCIV (Dec. 15, 1969), 4503-4.

2615   Fraser, M. A. C.   Libraries in Africa: a description of various aspects as practiced in West and South Africa.   Washington, D. C.:   Catholic University of America, 1968.   (Research paper, No. 23.)

2616   Freeman, M. L.   A Bibliography on teaching of librarianship
on Africa South of the Sahara and excluding South Africa.
Washington, D. C.:   Catholic University of America, 1969.
(Research paper, No. 81.)

2617   "Ghana."   In International Federation of Library Associations.
Conference, 1968, Frankfurt am Main.   Actes.   Proceedings,
Nijhoff, 1969, p. 249.
On the Ghana Library Association.

2618   "Ghana Library Association," Unesco Bull. Lib., XXIII (Sept.
1969), 275.

2619   Greer, R. C.   "National bibliography," Library Trends, XV
(Jan. 1967), 350-77.
Includes a useful table on the characteristics of current
national and trade bibliographical services in some 87
countries.

2620   Hackman, Martha L.   The Practical bibliographer.   Englewood Cliffs, New Jersey: Prentice-Hall, 1970.   118 p.
Examines principles and methods of various bibliographical compilations with specific examples of their
practical application.   Each chapter is followed by problems or projects and bibliography.

2621   Haines, Helen Elizabeth.   Living with books; the art of book
selection.   2nd ed.   New York: Columbia University Press,
1964.   610 p.   (Columbia University studies in library
service, No. 2.)   Reprint of the 1950 edition.   1st ed. 1935.

A classic work that has served for many years not only
as a buying list of essentials in academic and public
libraries, but also as a standard textbook for library school
courses in book selection.
Rev: Library Assoc. Rec., LIII (March 1951), 97-8.
Library Quarterly, XXI (July 1951), 218-9.

2622 Harris, John. Librarians for Ghana: a lecture. Legon:
Dept. of Library Studies, University of Ghana, 1970. 16 p.
(Occasional paper, No. 1.)
Surveys the early work by the British Council on library
training at Achimota; establishment of West African library
schools, including Ghana Library School, now superseded
by the Dept. of Library Studies; and the library education
in Ghana.

2623 _____. "Librarianship in West Africa," New Zealand
Libraries, XXIII (March 1960), 43-51.
The author, former Librarian of the University of
Ibadan and Director of the University of Ghana Library
School, is presently Vice-Chancellor of the University
of Benin, Nigeria.

2624 _____. "Notes on book preservation in West Africa,"
WALA News, II, No. 4 (1956), 102-5.

2625 _____. Patterns of library growth in English-speaking
West Africa. Legon: Dept. of Library Studies, University
of Ghana, 1970. 28 p. 15 tables. Bibliog. (Occasional
papers, No. 3.)
Valuable statistical information on the library development in Ghana, Nigeria and Sierra Leone, based upon data
obtained from questionnaire, correspondence, annual reports,
the Nigerian Libraries and the Ghana Library Journal. The
areas studied include the use of library, stock, expenditure
and staff, and the figures for 1967/68 are compared with
those of 1961/62.

2626 _____. "Presidential address," WALA News, II (Jan.
1955), 5-10; II, No. 3 (1956), 54-62; III (June 1959), 102-8.
Presidential address at the Conference of the West
African Library Association formed in 1953, comprising
librarians of English-speaking West Africa. The name of
the official organ of the Association, The West African
Libraries changed in January 1955 to WALA News, was
later superseded partly by the Ghana Library Journal, Oct.
1963+ and partly by the Nigerian Libraries, Feb. 1964+.

2627 Herrick, Mary D. "Bibliographical problems from new
countries in Africa," Coll. & Res. Lib., XXVIII (Sept.
1967), 347-50.

2627a Hiebert, R. E. , ed. Books in human development. Washing-
       ton, D. C. : Dept. of Journalism, American University,
       1965. 131 p.
              Report of the conference on the role of books in human
       development, Airlie, 1964, sponsored by the American
       University and the U. S. Agency for International Develop-
       ment.

2628   Hillway, Tyrus. Introduction to research. 2nd ed. Boston:
       Houghton-Mifflin, 1964. 308 p. 1st ed. 1956.
              A lucid presentation of the main principles and methods
       of research. Extensive bibliography. "Intended as an
       orientation to research in all fields, for knowledge is a
       seamless whole" (Preface).

2629   Horrocks, Stanley H. "UNESCO Seminar in Africa, " Library
       Assoc. Rec. , LXV (Sept. 1963), 122-4.

2630   "Indexing of West African periodicals, " WALA News, III
       (Feb. 1960), 178-80.

2631   "Intellectual freedom, " Library Trends, XIX (July 1970),
       1-168.
              Exhaustive examination of various aspects of one of the
       most controversial and misunderstood topics in library
       profession by well-informed librarians from different
       nationalities. The issue, entirely devoted to the topic, is
       introduced by its editor, Everett Moore, Assistant Univer-
       sity Librarian, University of California, Los Angeles.

2631a Johnson, Alfred Frederick. "The Place of libraries in
       national economic development, " Unesco Bull. Lib. , XVI,
       No. 5 (1962), 247-8.

2632   Jones, Ruth. "Forty-one years of African bibliography, "
       Africa, XLI (Jan. 1971), 54-6.
              A general survey with special reference to the quarterly
       bibliography in Africa, Journal of the International African
       Institute, and the African Abstracts also published by the
       Institute. Miss Jones, Librarian of the International
       African Institute in London, is widely known for her bib-
       liographical work on Africa.

2633   Kenworthy, Leonard S. "Library progress in Ghana, " Wil-
       son Lib. Bull. , XXXIV (Dec. 1959), 267-8.

2634   Kotei, S. I. A. "Some problems in Africana library classifi-
       cation. " In J. D. Pearson and Ruth Jones, eds. The Bib-
       liography of Africa. London: Cass, 1970, pp. 138-54.
              The author, a Ghanaian librarian, teaches in the De-
       partment of Library Studies, University of Ghana.

2635 Lancour, Harold. "Impressions of British West Africa,"
ALA Bull., LII (June 1958), 419-20.
Impressions of the cultural growth of Ghana, Gambia,
Nigeria and Sierra Leone during Dr. Lancour's survey of
libraries in those countries.

2636 _____. Libraries in British West Africa: a report of
a survey for the Carnegie Corporation of New York, Octo-
ber-November 1957. Urbana: University of Illinois Library
School, 1958. 32 p. (Occasional papers, No. 53.)
The survey was designed "to provide background material upon which the Corporation could evaluate the re-
quests for assistance for libraries coming from those
countries and as a basis for initiating projects designed
to further library development." An excellent study of
the library situation in Gambia, Ghana, Sierra Leone and
Nigeria, by the then Associate Director of the University
of Illinois Library School.
Rev: Library Rev., No. 131 (Autumn 1959), 203-4.

2637 "Library Statistics for West Africa," WALA News, IV (Oct.
1961), 22-4.
The tabulated report indicates that the Ghana Library
Board leads other West African libraries in the numbers
of readers and volumes of books, whereas the Ibadan
University Library leads in serials.

2637a Lottman, H. R. "American books in Ghana," Publishers'
Weekly, CCI (March 13, 1972), 43-5.

2637b _____. "Ghana enters the publishing age," Publishers'
Weekly, CCI (March 6, 1972), 34-6.

2638 Meyriat, Jean. "Services bibliographiques internationaux et
bibligraphie africaine." In J. D. Pearson and Ruth Jones,
eds. The Bibliography of Africa. London: Cass, 1970,
pp. 249-63.
In English and French. The author is Secretary-Gen-
eral of the International Committee for the Documentation of
the Social Sciences, and Director of the Literary of National Foundation of Political Science in Paris, France.

2639 Miller, Rosalind. "Librarians: a vanishing breed," Library
J., LXXXIX (Nov. 15, 1964), 4597-9.

2640 Momah, C. C. "Man-power needs of West African libraries
and possible solutions," WALA News, IV (Dec. 1961), 78-
85.

2641 Moon, Eric, ed. Book selection and censorship in the sixties.
New York: Bowker, 1969. 421 p.
Rev: Canadian Library J., XXVII (May 1970), 240-1.
J. Educ. Libr., X (Spring 1970), 316-7.

2642   Morton, Florrinell. "Accreditation in library education,"
        ALA Bull., LV (Nov. 1961), 876-9.

2642a   Murtagh, Donald David. Education for librarianship in
        Africa: a bibliography. Johannesburg: Dept. of Bibli-
        ography, Librarianship and Typography, University of the
        Witwatersrand, 1968. 32 p.
           385 numbered entries arranged by broad geographic area
        and by country, with an author index. The introduction
        surveys the status of library education in various African
        countries. Originally compiled as part of the requirement
        of Diploma in Librarianship, University of the Witwaters-
        rand, Johannesburg.

2643   Musiker, Reuben. "A World view of Africana," Library Mat.
        Afr., V (Nov. 1967), 48-55.
           Paper presented at the First South African Conference
        of Bibliophiles, Cape Town, 28th November 1966. Reviews
        major bibliographical activities in Europe and the United
        States.

2643a   Musisi, J. S. "Africa's need in librarianship," Assistant
        Librarian, LVIII, No. 12 (1965), 256-7.

2644   Odumosu, J. Olu. "After 10 years; the future of librarian-
        ship in West Africa," Library World, LXIV (June 1963),
        356+.

2645   _____. "Exchange programmes, not a Peace Corps:
        Africa's need in librarianship," Assistant Librarian, LVIII
        (June 1965), 102+.

2646   "Offor, Richard," Aslib Proceedings, XVI (Feb. 1964), 40;
        Library Assoc. Rec., LXVI (Feb. 1964), 89-90.
           An obituary.

2647   Overington, Michael A. The Subject departmentalized public
        library. London: The Library Association, 1969. 167 p.
           Rev: Library Rev., XXII (Winter 1969), 210. Library
        World, LXXI (Jan. 1970), 223.

2648   Panofsky, Hans E. "The role of microform in the acquisi-
        tion and bibliographic control of Africana." In J. D. Pear-
        son and Ruth Jones, eds. The Bibliography of Africa.
        London: Cass, 1970, pp. 286-300.
           Panofsky is Curator of Africana, Northwestern Univer-
        sity Library in U. S. A.

2648a   Plumbe, Wilfred J. The preservation of books in tropical
        and subtropical countries. Kuala Lumpur: Oxford Univer-
        sity Press, 1964. 72 p.

2648b _____ . Storage and preservation of books, periodicals
and newspapers in tropical climates: a select bibliography.
Rev. ed. Paris: UNESCO, 1964. 12 p. 1st ed. 1958.
164 entries arranged under five topics--Book preserva-
tion-general; Insect pests and their control; Fungi; Paper;
Protection of buildings.

2649 Rieger, Morris. "Gold Coast: archives reports, 1950-57,"
Amer. Arch., XXII (April 1959), 243-5.
Account of the National Archives of Ghana established in
1950.

2650 Spaulding, William E. and Datus C. Smith. Books for Ghana
and Nigeria. New York: Franklin Publications, 1962.
33 p.
A survey of the book trade.

2650a UNESCO. Book development in Africa; problems and perspectives. Paris, 1969. 37 p.
Part I consists of the report of the meeting of experts on
book development in Africa, Accra, 13-19 February 1968.
Part II includes paper prepared by the Secretariat of the
Economic Commission for Africa under title " Economic
implications of book development in Africa. "

(10) LIBRARIANSHIP--NATIONAL AND PUBLIC

2651 American Library Association. Public Library Association.
Standards Committee. Minimum standards for the public
library system, 1966. Adopted July 3, 1966, by members
of the Public Library Association. Chicago, 1967. 60 p.
(Chairman A. Chapman Parsons.)

2652 _____ . Subcommittee on Standards for Children's Service.
Standards for children's services in public libraries.
Chicago, 1964. 24 p. Bibliog.

2653 Bowler, Roberta, ed. Local public library administration.
Chicago: International City Manager's Association, 1964.
375 p. Bibliog.
"One of a series of 13 volumes on municipal administration published by the International City Managers'
Association. Each volume is a complete and separate
training and reference manual dealing with one field of
municipal administration ... intended to provide information for library administrators and the local government
officials on organization, management, services and program with the context of local government" (Foreword).
Although based on the American Library situation, the
bibliothecal principles and ideas discussed are quite applicable to other countries.

Rev: Library J., XC (Nov. 15, 1965), 4943-5. Wilson
Lib. Bull., XXXIX (Feb. 1965), 491-2.

2654 Cornelius, David. "On trek with the mobile library in
      Ghana," Unesco Bull. Lib., XII (Aug. /Sept. (1968)), 206-7.

2655 Danton, Joseph Periam, ed. The Climate of book selection;
      social influences on school and public libraries; papers
      presented at a symposium held at the University of Cali-
      fornia, July 10-12, 1958. With an introduction by J.
      Periam Danton. Berkeley: School of Librarianship, Uni-
      versity of California, 1959. 98 p.
           Rev: Library Quarterly, XXX (July 1960), 237.

2656 Dean, John, et al. "Public libraries and general library
      development; Anglophone West Africa, East Africa and
      Central Africa." In P. H. Sewell, ed. Five Years' Work
      in librarianship, 1961-65. London: Library Association,
      1968, pp. 303-14.

2657 Dobson, M. O. "Public libraries in the Gold Coast," Wilson
      Lib. Bull., XXVIII (Nov. 1953), 288-9; 291.
           Dobson was Deputy Chief Librarian, Gold Coast Library
      Board.

2658 Evans, Evelyn J. The Development of the public library
      services in the Gold Coast. London: The Library Asso-
      ciation, 1956. 32 p.
           Rev: Library Assoc. Rec., LVIII (July 1956), 287-8.
      Library Rev., No. 119 (Autumn 1956), 590-2.

2659 _____. "Public libraries in the Gold Coast," W. Afr. Lib.
      I, (Sept. 1954), 1-3.

2660 _____. "The public library and secondary school in Ghana,"
      W. Afr. J. Educ., IV (June 1960), 61-3.

2660a _____. "The Public library and the community," WALA
      News, III (June 1959), 147-56.

2661 _____. "Public library distribution techniques in Africa,"
      Indian Librarian, X (Sept. 1955), 62-7.

2662 Flood, Roy A. "Development of public library services in the
      Gold Coast," Library Assoc. Rec., LVIII (July 1956), 287-8.
           Review of Evelyn Evans' The Development of public
      library services in the Gold Coast (1956).

2663 _____. Public libraries in the colonies. London: Library
      Association, 1951. 45 p. (Library Association pamphlet,
      No. 5.)
           Rev: Libn. & Bk. World, XL (Dec. 1951), 259-60. Li-
      brary Rev., No. 103 (Autumn 1952), 454-5.

2664   Griffin, Ella.   A Study of the reading habits of adults in
       Ashanti, Southern Ghana and Trans-Volta Togoland.   Accra:
       Bureau of Languages, 1958?   93 p.

2665   Horrocks, Stanley H. and J. A. Hargreaves.   "Bookmobile
       operations over the world," Library Trends, IX (Jan. 1961),
       360-73.

2665a Knox-Hooke, S. A.   "The Law relating to public libraries in
       West Africa: a comparative study with the U K library
       laws," FLA Thesis, London, 1966.

2666   Middlemast, Kenneth.   "The Gold Coast Library Board and
       its contribution to literacy, particularly in the rural areas,"
       Advance, VIII (Oct. 1955), 13-14.

2667   _____.   "Public libraries in Ghana," Library J., LXXXII
       (Nov. 15, 1957), 2871-3.
             Obituary on Middlemast.   WALA News, II (Feb. 1958),
       190; III (March 1959), 81-3.

2668   _____ and Kenneth Scott.   "A Tropical regional library,"
       Library Assoc. Rec., LVIII (Jan. 1956), 5-11.
             The Sekondi Regional Library in the Gold Coast opened
       July 8, 1955.

2669   Offor, Richard.   "Development of public library services in
       the Gold Coast," Library Rev., No. 119 (Autumn 1956),
       490-2.

2670   Ofori, A. G. T.   "Library cooperation in Ghana: the public
       libraries point of view," Ghana Library J., I (Oct. 1964),
       60.
             Suggests that the Scandinavian library cooperation
       system should be adopted; bibliographical services improved
       and a bindery established.

2671   Ofori-Attah, Grace.   "Ghana librarian views children's work,"
       Library J., LXXXIII (Nov. 15, 1958), 3273-4; Jr. Lib., V
       (Nov. 1968), 9-10.

2672   _____.   "School libraries and children's libraries in
       Ghana," WALA News, III (July 1958), 34-41.

2673   Ogunsheye, F. Adetowun.   "Objectives and standards of
       practice for public libraries in West Africa, pt. 2."   In
       John Dean, ed.   Standards of practice for West African
       libraries.   Ibadan: Institute of Librarianship, University
       of Ibadan, 1969, pp. 53-65.
             Mrs. Ogunsheye is Professor of Library Studies, Uni-
       versity of Ibadan.

2674   Okorie, Kalu. "Objectives and standards of practice for
       public libraries in West Africa, pt. 1." In John Dean, ed.
       Standards of practice for West African libraries. Ibadan:
       Institute of Librarianship, University of Ibadan, 1969, pp.
       47-50.
              The Nigerian author is the first Director of Library
       Services for Eastern Nigeria.

2674a Simsova, Silva and M. MacKee. A Handbook of comparative
       librarianship. Hamden, Conn.: Archon Books, 1970. 413 p.
              An excellent manual for beginning students of comparative
       librarianship, it discusses in part one its basic purposes,
       methodology and problems arising from teaching it and in
       part two provides a comprehensive bibliography of area
       studies.
              Rev: Library Assoc. Rec., LXXII (May 1970), 218
       and 220. Library Quarterly, XL (Oct. 1970), 449-50.
       Library World, LXXI (May 1970), 353-4.

2675   Strickland, J. T. "Mobile libraries in Ghana," WALA News,
       III (July 1958), 17-25.
              Includes a map of branch libraries and book boxes. The
       author is former Deputy Director of the Ghana Library
       Services.

2676   _____. "Work in progress," Top of the News, XIV (May
       1958), 20-1.
              Children's library services in Ghana.

2677   Sydney, Edward. "New Central Library, Accra," Library
       Assoc. Rec., LVIII (Nov. 1956), 431-3.

2678-2679. [No entries.]

2680   UNESCO. Development of public libraries in Africa; the
       Ibadan Seminar. Paris, 1954. 153 p. French edition
       in 1955. 164 p.
              The seminar was held 27 July-21 August 1953. The
       immediate outcome of the seminar was the founding of the
       West African Library Association limited to the English-
       speaking West African countries with Nigeria, the Gold
       Coast and Sierra Leone on the executive committee.

2681   "UNESCO seminar on the development of public libraries in
       Africa," South Afr. Libr., XXI (April 1954), 115-8;
       Unesco Bull. Lib., VIII (Jan. 1954), E8-10.

2682   White, Ruth Margaret, ed. Public library policies--general
       and special. Chicago: American Library Association, 1960.
       109 p. (The Public library reporter, no. 9.)
              Statements of policies by various American librarians.

(10) LIBRARIANSHIP--SCHOOL AND TEACHER COLLEGE

2683 Allen, Joan. Organization of small libraries; a manual for
      educational institutions in tropical countries. London:
      Oxford University Press, 1961. 80 p.
          Written by former librarian of the Northern Nigeria
      Regional Library.
          Rev: Malayan Library J., II (April 1962), 114. WALA
      News, IV (June 1962), 127-8.

2684 American Library Association. "New goals for the school
      libraries," ALA Bull., LIV (Feb. 1960).
          The entire issue is devoted to school library standards.

2685 Crookall, Robert Egerton. School libraries in West Africa.
      London: University of London Press, 1961. 128 p.
          A practical handbook of school library organization.
          Rev: Malayan Library J., II (Oct. 1961), 19-20.

2686 Douglas, Mary Peacock. The Primary school library and
      its services. Paris: UNESCO, 1961. 103 p. Bibliog.
          (UNESCO manuals for libraries, 12.)
          Rev: Library Assoc. Rec., LXIV (July 1962), 264.
      Library J., LXXXVII (Feb. 15, 1962), 834.

2687 Fadero, Joseph Olatunji. "Objectives and standards of
      practice for school libraries in West Africa." In John
      Dean, ed. Standards of practice for West African libraries.
      Ibadan: Institute of Librarianship, University of Ibadan,
      1969, pp. 69-81.
          Fadero is librarian of the Federal School Library Ser-
      vice, Yaba, Lagos.

2688 Gunton, Dennis H. "The Role of the library in the teacher
      training college," Nigerian Libraries, V (Dec. 1969),102-10.

2689 _____. "The School library in West Africa," W. Afr. J.
      Educ., IV (June 1960), 52-5.

2690 Horrocks, Stanley H. "Public and school libraries and popu-
      lar education in Africa," UNESCO Bull. Lib., XV (Sept.
      1961), 259-62.

2690a Mensah Kane, J. J. "Secondary schools and training college
      libraries in Ghana," Ghana Library J., I, No. 2 (1964),
      27-31.

(10) LIBRARIANSHIP--UNIVERSITY AND SPECIAL

2691 Achimota College. Library. Achimota Library Catalogue.
      Achimota: Achimota Press, 1935. 264 p.

2692   Amedekey, E. Y.   "Current problems of university libraries
       in Ghana," Ghana Library J., I (Feb. 1964), 36-41.

2692a Asheim, Lester E.   "University libraries in developing
       countries," ALA Bull., LIX (October 1965), 795-802.
              Discusses the effects of limited indigenous publishing on
       the growth of the university library collections; library
       administration and organization; and the nature of library
       service.

2693   Association of College and Research Libraries.   Committee
       on Standards.   "Standards for college libraries," Coll. &
       Res. Lib., XX (July 1959), 274-80.

2694   Brown, Alberta L.   "The Measurement of performance and
       its relation to special library service," Special Libraries,
       I (Oct. 1959), 379-84.
              Paper presented at a General Session of the Special
       Libraries Association Convention, Atlantic City, New Jer-
       sey, in the United States, June 2, 1959.   Quantitative
       factors are the size, type and location of the library, its
       physical facilities and book collection.   Qualitative evalua-
       tion involves the staff qualifications and job performance.

2695   Carnovsky, Leon.   "Standards for special libraries; possi-
       bilities and limitations," Library Quarterly, XXIX (July
       1959), 168-73.

2696   Clapp, V. W. and R. T. Jordon.   "Quantitative criteria for
       adequacy of academic library collections," Coll. & Res.
       Lib., XXVI (Sept. 1965), 371-80.

2697   Danton, Joseph Periam.   "The Subject specialist in national
       and university libraries with special reference to book
       selection," Libri, XVII, No. 1 (1967), 42-58.
              A revision of a paper presented at the 32nd Session of
       the IFLA General Council, National and University Libraries
       Section, in The Hague, Sept. 1966.   Argues that book
       selection is one of the most professional aspects of librar-
       ianship, and distinguishes between "subject" and "area"
       specialist, concluding that the latter has an overall advan-
       tage over the former.   Dr. Danton is Professor of Librari-
       anship at the University of California, Berkeley.

2698   Dean, John.   "The African collection, University of Ghana
       Library," Ghana Library J., I (Oct. 1964), 71-4.

2699   _____.   "The Balme Library, University of Ghana: history,
       structure and development, 1948-1965," Nigerian Libraries,
       III (Aug. 1967), 79-82.

2700 _____. "Objectives of the college and school library,"
Nigerian Libraries, V (Dec. 1969), 78-82.
Paper presented at a workshop on teacher training col-
lege libraries, March 1968, Ibadan University.

2701 _____. "Organization and services of university libraries
in West Africa." In Miles Jackson, ed. Comparative and
international librarianship. Westport, Conn.: Greenwood
Press, 1970, pp. 113-37.

2702 Dipeolu, Jonathan O. "Objectives and standards of practice
for university libraries in West Africa." In John Dean, ed.
Standards of practice for West African libraries. Ibadan:
Institute of Librarianship, University of Ibadan, 1969, pp.
31-44.

2703 Dopson, Laurence. "The Medical libraries of West Africa,"
W. Afr. Rev., XXIV (Oct. 1953), 1050-2.

2704 Egger, E. and D. J. Urquhart. "Needs of special libraries,"
Unesco Bull. Lib., XII (Nov. /Dec. 1958), 254-60.

2705 Fischer, Herta D. "Special libraries in Ghana?" Special
Libraries, LX (Jan. 1969), 35-44.

2706 Gatliff, J. W. and S. Forman. "Inter-library loan policies
on dissertations and serial publications," Coll. & Res. Lib.
XXV (May 1964), 209-11.

2706a Gelfand, Morris A. University libraries for developing
countries. Paris: UNESCO, 1968. 157 p. (UNESCO
manuals for libraries, 14.)
Provides much technical information of immense value
to those concerned with administration of university libraries
in developing nations. The author is a distinguished University Librarian and UNESCO field expert in developing
countries.
Rev: J. Doc., XXIV (Sept. 1968), 215-6. Library
World, LXX (April 1969), 277-8.

2707 Guttsman, W. L. "Learned librarians and the structure of
academic libraries," Libri, XV, No. 2 (1965), 159-67.

2708 Hirsch, Felix E. "How can we implement the ALA standards
for college libraries?" Coll. & Res. Lib., XXII (March
1961), 125-9.
The standards established by the American Library
Association.

2709 [No entry]

2710 Havard-Williams, P. "The Student and the university
library," Library Assoc. Rec., LX (Sept. 1958), 269-72.

2711   Humphreys, Kenneth. "The Subject specialist in national
       and university libraries," Libri. , XVII, No. 1 (1967), 29-
       41.
            Paper presented by the Librarian of the University of
       Birmingham at the 32nd Session of the IFLA General
       Council, National and University Libraries Section, in The
       Hague, Sept. 1966.

2712   Lyle, Guy R. , et al.   The Administration of the college
       library. 3rd ed. New York: H. W. Wilson, 1961.   491 p.
       1st ed. 1944.
            "Aims at giving the student a simple, logical and self-
       contained introduction to all aspects of library administra-
       tion as they apply to college libraries and at doing this in
       a manner that will help him to get a clear picture of
       college library work in its entirety and as an integral part
       of the college educational program" (Preface).   Each chap-
       ter is followed by bibliography.   Written for American aca-
       demic libraries, but valuable to academic libraries else-
       where.   Lyle is Director of the Emory University Libraries
       in the U. S. A.
            Rev: Library J. , LXXXVI (Aug. 1961), 2636-7.   Li-
       brary Quarterly, XXXII (Jan. 1962), 93.

2713   Muller, Robert H.   "Research approach to university library
       problems," Coll. & Res. Lib. , XXIV (May 1963), 199-203.

2713a Neequaye, E. K.   "Library cooperation in special libraries,"
       Ghana Library J. , I (Oct. 1964), 56.

2714   Offor, Richard.   "The Development of university libraries in
       British overseas territories," Aslib. Proceedings, VI
       (Aug. 1954), 151-8.
            The Gold Coast, Nigeria, Khartoum and East Africa.

2715   _____ .   "University libraries in the British colonies and
       the Sudan," Libri, V, No. 1 (1954), 54-75.

2716   Ologundudu, V.   "The Needs of government and other special
       libraries in West Africa," WALA News, II (Jan. 1955), 11-
       13.

2717   Padmore the missionary; Osagyefo opens a new library in
       Accra to the memory of one of the greatest architects of
       African liberation.   Accra: Ministry of Information and
       Broadcasting, 1960.

2718   Pafford, J. H.   "Book selection in the university library,"
       UNESCO Bull. Lib. , XVII, No. 1 (1963), 12-16.

2719   Pitcher, G.   "The University of Science and Technology
       Library, Kumasi," Nigerian Libraries, III (Aug. 1967),

93-6.

The college attained university status in 1961, and its library was opened with the books from the teacher training Department in Achimota transferred to Kumasi in 1951.

2720   Rappaport, Philip. "Objectives and standards of practice for special libraries in West Africa." In John Dean, ed. Standards of practice for West African libraries. Ibadan: Institute of Librarianship, University of Ibadan, 1969, pp. 85-91.

The author is former Library Adviser to the Nigerian Federal Government.

2720a Rogers, Rutherford D. and David C. Weber. University library administration. New York: H. W. Wilson, 1971. 454 p.

"Designed to provide librarians and other academic personnel with a current treatment of the more important issues in the administration of a university library. The issues and problems dealt with are those which, in substantial degree, affect the economy of the library operation, its service to its clientele, the securing of adequate financial support, the impact of various matters on the staff, and external relations both on and off campus" (Preface). Subject index. Rogers is Librarian of Yale University and Weber is Director of Stanford University libraries.

Rev: Australian Library J., XX (Dec. 1971), 38-9. Library Assoc. Rec., LXXIII (Dec. 1971), 243-4. Library J., XCVI (Nov. 1971), 3579-80.

2721   Tetty, Charles. "Medical library services in English-speaking West Africa," WALA News, III (May 1960), 245-9.

2721a "University and special libraries in Ghana," Library World, LXIV (Feb. 1963), 214-7.

2722   Walker, Elise. "The University College of the Gold Coast Library," Library Assoc. Rec., LVI (May 1954), 166-70.

2723   Wasserman, Paul. "Measuring performance in a special library--problems and prospects," Special Libraries, XLIX (Oct. 1958), 377-82.

Dr. Wasserman is former Dean of Graduate Library School, University of Maryland in the U.S.A.

2724   Wilson, Louis Round and Maurice F. Tauber. The University Library; the organization, administration and function of academic libraries. New York: Columbia University Press, 1956. 641 p. (Columbia University Studies in Library service, No. 8.)

Rev: J. Doc., XII (Dec. 1956), 239-40. Library Quarterly, XXVI (Oct. 1956), 388-90.

2725 Young, R. D. E. "University library co-operation," Ghana
       Library J., I (Oct. 1964), 56.
            The proposed National Union Catalogue for Ghana would
       be unnecessary if Telex were installed to link the three
       universities. Stresses the need for a union catalog of
       periodicals; cooperation between the universities; installa-
       tion of photographic units in each library; and standardiza-
       tion of staff salaries.

(11) LINGUISTICS--GENERAL

2726 Akyea, E. Ofori. "A Study of some verbal art forms of
       Juaben--an Ashanti state," Master's Thesis, University of
       Ghana, 1967. 158 p.

2727 Amonoo, R. F. "Problems of Ghanaian 'Lingue Franche.'"
       In John Spencer, ed. Language in Africa. Cambridge:
       Cambridge University Press, 1963, pp. 78-95.

2728 Armstrong, Robert G. The Study of West African languages.
       Ibadan: Ibadan University Press for NISER, 1964. 74 p.
            An expanded version of an inaugural lecture delivered
       at the University of Ibadan on Feb. 20, 1964.

2729 Asamoa, E. A. "The Problem of language in education in
       the Gold Coast," Africa. (Lond.) XXV (Jan. 1955), 60-78.

2730 Barnard, G. L. Report on the use of English, (as the medium
       of instruction) in the Gold Coast. Accra: Govt. Printer,
       1956. 74 p.

2731 Berry, Jack. "The Madina Project, Ghana." In W. H.
       Whiteley, ed. Language use and social change. London:
       Oxford University Press for the International African
       Institute, 1971, pp. 318-33.
            One of the studies presented and discussed at the Ninth
       International African Seminar at University College, Dar es
       Salaam on Dec. 1968. A socio-linguistic study jointly
       sponsored by the Institute of African Studies, University
       of Ghana and the Department of Linguistics, North-Western
       University in the U. S., designed to determine "how many
       and what kinds of languages are currently spoken in Madina,
       by how many people and under what circumstances, and the
       attitudes and beliefs about languages held by the residents
       of Madina. "

2732 _____. "The Madina Project: socio-linguistic research in
       Ghana." In Gwendolen Carter and Ann Paden, eds.

Expanding Horizons in African studies. Evanston: North-western University Press, 1969, pp. 303-13.

2733 _____ . "Oral data collecting and Linguistics in Africa,"
J. Folklore Inst., VI, Nos. 2-3 (1969), 93-117.
With appendix by E. W. Stevick and comment by H. Wolff.

2734 _____ . The Place-names of Ghana. Accra: University
Bookshop, 1958. 190 p.
Problems of standardizing the Ghanaian place-names.

2735 _____ . "Structural affinities of the Volta River languages
and their significance for linguistic classification," Doc-toral Dissertation, London Univ., 1951/52.

2736 Brown, P. P. and J. Scragge. Common errors in Gold Coast
English: their cause and correction. London: Macmillan,
1950. 134 p.

2737 Cole, Desmond T. "African linguistic studies, 1943-1960,"
African Studies, XIX (1960), 219-29.

2738 Conference on the Study of Ghanaian Languages, University of
Ghana, Legon, 5-8 May 1968. Proceedings. Accra:
Ghana Publishing Corp., for Institute of African Studies,
Legon, 1968. 112 p.

2739 Dalby, D. "Provisional identification of languages in the
Polyglotta Africana," Sierra Leone Language Review, No.
3 (1964), 83-90.

2740 Dickens, K. J. "Orthography in the Gold Coast," Africa
(Lond.) VI, No. 3 (1933), 317-22.

2741 Djoleto, S. A. English practice for the African student.
London: Macmillan, 1967. 186 p.

2742 Fage, J. D. "Some notes on a scheme for the investigation
of oral tradition in the Northern Territories of the Gold
Coast," J. Hist. Soc. Nigeria, I, No. 1 (1956), 15-19.

2743 Ghana Bureau of Languages. Bibliography of works in
Ghana languages. Accra, 1967. 161 p.
Contains about 1200 entries, with titles also translated
into English and descriptive annotations. Arranged by
ethnic divisions. Analytical general index and index of
ethnic divisions.

2744 _____ . The Writing of Akan. Accra, 1962.

2745 Greenberg, Joseph H. "The Application of new world evidence
to an African linguistic problem," Mém. IFAN, XXVII
(1953), 129-31.

2746   . "Historical inferences from linguistic research in
Sub-Saharan Africa. " In Jeffrey Butler, ed. Boston University papers in African history. V. I. Boston: Boston
University Press, 1964, pp. 1-15.
Describes the principal methods by which inferences of
interest to the historian can be derived from linguistic
data and illustrates these methods by employing specific
examples from African languages.

2747   . "Historical linguistics and unwritten languages. "
In A. L. Kroeber, ed. Anthropology Today, Chicago, 1953,
pp. 265-86.

2748   . "Studies in African linguistic classification, I:
The Niger-Congo family, " Southwestern J. Anthrop. , V
(Autumn 1949), 79-100.

2749   . Studies in African linguistic classification. New
Haven: Campus Publishing Co. , 1955.

2750   Griffin, Ella. "Du matériel du lecture pour les habitants
du Ghana, " Rev. Int. Educ. Adul. J. , XV, No. 3 (1963),
138-44.

2751   Hair, P. E. "Collections of vocabularies of Western Africa
before the Polyglotta: a key, " J. Afr. Lang. , V, Pt. 3
(1966), 208-17.

2752   Harman, H. A. The New Script and its relation to the languages of the Gold Coast. Accra: Education Dept. , 1930.
43 p.

2753   Hartley, N. "Language and nation building--examples from
West Africa, " Incorporated Linguist, (Lond.) VIII (July
1969), 57-9.
Chiefly on the political and social impact of the Nigerian
ethnic and linguistic diversities on Nigeria, with a
sketchy mention of other West African states.

2754   Homburger, L. The Negro-African languages. London:
Routledge, 1949. 275 p.

2755   Jeffreys, M. D. "Some West African language borrowings
and lendings, " Africa, V (Oct. 1932), 503-9.

2756   . "Word borrowing" (from West African languages),
Nigeria, No. 21 (1940), 358-62.

2757   Kennedy, Jack Scott. "Language and communication problems
in the Ghanaian theatre, " Okyeame, IV (Dec. 1968), 103-9.

Linguistics   297

2758   . "The Use of language and the Ghanaian actors'
       technique," Research Review, IV, No. 2 (1968), 61-2.

2759 Kotey, Paul Francis. "Directions in Ghanaian linguistics:
       a brief survey." Paper presented at an African Faculty
       Seminar at Ohio University, Nov. 18, 1968. 15 p. (Papers
       in International Studies. Africa series, No. 2.)
          Reviews the current linguistic work in Ghana, concen-
       trating his paper on Twi, Ewe and Ga "principally because
       work on these languages is representative of work done on
       the others." Notes also that although greatest linguistic
       study has been focussed upon Ghana's five main languages--
       Twi, Ewe, Ga, Dagbani and Kassem, there are about
       sixty other languages.

2760 Ladefoged, Peter. Elements of acoustic phonetics. Edin-
       burgh: Oliver and Boyd, 1962. 118 p.

2761   . A Phonetic study of West African languages: an
       auditory-instrumental survey. 2nd ed. Cambridge: Cam-
       bridge University Press, 1968. 74 p. Bibliog. 1st ed.
       1964.

2762   . Three areas of experimental phonetics: stress
       and respiratory activity: the nature of vowel quality, units
       in perception and production of speech. London: Oxford
       University Press, 1967. 180 p. (Language and Language
       Learning 15.)

2763   . "The value of phonetic statements," Language,
       XXXVI, No. 3 (1960), 387-96.

2764 Okyne, Robert Richardson. Far and near. London: Univer-
       sity of London Press, 1967. 127 p. (English at work
       reader, No. 4.)

2765   . Tales and discoveries. London: University of
       London Press, 1967. 127 p. (English at work reader,
       No. 5.)

2766   . This modern world. London: University of Lon-
       don Press, 1967. 110 p. (English at work reader, No. 6.)

2767   . Three friends at school. London: University of
       London Press, 1967. 78 p. (English at work reader,
       No. 7.)

2768 Owiredu, P. A. "Proposal for a national language for
       Ghana," African Affairs, LXIII (April 1964), 142-5.
          Discusses the problems of choosing any of the Ghanaian
       principal languages as a national language stressing the
       fact that an attempted unification of Twi and Fante failed

owing to strong local feelings against it.   Suggests compulsory vernacular studies for all secondary schools.

2769 _____. "Towards a common language for Ghana," African Affairs, LVI (Oct. 1957), 295-9.
Reviews the problems of adopting one language as the official language, suggesting that while English could be recognized as the compulsory second language for use in inter-regional and external transactions, each of the five Regional Assemblies should select as the official language of its region any of these--Twi and Fante; Ga, Ewe and Dagbani.

2770 Painter, Colin. "The Distribution of Guang in Ghana, and a statistical pre-testing on twenty-five idolects," J. West Afr. Lang., VI (Jan. 1967), 25-78.

2771 Rattray, Robert Sutherland. "The Drum language of west Africa," J. Afr. Soc., LXXXVII (1923), 226-36; 302-16.

2772 Schneider, Gilbert D. West African pidgin-English: an historical over-view. Athens: Ohio University, Center for International studies, 1967. 23 p. (Papers in International studies, No. 8.)

2773 Siertsema, Bertha. A Test in phonetics: 500 questions and answers on English pronounciation and how to teach in West Africa. The Hague: Nijhoff, 1959. 94 p.

2774 Spencer, John, ed. The English language in West Africa. London: Longmans, 1971. 190 p.

2775 Storch, R. F. "Writing in Ghana," Universitas (Accra), II, No. 5 (1967), 148-51.

2776 Strevens, Peter. "Spoken English in the Gold Coast," Colonial Review (Sept. 1954), 207-8.

2777 Ward, Ida C. Report of an investigation of some Gold Coast language problems. London: Crown Agents, 1945. 74 p.

2778 _____. "Verbal tone patterns in West African languages," Bull. Sch. Orient. Afr. Stud., XII, Parts 3-4 (1948), 831-7.

2779 Welmers, William Everett and Ruth Sloan. A Preliminary survey of existing resources for training in African languages and linguistics. Washington, D.C.: Georgetown University Press, 1957. 145 p. Bibliog.

2780 Westermann, Diedrich Hermann. "African linguistic classification," Africa, XXII (1952), 250-6.

Review of Studies in African linguistic classification, by
J. H. Greenberg.

2781 _____. "A Visit to the Gold Coast," Africa (Lond.) I
(Jan. 1928), 107-11.
A report of author's visit to the Gold Coast in February
to April 1927, sponsored by the Gold Coast Government
and designed "to advise them regarding a common script
for the leading languages and related subjects." The languages concerned with are Akan, with its two main dialects,
Twi and Fante, Ga and Ewe.

2782 _____ and M. A. Bryan. Languages of West Africa. London: Oxford University Press, for the International African
Institute, 1952. 215 p.

2783 Wolff, Hans. "Subsystem typologies and area linguistics,"
Anthropological Linguistics, I, No. 7 (1959), 1-88.

(11) LINGUISTICS--EWE

2784 Ansre, G. "The grammatical units of Ewe; a study of
their structure, classes and systems," Doctoral Dissertation, London University, 1965/66.

2785 _____. "Reduplication in Ewe," J. Afr. Lang., II (1963),
128-32.

2786 _____. "The tonal structure of Ewe," Master's Thesis,
Hartford Seminary Foundation, 1961.

2787 Berry, Jack. The Pronunciation of Ewe. Cambridge, Eng.:
Heffer, 1951. 28 p.
Ewe is a language spoken by over a million people in
Ghana. This study guide is designed for the European
learner whom the author advises to concentrate first on
tone and strange consonants.

2788 Kropp, Mary Esther. "Adampe and Anfue dialects of Ewe in
the Polyglotta Africana," Sierra Leone Language Review,
No. 5 (1966), 116-24.

2789 Riebstein, P. E. Eléments de grammaire Ewe. Holland,
Mission Catholique Steyl, 1928. 132 p.

2790 Schober, Reinhold. "Die semantische Gestalt des Ewe,"
Anthropos, XXVIII (1933), 621-32.

2791 Westermann, Diedrich Hermann. Evefiafa (Ewe-English dictionary). Berlin: D. Reimer, 1928. 300 p.

2792 _____ . Die Ewe-Sprache in Togo: eine praktische Ein-
fuhrung. 2nd ed. Berlin: de Gruyter, 1961. 95 p.

2793 _____ . Gbesela Yeye (English-Ewe dictionary). Berlin:
D. Reimer, 1930. 348 p.

2794 _____ . A study of the Ewe language. Translated by A. L.
Bickford-Smith. London: Oxford University Press, 1930.
258 p.

2795 _____ . Worterbuch der Ewe-Sprache. Rev. ed. Berlin:
Akamedie-Verlag, 1954. 796 p. First published 1905.

2796 Wiegräbe, Paul. "Ewelieder," Afrika und Übersee, XXXVII
(Aug. 1953), 99-108; (Sept. 1954), 155-64.
Ewe songs with German text.

(11) LINGUISTICS--FANTE AND TWI

2797 Akrofi, C. A. Twi Kasa Mmara. 2nd ed. (Twi grammar
in Twi.) London: Longmans, 1960. 110 p. 1st ed.,
1937.

2798 _____ . Twi Mmebusem: Twi proverbs, with English
translations and comments. Kumasi: Presbyterian Book
Depot, 1958. 173 p.

2799 _____ and G. L. Botchey. English--Twi--Ga dictionary.
Accra: Waterville, 1968. 83 p.

2800 _____ and Eugen L. Rapp. A Twi spelling book. Accra:
Govt. Printer, 1938. 110 p.

2801 Amu, Ephraim. Twenty-five songs in the Twi language.
London: Sheldon Press, 1932. 91 p.

2802 Balmer, W. T. and F. C. Grant. A Grammar of the Fante-
Akan language. London: Atlantis Press, 1929. 223 p.

2803 Bartels, F. L. Fante word list with rules of spelling.
Cape Coast: Methodist Book Depot, 1944. 84 p.

2804 _____ and J. H. Annobil. Mfantse nkasafua dwumadzi: a
Fante grammar of function. 11th ed. Cape Coast: Methodist Book Depot, 1962. 182 p. 1st ed. 1946.

2805 Bellon, Immanuel. Twi lessons for beginners, including a
grammatical guide and numerous idioms and phrases. Rev.
ed. Accra: Presbyterian Book Depot, 1963. 76 p.

2806 Berry, Jack. English, Twi, Asante, Fante Dictionary. London: Macmillan, 1960. 146 p.

2807 _____. "A Note on Twi accents." In J. Lukas, ed. Afrikanistische Studien, 1955, 295-8.

2808 _____. "Vowel harmony in Twi," Bull. Sch. Orient. Afr. Stud., XIX (1957), 124-30.

2809 Boadi, L. K. "Comparative sentences in Twi-Fante," J. West Afr. Lang., III, No. 1 (1966), 39-46.

2810 _____. "Palatality as a factor in Twi vowel harmony," J. Afr. Lang., II (1963), 133-8.

2811 _____. "Some Twi phrase structure rules," J. West Afr. Lang., II, No. 1 (1965), 37-46.

2812 _____. "Some aspects of Akan deep syntax," J. West Afr. Lang., V (July 1968), 83-90.

2813 _____. "The syntax of the Twi verb," Doctoral Dissertation, London University, 1965/66.

2814 Brew, S. H. Practical Fanti Course. Cape Coast: Wesleyan Book Depot, 1917. 132 p.

2815 Christaller, Johann G. Dictionary of the Asante and Fante language called Tshi (Twi). Basel: Evangelische Missionsgesellschaft, 1933. 607 p. 1st ed. 1881.

2816 _____. A Grammar of the Asante and Fante language called Tshi based on the Akuapem dialect with reference to the other (Akan and Fante) dialects. Farnborough, Hampshire: Gregg International Publishers, 1964. 203 p.
       First published in 1875, by the Basel Evangelical Missionary Society. Primarily designed for missionaries and other Europeans, it has a long useful introduction on the languages and dialects of the Gold Coast (Ghana).

2817 Christensen, J. B. "The Role of proverbs in Fante culture," Africa (Lond.) XXVIII (July 1958), 232-43.
       Discusses proverbs of the Akan-speaking people among the Fante of the Central region of the Coastal Province of Ghana. The themes of these proverbs apply almost to all the Akan people. Aspects of the Fante culture are also chosen to illustrate the ways in which these proverbs are usually used.

2818 Coker, Increase H. Grammar of African names: an outline guide to the study and appreciation of African names selected from the Akan (Gold Coast) Yoruba, Ijaw, and Efik-

Ibibio language groups.   Lagos: Techno-Literary Works,
1954.   36 p.

2819   Dolphnyne, F. A.   The Phonetics and phonology of the verbal
piece in the Asante dialect of Twi.   London: School of
Oriental and African Studies, 1965.   302 p.

2820   Mason, C. I. and E. C. Bilson.   First stage in Fante reading.
Achimota: Achimota Press, 1936.   51 p.

2821   Matson, J. N.   "History in Akan words," Trans. Gold Coast
& Togoland Hist. Soc., II (1956), 63-70.

2822   Mead, Margaret.   "A Twi relationship system," J. Roy.
Anthrop. Inst., LXVII (July-Dec. 1937), 297-304.

2823   Methodist Book Depot.   Mfantse nkasafua nkyerekyerease:
interim Fante-English dictionary.   Cape Coast, 1955.   68 p.

2824   _____.   Twi grammar of function.   Cape Coast, 1950.
191 p.

2825   Mohr, A.   A Dictionary of English-Twi.   2nd ed.   Basel:
Basel Missionary Society, 1909.   247 p.

2826   Ofosu-Appiah, L. H.   "On translating the Homeric epithet and
simile into Twi," Africa (Lond.) XXX (Jan. 1960), 41-5.

2827   Rapp, Eugen L.   An Introduction to Twi.   Basel: Evengelische
Missionsgesellschaft, 1948.   119 p.   1st ed. 1936.

2828   Russell, J. D.   Fanti-English dictionary.   Cape Coast: Wesleyan Book Depot, 1910.   193 p.

2829   Schachter, Paul.   "Natural assimilation rules in Akan,"
Int. J. Amer. Ling., XXXV, No. 4 (1969), 342-55.

2830   _____ and Victoria Fromkin.   A Phonology of Akan:
Akuapem, Asante and Fante.   Los Angeles, University of
California, 1968.   (Working papers in phonetics, No. 9.)

2831   Stewart, John M.   "The analysis of the structure of the Fante
verb, with special reference to tone and glottalisation,"
Doctoral Dissertation, London University, 1962/63.

2832   _____.   "A note on Akan-centered linguistic acculturation,"
Research Review, III, No. 2 (1967), 66-73.

2833   _____.   "Some restrictions on objects in Twi," J. Afr.
Lang., II (1963), 145-9.

2834 _____. "Tongue root position in Akan vowel harmony,"
     Phonetica, XVI (1967), 185-204.

2835 _____. The typology of the Twi tone system. With com-
     ments by Paul Schachter and William E. Welmers. Legon:
     Institute of African Studies, 1964.

2836 Taylor, C. J. "Some Akan names," Nigerian Field, XVIII
     (1953), 34-7.

2837 U. S. Foreign Service Institute. Twi basic course, by J. E.
     Redder, et al. Washington, D. C. : Dept. of State, 1963.
     224 p. (Its basic course series.)
        "Designed to provide basic structures and vocabulary
     for the situation in which the foreigner is most likely to
     need Twi. " Includes a glossary.

2838 Welmers, William Everett. A Descriptive grammar of Fanti.
     Baltimore: Linguistic Society of America, 1946. 78 p.
     (Doctoral Dissertation, University of Pennsylvania.)

2839 Wohlgemuth, N. "Ein Fante-Tiermärchen, " Ethnos, V
     (1936), 128-32.

(11) LINGUISTICS--GA

2840 Ablorh-Odjidja, J. R. Ga for beginners, including grammar,
     notes and numerous idioms. Accra: Waterville, 1968.
     207 p.

2841 Akrofi, C. A. and G. L. Botchey. English--Twi--Ga diction-
     ary. Accra: Waterville, 1968. 83 p.

2842 Apronti, Eric Ofoe. "New orthographies for Ga and Dangme,"
     Research Review, VI, No. 1 (1969), 52-8.

2843 Armstrong, M. A New Ga reader. London: Oxford Univer-
     sity Press, 1931. 46 p.

2844 Bannerman, C. J. Ga grammar of function. New ed. Cape
     Coast: Methodist Book Depot, 1948. 168 p.

2845 Berry, Jack. Pronunciation of Ga. Cambridge, Eng. : Hef-
     fer, 1951. 24 p.
     Included for the beginner

2846 Fleischer, C. F. and M. B. Wilkie. "Specimens of folklore
     of the Ga-people in the Gold Coast, " Africa (Lond.), III,
     No. 3 (1930), 360-8.

2847   Ga Society. <u>Ga word list with rules of spelling.</u> 3rd ed.
       Cape Coast, 1946. 55 p.

2848   Kotey, Paul F. "The Ga adjectives: their significance for
       the theory of language universals," Master's Thesis,
       Harvard University, 1967.

2849   Kropp, Mary Esther. "An Analysis of the consonant system
       of Ga," <u>J. West. Afr. Lang.</u>, V (Jan. 1968), 59-61.

2850   _____. "A Comparative study of Ga and Adangbe with
       special reference to the verb." Doctoral Dissertation,
       London University, 1968. 328 p.

2851   _____. "The Morphology of the Ga aspect system," <u>J.
       Afr. Lang.</u>, V, Part II (1966), 121-7.

2852   Okunor, J. V. "Tone in the Ga verb," Master's Thesis,
       University of Ghana, 1964.

2853   Wilkie, M. B. <u>Ga grammar, notes and exercises.</u> London:
       Oxford University Press, 1930. 239 p.

(11)   LINGUISTICS--OTHER LANGUAGES

2854   Accam, T. N. <u>Adangbe vocabularies, including a Klama
       vocabulary.</u> Edited by M. E. Kropp. Legon: Institute
       of African Studies, University of Ghana, 1966. 75 p.
       (Local Studies Series, no. 2.)

2855   Apronti, Eric Ofoe. "The language of a two-year-old
       Dangme," <u>Ghana Journal of Child Development,</u> II, No. 1
       (1969), 19-29.

2856   _____. "A Phonetic and phonological study of the nominal
       piece in Adangme," Doctoral Dissertation, London Univer-
       sity, 1967. 2 v.

2857   Berry, Jack. "Some notes on the phonology of the Nzema
       and Ahanta dialects," <u>Bull. Sch. Orient. Afr. Stud.</u>, XVII,
       No. 1 (1955), 160-5.

2858   _____. "Some preliminary notes on Ada personal nomen-
       clature," <u>Afr. Lang. Stud.</u>, No. 1 (1960), 177-84.

2859   Blair, H. A. <u>Dagomba dictionary and grammar.</u> Accra:
       Govt. Printer, 1941. 151 p.

2860   Chamberlain, G. D. <u>A Brief Account of the Brissa language.</u>
       Accra: Govt. Printer, 1930. 53 p.

2861 Chinebuah, I.K. "The Category of number in Nzema," J. Afr. Lang., II (1963), 244-59.

2862 _____. "Consonant mutation in Nzema," J. West Afr. Lang., VII, No. 2 (1970), 69-84.

2863 _____. "A Phonetic and phonological study of the nominal piece in Nzema based on the candidate's own pronunciation," Master's Thesis, London University, 1963.

2864 Crouch, Marjorie. Collected field reports on the phonology of Vagala. Legon: Institute of African Studies, University of Ghana, 1966. 44 p.

2865 Dakuru, M.E. "The Adangme verb reconsidered," J. Afr. Lang., IX, Part I (1970), 19-26.

2866 _____. "Bowdich's Adampe word list," Research Review, V, No. 3 (1969), 45-9.
     Represents a southern Guan language with Adangme numbers.

2867 Fisch, R. Grammatik der Dagombasprache. (Dagbane) Berlin: G. Reimer, 1912. 79 p.

2868 Frajzyngier, Zygmunt. "An Analysis of the Awutu verb," Master's Thesis, University of Ghana, 1965. 82 p.

2869 Hintze, Ursula. "Untersuchungen zur sprachlichen Stellung der Nzema innerhalb der Akan Sprachen," Phil. Diss. Berlin, 1949. 137 p.

2870 Kennedy, Jack Scott. The Phonology of Dagaari. Accra: Institute of African Studies, University of Ghana, 1970.

2871 Kropp, Mary Esther. Adangme vocabularies. Accra: Institute of African Studies, University of Ghana, 1970.

2872 _____. "The Morphology of the Adangme verb complex," J. Afr. Lang., III, Part I (1964), 80-95.

2873 Lassig, Robert. "Die Kussassi-Sprache im West-Sudan," Phil. Diss. Berlin, 1928. 59 p.

2873a Painter, Colin. Gonja: a phonological & grammatical study. Bloomington: Indiana University Press, 1969. 523 p. (Indiana University publications, African series, Vol. 1.)

2874 Puplampu, D.A. Adangme manner of speech: a study of the Adangme language, parts 1 & 2. London: Macmillan, 1953. 112 p.

2875 _____. "The National epic of the Adangme," African
     Affairs, L (1951), 236-41.

2876 Richardson, Irvine. "The Role of tone in the structure of
     Sukuma," Doctoral Dissertation, London University, 1956.

2877 Shirer, W. L. Dagbane grammar. Tamale: Assemblies of
     God Mission, 1939. 89 p.

2878 Welman, Charles W. A Preliminary study of the Nzima
     language. London: Crown Agents, 1926. 113 p.

2879 Westermann, Diedrich Hermann. Die Sprache der Guang in
     Togo und auf der Golkuste und funf andere Togo-Sprachen.
     Berlin: D. Reimer, 1922. 268 p.

2880 Wilson, W. A. "Relative constructions in Dagbani," J. Afr.
     Lang., II (1963), 139-44.

2881 _____ and J. T. Bendor-Samuel. The Phonology of the
     nominal in Dagbani. Legon: Institute of African Studies,
     University of Ghana, 1965. 46 p.

(12) LITERATURE--GENERAL

2882 Armah, Ayi Kwei (Ghana). "An African fable," Présence
     Africaine, No. 68 (1968), 192-6.

2883 Armattoe, Raphael Ernest (Ghana). The Golden age of West
     African civilization, etc. Londonderry: Londonderry
     Sentinel for the Lomeshire Research Centre, 1945. 98 p.

2884 _____. Personal recollections of the Nobel Lauretian
     Festival of 1947. Londonderry: Lomeshire Research
     Centre, 1948. 62 p.

2885 Awoonor, Kofi (Ghana). "Changing role of the African writer,"
     Ghana Guardian, I (Oct. 1966), 9-14.

2886 _____. "Culture, literature and arts in Africa," New Time
     (Accra), No. 2 (Sept. 1967), 17-26.

2887 _____. "Fresh vistas for African literature," Afr. Rev.
     (Accra) I, (May 1965), 35+.

2888 _____. "Reminiscences of earlier days." In Per Wästberg,
     ed. The Writer in Modern Africa. Uppsala: Scan-
     dinavian Institute of African Studies, 1967, pp. 112-8.

2889 _____ . "Sources of Ghanaian literature," New Time
      (Accra) No. 3 (Oct. 1967), 29-30.

2890 Barker, W. H. and C. Sinclair. West African folk tales.
      London: Harrap, 1917. 184 p.
      Specially illustrative of the richness of imagery in
      African folklore.

2891 Banham, Martin and John Ramsaran. "West African writing,"
      Books Abroad, XXXVI (Autumn 1962), 371-4.

2892 Beier, Horst Ulli. Black Orpheus: an anthology of new
      African and Afro-American stories. Ikeja, Nigeria: Long-
      mans, 1964. 156 p.
      Rev: New African, IV (July 1965), 112. TLS (April
      29, 1965), 323.

2893 _____ . Introduction to African literature: an anthology
      of critical writing from Black Orpheus. Evanston, Ill.:
      Northwestern University Press, 1967. 272 p. Bibliog.

2894 Bol, Vincent P. and Jean Allary. Littératures et poèts
      noirs. Leopoldville: Bibliothèque de l'Etoile, 1964.
      Covers black writers in European writings, designed
      primarily as a teacher's guidebook. Too sketchy on
      American and West Indian authors.

2895 Brewer, J. Mason and H. O. Welbeck. "How the spider
      bought God's title and other spider tales from Ghana,"
      Int. Rev., XXXV (Sept. 1962), 188-93.

2896 Cartey, Wilfred, ed. Palaver; modern African writings.
      London: Nelson, 1970. 183 p.
      Rev: Africa Report, XVI (April 1971), 36-7.

2897 _____ . Whispers from a continent: the literature of
      contemporary black Africa. London: Heinemann, 1971.
      397 p. (Studies in African literature.)
      First published in 1969 by Random House, New York.
      Rev: Conch, II (Mar. 1970), 67-9.

2898 Dathorne, O. R. "African folktales as literature," Conch,
      II (Sept. 1970), 90-101.

2899 Dei-Anang, M. F. (Ghana). "A Writer's outlook," Okyeame,
      I (Jan. 1961), 40-3.

2900 Drachler, Jacob, ed. African heritage; intimate views of the
      black Africans from life, love, and literature. Preface by
      Melville J. Herskovits. New York: Crowell-Collier Press,
      1963. 286 p.

2901   Edwards, Paul, comp. <u>Through African eyes</u>. Cambridge:
       Cambridge University Press, 1966. 2 v. 102, 117 p.
       "Designed principally for African schools--Its main pur-
       pose is to help direct and increase reading for pleasure
       by offering samples of the lively and intelligent writings
       which have come from Africa. " Only prose selections
       with one by a Ghanaian, Solomon Attah-Ahuma, entitled
       "The Gold Coast and national consciousness. "

2902   Feuser, W. F.   "Beyond British cultural assumptions: the
       Ife Conference on African Writing in English, 16th-19th
       December, 1968, " <u>Afr. Act.</u>, XXXV-XXXVI (Feb. 1969),
       47-51.
       The author is Professor of Modern Languages, at the
       University of Ife, Nigeria.

2903   Finnegan, Ruth. <u>Oral literature in Africa.</u> London: Ox-
       ford University Press, 1970. 580 p.
       Rev: <u>African Notes</u>, VI, No. 2 (1971), 107-12.

2904   Gerard, Albert.   "Bibliographical problems in creative
       African literature, " <u>J. Gen. Educ.</u> (Chicago) XIX (1967),
       25-34.
       A comprehensive survey of various bibliographical
       studies and compilations on Africa, indicating their
       strengths and weaknesses, with suggestions for improve-
       ment.

2905   Ghana.   Ministry of Information. <u>Voices of Ghana: literary</u>
       <u>contributions to the Ghana Broadcasting System, 1955-1957.</u>
       Edited by Henry Swanzy. Accra, 1958.   266 p.
       Plays, poems and stories in English, including some
       brief biographical sketches.

2906   Goodwin, K. L. <u>National identity: papers delivered at the</u>
       <u>Commonwealth Literature Conference, University of Queens-</u>
       <u>land, Brisbane, 9th-15th August, 1968.</u> With an introduc-
       tion by A. N. Jeffares. London: Heinemann Educational
       Books, 1970. 219 p.
       Contents include the Development of national attitudes;
       Cultural exchange in literature and languages; The Novel
       and national identity; Poetry and national identity.   There
       are also reports of working parties on various problems of
       Commonwealth literature.

2907   Görög, Veronika.   "Toward a method of analysis of African
       oral literature; introduction to a selective, analytical bib-
       liography, " <u>Conch,</u> II (Sept. 1970), 59-68.

2908   Green, L. <u>Folktales and fairytales of Africa.</u> Morristown,
       New Jersey: Silver Burdett Co. , 1967. 96 p.
       Includes a chapter on Ghana.

2909 Grottanelli, V. L. "Nzema proverbs, " <u>Afrika und Ubersee,</u>
      LXXII (Feb. 1958), 17-26.

2910 Hodgkin, Thomas. "The Islamic literary tradition in Ghana."
      In <u>Islam in Tropical Africa: Studies presented at and dis-</u>
      <u>cussed at the Fifth International Seminar, Ahmadu Bello</u>
      <u>University, Zaria, January 1964.</u> London: Oxford Univer-
      sity Press, 1966, pp. 442-60.

2911 Izevbaye, David Sunday. "The Relevance of modern literary
      theory in English to poetry and fiction in English-speaking
      West Africa, " Doctoral Dissertation, Ibadan University,
      1968.

2912 Jablow, A. <u>An Anthology of West African folklore.</u> London:
      Thames & Hudson, 1962. 223 p.
      Classifies the stories into dilemma tales, love stories
      and riddles. Includes a collection of some proverbs.

2913 Jones, E. "The Decolonisation of African literature."
      Paper presented at the African-Scandinavian Writer's
      Conference, Stockholm, 6-9 February, 1967.

2914 _____. "African literature, 1966-1967, " <u>African Forum,</u>
      III (Summer 1967), 5-25.
      A bibliographic essay on the works of literature pub-
      lished during the period, noting that "too many of the new
      novels are little more than documentaries of African village
      life and customs--there is little new in verse and drama."

2915 _____. "Nationalism and the Writer. " In John Press, ed.
      <u>Commonwealth literature: unity and diversity in a common</u>
      <u>culture.</u> London: Heinemann, 1965, pp. 151-67.
      States that African writers despite their strong nation-
      alistic feelings may have to continue to use the colonial
      languages for their writings if they hope to gain a wide
      readership.

2916 Jones-Quartey, K. A. "The Gold Coast press, 1822-c. 1930,
      and the Anglo-African press, 1825-c. 1930, " <u>Research Re-</u>
      <u>view</u> (Legon) IV, No. 2 (1968), 30-46.

2917 _____. "Sierra-Leone and Ghana: nineteenth century
      pioneers in West African journalism, " <u>Sierra Leone Stud. ,</u>
      No. 12 (Dec. 1959), 230-44.

2918 Joslin, Mike. <u>Märchen von der Gold Küste: Gesammett</u>
      <u>und Aufgezeichnet.</u> München: Nymphenburger Verlagshand-
      lung, 1960. 207 p.

2919 Kesteloot, Lilyan. "Problems of the literary critic in Africa, "
      <u>Abbia,</u> No. 8 (Feb. -Mar. 1965), 29-44.

2920 Komey, Ellis Ayitey (Ghana) and Ezekiel Mphahlele, eds.
      Modern African Stories. London: Faber & Faber, 1964.
      227 p.
      Rev: African Forum, I (Fall 1965), 113-4.

2921 Kponkpongori, C. S. (Ghana) et al. Gonja proverbs. Edited by
      O. Rytz. Legon: Institute of African Studies, University
      of Ghana, 1966? 64 p. (Local studies series, No. 3.)

2922 Lindfors, Bernth. "Approaches to folklore in African lit-
      erature," Conch, II (Sept. 1970), 102-11.

2923 Makward, Edris. "African writers share basic themes and
      concerns: post-independence commitment, culture-conflict
      and quandry of the 'Been-to' cut across linguistic divisions,"
      Africa Report, XVI (Mar. 1971), 28-31.
      An excellent article stressing the fact that the themes
      of post-1950 African writers have been similar despite the
      linguistic and cultural differences among these writers.
      Gives examples of the works of some well-known African
      writers such as Chinua Achebe, Wole Soyinka, Ayi Kwei
      Armah, Lenrie Peters, William Conton, Hamidou Kane,
      etc.

2924 Meleod, A. L., ed. The Commonwealth pen: an introduction
      to the literature of the British Commonwealth. New York:
      Cornell University Press, 1961. 243 p.

2925 Moore, Gerald. The Chosen tongue; English writing in the
      Tropical World. London: Longmans, 1970.
      A critical study of selected African writers such as
      Wole Soyinka, J. P. Clark, Christopher Okigbo, etc.
      Rev: Africa Report, XVI (Jan. 1971), 37-8.

2926 _____. "Modern African literature and tradition," African
      Affairs, LXVI (July 1967), 246-7.

2927 Mphahlele, E. "African writing in English." Paper pre-
      sented at the International Symposium of African Culture,
      Ibadan, Nigeria, on December 1960.

2928 Nassau, Robert Hamill. Where animals talk: West African
      folklore tales. New York: Negro Universities Press, 1970.
      250 p.
      Reprint of the 1912 ed.

2929 Obiechina, Emmanuel N. "The Growth of written literature in
      English-speaking West Africa," Conch, I (Sept. 1969), 3-
      22.

2930 _____. "Transition from oral to literal tradition," Pré-
      sence Africaine, Eng. ed. No. 63 (1967), 140-61.

Examines various kinds of oral communication in African traditional societies by use of legends, riddles, proverbs, myths, etc.

2931   Okpaku, Joseph, ed. New African literature and the Arts. New York: Crowell, 1970. 359 p.
Edited and introduced by a Nigerian playwright-engineer and critic, it comprises works by Africans and non-Africans known for their contributions to African literature. Grouped under the headings--Essays. --Poetry. --Short Stories. --Drama and Films. --Music and Dance. --Art. Includes a short story by Christian Aidoo, Ghanaian playwright, and there is a section for biographical information on the contributors.

2932   Osei-Mensah, Grace (Ghana). Eight delightful folk tales. Accra: Waterville, 1965. 58 p.

2933   Pieterse, Cosmo and Donald Munro, eds. Protest and conflict in African literature. New York: Africana Publishing Corp., 1969. 127 p.
Different critics examine some selected works of well-known African writers, emphasizing similarities and dissimilarities. The four basic periods covered: 1890-1935, 1935-1940; 1940-1960; Post-independence. Includes biographical notes on the critics.

2934   Povey, John. "Canons of criticism for neo-African literature," African Proceedings, III (1966), 73-91.

2935   Press, John, ed. Commonwealth literature: Unity and diversity in a common culture. Extracts from the proceedings of a Conference held at Bodington Hall, Leeds, 9-12 September 1964 under the auspices of the University of Leeds. London: Heinemann, 1965. 223 p.
Contributors from different Commonwealth countries. Contents: Literature and environment; Inheritance and adaptation; Language and culture; English literature in multi-lingual societies; Communications and responsibility.

2936   Retel-Laurentin, Anne. "Structure and symbolism: an essay in methodology for the study of African tales," Conch, II (Sept. 1970), 29-53.

2937   Roscoe, Adrian A. Mother is gold; a study in West African literature. New York: Cambridge University Press, 1971. 272 p.

2938   Rutherfoord, Peggy. Darkness and light: An anthology of African writing. London: Faith Press, 1958. 208 p.
Prose and verse selections grouped by broad geographic areas with biographical information on the authors. Among

Ghanaians included are Kwame Nkrumah, R. E. Armattoe and Thomas Codjoe.

2939   Shelton, Austin J.   The African assertion: a critical anthology of African literature.   New York: Odyssey Press,
1968.   273 p.
Prose and verse selections in English and French
grouped topically.   A long useful introductory essay on
African literature, past and present--the impact of slavery,
missionary activities, colonialism and nationalism upon
African writings.   Includes selections from several works
by Ghanaians.

2940   _____.   "Behaviour and cultural values in West African
stories: literary sources for the study of cultural contact,"
Africa, XXXIV (Oct. 1964), 353-9.

2941   Sherlock, P. M.   Anansi the Spider Man: Jamaican folktales.
London: Macmillan, 1956.   86 p.
The stories are believed to have originated from Ghana.

2942   Stanislaus, Brother Joseph.   "The Growth of African literature: a survey of the works published by African writers
in English and French," Doctoral Dissertation, University
of Montreal, 1952.

2943   Storch, R. F.   "Writing in Ghana," Universitas, II No. 5
(1957), 148-51.

2944   Sutherland, Efua (Ghana).   The Roadmakers (picture essay).
Accra: Ghana Information Services, 1961.   80 p.

2945   Tibble, Anne, ed.   African-English literature: a short survey of prose and poetry up to 1965.   London: Peter Owen,
1965.   364 p.   Bibliog.

2946   Vernon-Jackson, Hugh.   More West African folk tales.   London: University of London Press, 1963.   2 v.

2947   Walsh, William.   A Manifold voice: studies in Commonwealth
literature.   London: Chatto & Windus, 1970.   218 p.
Rev: West Africa, No. 2759 (April 25, 1970), 461.

2948   Wrong, Margaret.   Across Africa.   London: International
Committee on Christian Literature for Africa (2 Eaton
gate, London, SW. 1.) 1940.   104 p.
Records the author's visit to Africa to investigate into
the need of literature for the natives, describing her impressions of Kenya, Uganda, the Sudan, Nigeria and the
Gold Coast (Ghana).

2949 _____ . Africa and the making of books, being a survey of
Africa's need of literature.   London: International Committee on Christian Literature for Africa, 1934.   56 p.
The state of African literature in 1933 when the author
toured Africa.

2950 Zell, Hans M.   "Bibliography," African Literature Today,
No. 1 (1968), 59-63.
Mainly concerned with creative writing, including critical
and reference works and anthologies.   Divided into 2 parts.
I. Periodical literature.   II. Books and pamphlets arranged
for the most part by country.

2951 _____ . "Bibliography," African Literature Today, No. 2
(Jan. 1969), 57-62.
The kinds of material listed and arrangement are similar to the ones published in number one of the same periodical in 1968.   Still does not indicate author's nationality.

2952 _____ . "Bibliography," African Literature Today, No. 3
(Sept. 1969), 56-62.
Grouped into 4 major parts covering books and periodical
articles.   I. Bibliographies and reference works.   II. Critical writings.   III. Anthologies.   IV. Works, with the
nationality of the author indicated.

2953 _____ . Writings by West Africans in print at December
1967.   New and rev. ed.   Freetown: Sierra Leone University Press, 1968.   31 p.
Lists 365 "In print" books originally published as a
guide to an exhibition held in Freetown in April 1967.
Covering creative, political and historical writings of
original nature, by English- and French-speaking West
Africans.   Includes Arabic selections, critical and reference works and anthologies.
Rev: West Africa, No. 2665 (June 29, 1968), 749-50.

(12) LITERATURE--DRAMA

2954 Acquaye, Saka (Ghana).   "The Language problem of the
developing African theatre, " African Arts, II, No. 1 (1968),
58-9.

2955 Aidoo, Christina Ama Ata (Ghana).   Anowa.   London: Longmans, 1970.   66 p.
Based upon a Ghanaian legend, the play tells the story
of a pretty girl who rejects suitors approved by her parents
and marries a man of her own choice, but later finds no
happiness.

2956 _____. The Dilemma of a Ghost. Accra: Longmans,
1965. 50 p.
Examines the cultural conflict that arises when a young
Ghanaian man who has studied in the United States returns
home with a black American wife.
Rev: African Forum, I (Summer 1965), 111-3. Books
Abroad, XL (Summer 1966), 358-9.

2957 Akyea, E. Ofori (Ghana). "The Atwia-Ekumf: Kodzidan--
an experimental African theatre," Okyeame IV (Dec. 1968),
82-4.

2958 Baker, D. S. "Shakespeare in Ghana." In Allardyce Nicoll,
ed. Shakespeare Survey, V. 16. Cambridge: Cambridge
University Press, 1963, pp. 77-82.

2959 Bame, K. N. "Comic play in Ghana," African Arts (Summer
1968), 30+.

2960 _____. "The Popular theatre in Ghana," Research Review
(Legon) III, No. 2 (1967), 34-8.

2961 Carpenter, P. "East and West: a brief view of theatre in
Ghana and Uganda since 1960," Makerere J., VIII (1963),
33-9.

2962 _____. "Theatre in East and West Africa," Drama (London) LXVIII (Spring 1963), 30-2.

2963 Danquah, Joseph (Ghana). Nyankonsem (Fables of the celes-
tial) Agoru bi a woakye mu abiesa; a play in three acts.
Done entirely in the Twi language (From Akan-Ashanti folk
tales, by R. S. Rattray). London: Longmans, Green,
1941. 56 p.

2964 _____. The Third woman: a play in five acts. London:
United Society for Christian Literature, 1943. 151 p.

2965 De Graft, John Coliman (Ghana). Sons and daughters. Lon-
don: Oxford University Press, 1964. 53 p. (Three
Crowns book.)
Family tensions engendered by conflicts between tradi-
tional and western values.
Rev: Black Orpheus, No. 19 (1966), 59-60. Books
Abroad, XXXIX (Summer 1965), 364. TLS (Aug. 13,
1964), 728.

2966 _____. Through a film darkly. London: Oxford University Press, 1970. 60 p. (Three Crowns books.)
First performed at the Ghana Drama Studio under the
title, Visitor from the past, in 1962, the play describes
the racial tensions in the lives of two married couples.

The author portrays his compatriots as possessing a mag-
nanimous capacity for racial acceptance.
Rev: Africa Report, XVI (May 1971), 40.

2967 Dei-Anang, Michael (Ghana). Cocoa comes to Mampong.
Brief dramatic sketches based on the story of Cocoa in
the Gold Coast, and some occasional verses.   Cape Coast
(Ghana): Methodist Book Depot, 1949. 47 p.

2968 _____. Okomfo Anokye's golden stool: a play in three
acts. Ilfracombe: Stockwell, 1960. 54 p.
Rev: W. Afr. Rev. (May 1960), 67.

2969 Edmonds, R. and I.C. Edmonds. "Playmakers in Africa,"
Inst. Int. Educ. News Bull. (New York) XXXIV (May
1959), 20-8.

2970 Fiawoo, F. K. (Ghana). The Fifth landing stage: a play in
five acts. (A free translation from the Ewe original.)
London: United Society for Christian Literature, 1943.
87 p.
Translated into several European languages, it describes
the social life and customs of Ewe "forefathers."

2971 Graham-White, Anthony. "A bibliography of African drama,"
Afro-Asian Theatre Bull., III (Oct. 1967), 10-24.

2972 _____. "J. B. Danquah, évolué playwright," J. New Afr.
Lit. Arts., (Fall 1966), 49-52.

2973 Hagan, W. B. "Saka Acquaye blends the arts in Ghana,"
Africa Report, XVI (Jan. 1971), 34-5.

2974 Herskovits, Melville J. "Dramatic expression among primitive peoples," Yale Review, XXXIII (1944), 683-98.

2975 Jones, Eldred. "A Note on the Lagos production of Christina
Aidoo's Dilemma of a Ghost," Bull. Assoc. Afr. Lit.
Eng. (Sierra Leone) II (March 1965), 37-8.

2976 Jones-Quartey, K. A. (Ghana). "The Problems of language
in the development of the African theatre," Okyeame, IV
(Dec. 1968), 95-102.

2977 Kay, Kwesi (Ghana). "Maama." In Cosmo Pieterse, ed.
Ten one-act plays. London: Heinemann Educational Books,
1968, pp. 231-53.
A play in four scenes set in ancient Gold Coast.

2978 Kedjanyi, John. "Observations on spectator-performer arrangement of some traditional Ghanaian performances,"
Research Review (Legon) II, No. 3 (1966), 61-6.

2979 Kennedy, Scott. "Language and communication in the Ghanaian
      theatre, " Okyeame, IV (Dec. 1968), 103-9.

2980 McHardy, Cecile. "The Performing arts in Ghana, " African
      Forum, I (Summer 1965), 113-7.

2981 Maesen, Albert. "African masks, " World Theatre, X (Spring
      1961), 31-40.

2982 Moore, Gerald. "The Arts in the new Africa, " Nigeria Maga-
      zine, No. 92 (March 1967), 92-7. Also in African Affairs,
      LXVI (April 1967), 140-8.
      All phases of art in Africa are discussed.

2983 _____. "Modern African literature and tradition, " African
      Affairs, LXVI (July 1967), 246-7.

2984 Morisseau-Leroy, F. "Ghanaian theatre mouvement, " World
      Theatre, XIV (Jan. 1965), 75-7.

2985 _____. "Le mouvement theatral au Ghana, " Int. Theatre
      Inf., nouvelle serie (Paris) XLVI (1965), 20-3.

2986 Nketia, Joseph Hanson Kwabena (Ghana). Ananwoma (Twi).
      London: Oxford University Press, 1951. 36 p. (Oxford
      Akan series.)

2987 Nyomi, C. K. (Ghana). Munyala Enelia (Ewe. The Fourth
      wise man). Accra: Bureau of Ghana Languages, 1959. 51 p.

2988 Ofori, Henry (Ghana). "The Literary Society. " In F. Litto,
      ed. Plays from black Africa. New York: Hill and Wang,
      1968, pp. 295-312.

2989 Povey, John F. "The First World Festival of Negro Arts at
      Dakar, " J. New Afr. Lit. Arts, No. 2 (Fall 1966), 24-30.

2990 _____. "West African drama in English, " Comp. Dr. I
      (Summer 1967), 110-21.

2991 Rea, C. J. "The Culture line: a note on Dilemma of a
      Ghost, " African Forum, I (Summer 1965), 111-3.
      A play by Christian Aidoo, Ghanaian playwright.

2992 Safo, G. N. (Ghana). Afrakoma (Twi). Accra: Scottish
      Mission Book Depot, 1955? 115 p.

2993 Soyinka, Wole. "Le Théâtre moderne negro-africain, "
      Premier Festival Mondial des Arts Nègres, Dakar, 1-24.
      Avril 1966. Colloque sur l'art nègre. Rapport. Tome I.
      Paris: Société Africaine de Culture, 1967, pp. 539-48.

2994 _____ . "Towards a true theatre," Nigeria Magazine, No.
75 (Dec. 1962), 58-60.

2995 Sutherland, Efua (Ghana). "Anansegoro; tu prêtas serment.
(You swore an oath; Anansegoro)." Présence Africaine,
No. 50. (1964), 221-36.
A play in one act.

2996 _____ . Edufa. London: Longmans, 1967. 65 p. Also
in Plays from black Africa, edited by F. Litto, New York,
1968, pp. 209-268.
A play in three acts. The story of a young educated
Ghanaian who brings tragedy on himself and his household
because of his inability to choose between western and
traditional values.

2997 _____ . "Edufa" (drama). Okyeame, III (Dec. 1966),
47-9.

2998 _____ . Foriwa: a play. Accra: State Publishing Corp.,
1967. 67 p.

2999 _____ . "Foriwa" (drama). Okyeame, II, No. 1 (1964),
40-7.

3000 _____ . Venture: two rhythm plays. Accra: Ghana Publishing House, 1968. 32 p.

3001 Tabi, R. A. (Ghana). Me nko me yam (Twi. I want it my
own way). Accra: Bureau of Ghana Languages, 1960.
51 p.

3002 Zeitlin, Arnold. "Ghana's young theatre," Theatre Arts,
XLVII (Nov. 1963), 65-7+.
The author who spent two years in Ghana working with
the American Peace Corps reviews the state and development of drama in Ghana, discussing the works of some
major Ghanaian dramatists such as Efua Sutherland, Saka
Acquaye and Joe de Graft.

(12) LITERATURE--FICTION

3003 Abruquah, Joseph Wilfred (Ghana). The Catechist. London: Allen & Unwin, 1965. 202 p.
Set in the late 19th and early 20th century and told in
the first person, it is a story of a man who remained a
lowly Catechist, although he should have become a powerful
preacher and a recognized figure in his society. He is
often transferred from one place to another but he still
manages to get his sons well educated.

Rev: Books Abroad, **XL** (Spring 1966), 228. J. New
Afr. Lit. Arts, (Fall 1967), 22-7. TLS (March 11, 1965),
201.

3004 _____. The Torrent. London: Longmans, 1968. 275 p.
A novel about a boy growing up in a fast changing society
of Ghana.
Rev: TLS (Mar. 20, 1969), 287.

3005 Adaye, J. J. (Ghana). Bere Adu! (Twi. Now it is the time).
Akpropong (Ghana): B. M. Press, 1913. 90 p.

3006 Aidoo, Christina Ata (Ghana). "A Gift from Somewhere,"
J. New Afr. Lit. Arts, (Fall 1966), 36-44.
A short story.

3007 Amartey, A. A. (Ghana). Adzenuloo (Ga-Riddles). Accra:
Bureau of Ghana Languages, 1961. 78 p.

3008 Anozie, Sunday Ogbonna. "Réalisme sociologique dans le
roman moderne Ouest-africain," Doctoral Dissertation,
Sorbonne, University of Paris, 1968. 400 p.

3009 _____. Sociologie du roman africain. Paris: Aubier-
Montaigne, 1970. 268 p.
English edition, entitled A Sociology of African novel,
by Northwestern University Press (forthcoming).
Rev: Conch, II (Sept. 1970), 114-21.

3010 Apraku, L. D. (Ghana). Aku Sika (Akuapem). Accra:
Bureau of Ghana Languages, 1957. 70 p.

3011 _____. A Prince of the Akans. London: Oxford University Press, 1964. 58 p.

3012 Armah, Ayi Kwei (Ghana). The Beautiful ones are not yet
born: a novel. Boston: Houghton-Mifflin, 1968. 215 p.
(African writers series.)
A story of a railway clerk in Ghana during the Nkrumah
regime, struggling against hard odds, especially against the
pressures put on him by his materialistic wife and mother.
Rev: West Africa, No. 2691 (Dec. 28, 1968), 1540-1.
N. Y. Times Bk. Rev., LXXIII (Sept. 22, 1968), 34. Nat.
Rev., XX (Nov. 5, 1968), 1120.

3013 _____. "Contact" (Story). New African, IV, No. 10
(Dec. 1965), 244-6.

3014 _____. Fragments. Boston: Houghton-Mifflin, 1970.
287 p.
A novel about a young African doctor dissatisfied with
the way things are being done in his country on his return

from abroad after several years of study. A problem of
post-independence Africa handled well.
Rev: Sat. Rev., LIII (Jan. 17, 1970), 40. New Republic, CLXII (Jan. 31, 1970), 24. Library J., XCIV
(Dec. 15, 1969), 4537.

3015 Ashton, Helen (Mrs. Arthur Jordon). Letty Landon. Lon-
don: Collins, 1951. 320 p.
A novel based upon Elizabeth Landon, a minor English
poet whose relationship with the Scottish governor of the
Gold Coast ends tragically only a few months after their
marriage.
Rev: Sat. Rev., XXXIV (Oct. 6, 1951), 34. TLS,
(Sept. 7, 1951), 561.

3016 Awoonor, Kofi (Ghana). The Earth, my brother; an allegorical
tale of Africa. Garden City, New York: Doubleday, 1971.
232 p.
Rev: Africa Report, XVI (Oct. 1971), 32-3.

3017 _____. "Just to buy corn, " (Story). Okyeame, II, No. 1
(1964), 22-30.

3018 Ballard, Martin. The Speaking drums of Ashanti. New York:
Longmans Young, 1970. 164 p.
A young boy, Simon, a fictional character, accompanies
the British Governor of Sierra Leone as his interpreter in
the struggle against the Ashanti slave traders. The setting
is real.

3019 Bediako, K. A. (Ghana). Don't leave me Mercy: echoes from
James Owusu's marriage life. Accra: Anowuo Educational
Publications, 1966. 116 p.
Provides some insight into Ghana's traditional marriage.

3020 _____. A Husband for Esi Ellua. Accra: Anowuo Educational Publications, 1967. 179 p.
A tragic love story.

3021 _____. Rebel. London: Heinemann Educational, 1969.
160 p. (African writers series, 59.)

3022 Blay, J. Benibengor (Ghana). After the wedding: a sequel
to Emelia's promise. Aboso, Ghana: Benibengor Book
Agency, 1945. 60 p.

3023 _____. Dr. Bengia wants a wife. London: Blackheath
Press, 1953. 23 p.

3024 _____. Emelia's promise and fulfillment. Accra: Waterville, 1967. 133 p.

3025 _____. Here and there stories. Accra: Bureau of
Ghana Languages, 1959. 24 p. (mimeographed)

3026 _____. Love in a clinic. Aboso: Benibengor Book
Agency, 1957. 28 p.
A short story.

3027 _____. Stubborn girl. Accra: Guinea Press, 1958.
22 p.

3028 Caute, David. At Fever pitch. London: Deutsch, 1959.
283 p.
The first novel of a British soldier who was born in
Egypt but served in the Gold Coast regiment where he
became well acquainted with French and British West
Africa.
Rev: Library J., (July 1961), 2489. Time, LXXVII
(June 2, 1961), 92.

3029 Conton, William F. The African. London: Heinemann,
1960. 213 p.
The story of a young mission-educated Hausa student
who goes to Britain where he picks a quarrel with a white
South African. He returns to his country, and soon after
he enters politics, becomes the Prime Minister of his
people. The author is a Sierra Leonean Headmaster of
a secondary school in Ghana.
Rev: Library J. LXXXV (Jan. 15, 1960), 300. N. Y.
Times Bk. Rev., (March 27, 1960), 42. TLS, (July 29,
1960), 485.

3030 Darko, D. Offei (Ghana). Friends today, enemies tomorrow.
Akropong (Ghana): Presbyterian Training College, 1959.
45 p.

3031 Dathorne, O. R. "The Beginnings of the West African novel,"
Nigeria Magazine, No. 93 (1967), 168-70.

3032 Descwu, P. M. (Ghana). The Three brothers, and other
stories. London: Longmans, 1951. 87 p.
The traditional stories of the Ewe.

3033 Djoleto, Amu S. (Ghana). The Strange man. London:
Heinemann Educational, 1967. 279 p. (African writers
series.)
Describes the life and times of old Mensa, a respectable
community member in Ghana.

3034 Donkor, Willie (Ghana). The Forbidden taste. Accra: Facts
& Fiction Agency, 1968. 72 p.

3035 _____. A Stab in my heart. Accra: Facts & Fiction
      Agency, 1968. 73 p.

3036 _____. The Troubles of a bachelor. Accra: The Author,
      1968. 73 p.

3037 Duodu, Cameron M. (Ghana). The Gab boys. London:
      Deutsch, 1967. 208 p.
        A novel about the social and political life in Ghana by
      a former editor of Ghana's Drum. The gab boys who
      derive their name from their gaberdine trousers are un-
      happy about their unemployment.
        Rev: New Statesman, (July 27, 1967), 123. TLS,
      (Aug. 17, 1967), 737.

3038 Efa, Edwin (Ghana). Asiemiri (Twi. Reminiscences of a
      hunter). London: Macmillan, 1950. 92 p.

3039 _____. Forosie (Twi). 2nd ed. Abetifi, Ghana: Metho-
      dist Book Depot, 1948. 122 p.

3040 Fielding, Ann. Ashanti blood. London: Heinemann, 1952.
      246 p.
        Story of a mining disaster in Ghana.

3041 Freshfield, Mark, pseud. (i. e. M. J. Field). The Stormy
      dawn. London: Faber & Faber, 1946. 191 p.
        Depicts mission education in Gold Coast's cocoa pro-
      ducing area.

3042 Gaunt, Mary and J. R. Essex. Arm of the leopard: a West
      African Story. London: Richards, 1904. 306 p.

3043 Gleason, Judith Illsley. This Africa; novels by West Africans
      in English and French. Evanston: Northwestern University
      Press, 1965. 186 p. Bibliog.
        A survey of the present state of fiction writing in West
      Africa, noting both its styles and traditions under specific
      literary themes as "Novels of the village," "Novels of the
      city," and "Novels of psychic life."
        Rev: Library J., XC (June 15, 1965), 2855. TLS
      (Dec. 30, 1965), 1209.

3044 Hamber, Thomas Rumsey. The Mine. London: Cassell,
      1953. 213 p.
        On a gold mine in Western Ghana.

3045 Hayford, Joseph Ephraim Casely (Ghana). Ethiopia Unbound:
      Studies in race emancipation. Edited by E. U. Essien-Udom.
      With an introduction by F. Nnabuenyi Ugonna. 2nd ed.
      London: Cass, 1969. 215 p. (Cass Library of African
      Studies. Africana modern library, no. 8.) 1st ed. 1911.

"Undoubtedly one of the most important contributions to
the literature of African nationalism. Although it is primarily a work of fiction and so properly belongs to the
field of African literature, it contains ideas that are indis-
pensable to all those interested in African Studies--As a
contribution to African literature, Ethiopia Unbound com-
bines the literary and religious function of Bunyan's Pil-
grim's Progress with the cultural significance of Arnold's
Culture and Anarchy" (Introduction).

3046   Hevi, Emmanuel John (Ghana). An African student in China.
       London: Pall Mall Press, 1964. 220 p. (Also published
       in Spanish, French, Chinese, and Portuguese.)
       An autobiographical novel.
       Rev: J. Asian. Stud., XXIV (Feb. 1965), 325.

3047   _____. Un étudiant africaine en Chine. Translated by
       Richard Walters. Paris: Editions Internationales, 1965.
       272 p.

3048   _____. Um estudiante Africano na China. Translated by
       A. C. Carvalho. São Paulo: Dominus, 1965. 206 p.

3049   _____. Un estudiante Africano en China. Translated by
       Cabino Pascual Arranz. Barcelona: Herder, 1965. 296 p.

3050   Hihetah, Robert Kofi (Ghana). "Throwing stories at lizards,"
       (a Story), Okyeame, II, No. 1 (1964), 31-3.

3051   _____. Painful road to Kodjebi. Accra: Anowuo Educa-
       tional Publications, 1967. 194 p.

3052   Huxley, Elspeth. The Walled city. London: Chatto & Windus,
       1947. 391 p.

3053   Knight, Brigid. I Struggle and I rise. London: Cassell,
       1946. 432 p.

3054   Konadu, Samuel Asare (Ghana). Come back Dora! A hus-
       band's confession and ritual. Accra: Anowuo Educational
       Publications, 1966. 218 p.

3055   _____. Night watchers of Korlebu. Accra: Anowuo Educa-
       tional Publications, 1967. 99 p.

3056   _____. Ordained by the oracle. Ibadan: Heinemann Educa-
       tional, 1969. 188 p. (African writer's series, No. 55.)

3057   _____. The Plawyer who bungled his life. Accra: Water-
       ville, 1965. 81 p.

3058 _____. Shadow of wealth. Accra: Anowuo Educational
Publications, 1966. 162 p.

3059 _____. Wizard of Asamang. Accra: Waterville, 1964.
90 p.

3060 _____. A Woman in her prime. London: Heinemann,
1967. 107 p.
The story of an Ashanti barren woman and her longing
for motherhood. She eventually achieves the fulfillment
of her desire and attributes that to her divine prayers. A
classic portrayal of the mental disposition of unmarried or
infertile woman in a traditional African society.
Rev: TLS (April 20, 1967), 325.

3061 Korsah, J. E. (Ghana). Kweku a oridzi ne dew. (Fanti.
Kweku is enjoying himself.) London: Longmans, 1937.
47 p. (Longmans Fante series.)

3062 Kwapong, D. O. (Ghana). Amansan nkabom nhyiam.
(Akuepem. The native unity's meeting.) Accra: Bureau
of Ghana Languages, 1961. 35 p.

3063 Kwei-Tsuru, N. M. (Ghana). Akwete Akwa. (Ga). Accra:
Scottish Mission Book Depot, 1955. 89 p.

3064 Lamptey, Jonas. The village in the trees. London:
Heinemann, 1955. 274 p.
A young mining engineer records his experiences in
Ashanti.

3065 Laurence, Margaret. This side Jordan. New York: St.
Martins Press, 1960. 304 p.
With its scene set in the Gold Coast just before it be-
came independent and the name changed to Ghana, it tells
the story of a school teacher torn, like other educated
Africans, between old tribal and modern forces.
Rev: Sat. Rev., XLIII (Dec. 10, 1960), 23. TLS
(Nov. 4. 1960), 705.

3066 Lautre, Maxine. "An Interview with Ama Ata Aidoo,"
Cult. Events Afr., No. 35 (Oct. 1967), i-iv.

3067 Mcdowell, Robert E. "Four Ghanaian novels," J. New Afr.
Lit. Arts, (Fall 1967), 22-7.
Includes discussion of The Catechist, by J. W. Abruquah;
The Narrow path, by Francis Selormey and A Woman in
her prime, by Samuel Konadu.

3068 Makward, Edris. "Negro-African novelists: a comparative
study of themes and influences in novels by Africans in
French and English," Doctoral Dissertation, Ibadan University, 1968.

3069 Mensah, Arthur (Ghana). Egya Awienze. (Nzema. Old man
      Awienze.) Accra: Bureau of Ghana Languages, 1934.
      21 p.

3070 Mickson, E. K. (Ghana). Now I Know. Accra: Pictorial Pub-
      lications, 1968. 72 p.

3071 _____. The Violent Kiss. Accra: Pictorial Publications,
      1968. 49 p.

3072 Moore, Gerald. "Mots anglais, vies africaines," Présence
      Africaine, No. 54 (1965), 116-26.
          Discusses the themes of the major novels of Chinua
      Achebe, Cyprian Ekwensi, Timothy Aluko and that of
      William Conton's first novel, The African, based upon his
      experiences in the Gold Coast. Examines also the appro-
      priateness of style and language used by these writers.

3073 Moore, Jane A. "The Middle Society: five orientations
      towards husband-wife roles in West African novels."
      Paper presented at the Annual Meeting of the African
      Studies Association, New York, November 1967. 23 p.

3074 Muskett, Netta. Flame of the forest. London: Hutchinson,
      1958. 240 p.

3075 Nii-Amarteifo, A. Vic. (Ghana). Bediaco (Twi). Accra:
      Bureau of Ghana Languages, 1962. 90 p.

3076 Nketia, Joseph Hanson (Ghana). Kwabena Amoa (Twi).
      London: Oxford University Press, 1953. 36 p. (Oxford
      Akan series.)

3077 Obeng, R. E. (Ghana). Eighteenpence. Ilfracombe: Stock-
      well, 1943. 167 p.
          Widely regarded as the first full length novel by a
      Ghanaian writer, it describes how a man succeeds in
      creating a huge fortune for himself by means of an only
      eighteen penny scythe.
          Rev: W. Afr. Rev. (April 1950), 393.

3078 Odoi, N. A. (Ghana). The Adventures of Esi Kakraba. Accra:
      Waterville, 1964. 55 p.

3079 Osae, Seth K. (Ghana). The Tears of a prostitute. Accra:
      The Author, 1968. 54 p.

3080 _____. Tears of a jealous wife. Accra: Advance Pub-
      lishing Co., 1968. 47 p.

3081 Porter, Dorothy. "Fiction by African authors: a preliminary
      checklist," Afr. Stud. Bull., V, No. 2 (May 1962), 54-66.

3082   Povey, John F.   "The Political themes in South and West
       African novels," Paper presented at the Annual Meeting of
       the African Studies Association, Philadelphia, Pennsylvania,
       Oct. 27-30, 1965.

3083   Rattray, Robert Sutherland.   The Leopard priestess.   New
       York: Appleton-Century, 1934.   224 p.
            The two West African lovers who are expecting a severe
       punishment at the hands of spirits for breaking four taboos
       are pardoned.
            Rev: N.Y. Times Bk. Rev., (April 28, 1935), 7.   TLS
       (Jan. 10, 1935), 20.

3084   Sam, Gilbert A. (Ghana).   A Christmastide tragedy.   Accra:
       Gilisam Publishing Syndicate, 1956.   12 p.   (Kanzar series,
       22.)

3085   _____ .   Love in the grave.   Accra: Gilisam Publishing
       Syndicate, 1959.   46 p.

3086   _____ .   Who Killed Inspector Kwasi Minta?   A crime-
       love story.   Accra: Gilisam Publishing Syndicate, 1956.
       26 p.   (Kanzaar series, 23.)

3087   Selormey, Francis. (Ghana).   The Narrow path.   London:
       Heinemann, 1966.   183 p.
            Kofi, son of an African school teacher in the Gold Coast
       of the 1920's, tells the story of his life with his harsh
       father and missionaries.
            Rev: New Statesman, (July 22, 1966), 136.   TLS
       (July 21, 1966), 629.

3088   Sey, K. Abaka (Ghana).   "A Father's salvation," (a Story).
       Présence Africaine, Eng. ed., No. 40 (1962), 65-70.

3089   Steen, Marguerite.   The Sun is my Undoing.   London: Col-
       lins, 1941.   1015 p.
            Slave trading in West Africa and the West Indies, and
       the activities of the English abolitionists.
            Rev: Sat. Rev., XXIV (Aug. 30, 1941), 7.   TLS
       (Oct. 4, 1941), 497.

3090   _____ .   Twilight on the floods.   London: Collins, 1950.
       704 p.
            The 1900 Bristol and the Gold Coast.

3091   Thomas, Elwyn.   Night of the Jassies.   London: Cape,
       1959.   222 p.
            A tribal uprising the Resident Commissioner has to face
       in West Guinea before independence.

3092 Tregidgo, P. S. "West African novels," Ghana Teachers' J.,
      No. 39 (July 1963), 8-11.

3093 Welman, John B. A Thorny wilderness. London: Black-
      wood, 1952. 292 p.
      Short stories.

3094 Wyllie, John. Riot. London: Secker & Warburg, 1954.
      256 p.

3095 Yeulett, M. The Graven image: West African stories.
      London: Lane, 1939. 206 p.

(12) LITERATURE--POETRY

3096 Acquaah, Gaddiel Robért. (Ghana). Oguaa aban. (Fanti Cape
      Coast castle.) London: Longmans, 1945. 46 p.

3097 Adali-Mortty, G. (Ghana). "Ewe poetry," Black Orpheus,
      No. 4 (Oct. 1958), 36-45.

3098 Ako, O. Dazi. (Ghana). The Seductive Coast: poems
      lyrical and descriptive from West Africa. London: Ouse-
      ley, 1909. 164 p.

3099 Appah, E. H. (Ghana). An Ode to Africa, and other verse.
      London: Stockwell, 1939.

3100 Armattoe, Raphael Ernest (Ghana). Between the forest and
      the sea; collected poems. Rev. enl. ed. Londonderry:
      Lomeshire Research Centre, 1952. 180 p. 1st ed. 1950.

3101 _____. Deep down the blackman's mind: poems. Ilfra-
      combe: Stockwell, 1954. 112 p.

3102 Awooner-Renner, Bankole. (Ghana). This Africa. With an
      introduction by J. B. Danquah and B. Sekyi. London: Cen-
      tral Books Ltd., 1943. 72 p.

3103 Awoonor, Kofi. (Ghana). Night of my blood. With an intro-
      duction by Ezekiel Mphahlele. Garden City, New York:
      Doubleday, 1971. 96 p.

3104 _____. Rediscovery, and other poems. Ibadan: Mbari
      Publications, 1964. 36 p.
      Rev: African Forum, I (Winter 1966), 121-3.

3105 _____ and G. Adali-Mortty, eds. (Ghana). Messages:
      poems from Ghana. London: Heinemann Educational
      Books, 1970. 200 p. (The African writers series, No.
      42.)

Among the Ghanaian poets included are J. De Graft, G.
Adali Mortty, A. Mensah, K. Awoonor, A. Armah, E.
Sutherland, A. Djoleto, C. Duodu, E. Komey.

3106   Bassir, Olumbe.   An Anthology of West African verse.
       Ibadan: Ibadan University Press, 1957.   68 p.
       A collection of poems by West African writers including
       Ghanaian poets: Efua Morgue, J. B. Danquah, Seth Cud-
       joe and R. E. Armattoe.   The compiler is a Nigerian Pro-
       fessor of Bio-Chemistry at the University of Ibadan,
       Nigeria.

3107   Beier, Horst Ulli.   African poetry: an anthology of traditional
       African poems.   Cambridge: Cambridge University Press,
       1966.   80 p.
       The poems all in English are grouped under the subjects:
       Religious songs; Death; Sorrow; Praise songs; Wars; Love;
       People; Animals, and Children's songs.   The selections
       taken from widely different tribes and cultures in Africa.
       Includes notes on the poems; sources of the poems and index
       of first lines.

3108   Blay, J. Benibengor. (Ghana).   Ghana sings.   Accra: Water-
       ville, 1965.   78 p.

3109   _____.   Immortal deeds.   A Book of Verse.   London:
       Stockwell, 1940.   31 p.

3110   _____.   King of the human frame.   Ilfracombe: Stockwell,
       1947.   31 p.

3111   _____.   Memoirs of the War.   Ilfracombe: Stockwell,
       1946.   32 p.

3112   _____.   Thoughts of youth.   Aboso (Ghana):   Benibengor
       Book Agency, 1961.   130 p.

3113   Braithwaite, Edward.   Masks: Poems.   London: Oxford
       University Press, 1968.   80 p.
       A collection of poems by a West Indian writer, dealing
       with his eight-year sojourn in Ghana.   The works are
       divided into six sections covering the period of the fall of
       ancient orders--the desecration and desolation, slavery and
       slave trade, exile in the new world, and present confusions.
       Includes a glossary of some of the Akan words used in the
       text.
       Rev: West Africa, No. 2677 (Sept. 21, 1968), 1099.

3114   Brew, Kwesi. (Ghana).   The Shadows of laughter.   London:
       Longmans, 1968.   67 p.
       A collection of poems by one of the leading Ghanaian poets.
       Rev: TLS (July 24, 1969), 836.

3115 Dei-Anang, Michael Francis (Ghana). Africa speaks: a col-
      lection of original verses. Accra: Guinea Press, 1959.
      99 p.
            Treats chiefly of life, patriotism and nature, reminiscent
      of the works of the classical poets, Horace and Vergil.

3116 _____. Ghana semi-tones: a collection of 18 new poems.
      Accra: Presbyterian Book Depot, 1962. 28 p.

3117 _____. Two faces of Africa; a collection of poems by
      M. F. Dei-Anang and his son. Accra: Waterville, 1965.
      (Africa's own library, No. 15.)

3118 _____. Wayward lines from Africa: a collection of poems.
      London: United Society for Christian Literature, 1946.
      47 p.

3119 _____ and Yaw Warren. Glory; poems on Ghana and
      Ghanaian life. With an introduction by Kwame Nkrumah.
      London: Heinemann, 1965. 69 p.

3120 Dubois, W. E. B. "Ghana calls" (poem). Freedomways, II
      (Winter 1962), 71-4.

3121 Hughes, Langston, ed. An African treasury: articles,
      essays, stories, poems by black Africans. New York:
      Crown, 1960.
            Includes poems by Ghanaians, A. Laluah, F. Parkes,
      M. Markwei, M. Dei-Anang.

3122 _____. Poems from black Africa. Bloomington: Indiana
      University Press, 1963. 158 p.
            The poems are grouped by country including those by
      Ghanaians.

3123 Jones, A. M. "African metrical lyrics," African Music, III,
      No. 3 (1964), 6-14.
            Lyrics in Ghana, Uganda and Zambia.

3124 Komey, Ellis Ayitey. (Ghana). "Africa: three poems on the
      African personality," W. Afr. Rev., (April 1960), 47.

3125 Kurankyi-Taylor, Dorothy. (Ghana). Reflected thoughts.
      Ilfracombe: Stockwell, 1959. 39 p.

3126 Mensah, Albert W. Kayper. (Ghana). The Dark wanderer:
      poems. Tubingen, Germany: Horst Erdmann Verlag, 1970.
      133 p.

3127 _____. "Light in jungle Africa," (poem). In John Reed,
      ed. A Book of African verse. London: Heineman, 1964.
      Also in Henry Swanzy, ed. Voices of Ghana, literary

contributions to the Ghana Broadcasting System, 1958.
The poem won the Margaret Wrong Prize in 1956.

3128   Moore, Gerald and H. U. Beier.   Modern poetry from Africa.
       Edited by Ronald Segal.   Harmondsworth: Penguin, 1963.
       192 p.   (Penguin African library AP 7.)
           The selections are grouped by country with a long in-
       troductory essay on African poetry.   There are biographical
       notes on the authors and index of first lines.   Includes
       poems by K. Brew, E. Komey and Kofi Awoonor (formerly
       George Awoonor-Williams).

3129   Nketia, Joseph Hanson. (Ghana)   "Akan poetry," Black
       Orpheus, No. 3 (May 1958), 5-28.

3130   _____.   Akwansosem bi (Twi. Some travel tales).   Accra:
       Scottish Mission Book Depot, 1953.   48 p.

3131   _____.   Apaee: poems recited by the Abrefo of the
       Asantehene on State occasions.   Legon: Institute of
       African Studies, University of Ghana, 1966.   34 p.

3132   _____.   Awonsem, 1944-1949.   (Twi. Poems.)   Cape
       Coast (Ghana):   Methodist Book Depot, 1952.   40 p.

3133   _____.   Ayan, v. 1, poetry of the atumpan drums of the
       Asantehene.   Legon: Institute of African Studies, Univer-
       sity of Ghana, 1966.   42 p.

3134   _____.   Funeral dirges of the Akan people.   New York:
       Negro Universities Press, 1969.   296 p.   Bibliog.
           Originally published in 1955.   Texts in English, Twi
       and Fante.

3135   Nutsuako, R. K. (Ghana)   Ewe poems and lyrics.   Accra:
       Presbyterian Press, 1967.   v. 1, 103 p.

3136   Parkes, F. Kobina. (Ghana)   Songs from the wilderness.
       London: University of London Press, 1965.   64 p.

3137   Reed, John and Clive Wake.   A Book of African verse.   Lon-
       don: Heinemann, 1964.   119 p.
           A selection of poems by Africans written in English to-
       gether with some translations of those written in French.
       Not drawn from the entire spectrum of Africa, nor is it
       quite representative of the traditional African poetry in the
       vernaculars.   Includes works by Ghanaian poets, R. Armat-
       toe, Kofi Awoonor, K. Brew, S. Cudjoe, A. Mensah and
       F. Parkes.
           Rev: TLS (June 11, 1964), 501.

3138 Sergeant, Howard, ed. Commonwealth poems of today. Lon-
      don: John Murray, for English Association, 1967. 288 p.
          An anthology of 250 poems from the commonwealth
      countries.
          Rev: Poetry Rev. (Lond.) (Summer 1967), 161. Alpha-
      bet (London) (Dec. 1968), 74.

3139 _____. New voices of the Commonwealth. London: Evans,
      1968. 208 p.
          A selection of poems by writers from various Common-
      wealth countries.

3140 _____. Poetry from Africa; Gabriel Okara, Gaston Bart-
      Williams, Kwesi Brew, David Rubadiri. Oxford: Pergamon
      Press, 1968. 101 p. (Pergamon poets, 2.)

3141 Serumaga, Robert. "George Awoonor-Williams interviewed,"
      Cult. Events Afr., No. 29 (April 1967), i-iii.
          An interview with a noted Ghanaian poet, currently
      known as Kofi Awoonor.

3142 Tibble, Anne, ed. African-English literature; a short survey
      and anthology of prose and poetry up to 1965. New York:
      October House, 1965.
          Includes poems by Kwesi Brew and Ellis Komey.
          Rev: Am. Bk. Collec, XVII (Oct. 1966) 3. Library
      J., XCI (April 1, 1966), 1898.

3143 Tolson, Melvin. "Three African poets," African Forum, I
      (Winter 1966), 121-3.
          A review of Icheke and other poems, by O. G. Nwanodi
      from Nigeria; Poems, by Lenrie Peters from Gambia;
      Rediscovery and other poems, by Kofi Awoonor.

3144 "West African voices," African Affairs, XLVIII (1949), 151-
      8.
          A BBC program on Igbo poetry, by D. C. Osadebay;
      Yoruba poetry, by E. L. Lasebikan, and Akan poetry by
      J. H. Nketia.

(13) MUSIC AND DANCE

3145 Akpabot, Samuel. "The Organization of the African orches-
      tra," J. New Afr. Lit. Arts, (June 1968), 74-6.
          An examination of African orchestra instrumentation by
      one of Nigeria's foremost composers and musicians.

3146   Akrofi, G. E.   "National drums and key-board music: a chal-
       lenge to Ghanaian composers," Music in Ghana, II (May
       1961), 61-6.

3147   Akuffo-Badoo, W. S.   "The Music of Kpa," Diploma Thesis,
       University of Ghana, 1967.   222 p.

3148   Amissah, Michael K.   "The Music of Ahanta Kundum,"
       Diploma Thesis, University of Ghana, 1965.   249 p.

3149   Amu, Ephraim.   "Choral music in the African idiom,"
       Music in Ghana, II (May 1961), 50-3.

3150   _____.   "How to study African rhythm," Gold Coast
       Teachers' J., VI, No. 2 (1954), 121-4.

3151   _____.   "Problems of notation: the symposium I.   The
       notation of pitch and rhythm," Music in Ghana, I (May
       1958), 54-60.

3152   _____.   Twenty-five African songs in the Twi language.
       Music and words.   London: Sheldon Press, 1932.   91 p.

3153   Aning, B. A.   "Adenkun--a study of the Akan female bands,"
       Diploma Thesis, University of Ghana, 1964.

3154   _____.   An Annotated bibliography of music and dance
       in English-speaking Africa.   Legon: Institute of African
       Studies, University of Ghana, 1967.   47 p.
       "Attempts to find out to what extent music and dance as re-
       lated, even interdependent, phenomena have been investi-
       gated."   Entries, comprising chiefly periodical articles,
       are grouped by country under four regional headings,
       with a general section.   Author index.

3155   _____.   "Factors that shape and maintain folk music in
       Ghana," Int. Folk Music Council Jl., XX (1968), 13-17.

3156   _____.   "Nnwonkoro: a study of stability and change in
       traditional music," Master's Thesis, University of Ghana,
       1969.

3157   Ankermann, Bernhard.   "Die afrikanischen Musikinstrumente,"
       Phil. F., Leipzig, 1901.   132 p.

3158   Antubam, Kofi.   "Arts of Ghana," United Asia, IX, No. 1
       (1957), 61-70.
       An interpretation of different Ghanaian dance gestures,
       and examination of the traditional concept of religion,
       social organization and Ghana's aesthetics, as revealed by
       Ghana's architecture, paintings, sculpture, etc.

3159   Armstrong, Robert G.   "Talking instruments in West Africa,"
        Explorations, No. 4 (Feb. 1955), 140-53.

3160   Asado, F. Onwona.   "An African orchestra in Ghana,"
        African Music, I, No. 4 (1957), 11-12.

3161   Asiama, S. D.   "Music and dancing in a Ghanaian community
        (Pokuase)," Diploma Thesis, University of Ghana, 1965.

3162   Atakora, Apea T.   "Mmoguo--song interludes in Akan folk
        tales," Diploma Thesis, University of Ghana, 1964.

3163   Ayi, C. K.   "The Music of Dipo custom (a puberty rite
        among the Shai)," Diploma Thesis, University of Ghana,
        1966.

3164   Azu, Enoch.   Adangme historical and proverbial songs.
        Accra: Govt. Printer, 1929.   136 p.
               Includes notation of solo, chorus and drum rhythms.

3165   Bansisa, Y.   "Music in Africa," Uganda Journal, IV (Oct.
        1936), 108-14.

3166   Beier, Horst Ulli.   "The Talking drums of Africa," African
        Music, I, No. 1 (1954), 29-31.

3167   Berntonoff, Deborah.   Dance towards the earth.   Translated
        by I. M. Lask.   Tel Aviv: Alityros Books, 1963.   233 p.
               Partly an ethnographic study of Ghana with an inter-
        pretative description of social dances.

3168   "Bertie Opoku, Ghana's dance artist," West Africa, No.
        2639 (Dec. 1967), 1669.

3169   Boateng, O. A.   Songs for infant schools.   (Twi)   London:
        Oxford University Press, 1948.   32 p.
               Gold Coast folk songs with melody and tonic sol-fa.

3170   Boulton, Laura C.   "West African music," Man, XXXVII
        (Aug. 1937), 130.
               Brief discussion of African music and musical instru-
        ments.

3171   Carrington, John F.   "African music in Christian worship,"
        Int. Rev. Missions, XXXVII (Aug. 1948), 198-205.

3172   Cudjoe, Seth D.   "Problems of notation, 3.   The notation of
        drum music," Music in Ghana, I (May 1958), 70-81.

3173   _____.   "The Techniques of Ewe drumming and the social
        importance of music in Africa," Phylon, XIV, (Sept. 1953),
        280-91.

3174 Dosoo, J. N. "Music in the middle schools," Music in Ghana,
        II (May 1961), 95-101.

3175 Dumm, R. W. "Boston: Unesco Arts Conference," Musical
        Courier, CLXIII (Dec. 1961), 37, 40.
        On Nigeria and Ghana.

3176 Fiagbedzi, Nissio S. "Sogbadzi: a study of Yeve music,"
        Diploma Thesis, University of Ghana, 1966.

3177 Fodeba, Keita. "La danse africaine et la scène," Présence
        Africaine, Nos. 14-15 (1957), 202-9.
        Background information on African music.

3178 Fortes, M. "Ritual festivals and social cohesion in the
        hinterlands of the Gold Coast," Amer. Anthrop., XXXVIII
        (Oct. /Dec. 1936), 590-604.
        Includes brief mention of the sacred Ginguan drums in
        the Namoos clan festival among the Tallensi.

3179 Frobenius, Leo. The Voice of Africa. London: Hutchinson,
        1913. 2 v. V. 1: 118 p. V. 2: 518 p.

3180 Gadzekpo, B. Sinedzi. "Making music in Eweland," W. Afr.
        Rev., XXIII (Aug. 1952), 817-21.

3181 Gbeho, Philip. "Africa's drums are more than tom-toms,"
        W. Afr. Rev., XXII (Oct. 1951), 1150-2.

3182 _____. "Beat of the master drum," W. Afr. Rev., XXII
        (Nov. 1951), 1263-5.

3183 _____. "Cross rhythm in African music," W. Afr. Rev.,
        XXIII (Jan. 1952), 11-13.

3184 _____. "The Indigenous Gold Coast music," Afr. Music
        Soc. Newsletter," I, No. 5 (June 1952), 30-4.
        Assesses the place of music and dance, as well as the
        role of the musicians and dancers in Ghana.

3185 _____. "Music of the Gold Coast," African Music, I, No.
        I (1954), 62-4.
        Chiefly background information.

3186 "Ghana's talking drums," W. Afr. Rev., XXX (May 1959),
        357-9.

3187 "Ghana's teacher of music," West Africa, (Nov. 3, 1956),
        871.
        Ephraim Amu.

3188 Harper, Peggy. "Conclusions reached ... on research into
      dance in Africa and on the use of traditional African dance
      in contemporary theatre and education," African Notes,
      (Jan. 1967), 46-9.

3189 Jenkins, Mildred Leona. "The Impact of African music upon
      the western hemisphere," Master's Thesis, Boston Uni-
      versity, 1942. 60 p.

3190 Jones, A. M. "African rhythm," Africa (London), XXIV (Jan.
      1954), 26-47.
          The author's experiences are drawn primarily from
      Northern Rhodesia (Zambia) but contain some principles
      that hold good for the Ewe people of Ghana.

3191 _____. Studies in African music. London: Oxford
      University Press, for the School of Oriental and African
      Studies, 1959. 2 v. V. 1: 308 p. Text. V. 2: 248 p.
      Music. 18 half-tone plates.
          Both volumes are interdependent. V. 1 consists of a
      series of essays on African music and contains some de-
      tailed commentaries on the contents of v. 2--a music
      book setting out scores of songs and dances. See West
      African Review (March 1961), 39+, for some comments by
      Ghanaian musicians, Philip Gbeho and Seth Gudjoe.

3192 Kinney, Sylvia. "A Profile on music and movement in the
      Volta Region, Part I," Research Review (Legon), III, No.
      1 (1966), 48-52.

3193 Kodzo, J. W. "Fighting mass apathy through band music,"
      Community Dev. Bull. (London), IV (March, 1953), 33-5.

3194 Kolinski, Mieczyslaw. "La Musica del Oeste Africano,"
      Rev. Estud. Musicales, I (Dec. 1949), 191-215.
          An analytical article with music notation.

3195 Ladzekpo, S. K. and H. Pantaleoni. "Takada drumming,"
      African Music, IV, No. 4 (1970), 6-31.

3196 Laing, E. "Scores and records of Ghanaian music," Music
      in Ghana, II (May 1961), 110-20.

3197 Laloum, C. and G. Rouget. "La Musique de deux chants
      liturgiques Yoruba," J. Soc. Afr. (Paris), XXXV, No. 1
      (1965), 109-39.
          Includes a phonodisc.

3198 Landeck, Beatrice. Echoes of Africa in folk songs of the
      Americas. New York: Mckay, 1961.

3199   Mensah, Atta A.   "The Akan church lyric," Int. Rev. Mis-
       sions, XLIX, No. 194 (1960), 183-8.

3200   _____ .   "The Guans in music: a historical study,"
       Master's Thesis, University of Ghana, 1966.   176 p.

3201   _____ .   "The Impact of western music on the musical
       traditions of Ghana," Composer, No. 19 (Spring 1966),
       19-22.

3202   _____ .   "Musicality and musicianship in North-Western
       Ghana," Research Review (Legon), II, No. 1 (1965), 42-5.

3203   _____ .   "The Polyphony of Gyil-gu, Kudzo and Awutu
       Sakuno," Int. Folk Music Council Jl., XIX (1967), 75-9.

3204   _____ .   "Problems involved in the 'arrangement' of folk
       music for Radio Ghana," Int. Folk Music Council Jl.,
       XI (1958), 83-4.

3205   _____ .   "Professionalism in the musical practice of
       Ghana," Music in Ghana, I (May 1958), 28-35.

3206   _____ .   "Writing African music for the keyboard," Music
       in Ghana, II (May 1961), 54-60.

3207   Merriam, Alan P.   "An Annotated bibliography of African
       and African derived music since 1936," Africa, XXI (Oct.
       1951), 319-29.
         Books and periodical articles divided into 2 parts.   I:
       121 entries of material personally examined by the author.
       II: 51 entries of material taken from other bibliographic
       sources.

3208   Moore, Carman.   "The Arts: Ghana's dance company
       sparkles in an effective blend of modern traditional,"
       Africa Report, XV (March 1970), 30-1.

3209   Nayo, Nicholas Z.   "Akpalu and his songs," Diploma Thesis,
       University of Ghana, 1964.

3210   _____ .   "The Use of folk songs in composition," Music in
       Ghana, II (May 1961), 67-9.

3211   Nketia, Joseph Hanson.   "African gods and music," Univer-
       sitas, IV, No. 1 (1959), 3-7.

3212   _____ .   African music in Ghana.   Evanston: Northwestern
       University Press, 1963.   148 p.   (Northwestern University,
       Evanston, Ill. African Studies, no. 11.)
         Presentation of African traditional music as practiced by
       different Ghanaian ethnic groups.   Appendix I: Bibliography.

Appendix II: Songs. Index of songs, tribal and regional maps.
    Rev: Amer. Anthrop., (June 1964), 699. Music Jl., XXII (Jan. 1964), 106.

3213   _____. "Akan poetry," Black Orpheus, No. 3 (May 1958), 5-27.

3214   _____. "Artistic values in African music," Composer, (Spring 1966), 16-19.

3215   _____. A Calendar of Ghana festivals. Accra: Arts Council of Ghana, n.d. (Unpublished manuscript.)

3216   _____. "Changing traditions of folk music in Ghana," Int. Folk Music Council Jl., XI (1959), 31-6.

3217   _____. "The Contribution of African culture to Christian worship," Int. Rev. Missions, XLVII (July 1958), 265-78.

3218   _____. "The Development of instrumental African music in Ghana," Music in Ghana, I (May 1958), 5-27.

3219   _____. Drumming in Akan communities of Ghana. London: Nelson, 1963. 212 p.
    A comprehensive survey of social implications of musical and poetic aspects of drumming in Akan society. Includes 9 music examples and 27 plates.
    Rev: J. Afr. Hist., V, No. 2 (1964), 334-5.

3220   _____. "Drums, dance and song," Atlantic Monthly, CCIII, No. 4 (1959), 67-72.
    Analysis of various kinds of music and their functions, and different types of instruments, such as drums, ideophones, wind and string instruments, etc.

3221   _____. Folk songs of Ghana. London: Oxford University Press for University of Ghana, 1963. 205 p.
    First in a series of publications intended to provide source material for performers, composers and students of African music.
    Rev: Amer. Anthrop., LXVII (Feb. 1965), 135.

3222   _____. Funeral dirges of the Akan people. Westport, Connecticut: Negro Universities Press, 1970. 296 p. Reprint of the 1955 edition.

3223   _____. "The Gramaphone and contemporary African music in the Gold Coast," Proceedings of the West African Institute of Social and Economic Research, 4th Annual Conference, Ibadan, 1956, pp. 191-201.

3224 _____. "Historical evidence in Ga religious music." In
J. Vansina, et al., eds. The historian in tropical Africa
(1964), pp. 265-80.

3225 _____. "The Ideal in African folk music: a note on
'Klama,'" Universitas, III (March 1958), 40-2.
Includes discussion of Adangme music and dance.

3226 _____. "Modern trends in Ghana music," African Music,
I, No. 4 (1957), 13-17.

3227 _____. Music in African cultures: a review of the meaning and significance of traditional African music. Legon:
Institute of African Studies, University of Ghana, 1966.

3228 _____. "Musicology and African music: a review of
problems and areas of research." In David Brokensha and
Michael Crowder, eds. Africa in wider world. New York:
Oxford University Press, 1967, pp. 12-35.

3229 _____. "Musik in Afrikanische Kulturen," Afrika Heute
(Bonn), June 1, 1966), 1-16.

3230 _____. "The Organization of music in Adangme society,"
African Music, II, No. 1 (1958), 28-30. Also in Univer-
sitas, III, No. 1 (1957), 9-11.
A general survey of musical practices among the
Adangme people.

3231 _____. Our drums and drummers. Accra: Ghana Publishing House, 1968. 48 p.

3232 _____. "Possession dances in African societies," Int.
Folk Music Council Jl., IX (1957), 4-9.

3233 _____. "The Problem of meaning in African music,"
Ethnomusicology, VI (Jan. 1962), 1-7.

3234 _____. "The Role of the drummer in Akan society,"
African Music, I, No. 1 (1954), 34-43.

3235 _____. "Traditional music of the Ga people," Universitas,
III, No. 3 (1958), 76-81; also in African Music, II, No. 1
(1958), 21-7.
Chiefly on the instrumental and vocal music.

3236 _____. "Yoruba musicians in Accra," Odu, VI (June 1958),
35-44.

3237 Onwona-Osafo, F. "An African orchestra in Ghana," African
Music, I, No. 4 (1957), 11-12.

3238   Opoku, Albert M.   "African dance drama," Music in Ghana,
        I (May 1958), 36-53.

3239   _____. Ghana dance ensemble.   Accra: Institute of Art
        and Sculpture, 1967.   1 v.

3240   _____. "Thoughts from the School of Music and Drama,
        Institute of African Studies, University of Ghana, Legon,"
        Okyeame, II, No. 1 (1964).
        The training and role of the dancer in Ghana.

3241   _____ and Willis E. Bell.   African dances: a Ghanaian
        profile: pictorial excerpts from the concerts of Ghanaian
        dances.   Legon: Institute of African Studies, University
        of Ghana, 1968.   40 p.
        Chiefly illustrated.

3242   Oppong, Christine.   "A Note on Dagomba chief's drummer,"
        Research Review (Legon), IV, No. 2 (1968), 63-5.

3243   Parrinder, E. G.   "Music in West African churches," African
        Music, I, No. 3 (1956), 37-8.

3244   Partos, Elizabeth and J. H. Nketia.   Chamber music in African
        idiom for violin and piano, Grade I.   Legon: Institute of
        African Studies, University of Ghana, 1967.   42 p.

3245   Peek, P.   "Record reviews: Ewe music of Ghana; music of
        Idoma of Nigeria," Ethnomusicology, XIV, No. 2 (1970),
        369-70.

3246   Pepper, M.   "Musique et pensée africaines," Présence
        Africaine, No. 1 (Oct. /Nov. 1947), 149-57.

3247   Price, J. H.   "A Bori dance in Accra," W. Afr. Rev. ,
        XXVIII, No. 352 (1957), 20-3.
        Describes a spirit dance, tracing its origin to Muslim
        and pagan communities of Southern Sudan.

3248   Reed, E. M.   "Music of West Africa, I.   Ashanti," Music
        and Youth, V (1925), 135-9.

3249   Riverson, Isaac, ed.   Akan songs.   New ed.   Cape Coast:
        Methodist Book Depot, 1954.   56 p.   Originally published
        as Songs of the Akan peoples, 1939.
        Piano score with tonic sol-fa.

3250   _____. "The Growth of music in the Gold Coast," Trans.
        Gold Coast & Togoland Hist. Soc. , I, Part IV, (1955),
        121-32.
        A historical survey of the development of music classified
        into three phases: Music in churches, schools and com-
        munity.

3251 _____ . "Problems of notation, II. Meter and rhythm,"
     Music in Ghana, I (May 1958), 61-9.

3252 _____ . The Teaching of music in primary schools. Accra:
     Methodist Book Depot, 1960. 52 p.

3253 Rodin, Paul and James Sweeney. African folk tales and
     sculpture. New York: Pantheon, 1952.

3254 Rohrbaugh, Lynn, ed. African songs. Delaware, Ohio:
     Cooperative Recreation Service, 1958.

3255 Smith, Edna M. "Musical training in tribal West Africa,"
     African Music, III, No. 1 (1962), 6-10.
     Examines the objectives and methods of music educa-
     tion for children in West African communities, and ob-
     serves that the traditional instruction is "based upon the
     principle of slow absorption of musical experience and
     active participation rather than formal teaching."

3256 _____ . "Popular music in West Africa," African Music,
     III, No. 1 (1962), 11-17.
     Critically analyzes instruments and music used for
     various West African popular dances. Emphasis is on
     recreation music with special reference to the Highlife,
     the most popular music in West Africa.

3257 Spriggs, Robert. "The Ghanaian highlife: notation and
     source," Music in Ghana, II (May 1961), 70-94.

3258 Stewart, J. L. "Northern Gold Coast songs," Afr. Music
     Soc. Newsletter, I (June 1952), 39-42.

3259 Titi-Lartey, E. O. "Kurunku--an Akan musical type (Fante),"
     Diploma Thesis, University of Ghana, 1965.

3260 Ward, William Ernest. "Gold Coast music in education,"
     Oversea Education, V, No. 2 (1934), 64-71.
     Discusses form, notation and rhythm of music and songs.

3261 Wiegräbe, Paul. "Ewelieder," Afrika und Ubersee, XXXVII,
     No. 3 (1953), 99-108; (Sept. 1954), 155-64.

3262 Williams, Drid. "The Dance of the Bedu moon," African
     Arts, (Autumn 1968), 18-21+.
     Describes the dancing of the Nafana people who live
     in the West-Central region of Ghana.

3263 Williamson, S. G. "The Lyric in the Fante Methodist Church,"
     Africa, XXVIII (April 1958), 126-34.

3264   Wilson, Charles B. "Work songs of the Fante fishermen,"
       Diploma Thesis, University of Ghana, 1966.

(14)   POLITICAL SCIENCE--NATIONALIST DEVELOPMENT

3265   Abdi, Getachew. "African nationalism; the role of political
       parties in African nationalism with special reference to
       its implications in Ghana," Doctoral Dissertation, Syra-
       cuse University, 1962.

3266   Afari-Gyan. "Nationalist ideology in the Gold Coast: some
       influence on its evolution from the beginnings of the proto-
       modern nationalist movement to 1950, as revealed in the
       indigenous newspaper press of the period," Master's
       Thesis, University of Ghana, 1969.   215 p.

3267   Ahuma, S. R. B. Attoh. The Gold Coast nation and national
       consciousness. With a new introduction by J. C. de Graft-
       Johnson. 2nd ed. London: Cass, 1971.   63 p.
              Rev. Ahuma's writings greatly influenced his contem-
       poraries and the Gold Coast Leader, the most influential
       newspaper of his day, founded by him in 1896 served as
       a springboard for nationalist agitation.

3268   Akyeampong, Henry Kwasi. The foundations of self-govern-
       ment: selected historic speeches on Ghana's independence.
       Accra: George Boakye Publishing Co., 1967.   51 p.

3269   Amamoo, Joseph G. The New Ghana: the birth of a nation.
       London: Pan Books, 1958.   145 p.

3270   Amu, Samir. Trois expériences africaines de développement,
       le Mali, la Guinée et le Ghana. Paris: Presses Uni-
       versitaires de France, 1965.   233 p.

3271   Apter, David Ernest. "The Development of Ghana nationalism,"
       United Asia, IX (1957), 23-30.

3272   Austin, Dennis. "Constitutional development of Ghana,"
       United Asia, IX (1957), 84-90.

3273   _____. Politics in Ghana, 1946-1960. New York: Oxford
       University Press, 1964.   459 p. (Institute of Commonwealth
       studies.)
              Chiefly on the rise of the Convention People's Party and
       its arrogation of total political power after independence.
              Rev: J. Mod. Afr. Stud., III (Aug. 1965), 301. Amer.
       Pol. Sci. Rev., LIX (Dec. 1965), 1007-8.

3274   Bankole, Timothy. Kwame Nkrumah; his rise to power.
       With a foreword by the Honourable Kojo Botsio. 2nd ed.
       Evanston: Northwestern University Press, 1963. 191 p.

3275   Bing, Geoffrey. Reap the whirlwind: an account of Kwame
       Nkrumah's Ghana from 1950-1960. London: Macgibbon &
       Kee, 1968. 519 p.
            Rev: Listener, LXXX (July 11, 1968), 52. TLS
       (June 6, 1968), 568.

3276   Boyon, Jacques. Naissance d'un état africain, le Ghana. La
       Gold Coast de la colonisation à l'indépendence. Paris:
       Colin, 1958. 274 p. (Cahiers de la Fondation Nationale
       des Sciences Politiques, 93.)

3277   _____. "Une idéologie africaine la Nkrumaisme," Rev.
       Fr. Sci. Pol., XIII (March 1963), 66-87.

3278   Bretton, Henry L. The Rise and fall of Kwame Nkrumah.
       New York: Praeger, 1966. 224 p.
            Rev: N. Y. Times Bk. Rev. (April 16, 1967), 24.
       TLS (June 8, 1967), 507.

3279   Busia, Kofi Abrefa. "Gold Coast and Nigeria on the road to
       self-government." In C. G. Haines, ed. Africa Today.
       Baltimore: Johns Hopkins University Press, 1955, pp.
       289-304.

3280   Coffee, Mary. "The Self-government movement in the Gold
       Coast, West Africa," Doctoral Dissertation, Harvard
       University, 1954. 153 p.

3281   "The Constitution Makers," West Africa, No. 2692 (Jan. 4.
       1969), 3.
            The meeting of Ghana's Constituent Assembly to discuss
       the proposals of the Constitutional Commission is considered
       by western observers as the first of its kind in Africa
       south of the Sahara.

3282   "Constitutional reform in the Gold Coast: the recommenda-
       tions of the Coussey Committee," J. Afr. Adm. (Jan. 1950),
       2-11.

3283   Crah, Linus Kwasi. Ghana national democracy: constitu-
       tionalism in the emergent nations with republican bi-
       cameral Legislature of freedom and justice for new States.
       London (34 Oxford Gardens, W. 4): Star Research (Publi-
       cations) Society, 1970. 72 p. (Ghana, opus 1).

3284   _____. Ghana state organism: theory of state and govern-
       ment containing an inquiry into the concept of statehood
       with special reference to the emergent nations. London:

Star Research (Publications) Society, 1970.   72 p.
(Ghana, opus 2.)

3285   Danquah, Joseph Boakye. Historic speeches and writings on
       Ghana. Compiled by H. K. Akyeampong. Accra: George
       Boakye Publishing Co. , 1966.   177 p.

3286   Davidson, Basil and Adenekan Ademola, eds.   The New
       West Africa: problems of independence.   Introd. by
       Ritchie Calder. London: Allen & Unwin, 1953.   184 p.
          Examination of the political and social changes in
       Ghana and Nigeria.

3287   De Graft Johnson, J. W.   Towards nationhood in West Africa:
       thoughts of young Africa addressed to young Britain.   With
       a new introduction by F. K. Drah. London: Cass, 1971.
       158 p.   New impression.

3288   Du Bois, W. E. B.   The Seventh son: the thought and writing
       of W. E. B. Du Bois.   Edited and with an introduction by
       Julius Lester. New York: Random House, 1971.   2 v.
       V. 1: 576 p.   V. 2: 815 p.
          Rev: Newsweek, LXXVIII (Aug. 23, 1971), 75, 77.

3289   Folson, B. G. D.   "The New Constitution of Ghana: some
       underlying principles, " Transition, VIII (June/July 1971),
       17-28.
          A reply to Twumasi's attack on the proposals for a new
       constitution put forward by the Constitutional Commission
       established after the coup of February 1966.

3290   Frimpong, J. H.   "The Joint Provincial Council of Paramount
       Chiefs and the Politics of independence in the Gold Coast, "
       Master's Thesis, University of Ghana, 1966.   123 p.

3291   Garvey, Marcus.   Collected papers and documents.   Edited
       by E. U. Essien-Udom and Amy Jacques Garvey. London:
       Cass.   (Forthcoming)
          Between 1916 and 1940 when he died, Garvey was the
       most passionate American advocate of a return of American
       blacks to Africa.

3292   _____ .   Philosophy and opinions of Marcus Garvey.   Com-
       piled by Amy Jacques Garvey. With a new introduction by
       E. U. Essien-Udom. 2nd ed. London: Cass, 1967.   2v.
       (Africana modern library.)
          Compiled from the speeches and articles of Marcus
       Garvey by his wife and originally published in two parts in
       1923 and 1926.
          Rev: West Africa, No. 2698 (Feb. 15, 1969), 182.

3293   Gerard, A. "Ghana: dominion, no. 8," Revue Nouvelle,
       XXV (April 1957), 437-46.

3294   "Ghana's blueprint for civilian rule," West Africa, No. 2644
       (Feb. 3, 1968), 120.
           Description of the 161 page document containing the
       constitutional recommendations of the 18 member commis-
       sion headed by Chief Justice Akuffo-Addo, under which
       Ghana should return to civilian rule.

3295   Goldsworthy, David. "Ghana's second republic," Australian
       Outlook, XXV (April 1971), 45-57.

3296   Greenwood, A. F. "Ten years of local government in Ghana,"
       J. Local Adm. Overseas (Jan. 1962), 23-8.

3297   Grewal, N. S. "Ghana's constitutional proposals," J. Asian
       Afr. Stud., II, No. 1 (1968), 69-79.

3298   "Guidelines for Ghana's constitution--1," West Africa, No.
       2695 (Jan. 23, 1969), 89.

3299   Halm, W. E. "Ghana's emergence as a self-governing
       country." In James Druff and Alan Manners, ed. Africa
       speaks. New York: Van Nostrand, 1961, pp. 62-70.

3300   Hansard Society for Parliamentary Government. What are
       the problems of parliamentary government in West Africa?
       The Report of a conference held by the Hansard Society
       for Parliamentary Government at St. Edmund Hall, Oxford,
       September 1957, under the Chairmanship of Geoffrey de
       Freitas, M. P., Hansard Society, London, 1958.   180 p.

3301   Heiting, Thomas James. "W. E. B. Du Bois and the develop-
       ment of Pan-Africanism, 1900-1930," Doctoral Dissertation,
       Texas Tech. University, 1969.   213 p.

3302   Hicks, Ursula. Development from below: local government
       and finance in developing countries of the Commonwealth.
       London: Oxford University Press, 1961.   349 p.

3303   Hopkins, A. G. "Economic aspects of political movements
       in Nigeria and the Gold Coast, 1918-1939," J. Afr. Hist.,
       VII, No. 1 (1966), 133-52.

3304   Horton, Africanus Beale. Letters on the political condition
       of the Gold Coast. New York: Humanities Press, 1970.
       178 p.   (Africana modern library.)
           Rev: Africa, XLII (Jan. 1972), 71-2.

3305   Jones-Quartey, K. A. B. "Anglo-African journals and jour-
       nalism in the nineteenth and early twentieth centuries,"

Trans. Hist. Soc. Ghana, IV (1959), 47-56.

3306 _____. "The Gold Coast press 1822-c.1930, and the
Anglo-African press 1825-c.1930, the chronologies," Research Review (Legon), IV, No. 2 (1968), 40-6.

3307 _____. "Press and nationalism in Ghana," United Asia,
IX (1957), 55-60.

3308 _____. "Thought and expression in the Gold Coast press,
1874-1930," Universitas, III, No. 3 (1958), 72-5; III, No.
4 (1958), 113-6.

3309 Juergensmeyer, J.C. "African presidentialism: a comparison of the 'Executive' under the constitution of the Federation of Nigeria, the Federal Republics of the Congo and
Cameroon and the Republics of Ghana, Chad, and the
entente," J. Afr. Law, VIII, No. 3 (1963), 157-77.

3310 Kimble, David. A Political history of Ghana: the rise
of Gold Coast nationalism, 1850-1928. New York: Oxford
University Press, 1963. 587 p.
    "A monumental and encyclopedic attempt to trace the
complex interaction of British, Fante and Ashanti in this
period."--John Flint, Nigeria and Ghana (1966).
    Rev: Amer. Hist. Rev., LXIX (1965), 462-3. J. Afr.
Hist., V (1964), 127-32.

3311 _____. "The rise of nationalism in the Gold Coast, 1908-
1928," Doctoral Dissertation, University of Ghana, 1960.
2 v.

3312 Kraus, J.G. "On the politics of nationalism and social change
in Ghana," J. Mod. Afr. Stud., VII (April 1969), 107-30.

3313 "Kwame Nkrumah." In Paul Sigmund, ed. The Ideologies of
the developing nations. New York: Praeger, 1967, pp.
251-61.
    Excerpts from Ghana: the autobiography of Kwame
Nkrumah (1957) and from Nkrumah's Consciencism:
philosophy and ideology for decolonization and development
(1964).

3314 Lee, J.M. "Parliament in republic Ghana," Parl. Affairs,
XVI (Fall 1963), 376-95.

3315 Legum, Colin. "The Passing of colonialism: action and
reaction in Ghana," Political Quarterly (July/Sept. 1958),
269-77.

3316 Nicholson, Marjorie. West African ferment. London:
Fabian Publications, 1950. 44 p.

3317   Nkrumah, Kwame. Axioms of Kwame Nkrumah: freedom
       fighters' edition. New and enl. ed. New York: Interna-
       tional Publishers, 169. 131 p.

3318   _____ . "Background to independence. " In P. E. Sigmund,
       ed. The Ideologies of the developing nations. Rev. ed.
       New York: Praeger, 1967, pp. 252-5.

3319   _____ . "Birth of my party, " United Asia, IX (1957),
       45-9.

3320   _____ . "Gold Coast's claim to independence, " United
       Asia (April 1955), 59-64.

3321   _____ . Handbook of revolutionary warfare: a guide to
       the armed phase of the African revolution. New York:
       International Publishers, 1968. 122 p.

3322   _____ . I Speak of freedom: a statement of African
       ideology. London: Heinemann, 1961. 291 p.
           A selection of Nkrumah's speeches and statements,
       interlaced with his own notes on Ghana's independence.
           Rev: Amer. Pol. Sci. Rev. , LVI (June 1962), 485.

3323   _____ . Motion for Gold Coast independence made by the
       Prime Minister in the Legislative Assembly of 3rd August,
       1956. Accra: Govt. Printer, 1956.

3324   _____ . "The movement for colonial freedom, " Phylon,
       XVI, No. 4 (1955), 397-409.

3325   _____ . Neo-colonialism: the last stage of imperialism.
       New York: International Publishers, 1965. 280 p.

3326   "Nkrumah's own story, " Africa Special Report, II (March 29,
       1957), 4-7.
           Chiefly autobiographical, throwing much light on his
       political philosophy and his struggle for Ghana's indepen-
       dence.

3327   Nsarkoh, J. K. Local government in Ghana. Accra: Ghana
       Universities Press, 1964. 309 p.

3328   Onipede, F. O. "African nationalism: a critical portrait, "
       Dissent, III (Summer 1956), 276-85.

3329   Padmore, George. The Gold Coast revolution: the struggle
       of an African people from slavery to freedom. London:
       Dobson, 1953. 272 p.
           Traces the rise of Gold Coast nationalism from the
       establishment of the Ashanti Confederacy through the emer-
       gence of Convention People's Party.

3330   Pao, C. Sheng. The Gold Coast delegates to Britain in 1934;
       the political background. Taipei & Taiwan: National
       Chengchi University, 1970. 42 p.

3331   Rathbone, Richard. "The Government of the Gold Coast after
       the Second World War, " African Affairs, LXVII (July 1968),
       209-26.

3332   Redmayne, Paul. Gold Coast to Ghana. London: Murray,
       1957. 48 p.

3333   Robinson, Kenneth. "Constitutional autochthony in Ghana, "
       J. Commonwealth Pol. Stud., I (Nov. 1961), 41-55.

3334   Royal Institute of International Affairs, Ghana: a survey of
       the Gold Coast on the eve of independence. London, 1957.
       62 p.

3335   Sampson, Magnus J. West African leadership. Public
       speeches of J.E. Casely Hayford. New York: Humanities
       Press, 1961. 160 p.

3336   Traber, Michael. "The Treatment of the Little Rock, Arkan-
       sas, school integration incident in the daily press of the
       Union of South Africa, West Nigeria and Ghana, from
       Sept. 1 to Oct. 1, 1957, " Doctoral Dissertation, New York
       University, 1960.

3337   Uwanaka, Charles. The Story of Ghana independence. Lagos:
       Pacific Printing and Publishing Works, 1957. 56 p.

3338   Wallerstein, Immanuel M. "The Emergence of two West
       African nations: Ghana and the Ivory Coast, " Doctoral
       Dissertation, Columbia University, 1959. 360 p.

3339   _____ . The Road to independence: Ghana and the Ivory
       Coast. London: Mouton, 1964. 200 p.
                Rev: Amer. Hist. Rev., LXXI (Oct. 1965), 269.   TLS
       (Sept. 16, 1965), 813.

3340   Walter, Gerhard. Goldküste wird Ghana. Berlin: Rütten &
       Loening, 1961. 145 p. (Taschenbuch Geschichte.)

3341   Wiseman, H.V. "The Gold Coast, from executive council to
       responsible cabinet, " Parl. Affairs, X, No. 1 (1956/57),
       27-35.

(14)   POLITICAL SCIENCE--STRUCTURES, PROCESSES, ETC.

3342   Adu, A. L. The Civil service in new African states. New
       York: Praeger, 1965. 242 p.

Describes the operations of civil service in former
British colonies in Africa and the relevant administrative
adaptations made since independence, with special attention
to the structure, staff, internal administration, policy
making and financial control of the civil service: The
author is former Head of Ghana's Civil Service.
Rev: Africa, XXXV (July 1965), 331. Pol. Sci. Q.,
LXXX (Dec. 1965), 673.

3343 African Bibliographic Center. Ghanaian politics and government, 1960-1962: a selected current reading list. Washington, D. C., 1964. 4 p.

3344 Afrifa, Akwasi A. The Ghana coup, 24th February 1966.
New York: Humanities Press, 1966. 144 p.
A detailed background story of the overthrow of the
Nkrumah regime by one of the main participants. Con-
tends that the military force remains the only effective
means of ending corrupt governments in Africa.
Rev: J. Asian Afr. Stud., IV (April 1969), 157-8.
TLS (Jan. 12, 1967), 22.

3345 _____. "Returning Ghana to civilian rule: the plans of
the National Liberation Council," Round Table, LVII (Oct.
1967), 380-4.

3346 Agarwala, C. B. "The Government of Ghana," Foreign
Affairs Rpts. (Aug. 1960), 87-95.

3347 Ake, C. "Charismatic legitimation and political integration,"
Comp. Stud. Soc. Hist., IX (Oct. 1966), 1-3.

3348 Akita, J. M. "The Transfer of the seat of government from
Cape Coast to Accra," Gold Coast Teachers' J., I (1956),
42-7.

3349 Akyea, L. E. The Buem-Krachi District Council. Accra:
Guinea Press, 1960. 52 p.

3350 Alexander, H. T. African tight rope: my two years as
Nkrumah's Chief of Staff. New York: Praeger, 1966.
152 p.
A Major-General and Ghana's Chief of Staff, 1960-61,
describes his resentment of African politicians using
the armed forces for political purposes and explains his
role in the Congo Crisis, as a leader of the Ghanaian
military contingent.
Rev: N. Y. Rev. Bks., VI (June 23, 1966), 11. TLS
(Dec. 23, 1965), 1191.

3351 Aligwekwe, Iwuoha E. "The Ewe and Togoland problem: a
case study in the paradoxes and problems of political

transition in West Africa," Doctoral Dissertation, Ohio
State University, 1960.

3352   Amamoo, J. G.   "The Rise and fall of Kwame Nkrumah,"
       African World, LXIV (April 1966), 4-6.

3353   Ampah, E. B. K.   The Tears of Dr. Kwame Nkrumah: the
       rise of the Convention People's Party.   Cape Coast: Pro-
       spect Printing Press, 1951.   29 p.

3354   Andoh, A. S. Y.   The Development of local government on
       Ghana, 1: background to local government ordinance of
       1951.   Legon: Institute of African Studies, University
       of Ghana, 1967.   21 p.

3355   _____.   The Development of local government in Ghana,
       2: the structure of local government, 1951-1966.   Legon:
       Institute of African Studies, University of Ghana, 1967.
       20 p.

3356   _____.   "Local government and local development in
       Ghana," Insight, II (Feb. 1967), 42-7.

3357   _____.   The Structure of local government, 1951-66.
       3: The Development of social welfare and community
       development and the village development committee.   Legon:
       Institute of African Studies, University of Ghana, 1967.
       18 p.

3358   Ankomah, Kofi.   "Reflections on administrative reform in
       Ghana," Int. Rev. Adm. Sci., XXXVI, No. 4 (1970),
       299+.

3359   Ankrah, J. A.   "Broadcast to the nation: excerpts from
       'The rebirth of Ghana--the end of tyranny.'"   In P. E.
       Sigmund, ed.   The Ideologies of the developing nations.
       New York: Praeger, 1967, pp. 263-8.

3360   _____.   "100 Days in Ghana," Africa Report, XI (June
       1966), 21-3.
            General Ankrah, Chairman of Ghana's National Libera-
       tion Council, in a radio broadcast, reviews his govern-
       ment's achievements in their first hundred days in office.

3361   Anthony, Seth.   "The State of Ghana," African Affairs,
       LXVIII (Oct. 1969), 337-8.
            An abridged version of the talk given by Ghana's High
       Commissioner in Britain, to the Royal African Society
       and the Royal Commonwealth Society on May 1, 1969.

3362   Apter, David.   Ghana in transition.   New York: Atheneum,
       1963.   432 p.

Revision of his book, The Gold Coast in transition (1955)
by Princeton University Press, based on his doctoral dissertation, Princeton University, 1954. Analysis of the
economic, social and political problems in establishing
western democratic institution and procedures in such a
tribal society as Ghana.

3363 _____ . The Politics of solidarity in Ghana. Berkeley:
Committee for African Studies, Institute of International
Affairs, University of California, 1966. 315 p.

3364 _____ . "The Role of traditionalism in the political
modernization of Ghana and Uganda," World Politics, XIII,
No. 1 (1960), 45-68.
The impact of ethnic or tribal provincialism on the
national politics of both countries.

3365 _____ . "Some economic factors in the political development of the Gold Coast," J. Econ. Hist., XIV (Oct. 1954),
409-27.

3366 _____ and Robert A. Lystad. "Bureaucracy, party, and
constitutional democracy: an examination of political role
systems in Ghana." In Gwendolen Carter and William O.
Brown, eds. Transition in Africa: studies in political
adaptation. Boston: Boston University Press, 1958, pp.
16-43.

3367 Arden-Clarke, Charles N. "Eight years of transition,"
African Affairs, LVII (Jan. 1958), 29-37.

3368 _____ . "Gold Coast into Ghana: some problems of
transition," Int. Affairs, XXXIV (Jan. 1958), 49-56.

3369 Arhin, P.K. "Factors in Ashanti political expansion, (1700-
1830)," B. Litt.'s Thesis, Oxford University, 1965/66.

3370 Asante, S.K.B. "Towards the future in Ghana," African
Affairs, LVII (Jan. 1958), 52-7.

3371 Austin, Dennis. "Elections in an African rural area,"
Africa, XXXI (Jan. 1961), 1-18.
On Kaseena and Nankanni peoples of Ghana.

3372 _____ . Ghana observed: collected papers on Ghana
politics and related essays. London: Cass. (forthcoming)
Comprises seminar papers, articles and monographs
written between 1958 and 1970, on the Ghanaian politics.
The Convention People's Party rule under Nkrumah, the
military coup of February 1966 and subsequent return to
civilian rule are examined. There are also some articles
on the Organization of African Unity, South Africa and the
Commonwealth.

3373   _____ . "Ghana since independence," World Today (Oct.
           1961), 424-35.

3374   _____ . "Opposition in Ghana, 1947-1967," Govt. Opp.,
           II (July/Oct. 1967), 539-55.

3375   _____ . "Progress in Ghana," International Journal, XXV,
           No. 3 (1970), 594-602.
                Discussion of the Busia's political philosophy, writings
           and government.

3376   _____ . "Return to Ghana," African Affairs, LXIX (Jan.
           1970), 67-71.
                Talk given at the Royal African Society, London, on
           October 1, 1969. Criticizes a single political party al-
           lowed between 1957 and 1964 in Ghana and regards Busia's
           government as "a very capable government, under a very
           democratic leader."

3377   _____ . "The Working committee of the United Gold Coast
           Convention," J. Afr. Hist., II, No. 2 (1961), 273-97.

3378   Ayisi, Eric O. "Ghana and the return to parliamentary
           government," Political Q., XLI (Oct./Dec. 1970), 432-43.

3379   Barkan, Joel David. "African university students and social
           change: an analysis of student opinion in Ghana, Tanzania
           and Uganda," Doctoral Dissertation, University of Cali-
           fornia, Los Angeles, 1970. 382 p.
                African students are likely to contribute to the develop-
           ment of their countries more "as agents of the established
           bureaucratic and political order than as agents of innovation
           and change," because hardly any of them is ready to play
           intrepreneurial roles whose reward is not considered com-
           mensurate with the risks involved.

3380   _____ . Elite perception and political involvement of uni-
           versity students in Ghana, Tanzania and Uganda. New York:
           African Studies Association, 1968. 26 p.

3381   Barker, Peter. Operation cold chop: the coup that toppled
           Nkrumah. Accra: Ghana Publishing Corp., 1969. 210 p.

3382   "Behind the scenes in Ghana: rise and fall of Tawia Adamfio,
           President's prestige enhanced," African World (Nov. 1962),
           21.

3383   Bennett, George. "The Gold Coast general election of 1954,"
           Parl. Affairs, VII (Autumn 1954), 430-9.

3384   Boateng, E. A. "Politics and education," an expanded version
           of an open lecture delivered at the 19th Annual New Year

School of the Institute of Adult Education of the University
of Ghana, at Commonwealth Hall, Legon, on 27th Dec.
1967.   19 p.

3385   Bosompen, J. E. Y.   The Legislative Assembly of the Gold
Coast.   Accra: The Author, 1955.   70 p.

3386   Bretton, Henry L.   "Current political thought and practice
in Ghana, " Amer. Pol. Sci. Rev. , LII (March 1958), 46-63.

3387   Brown, Paul S.   "Patterns of authority in West Africa, "
Africa, XXI, No. 4 (1951), 261-74.

3388   _____.   "Political organization and laws in West Africa, "
Master's Thesis, University of Chicago, 1948.   147 p.
Compares West African political systems.

3389   _____.   "A Study in authority in indigenous West African
societies, " Doctoral Dissertation, London University, 1951.

3390   Busia, Kofi Abrefa.   Africa in search of democracy.   New
York: Praeger, 1967.   189 p.
Rev: TLS (Nov. 2, 1967), 1033.   West Africa, No. 2636
(Dec. 9, 1967), 1575.

3391   _____.   Position of the chief in the modern political
system of Ashanti: a study of the influence of contem-
porary social changes on Ashanti political institutions.
London: Oxford University Press for the International
African Institute, 1951.   233 p.
Originally submitted as doctoral dissertation, Oxford
University.

3392   _____.   "The Prospects for parliamentary democracy in
the Gold Coast, " Parl. Affairs, V (Autumn 1952), 438-44.

3393   Card, Emily and Barbara Callaway.   "Ghanaian politics:
the elections and after, " Africa Report, XV (March 1970),
10-15.
Tribal tension poses a serious obstacle to effective
government by Busia, judging by the region-by-region study
of the voting patterns during the 1969 elections.

3394   Chauvel, J. F.   "Le Ghana, ou la tentation de l'Occident, "
Revue de Paris, LXXIII (April 1966), 74-9.

3395   Cheng, S. C.   "Schemes for the federation of the British
empire, " Doctoral Dissertation, Columbia University, 1931.

3396   "Clay-foot redeemer: Nkrumah, " America, CXIV (March 12,
1966), 344.

3397   Cohen, D. L.   "The Convention People's Party of Ghana: its
       organization and function," Doctoral Dissertation, Birming-
       ham University, 1970.   320 p.
           The author is Professor of Political Science, Makarere
       University, Uganda.

3398   Coleman, James S.   "A Survey of selected literature on the
       government and politics of British West Africa," Amer.
       Pol. Sci. Rev., XLIX (Dec. 1955), 1130-55.

3399   Craig, J. A.   "Ghana's general election," World Today, XXV
       (Oct. 1969), 428-36.

3400   Cruise O'Brien, Conor.   "Two addresses."   In Conor Cruise
       O'Brien.   Writers and Politics.   New York: Pantheon
       Books, 1965, pp. 239-59.
           The former Vice-Chancellor of the University of Ghana,
       in these two addresses on Ghana, stresses the need to in-
       sulate institutions of higher learning from political con-
       tagion with which the University of Ghana was infected
       during the Nkrumah regime.

3401   Cudjoe, Seth D.   Aids to African autonomy: a review of
       education and politics in the Gold Coast.   London: College
       Press, 1950.   62 p.

3402   Dei-Anang, Michael.   Ghana resurgent.   Accra: Waterville,
       1964.   248 p.
           A political and social history of Ghana.

3403   Dove, G. F. K.   "The Political philosophy of Kwame Nkrumah,"
       Master's Thesis, Howard University, 1955.   87 p.

3404   Dowse, Robert E.   "Ghana: one party or totalitarian?"   Brit.
       J. Soc., XVIII (Sept. 1967), 251-68.

3405   Drake, St. C.   "Prospects for democracy in the Gold Coast,"
       Ann. Amer. Acad. Pol. Soc. Sci., CCCVI (July 1956),
       78-87.

3406   _____.   "Traditional authority and social action in former
       British West Africa," Human Organization, XIX (Fall 1960),
       150-8.

3407   Dubois, Victor D.   Military rule and its repercussions in
       West Africa.   New York: American Universities Field
       Staff, 1969.   (West African series, v. 12, no. 6.)

3408   Dumor, E. E.   "Legitimacy and political participation [in
       Ghana], 1949-1960," Master's Thesis, University of Ghana,
       1969.

3409 Duodu, Cameron. "Ghana since Nkrumah," Listener, LXXVIII
      (Oct. 19, 1967), 499-500.

3410 Dzirasa, Stephen. Political thought of Dr. Kwame Nkrumah.
      Accra: Guinea Press, 1962. 133 p.

3411 Edu, John E. The Amazing story of the C. P. P.   Accra:
      New Gold Coast Publishing Co., 1954. 47 p.

3412 Effah-Apenteng, Victor. "Gold Coast politics: the federalist
      agitation, 1954-57," Master's Thesis, University of Ghana,
      1970.

3413 Efrat, E. S. "The Application of federalism to emergent
      states in West Africa," Doctoral Dissertation, University
      of Texas, 1961.

3414 Erzuah, J. B. "Comparative study of constitutional and
      administrative structures in Ghana," Civilisations, XIV,
      Nos. 1-2 (1964), 85-91.
      Summary in French.

3415 Esseks, John D. "Government and indigenous private enter-
      prise in Ghana," J. Mod. Afr. Stud., IX (May 1971), 11-
      29.

3416 _____. "Political independence and economic decoloniza-
      tion; the case of Ghana under Nkrumah," Western Pol. Q.,
      XXIV (March 1971), 59-64.

3417 Fagen, Richard. "Politics and communication in the new
      states: Burma and Ghana," Doctoral Dissertation, New
      York University, 1963.

3418 Feit, Edward. "Military coups and political development:
      some lessons from Ghana and Nigeria," World Politics,
      XX (Jan. 1968), 179-93.

3419 _____. "The Rule of the 'iron surgeons' military govern-
      ment in Spain and Ghana," Comp. Pol., I (July 1969),
      485-97.

3420 Finlay, David J. "Students and politics in Ghana,"
      Daedelus (Winter 1968), 51-69.

3421 Fitch, Bob and Mary Oppenheimer. Ghana: end of an illu-
      sion. New York: Monthly Review Press, 1966. 130 p.
      A readable, analytical political history of Ghana, de-
      lineating the events leading to the overthrow of Nkrumah in
      February 1966, and exploding several long-existing myths
      about the recent political history of Ghana.
      Rev: Amer. Pol. Sci. Rev., LXI (Sept. 1967), 827.

J. Asian Afr. Stud., II (July/Oct. 1967), 279-80.

3422   Folson, Kweku. "An African tragedy: Kwame Nkrumah and
       Mr. Bing (Q. C.)," Encounter, XXXIII (July 1969), 35-43.

3423   Garigue, P. "An Anthropological interpretation of changing
       political leadership in West Africa," Doctoral Dissertation,
       London University, 1952/53.

3424   Garrison, Lloyd. "Portrait of Nkrumah as dictator," N.Y.
       Times Magazine (May 3, 1964), 15, 108-11.
       Considers Nkrumah's government as autocratic and
       resentful of the U.S.

3425   Ghana. Commission on Regional Assemblies. Regional
       assemblies. Accra: Govt. Printer, 1958. 228 p.

3426   Ghana. Ministry of Information. Osagyefo President Kwame
       Nkrumah makes plea for political union of Africa at Addis
       Ababa (Ethiopia) Summit Conference, May 24, 1963. 18 p.

3427   _____. The Rebirth of Ghana; the end of tyranny. Accra,
       1966. 56 p.
       The overthrow of the Nkrumah regime on February 24,
       1966 considered as an end to dictatorship in Ghana. In-
       cludes proclamations, biographies, broadcasts and state-
       ments by the new government leaders.

3428   "The Gold Coast general election, 1951," J. Afr. Adm.
       (April 1951), 65-77.

3429   Goody, John Rankine. "Consensus and dissent in Ghana,"
       Pol. Sci. Q., LXXXIII (Sept. 1968), 337-52.

3430   Grundy, Kenneth. "Theories and ideologies of West African
       underdevelopment and development," Doctoral Dissertation,
       Pennsylvania State University, 1963.

3431   Gutteridge, William. "Military elites in Nigeria and Ghana,"
       African Forum, II (Summer 1966), 36-41.

3432   Hailey, Lord. Native administration in the British African
       territories, Part 3: West Africa, Nigeria, Gold Coast,
       Sierra Leone, and Gambia. London: H. M. S. O., 1950-3.
       5 v.

3433   Harris, R. L. "The Effects of political change on the role
       set of the senior bureaucrats in Ghana and Nigeria," Adm.
       Sci. Quarterly, XIII (Dec. 1968), 386-401.

3434   Hatch, John. "Policies and politics in the Gold Coast,"
       Africa South, I (Oct. /Dec. 1956), 107-15.

3435 Hoepli, Nancy L., ed. West Africa Today. New York:
      H. W. Wilson, 1971. 197 p. (The reference shelf Vol.
      42, No. 6.)
         Excerpts almost entirely from newspapers and periodicals,
      topically grouped. Contents include West Africa comes of
      age, --The politics of independence, --Nigeria: secession
      and survival, --West Africa's economy, --Africa, the United
      States and the future. Each selection is preceded by
      editor's introduction.

3436 Huntington, Samuel P. "Political development and political
      decay," World Politics, XVII (April 1965), 386-403.

3437 _____. Political order in changing societies. New Haven:
      Yale University Press, 1968. 488 p.
         Written under the auspices of the Center for Political
      Affairs, Harvard University, and delivered in part as the
      Henry L. Stimson Lectures, Yale University.

3438 Huxley, Elspeth. "Rope that hanged Nkrumah," National
      Review, XVIII (March 22, 1966), 268-70.

3439 Ikoku, Samuel G. Le Ghana de Nkrumah. Trans. from the
      English by Yves Bénot. Paris: Maspero, 1971. 244 p.
      (Cahiers libres, 197-198.)

3440 "J. A. Ankrah." In Paul Sigmund, ed. Ideologies of the
      developing nations. New York: Praeger, 1967, pp. 262-8.
         An excerpt from the broadcast of Lt. General Joseph
      Ankrah to the nation 4 days after the fall of Nkrumah, con-
      tained in The Rebirth of Ghana--the end of tyranny (1966).

3441 Jenkins, Amelia V. "The Role of culture and power conflict
      in the development of the African state of Ghana," Doctoral
      Dissertation, New York University, 1962.

3442 Jordon, Robert S. Government and power in West Africa.
      New York: Africana Publishing Corp., 1969. 336 p.

3443 Katako, Joseph Yao. "Education and training of civil ser-
      vants in the governments of Ghana and the United States
      of America: a comparative study," Doctoral Dissertation,
      Syracuse University, 1970. 339 p.

3444 Kay, Geoffrey and S. Hymer. Political economy of coloni-
      alism in Ghana: a collection of documents and statistics,
      1900-1960. New York: Cambridge University Press, 1972.

3445 Keller, Gerda. "Die politischen Einrichtungen der Ewe in
      Togo und ihre Beeinflussung durch die Goldküste." Phil. F.,
      Berlin, 1944.

3446   Kerstiens, Thom.   The New elite in Asia and Africa: a
       comparative study of Indonesia and Ghana.   New York:
       Praeger, 1966.   282 p.
          Rev: Choice, III (Nov. 1966), 821.

3447   Kilson, Martin.   "Elite cleavage in African politics: the case
       of Ghana, " J. Int. Affairs, XXIV, No. 1 (1970), 75-83.

3448   _____.   Tensions and dynamics of African single-party
       systems: case of the erstwhile Convention People's Party.
       Cambridge: Dept. of Government, Harvard University,
       1968.   12 p.

3449   Kimble, David.   The Machinery of self-government.   London:
       Penguin Books, 1953.   124 p.   (Penguin's West African
       series.)

3450   Kotei, S. I. A.   "Politics and government in West Africa: a
       select annotated bibliography, 1955-1965; Vol. 1: political
       processes.   Vol. 2: government, " Master's Thesis, Univer-
       sity of Ghana, 1966.   2 v.

3451   Kraus, Jon G.   "Ghana: the coup as mechanism of political
       change, "   Paper presented at the 9th Annual Meeting of
       the African Studies Association, Bloomington, Indiana Uni-
       versity, 26-29 October, 1966.
          Examination of the work of the Military Government and
       its pledge to hand over power rapidly to a democratically
       constituted civilian government.

3452   _____.   "Ghana without Nkrumah--II: the men in charge, "
       Africa Report, XI (April 1966), 16-20.
          The military officers and other participants of the coup
       that ousted Nkrumah from office.

3453   _____.   "Ghana's new 'corporate parliament, '" Africa
       Report, X (Aug. 1965), 6-11.
          Political changes between 1956 and 1965.

3454   Leader, Shelah Gilbert.   "Military professionalism, inter-
       vention and the disposition to intervene in Ghana and Mali, "
       Doctoral Dissertation, State University of New York, 1971.
       234 p.
          Contends that African army officers generally are
       professional by western standards and that their elite self-
       image which induces them to oust politicians and rule in
       their place is their most professional quality.

3455   Lefever, Ernest W.   Spear and scepter: army, police and
       politics in tropical Africa.   New York: Brookings Insti-
       tute, 1971.

3456   Legum, Colin. "Ghana's return to democracy," Round Table,
       LX (Jan. 1970), 27-33.

3457   Lejeune, E. "Principes et limites du Nkrumahisme,"
       Remarques Africaines (Bruxelles), VIII, No. 268 (1966),
       232-45.

3458   "Letter on the Ghana coup that overthrew K. Nkrumah govern-
       ment in 1966," Freedomways, VI (Spring 1966), 152-8.

3459   Lewis, W. Arthur. Politics in West Africa. New York:
       Oxford University Press, 1965. 98 p.
       Analysis of the power structure in 13 independent West
       African states.
       Rev: Africa Report, XI (June 1966), 64. Amer. Pol.
       Sci. Rev., LXI (Dec. 1967), 115.

3460   McQuade, L. C. "The Showplace of black Africa," Yale Re-
       view, XLIX (Dec. 1959), 215-29.

3461   MacRae, D. G. "Nkrumahism: past and future of an ide-
       ology," Govt. Opp., I (July/Sept. 1966), 535-45.

3462   Mair, L. P. "Traditional authorities in Gold Coast local
       government," West Africa, No. 2023 (1955), 1140-1.

3463   Manu, Yaw. "The Transformation of internal political
       power in Ghana," Doctoral Dissertation, New York Univer-
       sity, 1965. 298 p.
       Reviews the role of chieftaincy, the traditional structure
       of authority in Ghana, in the light of the existing political
       parties.

3464   Markovitz, Irving. "Ghana without Nkrumah--I: the winter
       of discontent," Africa Report, XI (April 1966), 10-15.
       The reasons for the coup against Nkrumah.

3465   Marvin, D. K. "A Conceptual scheme for use in study of
       African political systems in transition," Doctoral Disserta-
       tion, Northwestern University, 1957.

3466   Mercier, Paul. "On the meaning of tribalism in black Africa."
       In Pierre L. Van den Berghe, ed. Africa: social prob-
       lems of change and conflict. San Francisco: Chandler,
       1965, pp. 483-501.

3467   Miller, Norman W. "The Political survival of traditional
       leadership," J. Mod. Afr. Stud., VI (Aug. 1968), 183-98.

3468   Munger, Edwin S. African field reports, 1952-1961. Cape
       Town: Struik, 1961. 808 p.
       The reports of the American Universities Field Staff.

3469 Newbury, Colin. The West African Commonwealth. Durham:
      Duke University Press, 1964. 106 p.

3470 Nkrumah, Kwame. Class struggle in Africa. New York:
      International Publishers, 1970. 96 p.
         Attributes most of the African political problems to
      foreign interests, opposes the growth of an African middle
      class and denounces neo-colonialism.
         Rev: Library J., XCVI (March 1, 1971), 841.

3471 _____. "Nkrumah's goals for Ghana: address, Dec. 22,
      1961," Africa Report, VII (Jan. 1962), 13-14+.

3472 _____. Politics are not for soldiers: an address by
      Kwame Nkrumah to cadets of the military academy.
      Accra: Govt. Printer, 1961.

3473 Nwani, Okonkwo. "Economics and politics in modern Africa
      --and the fall of Nkrumah," Negro Digest, XVIII (May
      1969), 35-41+.

3474 Nwanodi, N. "Problems of elections and representation in
      British West African colonies," B. Litt.'s Thesis, Oxford
      University, 1957/58.

3475 Nyalander, C. T. "Ghana--my country; address," Canadian
      Geogr. J., LXIV (April 1962), 134-46.

3476 Ocran, A. K. A Myth is broken: an account of the Ghana
      coup d'état of 24th February 1966. New York: Humanities
      Press, 1969. 104 p.

3477 Omari, T. Peter. Kwame Nkrumah: the anatomy of an
      African dictatorship. Preface by Justice Nii Amaa Ollenu.
      New York: Africana Publishing Corp., 1970. 229 p.
      Bibliography.
         A penetrating study of Nkrumah, the man, his policies
      and his political methods, providing at the same time a
      lucid account of the constitutional and political history of
      the Gold Coast colony and the emergence of the elite.
         Rev: Choice, VIII (July 1971), 720. Library J.,
      XCVI (May 15, 1971), 1718.

3478 Osei, G. K. The Spirit and the structure of Nkrumah's Con-
      vention People's Party. London: The Author, 1962. 48 p.

3479 Owusu, Maxwell. Uses and abuses of political power: a
      case study of continuity and change in the politics of
      Ghana. Chicago: University of Chicago Press, 1970.
      364 p.
         Rev: Africa Report, XVI (Oct. 1971), 36.

3480 Owusu, Seth Amoako. "Political institutions of the coastal
      areas of the Gold Coast as influenced by European contact,"
      Doctoral Dissertation, University of Chicago, 1954.

3481 Page, Bruce. "Messiah and mug," Sunday Times Magazine
      (March 5, 1967), 6-17.
      On Kwame Nkrumah.

3482 Parenti, Michael. "Ethnic politics and the persistence of
      ethnic identification," Amer. Pol. Sci. Rev., LXI (Sept.
      1967), 717-26.

3483 Passin, Herbert and K. A. Jones-Quartey, eds. Africa:
      the dynamics of change. Ibadan: Ibadan University Press,
      1963. 262 p.

3484 Paterson, Adolphus A. "Why Africa needs a free press,"
      Africa Report, XVI (April 1971), 22-4.
      The Ghanaian journalist stresses the educational role
      of the press, especially the newspapers in a democratic
      state, and argues that the freedom of the press is impos-
      sible when controlled by the government, as was the case
      in Ghana during the Nkrumah regime.

3485 "Personalities and politics in Ghana: 3," West Africa, No.
      2714 (June 7, 1969), 635.
      Speculations about the possible candidates to assume
      the civilian leadership on the military's surrender of
      power.

3486 "Philosophers and kings: studies in leadership," Daedalus,
      XCVII, No. 3 (1968), 683-1082.
      Includes studies on Bismarck, de Gaulle, Gandhi, New-
      ton and Nkrumah.

3487 Price, J. H. "How democracy works in Ghana," Universitas,
      IV, No. 4 (1960), 105-6.

3488 Price, Robert M. "Military officers and political leadership:
      the Ghanaian case," Comp. Pol., III (April 1971), 361-
      79.

3489 Reitsch, Hanna. Ich flog für Kwame Nkrumah. Munich:
      Lehman, 1968. 219 p.

3490 Roberts, Margaret. "Ghana's three power groups: The Na-
      tional Liberation Council under General Ankrah, the United
      Party under Dr. K. A. Busia and the businessmen's--
      politicians' alliance under Komla Gbedemah," Venture
      (May 1968), 15-18.

3491 Rothenberg, Georg. "Das Experiment Ghana, " Zukunft, Nos.
      9-10 (1967), 29-33.

3492 Royal Institute of International Affairs. Ghana: a brief
      political and economic survey. London, 1957. 65 p.

3493 Sadler, J. R. "West Africa: searches for stability, " Mili-
      tary Review, XLIX (Nov. 1969), 28-38.

3494 Sale, J. Kirk. "Loneliness and Kwame Nkrumah, " N. Y.
      Times Magazine (June 27, 1965), 20-2+.

3495 Sanders, Charles L. "Kwame Nkrumah: the fall of a
      Messiah, " Ebony, XXI (Sept. 1966), 138-46.

3496 Sarpong, Peter. "Tribalism and national unity, " Insight
      and Opinion, III, No. 4 (1968), 11-15.

3497 Schacter, Ruth. "Single party systems in West Africa, "
      Amer. Pol. Sci. Rev. , LV (June 1961), 294-307.

3498 Segbawu, Courage M. K. "Some political ideas of Kwame
      Nkrumah, " Master's Thesis, University of Ghana, 1968.

3499 Shram, John R. "Chieftaincy and politics in independent
      Ghana, " Master's Thesis, University of Ghana, 1967.
      102 p.

3500 Sigmund, P. "Nkrumah, Charisma fails, " Commonweal,
      LXXXIV (April 1, 1966), 50-2.

3501 Snowiss, Leo M. "Democracy and control in a changing
      society: the case of Ghana, " Doctoral Dissertation, Uni-
      versity of Chicago, 1960.
          Examines the intensive use of ideology and control of
      voluntary organizations by the Ghanaian Government to
      preserve political stability at a period of rapid social
      change and economic advancement.

3502 Sodipo, J. O. "Aristotle's doctrine of the evolution of society
      with special reference to the First Book of the Politics;
      together with a consideration of the relevance of this doc-
      trine to recent developments of communities in West Africa, "
      Doctoral Dissertation, Durham University, 1964.
          The author is Professor and Head, Dept. of Religious
      Studies and Philosophy, University of Ife, Nigeria, and editor
      of Second Order; an African Journal of Philosophy.

3503 Soglo, N. Essai de typologie des systems politiques pre-
      coloniaux en Afrique occidentale. Paris: Faculté de
      Droit et de Sciences, Université de Paris, 1969.
          A legal and historical study of the political societies of
      pre-colonial West Africa.

3504 The Spark Accra. Eds. Some essentials of Nkrumaism.
      London: Panaf Books, 1970.

3505 Symonds, Richard. The British and their successors: a
      study in the development of the government services in the
      new states. Evanston: Northwestern University Press,
      1966. 286 p.

3506 Taylor, Don. Africa: the portrait of power. London:
      Robert Hale, 1967. 191 p.

3507 Tiger, Lionel Samuel. "Bureaucracy and charisma in
      Ghana, " J. Asian Afr. Stud., I (Jan. 1966), 13-26.

3508 _____. "Bureaucracy in Ghana and the civil service, "
      Doctoral Dissertation, London University, 1962. 313 p.

3509 _____. "Ghana: a charismatic nation, " Current History,
      XLV (1963), 335-40.

3510 _____. "Nkrumah's Ghana and the theory of charisma, "
      Bull. Afr. Stud. Canada, II, No. 1 (Nov. 1964), 2-10.

3511 Timothy, E. Bankole. Kwame Nkrumah: his rise to power.
      With a foreword by Kojo Botsio. London: Allen & Unwin,
      1955. 201 p.
      Rev: TLS (Jan. 6, 1956), 4.

3512 Tixier, G. "Le parti de la Convention du Peuple du Ghana, "
      Penaut, LXXIV, No. 701 (1964), 167-78.

3513 Turner, G. C. "Color rulers: Kwame Nkrumah, " Negro
      Hist. Bull., XXV (March 1, 1962), 136-7.

3514 "Twelve years of Ghana, " West Africa, No. 2700 (March 1,
      1969), 229-30.
      Reviews Ghana's economic and political conditions
      from 1957 to March 6, 1969.

3515 Van Lare, William Bedford. The Rise and fall of Kwame
      Nkrumah and its impact on the rest of Africa. Accra:
      Ghana State Publishing Corp., 1967. 30 p.
      A speech originally delivered before the United Nations
      Club of Queen's University, Kingston, Ontario, on March 1,
      1967.

3516 Vanhanen, Tatu. "On the conditions of multi-party system in
      ten Commonwealth countries, " J. Commonwealth Pol. Stud.,
      VIII, No. 1 (1970), 40-53.
      A study of the success and failure of the British Parlia-
      mentary procedure in India, Pakistan, Ceylon, Ghana, Ma-
      laysia, Nigeria, Tanzania, Jamaica, Trinidad and Tobago
      and Uganda.

3517 Wallerstein, I. "Ghana as a model," Africa Report, XII
      (May 1967), 43-6.

3518 Ward, William Ernest. Government in West Africa. London:
      Allen & Unwin, 1965. 269 p.

3519 _____. "Tribalism in Ghana: tribalism is unlikely to
      trouble the new regime in Ghana," Venture, XVIII (June
      1966), 22-6.
      An overly optimistic observation belied by the subsequent
      political events in Ghana.

3520 Weiner, Myron. "Political integration and political develop-
      ment," Ann. Amer. Acad. Pol. Soc. Sci. (March 1965),
      52-64.

3521 Welch, Claude E. "Ghana: the politics of military with-
      drawal," Current History, LIV (Feb. 1968), 95-100.

3522 _____. "The Growth of political consciousness among the
      Ewe," Paper presented at the Meeting of the American
      Anthropological Association, November 1965.
      With emphasis on immediate post-World War II period,
      he examines the factors conducive to the political awaken-
      ing of the Ewe people of Togo and Southeastern Ghana.

3523 _____. "Return to civilian rule in Ghana," Current His-
      tory, LVI (May 1969), 286-91.
      On September 29, 1969 the National Liberation Council
      handed over power to a democratically constituted govern-
      ment, which ironically was deposed by another military
      coup on January 13, 1972.

3524 _____. "Shifting authority in West Africa," Current His-
      tory, L (March 1966), 153-8.
      Analysis of the different methods employed by the leaders
      of 14 independent West African states to promote national
      unity and economic development.

3525 Wolfinger, Raymond E. "The Development and persistence
      of ethnic voting," Amer. Pol. Sci. Rev., LIX (Dec. 1965),
      896-908.

3526 Wright, George. "Comparison of the function of the press
      of Ghana and Nigeria," Thesis for a certificate, Institute
      of African Studies, Columbia University, 1966.
      A comparative study of the historical development of
      the press in both countries, 1850-1945 and its relationship
      to the existing political structures.

3527 Zolberg, Aristide. Creating political order: the party states
      of West Africa. Chicago: Rand McNally, 1966. 168 p.

(Studies in political change.)
Rev: Amer. Pol. Sci. Rev., LIX (Sept. 1967), 820.
World Politics, XX (Oct. 1967), 128.

3528 _____. "Patterns of national integration," J. Mod. Afr.
Stud., V (Dec. 1967), 449-67.

3529 _____. "Structure of political conflict in the new states
of tropical Africa," Amer. Pol. Sci. Rev., LXII (March
1968), 70-87.

(14) POLITICAL SCIENCE--FOREIGN POLICY

3530 Addo, Max. Ghana's foreign policy in retrospect. Accra:
Waterville, 1967. 49 p.

3531 Adu, A. L. "Post-colonial relationships: some factors in
the attitudes of African states," African Affairs, LXVI
(1967), 295-309.
The common desire of black African states for economic development, political and internal social stability,
and their united front against the white supremacist South
Africa are conducive to African unity.

3532 All African people's conference: speeches by the Prime Minister of Ghana at the opening and closing sessions on
December 8th and 13th, 1958. Accra: Govt. Printer, 1958.

3533 Amamoo, Joseph G. "Ghana and the western democracies,"
African Affairs, LVIII (Jan. 1959), 54-60.
Ghana's relations with African and non-African nations
following her independence on March 6, 1957.

3534 Armah, Kwesi. Africa's golden road. With a foreword by
Jomo Kenyatta. London: Heinemann, 1965. 292 p.
A discussion of Nkrumah's political philosophy and
policies--the one-party system, non-alignment and unitary
continental African State--by Ghana's former High Com-
missioner in London.
Rev: Amer. Pol. Sci. Rev., LXI (March 1967), 210.
TLS (March 17, 1966), 227.

3535 Austin, Dennis. "The Uncertain frontiers: Ghana--Togo,"
J. Mod. Afr. Stud., I (June 1963), 139-45.

3536 Beichman, Arnold. "Western socialists and Ghana," Transition (April/May 1967), 28-9.

3537 Binder-Krauthoff, Kristine. Phasen der Entkolonialisierung
eine Analyse kolonial--politischer Relikte in Afrika auf der
Grundlage historischer Prozesse in Ghana und der

<u>Elfenbeinküste</u>.   Berlin: Duncker & Humblot, 1970.   185 p.

3538   Busia, Kofi Abrefa.   <u>The Challenge of Africa.</u>   New York:
       Praeger, 1962.   150 p.
           Four basic challenges in Africa--"challenge of culture,
       colonial experience, common humanity and morality, and
       responsible emancipation."
           Rev: <u>Library J.</u>, LXXXVII (Dec. 15, 1962), 4554.

3539   Cone, L. Winston.   "Ghana's African and world relations,"
       <u>India Quarterly</u>, XVII (July/Sept. 1961), 258-76.

3540   Crutcher, John Richard.   "Political authority in Ghana and
       Tanzania: the Nkrumah and Nyerere regimes," Doctoral
       Dissertation, University of Notre Dame, 1968.   510 p.
           A comparative study of the two socialist systems,
       noting how each is trying to reconcile African tradition
       with the modernity of the colonial masters.

3541   Debrah, E. M.   "Understanding Ghana," <u>Social Science,</u>
       XXXVI (1961), 231-8.

3542   _____.   "Will most uncommitted nations remain uncom-
       mitted?" Ann. Amer. Acad. Pol. Soc. Sci., CCCXXXVI
       (July 1961), 83-97.
           An address, April 15, 1961, with questions and answers.

3543   DeLancey, Mark W.   "The Ghana-Guinea-Mali Union: a bib-
       liographic essay," <u>Afr. Stud. Bull.</u>, IX (Sept. 1966), 35-
       51.
           The Union of Independent African States (UIAS) founded
       in 1958 comprising the three states was declared void in
       1963 by Guinean President Sekou Touré.

3544   "Dr. Nkrumah and the Americans," <u>Tablet,</u> CCXIV (Dec. 31,
       1960), 1210.

3545   Dowse, Robert E.   <u>Modernization in Ghana and the U. S. S. R.:</u>
       <u>a comparative study.</u>   New York: Humanities Press, 1969.
       107 p.   (Library of political studies series.)
           Rev: <u>Choice,</u> VI (Jan. 1970), 1656. <u>TLS</u> (Sept. 4,
       1969), 972.

3546   Drake, St. Clair.   "Nkrumah's advisor backs 'dynamic na-
       tionalism' as alternative to communism in Africa," <u>Africa</u>
       <u>Special Report,</u> III (April 1958), 5-8.
           The West Indian writer and theoretician, George Pad-
       more, whose prolific writings on Pan-Africanism helped
       shape Ghanaian domestic and foreign policies was Nkrumah's
       Advisor on African Affairs.   Strongly critical of Commu-
       nism and equally distrustful of the western tradition, he
       urges Pan-Africanism as an "ideological alternative to

Communism on the one side and tribalism on the other."
An excellent article reflecting the political views of both
Padmore and Nkrumah.

3547 Du Bois, W. E. B.   The World and Africa: an inquiry into
the part which Africa has played in world history.   Enl.
ed.   New York: International Publications Service, 1965.
352 p.

3548 Duignan, Peter.   "Pan-Africanism: a bibliographic essay, "
African Forum, I (Summer 1965), 105-7.
An essay in three phases: The American reaction to
racism, 1900-1945; Pan-Africanism, 1945-1958; The dream
of continental unity after Ghanaian independence in 1957.

3549 Folson, B. G. D.   "The Communist view of colonialism--an
African interpretation. "   In K. London, ed.   New nations
in a divided world.   New York: Praeger, 1964, pp. 45-56.

3550 "Ghana, Guinea, Mali formalize their union, " Africa Report,
VI (Aug. 1961), 11.
The formalization of the charter of the Union of African
States comprising the three nations in November 1958.

3551 "Ghana and the Commonwealth: the politics of a single-party
state, " Round Table (Dec. 1964), 30-9.

3552 "Ghana's collusion with imperialism, " Curr. Dig. Soviet Pr. ,
XIX (Dec. 6, 1967), 17-18.
Critical of the military leaders that ousted Nkrumah for
their anti-Soviet attitudes.

3553 Mazrui, Ali.   "Nkrumah: the Leninist Czar, " Transition,
VI, No. 26 (1966), 9-17.

3554 Megahed, H. T.   Socialism and nation-building in Africa: the
case of Mali, 1960-68.   Budapest: Centre for Afro-Asian
Research, Hungarian Academy of Sciences, 1970.   41 p.

3555 Meyers, Albert J.   "Back from the brink of communism in
Ghana... " U. S. News and World Report, LXI (Aug. 22,
1966), 88-9.
Praises the military that toppled the Nkrumah regime
for its efforts to restore sound economic policy for Ghana
and stamp out any Communist traces from the country.

3556 Mohan, Jitendra.   "Ghana, the Congo and the United Nations, "
J. Mod. Afr. Stud. , VII (Oct. 1969), 369-406.

3557 Newbury, Colin W.   "Military intervention and political
change in West Africa, " Africa Quarterly, VII (Oct. /Dec.
1967), 215-21.

3558 Nkrumah, Kwame. Africa must unite. New York: Praeger,
      1963. 229 p.
          The Ghanaian President until February 1966 presents
      his program for political and economic union of Africa.
          Rev: N.Y. Times Bk. Rev. (Oct. 27, 1963), 24. TLS
      (June 28, 1963), 469.

3559 _____. "African prospect," Foreign Affairs, XXXVII
      (1958), 45-53.

3560 _____. "Ali Mazrui's Nkrumah: a case of neo-colonial
      scholarship," Freedomways, VII (Spring 1967), 170-4.

3561 _____. Challenge of the Congo. New York: International
      Publishers, 1967. 304 p.
          Charges that the foreign interference in the Congo con-
      tinued even after independence.
          Rev: Sat. Rev., L (March 25, 1967), 28.

3562 _____. Consciencism, philosophy and ideology for de-
      colonization. Rev. ed. New York: Monthly Review
      Press, 1970. 122 p. 1st ed. 1965.
          Rev: Freedomways, VI (Winter 1966), 53-9. Negro
      Digest, XIV (June 1965), 51-2.

3563 _____. Dark days in Ghana. New ed. New York: In-
      ternational Publishers, 1969. 219 p. 1st ed. 1968.
          States that the military coup that deposed him was
      counter-revolutionary, inspired by imperialists and a
      serious tactical set-back to African revolutionary struggle
      to divest itself of all vestiges of colonialism.
          Rev: West Africa, No. 2666 (July 6, 1968), 776.

3564 _____. "Dawn of a united Africa," Negro Digest, XIII
      (Nov. 1963), 86-91.

3565 _____. Hands off Africa: some famous speeches with a
      tribute to George Padmore. Accra: Ministry of Local
      Govt., 1960. 62 p.

3566 _____. Towards colonial freedom: Africa in the struggle
      against world imperialism. London: Heinemann, 1962.
      45 p.
          A collection of his political writings while a student in
      the U.S. in 1942, published as result of his subsequent
      racial experiences in Britain in 1945.

3567 _____. Voice from Conakry. London: Panaf Publications,
      1967. 73 p.
          Broadcasts, made to the Ghanaian people between March
      and December 1966 on Radio Guinea's "Voice of Revolution,"
      attempt to vindicate Nkrumah's regime, attributing the first

coup to the machinations of "local reactionaries, imperialists and neo-colonialists" and urge his compatriots to resist the military rule.

3568 _____. "What Nkrumah said to the U.S. Senate." In Langston Hughes, ed. An African Treasury: articles, essays and poems. New York: Crown, 1960, pp. 75-6.

3569 _____. "The White man's future in Africa," Negro Digest, X (June 1961), 36-41.

3570 "Nkrumah's school for subversion," Atlas, XII (Dec. 1966), 20-2.
    The Military Government's claim to be in possession of some documents on Nkrumah's plan to subvert all of Africa with the aid of some Chinese trained agents.

3571 O'Connell, James. "Senghor, Nkrumah and Azikiwe: unity and diversity in the West African state," Nigerian J. Econ. Soc. Stud., V, No. 1 (1963), 77-93.

3572 Padmore, George. Africa and world peace. London: Secker & Warburg, 1937. 285 p.

3573 _____. Africa: Britain's empire. London: Dobson, 1949. 266 p.

3574 _____. "Pan-Africanism and Ghana," United Asia, IX, No. 1 (1957), 50-4.

3575 _____. Pan-Africanism or Communism? The coming struggle for Africa. London: Dobson, 1956. 463 p.

3576 Phillips, John. Kwame Nkrumah and the future of Africa. New York: Praeger, 1960. 272 p.

3577 Pirro, Ellen. "A Computer analysis of African political ideology: Ghana and Guinea," Doctoral Dissertation, Yale University, 1968. 559 p.
    The study, based on Kwame Nkrumah and Sekou Touré, indicates Ghana's political approach was pragmatic and Guinea's idealistic.

3578 Price, R.M. "Theoretical approach to military rule in new States: reference-group theory and the Ghanaian case," World Politics, XXIII (April 1971), 399-430.

3579 Quaison-Sackey, Alex. "Africa and United Nations: observations of a Ghanaian diplomat," African Forum, I (Summer 1965), 53-68.

3580 _____. Africa unbound: reflections of an African statesman. With a foreword by Dr. Kwame Nkrumah. London:
Deutsch, 1963. 174 p.
   A lucid but autobiographical attempt to expound "African
personality" by Ghana's former Permanent Representative
to the United Nations and U. N. General Assembly President.
   Rev: Ann. Amer. Acad. Pol. Soc. Sci., CCCLI (Jan.
1964), 227. Library J., LXXXVIII (July 1963), 2712.

3581 Reed, David. "Ghana: Communism's new foothold in Africa, "
Readers' Digest, LXXXV (July 1964), 202-7+.

3582 Schildkrout, E. "Strangers and local government in Kumasi, "
J. Mod. Afr. Stud., VIII (July 1970), 251-69.

3583 Skurnik, W. A. E. , ed. African political thought, Lumumba,
Nkrumah and Touré. Denver: University of Denver, 1968.
147 p. (Monograph series in World Affairs, nos. 3 & 4.)
"The Political ideology of Nkrumah, " by K. W. Grundy.

3584 _____. "Ghana and Guinea, 1966: a case study in inter-
African relations, " J. Mod. Afr. Stud., V (Nov. 1967),
369-84.
   Despite both countries' abortive political entente in 1958,
their relations have deteriorated since the fall of Nkrumah
in February 1966, who lived in self-imposed exile in
Guinea until his death on April 27, 1972.

3585 Stahn, E. Kommunistische Modelle fur Afrika? Ghana und
Guinea. Hanover: Verlag fur Literatur und Zeitgeschehen,
1964. 192 p.

3586 Thompson, Vincent Bakpetu. Africa and unity: the evolution
of Pan-Africanism. With a foreword by Basil Davidson.
London: Longman, 1969. 412 p.
   A study of the African efforts at political and economic
unity by a Nigerian scholar.
   Rev: African Affairs, LXX (Jan. 1971), 84-5. Amer.
Hist. Rev., LXXV (Oct. 1970), 1755.

3587 Thompson, Willard Scott. Ghana's foreign policy 1957-65:
diplomacy, ideology and the new state. Princeton: Princeton University Press, 1969. 462 p.
   Rev: African Affairs, LXX (April 1971), 185-6. West
Africa, No. 2741 (Dec. 13, 1969), 1509-11.

3588 _____. "Ghana's foreign policy under military rule, "
Africa Report, XIV (May/June 1969), 8-13.

3589 _____. "New directions in Ghana, " Africa Report, XI
(Nov. 1966), 18-22.
   Specifies the goals of the Military Government that

toppled Nkrumah, emphasizing its future foreign policy.

3590 _____. "Non-alignment in the third world: the record of Ghana," Orbis, II (Winter 1968), 1233-55.

3591 U. S. Congress. Senate. Committee on the Judiciary. Sub-committee to Investigate the Administration of the Internal Security Act and other Internal Security Laws. Ghana students in the United States oppose U. S. aid to Nkrumah; staff conferences Aug. 29, 1963 and Jan. 11, 1964. With an introduction by Senator Thomas J. Dodd. Washington, D. C., 1964. 104 p. (88th Congress, 2nd session.)

3592 _____. Is U. S. money aiding another communist state? Hearing, Dec. 3, 1962. Testimony of K. A. Busia. Washington, D. C., 1963. 165 p.
A hearing on Nkrumah's socialist ideas and communist associations.

3593 Warner, D. Ghana and the new Africa. London: Muller, 1960. 181 p.

3594 Waterman, Peter. "Marxist critiques of Nkrumah's Ghana," Nigerian Opinion, VII, Nos. 7-9 (1971), 85-8.

3595 Welch, Claude E. Dream of unity: pan-Africanism and political unification in West Africa. Ithaca, New York: Cornell University Press, 1966. 396 p.
Examines the four attempts to form political unions between English- and French-speaking West African countries, namely the Ewe unification movement; the formation of the Federal Republic of Cameroon; "Senegambia"; and the Ghana-Guinea-Mali "Union of African States."
Rev: Amer. Hist. Rev., LXXII (Jan. 1967), 657.
Amer. Pol. Sci. Rev., LXI (Sept. 1967), 839.

3596 Zartman, Ira William. International relations in the new Africa. London: Prentice-Hall, 1966. 175 p.
The intra-African relations of Northern and Western states of Africa, with special reference to their policy decision-making machinery, foreign policy experiments and their basic goals.
Rev: Choice, III (Dec. 1966), 962.

3597 _____. "The Politics of boundaries in North and West Africa," J. Mod. Afr. Stud., III, No. 2 (1965), 155-73.

(15)   RELIGION AND PHILOSOPHY

3598   Agbley, Seth. "The Origin of idols," Ghana Bull. Theol.,
       I (Dec. 1959), 3-11.

3599   Akesson, Sam K. "The Akan Concept of the soul," African
       Affairs, LXIV (Oct. 1965), 280-91.

3600   _____. "The Secret of Akom (in Ashanti)," African
       Affairs, XLIX, No. 196 (1950), 237-46; No. 197 (1950),
       325-33.
           A study by a Methodist Minister based on the informa-
       tion given by a Christian convert. Includes a discussion
       of spirit possession as symptomatic of a call of the pos-
       sessed to priesthood; the function of the priest as a mid-
       dleman between the spirits and the possessed; use of cer-
       tain medicinal lotions extracted from plants on the possessed.

3601   Alleyne, Cameron. Gold Coast at a glance, especially adapted
       to missions study classes. New York: Hunt Printing Co.,
       1931. 143 p.

3602   Amissah, S. H. "The Present position and problems of the
       Churches in Africa." In Consultation Digest. Geneva:
       World Council of Churches, 1965, pp. 45-51.

3603   Ampofo, Oku. "The Traditional concept of disease, health
       and healing, with which the Christian Church is confronted,"
       Ghana Bull. Theol., III (June 1976), 6-7.

3604   Amu, Ephraim. "The position of Christianity in modern
       Africa," Int. Rev. Missions, XXIX (Oct. 1940), 477-85.

3605   Ansay, J. K. The Centenary history of the Larteh Presby-
       terian Church, 1853-1953. Larteh: Presbyterian Church,
       1955. 111 p.

3606   Armattoe, Grant Raphael Ernest. "Epe-Ekpe," African
       Affairs, L (Oct. 1951), 326-31.
           New Year cult of the Glidji Ewe.

3607   Armstrong, Charles W. The Winning of West Africa. Lon-
       don: Wesleyan Methodist Missionary Society, 1920. 64 p.
           Chapter IV summarizes the work of the Prophet Harris
       in Ghana.

3608   Arthur J. B. "The Christian faith and African culture, es-
       pecially its liturgical expression," Ghana Bull. Theol., II,
       No. 2 (1962), 1-12.

3609   Aryee, A. F.   "Christianity and polygamy in Ghana: the role
       of the Church as an instrument of social change," Ghana J.
       Soc., III, No. 2 (1967), 98-105.

3610   Asamoa, E. A.   "The Christian Church and African heritage,"
       Int. Rev. Missions, XLIV (July 1955), 292-301.

3611   _____.   "The Influence of fetichism," In Christianity and
       African culture.   Accra: Christian Council, 1955, pp. 39-
       45.

3612   Ashanin, C. B.   "The Social significance of religious studies
       in West Africa," Universitas, IV (Dec. 1959), 9-11.

3613   Assuon, B. K.   "Religion and social change among the
       Ahanta of Ghana," Master's Thesis, University of Ghana,
       1970.

3614   Baeta, Christian G.   "Aspects of religion."   In W. Birming-
       ham, et al., eds.   A Study of Contemporary Ghana, v. 2.
       Evanston: Northwestern University Press, 1967, pp. 240-
       50.
           Historical analysis of Ghana's traditional, Islamic and
       Christian religions.

3615   _____.   "The Challenge of African culture to the church
       and the message of the church to African culture."   In
       Christianity and African culture.   Accra: Christian
       Council, 1955, pp. 51-61.

3616   _____.   "Challenge of the Ghana Church Union proposals,"
       Ref. Presb. World, XXVIII (June 1964), 69-74.

3617   _____.   Christianity in tropical Africa: studies presented
       and discussed at the Seventh International African Seminar,
       University of Ghana, April 1965.   With a foreword by
       Daryll Forde.   London: Oxford University Press for the
       International African Institute, 1968.   449 p.
           Includes several articles on Ghana.

3618   _____.   "Conflict in mission: historical and separatist
       Churches."   In Gerald Anderson, ed.   The Theology of
       the Christian mission.   New York: McGraw Hill, 1961,
       pp. 290-9.

3619   _____.   "Is there still a role for European and American
       missionaries in Africa," Central Africa, LXXXI (Jan. 1963),
       12, 15.

3620   _____.   Prophetism in Ghana: a study of some "spiritual"
       churches.   London: S. C. M. Press, 1962.   169 p.
           Originally submitted as doctoral dissertation, London

University, 1959. A study by a Ghanaian theologian of
nine independent churches in Ghana, three of which are
outgrowths of Nigerian Aladura churches. Churches studied
include the Church of the Twelve Apostles; Musama Disco
Christo Church; The Savior Church and the Apostolic
Revelation Society.

3621 Bane, Martin. Catholic pioneers in West Africa. Dublin:
      Clonmore & Reynolds, 1956. 220 p.

3622 Bartels, Francis L. "Jacobus Eliza Johannes Capitein,
      1719-47, " Trans. Hist. Soc. Ghana, IV, Part I (1959),
      3-13.

3623 _____. The Roots of Ghana Methodism. Cambridge:
      Cambridge University Press, 1965. 368 p.
      Rev: Trans. Hist. Soc. Ghana, VIII (1965), 172-6.

3624 Beecham, John. Ashantee and the Gold Coast: being a
      sketch of the history, social state, superstitions of the
      inhabitants of these countries with a notice of the state
      and prospects of Christianity among them. London: Daw-
      sons, 1968. 378 p. (Colonial history series.)
      First published 1841. An attempt by a leading member
      of the Methodist Society to stimulate interest in missionary
      work.

3625 Beetham, T. A. Christianity and the New Africa. London:
      Pall Mall, 1967. 206 p.
      Topics discussed include the coming of Christianity to
      Africa; the weakness and strength of the church at the
      coming of national independence; and the challenge facing
      the church and principles of its response. 4 appendices:
      I. Statistical notes. II. Distribution of the Churches
      in Sub-Saharan Africa. III. All-Africa Conference of
      churches. IV. Organization of Christian cooperation in
      Africa. Maps, bibliography and index.

3626 _____. "Ghana. " In Stephen Neill, et al. , eds. Concise
      dictionary of the Christian World Mission. New York:
      Abingdon Press, 1971, pp. 225-7.
      Gives statistical figures of various religious sects, mis-
      sionaries and their activities and educational impact.

3627 Belshaw, Harry. "Church and state in Ashanti, " Int. Rev.
      Missions, XXXV (Oct. 1946), 408-15.

3628 _____. Facing the future in West Africa. London:
      Cargate Press, 1951. 128 p.

3629 _____. "Religious education in the Gold Coast, " Int. Rev.
      Missions, (July 1945), 267-72.

3630 Bentley, Muriel. "Philip Quaque," Church Quarterly Review,
      CLXVII (April/June 1966), 151-65.
          First African chaplain at Cape Coast. See also the
      biography section.

3631 "The Bond, African priest and his people, picture story."
      Sign, XXXIX (July 1960), 43-7.

3632 Braun, Richard and Gertrude Braun. Letters from Ghana.
      Philadelphia: Christian Education Press, 1959. 154 p.

3633 Bruce, Ernest. "I grew up with history," African Challenge
      (Lagos, Nigeria) (April 1957), 6-10.
          A Ghanaian Methodist Minister recounts his personal
      reminiscences of Prophet Harris.

3634 _____. "Reminiscences of Ghana Methodism." In Founda-
      tion Conference. Cape Coast: Mfantsipim Press, 1961,
      pp. 23-7.

3635 Burke, F. L. and F. J. McCreanor. Training missionaries
      for community development; a report on experiences in
      Ghana. Princeton, New Jersey: Jill de Grazia, 1960.
      86 p.
          Also published in Italian by Ingran, Roma, 1960. 123 p.

3636 Busia, Kofi Abrefa. "Ancestor worship, libation, stools,
      festival." In Christianity and African culture. Accra:
      Christian Council, 1955, pp. 17-23.

3637 _____. "Freedom and unity in Christ-in society," Int.
      Rev. Missions, LII (July 1963), 447-52.

3638 _____. "Has Christian faith been adequately presented,"
      Int. Rev. Missions, L (Jan. 1961), 86-9.

3639 _____. Urban churches in Britain: a question of rele-
      vance. London: Lutterworth Press, 1966. 175 p.

3640 Butt-Thompson, F. W. West African secret societies: their
      organizations, officials and teaching. London: Witherby,
      1929. 320 p.

3641 Carstairs, G. M. "A View from the Shrine," Listener (Lon-
      don), LXIV (Mar. 2, 1961), 387-9.
          A comparison of modern West African shrines with
      those of India.

3642 Cerulli, E. "La Setta dei carriers. Sincretisme religiose
      pagano-Cristiano nel Ghana," Stud. Mat. Storia Rel. (Rome),
      XXXIV, No. 1 (1963), 27-59.

3643 Champagne, Emery. "La religion des noirs du Norel de la
      Gold Coast," Anthropos, XXIII (1928), 851-60.

3644 Champagne, Gabriel. Catholic hymnal. Accra: Diocese of
      Tamale, 1965. 73 p.

3645 Ching, Donald Stanley. Ivory tales. London: Epworth Press,
      1950. 126 p.
      Includes an account of Prophet Harris.

3646 _____. A Plain account of Christian experience. London:
      Epworth Press, 1947. 63 p.

3647 _____. They do likewise. A survey of Methodist medical
      missions in Africa. London: Cargate Press, 1951.
      130 p.

3648 Christensen, James Boyd. "Adaptive functions of Fanti
      priesthood." In W. Bascom and M. Herskovits, eds.
      Continuity and change in African cultures. Chicago: Uni-
      versity of Chicago Press, 1959, pp. 257-78.
      A brief analysis of the impact of Christianity upon
      traditional Fanti religion. Includes a discussion of "new
      cults."

3649 _____. "The Tigare cult of West Africa," Papers of the
      Michigan Academy of Science, Art and Letters, XXXIX
      (1954), 389-98.
      A neo-pagan cult.

3650 Christian Council of the Gold Coast. Report on common
      beliefs with regard to witchcraft. Accra: Scottish Mis-
      sion Book Depot, 1932. 8 p.

3651 Cooksey, J. J. and A. Mcleish. Religion and civilizations
      in West Africa; a missionary survey of French, British,
      Spanish and Portuguese West Africa, with Liberia. London:
      World Dominion Press, 1931. 277 p.

3652 Creedy, L. A. "News of the churches; Presbyterian Church
      of Ghana," Ref. Presb. World, XX (Dec. 1968), 173.

3653 Danquah, Joseph B. The Akan doctrine of God: a fragment
      of Gold Coast ethics and religion. With an introduction
      by Kwesi A. Dickson. 2nd ed. London: Cass, 1968.
      206 p. 1st ed. 1944.
      The author states, "Akan religious doctrine knows only
      one God. Everything else found in the land, in the form
      of religion, is nothing else but superstition ... the cults
      of the private man desirous to satisfy the natural craving
      for religion, should not be ascribed to the Akan as their

racial or natural conception of God." A glossary of Akan
words.
Rev: J. Asian Afr. Stud., IV (Oct. 1969), 320.

3654 Debrunner, Hans W. A Church between colonial powers; a
study of the church in Togo. Translated by Dorothea M.
Barton. London: Lutterworth Press, 1965. 368 p.
(World studies of churches in mission.)

3655 _____. A History of Christianity in Ghana. Accra: Waterville, 1967. 375 p. Bibliog.

3656 _____. "The Moses of the Presbyterian Church: an historical meditation on Rev. Andreas Riis (1804-1854)," Ghana
Bull. Theol., I (Dec. 1957), 10-16; I (June 1958), 12-20.

3657 _____. "Notable Danish chaplains on the Gold Coast,"
Trans. Gold Coast & Togoland Hist. Soc., II, Part 1
(1956), 13-29.
Wilhelm Johann Mueller, Johann Rask and H.C. Monrad.

3658 _____. "A note on the Asonu cult in Nzima, Ghana,"
Africa, XXXII (Oct. 1962), 393.

3659 _____. Witchcraft in Ghana; a study on the belief in
destructive witches and its effect on the Akan tribes. 2nd
ed. Accra: Presbyterian Book Depot, 1961. 213 p.
Rev: Int. Rev. Missions, L, No. 198 (1961), 139.

3660 _____, et al. "Early Fante Islam," Ghana Bull. Theol.,
I (Dec. 1959), 22-33.

3661 Desai, Ram, ed. Christianity in Africa as seen by Africans.
Denver: Alan Swallow, 1962. 135 p.
Includes K.A. Busia's "Christianity and Ashanti" and
J.H. Nketia's "The Contribution of African culture to
Christian worship."

3662 Dickson, Kwesi A. The History and religion of Israel.
Darton: Longmann & Todd, 1968. 519 p.

3663 _____. "The Methodist Society: a section," Ghana Bull.
Theol., II (June 1962), 1-7.

3664 _____ and Paul Ellingworth, eds. Biblical revelation and
African beliefs. London: Lutterworth Press, 1969. 191 p.
Papers presented at a consultation of African theologians
held at Immanuel College, Ibadan, Nigeria, January 1966
under the auspices of the All-Africa Conference of
Churches.

3665   Dovlo, C. K.   Christianity and family life in Ghana.   Accra:
        Waterville, 1967. 55 p.

3666   Drayton, Thomas.   Wo dofo bi adi kan (Akuepem-Twi.   Life
        beyond the death with evidence.)   Translated from the
        English by E. F. Andrews-Ayeh.   Accra: Bureau of Ghana
        Languages, 1960. 98 p.

3667   Dretke, J. P.   "The Muslim community in Accra: a his-
        torical survey," Master's Thesis, University of Ghana,
        1968. 187 p.

3668   "Einige Abstraktbildungen des Ewe im Neuen Testament,"
        Die Bibel in der Welt, IX (1966), 72-9.

3669   Evans, H. St. John T.   "The Akan doctrine of God."   In
        Edwin William Smith, ed.   African ideas of God.   London:
        Lutterworth, 1944, pp. 241-59.

3670   Evans-Pritchard, E. E.   Theories of primitive religion.
        London: Oxford University Press, 1965. 140 p.
            Examination of various theories propounded to explain
        the religions of primitive people, and implicitly, of re-
        ligions in general.

3671   Ezeanya, Stephen Nweke.   "Oaths in the traditional religion
        of West Africa," W. Afr. Rel., No. 7 (1967), 1-10.
            The Author, a Nigerian theologian, is a Lecturer in
        Religion, University of Nigeria, Nsukka.

3672   Fiawoo, D. K.   "Ancestral worship among the Ewe-speaking
        people of Southern Ghana: a study in religious change,"
        Ghana J. Soc., V (Oct. 1969), 18-22.
            Ancestor cults are based on lineage and clans rather
        than chiefdoms, and Pagans and Christians almost equally
        believe in the ancestors.

3673   _____.   "From cult to church: a study of some aspects
        of religious change in Ghana," Ghana J. Soc., IV (Oct.
        1968), 72-87.

3674   _____.   "The influence of contemporary social changes on
        the magico-religious concepts and organization of the
        Southern Ewe-speaking people of Ghana," Doctoral Disserta-
        tion, Edinburgh University, 1959.

3675   _____.   "Urbanization and religion in Eastern Ghana,"
        Soc. Rev., VII (July 1959), 83-97.

3676   Field, Margaret Joyce.   "Ashanti and Hebrew Shamanism,"
        Man, LVIII, No. 7 (1958), 14.
            Similarity of Ashanti to Hebrew Shamanism.

3677 _____. "Mental disorder in rural Ghana," J. Mental Sci.,
CIV, No. 437 (1958), 1043-51.
Discusses different religious shrines and their functions;
spirit possession of Ashanti priests and Ga women.

3678 _____. Religion and medicine of the Ga people.   Accra:
Presbyterian Book Depot, 1961.   214 p.
Reprint of the 1937 edition by Oxford University Press.
Public religious worship in 7 communities; principles and
practices of magic and medicine, and spirit possession.

3679 _____. "Some new shrines of the Gold Coast and their
significance," Africa, XIII (April 1940), 138-49.
Various kinds of shrines; the treatments they give;
official attitude towards the shrines and spirit possession
by the female attendants of the shrines.

3680 _____. "Witchcraft as a primitive interpretation of mental
disorder," J. Mental Sci., CI, No. 425 (1955), 826-33.

3681 Fisher, Humphrey. "Planting Ahmadiyya in Ghana," West
Africa, No. 2226 (Jan. 1960), 121.
Establishment of Moslem faith.

3682 Fortes, Meyer. Oedipus and Job in West Africa.   Cambridge:
Cambridge University Press, 1959.   81 p.

3683 _____. "Pietas in ancestor worship," J. Roy. Anthrop.
Inst., XCI, No. 2 (1961), 166-91.

3684 Froehlich, J.C. Animismes, les religions paiennes de
l'Afrique de l'Ouest. Paris: Editions de l'Orante, 1964.
255 p. (Coll. Lumière et nations.)

3685 Gaba, Christian Robert. "Anlo traditional religions: a study
of the Anlo traditional believers' concept of and communication with the 'Holy,'" Doctoral Dissertation, London University, 1965.   495 p.

3686 _____. "Sacrifice in Anlo religion," Ghana Bull. Theol.,
III (Dec. 1968), 13-19; (Dec. 1969), 1-7.
The two principal sacrifices are "dzu" sacrifices in
form of a gift to nourish the holy and "nuxe" sacrifice
chiefly to placate the angry holy. These sacrifices are,
on the whole, intended for the ancestors and lesser gods.

3687 Gartlan, J. "Christening of pagan customs in Ghana,"
Catholic World, CXC (Nov. 1959), 101-6.

3688 Ghana. Church Union Committee. Proposed constitution of
the United Church. Accra, 1967.   70 p.

3689   "Ghanaian studies for priesthood," Sepia, II (Aug. 1962),
       59-61.

3690   Gildea, R. Y.   "Religion in the Ashanti Province of Ghana,"
       Social Science (Winfield), XXXVIII (Oct. 1963), 209-12.

3691   Grau, Eugene.   "The Evangelical Presbyterian Church of
       Ghana," Doctoral Dissertation, Hartford Seminary Founda-
       tion, 1964.

3692   _____.   "The German Protestant heritage of the church
       in Ghana, 2," Ghana Bull. Theol., III (June 1968), 14-22.

3693   _____.   "Missionary policies as seen in the work of mis-
       sions with the evangelical Presbyterian Church, Ghana."
       In C. G. Baeta, ed.   Christianity in tropical Africa.   Lon-
       don: Oxford University Press, 1968, pp. 61-78.
       Considers the church sympathetic to the traditional
       African society.

3694   Grottanelli, Vinigi L.   "Asonu worship among the Nzema:
       a study in Akan art and religion," Africa, XXXI (Jan. 1961),
       46-60.

3695   _____.   "Gods and mortality in Nzema polytheism," Ethnol-
       ogy, VIII, No. 4 (1969), 370-405.
       Concerned chiefly with the interrelationships between
       religious beliefs and behavior patterns in this polytheistic
       Akan tribe of Ghana.

3696   _____.   "Pre-existence and survival in Nzema beliefs,"
       Man, LXI (Jan. 1961), 1-5.

3697   Groves, Charles Pelham.   The Planting of Christianity in
       Africa.   London: Lutterworth Press, 1964.
       4 v.   Reprint of the 1948-1958 edition.   v. 1 to 1840.
       v. 2: 1840-1878.   v. 3: 1878-1914.   v. 4: 1914-1954.

3698   Hagan, G. P.   "Some aspects of Akan philosophy," Master's
       Thesis, University of Ghana, 1964.

3699   Haliburton, Gordon M.   "The Anglican Church of Ghana and
       the Harris movement of 1914," Bull. Soc. Afr. Church
       Hist. (Nsukka, Nigeria), I (Dec. 1964), 101-6.
       On John Swatson, an evangelist in West Ghana, who was
       influenced by Prophet Harris.

3700   _____.   "The Late Sampson Oppong, Ashanti Prophet,"
       W. Afr. Rel., (Nsukka, Nigeria), No. 5 (Feb. 1966), 1-3.
       An obituary.

3701 _____. "The Prophet Harris and the Methodist Church,"
Paper presented at an African History Seminar, School of
Oriental and African Studies, February 1963, 8 p. (mimeo-
graphed)
Methodist reactions to the influence of Prophet Harris in
Apoloma, 1914-1926.

3702 Harker, F.D. The Church is there. Edinburgh: The Church
of Scotland Foreign Mission Committee, 1964.

3703 Hartenstein, Karl. Anibue: die "Neue Zeit" auf der Gold-
kuste und unsere Missions ausgabe. Stuttgart: Evangelische
Missionsverlag, 1932.

3704 Heman-Ackah, David. Marriage problems in Ghana. Rev.
ed. Accra: The Author, 1961. 127 p. First published
1938.

3705 Holas, B. "Organizations socio-religieuses en Afrique noire,"
Bull. IFAN, (B), XVI, Nos. 1-2 (1964), 40-70.

3706 Howells, William. The Heathens: primitive man and his
religions. Garden City, New York: Doubleday, 1948.
306 p.
Spirit possession and its relation to disease and medicine, with examples from different cultures; for example,
the Ga people of Ghana.

3707 Hulsen, C. Unbaptized infants. Cape Coast: Catholic Mission Press, 1965. 236 p.

3708 Ilogu, Edmund C. "Religion and culture in West Africa,"
Theology Today, XX (1963), 53-60.
The author is a Nigerian theologian and Head of the
Dept. of Religion at the University of Nigeria, Nsukka.

3709 "The Influence of religion on language." In Proceedings of
the First International Congress of Africanists, Accra,
1962. London, 1964, pp. 115-23.

3710 Jahoda, Gustav. "Traditional healers and other institutions
concerned with mental illness in Ghana," Int. J. Soc.
Psychiatry, VII, No. 4 (1961), 245-68.
Considers a prayer healing church as an innovative
social institution to deal with new social problems.

3711 James, E.O. "The Withdrawal of the 'High God' in West
African religion," Man, LXII (July 1962), 106.

3712 Johnson, W.R. "A Consideration of the Ashanti religion in
the light of some concepts suggested by Robin Horton,"
Master's Thesis, London University, 1963/64.

3713 Kiev, Ari, ed. Magic, faith and healing: studies in primi-
      tive psychiatry today. New York: The Free Press, 1964.
      475 p.
      Nineteen studies conducted by authorities in psychiatry,
      social anthropology and psychology in different countries
      on healing practices and beliefs relating disorders. Dr.
      Kiev is Research Associate in Psychiatry, Columbia Uni-
      versity College of Physicians and Surgeons.

3714 Kilson, Marion. Kpele Lala: Ga religious signs and sym-
      bols. Cambridge, Mass.: Harvard University Press, 1970.

3715 King, Noel Q. Religions of Africa. New York: Harper,
      1970. 116 p.
      Chiefly on the traditional religions of Akan, Yoruba, Nuer,
      Acholi, Buganda, and Ankole.
      Rev: Africa Report, XVI (Oct. 1970), 36-7.

3716 Kittler, Glenn D. The White Fathers. London: W. H.
      Allen, 1957. 319 p.
      On Northern Ghana.

3717 Krass, A. "Towards a more indigenous liturgy," Ghana
      Bull. Theol., III (Dec. 1969), 20-8.

3718 Laing, George E. "Libation: some notes on letters,"
      Ghana Bull. Theol., I (Dec. 1958), 2-3.

3719 Latourette, Kenneth Scott. The Christian World mission in
      our day. New York: Harper, 1954. 192 p.

3720 _____. Christianity in a revolutionary age; a history of
      Christianity in the nineteenth and twentieth centuries. New
      York: Harper, 1958-62. 5 v.

3721 Levtzion, Nehemia. Muslims and chiefs in West Africa: a
      study of Islam in the Middle Volta Basin in the pre-colonial
      period. Oxford: Clarendon Press, 1968. 228 p.

3722 Mctorkle, W. F. The Assemblies of God of Ghana: Constitu-
      tion and laws. Accra: Assemblies of God Mission, 1968.
      66 p.

3723 Madden, A. F. "The Attitudes of the evangelical to the
      Empire and imperial problems, 1820-1850," Doctoral Dis-
      sertation, Oxford University, n. d.

3724 Marshall, M. J. "Christianity and nationalism in Ghana,"
      Master's Thesis, University of Ghana, 1965.

3725 Mauny, Raymond. "Ancient Capital of the land of gold,"
      Practical Anthropology, VIII (May/June 1961), 135-8.

3726 _____ . "Le judaisme, les juifs et l'Afrique occidentale,"
Bull. IFAN, XI (Juil-Oct. 1959), 354-78.

3727 Maxwell, Arthur S. Your bible and your priceless treasures
in the Holy scriptures. Accra: Advent Press, 1966.
302 p.

3728 Maxwell-Lawford, F. Catholics at Achimota: an account of
the first six years. Achimota: Achimota College Press,
1933. 25 p.

3729 Mbiti, John S. African religions and philosophy. New York:
Praeger, 1969. 290 p. Bibliog.
Examines African concepts of the nature and works of
God, religious attitudes toward birth and childhood, initia-
tion and puberty, marriage and procreation, death, the
concepts of evil, ethics and justice; the place of medicine
men, rainmakers, priests in African societies, etc. Index
of authors, index of peoples and languages, subject index
and bibliography. Dr. Mbiti, a Protestant theologian from
Kenya, is Professor and Head of the Dept. of Religious
Studies, Makerere University College, Uganda.
Rev: Library J., XCIV (Aug. 1969), 2795. TLS
(March 5, 1970), 261.

3730 _____ . "Christianity and traditional religions in Africa,"
Int. Rev. Missions, LIX, No. 236 (1970), 430-40.

3731 _____ . Concepts of God in Africa. New York: Praeger,
1970. 348 p. Bibliog.
"This book presents a portion of [African] traditional
religious and philosophical wisdom, gathered from over
two hundred and seventy different peoples [tribes]. The
subject is God both alone and in relation to the Universe
of Spiritual beings, man, animals, plants, natural object,
and phenomena" (Preface). Index of subjects, list of
African peoples, their countries and names for God.
Rev: Choice, VII (Nov. 1970), 1242. Library J.,
XCV (Feb. 1, 1970), 501.

3732 _____ . New Testament eschatology in an African background: a study of the encounter between New Testament
theology and African traditional concepts. London: Oxford
University Press, 1971. 244 p.

3733 McNulty, J. "Credit unions in Northern Ghana: the church
goes to the people," Month, XXIV (Oct. 1960), 255-8.

3734 Mensah, Annan Attah. "The Akan church lyric," Int. Rev.
Missions, XLIX (April 1960), 183-8.

3735   The Methodist Church of the Gold Coast.   "I will build my
       Church:" the report of the Commission appointed by the
       Synod of the Methodist Church, Gold Coast, to consider
       the life of the Church.   Stalbans: Campfield Press, 1948.
       171 p.

3736   _____.   Synod discussion of the report of the Commission
       on the life of the Church.   Accra: Methodist Book Depot,
       1949.

3737   Meyerowitz, Eva Lewin.   The Akan of Ghana: their ancient
       beliefs.   London: Faber & Faber, 1958.   164 p.
           Customs and religious beliefs of the Akan people.

3738   _____.   "Concepts of the soul among the Akan of the Gold
       Coast," Africa, XXI (Jan. 1951), 24-31.

3739   _____.   The Divine kingship in Ghana and ancient Egypt.
       London: Faber & Faber, 1960.   260 p.
           Traces the cults of the Pharoahs among the Akan.

3740   _____.   The Sacred state of the Akan.   London: Faber &
       Faber, 1951.   222 p.   101 plates.
           Rev: Africa, XXII (Oct. 1952), 360-8.

3741   Milligan, Robert H.   The Fetish folk of West Africa.   New
       York: A. M. S. Press, 1970.   328 p.

3742   Mobley, Harris W.   The Ghanaians' image of the missionary:
       an analysis of the published critiques of Christian mis-
       sionaries by Ghanaians, 1897-1965.   Leiden: Brill, 1970.
       181 p.   (Studies on religion in Africa, v. 1.)
           Originally submitted as doctoral dissertation, Hartford
       Seminary Foundation, 1966.

3743   Nassau, Robert Hamill.   Fetichism in West Africa: forty
       years' observation of native customs and supersititions.
       New York: Universities Press, 1969.   389 p.   Reprint of
       the 1904 edition.

3744   Neill, Stephen Charles.   Colonialism and Christian mission-
       aries.   New York: McGraw-Hill, 1966.   445 p.

3745   Nimako, S. Gyasi.   The Christian and funerals.   Cape Coast:
       Methodist Book Depot, 1954.   94 p.

3746   Nketia, Joseph Hanson K.   "Birth, puberty and death."   In
       Christianity and African culture.   Accra: Christian Coun-
       cil, 1955, pp. 24-38.

3747   _____.   "The Contribution of African culture to Christian
       worship, " Int. Rev. Missions, XLVII (Oct. 1958), 265-78.

3748 _____. "Possession dances in African society," Int. Folk
Music Council Jl., IX (1957), 4-9.

3749 Parrinder, Edward Geoffrey. African traditional religion.
London: Hutchinson, 1954. 160 p.

3750 _____. "Divine Kingship in West Africa," Numen, III,
No. 2 (1956), 111-21.

3751 _____. The Faiths of mankind: a guide to the world's
living religions. New York: Crowell, 1964. 206 p.
British title: The World's living religions.

3752 _____. "The Religious situation in West Africa," African
Affairs, LIX (Jan. 1960), 38-42.
Includes a brief description of independent religious
movements and their mixture of pagan and Old Testament
elements.

3753 _____. West African religion: a study of the beliefs and
practices of Akan, Ewe, Yoruba, Ibo and kindred peoples.
London: Epworth Press, 1961. 203 p. Bibliog.
A comparative study by the first lecturer in Religious
Studies, University of Ibadan, Nigeria. Examines temples
and forms of worship; priests and attendants, possession
dances, spirit possession and mediumship.

3754 _____. Witchcraft: European and African. London:
Faber & Faber, 1963. 215 p.

3755 _____. Worship in the world's religions. New York:
Association Press, 1961. 239 p.

3756 Parsons, Robert T. The Churches and Ghana society, 1918-
1955: a survey of the work of three Protestant mission
Societies and the African Churches which they established
in their assistance to the societary development. Leiden:
E. J. Brill, 1963. 240 p.

3757 _____. Some problems in the integration of Christianity
and African culture in Ghana, 1918-1955. Accra: University of Ghana, 1962.
First International Conference of Africanists, Dec. 11-
18, 1962.

3758 Paternot, Marcel. Lumière sur la Volta, chez les Dagari.
Paris: Association des Missionaires d'Afrique, 1953.
254 p.

3759 Pfann, Helene M. A Short history of the Catholic Church in
Ghana. Cape Coast: Catholic Mission Press, 1965.
172 p.

3760 Phillips, J. B. "Social and religious symbolism in certain
      Akan chiefdoms, " B. Litt. 's Thesis, Oxford University,
      1963.

3761 Platt, William J. From fetish to faith. London: Living-
      stone Press, 1935. 159 p.
      West African church history.

3762 Quarcoo, A. K. "The Ancestors in Ghanaian religious and
      social behaviour, " Research Review, III, No. 2 (1967),
      39-50.

3763 _____. "A Debut of Ghanaian traditional visual art into
      liturgical art of the Christian Church of Ghana, " Research
      Review, IV, No. 3 (1968), 53-64.

3764 _____. "A Note on the ancestor cult in Ghana, " Research
      Review, III, No. 1 (1966), 74-8.

3765 Rattray, Robert Sutherland. Religion and art in Ashanti.
      With chapters by G. T. Bennett, Vernon Blake, H. Dudley
      Buston, R. R. Marett, C. G. Seligman. New York: Oxford
      University Press, 1959. 432 p. (Oxford reprint series.)
          Reprint of the 1927 edition. Primarily on pottery and
      aesthetics.

3766 "Rededication and prophetism in Ghana, " Cahiers Etud. Afr.,
      X (1970), 228-305.

3767 Ringwald, Walter. Die Religion der Akanstämme und das
      Problem ihrer Bekehrung. Stuttgart: Evang. Missions-
      verlag, 1952. 358 p.

3768 _____. Stafette in Afrika: der Weg einer jungen Kirche
      in Ghana. Stuttgart: Evang. Missionsverlag, 1957.
      92 p.

3769 Sackey, Isaac. "A Brief history of the A. M. E. Zion Church,
      West Gold Coast District, " Ghana Bull. Theol., I, No. 3
      (1957), 16-20.
          The Ghanaian clergyman describes the "Ethiopian" type
      of independent church founded under American sponsorship
      in the Gold Coast in 1903.

3770 Sawyerr, Harry. "Christian evangelistic strategy in West
      Africa: reflecting in the Centenary of the Consecration of
      Bishop Adjayi Crowther on St. Peter's Day, 1864, " Int.
      Rev. Missions, LIV (July 1965), 343-52.
          The installation of the Nigerian missionary as the first
      Bishop of the Niger Diocese.

3771 _____. God: ancestor or Creator? Traditional belief in
       Ghana; Nigeria, and Sierra Leone. London: Longmans,
       1970. 118 p.

3772 Shelton, Austin J. "On recent interpretations of 'Deus
       Otiosus' the withdrawn God in West African psychology,"
       Man, LXV, No. 55 (1964), 53-4.

3773 _____. "Le principe cyclique de la personalité africaine,"
       Présence Africaine, No. 45 (1963), 98-104.

3774 Smith, Edwin William. African beliefs and Christian faith.
       London: Lutterworth Press, 1944. 192 p.

3775 _____. African ideas of God: a symposium. 2nd ed.
       revised and edited by E. G. Parrinder. London: Edinburgh
       House Press, 1961. 308 p.

3776 _____. "Religious beliefs of the Akan," Africa, XV (Jan.
       1945), 23-9.

3777 Smith, Noel. The Presbyterian Church of Ghana, 1835-1960:
       a younger church in a changing society. London: Oxford
       University Press, 1966. 304 p.
       Originally submitted as doctoral dissertation, Edinburgh
       University, 1964, it refers to Ghanaian separatist churches.

3778 Sodipo, J. O. "Aristotle's doctrine of the evolution of society
       with special reference to the First Book of the Politics,
       together with a consideration of the relevance of this
       doctrine to recent developments of communities in West
       Africa," Doctoral Dissertation, Durham University, 1964.
       The author is a Nigerian classical philosopher.

3779 Southon, A. E. Gold Coast Methodism; the first hundred
       years 1835-1935. Accra: Methodist Book Depot, 1934.
       158 p.
       Begins with Joseph Dunwell's arrival at Cape Coast on
       New Year's Day, 1835 and includes the story of Thomas
       Birch Freeman and Dr. Aggrey.

3780 Spieth, Jakob. Die Religion der Eweer in Sud-Togo. Leipzig:
       Dietrich'sche Verlagsbuchhandlung, Theodor Weicher, 1911.
       316 p.

3781 Stoevesandt, G. "The sect of the Second Adam on the Gold
       Coast," Africa, VII (Oct. 1934), 479-82.
       The story of a small defunct community that once
       existed in the early 1900's near the village Nkwakubio with
       Ewe as a predominant language.

3782   Swithenbank, Michael. Ashanti fetish houses. Accra: Ghana
       Universities Press, 1969. 68 p.

3783   Tauxier, Louis. Religion, moeurs et coutumes des Agnis
       de la Côte d'Ivoire. Paris: Geuthner, 1932. 255 p.
       (Etudes Soudanaises.)

3784   Tildsley, Alfred. The Remarkable work achieved by Rev.
       Dr. Mark C. Hayford in promotion of the spiritual and
       material welfare of the natives of West Africa, and proposed
       developments. London: Morgan & Scott, 1926. 36 p.

3785   Trimingham, John Spencer. The Christian Church and Islam
       in West Africa. London: S.C.M. Press, 1956. 64 p.
       (I.M.C. research pamphlets, no. 3.)

3786   _____. A History of Islam in West Africa. London: Ox-
       ford University Press, for University of Glasgow, 1962.
       272 p.
               The historical background to Islam in West Africa (1959)
       by the same author, who is the Secretary of the Church
       Missionary Society in the Sudan.

3787   _____. Islam in West Africa. London: Oxford University
       Press, 1959. 272 p.
               "A phenomenological study of the religious life of West
       African Muslims" (Preface). The spread of Islam: and
       the interaction between the religion and the African society.

3788   Turner, Harold W. "The Catechism of an independent West
       African Church, " Sierra Leone Bull. Rel., II (Dec. 1960),
       45-57.
               Analyzes a text from the Church of the Lord Aladura,
       comparing it with two Ghanaian and two Kimbanguist
       catechisms.

3789   _____. "The Church of the Lord: the expansion of a
       Nigerian independent church in Sierra Leone and Ghana, "
       J. Afr. Hist., III, No. 1 (1962), 91-110.

3790   _____. "The Litany of an independent West African
       church, " Sierra Leone Bull. Rel., I (Dec. 1959), 48-55;
       also in Practical Anthropology, VII (Nov./Dec. 1960),
       256-62.
               Analysis of a Church of the Lord (Aladura) text.

3791   _____. Profile through preaching: a study of the ser-
       mon texts used in a West African independent church.
       London: Edinburgh House Press, 1965. 88 p.
               The Church of the Lord (Aladura). Contains visual
       profiles based on the analysis of 8,000 texts and compares
       them with Anglican theological ideas.

3792 _____ . "Searching and syncretism: a West African documentation, " Int. Rev. Missions, XLIX (April 1960), 189-
94; also in Practical Anthropology, VIII (May/June 1961),
106-10.
Analyzes the religious literature in the possession of an
Aladura Church.

3793 Verstraelen, F. J. Christians in Ghanaian life. Accra:
National Catholic Secretariat, 1968. 119 p.

3894 Villiers, A. Les Serpents de l'Ouest Africain. Dakar:
IFAN, 1950. 146 p. (Initiations Africaines, no. 2.)
A chapter, "Serpents and man, " deals with attitudes
of various West African tribes towards serpents.

3795 Ward, Barbara E. "Some observations on religious cults
in Ashanti, " Africa, XXVI (Jan. 1956), 47-61.
Dissatisfaction with the Ashanti Church; new religions
and Witch Cults in the 1940's.

3796 Webster, James Bertin. "Source material for the study of
the African Churches, " Bull. Soc. Afr. Church Hist. , I
(Dec. 1963), 41-9.

3797 Wiegräbe, P. "Un nouveau culte indigène à la côte d'Or, "
J. Miss. Evang. (Paris), V (Oct. 1950), 378-80.
The Tigare cult in Ghana.

3798 Wilkie, A. W. "An Attempt to conserve the work of the
Basel Mission to the Gold Coast, " Int. Rev. Missions
(Jan. 1920), 86-94.

3799 Wilks, Ivor. "The Growth of Islamic learning in Ghana, "
J. Hist. Soc. Nigeria, II (Dec. 1963), 409-17.

3800 _____ . "Islam in Ghana history: an outline, " Ghana
Bull. Theol. , II, No. 3 (1962), 20-8.

3801 _____ . The Tradition of Islamic learning in Ghana. Accra:
University of Ghana, 1962. 5 p.
First International Congress of Africanists, Dec. 11-18,
1962. Doc. /51.

3802 Williamson, S. G. Christ or Muhammad? Cape Coast:
Methodist Book Depot, 1953. 64 p.

3803 _____ and Kwesi Dickson, eds. Akan religion and the
Christian faith: a comparative study of the impact of two
religions. Accra: Ghana Universities Press, 1965. 186 p.

3804 Wilson, J. Michael. Christian marriage. New ed. Accra:
Presbyterian Book Depot, 1961.

3805   Wiltgen, R.M.   Gold Coast mission history, 1471-1880.
        Techny, Ill.: Divine Word Publications, 1956. 182 p.
        The spread of Roman Catholicism from the Portuguese
        arrival to the founding of the Society of African Missions.

3806   Wrong, Margaret.   "The Church's task in Africa South of
        the Sahara," Int. Rev. Missions (April 1947), 206-31.
        The author was Secretary of the International Committee
        on Christian Literature in Africa.

3807   Yates, Walter.   "The History of the A.M.E. Zion Church in
        West Africa, Liberia, and the Gold Coast (Ghana),"
        Master's Thesis, Hartford Seminary Foundation, 1963.

(16) SOCIOLOGY

3808   Ackah, C.A.   "Social stratification in Ghana," Ghana J. Soc.,
        V, (Oct. 1969), 1-7.

3809   Acquah, Ione.   Accra survey: a social survey of the capital
        of Ghana formerly called the Gold Coast.   London: Lon-
        don University Press, 1958.   176 p.

3810   Addo, Nelson Otu.   "Assimilation and absorption of African
        immigrants in Ghana," Ghana J. Soc., III (Feb. 1967),
        17-32.

3811   _____.   "Demographic and socio-economic aspects of
        Madina, an Accra suburb," Ghana J. Soc., II (Oct. 1966),
        1-7.

3812   _____.   "Demographic aspects of urban development in
        Ghana in the twentieth century."   Paper presented at the
        First African Population Conference, Ibadan, January 3-
        7, 1966.

3813   _____.   "Spatial distribution and ecological patterns among
        the foreign population in Ghana," Ghana J. Soc., IV (Feb.
        1968), 19-35.

3814   Addo, J.S.   "The Rehabilitation service in Ghana, 1961-
        1964," Advance (Jan. 1964), 25-7.

3815   Adjei, Ako.   "Imperialism and spiritual freedom: an African
        view," Amer. J. Soc., L (Nov. 1944), 189-98.

3816   Aldous, Joan.   "Urbanization, the extended family and kin-
        ship ties in West Africa," Social Forces, XLI (1962), 6-12.

3817   Ametewee, V. K.   "Inter-tribal marriage in Ghana: a func-
       tional analysis," Oguua Chronicle (Cape Coast), I, No. 2
       (1966), 31-3.

3818   Amoah, S. A.   "Ghanaian university students: a sociological
       study of an incipient elite," Master's Thesis, University
       of Ghana, 1969.

3819   Ansah, M. P.   "Akwamu: a study of its social and cultural
       institutions and their diffusion," Master's Thesis, Univer-
       sity of Ghana, 1968.   246 p.

3820   Assimeng, J. Max.   "A Sociological analysis of the impact
       and consequences of some Christian sects in selected
       African countries," Doctoral Dissertation, Oxford Univer-
       sity, 1968.   583 p.

3821   _____.   "Status and cultural revival: pursuit of 'the good
       old days,'" Ghana J. Soc., V (Feb. 1969), 8-14.
               "Seeks to delineate some of the sociological and psycho-
       logical factors which determine the acceptance or rejection
       of cultural motivations in social systems."

3822   Ballard, C. A.   "The Contemporary youth movement in Ghana:
       a comparative study of the Ghana Young Pioneers and other
       youth groups," Master's Thesis, University of Ghana, 1966.
       203 p.

3823   Banton, Michael.   "The Restructuring of social relationships."
       In A. Southall, ed.   Social change in modern Africa.   Lon-
       don: Oxford University Press, 1961, pp. 13-25.

3824   Beattie, J. H. M.   "Checks on the abuse of political power in
       some African states," Sociologus, IX (1959), 97-115.

3825   Beckett, W. H.   Akokoaso: survey of a Gold Coast village.
       London: School of Economics and Political Science, 1944.

3826   Bellamy, J.   "African elites--a study of Ghana," Marxism
       Today, II (Feb. 1967), 37-43.

3827   Birmingham, Walter, et al., eds.   A Study of contemporary
       Ghana.   V. 2. Some aspects of social structure.   Evanston:
       Northwestern University Press, 1967.   271 p.
               Rev: Amer. J. Soc., LXXIV (July 1968), 95-6.   Choice,
       V (Nov. 1968), 1173.

3828   Boakye, Isaiah.   "Some aspects of the social organizations of
       the fishing villages on Lake Bosumtwi," Master's Thesis,
       University of Ghana, 1965.

3829   Brokensha, David. "Kofi in search of a job," Odu, New series, I
        (April 1969), 71-84.
        Problems of unemployment for a young Ghanaian school-
        leaver.

3830   _____. "Socialism and one-party governments." (Ghana
        and Tanzania). In David Brokensha and Peter Hodge.
        Community development: an interpretation. San Francisco:
        Chandler, 1969, pp. 155-9.
        Contrasts the effects of socialist systems of government
        under Nkrumah and Nyerere on the community development
        programs in Ghana and Tanzania.

3831   _____. Tutu survey. Legon: Institute of Education,
        University of Ghana, 1961. 23 p.

3832   _____. "Volta resettlement and anthropological research,"
        Human Organisation, XXII (Winter 1963/64), 286-90.

3833   _____ and P. T. W. Baxter, eds. Egya survey. Legon:
        Institute of Education, University of Ghana, 1960. 116 p.

3834   _____ and Peter Hodge. Community development: an
        interpretation. San Francisco: Chandler Publishing Co.,
        1969. 222 p. (Chandler publication in social and eco-
        nomic change.)
        Examines different community development programs in
        Africa, South-East Asia and Middle East, noting their
        strengths and weaknesses and the effect of the country's
        political system on them. In pp. 78-84, it compares
        community development training in Ghana and India.

3835   Brown, C. K. "Social development of the pre-school children,"
        (Ghana), Master's Thesis, University of Ghana, 1969.

3836   Busia, Kofi Abrefa. "The Conflict of cultures: a plea for
        patience," Atlantic Monthly, CCIII (April 1959), 81-4.
        Many of the problems of social change in West Africa
        arise from people's desire to simulate cultures different
        from their own.

3837   _____. "The Present situation and aspiration of elites
        in the Gold Coast," Int. Soc. Sci. Bull., VIII (1956),
        424-31.

3838   _____. Report on a social survey of Sekondi-Takoradi.
        London: Crown Agents, 1950. 164 p.

3839   _____. "Social survey of Sekondi-Takoradi." In Social
        implications of industrialisation and urbanization in Africa
        South of the Sahara. Paris: UNESCO, 1956, pp. 74-86.

3840 _____ . "Some aspects of the relation of social conditions to
human fertility in the Gold Coast." In F. Lorimer, et al., eds.
Culture and human fertility, Paris: UNESCO, 1954, pp. 341-50.

3841 Caldwell, John C. African rural-urban migration; the movement to Ghana's towns. New York: Columbia University
Press, 1969. 257 p.
      General movements to the towns; the pattern of rural-
urban migration; the definition of rural-urban migrant;
rural-urban links; role of migration, etc.
      Rev: Ann. Amer. Acad. Pol. Soc. Sci., CCCXCI
(Sept. 1970), 222. Choice, VII (March 1970), 156.

3842 _____ . "Determinants of rural-urban migration in Ghana,"
Pop. Stud., XXII (Nov. 1968), 361-78.

3843 _____ . "The Erosion of the family: a study of the fate
of the family in Ghana," Pop. Stud., XX, No. 1 (July
1966), 5-26.

3844 _____ . "Family formation and limitation in Ghana: a
study of the residents of communally superior urban areas."
In Bernard Berelson, et al., eds. Family planning and
population programs: a review of world developments.
Chicago: University of Chicago Press, pp. 595-613.

3845 _____ . "Fertility attitudes in three economically con-
trasting rural regions of Ghana," Econ. Dev. Cult. Change,
XV, (Jan. 1967), 217-38.

3846 _____ . "Fertility differentials as evidence of incipient
fertility decline in a developing country: the case of
Ghana," Pop. Stud., XXI (July 1967), 5-22.

3847 _____ . Population growth and family change in Africa:
the new urban elite in Ghana. Canberra: Australian
National University Press, 1968. 222 p.
      The study conducted in 1962-63 on family and shifts in
social values in Ghana's major towns.
      Rev: Am. Soc. Rev., XXXIV (April 1969), 298. Ann.
Amer. Acad. Pol. Soc. Sci., CCCLXXXI (Jan. 1969), 187.

3848 _____ . "Study of age misstatement among young children
in Ghana," Demography, III, No. 2 (1966), 477-90.

3849 Chambers, Robert, ed. The Volta resettlement experience.
London: Pall Mall, 1970. 286 p.
      Rev: J. Mod. Afr. Stud., IX (May 1971), 143-6.
West Africa, No. 2759 (1970), 459-60.

3850 Christensen, J. B. "Problems of a society in transition,"
United Asia, IX (Feb. 1957), 15-22.
      On Ghana.

3851   Christian, A.   "The Place of women in Ghana society,"
       African Women, III (Dec. 1959), 57-9.

3852   Clarke, E.   "The Sociological significance of ancestor wor-
       ship in Ashanti," Africa, III, No. 4 (1930), 431-71.

3853   Clignet, Remi and Philip Foster.   "Potential elites in Ghana
       and the Ivory Coast: a preliminary comparison," Amer.
       J. Soc., LXX (Nov. 1964), 349-62.

3854   Cookson, Claude E.   "The Gold Coast hinterland and the
       negroid race," J. Afr. Soc., XIV (April 1915), 298-307.

3855   Crabtree, A. I.   "Marriage and family life amongst the
       educated Africans of the Gold Coast," Master's Thesis,
       London University, 1950.

3856   De Graft-Johnson, K. E.   "The Evolution of elites in Ghana."
       In Peter C. Lloyd, ed.   The new elites of tropical Africa.
       London: Oxford University Press, 1966, pp. 104-17.

3857   _____.   "Social control in a changing society," Ghana J.
       Soc., I (July 1965), 47-55.
       On Ghana.

3858   _____.   "The Place of sociology in an integrated social
       science curriculum for modern Africa," Ghana J. Soc., II
       (Oct. 1966), 29-35.

3859   Dow, Thomas E.   "Fertility and family planning in Africa,"
       J. Mod. Afr. Stud., VIII (Oct. 1970), 445-57.

3860   Drake, St. Clair.   "Social surveys in Ghana," Advance, XXIX
       (July 1959), 5-18.

3861   _____ and T. Peter Omari.   Social work in West Africa:
       report of the Seminar on Social Work in West Africa held
       at Legon, Ghana, August 1962.   Accra, 1962.   142 p.

3862   Drew, J. B., et al.   Village housing in the tropics, with
       special reference to West Africa.   London: Lund
       Humphries, 1947.   134 p.

3863   Dubb, A. A., ed.   The Multi-tribal society: proceedings of
       the Sixteenth Conference of the Rhodes-Livingstone Institute
       held at the Oppenheimer College for Social Service, Lusaka,
       February, 1962.   Lusaka, Zambia, 1962.   165 p.

3864   du Sautoy, P.   "Community development and problems at
       resettlement schemes," Comm. Dev. J., IV (July 1969),
       143-50.

3865 _____. Community development in Ghana. London: Oxford University Press, 1958. 209 p.

3866 _____. "Community development programmes in Nigeria,
Ghana and Sierra Leone," Dev. Civil., No. 21 (March
1965), 25-31.

3867 _____. The Organization of a community development
programme. London: Oxford University Press, 1962.
156 p.

3868 Egblewogbe, E. Y. "Games and songs as an aspect of
socialization of Ewelans," Master's Thesis, University
of Ghana, 1967. 168 p.

3869 Fiawoo, D. K. "The Social environment and heights and
weights of Ghanaian children," Ghana J. Child Dev., I
(Jan. 1968), 63-94.

3870 _____. "Urbanization and religion in Eastern Ghana,"
Soc. Rev., VII (July 1959), 83-97.

3871 Field, Margaret Joyce. Search for security; an ethno-
psychiatric study of rural Ghana. Evanston: Northwestern University Press, 1960. 478 p. (African
studies, no. 5.)
    A clinical but ethnographic study of mental illness in
Ghana by a British psychiatrist, based chiefly on her
observation of 146 cases of mentally disturbed people who
go to the shrines, seeking the medical aid of native
doctors.
    Rev: Amer. Anthrop., LXIII (April 1961), 435. New
Statesman, LX (Sept. 3, 1960), 314-5.

3872 Fortes, Meyer. "A Demographic field study in Ashanti."
In Frank Lorimer, ed. Culture and human fertility.
Paris, 1954, pp. 253-339.

3873 _____. "Some aspects of migration and mobility in
Ghana," J. Asian Afr. Stud., VI (Jan. 1971), 1-20.

3874 _____. "Time and social structure: an Ashanti case
study." In Meyer Fortes, ed. Social structure: studies
presented to A. R. Radcliffe-Brown. London: Oxford
University Press, 1949, pp. 54-84.

3875 _____, et al. "Ashanti survey, 1945-46; an experiment
in social research," Geogr. J., (Oct. /Dec. 1947), 149-79.
    Geographical, economic, anthropological and social
aspects of the survey, with indications of methods used
and problems encountered.

3876 _____ and Doris Mayer. "Psychosis and social change
      among the Tallensi of Northern Ghana," Cahiers Etud.
      Afr., VI, No. 21 (1966), 5-40.
           Cultural and social context, by Fortes, an anthropolo-
      gist, and psychiatric observations, by Mayer, a psychiatrist.

3877 Friedlander, D. "Measuring fertility in Ghana." Paper pre-
      sented at the First African Population Conference, Ibadan,
      January 1966.

3878 Gardiner, Robert Kweku Attah. A World of peoples. New
      York: Oxford University Press, 1966. 93 p. (The Reith
      lectures, 1965.)

3879 _____ and H.O. Judd. The Development of social adminis-
      tration. 2nd ed. London: Oxford University Press, 1959.
      208 p.

3880 George, Sister Aquin O'Connor. "The Status of women in
      selected societies of West Africa: a study of the concept
      in law and in practice," Doctoral Dissertation, New York
      University, 1960.

3881 Ghana. Ministry of Housing. Accra: a plan for the town.
      Accra: Govt. Printer, 1958. 137 p.

3882 Ghana Government. White paper on marriage, divorce and
      inheritance. Accra: Govt. Printer, 1962. 7 p.
           Proposals to reform legal marriage system to conform
      with the traditional one.

3883 Gil, B. "Immigration into Ghana and its contribution to
      skill." Paper presented at the United Nations World
      Population Conference, Belgrade, 1965, and printed in
      United Nations World Population Conference, 1965, IV,
      New York, 1967.

3884 Golding, P.T.F. "Some methodological problems of the
      social survey in a developing West African state, Ghana,"
      Master's Thesis, London University, 1963.

3885 Goody, Esther. "The Fostering of children in Ghana: a
      preliminary report," Ghana J. Soc., II (Feb. 1966), 26-33.

3886 Goody, John Rankine. "Class and marriage in Africa and
      Eurasia," Amer. J. Soc., LXXVI (Jan. 1971), 585-603.

3887 _____. "Inheritance, property and marriage in Africa
      and Eurasia," Sociology, III (1969), 55-76.
           Compares the systems of inheritance in Africa and
      Eurasia, with special reference to devolution of property
      and marriage systems.

3888 _____ . Technology, tradition and the state of Africa.
New York: Oxford University Press, 1971. 88 p.
A study of the impact of technology on various African
societies, based on the thesis that "the nature of 'indigenous'
African social structure, especially in its political aspects,
has been partly misunderstood because of a failure to appreciate certain basic technological differences between Africa
and Eurasia." Extensive bibliography and good index.

3889 Gordon, James. "Rural sociology and economics in relation
to agricultural development in West Africa: an annotated
bibliography," Ghana J. Agr. Sci., I, Part 2 (1968),
173-8.

3890 Haggan, Hannah, ed. Courtesy for boys and girls. Anowuo
Educational Publications, 1966. 60 p.

3891 Hamilton, Ruth Simms. "Urban social differentiation and
membership recruitment among selected voluntary associations in Accra, Ghana," Doctoral Dissertation, Northwestern University, 1966.
Based on the interviews with 500 participants from 27
voluntary associations in Accra, representing three principal types--benevolent-friendly societies; church related
groups; and political groups of the former Convention
People's Party, the study is designed to ascertain how
far these participants and their organizations reflect social
changes in the larger society.

3892 Hart, Keith. "Migration and tribal indentity among the
Frafras of Ghana," J. Asian Afr. Stud., VI (Jan. 1971),
21-36.
The migratory tendencies of this tribal enclave in
Voltaic area of what is now mostly Northern Ghana.

3893 Heman-Ackah, David. Marriage problems in Ghana. Rev.
ed. Accra: The Author, 1961. 127 p. 1st ed. 1938.

3894 Hodge, Peter. "The Development of welfare policy and
practices in Ghana, 1901-57," Master's Thesis, Nottingham University, 1965/66.

3895 _____ . "The Ghana workers brigade: a project for
unemployed youth," Brit. J. Soc., XV (June 1964), 113-28.

3896 _____ . "Time and change in Ghana," Comm. Dev. J.,
IV (Oct. 1969), 190-7.
Lack of community development programs immediately
before and after the fall of the Nkrumah regime owing to
Ghana's financial straits. Advocates initiation of effective
programs.

3897 _____ . Social administration in the political kingdom--the
Ghanaian experience. London: Routledge and Kegan Paul,
1969. 300 p.

3898 Holzer, J. Seasonality of vital events in selected towns of
Ghana. An analysis of registration data relating to the
period, 1956-1960. Accra: Institute of Statistics, University of Ghana, 1966. 146 p. (Monograph series, No. 1.)

3899 Hue, Nguyen Thi. "Training for community development: a
comparative study of national programs in Ghana, India
and the Philippines," Doctoral Dissertation, University of
Michigan, 1962.

3900 Hunter, John M. "The Clan of Nangodi," Africa, XXXVIII
(Oct. 1968), 377-412.

3901 _____ . "The Social roots of displaced settlement in
Northern Ghana," Ann. Assn. Amer. Geog., LVII (June
1967), 338-49.

3902 Ijomah, B. I. C. "The Problem of quantitative research in
Africa," Conch, III (March 1971), 14-32.

3903 Jahoda, Gustav. "Aspects of westernization: a study of
adult class students in Ghana," Brit. J. Soc., XII (Dec.
1961), 375-86.

3904 _____ . "Boys' images of marriage partners and girls'
self-images in Ghana," Sociologus, VIII, No. 2 (1958), 155-
69.

3905 _____ . "Child animism: II. A Study in West Africa,"
J. Soc. Psych., XLVII, No. 2 (1958), 213-22.

3906 _____ . "Geometric illusions and environment: a study
in Ghana," Brit. J. Psych., LVII (1966), 193-9.

3907 _____ . "Immanent justice among West African children,"
J. Soc. Psych., XLVII, No. 2 (1958), 241-8.
Deals with Ghanaian children.

3908 _____ . "A note on Ashanti names and their relation to
personality," Brit. J. Psych., XLV (1954), 192-5.

3909 _____ . "Social aspirations, magic and witchcraft in
Ghana: a social psychological interpretation." In P. C.
Lloyd, ed. The New elites of tropical Africa. London:
Oxford University Press, 1966, pp. 199-215.

3910 _____ . "The Social background of a West African student
population," Brit. J. Soc., VI, No. 1 (1955), 71-9.

3911 _____. White man: a study of the attitudes of Africans
      to Europeans in Ghana before independence. London: Ox-
      ford University Press, 1961. 144 p.
      A great psychological impact was made on the Ghanaians
      by Europeans whose culture they assimilated.

3912 Jane, Sister S. "The Girl problem in Ghana," Worldmission,
      XII (Fall 1961), 72-9.

3913 Jones-Quartey, Pearl W. "Voluntarism in Ghana," Ghana J.
      Soc., V, (Oct. 1969), 8-10.
      Voluntarism imported from Europe; problems of develop-
      ing YWCA and its membership are examined.

3914 Karikari, K. A. "University adult education in Ghana--a
      historical survey," Ghana J. Soc., V, (Oct. 1969), 11-17.
      The university adult course was introduced in 1947.

3915 Kelly, Gail Margaret. "The Ghanaian intelligensia," Doctoral
      Dissertation, University of Chicago, 1959.

3916 Kilson, M. D. "Continuity and change in the Ga residential
      system," Ghana J. Soc., III, No. 2 (1967), 81-97.

3917 _____. "Variations in Ga culture in Central Accra,"
      Ghana J. Soc., III (Feb. 1967), 33-54.

3918 Klingshirn, A. "Some aspects of socialization in a Ghanaian
      town: a descriptive study of child rearing practices at
      Larteh," Master's Thesis, University of Ghana, 1964.

3919 Kirchherr, E. C. "Tema, 1951-1962: the evolution of a
      planned city in West Africa," Urban Studies, V (June 1968)
      207-17.

3920 Kuoh, T. "Women's place is in the world, not in the home;
      interview by M. B. Cissey," Atlas, XX (Feb. 1971), 39.

3921 Kuper, Hilda, ed. Urbanization and migration in West
      Africa. With an introduction by Hilda Kuper. Los Angeles:
      University of California Press, 1965. 227 p.
      Rev: African Forum, I (Spring 1966), 119-21. Amer.
      Anthrop., LXVIII (Aug. 1966), 1026. Int. Labour Rev.,
      XCIII (June 1966), 685.

3922 Kwaw-Yankson, A. "Prestige seeking in a changing society,"
      Oguaa Chronicle, (Cape Coast) I, No. 2 (1966), 20-5.

3923 Lambo, T. Adeoye. "Malignant anxiety: a syndrome asso-
      ciated with criminal conduct in Africans," J. Mental Sci.,
      CVIII (1962), 256-64.

3924 _____. "Socio-economic change and its influence on the
      family, with special emphasis on the role of women: a
      socio-psychological evaluation, " Ibadan, No. 26 (Feb. 1969),
      30-5.

3925 Larkin, F., et al. "Differentiation of households in a
      Ghanaian community, " J. Marriage Fam., XXXII (May
      1970), 304-14.

3926 Le Moal, G. "Un aspect de l'émigration: la fixation de
      Voltaïques du Ghana, " Bull. IFAN, XXII, Nos. 3-4 (1960),
      446-54.

3927 Little, Kenneth Lindsay. "The African elite in British West
      Africa. " In A. W. Lind, ed. Race relations in world per-
      spective, Honolulu, 1955, pp. 263-88.

3928 _____. Some contemporary trends in African urbanization.
      Evanston: Northwestern University Press, 1966. 15 p.
      (Melville J. Herskovits memorial lecture, 2.)
      Delivered under the auspices of the Program of African
      Studies, Northwestern University, on April 20, 1965.

3929 _____. "Some urban patterns of marriage and domesticity
      in West Africa, " Soc. Rev., VII, No. 1 (1959), 65-82.

3930 _____. "The Urban role of tribal associations in West
      Africa, " Afr. Stud., XXI (1962), 1-9.

3931 _____. West African urbanization: a study of voluntary
      associations in social change. London: Cambridge Univer-
      sity Press, 1965. 179 p. Bibliog.
      Tribal associations and syncretic cults; modern associa-
      tions in the migrant and urban community; the rise of the
      young men; position of women; ethnicity and social class.
      Rev: African Forum, I (Spring 1966), 122-3. Amer.
      Anthrop., LXVIII (Aug. 1966), 1026.

3932 _____. "West African urbanization as a social process. "
      In William John Hanna, ed. Independent black Africa; the
      politics of freedom. Chicago, 1964, pp. 137-49.

3933 Lubeck, Paul. Patterns of assimilation of Hausa families
      in Dagomba. Interdisciplinary seminar in field methods,
      summer 1968. Evanston: Institute of African Studies,
      Northwestern University, 1968. 55 p. (Yendi project,
      no. 4.)

3934 Mckissack, I. J. "The Social values of Ghanaian adolescents, "
      Ghana J. Soc., IV (Oct. 1968), 109-17.

3935   McMullan, M.   "A Theory of corruption based on a consideration of corruption in the public service and Governments
of British Colonies and ex-colonies in West Africa," Soc.
Rev., IX (July 1961), 181-201.

3936   McNulty, Michael L.   "Urban centers and the spatial pattern
of development in Ghana," Doctoral Dissertation, Northwestern University, 1966.

3937   _____.   "Urban structure and development: the urban
system of Ghana," J. Dev. Areas, III (Jan. 1969), 159+.

3938   Mends, E. H.   "Some aspects of periodic ritual ceremonies
of the Anomabo Fante," Ghana J. Soc., V (Feb. 1969),
39-48.

3939   Mills-Odoi, D. G.   "The La family and social change,"
Master's Thesis, University of Ghana, 1967.   214 p.

3940   Moscati, Roberto.   "Osservazioni sulle caratteristiche e
la dinamica delle elites nella Republica del Ghana," Studi
di Sociologia (Milano), V, No. 1 (1967), 14-37.
The concept of African elites, illustrated by the Ghanaian
case, implies a gap between educated and uneducated people,
ignoring the existence of the political middle class.

3941   Newkirk, G.   "Ghanaian women's perception of the ideal
child," J. Home Econ., LIX (April 1967), 271-4.

3942   Nukunya, G. K.   "The Yewe cult among Southern Ewe-speaking
people of Ghana," Ghana J. Soc., V (Feb. 1969), 1-7.

3943   Ogun, G. E.   "Multivariate analysis of the physical measure-
ments of various groups of people in Ghana," Master's
Thesis, University of Ghana, 1970.

3944   Omari, T. Peter.   "Changing attitudes of students in West
African society towards marriage and family relationships,"
Brit. J. Soc., XI (1960), 197-210.

3945   _____.   Marriage guidance for young Ghanaians.   With a
foreword by Dr. Charles O. Easmon.   London: Nelson,
1962.   148 p.

3946   _____.   "Role expectation in the courtship situation in
Ghana," Social Forces, XLII (Dec. 1963), 147-56.

3947   Oppong, Christine.   "Some sociological aspects of education
in Dagbon: a functional analysis of some of the factors
influencing recruitment to and assumption of a number of
adult roles in a traditional Northern Ghanaian Kingdom,"

Master's Thesis, University of Ghana, 1965.

3948   Opuku-Ampomah, J. K. "Introducing an Ashanti girl into womanhood," Ghana Notes & Queries, No. 2 (May/Aug. 1961), 7-9.

3949   Osae-Addo, Gladys and Honor Ward. Newtown families: a book for parents who love their children. Kumasi: African Christian Press, 1967. 96 p.

3950   Osei-Kofi, Ebenezer. The Family and social change in Ghana. Göteberg: Sosiologiska Institut vid Göteborgs Universitet, 1967. 62 p.

3951   Oyedipe, F. P. A. "Some sociological aspects of the Yoruba family in Accra," Master's Thesis, University of Ghana, 1967. 247 p.

3952   Peil, Margaret. "Aspirations and social structure: a West African example," Africa, XXXVIII (Jan. 1968), 71-8.
Paper presented at the Annual Meeting of the American Sociological Association, Miami, Florida, August 1966.
An analysis of the study designed "to find out whether there has been any change in the traditional demand for clerical jobs and what the employment problems of primary school leavers are."

3953   _____. "Ghanaian university students: the broadening base," Brit. J. Soc., XVI (March 1965), 19-28.

3954   _____. "Middle school leavers; occupational aspirations and prospects," Ghana J. Soc., II (Feb. 1966), 7-16.

3955   _____. "Reactions to estate housing; a survey of Tema," Ghana J. Soc., IV (Feb. 1968), 1-18.

3956   _____. "The Expulsion of West African aliens," J. Mod. Afr. Stud., IX (Aug. 1971), 205-29.

3957   Pfeffer, K. H. Ghana Menschlich-soziale Grundlagen für die wirtschaftliche Entwicklung eines jungen Staatswesens. Hamburg: Verlag Weltarchiv, 1961. 81 p.

3958   Poku, K. "Traditional roles and peoples of slave origin in modern Ashanti--a few impressions," Ghana J. Soc., V (Feb. 1969), 34-8.

3959   Polgar, Steven. "Akan clerks: a study of an intermediate non-localized group in a situation of culture change," Doctoral Dissertation, University of Chicago, 1956.

3960   Pool, D. I.   "The Ghana fertility survey." Paper presented
       at the First African Population Conference, Ibadan, Janu-
       ary, 1966.

3961   _____.   "A Note on a demographic sample survey for the
       study of factors affecting fertility in Ghana," Africa,
       XXXVII (July 1967), 327-34.

3962   _____.   "The Number and type of conjugal unions as cor-
       relates of levels of fertility and attitudes to family limita-
       tion in Ghana." Paper presented at the Annual Meeting of
       the Population Association of America, Boston, 18-20,
       April, 1968.

3963   Pratt, Mildred.   "A Study of the development of social wel-
       fare in a selected group of African countries: Ghana,
       Sierra Leone, Kenya and Tanzania," Doctoral Dissertation,
       University of Pittsburgh, 1969.   257 p.
       A descriptive analysis of the development of social wel-
       fare institutions in the countries from the British colonial
       era through independence.

3964   Quarcoo, A. K.   "Processes of social control among the Shai
       (Dangme)," Master's Thesis, University of Ghana, 1965.
       163 p.

3965   Robertson, A. F.   "African and European social clubs in
       rural Ghana," Race, XII (Oct. 1970), 207-18.

3966   Rollings, P. J.   "Origins and careers of Legon sociology
       graduates," Ghana J. Soc., III (Feb. 1967), 55-64.

3967   Rouch, Jean.   "Migrations au Ghana," J. Soc. Africanistes,
       XXVI, Nos. 1-2 (1956), 33-196.

3968   _____.   Notes sur les migrations en Gold Coast: premier
       rapport de la mission effectuée en Gold Coast de mars à
       dec., 1954.   Accra, 1954.   103 p.

3969   _____.   "Second generation migrants in Ghana and the
       Ivory Coast." In A. W. Southall, ed. Social change in
       modern Africa. London: Oxford University Press, 1961,
       pp. 300-4.

3970   Salami, B. A.   "Some aspects of urbanization in the mining
       towns of Ghana, with special reference to housing conditions
       in Akwatia," Master's Thesis, Kumasi University of Science
       and Technology, 1968.   130 p.

3971   Sellnow, Irmgard.   "Soziologische und okonomische Aspekte
       des inner-afrikanischen Handels und Handwerks: ein Beitrag
       zur Geschichte der Hausa-enklaven in Ghana," Mitt. Inst.
       Orient. (Berlin), XIV, No. 1 (1968), 1-27.

3972   Tay, Janet.   "The National Women's Training Centre,
       Panfrokrom, " African Women, V, No. 1 (Dec. 1962), 1-3.

3973   Tiger, L.   "Bureaucracy and charisma in Ghana, " J. Asian
       Afr. Stud., I (Jan. 1966), 13-26.

3974   _____.   "Ghanaian politics and social change, " Int. J.
       Comp. Soc., VII (March 1966), 227-36.

3975   United Nations.   Technical Assistance Programme.   Housing
       in Ghana.   New York, 1957.   220 p.
              Reviews the sociological, financial and physical problems
       of housing in the urban areas.

3976   _____.   Report on housing in the Gold Coast.   New York,
       1956.   174 p.

3977   Verstraelen, F.J.   "Catholic missionaries, marriage and
       family life in Ghana: a socio-historical study (1880-1960)
       with special reference to the coastal Akan, " Master's
       Thesis, University of Ghana, 1969.

3978   Voluntary Workcamps Association.   Chichiwere: voluntary
       workcamps for West Africa.   Accra: Guinea Press, 1958?
       144 p.

3979   Wallerstein, Immanuel.   "Class, tribe and party in West
       African politics, " Proceedings of the Fifth World Congress
       of Sociology, held in Bari, Italy, in 1962.

3980   _____.   "Ethnicity and national integration in West Africa, "
       Cahiers Etud. Afr., III (1960), 129-39.

3981   _____ and M. Hechter.   "Social rank and nationalism; some
       African data, " Public Opinion Q., XXXIV (Fall 1970), 360-
       70.

3982   Weinberg, S. Kirson.   "Juvenile delinquency in Ghana: a
       comparative analysis of delinquents and non-delinquents, "
       J. Crim. Law (Dec. 1964), 471-81.

3983   _____.   " 'Mental hearing' and social change in West Africa, "
       Social Problems, XI (Winter 1964), 257-69.

3984   _____.   "Urbanization and male delinquency in Ghana, "
       J. Res. Crim. Delinq., (July 1965), 85-94.

3985   "Women's work, " Advance (Oct. 1965), 1-32.
              Discussion by different contributors of problems of
       women's organization in rural and urban areas--recruit-
       ment and training of organizers.

3986   Wyllie, Robert. "Ghanaian university students: a research
       note," Brit. J. Soc., XVII (Sept. 1966), 306-11.

(17) JUVENILE LITERATURE

3987   Acquaye, Alfred Allotey. Children of West Africa. London:
       Oak Tree Press, 1968. 96 p.

3988   Acquaye, Saka. Obadzeng goes to town. London: Evans,
       1965. 30 p. (Plays for African schools.)

3989   Adams, David Thickens. An Elementary geography of the
       Gold Coast. 3rd ed. London: University of London Press,
       1941. 240 p.
       Designed for elementary and secondary schools, it sur-
       veys physical, sociological and economic aspects of the
       Gold Coast.

3990   Addison, John. Ancient Africa. New York: John Day,
       1971. 48 p.

3991   Addo, Peter Eric. Ghana folk tales--Ananse stories from
       Africa. Jericho, New York: Exposition Press, 1968.
       51 p.
       A collection of sixteen tales, thirteen of which involve
       Ananse (the Spider)--the virtuous but greedy trickster.
       Three main themes embodied in these tales: the value
       of knowledge; proper education for children; and the im-
       portance of good social behavior.
       Rev: Afr. Stud., XXX, no. 1 (1971), 65-6.

3992   Addy, E. A. Ghana history for primary schools. Book 1:
       1450-1800. London: Longmans, 1958. 90 p.

3993   _____ . Ghana history for primary schools. Book 2:
       1800-1957. London: Longmans, 1960. 97 p.

3994   Africa: an annotated list of printed materials suitable for
       children, selected and annotated, by a Joint Committee
       of the American Library Association, Children's Services
       Division and the African-American Institute, Information
       Centre on Children's Cultures. Chicago, 1968. 76 p.
       Rev: Top of the News, XXVI (Nov. 1969), 88-9.

3995   Agadzi, Anna. From poverty to prosperity. Accra: Ad-
       vance Press, 1968. 25 p.

3996 Al Hassan, Susan. Asana and the magic calabash. Accra:
      Longmans, 1963. 24 p. (Stories for Africa.)

3997 Ames, Sophia Ripley. Nkrumah of Ghana. Chicago: Rand
      McNally, 1962. 184 p.
        The biography of the former President of Ghana.
        Rev: Sat. Rev., XLIV (Nov. 11, 1961), 55.

3998 Appiah, Peggy. The Children of Ananse. Illus. by Mora
      Dickson. London: Evans, 1968. 176 p.

3999 _____. The Pineapple child, and other tales from Ashanti.
      Illus. by Mora Dickson. London: Duetsch, 1969. 173 p.
        A collection of Ghanaian folktales.
        Rev: West Africa, No. 2737 (Nov. 15, 1969), 1373.

4000 _____. A smell of onions. London: Longmans, 1971.
      84 p.
        A novel.

4001 _____. Tales of an Ashanti father. Illus. by Mora Dick-
      son. London: Deutsch, 1967. 157 p.

4002 Arbuthnot, Mary Hill. Children and books. 3rd ed. Chicago:
      Scott Foresman, 1964. 688 p. 1st ed. 1947.
        An important reference work primarily designed as a
      textbook for children's literature courses in English and
      Education Departments and library schools in the United
      States. Evaluatively analyzes various children's books
      and audio-visual materials organized in five major parts
      topically subdivided. Each section is followed by problems,
      projects and extensive bibliography. For example, Chapter
      1 discusses seven basic needs of children and Chapter 2,
      criteria for selecting children's books and selection aides.
      Directory of publishers; a guide to pronunciation; author,
      illustrator, subject and title indexes. Although American-
      slanted it should be valuable to anyone working with
      children's library collection.

4003 Berry, John P. Africa speaks: a prose anthology. London:
      Evans, 1970. 120 p.
        Includes summary questions.

4004 Blay, J. Benibengor. Tales for boys and girls. London:
      Macmillan, 1966. 44 p.

4005 Bleeker, Sonia. The Ashanti of Ghana. New York: Morrow,
      1966. 160 p.
        A semi-fictionalized description of the daily life, culture,
      government of the Ashanti; tracing the Ashanti history from
      the European establishment of a gold and slave trade with

the West Coast natives up to the Ghanaian independence.
Rev: Library J., XCI (Oct. 15, 1966), 5222.

4006 Bown, Lalage. "Children's books from Africa," Interracial
Books for Children, II (Spring 1970).
A survey of juvenile works published by African and
British publishers, written mostly by Africans and re-
flecting "the genuine atmosphere of African life." The
author teaches at the University of Zambia.

4007 Brooks, Lester J. Great civilisations of ancient Africa.
New York: Four Winds, 1970. 304 p.

4008 Courlander, Harold and George Herzog. The Cow-tail switch
and other West African stories. New York: Holt, 1947.
143 p.
Delightful folktales drawn from various West African
countries. Some attempt to explain the natural phenomena;
others comment on social values and relationships.

4009 _____ and Albert K. Prempeh. The Hat-shaking dance
and other tales from Ghana. New York: Harcourt, Brace
& Jovanovich, 1957. 115 p.

4010 Davidson, Basil. Discovering our African heritage. Boston:
Ginn, 1971. 278 p.

4011 De Graft-Hanson, J. O. The Secret of Opokuwa: the success
story of the girl with a big state secret. Accra: Anowuo
Educational Publications, 1967. 72 p.
An exciting adventure of three children with the scene set
in a Ghanaian village.

4012 Dick, John. African forum: a comprehension and composition
book for African secondary schools. Cambridge: Cambridge
University Press, 1968. 101 p.
Extracts from the works of writers of various nation-
alities to help students talk and write about their local
experiences.

4013 Dietz, Betty and Michael B. Olatunji. Musical instruments
of Africa: their nature, use, and place in the life of a
deeply musical people. New York: John Day, 1965.
115 p.
A popularized work intended for teenagers by Professor
Dietz of Brooklyn College, New York, and Olatunji, a
Nigerian student in the United States. Well illustrated and
includes a guide to pronunciation, bibliography and an index.
Rev: Library J., XC (April 15, 1965), 2030.

4014 Dorliae, Peter G. Animals mourn for Da Leopard, and
other West African tales. Illus. by S. Irein Wanboje.

Indianapolis: Bobbs-Merrill, 1970.   68 p.
Ten tales and proverbs introducing popular West African
folk characters.

4015   Dzovo, Emmanuel Victor. Salami and Musa: a story.
London: Longmans, 1967.   72 p.

4016   Edwards, Paul Geoffrey, ed.   Through African eyes.   Cambridge: Cambridge Press, 1966.   2 v.
"Designed principally for African schools--its main
purpose is to help to direct and increase reading for
pleasure by offering samples of the lively and intelligent
writing which has come from Africa" (Preface).   Edwards
is Senior Lecturer in English at the University of Edinburgh.

4017   _____.   West African narrative: an anthology for schools.
Edinburgh: Nelson, 1963.   252 p.
Extracts from the works of West African authors with
varied interests, known and obscure, covering different
kinds of writings in different periods, including eighteenth
and nineteenth centuries.

4018   Elliot, Geraldine. The Long grass whispers: African folk
tales. New York: Schocken Books, 1970.   142 p.

4019   Eskelund, Carl and K. Eskelund. Bamburu, boy of Ghana,
in West Africa. London: Methuen, 1958.   46 p.

4020   Fage, J. D. , ed. Africa discovers her past. London: Oxford University Press, 1970.   96 p.

4021   Finkley, Sylvia C. Africa in early days. New York: Odyssey Press, 1969.   85 p.

4022   Freestone, Basil. Osei Tutu: the leopard owns the land.
London: Dobson, 1968.   183 p.   (People from the past
series.)
Tells about a man who assembled the tales of the
Ashanti.

4023   Gidal, Sonia and Tim. My village in Ghana. New York:
Pantheon, 1970.   74 p.
A vivid description of life in an Ashanti village.   Well
illustrated.
Rev: Library J. , XCV (June 15, 1970), 2308.   Sat.
Rev. , LIII (April 18, 1970), 37.

4024   Haskett, Edythe Rance. Some gold, a little ivory; country
tales from Ghana and the Ivory Coast. New York: John
Day, 1971.   126 p.

4025 Hoh, Israel Kafu. Prodigal brothers. London: Evans, 1967.
      29 p. (Plays for African schools.)

4026 Kaye, Geraldine. Great day in Ghana: Kwasi goes to town.
      Illustrated by Valerie Herbst. New York: Abelard-Schu-
      man, 1962. Unpaged.
      On the social life and customs in Ghana.

4027 Kittler, Glenn. Let's travel in Nigeria and Ghana. Edited
      by Darlene Geis. New ed. Chicago: Children's Press,
      1965. 85 p. (A Let's travel book: people and places.)
      1st ed. 1962 under title: A Colorslide tour of Nigeria and
      Ghana.

4028 Lacy, Leslie Alexander. Black Africa on the move. New
      York: Watts, 1969. 63 p.

4029 Marshall, Anthony D. Africa's living arts. New York:
      Watts, 1970. 96 p.

4030 Moore, Jane Anne. Cry sorrow, cry joy! Selections from
      contemporary African writers. New York: Friendship,
      1971. 224 p.

4031 Mutiso, Gideon-Cyrus. Messages: an annotated bibliography
      of African literature for schools. Upper Montclair, New
      Jersey: Montclair State College Press, 1970.

4032 Neville, C. J. Salifu the detective. 2nd rev. ed. London:
      Macmillan, 1957. 185 p. 1st ed. 1950.
      An adventure novel about a boy in the North of the Gold
      Coast (Ghana).

4033 Nickel, Helmut. Arms and armour in Africa. New York:
      Atheneum, 1971. 58 p.

4034 Niven, Cecil Rex. The Lands and peoples of West Africa:
      Gambia, Sierra Leone, Ghana and Nigeria. 2nd ed. New
      York: Macmillan, 1961. 84 p. (The lands and peoples
      series.) 1st ed. 1958 under title: The Land and people
      of West Africa.

4035 Nwoga, Donatus Ibe, ed. West African verse: an anthology,
      chosen and annotated. London: Longmans, 1967. 242 p.
      Selected works of some twenty West African poets de-
      signed for secondary schools, with biographical and critical
      notes on the authors. Dr. Nwoga is the Head of the English
      Department, University of Nigeria.

4036 Ott, A. and J. J. Adaye. English for Twi boys and girls.
      Kumasi: Basel Mission Book Depot, 1957. 187 p.

4037   Owusu, Martin. "The Story of Ananse told," Okyeame, IV
       (Dec. 1968), 51-60.

4038   Parsons, D. St. John. Our poets speak. New York: Afri-
       cana Publishing Corp., 1971. 64 p. First published in
       1966 by University of London Press.
           An anthology of poems with varied themes and style,
       selected from works of noted African poets. Designed for
       secondary schools, it includes biographical notes on the
       authors and other noteworthy points.

4039   Powell, Erica. Kwame Nkrumah of the new Africa. Adapted
       from Ghana, the autobiography of Kwame Nkrumah. Trans.
       from the French by C. L. Patterson. London: Nelson,
       1961. 68 p.

4040   Ridout, Ronald. English for schools and colleges in West
       Africa, Book 3. Lagos: Macmillan, 1969. 248 p.
           For more advanced secondary school students.

4041   _____. English for schools and colleges in West Africa:
       an introductory book. Lagos: Macmillan, 1968. 131 p.

4042   Sale, J. Kirk. Land and people of Ghana. Philadelphia,
       Pennsylvania: Lippincott, 1963. 159 p. (Portraits of the
       nations series.)

4043   Schloat, G. Warren. Kwaku, a boy of Ghana. New York:
       Knopf, 1962.
           A novel about daily life of a small boy living in Tema,
       seaport in Ghana--his experiences in his home and at
       school.
           Rev: Commonweal, LXXVII (Nov. 16, 1962), 210.
       Library J., LXXXVIII (Jan. 15, 1963), 342.

4044   Stejskal, Vaclau. "Children's literature and education,"
       Ghana Teachers' J., No. 53 (Oct. 1966), 47-54.

4045   Sutherland, Efua Theodora. Playtime in Africa. Photos
       by Willis E. Bell. London: Knight & Truscott, 1960.
       62 p.

4046   Theobald, Robert, ed. The New nations of West Africa.
       New York: Wilson, 1960. 179 p. (The reference shelf,
       v. 32, no. 2.)
           Thirty-three articles by British and American writers
       that appeared in various leading newspapers describe the
       political, economic and social problems of the West African
       nations before independence.

4047   Watts, Margaret E., ed. The New generation: prose and
       verse from the secondary schools and training colleges

of Ghana. Accra: State Publishing Corp., for the Ghana
Association of Teachers of English, 1967.   58 p.

(D) OFFICIAL PUBLICATIONS

Many official publications on specific subjects have already been
entered under the applicable subjects in the preceding classified
sections.   The publications listed below are grouped into three
headings: The Gold Coast; Ghana and Great Britain.   Entries
under each heading are arranged by author or the issuing government
agency.   Works published by the same agency follow an annalistic
arrangement--by the year of publication, and not in strict chronological order, for it has not been possible to ascertain the exact
days and months for all the publications issued the same year.
Thus publications appearing the same year and issued by the same
government agency are arranged alphabetically by title.   Dates of
publication precede each title entry.

(1) THE GOLD COAST

4048   Gold Coast.   Census Office. 1932.   The Gold Coast, 1931; a
       review of conditions in the Gold Coast in 1931 as compared
       with those of 1921, based on figures and facts collected by
       the Chief Census Officer of 1931, together with a historical,
       ethnographical, and sociological survey of the people of the
       country.   Accra. 265 p.
           The Chief Census Officer, Allan Wolsey Cardinall, later
       published Bibliography of the Gold Coast (1932) as a com-
       panion volume to this census report.
           Rev: Africa, VII (Jan. 1934), 60-9.

4049   _____ . 1932.   The Gold Coast, 1931; appendices contain-
       ing comparative and general statistics of the 1931 census.
       Accra.   246 p.

4050   _____ . Education Dept. 1951.   Accelerated Development
       Plan for Education, 1951.   With a foreword by Kojo Botsio,
       Minister of Education and Social Welfare.   Accra: Govt.
       Printer.   23 p.

4051   _____ . 1953.   Progress in education in the Gold Coast.
       Accra.   20 p.

4052   _____ . Dept. of Social Welfare and Community Develop-
       ment. 1952.   Literacy campaign.   Accra: West African
       Graphic Co.   52 p.

410

4053 _____ . 1955. Problem children of the Gold Coast.
      Accra.   28 p.

4054 Gold Coast. Government. 1918. Report of the Commission
      of Enquiry into the claims of certain chiefs of the Ayan to
      be Head Chief of an Ayan Division. London: Waterloo.
      37 p. (Sessional paper No. 6 of 1917/18.)

4055 _____ . 1921. Further correspondence relating to the
      National Congress of British West Africa, together with
      the Governor's [Guggisberg] speech at the Legislative
      Council meeting on 27th April, 1921. Accra. 17 p.
      (Sessional paper No. 10 of 1920/21.)

4056 _____ . 1922. Report by the Director of Education
      [D. J. Oman] on his visit to educational institutions in the
      United States. Accra. 32 p.

4057 _____ . 1923. Report of the Town Councils Committee
      on the Constitution and Working of the Existing Town
      Councils in the Colony. Accra. 95 p. (Sessional paper
      No. 17 of 1922/23.)

4058 _____ . 1925. Despatches from his Excellency the
      Governor [Guggisberg] to the Secretary of State of the
      Colonies on the system of education, organization, cost
      of buildings and equipment and annual cost and revenue
      of Achimota College and School. Accra. 26 p. (Ses-
      sional paper No. 9 of 1925/26.)

4059 _____ . 1928. Papers relating to a project for the con-
      struction of a railway between Kumasi and the Northern
      Territories of the Gold Coast. Accra. 109 p. (Ses-
      sional paper No. 23 of 1927/28.)

4060 _____ . 1929. Despatches relating to a project for the
      construction of a railway between Kumasi and the Northern
      Territories of the Gold Coast. Accra. 23 p. (Sessional
      paper No. 16 of 1929/30.)

4061 _____ . 1930. Correspondence relating to the installation
      of an electric light and power plant at Cape Coast. Accra.
      12 p. (Sessional paper No. 13 of 1930/31.)

4062 _____ . 1930. Correspondence relating to the revision of
      the initial rates of salary in the African civil service.
      Accra. 31 p. (Sessional paper No. 1 of 1930/31.)

4063 _____ . 1930. Despatches from the Secretary of State
      relating to the proposal to establish a Medical College in
      the Gold Coast, together with regulations and conditions
      for the award of Government scholarships to African

students for the purpose of studying medicine in the United Kingdom. Accra. 8 p. (Sessional paper No. 16 of 1930/31.)

4064   . 1930. Scheme for the reorganization of the Government Technical School. Accra. (Sessional paper No. 2 of 1930/31.)

4065   . 1931. Address delivered by His Excellency the Acting Governor on the occasion of the Opening of the 1931-32 session of the Legislative Council. Accra.

4066   . 1932. Report of the Committee Appointed in 1932 by the Governor of the Gold Coast Colony to Inspect the Prince of Wales's College and School, Achimota. Letchworth, Herts: Garden City Press. 80 p. (H.S. Newlands, Chairman.)

4067   . 1934. Report of the Advisory Committee on Education in the Colonies on the Educational Function of Local Bodies in the Tropical African Dependencies. Accra. (Sessional paper No. 8 of 1934.)

4068   . 1935. Papers relating to the restoration of the Ashanti Confederacy. Accra. 115 p.

4069   . 1939. Report of the Committee Appointed in 1938 by the Governor of the Gold Coast Colony to Inspect the Prince of Wales College, Achimota. Accra. 154 p. (A.W. Pickard--Cambridge, Chairman.)

4070   . 1943. Report of the Education Committee, 1937-41, to Examine the Existing Educational System in the Gold Coast. Accra. 32 p.

4071   . 1944. Address delivered by His Excellency the Governor, Sir Alan Cuthbert Maxwell Burns, K.C.M.G., on the occasion of the opening of the 1944 session of the Legislative Council, 13th March, 1944. Accra. 38 p.

4072   . 1944. Statement on government's policy regarding the appointment of African candidates to the senior posts of the various Government Departments. Accra. (Sessional paper No. 1 of 1944.)

4073   . 1945. Address delivered by His Excellency the Governor, Sir Alan Cuthbert Maxwell Burns, K.C.M.G., on the occasion of the opening of the 1945 session of the Legislative Council, 6th March, 1945. Accra. 38 p.

4074   . 1946. Despatch on higher education in West Africa, by the Secretary of State for the Colonies. Accra. (Sessional paper No. 4 of 1946.)

4075   . 1947. Report of the Commission of Enquiry into the Representations made by W. E. Conway and others Repudiating Allegations in the Report of the Commission of Enquiry into the Conduct and Management of the Supplies and Customs Departments. Accra. 144 p. (Extraordinary gazette No. 64 of 1947.)

4076   . 1947. Revised conditions of service for the Gold Coast civil services, 1946. 73 p. (Its sessional paper No. 1 of 1947.)

4077   . 1947. Report of the Committee on the Scale of Emoluments Applicable to Teachers in Non-Government Institutions. Accra. 20 p. (Sessional paper No. 6 of 1947.)

4078   . 1949. The Gold Coast; a brief description for presentation at the Gold Coast stand, British Industries Fair, 1949. Accra. 32 p.

4079   . 1949. Report to His Excellency the Governor by the Committee on Constitutional Reform, 1949. London: H. M. S. O. 104 p. (Colonial No. 248.) (Chairman, J. H. Coussey.)

4080   . 1950. Supplement to the report of the Select Committee of the Legislative Council on the Africanization of the Public Service. Accra. 70 p. (Sessional paper 4 of 1950.)

4081   . 1951. Report of the Select Committee Appointed to Make Recommendations Concerning Local Government in Ashanti. Accra. 64 p.

4082   . 1953. Gold Coast Government on the report of the Broadcasting Commission. Accra. 16 p.

4083   . 1953. Report of the Commission of Enquiry into Representational and Electoral Reform. Accra. 32 p. (Sessional paper, No. 1 of 1953.) (Chairman: Mr. Justice Van Lare.)

4084   . 1954. A Statement on the programme of the Africanisation of the public service. Accra: Govt. Printer. 76 p.

4085   . 1955. Report of the Select Committee on Federal System of Government and Second Chamber for the Gold Coast, together with the proceedings of the Committee, minutes of evidence and an appendix. Accra. 198 p. (Chairman: C. H. Chapman.)

4086   . 1956. Constitutional proposals for Gold Coast
        independence and statement on the report of the Constitu-
        tional Adviser and the report of Achimota Conference.
        Accra. 1956. 7 p.

4087   . 1956. Government proposals in regard to the
        future constitution and control of statutory boards and
        corporations in the Gold Coast Report of the Commission
        of Enquiry into the affairs of the Cocoa Purchasing Com-
        pany Limited. Accra. 73 p.

4088   . 1956. The Government's revised constitutional
        proposals for Gold Coast independence. Accra. 18 p.

4089   . 1956. Report of the Preparatory Commission on
        the Volta River Project. London: H. M. S. O. 3 vols.
                V. 1. presented by R. G. A. Jackson. V. 2. contains
        appendices. V. 3. includes engineering report made to
        the Preparatory Commission by Sir William Hal Row.

4090   . 1956. Report on the use of English (as the
        medium of instruction) in the Gold Coast schools. Accra.
        70 p. (Director of the study: G. L. Barnard.)

4091   Gold Coast. Laws, Statutes, etc. 1920. The Laws of the
        Gold Coast Colony containing the ordinances of the Gold
        Coast Colony and the orders, proclamations, rules, regu-
        lations and by-laws--in force on 31st day December 1919--
        Rev. ed. London: Stevens.

4092   . 1951. Laws of the Gold Coast. Rev. ed. Accra:
        Govt. Printer. 5 vols.

4093   . 1951. Local Government Ordinance. Accra.
        65 p. (Its No. 29, 1951.)

4094   . 1952. Municipal Councils Ordinance, 1952.
        Accra. 78 p.

4095   . 1952-54. Laws of the Gold Coast. Supplement.
        Accra: Govt. Printer. 2 v.

4096   . 1954. Laws of the Gold Coast. Rev. ed. Accra.
        Vols. 6-9.

4097   . 1956. Handbook for native courts in the colony.
        Acra. 63 p.

4098   Nkrumah, Kwame. 1956. Revised constitutional proposals:
        speech delivered in the Legislative Assembly on November
        12th 1956. London. 14 p.
                (Supplement to the Gold Coast Colony today, v. 1, No.
        24, Dec. 5, 1956.)

(2) GHANA

4099 Ghana. Broadcasting Corporation. 1966. Our destiny in
      our hands; news commentaries from Radio Ghana, Febru-
      ary 24, 1966. Accra. Ministry of Information. 26 p.

4100 _____. Census Office. 1960. Manuals for census offi-
      cers and enumerations of the 1960 census. Accra. 8 vols.

4101 _____. Central Bureau of Statistics. 1961. Import and
      export list (to come into force on 1st Jan. 1961). Accra.
      52 p.

4102 _____. 1968. Educational Statistics, 1963-64: secondary
      schools, teacher training colleges, commercial/technical
      institutes. Accra. 187 p.

4103 _____. Embassy (Brazil) 1968. Aspectos de cultura de
      Gana. Rio de Janeiro. 36 p.

4104 _____. Government. 1957. Report of the Commission
      Appointed to Enquire into Salaries and Wages of the Civil
      Service and Non-Government Teaching Service. Accra.
      78 p.

4105 _____. 1958. Proposed scheme for international service
      of the Ghana Broadcasting System, by A. L. Pidgeon and
      J. L. Marshall. Accra. 22 p.
      A report by officers of the Canadian Broadcasting
      Corporation.

4106 _____. 1958. Report of the Commission Appointed to
      Enquire into the Affairs of the Kumasi State Council and
      the Asanteman Council. Accra. 141 p. (Commissioner,
      Mr. Justice Sarkodee-Adoo.)

4107 _____. 1959. Interim report of the Commission of En-
      quiry into the Working and Administration of Present
      Company Law. Accra. (Commissioner, L. C. B. Gower.)

4108 _____. 1959. Proceedings and report of the Commission
      Appointed to Enquire into the Matters Disclosed at the
      Trial of Captain Benjamin Awhaitey before a Court-Martial
      and the Surrounding Circumstances, with the Minutes of
      Evidence Taken before the Commission, January-March,
      1959. Accra. 506 p. (Chairman: G. Granville Sharp.)

4109 _____. 1959. Statement by the Government on the report
      of the Commission Appointed to Enquire into the Matters
      Disclosed at the Trial of Captain Benjamin Awhaitey before
      a Court-Martial and the Surrounding Circumstances. Accra.
      50 p.

4110 _____. 1959? Second Development Plan, 1959-64. Accra:
124 p.

4111 _____. 1960. Correspondence exchanged between Kwame
Nkrumah and the leaders of the Republic of the Congo on
the situation. Accra. 26 p.
Covers the period, July 13-Oct. 10, 1960.

4112 _____. 1960. Government statement on the report on a
television service, by R. D. Cahoon and S. R. Kennedy of
the Canadian Broadcasting Corporation. Accra. 3 p.
(W. P. No. 4/60.)
The report was submitted to the Government in 1959.

4113 _____. 1960. Proceedings, official report of the Con-
stituent Assembly, 14th March-29th June, 1960. Accra.
420 p.

4114 _____. 1961. Final Report of the Commission of Enquiry
into the Working and Administration of the Present Company
Law of Ghana. Accra. 325 p.

4115 _____. 1961. Presidential address by Osagyefo Dr.
Kwame Nkrumah, President of the Republic of Ghana to
the resumed session of the 15th General Assembly of the
United Nations, New York, 7th March 1961. New York.
49 p.

4116 _____. 1961. Report of the Commission Appointed to
Enquire into the Insolvency Law of Ghana. Accra. 272 p.
(Chairman: A. Adomakoh.)

4117 _____. 1961. Report of the Committee on the Education,
Rehabilitation and Employment of Disabled People in Ghana.
Accra. 23 p. (Chairman: John Wilson.)

4118 _____. 1961. Report of the Commission on University
Education, December 1960-January 1961. Accra. 43 p.
(Chairman: Kojo Botsio.)

4119 _____. 1961. Statement by the Government on the report
of the Commission on University Education, December
1960-January 1961. Accra: Govt. Printer. 7 p. (W. P.
No. 5/61.)

4120 _____. 1961. Statement of the Government on the recent
conspiracy (allegation that opponents of Nkrumah's taxation
proposals had plotted to assassinate him and overthrow the
government). Accra. 50 p.

4121 _____. 1961. Survey of high-level manpower in Ghana,
1960. Accra: Ministry of Information. 62 p.

4122   _____. 1961. The Volta River Project. Statement by
          the Government of Ghana, 20th Feb. 1961. Accra. 99 p.

4123   _____. 1961. White paper on marriage, divorce and in-
          heritance. Accra. 5 p. (W. P. No. 3/61.)

4124   _____. 1962. Education Act, 1961. (Eighty-seventh
          Act of the Parliament of the Republic of Ghana) Accra:
          State Publishing Corporation, Printing Division. 16 p.
          The legalization of the compulsory education; specifi-
          cation of the duties of local education authorities and
          teachers' position and organization.

4125   _____. 1962. Report of the Commission of Enquiry into
          the Operation of Rent Control Ordinance. Accra. 99 p.
          (Ministry of Communications and Works, No. 2 of 1962.)
          (Chairman: S. A. Kwaku Bonsu.)

4126   _____. 1963. A Memorandum in regard to Southern
          Rhodesia submitted to Security Council on the 2nd August,
          1963. Accra. 84 p. (W. P. No. 4/63.)
          The position of Ghana on the Rhodesian issue put before
          the Security Council of the United Nations.

4127   _____. 1963. Report of the Commission Appointed to
          Enquire into the Circumstances which led to the Payment
          of 28,545 pounds to Colledge (Cocoa) Limited as Compen-
          sation for Land Acquired for the Achiesi-Kotoku Railway.
          Accra. 39 p.

4128   _____. 1964. Seven-year Development Plan, 1963/64-
          1969/70. Accra. 305 p.

4129   _____. 1966. Report of the Committee of Enquiry on
          the Local Purchasing of Cocoa. Accra. (Chairman:
          J. C. De Graft-Johnson.)

4130   _____. 1966. Statement on Southern Rhodesia by the
          President and Government of Ghana, Oct. 1965. to January
          1966. Accra: Publicity Secretariat for the Ministry of
          Foreign Affairs. 25 p.
          Statements by President Kwame Nkrumah.

4131   _____. 1967. Report of the Commission on Enquiry into
          Irregularities and Malpractices in the Grant of Import
          Licenses. Accra: Ministry of Information. 476 p.

4132   _____. 1967. Report of the Commission of Enquiry,
          University of Science and Technology. Accra. 315 p.

4133   _____. 1967. Report of the Commission of Enquiry on
          the Commercial Activities of the Erstwhile Publicity

Secretariat, and White Paper on the Report.   Accra.
122 p.

4134 _____. 1967. Report of the Committee of Experts to
Advise on the Future of the Ghana Academy of Sciences.
Accra. 63 p.

4135 _____. 1967. Report of the Commission on the Structure
and Renumeration of the Public Services of Ghana.   Accra:
Ministry of Information.   99 p.   (Chairman: Mr. Justice
G. C. Mills-Odoi.)

4136 _____. 1968. Memorandum on the Proposals of the
Constitutional Commission for a Constitution for Ghana.
Accra: State Publishing Corporation, Printing Division.
161 p.   (Chairman: Mr. Justice Akufo-Addo.)

4137 _____. 1968. Report of the Commission of Enquire
into Electoral and Local Government Reform.   Accra.
3 parts.   (Chairman: Mr. J. B. Siriboe.)

4138 _____. 1968. Report of the Commission Appointed to
Enquire into the Manner of Operation of the State Housing
Corporation.   Accra: Ministry of Information.   335 p.
(Chairman: David Samson Effa.)

4139 _____. 1968. Report of the Committee Appointed to
Enquire into the Manner of Operation of the State Dis-
tilleries Corporation.   Accra.   97 p.   (Chairman: Mr.
J. O. T. Agyeman.)

4140 _____. 1968. Report of the Committee of Enquiry into
the State Furniture and Joinery Corporation.   Accra:
Ministry of Information.   157 p.   (Chairman: Mr. S. A. X.
Tsegah.)

4141 _____. 1969. Population planning for national progress
and prosperity; Ghana population policy.   Accra.   23 p.
Preface by E. N. Omaboe, Commissioner for Economic
Affairs.

4142 _____. 1969. Report of Sowah Commission of Enquiry
into the assets of Specified persons.   Accra: Ministry of
Information.   207 p.

4143 _____. 1969. White paper on the report of Manyo-Plange
Commission of Enquiry into the Assets of Specified Persons.   Accra-Tema.   (Its W. P. No. 11/69.)

4144 _____. 1969. White paper on the report of the Committee Appointed to Investigate All Aspects of the Health
Needs of Ghana.   Accra-Tema.   12 p.   (Its W. P. No.
15/69.)

4145 _____. 1969. White paper on the second report of Sowah
Commission of Enquiry into Assets of Specified Persons.
Accra: Ministry of Information. 11 p. (Its W. P. No.
16/69.)

4146 _____. 1969. White paper on the third report of the
Jiagge Commission of Enquiry into the Assets of Specified
Persons. Accra: Ministry of Information. 4 p.

4147 _____. Ministry of Education, 1957. Education in Ghana;
text of speech given to the Ghana Parliament on June 13,
1957, by the Minister of Education. Washington, D. C.
Information Office, Embassy of Ghana. 10 p.

4148 _____. 1959. First Seminar on the Writing of School
Text-books for Ghana; the background papers. Accra:
Bureau of Ghana Languages. 64 p.

4149 _____. 1960. The Duke in Ghana: a pictorial record
of the visit to Ghana of His Royal Highness the Prince
Philip, Duke of Edinburgh, in 1959, together with the collected speeches made by his Royal Highness, by the Prime
Minister of Ghana and others. Accra. 36 p.

4150 _____. Information Services Dept. 1958. Ghana is reborn, 6th March 1957, by Lionel Birch. London: Neame.
106 p.

4151 _____. 1966. Ghana reborn. New York: Ghana Information Services. 68 p.

4152 _____. 1967. Outline of Government economic policy.
New York. 10 p.

4153 _____. Laws, Statutes, etc. 1960. The Civil Service
Act, 1960 and the Civil Service Regulations, 1960.
Accra. 39 p.

4154 _____. 1961. Index to the Acts and Ordinances with
chronological table, in force on 31st March, 1961. Accra.
127 p.

4155 _____. Ministry of Information, 1960. Press handbook;
inauguration of the Republic of Ghana. Accra: Ghana
Information Service. 35 p.

4156 _____. 1962. Ghana Republic souvenir. Accra. 55 p.
Contents: Towards the Republic.--The new constitution;
the end of an epoch;--Republic Day.--Days of celebration.
--In honour of the past.

4157 _____. 1966. Nkrumah's subversion in Africa: documentary evidence of Nkrumah's interference in the affairs
of other African states. Accra. 91 p.

4158 _____. 1966. The Rebirth of Ghana; the end of tyranny.
Accra. 56 p.
        Considers the deposition of Kwame Nkrumah as the end
of dictatorship in Ghana.

4159 _____. 1967. Dr. J. B. Danquah: detention and death
in Nsawam Prison. Extracts from evidences of witnesses
at the Commission of Enquiry in Ghana prisons. Accra.
212 p.

4160 _____. 1967. Duplicité de Nkrumah sur l'Afrique. Accra.
139 p.

4161 _____. 1967. Nkrumah's subversion in Africa; documentary evidence of Nkrumah's interference in the affairs
of other African states. Accra. 91 p.

4162 _____. 1968. M. E. Obetsebi-Lamptey; sa detention et
sa mort à la prison de Nsawam; extraits de depositions
de temoirs à la Commission de enquete Concernant les
prisons du Ghana. Accra. 57 p.

4163 _____. 1968. Two years after liberation: a review of
the second year of liberation. Accra. 38 p.

4164 _____. National Economic Committee. 1967. Ghana's
economy and aid requirements in 1967. Accra. 43 p.

4165 _____. Office of the Government Statistician. 1960.
Survey of cocoa producing families in Ashanti, 1956-57.
Accra. 112 p. (Statistical and economic papers, No. 7.)

4166 _____. Office of the Government Statistician. 1961.
Index to the import and export list (to come into force on
1st January, 1961). Accra. 75 p.

4167 _____. Town and Country Planning Division. 1958. Accra,
a plan for the town; the report for the Ministry of Housing.
With a foreword by Kwame Nkrumah.

4168 _____. United Party. 1959. In defense of Ghana; a
statement by the National Executive of the United Party
on the Granville Sharp Commission's reports and the
Government's white paper on the report. Accra. 35 p.

4169 International Labour Office. 1961. Report to the
Government of Ghana on the establishment of a national
apprenticeship system. Geneva. 53 p.

4170 _____ . 1962. Report to the Government of Ghana on the organization of a national system of vocational guidance. Geneva. 65 p.

4171 _____ . 1966. Report to the Government of Ghana on the introduction of a provident fund and pension scheme. Geneva. 80 p.

4172 Nkrumah, Kwame. 1957. Ghana's policy at home and abroad; speech given in the Ghana Parliament, August 29, 1957. Washington, D.C.: Information Office, Ghana Embassy. 14 p.

4173 _____ . 1958. Foreign policy; a statement made in the National Assembly on 3rd September 1958. Washington, D.C., Information Section, Embassy of Ghana. 7 p.

4174 _____ . 1960. Address to the 15th session of the General Assembly of the United Nations. Accra: Ghana Information Services, 1960. 22 p.

4175 _____ . 1960. Collection of speeches delivered during the Republic celebrations 30th June-4th July, 1960. Accra. 15 p.

4176 _____ . 1960. Peace! The world from African eyes: address of Osagyefo Dr. Kwame Nkrumah, President of the Republic of Ghana to the 15th session of the United Nations General Assembly, Sept. 23, 1960. Accra. 27 p.

4177 _____ . 1961. Building a socialist state: an address to the C.P.P. study group, April 22, 1961. Accra. 12 p.

4178 _____ . 1961. Osagyefo speaks; two addresses given during the first anniversary of the inauguration of the Republic of Ghana. Accra: Govt. Printer. 8 p.

4179 _____ . 1962. Address to mark the opening of the First International Congress of Africanists on December 12th, 1962. Accra. 12 p.

4180 _____ . 1963. Torch bearers; address at the opening of the Second Conference of African Journalists held in Accra on 11th Nov. 1963. Accra. 17 p.

(3) GREAT BRITAIN

4181 Great Britain. Central Office of Information. Reference Division. 1947. Local self-government in British West Africa. London. 17 p. (Typescript)

4182   _____ .   1957.   The Making of Ghana.   London.   46 p.
(Reference pamphlet, 19.)

4183   _____ .   Colonial Office.   1938.   Report of the Commission on the marketing of West African cocoa.   London.
221 p.   (Cmnd. 5845.)   (Chairman: William Nowell.)

4184   _____ .   1945.   Report of the Commission on Higher
Education in West Africa.   London.   (Cmnd. 6655.)

4185   _____ .   1947.   Report of the Commission on the Civil
Services of British West Africa, 1945-46.   London.
189 p.   (Chairman: Sir Walter Harragin.)

4186   _____ .   1948.   Annual report on the Gold Coast for the
year 1946.   London.

4187   _____ .   1948.   Report of the Commission of Enquiry into
Disturbances in the Gold Coast, 1948.   London.   103 p.
(Watson Report.)

4188   _____ .   1948.   Statement by H. M. Government on the
report of the Commission of Enquiry into the Disturbances
in the Gold Coast, 1948.   London.   19 p.

4189   _____ .   1949.   Gold Coast.   Statement of His Majesty's
government on the report of the Committee on Constitutional
Reform; despatch of 14th Oct. 1949 from the Secretary of
State.   London.   11 p.   (Colonial No. 250.)

4190   _____ .   1952.   An Economic Survey of the colonial territories, vol. 3: The Gambia, the Gold Coast, Nigeria
and Sierra Leone, and St. Helena.   London.   103 p.

4191   _____ .   1956.   Report to the General Assembly of the
United Nations on Togoland under United Kingdom administration for the year 1955.   London.   198 p.

4192   _____ .   1957.   Britain and the Gold Coast: the dawn of
Ghana.   London.   41 p.

4193   _____ .   1957.   The proposed constitution of Ghana, presented by the Secretary of State for the Colonies to Parliament Feb. 1957.   London.   10 p.

(E) NEWSPAPERS AND PERIODICALS

(1) SELECT GHANAIAN NEWSPAPERS

4194 Business Weekly. Accra: Business Publications. (Ring Road West, P. O. Box 2351). Weekly.
An independent paper in English.

4195 Daily Graphic. Accra: Graphic Corporation. (Brewery Road, P. O. Box 742). Daily.
Independent and the most widely read newspaper in Ghana. Printed in English and very strong in international news.

4196 The Evening News. Accra: Guinea Press Ltd. (Ring Road West, P. O. Box 2638). Daily.
In English.

4197 The Ghanaian Times. Accra: Guinea Press Ltd. (Ring Road West, P. O. Box 2638). Daily.
A government newspaper in English.

4198 New Ashanti Times. Obuasi: Ashanti Gold Fields Corporation Ltd. (P. O. Box 9). Weekly.
The organ of the Ashanti Gold Fields Corporation. A largely non-political newspaper in English with emphasis on the economic development of Ghana; second in quality to Daily Graphic.

4199 The Standard. Cape Coast: Archdiocese. (Catholic Mission Press, P. O. Box 60). Weekly.

4200 Sunday Mirror. Accra: Graphic Corporation. (Brewery Road, P. O. Box 742). Weekly.
A government paper in English.

4201 Weekly Spectator. Accra: Guinea Press Ltd. (Ring Road West, P. O. Box 2638). Weekly.
A government paper in English.

(2) SELECT GHANAIAN PERIODICALS

4202 African Woman, v. 1+, 1961+. Accra. Monthly.

4203   The African Worker; le travailleur africain, v. 1, No. 1+,
       1961+. Accra: African Affairs Division. Semi-monthly.

4204   The Economic Bulletin of Ghana, v. 1+, 1957+. Legon:
       Economic Society of Ghana. Quarterly. 1957-61, Monthly.
       1962+, Quarterly.

4205   Ghana. University. Institute of African Studies. Research
       Review, v. 1, No. 1+, 1965+. Legon. Three times a
       year.
       Includes reports on current research done by people
       associated with the University, specifying unique items of
       research.

4206   Ghana Bulletin of Theology, v. 1, No. 1+, 1964+. Legon:
       Dept. for the Study of Religions, University of Ghana.
       Semi-annual.

4207   Ghana Cultural Review, v. 1+, March 1965+. Accra: Divi-
       sion of Higher Education, Dept. of Art and Culture.
       Quarterly.

4208   Ghana Foreign Affairs, v. 1, No. 1+, Dec. 1960+. Accra:
       Ministry of Foreign Affairs. Quarterly.

4209   Ghana Geographical Association. Bulletin, v. 1+, 1956+.
       Accra. Semi-annual.

4210   Ghana Guardian, v. 1, No. 1+, Oct. 1966+. Accra: West
       African Publications Service. Monthly.

4211   Ghana Journal of Child Development, v. 1, No. 1+, June
       1968+. Legon, Child Development Unit, Dept. of Soci-
       ology, University of Ghana. Semi-annual.

4212   The Ghana Journal of Sociology: a review of research on
       West African Society, v. 1+, 1965+. Legon: Dept. of
       Sociology, University of Ghana. Semi-annual.

4213   Ghana Library Journal, v. 1, No. 1+, Oct. 1963+. Accra:
       Ghana Library Association. Three times a year. (Irregu-
       lar)
       Contains articles on the development of librarianship in
       Ghana. Supersedes in part WALA News.

4214   Ghana News, v. 1, No. 1+, 1963+. Washington: Embassy
       of Ghana. Monthly.

4215   Ghana Notes and Queries, No. 1+, 1961+. Legon: Historical
       Society of Ghana. Irregular.
       Emphasis is on archaeology and history.

4216   Ghana Review, v. 1, No. 1+, June 1961+. Accra: Ghana
       Information Services. Monthly. (Irregular)
       Title varies: Ghana Reconstructs.

4217   Ghana Teachers' Journal, May 1952+. Accra. Three times
       a year.

4218   Ghana Today, v. 1, No. 1+, March 1957+. Accra: In-
       formation Dept., Ministry of External Affairs. Bi-weekly.

4219   Ghana Trade Journal, v. 1+, June 1959+. Accra: Business
       Publications. Monthly.
       "Ghana's oldest magazine for trade, commerce, indus-
       try and finance."

4220   Insight and Opinion: quarterly for current African writing, v. 1+,
       March 1966+. Accra: Nanonom Publishers. Quarterly.
       Contains articles on current events, including film and play
       reviews.

4221   Journal of Management Studies, v. 1, No. 1+, June 1966+.
       Legon: School of Administration, University of Ghana.
       Irregular.

4222   Legon Observer, v. 1+, No. 1+, July 1966+. Legon:
       Dept. of Political Science, University of Ghana. Bi-
       weekly.
       The organ of the Legon Society on National Affairs.

4223   New Era, No. 1+, Oct. 1968+. Monthly.
       "A magazine for emergent Ghana."

4224   Transition, v. 1, No. 1+, 1961+. Accra: Transition Ltd.
       in association with the International Association for Cul-
       tural Freedom (Paris). Irregular.
       An important, well edited journal, until October 1968
       was published in Kampala, Uganda, where the editor,
       Rajat Neogy was imprisoned by the Obote government for
       seditious publication. Emphasis is on creative writing
       and politics. The Ghana address: Airport P. O. 9063,
       Accra.

(F) DIRECTORY OF PUBLISHERS, BOOKSELLERS, ETC.

This select list of principal publishers in Ghana includes research institutes and university bookstores that act as distributing agencies for their university or institute.   Included are the Ghanaian branches of some major British publishers that at times produce works under a separate imprint for local consumption, and also indicated where known are the other British and American distributors.

4225   Aburi Printing Works Ltd.
P. O. Box 325
Aburi

4226   Anowuo Educational Publications
2R McCarthy Hill
Accra
(Some titles obtainable from Humanities Press, New York.)

4227   Benibengor Book Agency
P. O. Box 40
Aboso

4228   Bureau of Ghana Languages
Ghana Information Services
Weija Road
Accra

4229   Catholic Mission Press
Royal Lane
P. O. Box 60
Cape Coast

4230   Gasarm Partners
P. O. Box 988
Accra

4231   Ghana Book Suppliers Agency
P. O. Box 3994
Accra

4232   Ghana Graphic Company Ltd.
P. O. Box 742
Accra

4233   Ghana State Publishing Corporation
       P. O. Box 4348
          Accra

4234   Ghana Trade Journal
       P. O. Box 2351
          Accra

4235   Ghana Universities Press
       P. O. Box 4219
          Accra
          (Oxford University Press publishes some titles on their
          behalf.)

4236   Government Printing Dept.
          Accra

4237   Guinea Press Ltd.
       King Road West
       P. O. Box 2638
          Accra

4238   Institute of African Studies
       University of Ghana
          Legon

4239   Longmans Green & Co. Ltd.
       P. O. Box 2051
          Accra

4240   Methodist Book Depot
       Atlantis House
       Commercial Street
       P. O. Box 100
          Cape Coast

4241   Mfantsiman Press Ltd.
       Old Market Street
       C. 19/3
          Cape Coast

4242   Moxon Paper Backs
       P. O. Box M 160
          Accra

4243   New Africa Publications
       P. O. Box 2052
          Accra

4244   Ofori & Sons
       P. O. Box 73
          Accra

4245   Presbyterian Book Depot
        P. O. Box 195
            Accra

4246   Reliance Book Depot
        P. O. Box 989
            Accra

4247   Scottish Mission Printing Press
        P. O. Box 3075
            Accra

4248   Secretariat for an Encyclopaedia
        P. O. Box 2797
            Accra

4249   Simpson's Book Service
        Lutterodt Street
        P. O. Box 1216
            Accra

4250   Spark Publications Ltd.
        P. O. Box M 171
            Accra

4251   Thomas Nelson & Sons Ltd.
        P. O. Box 2187
            Accra

4252   University Bookshop
        University of Ghana
        P. O. Box 1
            Legon

4253   University College Bookshop
        University College
            Cape Coast

4254   University of Science and Technology
            Kumasi

4255   Vox Populi Press
        P. O. Box 1496
            Accra

4256   Waterville Publishing House
        P. O. Box 195
            Accra

4257   West African Bookshop
        P. O. Box 256
            Accra

4258   West African Trade Union Information & Advisory Centre
       Selwyn Market Street, D 794/3
       P. O. Box 70
           Accra

Book Trade Organization

4259   Ghana Booksellers Association
       P. O. Box 899
           Accra

4260 Abbia, No. 1+, Feb. 1963+. Yaoundé, Cameroun.
Quarterly. (irregular)
"Cameroon Cultural Review" in English, French or
indigenous languages, sponsored by the Education Ministry of the Federal Republic of Cameroon.

4261 Africa; journal of the International African Institute, v. 1+,
1928+. London. Quarterly.
Strong in African ethnology, sociology and linguistics.
Includes book reviews and extensive bibliography. Text
in English, French or German.

4262 Africa, No. 1+, 1942+. Madrid: Instituto de Estudios
Africanos. Monthly.
Of general interest with emphasis on Spanish Africa.
Book reviews and bibliography.

4263 Africa; revista trimestrale di studi e documentazione, v. 1+,
1946+. Roma: Le Edizioni Africana. Quarterly.
Studies of a general interest and extensive documentation of books and periodical articles.

4264 Africa Digest, v. 1+, July 1953+. London. Bimonthly.
Summaries and articles of current interest, and includes
extracts from newspapers and periodicals.

4265 Africa Institute. Bulletin, v. 1+, Feb. 1963+. Pretoria.
Monthly.
Editions in English and Afrikaans. Includes book
reviews.

4266 Africa Quarterly: journal of Indian Council for Africa, v. 1+,
April/June 1961+. New Delhi. Quarterly.
Contains articles on contemporary African affairs.

4267 Africa Report, v. 1+, July 1956+. Washington, D.C.,
African-American Institute. Monthly except July, August
and September.
Scholarly articles on current events in Africa--political,
economic, literary, social, historical, etc. Includes book
reviews and annual index.

4268   Africa Research Bulletin, v. 1+, 1964+.   Exeter, Eng. :
        Africa Research Ltd.   Monthly.
            Series A: Political, social and cultural.   Series B:
        Economic, financial and technical.

4269   Africa Today, v. 1+, 1954+.   Denver: Graduate School of
        International Studies, University of Denver.   Bimonthly.
            Articles on the problems of African international rela-
        tions and on the political, social and economic aspects of
        Africa.

4270   African Arts/Arts d'Afrique, v. 1, No. 1+, Autumn 1967+.
        Los Angeles: African Studies Center, University of Cali-
        fornia.   Quarterly.
            "Magazine devoted to the graphical, plastic, performing
        and literary arts of Africa, traditional and contemporary. "

4271   African Abstracts, quarterly review of articles appearing in
        current periodicals, v. 1+, 1950-1972. London: International
        African Institute. Quarterly. Ceased publication Oct. 1972.
            Very strong in ethnology, linguistics and history.   Also
        issued in French under title Analyses Africanistes, by
        Centre d'Analyse et de Recherche Documentaire pour
        l'Afrique Noire, Paris.

4272   African Affairs, journal of the Royal African Society, Lon-
        don, v. 1, No. 1+, Oct. 1901+.
            Scholarly articles on African studies, book reviews
        and specially compiled bibliographies.   Includes an annual
        index.

4273   African Law Digest, v. 1+, 1956+.   New York: African
        Law Center, Columbia University.   Quarterly.
            "A compilation, in digest form, of the significant legis-
        lation, administrative regulations and notices of the states
        and territories of Africa together with notes and other
        items of interest. "   Items, grouped by country, are taken
        from government gazettes and official journals.   Quarterly
        and cumulative annual indexes.

4274   African Literature Today, No. 1+, 1968+. Oxford, Eng. :
        Heinemann Educational Books. Semi-annual.

4375   African Music, journal of the African Music Society, v. 1,
        No. 1+, 1954+. Roodeport, South Africa.   Annual.
            In English and French.   Includes musical texts and
        supersedes the earlier Newsletter of the Society.   Covers
        Africa south of the Sahara; very strong in Bantu music.

4276   African Studies, v. 1+, March 1942+.   Johannesburg: Wit-
        watersrand University Press.   Quarterly.

Devoted to the study of African culture, government
and languages.   Includes book reviews and bibliography.

4277   African Studies Review, v. 1+, April 1958+.   Ann Arbor, Mich:
         African Studies Center, Michigan State University, for the
         African Studies Association.   Three times a year.
            A scholarly journal superseding African Studies Bulletin
         with a historical, sociological and anthropological emphasis.
         Extensive book reviews.

4278   Africana Library Journal; a quarterly bibliography and news
         bulletin, v. 1, No. 1+, 1970+.   New York: Africana Pub-
         lishing Corporation.   Quarterly.
            Devoted to African studies, arts and literature.   Includes
         bibliographic essays, book reviews with emphasis on new
         reference works, news of bibliographic development in
         Africa and biographies of African scholars.   Its special
         feature is the inclusion of carefully compiled bibliography,
         geographically arranged.   A "must" for all libraries in-
         terested in African publications.
            Rev: South African Libraries, XXXVIII (April 1971),
         342.

4279   Cahiers d'Etudes Africaines, v. 1+, 1960+.   Paris: Mouton.
         Quarterly.
            Emphasis is on the social sciences.

4280   Canadian Journal of African Studies; Journal Canadien des
         Etudes Africaines, v. 1+, Mar. 1967+.   Montreal: Loyola
         College for the committee on African studies in Canada.
         Semi-annual.
            "Journal devoted to African research in the humanities
         and social science."   Text in English and French.

4281   Comparative Education Review, v. 1+, June 1957+.   New
         York: Three times a year.
            Official organ of the Comparative Education Society.   A
         scholarly journal; frequently carrying well-annotated bib-
         liography classified by broad geographic areas, including
         Africa.

4282   Cultural Events in Africa, No. 1+, Dec. 1964+.   London:
         Transcription Centre.   Monthly.
            Devoted to news of cultural events in Africa and abroad,
         with emphasis on the creative writings, films, radio, tele-
         vision, etc.   Articles, notices of forthcoming and recent
         publications.

4283   Current Anthropology, v. 1+, 1960+.   Chicago.   Five times
         a year.
            "Sponsored by the Wenner-Gren Foundation for Anthro-
         pological Research."   Includes annual cumulative indexes.

4284   Current Bibliography on African Affairs, v. 1+, 1962+.
       New York: Greenwood Periodicals for the African Bib-
       liographic Center. Monthly.
           Includes documents published by governments and inter-
       national organizations, scholarly books, periodical articles,
       book reviews and announcements of forthcoming publications.
       Author index.

4285   English Studies in Africa, v. 1+, March 1958+. Johannes-
       burg: Witwatersrand University Press. Semi-annual.
           Includes critical articles, book reviews, bibliographical
       essays.
           An annual bibliography, "Select bibliography; books and
       articles on English language and literature published or
       written in South Africa," by M. E. Farmer, appears in
       the Sept. issue.

4286   Génève-Afrique: Acta Africana, v. 1+, 1962+. Geneva:
       Institute Africain de Génève. Semi-annual.
           In English and French. Emphasizes African foreign
       relations, history and culture. Includes abstracts, book
       reviews and bibliography.

4287   International Centre for African Economic and Social Docu-
       mentation. Bulletin d'information sur les recherches dans
       les sciences humaines concernant l'Afrique. Bulletin of
       Information and Current Research on Human Sciences Con-
       cerning Africa, No. 1+, 1963+. Bruxelles: C. 1. D. E. S. A.
       Irregular.
           A very valuable source on Africa for research proposed,
       in progress or completed. Includes the address of the
       author, date of completion, publisher and date where known.
       Institution, topical and geographic indexes.

4288   Jeune Afrique, No. 1+, Oct. 1962+. Paris: Presse Afri-
       caine. Weekly.
           A French language periodical with emphasis on African
       foreign affairs. Also issued in New York.

4289   Joint Acquisitions List of Africana, v. 1, No. 1+, 1962+.
       Evanston: Africana Dept. , Northwestern University
       Library. Bimonthly.
           Lists titles reported cataloged in major African collec-
       tions in the U. S. and abroad, and each issue consists of
       titles published during the current year and the five pre-
       ceding ones. Includes some doctoral dissertations.

4290   Journal of Administration Overseas, v. 1+, 1962+. London:
       Ministry of Overseas Development, Administrative Services
       Branch. Quarterly.
           Articles on various aspects of administration overseas,
       especially in developing nations.

4291 Journal of African and Asian Studies, v. 1+, Autumn 1967+.
Delhi: Dept. of African Studies, University of Delhi.
Semi-annual.
A scholarly journal with numerous bibliographical foot-
notes and book reviews.

4292 Journal of African History, v. 1+, 1960+. London: Cambridge University Press. Three times a year.
A scholarly journal in English or French. Includes
book reviews.

4293 Journal of African Languages, v. 1+, 1962+. Hertford, Eng.:
Mimram Books. Three times a year.
Scholarly articles in English, French and German on
African linguistics and philology.

4294 Journal of African Law, v. 1+, Spring 1957+. London:
Butterworth. Three times a year.
Journal of the International African Law Association,
containing scholarly articles on major aspects and themes
of African legal developments.

4295 Journal of Asian and African Studies, v. 1+, Jan. 1966+.
Leyden, Netherlands. Quarterly.
A scholarly journal edited at York University, Toronto.

4296 Journal of Commonwealth Literature, No. 1+, Sept. 1965+.
London: Heinemann Educational Books and the University
of Leeds. Semi-annual.
Reviews creative writing in English from Commonwealth
countries except Britain. Includes bibliography geographically
arranged.

4297 Journal of Commonwealth Political Studies, v. 1+, Nov. 1961+.
Leicester: Leicester University Press. Semi-annual.
A scholarly journal. Includes book reviews.

4298 Journal of Developing Areas, v. 1+, Oct. 1966+. Macomb:
Western Illinois University. Quarterly.
In English or French.

4299 Journal of Modern African Studies, v. 1+, Mar. 1963+.
London: Cambridge University Press. Quarterly.
A scholarly journal with emphasis on politics, history
and economics. Book reviews and bibliographical essays.

4300 Journal of Religion in Africa; Religion en Afrique, v. 1+,
1967+. Leiden: E. J. Brill. Three times a year.

4301 Journal of West African Languages, v. 1+, 1964+. London:
Cambridge University Press in association with the Institute of African Studies, University of Ibadan. Semi-annual.

Scholarly articles on West African languages.

4302 Mawazo, v. 1+, No. 1+, June 1967+. Kampala: Faculty of
Arts and Social Sciences, Makerere University College.
Semi-annual.
Supersedes Makerere journal, which ceased publication
in 1966.

4303 Mizan: USSR--China--Asia, v. 1+, 1959+. London: Central
Asian Research Centre. Bimonthly.
Reviews Sino-Soviet policies towards developing nations,
using Soviet writings on these areas as primary source for
Soviet views.

4304 Pan-African Journal, v. 1, No. 1+, 1968+. New York.
Quarterly.
"Aimed at promoting African scholars' expressions and
thoughts on poetry, literature, music, political, social and
economic matters of Africa, as well as that of African
unity. "

4305 Présence Africaine; revue culturelle du monde noir, No. 1+,
Nov. /Dec. 1947+. Paris. Quarterly.
Scholarly articles in English and French. Includes book
reviews.

4306 Race: The Journal of the Institue of Race Relations, v. 1+,
Nov. 1959+. London: Oxford University Press. Quarterly.
Articles on world race relations.

4307 Research in African literatures, v. 1+, 1970+. Austin:
English Dept. , University of Texas. Semi-annual.
Published as the official organ of both the African Literature Committee of the African Studies Association,
U. S. A. and the African Literatures Seminar of the Modern
Language Association. Includes all forms of oral and written
African literature, with emphasis on biographical, historical
and theoretical articles, surveys of published research, on
individual topics. Book reviews, bibliographies, discogra-
phies and filmgraphies and descriptions of university courses
are included in different issues.

4308 Revue Française d'Etudes Politiques Africaines, No. 1+,
1966+, Dakar: Société Africaine d'Edition.
Title varies: 1966-67, Le Mois en Afrique: revue
française d'études politiques africaines.

4309 West Africa, v. 1+, Feb. 1917+. London: Overseas Newspapers. Weekly.
Contains a wide range of articles on art, literature,
economics, politics and social problems.

MAJOR SOURCES CONSULTED

ABC pol. sci.; advance bibliography of contents: political science and government (Santa Barbara, California).

Abrash, Barbara. Black African literature in English since 1925: works and criticism (1967).

Abstracts in anthropology (Westport, Conn.).

Africa; journal of International African Institute (London).

African Bibliographic Center. A Current bibliography on African affairs (New York).

African abstracts (London).

African Affairs (London).

African notes (Ibadan).

African studies bulletin (Boston).

Africana Library Journal (New York).

Alderfer, Harold F. A Bibliography of African government, 1950-1966 (Jefferson City, Penn.: 1967).

Aning, B. A. An Annotated bibliography of music and dance in English-speaking Africa (Legon, 1967).

Art index (New York).

Behn, Hans Ulrich. Die Presse in Westafrika (Hamburg, 1968).

Biblio (Paris).

Bibliografia nazionale italiana (Florence, Italy).

Bibliographie ethnographique de l'Afrique Sud-Saharienne (Tervuren, Belgium).

Book review digest (New York).

Book review index (Detroit).

Boston University. Library. Catalog of African government documents and African area index (1960).

_____. List of French doctoral dissertations on Africa, 1884-
1961 (1966).

British education index (London).

British Museum. Dept. of Printed Books. General catalogue of
printed books (London).

British national bibliography (London).

Bulletin of information on current research on human sciences
concerning Africa (Brussels).

Business periodicals index (New York).

C. C. T. A. Inventory of economic studies concerning Africa south
of the Sahara (London, 1960).

California. University Library (Berkeley). Author-title catalog
(Boston: G. K. Hall, 1963).

California. University Library (Los Angeles). Dictionary catalog
of the University Library, 1919-1962 (Boston: G. K. Hall,
1963).

California. University Library (Santa Barbara). Catalog (Santa
Barbara).

Canadian periodical index (Ottawa).

Cardinall, A. W. Bibliography of the Gold Coast (1932).

The Catholic periodical and literature index (Haverford, Penn.).

Council for Old World Archaeology. COWA Surveys and bibliographies (Cambridge, Mass.)

Cumulative book index (New York).

Current index to journals in education (New York).

Deutsche Dissertationen über Afrika: ein Verzeichnis für die Jahre,
1918-1959 (Bonn).

Deutsches Bücherverzeichnis (Leipzig).

Dissertation abstracts: Abstracts of dissertations and monographs
in microfilm (Ann Arbor, Mich.).

Dolan, Eleanor. Higher education in Africa south of the Sahara:
    Selected bibliography, 1945-61 (Washington, D.C., 1961).

Drake, H. A Bibliography of African education south of the Sahara
    (Aberdeen, 1942).

Economic abstracts (The Hague).

Education index (New York).

Essay and general literature index (New York).

Gaskin, L.J.P. A Bibliography of African art (1965).

_____. A Select bibliography of music in Africa (1965).

Geographical abstracts (London).

Ghana national bibliography (Accra).

Gildea, Ray. Nationalism and indirect rule in the Gold Coast,
    1900-1950 (New York, 1964).

Glazier, Kenneth. Africa south of the Sahara: A select and
    annotated bibliography, 1964-1968 (Stanford, Cal., 1969).

Hanna, William John and Judith Hanna. Politics in black Africa:
    A selective bibliography of relevant periodical literature (East
    Lansing, Mich., 1964.)

Hanson, John W. and Geoffrey Gibson. African education and
    development since 1960: A select and annotated bibliography
    (East Lansing, Mich., 1966).

Historical abstracts (Santa Barbara, Cal.).

Index to foreign legal periodicals (London).

Index to legal periodicals (New York).

Index to periodical articles by and about negroes (Boston).

Index to periodical articles related to law (Dobbs Ferry, N.Y.)

Index to religious periodical literature (Chicago).

Index to selected periodicals (Boston).

An Index to the book reviews in the humanities (Williamston, Mich.)

Index translationum (Paris).

International bibliography of historical sciences (Paris).

International bibliography of the social sciences; anthropology,
      economics, political science and sociology... (London).

International political science abstracts (Oxford).

Internationale Bibliographie der Zeitschriften-Literatur aus allen
      Gebieten den Wissens (Osnabruck).

Jahn, Janheinz. A Bibliography of neo-African literature from
      Africa, America and the Caribbean (1965).

_____ and Claus Peter Dressler. Bibliography of creative
      African writing (Nendeln, 1971).

Johnson, A. F. A Bibliography of Ghana, 1930-1961. (Evanston,
      Ill., 1964).

Joint acquisitions list of Africana (Evanston, Ill.).

Karal, Gulgun. African legal and constitutional materials: An
      annotated bibliography (Los Angeles: University of California,
      1969).

Klingelhofer, E. L. A Bibliography of psychological research and
      writings on Africa (Uppsala, 1967).

Kotei, S. I. A. The Akan of Ghana: A select bibliography (Accra,
      1963).

Library and information science abstracts (London).

Library literature (New York).

London. Commonwealth Institute. The Commonwealth in Africa:
      An annotated list (1969).

Matthews, Daniel, ed. Current themes in African historical
      studies: A selected bibliographical guide to resources for
      research in African history (Westport, Conn.: Negro Uni-
      versities Press, 1970).

Mitchell, Robert Cameron and Harold W. Turner. A Bibliography
      of modern African religious movements (Evanston, Ill., 1966).

Modern Language Association of America. MLA international bib-
      liography of books and articles on the modern languages and
      literatures (New York).

The Music index (Detroit).

National Book League, London. Creative writing from black Africa (1971).

New York. Missionary Research Library. Books about Africa south of the Sahara, 1958-1962: A reading list (New York, 1963).

Paricsy, Pal. A New bibliography of African literature (Budapest, 1969).

Parker, Franklin. African education: A bibliography of 121 U.S.A. doctoral dissertations (Washington, D.C., 1965?).

Peabody Museum of Archaeology and Ethnology, Harvard University. Author and subject catalogues of the Library (Boston, 1963).

Pearson, J.D. and Ruth Jones, eds. The Bibliography of Africa (London, 1970).

Population index (Princeton, N.J.).

Public Affairs Information Service. Bulletin (New York).

Ramsaran, John A. New approaches to African literature: a guide to negro-African writing and related subjects. 2nd ed. (Ibadan, 1970).

Readers' guide to periodical literature (New York).

Repertoire d'art et d'archéologie (Paris).

Sasnett, Martena and Inez Sepmeyer. Educational systems in Africa: interpretations for use in the evaluation of academic credentials (Berkeley, Cal., 1966).

Social sciences and humanities index (New York).

Sommer, John W. Bibliography of African geography (Hanover, N.H., Dartmouth College, 1965).

South African Public Library. A Bibliography of African bibliographies, covering territories south of the Sahara. 4th ed. (1961).

Standing Conference on Library Materials on Africa. Theses on Africa accepted by universities in the United Kingdom and Ireland (Cambridge).

_____. United Kingdom publications and theses on Africa (Cambridge).

Subject guide to books in print, 1971 (New York).

Ulrich's international periodicals directory. 14th ed. (New York).

U.S. Dept. of the Army. Africa: problems and prospects (Washington, D.C., 1967).

U.S. Dept. of Health, Education and Welfare. Office of Education. Bureau of Research. Research in education (Washington, D.C.).

U.S. Dept. of State. Bureau of Intelligence and Research. External research list. Africa: A list of current social science research by private scholars and academic centers (Washington, D.C.).

U.S. Foreign Service Institute. Africa, sub-Sahara; A selected functional bibliography (Washington, D.C., 1967).

U.S. Library of Congress. Library of Congress and National Union catalog. Author lists, 1942-62. (Washington, D.C.).

_____. Library of Congress. Catalog. Books: subjects (Washington, D.C.).

_____. National Union catalog (Washington, D.C.).

U.S. Library of Congress. General Reference and Bibliography Division. African libraries, book production and archives: A list of references. Compiled by Helen Conover (1962).

_____. Ghana: A guide to official publications, 1872-1968 (Washington, D.C., 1969).

_____. A list of American doctoral dissertations on Africa (Washington, D.C., 1962).

_____. Sub-Saharan Africa: A guide to serials (Washington, D.C., 1970).

United States and Canadian publications on Africa (Stanford, Cal.)

Walford, A.J. Guide to reference material. 2nd ed. v. 2-3 (London, 1968 & 1970).

Winchell, Constance. Guide to reference books. 8th ed. (Chicago, 1967).

Zaretsky, Irving I. Bibliography on spirit possession and spirit mediumship (Berkeley, Cal., 1966).

Aidoo, Christina Ama Ata
2955-2956, 3006
Aidoo, J. E. 2355
Ainslie, Rosalynde 479
Aiyepeku, Wilson O. 141
Ajayi, J. F. A. 2011-2013
Ake, C. 3347
Akesson, Sam K. 591, 3599-
3600
Akinjogbin, Isaac A. 2014
Akinola, G. A. 2015
Akita, J. M. 1056, 2016, 2578,
3348
Ako, O. Dazi 3098
Akpabot, Samuel 3145
Akpan, Moses E. 239
Akrofi, C. A. 592, 2797-2800,
2841
Akrofi, G. E. 3146
Akpropong Presbyterian Boys
Middle School 1524
Akuamoa, R. 1241
Akuffo-Badoo, W. S. 3147
Akwawuah, K. A. 1242
Akyea, E. Ofori 2726, 2957
Akyea, L. E. 3349
Akyeampong, Henry Kwasi
593, 1064, 3268
Alderfer, Harold F. 89, 240-
241
Aldous, J. 594, 3816
Alexander, H. T. 3350
Al Hassan, Susan 3996
Alicoe, T. 595
Aligwekwe, Iwuoha E. 3351
Alimen, H. 767
Allary, Jean 2894
Allen, Joan 2683
Alleyne, Cameron 3601
Allison, Philip 924
Allott, Antony N. 2357-2370
Alman, Miriam 4
Almond, Gabriel Abraham 242-
243
Altbach, Philip G. 101
Amamoo, Joseph G. 3269,
3352, 3533
Amartey, A. A. 3007
Amedekey, E. Y. 549, 2579,
2692
Amegashie, Evans 1052
Amegashie, R. S. 1243, 1364
Amenumey, D. E. 2017-2019

American Library Association
2651-2652, 2684
American Universities Field
Staff 30
Ames, Sophia R. 3997
Ametewee, V. K. 3817
Ameyaw, Kwabena 2260
Amin, Samir 1113
Amissah, A. N. E. 2371-2372
Amissah, Michael K. 3148
Amissah, S. H. 1525, 3602
Amoa, R. K. 1114
Amoah, F. E. 1777
Amoah, S. A. 3818
Amonoo, R. F. 2727
Amoo, J. W. A. 596
Ampah, E. B. K. 3353
Ampah, Sampson Kofi 1244
Ampofo, Oku 3603
Amu, Ephraim 2801, 3149-
3152, 3604
Amu, Samir 3270
Anang, J. L. 1778-1779
Andah, E. 1780
Anderson, Gerald H. 1406
Anderson, James Norman
2373-2375
Anderson, John D. 2019a
Anderson, M. M. 777
Anderson, Rosa Claudette 1961
Andic, Fuat 244, 1407
Andic, Suphan 1407
Andoh, A. S. Y. 3354-3357
Andrain, Charles Franklin 245-
246
Andreski, Stanislav 247
Anene, F. K. 1526
Aning, B. A. 3153-3156
Anipa, Seth E. 1781
Ankermann, Bernhard 3157
Ankomah, Kofi 3358
Ankrah, J. A. 3359-3360
Anomako III, Nana Kodwo 597
Anozie, Sunday Ogbonna 3008-
3009
Anquandah, J. 768
Ansah, M. P. 2261, 3819
Ansay, J. K. 3605
Ansere, J. K. 1408
Ansre, G. 2784-2786
Anstey, R. T. 2020
Anthony, Seth 3361
Anti, A. A. 2261a

445

Barbour, K. M. 1784
Barclays Bank, D. C. O. 1119
Bareau, P. 1246
Barkan, Joel David 3379-3380
Barker, Peter 3381
Barker, W. H. 1537, 2890
Barnard, G. L. 2730
Barnes, Leonard 251
Bartels, F. L. 1108, 1538-
    1539, 2803-2804, 3622-3623
Bartlett, Vernon 1120
Barton, Frank 482
Barton, T. 1540
Bascom, William 483, 930
Bassa-Quansah, Y. 1541
Bassir, Olumbe 3106
Bateman, Merrill J. 1247-
    1249
Baty, Thomas 2386
Bauer, P. T. 312
Baum, E. 252
Baxter, P. T. W. 3833
Beal, R. E. 1250
Beattie, John H. 179, 3824
Bebey, Francis 484
Beckett, W. H. 604, 3825
Bederman, Sanford Harold 102
Bediako, K. A. 3019-3021
Beeby, C. E. 386, 1542
Beecham, John 2269, 3624
Beetham, T. A. 1074, 3625-
    3626
Behn, Hans Ulrich 538
Behrman, J. R. 1411
Beichman, Arnold 3536
Beier, Horst Ulli 605, 931,
    2892-2893, 3107, 3128, 3166
Beling, Willard A. 253
Bell, M. J. 254
Bell, Willis E. 3241
Bellamy, J. 3826
Bellon, Immanuel 2805
Belshaw, Harry 1543, 3627-
    3629
Bending, H. B. 1544
Benet, Yves 255
Benge, Ronald Charles 141a,
    2587-2587b
Benneh, George 1785-1786
Bennett, George 3383
Bennion, Francis A. 2387
Bentley, Muriel 3630
Bentsi-Enchill, Kwamena 2388-
    2390

Benveniste, Guy 6, 387
Berg, Elliot 256
Berg, E. J. 1252
Berge, François 2026
Berman, Sanford 2588-2589
Bernard, Laureat J. 1534
Berntonoff, Deborah 3167
Berrian, Albert H. 485
Berry, B. J. 1121
Berry, Jack 607, 932, 2731-
    2735, 2787, 2806-2808, 2845,
    2857-2858
Berry, John P. 4003
Besterman, Theodore 31
Bevans, Charles I. 2391
Bevin, H. J. 1122, 2027
Beyer, Barry K. 115, 388
Biaku, C. Y. 1787
Bibby, John 1544a, 1680
Bibliothèque du Musée de
    l'Homme, Paris 33
Biebuyck, Daniel 933
Bienen, Henry 257-258
Bilson, E. C. 2820
Binder-Krauthoff, Kristine
    3537
Bing, Geoffrey 2028, 3275
Biobaku, Saburi O. 1545
Bipoum-Woum, Joseph-Marie
    259
Birmingham, C. S. 2393
Birmingham, David 2029
Birmingham, R. L. 2393
Birmingham, W. B. 1123-1124,
    1253, 1412
Birmingham, Walter 3827
Birthwhistle, Norman Allen
    1075-1076, 1546
Bissue, Isaac 1125
Bittle, William E. 608
Blair, H. A. 639, 2859
Blake, John W. 2030-2032
Blay, J. Benibengor 3022-
    3027, 3108-3112, 4004
Bleeker, Sonia 4005
Bloomfield, B. C. 34
Bloomfield, Valerie 2590
Blumenfeld, F. Y. 260, 389
Blumer, B. C. 1547
Blunt, M. E. 1365
Boadi, L. K. 2809-2813
Boahen, Albert Adu 2033-
    2038, 2242, 2270

447

Butts, Patricia 39
Butwell, Richard 266
Bwasty-Semme, A. 1414
Byl, Adhemar 1131

Cadbury, L. J. 1964
Caldwell, John C. 617, 1132-1133, 1559, 1802-1804, 3841-3848
Callaway, Barbara 3393
Calvocoressi, D. S. 780-785
Campbell, Alexander 1965
Canham, Peter 2275
Cann, G. L. 1805
Cantor, David 1254
Carbon Ferrière, Jacques de 1415-1416
Card, Emily 3393
Cardinall, Allan Wolsey 554, 618-620, 788-790, 1966
Carey, Margaret 185
Carlston, Kenneth S. 186
Carney, David Edward 1134
Carnovsky, Leon 2695
Carpenter, P. 2961-2962
Carrington, John F. 3171
Carstairs, G. M. 3641
Cartensen, Edward 1063
Carter, G. F. 786
Carter, Gwendolen M. 145
Carter, P. J. 787, 937
Cartey, Wilfred 2896-2897
Cartland, G. B. 2052
Cary, Joyce 2053
Casson, Stanley 791
Caughey, Robert R. 299
Caute, David 3028
Cave, R. M. 2054
Cell, John W. 394
Cerulli, E. 3642
Cervenka, Zdenek 267
Cerych, Ladislav 1560
Chabas, Bernard 395
Chamberlain, G. D. 2860
Chambers, David S. 2124
Chambers, Robert 1136, 3849
Champagne, Emery 3643
Champagne, Gabriel 3644
Chantal, J. de 2592a
Chantler, Clyde 568, 2055
Chaplin, B. H. 1561-1562
Chapman, Daniel 1563

Chapman, Eddie 1967
Chard, C. S. 792
Chardey, F. 621
Chasin, Doris H. 1564
Chauvel, J. F. 3394
Cheng, S. C. 3395
Chesswas, John D. 396
Chicorel, Marietta 121
Chinebuah, I. K. 2861-2863
Ching, Donald S. 3645-3647
Chirgwin, A. M. 1043
Chorley, R. J. 1806
Christaller, Johann G. 2815-2816
Christensen, Erwin O. 938
Christensen, James Boyd 622-624, 1417, 2817, 3648-3649, 3850
Christian, A. 2399, 3851
Christian Council of the Gold Coast 3650
Chukura, Olisa 2400
Church, R. J. H. 1136, 1807-1810
Cissé, D. 1137
Clapp, V. W. 2696
Claridge, William W. 2276
Clark, Alden H. 2592b
Clark, J. D. 793-797
Clark, Violet E. 1565
Clarke, David L. 798
Clarke, E. 3852
Clarke, F. A. 2137
Clarke, John Heinrik 1968, 2056-2057
Clarke, K. W. 627
Clausen, Wolfgang 2058
Clignet, Remi 187, 1566, 3853
Cloete, Stuart 1969
Clottey-Atukwei, St. John
  see Clottey, St. John Atukwei
Clottey, St. John Atukwei 1255
Cobb, F. W. 1567
Cochraine, T. W. 1811
Cockburn, C. 939
Coffee, Mary 3280
Cofie, J. 1812
Cohen, Abner 625
Cohen, D. L. 3397
Coker, Increase H. 2818
Cole, Desmond T. 2737
Cole, Herbert M. 956a

448

George, Claude 2114
Georges, Hardy 959
Gerard, Albert 2904, 3293
Gerbrands, Adrianus Alexander 960
Gertzel, Cherry J. 2115-2116
Gevoud, R. G. 1158
Ghana. Broadcasting Corporation 4099; Capital Investments Board 1379; Census Office 4100; Central Bureau of Statistics 540, 1159-1161, 1445, 4101-4102; Centre for Civic Education 1603; Church Union Committee 3688; Cocoa Marketing Board 1443-1444; Commission on Regional Assemblies 3425; Commission on University Education 1604; Embassy (Brazil) 4103; Government 1609, 2117, 3882, 4104-4146; Information Services 4150-4152; Mineworkers Union 1270a; Ministry of Education 1605-1606, 4147-4149; Ministry of Housing 3881; Ministry of Information and Broadcasting 541, 1162, 1162a, 1607, 1842-1845, 2905, 3426-3427, 4155-4163; Ministry of Trade and Industry 542, 1447; National Archives 2432a; National Economic Committee 4164; Office of the Government Statistician 4165-4166; Official Planning Commission 1163; People and Cities Workshop 1846; Town and Country Planning Division 4167; Trades Union Congress 1272; United Party 4168; University. Institute of African Studies 2296-2297; University Advisory Committee 1608
Ghana Academy of Arts and Sciences 570
Ghana National Association of Teachers 1610
Ghanatta, Y. Boakye 1087
Gibson, Geoffrey W. 109
Gibson, Gordon D. 663
Gidal, Sonia 4023

Gidal, Tim 4023
Gil, B. 3883
Gilbert, D. A. 1848
Gildea, Ray Y. 1167, 3690
Gilissen, John 2436
Gill, J. Withers 664
Gillespie, W. H. 2119, 2437
Gillis, Frank 126
Glazier, Kenneth M. 43, 47-48
Gleason, Judith Illsley 3043
Gleave, M. B. 1849, 1959
Glickman, Harvey 94, 289
Glover, B. K. 1850
Gluckman, Max 290, 665-665a, 2438
Goble, P. L. 1851
Godfrey, E. M. 1168, 1277
Godwin, G. 961
Goff, Henry 133
Gold Coast. Census Office 4048-4049; Dept. of Social Welfare and Community Development 1614, 4052-4053; Education Dept. 4050-4051; Government 1616, 2120-2121, 2439, 4054-4090; Public Relations Dept. 1279; Survey Dept. 1852; University College 1615
Golding, P. T. F. 3884
Goldsworthy, David 3295
Goldwater, Robert 962-964
Gollo, F. K. 2440
Goodall, George 1853-1854
Goodwin, A. J. 842
Goodwin, K. L. 2906
Goody, Esther 666, 677, 3885
Goody, Jack
    see Goody, John Rankine
Goody, John Rankine 667-678, 1617, 2044, 2122-2123, 2298, 3429, 3886-3888
Gordon, J. 1281, 2299, 3889
Gordon, Sara Lee 1169
Gormerly, Patrick J. 291
Görög, Veronika 2907
Gorst, Sheila 1170
Gould, Peter R. 1855-1856
Gower, L. C. B. 2441
Graft, John Coliman de
    see De Graft, John Coliman
Graham, C. K. 1618

Graham-White, Anthony 2971-2972
Grant, F. C. 2802
Grau, Eugene 3691-3693
Gray, Richard 843, 2124
Great Britain. Admiralty. Hydrographic Dept. 1857; Board of Trade 1171, 1451; Central Office of Information 2125, 4181-4182; Colonial Office 1619-1620; 2126-2129, 2300, 2442, 4183-4193; Commonwealth Secretariat 417; Meteorological Office 1858-1859; War Office 2130
Green, L. G. 1976, 2908
Green, Reginald Herbold 292-293, 1172-1173, 1282-1283
Greenaway, F. 965
Greenberg, Joseph H. 2745-2749
Greene, Fred 294
Greenough, Richard 1621
Greenstreet, D. K. 1174
Greenstreet, M. 1284
Greenwood, A. F. 3296
Greer, R. C. 2619
Gregory, Robert G. 418
Grewal, N. S. 3297
Griffin, Ella 1622-1624, 2664, 2750
Griffith, William B. 1079, 2444-2445
Grindal, Bruce T. 1624a
Grobel, L. 966
Grottanelli, V. L. 967, 2909, 3694-3696
Grove, David 968, 1175, 1860-1861
Grove, J. M. 1862
Groves, Charles P. 3697
Grundy, Kenneth W. 1176, 3430
Guggisberg, Frederick Gordon 1625-1627, 2131-2132
Gunther, John 1098, 1977
Gunton, Dennis H. 2688-2689
Gutkind, Peter Claus 49
Gutteridge, William 295-297, 3431
Guttsman, W. L. 2707
Gwasi-Twum, K. 1863
Gyando, S. O. 2446-2447
Gyasi, E. M. 1285

Gyasi-Twum, K. 1286

Hachten, William A. 493-494
Hackman, Martha L. 2620
Hagan, G. P. 2448, 3698
Hagan, W. B. 1041, 2973
Haggan, Hannah 3890
Haggett, P. 1806
Hailey, Lord 3432
Haines, Helen Elizabeth 2621
Hair, P. E. 2751
Hale, S. 969
Haliburton, G. M. 2133, 3699-3701
Hall, Peter 1082
Hall, Veronica 121
Hall, W. M. 680
Halleran, T. 681
Hallett, Robin 1177, 1978
Halm, W. E. 3299
Hamber, Thomas R. 3044
Hamdan, G. 1864
Hamilton, Ruth Simms 3891
Hamrell, S. 198
Hance, William A. 199, 419, 1178
Hanna, Judith Lynne 95, 200, 495-497
Hanna, William J. 95, 200, 298
Hannah, Harold Winford 299, 421
Hannigan, A. St. J. 682-683, 2449-2454
Hansard Society for Parliamentary Government (London) 3300
Hanson, John W. 109, 422
Hargreaves, John D. 2134
Harman, H. A. 575, 2752
Harper, Charles H. 684
Harper, Peggy 3188
Harris, F. J. 201
Harris, John 2622-2626
Harris, P. B. 300
Harris, Richard L. 1179, 3433
Hart, Keith 1386, 3892
Hart, Thomas A. 1628
Hartley, N. 2753
Harvey, William B. 2455-2459

454

Haskett, Edythe R. 4024
Hatch, John 420, 3434
Hauser, A. 1287
Havard-Williams, P. 2710
Havinden, M. A. 1865
Hawkins, E. K. 1453-1455
Hayford, Casely 685, 2135-
2136, 2301, 2460, 3045
Hayward, D. H. 1866, 1891
Hayward, Fred M. 1629
Haywood, A. 2137
Hazlewood, Arthur 301, 1456-
1457
Head, L. L. 2461
Heath, R. G. 1288
Hedges, R. Y. 2462
Heidelberg, W. 2463
Heigham, J. B. 1289
Heine, Bernd 498
Heiting, Thomas James 3301
Hellawell, R. 2464
Helly, D. O. 2138
Heman-Ackah, David 3704,
3893
Hempstone, Smith 302
Herbert, A. 1630
Herdeck, Donald E. 12
Herrick, Mary D. 2627
Herskovits, F. S. 686
Herskovits, Merville 686, 2974
Herzog, George 4008
Hevi, Emmanuel J. 3046-3049
Hewitt, Arthur Reginald 50
Heydon, J. D. 2465
Hicks, Ursula K. 1458, 3302
Hiebert, R. E. 2627a
Higson, F. G. 1867
Hihetah, Robert Kofi 3050-51
Hill, Polly 1290-95, 1460-64
Hilliard, F. H. 1631
Hilling, D. 1465, 1868-1869
Hillway, Tyrus 2628
Hilton, Thomas Eric 1296, 1870-
1879
Hinchliffe, J. Keith 1632
Hinderling, P. 844, 970
Hintze, Ursula 2869
Hirsch, Felix E. 2708
Hodge, Peter 1633, 3834,
3894-3897
Hodgkin, Thomas 2910
Hodson, Arnold E. 2139
Hoebel, E. Adamson 2466-2467

Hoehn, R. Philip 51
Hoepli, Nancy L. 3435
Hoh, Israel Kafu 4025
Holas, B. 3705
Holden, J. J. 2140
Holdsworth, Mary 52
Holland, D. C. 2468
Hollander, E. D. 1297
Holt, C. R. 1084
Holzer, Jerry 1880, 3898
Homburger, L. 2754
Hone, Ralph 2469
Hood, Harrison 774
Hoon, N. M. 1634
Hooper, Everett E. 2141
Hoorweg, J. C. 109a
Hopkins, Antony Gerald 1180-
1183, 2142, 3303
Hopkins, Keith 303
Hornby, William Frederic 423
Horrocks, Stanley H. 2628,
2665, 2690
Horrut, C. Frédéric 424
Horton, James Africanus
2302, 3304
Hoselitz, Berthold Frank 53
Hovet, Thomas 304
Howard, C. 1979
Howard-Bennett, Rosemary
1085
Howard University. Library.
The Moorland Foundation
54
Howe, R. W. 1466, 1980
Howells, William 3706
Howitt, William 2143
Hoyle, B. S. 1869
Huber, Hugo 687-692, 971
Hue, Nguyen Thi 3899
Huff, Curtis E. 305
Hughes, Langston 499, 3121-
3122
Hugot, Henry J. 425
Hull, May 972
Hulman, Diana 1881
Hulsen, G. 3707
Humphreys, Kenneth 2711
Hunter, John M. 693, 1298,
1882-1891, 3900
Huntington, Samuel P. 3436-
3437
Hurd, G. E. 1635
Huszar, Luszlo 968, 1861

Krishnamurthy, S. 323
Kropp, Mary E. 2788, 2849-
2851, 2871-2872
Kuczynski, R. R. 1900
Kuivi, P. Y. 1901
Kullas, H. 2308
Kumah, John Kweku 2309-2310
Kumasi. University of Science
and Technology. Dept. of
Art Education 1656
Kuoh, T. 3920
Kuper, Hilda 324, 3921
Kuper, Leo 324
Kurankyi-Taylor, D. 3125
Kutscher, Gerdt 978
Kwabena-Nketia, Joseph Hanson
see Nketia, Joseph Hanson
Kwaku, William A. 1054
Kwamena-Poh, M. A. 2311-2311a
Kwapong, Alexander A. 850,
1657-1660, 2158
Kwapong, D. O. 3062
Kwaw-Swanzy, B. E. 2159
Kwaw-Yankson, A. 3922
Kwei-Tsuru, N. M. 3063
Kyerematen, A. A. 698, 979-
980, 2311b, 2483

La-Anyane, S. 1197, 1902
Labouret, Henri 699
Lacour-Gayet, Robert 432
Lacouture, Jean 204
Lacy, Leslie A. 1070, 1099,
1306, 2160, 4028
Ladefoged, Peter 2760-2763
Ladzekpo, S. K. 3195
Laing, E. 3196
Laing, George E. 3718
Laloum, C. 3197
Lambo, T. A. 205, 981, 3923-
3924
Lamptey, Jonas 3064
Lancour, Harold 2635-2636
Landeck, Beatrice 507, 3198
Landheer, Bartholomeus 151a
Lang, D. M. 508
Lantis, Margaret 700
Larkin, F. 3925
Lassig, Robert 2873
Latham, Norah 2161
Latourette, Kenneth S. 3719-3720
Laude, Jean 509

Laurence, Margaret 3065
Lautre, Maxine 3066
Lavroff, D. G. 2484
Lawrence, A. W. 851-853, 982,
2162-2163
Lawson, R. M. 1198-1200, 1307-
1310, 1472, 1903
Leader, Shelah G. 3454
Leakey, Louis Seymour 206-207
Learoyd, F. G. 1661
Lee, Douglas H. 1904
Lee, J. M. 325, 433, 2485,
3314
Lefever, Ernest W. 3455
Legassick, Martin 2312-2313
Legum, Colin 208, 326, 3315,
3456
Legvold, Robert 327
Lejeune, E. 3457
Le Moal, G. 3926
Leuzinger, Elsy 983
Lever, A. W. 2164
Levtzion, Nehemia 2165-2166,
2314, 3721
Levy, Mildred B. 1312
Lewis, Leonard John 434-435,
1662-1671
Lewis, Roy 436
Lewis, William Arthur 1313-
1314, 3459
Lieck, A. 2487
Lindfors, Bernth 130, 510,
2922
Line, Maurice B. 152
Lippmann, M. 984
Little, Kenneth L. 3927-3932
Liveright, A. A. 1672
Livingstone, Ian 1208
Lloyd, Alan 2315
Lloyd, Joan E. 511
Lloyd, Peter C. 210
Lloyd, Peter J. 328
Lochner, Norbert 1053
Lofchie, M. F. 328a
Loken, R. de L. 329
London. University. School of
Oriental and African Studies
854
Long, Richard A. 485
Lottman, H. R. 2637a-2637b
Lovens, M. 2488
Loveridge, A. J. 435, 2489
Lubeck, Paul 3933

Lugard, Frederick 1673
Lury, D. A. 1215
Luttwak, Edward 14
Lyle, Guy R. 2712
Lynes, J. 2490
Lystad, Mary H. 701, 985
Lystad, Robert 211, 702, 3366

Maas, J. van Lutsenburg 1677
Mabey, S. J. 1436
Mabileau, Albert 437
McAree, James 58
Macartney, William M. 1044
Macaulay, B. 2491
McCall, Daniel F. 703, 1473,
  1905, 2167-2168
McClain, W. T. 2492
McCowan, A. 704
McCreanor, F. J. 3635
MacDonald, G. 577, 1315
Mcdowell, Robert E. 3067
McElligott, Theresa E. 1674
McEvoy, Catherine 1675
McEwen, Frank 986
McGee, Terence Gary 212
McGowan, Patrick J. 97
McGregor, Gordon Peter 511a
McHardy, Cecile 2980
McIntyre, William D. 2169-70
McKay, Vernon 330
McKee, M. 34, 2170a, 2674a
McKissack, I. J. 3924
MacKnight, V. R. 59
Mcleish, A. 3651
McLeod, M. D. 705
McMullan, M. 3935
McNown, John C. 438
McNulty, J. 3733
McNulty, Michael L. 1906-
  1907, 3936-3937
Macphee, Alan 1201
McQuade, L. C. 3460
MacRae, D. G. 3461
Mctorkle, W. F. 3722
McWilliam, Henry 1676
Madden, A. F. 3723
Maesen, Albert 2981
Maginat, M. 331
Mai, Erwin 1316
Mair, Lucy P. 2493, 3462
Maistriaux, Robert 213
Makeba, Miriam 512

Makward, Edris 2923, 3068
Malclès, Louise-Noëlle 60
Manoukian, Madeline 706-708
Manshard, Walther 1202, 1908-
  1909
Mante, E. F. G. 1910
Manu, Yaw 3463
Maquet, Jacques 5, 214-215,
  331a
Marais, H. C. 109a
Mardeck, H. 2494
Marie Louise, Princess 578
Markovitz, I. L. 513, 3464
Maroix, Jean Eugene 2171
Marriott, H. P. 775
Marshall, Anthony D. 4029
Marshall, M. J. 3724
Martin, Eveline C. 2172-2173
Martin, G. B. 2174
Martin, Jane 98
Marvill, R. O. G. 2175
Mason, C. I. 2820
Mate-Kole, Azzu 2317
Mathewson, R. D. 855-859
Matson, J. N. 2316, 2495-
  2496, 2821
Matthews, Daniel G. 61, 112
Matthews, Ronald 332
Matthews, Sharlynn E. 15
Mauny, Raymond 860-863,
  2176, 3725-3726
Maxwell, Arthur S. 3727
Maxwell, Leslie F. 2497
Maxwell-Lawford, F. 3728
Mayer, Doris 3876
Mayer, Emerico Samassa 579,
  2177
Mazrui, Ali A. 333, 3553
Mbaeyi, Paul M. 2178
Mbiti, John S. 3729-3732
Mboya, Tom J. 334
Mead, Margaret 709, 2822
Meauze, Pierre 987
Meek, Charles Kingsley 710,
  2498-2499
Megahed, H. T. 3554
Melady, Thomas Patrick 16
Meleod, A. L. 2949
Mellor, M. 1911
Mendes, Joao 335
Mends, E. H. 3838
Menezes, Carmen F. 1318
Mensah, Albert W. 3126-3127

459

Mensah, Arthur 3069
Mensah, Atta A. 3199-3206, 3734
Mensah, Godwin 1679
Mensah, Isaac Ackom 1317, 2500
Mensah, P.J. 1912
Mensah-Brown, A.K. 711, 2501-2503
Mensah Kane, J.J. 2690a
Menzel, Brigitte 988
Mercier, Paul 3466
Mercier, Roger 131
Meredith, Henry 1989
Merklinghaus, S. 1203
Merriam, Alan P. 126, 132, 514, 3207
Metcalfe, George E. 1091, 2179-2181
Methodist Book Depot 2823-2824
The Methodist Church of the Gold Coast 3735-3736
Mettle, M.A. 2504
Meyerowitz, Eva Lewin 712-715, 864, 989, 2318-2322, 3737-3740
Meyers, Albert J. 3555
Meyriat, Jean 437, 2638
Mickson, E.K. 3070-3071
Middlemast, Kenneth 2667-2668
Middleton, John 179
Migeod, F.W. 865-867, 1913
Miller, Andrew 1680
Miller, J.D.B. 440
Miller, Norman N. 216, 3467
Miller, Rosalind 2639
Milligan, Robert H. 3741
Mills-Odoi, D.G. 3939
Milne, E.M. 1319
Milner, Alan 2505
Miner, Horace 153
Miracle, M.P. 868, 1391
Misfud, F.M. 2506
Mitchell, Robert C. 86
Mitchison, N.H. 716, 1681, 1990
Moberly, F.J. 2182
Mobley, Harris W. 3742
Mohan, Jitendra 3556
Mohr, A. 2825
Mohr, R. 717

Molnos, Angela 154
Momah, C.C. 2640
Monti, Franco 990
Montmard, André 2183
Montoy, Louis 395
Moon, Eric 2641
Moore, Carman 3208
Moore, Clark 155
Moore, Gerald 515-516, 2925-2926, 2982-2983, 3072, 3128
Moore, Jane A. 3073, 4030
Moran, William E. 6
Morel, Edmund Dene 2184-2185
Morgan, W.B. 1914-1915
Morisseau-Leroy, F. 2984-5
Morrison, Gresham 1682
Mortimer, C.T. 1683
Morton, Florrinell 2642
Morton, G. 1684
Moscati, Roberto 3940
Moseley, Maboth 1092, 2323
Mosley, Nicholas 1991
Mosely, Philip E. 336
Moumouni, Abdou 441
Moxon, James 1392
Mphahlele, Ezekiel 517-520, 2920, 2927
Muller, Robert H. 2713
Mullin, Joseph 217
Mumford, W. Bryant 1685
Mundy-Castle, A.C. 1686
Munger, Edwin S. 113, 1687, 1916, 3468
Munier, H. 1688
Munro, Donald 2933
Murphy, John D. 133
Murtagh, Donald David 2642a
Musgrove, F. 1917
Musiker, Reuben 2643
Musisi, J.S. 2643a
Muskett, Netta 3074
Musson, M. 1045
Mutiso, Gideon-Cyrus 521, 4031
Mwase, George Simon 442
Myatt, Frederick 2324

Nader, Laura 337
Nagel, Ronald 249
Namasivayam, S. 2507
Nantwi, Emmanuel K. 2508

Naseem, Ahamad 1474
Nassau, Robert Hamill 1992,
2928, 3743
Nathan, Matthew 2186-2187
National Book League, London
62-63
Nayo, Nicholas Z. 3209-3210
N'Diaye, Jean Pierre 443
Neal, James 1094
Neequaye, E. K. 2713a
Neill, Stephen Charles 218-
220, 3744
Nevermann, Hans 1024
Neville, C. J. 4032
New York. Museum of Primi-
tive Art 991
New York Public Library 64
Newbury, Colin W. 2188-2191,
3469, 3557
Newkirk, G. 3941
Newlands, H. S. 869
Newton, Peter 423
Nez, George 1320
Nicholson, Marjorie 1321, 3316
Nicholson, Stanley A. 1394
Nickel, Helmut 4033
Nicol, Davidson 338
Niculescu, B. M. 1475, 1690
Nii-Amarteifo, A. V. 3075
Nii Kwabena Bonne III 1089
Nikoi, Amon 2192
Nimako, S. Gyasi 3745
Nitsche, K. 1204
Niven, Cecil 1046, 1918, 4034
Nketia, Joseph Hanson K. 1691,
2986, 3076, 3129-3134, 3211-
3236, 3244, 3746-3748
Nkrumah, Kwame 1100, 1692-
1693, 2193, 2510, 3317-
3325, 3470-3472, 3556-3569,
4098, 4172-4180
Norman, Leys 1694
Northrop, F. S. C. 2511
Northwestern University. Evan-
ston, Ill. Library 65
Nottingham, John 339
Nsarkoh, J. K. 3327
Nsiah, M. E. K. 1322, 1919
Nukunya, G. K. 718, 3942
Nunoo, R. B. 870-872
Nutsuako, R. K. 3135
Nwabara, S. N. 2199
Nwafor, M. O. E. 2194

Nwani, Okonkwo 3473
Nwanodi, N. 3474
Nwoga, Donatus Ibe 4035
Nworah, Kenneth Dike 2195
Nwosu, S. N. 1695
Nyalander, C. T. 3475
Nyarko, K. A. 1920
Nyerere, Julius K. 340
Nyomi, C. K. 2987
Nypan, Astrid 1476-1477
Nystrom, Bradley 110

Obeng, H. B. 1205
Obeng, R. E. 3077
Obeng-Addae, H. E. 1047
Obichere, Boniface I. 2196
Obiechina, Emmanuel N. 2929-
2930
Oboli, Herbert O. 1921
O'Brien, Conor Cruise
see Cruise O'Brien, Conor
Obumselu, Mrs. C. D. 719
O'Connell, James 3571
O'Connor, A. M. 444, 1922-
1923
Ocrah, Modibo T. 2514
Ocran, A. K. 3476
Oddoye, D. E. M. 720
Odita, Emmanuel Okechukwu
992-994
Odoi, N. A. 1696, 3078
Odumosu, J. Olu 2644-2645
O. E. C. D.
see Organization for Econom-
ic Cooperation and Develop-
ment
Offonry, H. K. 721
Offor, Richard 2669, 2714-
2715
Ofori, A. G. T. 2670
Ofori, Henry 2988
Ofori-Amankwah, E. H. 2512
Ofori-Attah, Grace 2671-2672
Ofori-Boateng, J. 2513
Ofosu-Appiah, L. H. 1697-
1700, 2826
Ogun, G. E. 3943
Ogunsheye, F. A. 1924, 2673
Ogwurike, C. 2515
Ojo, Gabriel J. 1925-1927
Okigbo, Pius 1206
Okina, A. 1701

Steel, D. 2553
Steel, R. W. 1946
Steen, Marguerite 3089-3090
Stein, J. L. 1222
Stejskal, Vaclau 1733, 4044
Stengers, Jean 2227
Sterling Editors 1947
Stevenson, Robert F. 360
Stewart, Charles C. 2228
Stewart, J. L. 3258
Stewart, J. M. 2333
Stewart, John M. 2831-2835
Stockade, F. A. 1223
Stoevesandt, G. 3781
Stokke, O. 530
Stoneman, Elvyn 18
Storch, R. F. 2775, 2943
Strain, W. H. 1734
Strasburg, P. A. 1497
Stratmon, David L. 1735
Streeten, Paul 1399
Strevens, Peter 2776
Strickland, J. T. 2599, 2675-2676
Stride, G. T. 2229
Strong, T. H. 1224-1225
Struchen, P. 2230
Stultz, Newell M. 278
Sufrin, Sidney 100, 361
Sullivan, George Edward 1736
Sulton, Francis 1737
Sutherland, Carol H. 1015
Sutherland, Efua 2000, 2944, 2995-3000, 4045
Swanzy, H. 1498
Sweeney, James 3253
Swithenbank, Michael 1016, 3782
Sydney, Edward 2677
Sydow, Eckart Von 1017
Symonds, Richard 3505
Szentes, T. 362
Szereszewski, R. 1226-1228

Taafe, E. J. 1948
Tabi, R. A. 3001
Tait, David 749-750
Tamakloe, Alexander A. 1949
Tamakloe, E. F. 751-752
Tamers, M. A. 898
Tanburn, E. 1343
Tauber, Maurice F. 2724

Taubert, Sigfred 23
Tauxier, Louis 3783
Tay, Janet 3972
Taylor, Alan R. 165, 1738-1739
Taylor, C. J. 2836
Taylor, Don 3506
Taylor, Sidney 24
Telli, Diallo 363
Tenkorang, S. 2231, 2334
Terrisse, A. 1018
Tettegah, J. K. 1344
Tetteh-Lartey, A. C. 1740
Tetty, Charles 2721
Textor, Robert 1741
Théberge, P. A. 1499
Theobald, Robert 1742, 4046
Thomas, Benjamin E. 105, 1950
Thomas, Elwyn 3091
Thomas, H. B. 2554
Thomas, Louis Vincent 228, 753
Thompson, L. A. 147
Thompson, R. F. 1019
Thompson, Vincent Bakpetu 3586
Thompson, Willard S. 3587-3590
Thornton, A. P. 468-469
Thoyer, J. R. 2555
Thurnher, Majda Theresia 229
Tibble, Anne 531, 2945, 3142
Tiffin, John 1568
Tiger, L. S. 1346, 3507-3510, 3973-3974
Tildsley, Alfred 3784
Timothy, Bankole 1106, 3511
Tinbergen, Jan 470
Titi-Lartey, E. O. 3259
Tixier, Gilbert 2556, 3512
Tolman, L. E. 117
Tolson, Melvin 3143
Tordoff, William 2334a-2336
Touval, Saadia 467
Traber, Michael 3336
Trachtman, Lester 1347-1349, 2557
Tranakides, G. 2232
Traore, Diawa-Mory 1350
Tregidgo, P. S. 3092
Trent, Richard D. 1744-1745
Trevor, Coombe 377

Trimingham, John Spencer
3785-3787
Trowell, Kathleen M. 1021-1024
Tufuo, J. W. 754
Turkson, R. B. 2558
Turner, G. C. 3513
Turner, Harold W. 86, 3788-
3792
Turner, V. 471
Turton-Hart, Francis 1351, 1951

Uche, U. U. 2559-2560
Uchendu, Victor C. 755-756
Udoma, E. Udo 2233
Ukpabi, S. C. 2234-2235
Underwood, Leon 1024a-1026
UNESCO
see United Nations Education-
al, Scientific and Cultural
Organization
United Africa Company 1352,
1501
United Nations 1230; Commis-
sion on the Status of Women
230; Economic Commission
for Africa 25, 364, 1229,
1353; Technical Assistance
Programme 3975-3976;
Trusteeship Council 2236
United Nations Educational,
Scientific and Cultural
Organization 26, 472, 1745a,
2650a, 2680
U. S. A. I. D.
see U. S. Agency for Interna-
tional Development 366
U. S. Board on Geographic
Names 1952; Congress.
Senate. Committee on Judi-
ciary 3591-3592; Dept. of
Agriculture 1401; Dept. of
Army 70, 547, 1354; Dept.
of Labor 1355; Foreign Ser-
vice Institute 2837; Library
of Congress. General Refer-
ence and Bibliography Divi-
sion 71-75, 566; Library of
Congress. Music Division
138; Library of Congress.
Serial Division 76
University of Ife. Institute of
African Studies 2561

Unoh, S. O. 473
Urquhart, D. J. 2704
Urquhart, Duncan H. 1356-7
Uwanaka, Charles 3337

Van Dantzig, Albert 2337
Van Dyck, C. 757-758
Vane, M. 2001
Vanhanen, Tatu 3516
Van Lare, William B. 3515
Van Rensburg, P. 474
Vansina, Jan 475, 2074
Varley, Douglas H. 139, 166-8
Varley, William 1953, 2237
Verba, Sidney 242
Vernon-Jackson, Hugh 2946
Verstraelen, F. J. 3793, 3977
Vieyra, Paulin S. 532
Villiers, A. 3894
Vlach, John M. 1748
Volta River Authority 1358
Volta River Preparatory Com-
mission 1402
Voluntary Workcamps Associa-
tion (Accra) 3978

Wagner, F. E. 100
Wake, Clive 3137
Wakely, Patrick I. 1749
Walford, Albert J. 78
Walker, Elise 2722
Walker, F. Deaville 1077
Wallbank, T. W. 1750
Wallenberg, Erik 1359
Wallerstein, Immanuel 367-
368, 2238-2239, 3338-3339,
3517, 3979-3981
Walsh, William 2947
Walter, Gerard 3340
Wanner, Gustaf Adolf 1502
Ward, Barbara
see Jackson, Barbara Ward
Ward, Honor 3949
Ward, Ida C. 2777-2778
Ward, W. E. F. 1072-3, 1752-
1754, 2240-2241, 3260, 3518-
3519
Warner, D. 2002, 3593
Warren, Dennis M. 566a
Warren, Fred Anthony 533
Warren, Lee 533

Wright, George   3526
Wright, Giles Robert   1360
Wright, Harrison   1078
Wright, Richard   2004-2005
Wrong, Margaret   2948-2949,
    3806
Wyllie, John   3094
Wyllie, R. W.   1768-1769, 3966
Wyndham, Hugh Archibald
    2255-2256

Yankah, J. T. N.   1770
Yankey, David Beikwaw   1361
Yannoulis, Y.   1507
Yates, Barbara   118-119
Yates, Walter   3807
Yegbe, J. B.   2257-2258
Yeulett, M.   3095
York, R. N.   785, 918-923
Young, R. D. E.   2725
Younger, Kenneth   1362

Zabel, Shirley   2576
Zahan, Dominique   232
Zaretsky, Irving I.   88
Zartman, Ira William   3596-
    3597
Zavolloni, Marisa   321
Zeitlin, Arnold   1771, 3002
Zell, Hans M.   140, 2950-2953
Zemba, Lydia Verona   582
Ziegler, Jean   233, 376
Zolberg, Aristide   569, 3527-
    3529
Zwernemann, Jurgen   1031